CULTURE AND EXPERIENCE

by

A. Irving Hallowell

WITHDRAWN

WAVELAND
PRESS, INC.
Prospect Heights, Illinois

For information about this book, write or call:
Waveland Press, Inc.
P.O. Box 400
Prospect Heights, Illinois 60070
(312) 634-0081

The designs for the chapter openings were adapted from *The Crafts of the Ojibwa* by C. A. Lyford, a publication of the Education Division, U.S. Office of Indian Affairs.

ISBN 0-88133-368-9

Printed in the United States of America

7 6 5 4 3 2 1

Preface to the Paperback Edition

IT IS WELL OVER A DECADE SINCE THE PAPERS IN THIS VOLUME, SOME OF WHICH go back thirty years, were selected and arranged around their central theme, "culture and experience." The interested reader might, therefore, be curious about what further thoughts I have had on the same subject and their relation to current developments in anthropology, biology, and psychology. As a matter of fact, my recent writings form an integral continuity with these papers.

The theme of the first chapter of Part I, "Personality Structure and the Evolution of Man," has been extended and elaborated in a number of my later publications: "The Structural and Functional Dimensions of a Human Existence" (*Quarterly Review of Biology*, XXI, No. 2, 1956); "Behavioral Evolution and the Emergence of the Self," in B. J. Meggers (ed.), *Evolution and Anthropology: A Centennial Appraisal* (Anthropological Society of Washington, 1959); "Self, Society and Culture in Phylogenetic Perspective," in Sol Tax (ed.), *Evolution after Darwin* (Vol. 2, *The Evolution of Man* [Chicago, 1960]); "The Protocultural Foundations of Human Adaptation," in S. L. Washburn (ed.), *Social Life of Early Man* (Chicago, 1961); "Personality, Culture and Society in Behavioral Evolution," in S. Koch (ed.), *Psychology: A Study of a Science* (New York, 1963); "Hominid Evolution, Cultural Adaptation and Mental Dysfunctioning," in *Transcultural Psychiatry* (Ciba Foundation Symposium, London, 1965).

The framework of these papers is *behavioral evolution*, a more inclusive perspective than that provided by physical anthropology (morphology) and archeology alone. It emphasizes the continuities as opposed to the discontinuities between man and the non-hominid primates. The organic, psychological, social, and cultural dimensions of the evolutionary process are taken into account as they are related to underlying conditions necessary for a human level of existence. Biologists, too, have become interested in behavioral evolution. For example, Anne Roe and G. G. Simpson (eds.), *Behavior and Evolution* (New Haven, 1958), and B. G. Campbell, *Human Evolution* (Chicago, 1966). Particularly important is the emergence in the course of hominid evolution of an ego structure, the foundation of man's development of a capacity for self-awareness and self-objectification. This is a necessary level of functioning in all socio-cultural systems of man. See, for example, T. Dobzhansky, *Mankind Evolving* (New Haven, 1962), pp. 337 ff., and E. and W. Menaker, *Ego in Evolution* (New York, 1965).

Behavioral evolution also involves the gradual development of cultural adaptation from an earlier level at which only the preconditions of such development are present in the earliest hominids and other primates. In other words, as Dobzhansky says (*op. cit.*, p. 18), "Human evolution has two components, the biological or organic, and the cultural or superorganic. These components are neither mutually exclusive nor independent, but interrelated and interdependent. Human evolution cannot be understood as a purely biological process, nor can it be adequately described as a history of culture. There exists a feedback between biological and cultural processes." This viewpoint excludes any concept of a macro-mutational, or "critical point," theory of the beginnings of culture. Further discussions of this are: C. Geertz, "The Transition to Humanity," in Sol Tax (ed.), *Horizons of Anthropology* (Chicago, 1964); M. F. Ashley Montagu (ed.), *Culture and the Evolution of Man* (Oxford, 1962), and C. H. Waddington, *The Ethical Animal* (New York, 1961).

A *protocultural stage* is thus indicated, with, in the course of time, the psychological restructuralization that led to ego development at some stage later than the earliest hominid differentiation. Recent studies that have contributed to our knowledge of the protocultural phase of human evolution have been the field investigations of non-human primates in their wild state. See I. DeVore (ed.), *Primate Behavior, Field Studies of Monkeys and Apes* (New York, 1965) and S. L. Washburn, *op. cit.*

Another development is the recent interest of psychological, particularly psychoanalytic, theorists in "ego psychology" and the "structural theory." See H. Hartmann, *Essays on Ego Psychology* (New York, 1964) and J. A. Arlow and C. Brenner, *Psychoanalytic Concepts and the Structural Theory* (New York, 1964). One of the consequences of this development is that the "recapitulation theory" (Chap. 2) is no longer dominant in psychoanalytic thought.

Among psychologists, too, the use of the Rorschach Test in personality and culture studies (Chap. 31) has been reviewed. Gardner Lindzey has made a highly critical appraisal of the use of this technique by anthropologists in his *Projective Techniques and Cross-Cultural Research* (New York, 1961).

Part II, "World View, Personality Structure, and the Self: The Ojibwa Indians," I have further developed in a more integrated presentation of the Ojibwa world view as a "great society" of "persons." "Ojibwa Ontology, Behavior and World View," in S. Diamond (ed.), *Culture in History* (New York, 1960). Also "The Ojibwa World View and Disease," in I. Galston (ed.), *Man's Image in Medicine and Anthropology* (New York, 1963), and "The Role of Dreams in Ojibwa Culture," in G. E. von Grunebaum and R. Caillois (eds.), *The Dream and Human Societies* (Berkeley, Calif., 1966). My approach has been "emic" rather than "etic," that is, from within the cultural system rather than from without. See also, D. French, "The Relationship of Anthropology to Studies in Perception and Cognition," in S.

iv

Koch (ed.), *Psychology: A Study of a Science* (Vol. 6, *Investigations of Man as Socius* [New York, 1963]) and W. C. Sturtevant, "Studies in Ethnoscience," in A. K. Romney and R. G. D'Andrade (eds.), *Transcultural Studies in Cognition* (*American Anthropologist*, LXVI, No. 3, Part 2, 1964). This ethnoscience, or ethnosemantic, approach has been specifically applied to the Ojibwa of Minnesota by Mary B. Black in her doctoral dissertation at Stanford University, *An Ethnoscience Investigation of Ojibwa Ontology and World View*, 1967. Taking my data as hypotheses to be tested, she has arrived at conclusions more refined than but closely parallel to my own.

While the effects of the impact of white culture on the Indian (Part IV) has been voluminously treated in the literature, acculturation is actually a two-way street. I have dealt with this reverse situation in two articles: "The Backwash of the Frontier: The Impact of the Indian on American Culture," in W. D. Wyman and C. B. Kroeber (eds.), *The Frontier in Perspective* (Madison, Wisconsin, 1958) and "The Impact of the American Indian on American Culture" (*American Anthropologist*, LXIX, No. 2, 1957). Related to these articles is one on the phenomenon of "transculturalization," as I have called it. It is an attempt to deal with the neglected topic of the subsequent lives of white persons who as captives were brought up as Indians, or who voluntarily left their own white group to lead the life of Indians. "American Indians, White and Black: The Phenomenon of Transculturalization" (*Current Anthropology*, IV, 1963, pp. 519–31). "Indianization" was typical of frontier America and has been treated widely by novelists. "Transculturalization" is, of course, world wide, one aspect of culture contact anywhere. See, for instance, "Beachcombers and Castaways" by H. E. Maude, a historical treatment of transculturites in the Pacific (*Journal of the Polynesian Society*, LXXIII, No. 3, 1964, pp. 254–93).

A. IRVING HALLOWELL

Philadelphia
June, 1967

v

Preface

Fᵢᵣₛₜ OF ALL I WISH TO EXPRESS MY APPRECIATION TO THE PHILA-delphia Anthropological Society for promoting the publication of this volume and, in particular, to the officers of the Society and members of the Publication Committee who have devoted so much time and thought to it. It was their idea that, since many of my papers which dealt with problems on the borderline between anthropology and psychology were scattered about in various periodicals, it might be useful to have them brought together and republished in a single volume.

It was neither desirable nor practical, however, to include all these papers; the major question then was what to select and what to omit and how to organize the articles selected. I did not wish to republish a series of papers arranged in chronological order, unedited and with no central focus. My choice of papers has been highly selective, and the material as it now stands has been organized around a series of problems I have dealt with from time to time, along with relevant data collected in the field. All of the previously published papers chosen for inclusion have been edited and some cutting, to eliminate repetitions, has been done. Besides this, some unpublished material has been added: Chapters 5 and 18, sketching the ethnohistorical background of the Northern Ojibwa (Berens River Saulteaux) and the Lac du Flambeau Ojibwa, specially prepared for this volume; Chapter 9, "Cultural Factors in Spatial Orientation"; and Chapter 17, the introduction to Part IV on problems in studying the psychological dimension of culture change. In content, the chapters range from those of the most general and theoretical nature to those which embody concrete observations on Ojibwa culture and behavior relevant to the general problems discussed. Except in two instances (Chapters 2 and 19), the titles of previously published articles have been retained.

The title of the volume, *Culture and Experience,* is intended to suggest an underlying theme which, I believe, will be apparent throughout. For a long time it has seemed to me that, sooner or later, anthropology will have to come to closer grips with a central problem towards which many of its data converge: it should be possible to formulate more explicitly the necessary and sufficient conditions that make a human existence possible and which account for the distinctive quality of human experience. A human level of existence implies much more than existence conceived in purely organic terms. Even if a naturalistic frame of reference is fully accepted, physical anthropology cannot give a complete answer to this question. The unique qualitative aspects of a human existence that arise out of conditions of human experience which are not simple functions of man's organic status alone, and that have variable as well as constant features, must be thoroughly explored in all their ramifications and given more explicit formulation.

Perhaps Franz Boas had some such problem in mind when he commented that one of the central questions of anthropology "was the relation between the objective world and man's subjective world as it had taken form in different cultures." At any rate, it seems to me that although we now know a great deal about man's organic status, seen in evolutionary perspective, about his capacity for the symbolic transformation and articulation of experience, and the wide variations in his sociocultural mode of life, the full significance of this knowledge cannot be brought to a logical focus without reference to an implicit psychological dimension. For a human level of existence not only necessitates a unique biological structure and a sociocultural mode of life; it necessitates a peculiar and distinctive kind of psychological structuralization, characterized by a level of personal adjustment and experience in which a unique and complex integration occurs between responses to an "outer" world of objects and events and responses to an "inner" world of impulse, fantasy, and creative imagination. Besides this, a human existence is one in which potentialities for readjustment, reorientation, change, are constantly present. (Cf. Hallowell, 1953a.*)

Part I, *Culture and Personality Structure,* contains papers which are the most general and theoretical in nature. The first of these discusses questions pertaining to the ultimate roots of human culture and personality structure viewed in the broad horizons of behavioral evolution. The second paper, "The Recapitulation Theory and Culture," is critical in nature. It is included because of the enormous influence the theory of recapitulation exerted in the heyday of evolutionary theory and later in psychoanalytic theory. By means of it phylogenetic processes and events could be brought into the same frame of reference as ontogenetic development in not only the prenatal but the postnatal period, and stages in cultural evolution could be related to stages in the development of the human individual. When combined with the theory of the inheritance of acquired characteristics, the determining conditions and consequences of the acquisition and transmission of culture were given a biological weighting quite different from that now generally assumed in theories of learning and personality formation. The role that the recapitulation theory played in Freud's thinking cannot be minimized; but he was not

---

*All references indicated by year and serial letter are to items in the Hallowell Bibliography at the end of the volume.

alone. Sir James G. Frazer adhered to it, as did J. M. Baldwin and G. Stanley Hall among psychologists. (See Hallowell, 1954a.)

The Rorschach paper deals with more than technical problems. In it I have tried to bring to a common focus certain aspects of personality and culture theory, contemporary theories of perception, and some assumptions inherent in the Rorschach Test as a psychological instrument. An extended version of this paper will appear in Bruno Klopfer, and others, *Developments in the Rorschach Technique,* II. *Fields of Application* (Yonkers-on-Hudson: World Book Co., 1955). It was written in 1952 and supersedes an earlier survey of the use of the Rorschach Test in anthropology (Hallowell, 1945b).

The last paper in this section, "The Self and Its Behavioral Environment," was completed in September 1951 and submitted to the late Geza Roheim for inclusion in Volume IV of *Psychoanalysis and the Social Sciences.* Since this volume had not gone to press at the time of his death (1953), it was withdrawn and subsequently published, with minor revisions, in *Explorations* (March 1954). (I mention these details because explicit reference to the expected source of original publication unfortunately has appeared in print.) As published in *Explorations,* the paper included the section on "The Ojibwa Self" which in this volume is Chapter 8 (Part II). The paper elaborates a generic aspect of the psychological structure of man on which I laid some stress in "Personality Structure and the Evolution of Man." But in addition it sets forth certain basic orientations, found in all cultures, which seem to be functionally related to the dominant ego-centered processes in human beings and are likewise inherent in the functioning of any human society.

Part II, *World View, Personality Structure, and the Self: The Ojibwa Indians,* groups together previously published material which epitomizes some of the most salient characteristics of the Ojibwa world as conceptualized and experienced by the individual. This part is prefaced, however, by a brief and broad-gauged ethnohistorical account of the Ojibwa as an ethnic group with special reference to the position of the Berens River people who so constantly reappear in the chapters of this volume. For the Ojibwa, in general, full ethnographic details must be sought in the sources listed in George P. Murdock's *Ethnographic Bibliography of North America* (Behavioral Science Bibliographies [2nd ed., New Haven: Human Relations Area Files, 1953]). For the Berens River Ojibwa other articles of mine contain considerable ethnographic information. In most of my articles I have used the term Saulteaux for these people since this is their most usual designation in Canada, including references in official documents. In Chapter 5 I have discussed the synonymy of Ojibwa designation which occasionally has caused some confusion.

One of the questions that has arisen in the course of personality and culture studies is how far specific personality constellations may transcend local ethnic units and be characteristic of the people in considerably wider regions (Hallowell, 1953a, pp.606-7). In "Some Psychological Character- istics of the Northeastern Indians," reprinted here as Chapter 6, I raised this question in concrete form and assembled data that strongly indicate that the Ojibwa in most respects exhibit psychological characteristics shared by other Indians of the Eastern Woodland Culture Area in former times. Recently, John J. Honigmann in his book, *Culture and Personal- ity* (New York, 1954, p. 334), has suggested "that a relatively homo- geneous personality can be discerned in the vast coniferous forest zone extending from northeastern Canada to western Alaska." Several articles of mine written in the thirties (Hallowell, 1936a, 1939a) contain some additional case material on the Ojibwa.

Part III, *The Cultural Patterning of Personal Experience and Be- havior,* includes articles which, although documented for the most part by observations on the Ojibwa, are keyed to categories of general human experiences and behavior. In a chapter, "Culture and Behavior," con- tributed to the *Handbook of Social Psychology,* edited by Gardner Lindzey (Addison-Wesley Press, 1954), Clyde Kluckhohn has organized his survey of the pertinent anthropological literature under such broad headings as Sexual Behavior, Perception, Cognition, Affect, "Abnormal" Behavior, Evaluative Behavior, etc. A number of chapters in this part have reference to the same categories. Although I have omitted a paper on "Cultural Factors in the Structuralization of Perception" (Hallowell, 1951a), Chapters 9, 10, 11, on spatiotemporal orientation and measure- ment, while concerned more essentially with the cognitive aspects of hu- man behavior, naturally involve perceptual experience as well. The inter- relations of affective experience, culture, and behavior are the major focus of Chapters 13, 14, and 15. In Chapter 16 sexual behavior is considered in relation to culturally defined norms of conduct on the one hand, and actual behavior on the other, particularly the kind of psychological affects that occur in cases of deviation and their relation to the operation of social sanctions. Chapter 14 deals with the latter theme from a more inclusive point of view.

Chapter 12, "The Nature and Function of Property as a Social Insti- tution," originally appeared in a periodical that had a very short run and has been defunct for many years. In it I deal with property rights as dis- tinctive human phenomena, characteristic of all human societies, no matter how varied in patterning they may be. To my mind, one of the universal functions of all systems of property rights is to orient the indi- viduals of a given society towards a complex set of basic values which are necessary to its functioning. This kind of value orientation is just as crucial in relation to the motivations and interpersonal adjustments of the indi- vidual as are the values associated, for example, with sexual behavior or religious behavior. "Property rights are not only an integral part of the economic organization of any society; they are likewise a coordinating factor in the functioning of the social order as a whole."

Part IV, *The Psychological Dimension in Culture Change,* includes a preliminary orientation to a very broad and complex problem, as well as the results of a field study undertaken at Lac du Flambeau in 1946. The special feature of the latter was the use made of projective tests and the analysis of the results obtained to probe the psychological depth of the effects of acculturation upon the life adjustment of the Indian population. Since such tests had not been used previously (except by myself) in trying to investigate the psychological dimension of culture change, the study must be considered as highly experimental. While its results have yet to be finally appraised, the subsequent use of the Rorschach by George R. Spindler, in an investigation of acculturation in relation to personal adjustment on the Menomini Reservation, indicates the kind of potentialities inherent in projective techniques when used systematically in a well-designed project.

Melford E. Spiro participated in the earliest planning stage of this volume, and he was good enough to look over my papers with a critical eye and make suggestions regarding those he thought should be included and excluded. I am greatly indebted to him for this, and to my colleague Loren C. Eiseley for his keen interest in the project and the opportunity I have had of discussing many practical details with him at every stage in the preparation of the manuscript. But it is impossible to express the debt I owe to my wife, Maude F. Hallowell. It was she who assumed the responsibility of carefully reading all the papers I set aside for possible republication and who assisted me in arriving at the final selection and the plan of organization. And upon her, too, fell the entire responsibility of editing the manuscript.

A. IRVING HALLOWELL

Philadelphia
March 1954

Acknowledgments

Grateful acknowledgment is due the following authors, publishers, and periodicals for permission to reprint papers of the author and other copyrighted material that originally appeared in their publications:

American Anthropologist

American Journal of Orthopsychiatry

American Sociological Review

Columbia University Press

Explorations

Houghton Mifflin Company

Journal of Projective Techniques

Journal of the Royal Anthropological Institute of Great Britain and Ireland

Journal of Social Psychology

McGraw-Hill Book Company, Inc.

Psychiatry

Dr. Howard Spoerl

Robert S. Peabody Foundation for Archaeology

The Woods Schools

World Book Company

Yale University Press

Phonetic Key

In the rendering of native Ojibwa words which appear in this book, I have approximated the *Phonetic Transcription of Indian Languages* (Smithsonian Miscellaneous Collections LXI, No. 6, 1916), recommended by a committee of the American Anthropological Association. I have not, however, followed all the refinements indicated. For the general reader it is hoped that the symbols used for the following sounds will make the Indian words sufficiently pronounceable:

Vowels	Consonants
a, as in *father*	c, approximates *sh* in *ship*
ä, as in *hat*	j, approximates *z* in *azure*
e, as *a* in *fate*	tc, approximates *ch* in *church*
ī, as in *pique*	dj, approximates *j* in *judge*
o, as in not (ǫ, *nasalized*)	
u, as in *rule*	
α, as *u* in *but*	

' breathing, concluding syllable after a vowel

′ (acute) and ` (grave) indicate major and secondary stress accents, respectively

Contents

Part I. Culture, Personality, and Experience

Part II. World View, Personality Structure, and the Self: The Ojibwa Indians

Part III. The Cultural Patterning of Personal Experience and Behavior: The Ojibwa Indians

xiii

Part IV. The Psychological Dimension in Culture Change

ABOUT THE NOTES

The notes will be found on pages 367 to 429. In the note section, at the upper right-hand corner of each recto page and the upper left-hand corner of each verso page, will be found boldface numbers indicating the pages of the text to which the notes on these two pages refer.

PART I

Culture, Personality, and Experience

Chapter 1 - Personality
Structure and the Evolution
of Man*

THE REJECTION OF ANY THEORY OF UNILINEAR CULTURAL EVOLUTION
seems to have led to a declining interest in all problems of cultural evolution as well as in any *inclusive* approach to what was once considered a
central problem of anthropology—the evolution of man. It almost appears
as if, in recent years, we had tagged the problem of human evolution as an
exclusively biological problem. Or, perhaps more accurately, a problem
that centers around the morphology of the primates in relation to the
emergence of creatures that can be identified as true hominids. Other
orders of continuity and differentiation that human evolution implies
have dropped out of the picture, although in the nineteenth century they
were the focus of considerable interest. We have even tended to leave the
definition of man in the hands of the physical anthropologist. Does this
mean that we are all agreed that the only criteria of human status are
morphological criteria? Are there no others of any importance? Is even
the question of human evolution in its inclusive aspects of no interest to
those of us who are not physical anthropolgists?

It is paradoxical, I think, that whereas opponents of human evolution in the nineteenth century were those who naturally stressed evidence
that implied discontinuity between man and his primate precursors, anthropologists of the twentieth century, while giving lip service to organic
evolution have, by the special emphasis laid upon culture as the prime human differential, once again implied an unbridged gap between ourselves
and our animal forebears. Yet continuity as well as differentiation is of
the essence of any evolutionary process. So where, may we ask, do the
roots of culture lie at the prehuman level? Even the concept of human
nature in the minds of some has become relativistic—relativistic, that is,
to the particular cultural form through which it is empirically manifest.
But if this is so, what is the emergence of a cultural mode of adaptation
a function of? Surely not of a subhuman nature, since other primates,
whatever their distinctive natures, did not evolve a cultural mode of
existence.

*Presidential address, the American Anthropological Association, 1949; reprinted from *Amer-
ican Anthropologist,* LII (April-June 1950).

1. PERSONALITY STRUCTURE AND THE EVOLUTION OF MAN

What has happened, of course, is that the human paleontologist, expert in biology, has concentrated on the morphology, locus, and succession of early hominids and related forms. And in recent years new discoveries have kept him extremely busy. The prehistoric archeologist, on the other hand, has concentrated on the forms, distribution, and succession of the objects from which the early cultures of man can be inferred. Neither has been directly concerned with *behavioral evolution,* an area which lies somewhere between the morphological facts and the material cultural evidence of man's existence. In other words, human evolution has been mainly approached through two lines of evidence: (1) skeletal remains, fragments of an organic structure which is only one of the material *conditions* of behavior; (2) the material products of human activity. Consequently, it is easy to understand how it has come about that man's human status has so often been characterized in terms of one or more criteria derived from these sources alone: the structure of the brain case, teeth, pelvis, foot, for instance, or the use of tools.

But there is an obvious difference between these two indicative categories of a human status when viewed evolutionally. The material evidence of organic structure can be related to the morphological traits of other primates, including those of an earlier temporal period, and facts about both continuity and differentiation can be stated. The contrary is true of the material cultural remains. *Their* only connections can be traced *forward,* not backward. So while they may be an index to the presence of man, tools tell us little about the steps in his evolution. If we wish to get behind the tool, as it were, we have to ask questions which neither the archeologist nor the physical anthropologist can answer by a direct appeal to his data. Tool-making is a specific product of behavior and what we have to know in order to explain the making and using of tools by one creature and not another is the kind of psychobiological structure that is a necessary condition of tool-making.[1] In this particular case we know that while, under certain conditions, individual chimpanzees have been observed to construct tools, tool-making and using is not an attribute of chimpanzee society. Neither is it traditional in any other infrahuman primate society. The problem becomes perplexing from the standpoint of human evolution since what we would like to know is whether there is any inner continuity between the processes which make it possible for an infrahuman primate to make and use tools and tools as a characteristic feature of human cultural adaptation. In order to gain any understanding of this problem a deeper question must be faced. It was propounded in the nineteenth century as the evolution of mind, the emergence of the human mind being conceived as the flowering of a long process.

No wonder some of those who reflected on this question, but who had chiefly the facts of comparative anatomy as their data, sincerely felt like St. George Mivart that such facts "re-echo the truth of long ago pro-

3

claimed by Buffon, that material structure and physical forces can never alone account for the presence of mind."[2] In this, of course, they were essentially right. In fact Mivart, a prolific and widely read writer, stated the problem very well in 1874. He says,

Man being, as the mind of each man may tell him, an existence not only conscious, but conscious of his own consciousness; one not only acting on inference, but capable of analyzing the process of inference, a creature not only capable of acting well or ill, but of understanding the ideas "virtue" and "moral obligation," with their correlatives freedom of choice and responsibility—man being all this, it is at once obvious that the principal part of his being is his mental power.

> In nature there is nothing great but man,
> In man there is nothing great but mind.

We must entirely dismiss, then, the conception that mere anatomy by itself can have any decisive bearing on the question as to *man's nature and being as a whole*. To solve this question, recourse must be had to other studies; that is to say, to philosophy, and especially to that branch of it which occupies itself with mental phenomena—psychology.

But if man's being as a whole is excluded from our present investigation [he goes on to say] man's body considered by itself, his mere "massa corporea," may fairly be compared with the bodies of other species of his zoological order, and his corporeal affinities thus established.[3]

It is clear from this quotation that to Mivart an inclusive approach to the evolution of man required that some consideration be given man's psychological evolution. Nevertheless he himself felt impelled to adopt a more exclusive approach: he kept to the material evidence. In the background of Mivart's thinking as well as that of others reflecting on problems of human evolution in the post-Darwinian period and long thereafter, there persisted the old metaphysical dualism of Descartes, the mind-body dichotomy. Psychologists and philosophers were almost forced to wrestle with the mind-body problem in some form, while anthropologists of the same period were content to deal with the material evidence of evolution and leave them to labor undisturbed.[4] But, however phrased, the problem of "mental" evolution still remains[5]: for neither the facts of organic structure in themselves, nor any reconstruction of behavioral evolution exposes the differential factors that ultimately led to the transformation of a subhuman society into a human society with an expanding cultural mode of adaptation. Consequently, some reconceptuaiization of the whole problem seems in order and I think we already have moved in that direction. It is no longer adequate, for example, to identify mind with mental traits such as consciousness, reason, intelligence, or, even more vaguely, with some sort of quantitative variable such as "mental power," which one then attempts to trace up or down the phylogenetic scale. Yet in the recent discussions of the Australopithecines one well-known authority on primate morphology employs both "mental power" and "intelligence" as conceptual indices for inferring the superior capacities of the Australopithecine over the chimpanzee and gorilla. It is even suggested that the superior "mental power" of the former accounts

4

for the fact that they were able to hunt and kill baboons. Since these creatures were reportedly evolving in the human direction one may seriously ask whether such an index of mental power involves much more in principle than the mental equipment of cats for killing rats![6]

As K. S. Lashley has recently pointed out,

The interest of early students of comparative psychology was in finding the origin of human mental *traits*. Darwin and Romanes could point out behavior of animals which suggested similarity of emotional character, memory, and intelligence to that of man, and could show the similarity increased with increasing bodily similarity to man. They could not specify what was changing in evolution or the nature of the steps between different levels of behavior. We are in a scarcely better position today. It is not possible to classify unit factors in behavior and to trace the development of distinct entities, as one may trace the evolution of the heart, the gill arches, or the limbs. For such a classification it is necessary to know the mechanisms by which the behavior is produced and to trace the evolution of these mechanisms. [Italics ours.][7]

Recent developments in personality psychology incline me to believe that we can be more optimistic than Lashley implies. For in man we must not only consider intrinsic mechanisms, but a structural basis of behavior which is also rooted in the gregarious nature of the primates and the potentialities offered for the socialization of individual experience. In recent years the concept of personality structure, whose genesis lies in social interaction, offers the beginnings of a conceptual resolution of the old mind-body dichotomy, while, at the same time, it relates the individual to his social setting. The assumption is that the individual functions as a psychobiological whole, as a total personality. Behavior has a structural basis, but this structuralization has arisen in experience and cannot, therefore, be reduced to an inherited organic structure. "Intelligence," "reason," or other mental traits then become specific functions of the personality structure. Thus, the distinctive psychological organization of the human being, whether described as mind or personality structure, is just as much a function of his membership in a social group as it is a function of his inherited organic equipment.[8]

From the standpoint of human evolution, then, both a social matrix of conduct *and* the expansion of the cortex are among the necessary conditions for the emergence of a *human* mind or a human personality structure. Just as bodily evolution and mental evolution cannot be separated, neither can psychological structuralization and the social evolution of mankind. To behave humanly as an adult the individual must become psychologically organized in a socialization process. His biological equipment is only *one* of the conditions necessary for this. Social or sensory isolation is a fatal handicap. Hence, it seems reasonable to suppose that the emergence of culture as a prime attribute of *human* societies must be somehow connected with a novel psychological structure rooted in the social behavior of the gregarious primate that gave rise to man. It is at this point that organic evolution, behavioral evolution, and the old problem of mental evolution come to a common focus.

Consequently, the achievement of a human status in the evolutionary process, when taken inclusively, is not to be conceived as a simple function of the possession of specific organic traits—brain size, foot structure, or some specific psychological traits such as intelligence, but as a total *psychobiological* adjustment that implies an overlaid psychological structure functionally integrated with organic structure. And just as in biology it is axiomatic that new structures give rise to new forms of behavior, the same principle applies here. The question is not what kind of biological structure makes a hominid, but what kind of psychobiological structure not only makes a man but at the same time accounts for human society and culture. In other words, human evolution is not just a biological problem, or a problem of cultural origins, or a problem that involves the development of a human mind. It is one of the central problems that must be grappled with if we are fully to understand man's uniqueness, the total conditions underlying his evolution, and his capacities for cultural achievement.

But can we in our present state of knowledge make any inferences regarding the generic characteristics of man's novel personality structure? It seems to me that what we already know about the personality structures of human beings, whether considered in their individual or group aspects, suggests that they may be regarded as specific forms of a *generic* psychic structure in man that clearly differentiates him from related primates, as well as from other animals. This structure is the foundation of man's specialized form of adaptation as a species as well as the basis of his personal adjustment as an individual. Consequently, it is just as important a factor in determining his human status as is the structure of his teeth or his feet. It is, in fact, the key to his human nature and the psychodynamics of his adjustment to life, just as his feet are a key to the biodynamics of his terrestrial adaptation. And just as we may say that in terms of morphological taxonomy man belongs to a zoological family, in terms of a taxonomy of levels of psychodynamic adjustment man is characterized by a unique psychic structure the generic form of which we have only begun to discern in the common features that underlie the range and variation of personality structures that have been empirically investigated in recent years.

To begin with, from all our observations of man after he has reached a fully human estate, we must infer that the psychobiological structure underlying this new level of adjustment is one which, while permitting the transcendence of an infrahuman level, by no means cuts man off from his animal heritage. On the contrary, the psychological evolution of man conforms to the principle of continuity and differentiation that we find in all organic evolution. Man functions on two levels at once, and, under certain conditions tends to regress. Indeed, this possibility is intrinsic to

6

the nature of man since from the standpoint of psychodynamics his adjustment is not a simple function of organic structure but of personal experience and behavioral environment as well.

The cognitive aspects of man's transcendence of his animal heritage always has proved impressive and gave rise to the oversimplified characterization of man as a "rational" animal. But as far back as the eighteenth century, Swift writing to Pope (1725) said, "I have got material towards a treatise proving the falsity of that definition *animal rationale* and to show it would be only *rationis capax*,"[9] i.e., capable of reason. Today we are able to discern more clearly than before that whatever "rationality" man may possess it is not a unitary mental trait; nor a function that can be contrasted with, or divorced from, other aspects of man's personality organization such as feeling and emotion. From an evolutionary point of view, however, it is one of the major indices to man's capacity for the transcendence of the immediate, local, time- and space-bound world of the other primates who lack the capacity for dealing effectively with objects and events outside the field of direct perception. Man, too, deals with present objects and events but, in addition, he is capable of adjusting his behavior to past and future objects and events. In a more technical psychological sense this means that the psychobiological structure that the hominid evolved is one in which intervening variables which mediate between immediate stimuli and overt behavior came to play a more primary role. Such intervening variables include unconscious processes such as dreams, as well as conscious operations like thinking and reasoning "whereby the remote as well as the immediate consequences of an impending overt action are brought into the psychological present, in full force, so to say, and balanced and compared."[10]

The common denominator of these intervening variables that so intimately link his "inner world" with his adjustment to the outer world and his fellow man is the symbolic or representative principle. This simply means that at the level of human adjustment the *representations* of objects and events of all kinds play as characteristic a role in man's total behavior as does the direct *presentation* of objects and events in perception. Thus skill in the manipulation of symbols is directly involved with the development of man's rational capacities. But symbolization is likewise involved with all other psychic functions—attention, perception, interest, memory, dreams, imagination, etc. Representative processes are at the root of man's capacity to deal with the abstract qualities of objects and events, his ability to deal with the possible or conceivable, the ideal as well as the actual, the intangible along with the tangible, the absent as well as the present object or event, with fantasy and with reality. Every culture as well as the personal adjustment of each individual gives evidence of this, both at the level of unconscious as well as conscious processes. Then, too, symbolic forms and processes color man's motivations, goals, and his affective life in a characteristic way. They are as relevant to an understanding of his psychopathological as of his normal behavior. If man's ancestors had remained *literal* realists like other animals, the hominid as we know him would never have evolved. Consequently, one of the basic questions which a consideration of the generic aspects of man's psychobiological structure involves is the root of man's capacity for the symbolic transformation of experience.[11] I do not intend to go into this difficult question here but, among other things, it would appear to involve the transition from capacities for *intrinsic* representative processes in animals below man, to the creation when we reach the human level of *extrinsic* symbolic systems. An animal for whom intrinsic symbolization is possible "is capable of carrying away with it from a situation . . . some inner change or state which 'stands for' the response which it will later make when it reencounters the same situation."[12] In other words, a central process is involved which functions as a substitute for actual sensory cues. Imagery would be a concrete example. But there is no way of directly projecting or communicating intrinsic symbolic processes. For this to occur, some media that can be externalized by the organism must be employed. Extrinsic symbolization, then, involves the operation of the representative principle on a higher and more complex level since socially communicable media may take on conventionalized representative functions. Thus symbols of this category can be responded to not only by the organism itself but by other organisms to whom the socially significant symbol is communicated. By means of a drawing, vocalization, or perhaps even by gestures, I can make *you* acquainted with *my* dream. Consequently, in the case of man, extrinsic symbolic systems functioning through vocal, graphic, plastic, gestural, or other media made it possible for groups of human beings to share a common meaningful world. A meaningful world in man being, in part, symbolically mediated implies a *cultural* milieu which becomes inextricably meshed with the world as biologically and physically constituted.

While the expansion of the cortex was undoubtedly *one* of the necessary conditions that made possible the increasing importance of intervening variables, and while the social transmission of extrinsic forms of symbolization implies learning, these conditional factors alone do not explain the evolution of extrinsic symbolization itself, nor the diversity of the systems that eventually arose. But I think it is quite clear that culture is unthinkable without extrinsic symbolization as a prime condition— speech, of course, being only one of the prime symbolic forms. However, since man's ancestors were a gregarious species, the matrix of such a step and the expansion and elaboration of its manifold possibilities must be conceived as a social matrix. From this the psychobiological structure that evolved cannot be dissociated. Thus at the human level of adjustment intervening variables became the integrative focus of intrinsic representative processes *and* socially transmissible extrinsic symbolic systems, at both conscious and unconscious levels.

Turning now to this social setting of the behavioral evolution of man, what reasonable deductions can be made with respect to the question of continuity and differentiation in this frame of reference that is relevant to our central problem? The socialization process, I think, gives us an important lead. For at both the human and subhuman levels we not only have parents and their offspring in continuous social interaction, we have single births and a considerable period during which the young are dependent. Now such dependence not only implies the need for care on the part of infants, it implies a power of life and death over the infant. There is also a common requirement at both levels—each new individual added to the group as a dependent infant must undergo a process of socialization under the direct influence of adults and subject to their demands. Carpenter says, for example,

A given number of monkeys and apes does not make or equal what I have been calling a group. Suppose we try this experiment: Raise in isolation animals of the species, but of the right sex and age to compose a group which meets the requirements of the formula for the average group characteristic of a species. These individuals will then be released together. What will happen? Some may so fear others that they flee. Some will be antagonistic and fight. Others will form into groups and remain together, as had been hoped or predicted, into a single organization. Why? Even though the social drives are operative and social incentives are present, the monkeys have not been conditioned to each other. They have not been socialized—i.e., they have not learned to make fitting responses to each other as complexes of stimuli. What is lacking is what I have called *integration*.

Social integration is conceived to begin with birth and to involve definable processes of social learning and adjustment. These processes are organic and involve the expressions and satisfactions of physiological drives. From one viewpoint, effective social integration of an individual conditions it in a manner to make it responsive to the communicative acts, motor expressions including gestures, and vocalizations. These communicative acts, involving specific stimuli patterns and fitting responses, constitute the core of group coordination. Let it be remembered that the stimulus aspects of communicative acts cannot be operative except on a background of social integration—i.e., animals which are conditioned to each other.[13]

We may assume, therefore, that the socialization process and the adjustment through learning that it implies links man with his primate forebears. But, even if it should turn out that we are able to ascertain that certain common habits in the subhuman primate are not only learned but socially transmitted, I do not think this fact alone would change the psychobiological status of the primates.[14] It would only be a small step in the human direction, a necessary but not a sufficient condition for the advance to the human level. For it seems quite apparent from the empirical evidence that inter-individual adjustment in the infrahuman primates is confined to responses to signs and signals. So far as symbolic processes are involved at all they are confined to the intrinsic type, the type of representative process that under adequate conditions of motivation enables a chimpanzee to make a tool or solve other problems. The young primate responds to tutelage, or discipline if you will, that is mediated from outside himself, and while he forms habit patterns on this basis that enable him to play the simple roles demanded of him in the group, there is no higher level of psychobiological integration. For example, he could never be trained to abhor incest.

The shift that occurred from this simple level of adjustment to one in which, through the mediation of extrinsic symbols, a higher level of integration could be reached is the crux of the problem of psychobiological evolution in the case of the hominid. Nevertheless, we must not lose sight of the continuity that was maintained from the ape level to man. For at the human level, too, and particularly in the earliest stages of the socialization of the individual relatively simple conditioning processes are likewise operative along with more complex levels of learning. What, then, are the special features of this higher level of integration that make it possible for man to function differently from any other animal, to act in ways denied to them? In a highly epitomized form it seems to me that these are:

First, the emergence of a dominant integrative center of the personality and consequently the development of ego-centered processes which permit man to become an object to himself. Associated with this new level of organization we have such universal characteristics of the human being as self-consciousness, self-identification and reference, self-evaluation, self-stimulation, self-control, the possibility of relating one's contemplated or actual conduct to traditional ideals and values, etc. The fact that every human social order operates as a moral order is, among other things, contingent upon man's becoming an object to himself. Together with man's capacity for self-direction and self-control the foundation is laid for holding the adult individual in all societies morally responsible for his overt actions and, in some societies, even for conduct that occurs in dreams, that is, at the level of intrinsic symbolization.

As a result of self-objectification human societies become social orders of conscious selves, in contrast with the societies of other primates where the development of ego-centered processes as part of the psychobiological structure of the individual do not become salient. In fact, when viewed from the standpoint of this peculiarity of man, cultures may be said to be elaborated systems of meaning which, in an animal capable of self-awareness, implement a type of adaptation which makes the role of the human being intelligible to himself, both with reference to an articulated universe and to his fellow men.

Secondly, what is perhaps even more significant and interesting is that, in addition to man's capacity for consciously evaluating his own acts and directing his own conduct, we now know that impulses and fantasies of which he is not aware are unconsciously evaluated for him. That is to say, his emotional nature becomes structuralized in such a way that anxiety, guilt, and depression become indices to the integrative level

10

reached by the personal adjustment of the individual in relation to the symbolically expressed and mediated norms of his society. This peculiarity of man involves, of course, the Freudian concept of the superego as part of the personality structure of man.

What I should like to stress here without going into the moot points of a complex matter is the positive theoretical value of such a construct. It permits a deeper insight into one of the psychological mechanisms involved in the direct transmission of culture values, while, at the same time, it helps to explain how an enhancement of ego development in man, who has remained so closely bound to his animal heritage through biologically rooted impulses, has been able to create and maintain effective social orders geared to highly diverse institutions and value systems. For, while, on the one hand, the superego functions as a kind of brake upon the ego, on the other, it facilitates the positive relations of the individual to socially sanctioned ideals and even the creation of new values. Without this ontogenetically rooted and largely unconscious aspect of the personality structure of man it is difficult to explain a great many things in the operation of human society and culture.

Going back once again to the seventeenth- and eighteenth-century thinkers who speculated about the nature of man and society we can well appreciate one of their major difficulties. They understood quite well the egotistical impulses of man, but they also had to account for a functioning social order. Hence they were driven to postulate certain *innate* moral qualities in man—whether good or bad. On the other hand, they had to invoke some form of "social contract" to bring men together and governmental institutions with coercive powers to influence man from outside himself. Even today we are apt to get into difficulties if we *only* conceptualize the transmission of culture in terms of socially acquired habits, or stress too much the outward coercive power of institutions as the mainstays of an effective social order. The concept of the superego as an intrinsic part of the psychobiological structure of man bridges the gap between the "inner" man, the social order, and cultural tradition.

That both the ego and the superego are structuralized in the socialization process is now a general assumption. How this takes place would divert us into the complications of the theory of personality genesis. But there is no doubt that both intrinsic and extrinsic symbolizations enter into this very intricate process. Man could hardly have become an object to himself without the use of symbolic means, particularly in view of the fact that the ego has to be built up from a level of crude, unorganized needs and desires. This is what Freud implied when he wrote, "Where id was, there shall ego be."[15] To what extent we have ego development in animals below man is a question that needs further examination. If we assume a complete break from lower primate to man we open another gap and another "mystery."[16] Symbolization also enters into the con-

11

comitant development of a superego in man. When Freud, referring to this facet of the personality structure, says that the long dependence of the child upon parents "leaves behind it a precipitate, which forms within his ego a special agency in which this parental influence is prolonged,"[17] he is, of course, speaking metaphorically. What is meant in a more literal sense is that by some central symbolic process in the organism attitudes, qualities or other aspects of the parents become represented in a parental "imago." But as Freud himself clearly points out this is only the beginning of superego structuralization in the individual. In time, he says, the superego "takes over contributions from later successors and substitutes of his parents, such as teachers, admired figures in public life, or high social ideals."[18] "Takes over" implies identification with such personages and integration of their qualities or what they stand for into the personality through the operation of symbolic processes. And the further taking over of "high social ideals" points to the possibility of the development of a superego which transcends identifications with actual or ideal personalities, one that is identified with unmediated abstract ideals.

I need not point out, I think, that in the early stages of the child's development in every society conflicts arise between the impulses of the individual and the demands of parents or cultural surrogates.[19] These conflicts have to be resolved. The significant human fact is that instead of these conflicts becoming externalized and resolved on that basis, they may be resolved for better or for worse, by unconscious repression. That is to say, certain impulses may never reach ego-awareness because the symbolic representations of them are excluded. Consequently the individual cannot deal with them through any external mode of adjustment because he is unaware of such impulses.

Thus, such processes as symbolization, identification, conflict, repression, etc., are some of the major mechanisms through which man becomes psychobiologically structured in the socialization process. They are intrinsic to the psychodynamics of human adjustment. Indeed, they are far more characteristic processes than learning which is, of course, a mode of adaptation shared not only with other primates, but with animals far lower on the phylogenetic scale. Consequently, there is nothing particularly human about learning per se. The "Law of Effect" does not apply to man alone. What is unique is the role which symbolization plays in the learning process and the contingence of the other mechanisms we have mentioned upon it. All of these together permit a higher order of integration and flexibility in human behavior. As Mowrer says,[20] "Living organisms which are unable to employ symbols versatilely are doomed to relative fixity of response, which, in the case of responses which have both remote and immediate consequences, is almost certain to result in a failure of 'integration.' " It has also been pointed out that loss of flexibility in personal adjustment is one of the key problems in the psychopathological aspects of human behavior.[21] Thus, the transmission of culture, if realistically viewed, must be thought of not as the acquisition through a simple conditioning process, of habits or cultural traits as they appear in our descriptive ethnographic accounts, but as part of a very complicated and symbolically mediated learning process in which mechanisms like conflict and repression play their role in the total integrative structure that we call the human personality.

Traditional terms like the "psychic unity" of man or "human nature" which have been somewhat emptied of their original meaning become genuinely significant again if we mean a primate whose level of adjustment implies such processes and mechanisms. As Roheim once remarked, "The most basic of all basic personalities is the one connected with the fact that we are all human."[22]

The generic psychobiological structure of man I have attempted to outline here is one that does not require any particular system of extrinsic symbolization as its medium. Just as biological structures once evolved in a rudimentary form possess potentialities for development and differentiation, so did the fundamental pattern of human psychological organization. Cultures could arise in which the significance of objects and events in the surrounding world, man's relation to man and the potential range of personal experience could be given different valences. Man's world became one that was not simply given. It was constantly molded by his interaction with it. Through the manner in which he represented it to himself it further became meaningful to him. But once a particular cultural system became established, a mode of life to which future generations had to adjust became perpetuated. The individual was forced to make his personal adjustment to life by means of the symbolic system provided by his society. But no culture frees the infant from the fundamental conflict arising from the biologically rooted impulses on the one hand, and the demands of parents or parent surrogates on the other, nor the need for some internal resolution of such conflicts. But the demands of the parents and the manner in which children are handled are not identical in all societies; hence the crucial importance of the socialization process in relation to the differential strains and stresses that account for the personality structure under one set of conditions as compared with another. What personality and culture studies have done is to demonstrate how important such differences are. When we have more knowledge of the range and variation in the human personality structure in relation to major provincial determinants we shall be able to state with more precision what is common to man everywhere. By that time we may be able to construct a better picture of the psychobiological structure of man as an evolving primate.

Chapter 2 - The Recapitulation Theory and Culture*

R EVITALIZED INTEREST IN ANIMAL MENTALITY, CHILD MENTALITY, AND the mentality of primitive man, all received their modern impetus from a common source: the concept of evolution. As a consequence of Darwin's work, evolution at once became the skeleton key by means of which attempts were made to unlock, and sometimes to force, new and untried doors of knowledge. Stages of evolutionary development soon were postulated for physical, biological, cultural, and mental phenomena. All kinds of analogies were drawn, new continuities envisaged, and underlying laws of development sought.

In order to interpret and coordinate the immense diversity of observations that seemed to support this evolutionary scheme, it was inevitable that auxiliary hypotheses and assumptions should arise. And it was inevitable, too, that they should be applied to the other spheres where evolutionary postulates were thought to be applicable, namely, the cultural and the mental.

Important among these hypotheses is Haeckel's "biogenetic law," based on embryological observations. It had long been noted[1] that structural features in the embryonic development of individual organisms sometimes closely resembled those that appeared in adult individuals of lower organic forms. Since Darwin's theory of evolution was based on the postulate that deep-seated resemblances in the structure of animals were indices to blood relationship, these embryonic facts were given a new interpretation that supported the evolutionary hypothesis. Because embryonic features in some instances appeared in the individual organism in the same order in which they arose in the ancestral series, this recapitulation of phyletic structures in the prenatal period was formulated as a "biogenetic law." It linked the early maturational stages of the individual with former stages in the development of the species. Some enthusiasts even claimed that observations upon reputed recapitulatory stages in the individual provided sufficient evidence for making phylogenetic deductions in the absence of paleontological records.

Thus the recapitulation hypothesis, popularized in the phrase "onto-

*Originally published as "The Child, the Savage and Human Experience," in *Proceedings of the Sixth Institute on the Exceptional Child* (Woods School, Langhorne, Pa., 1939), pp. 8-34.

14

geny repeats phylogeny," offered an hypothesis by means of which new data could be assembled both in support of the evolutionary theory and as a demonstration of it. It was not long, for example, before some zoologists extented the application of the theory beyond the embryonic period. Attention was called to behavioral phenomena in the postnatal phase of development which were thought to exhibit evidence of recapitulation.

Contemporaneously with the formulation and application of the recapitulation hypothesis, some anthropologists of the late nineteenth century were attempting to apply the biological concept of evolution to nonbiological phenomena. It was thought that human culture had evolved through a unilinear series of stages culminating in occidental civilization. Hence the aboriginal peoples that still survived represented arrested stages of cultural development that the more advanced races had passed through.

Usually the backwardness of these savage peoples, implicitly, if not explicitly, was interpreted as an index of their limited mental capacities. Hence, the idea of different levels of mental development within the human race as a whole was supported by anthropology, despite the fact that there was no direct evidence that this was true and that the stages of evolutionary cultural development postulated were arrived at by analogical reasoning rather than by actual historical investigation.

But this interpretation coordinated perfectly with a general scheme of mental evolution conceptualized in broad genetic terms. It was thought that mental development paralleled the organic in the hierarchy of evolutionary stages beginning with the lowest stages of animal mind and gradually ascending to human mind; the latter, in turn, developing through a succession of stages in the history of the race to the apex reached by the adult "rational" mind of occidental man.

It only remained for a genetically oriented psychology to relate the notion of cultural stages in the evolution of the race to maturational phases in the development of the individual in order to complete a schema which, at the human level, made savage mentality and child mentality directly comparable. Basically, this was accomplished by taking the cue from zoologists and extending the theory of recapituation to the *postnatal* behavioral development of the child. In the newborn infant, for example, the grasping reflex was interpreted as a simian phase in development as well as proof of the arboreal ancestry of man.[2] Recently Hrdlicka has interpreted the fact that children sometimes run on all fours like quadruminous primates in terms of the recapitulation hypothesis.[3] The interpretation of subsequent behavior patterns and modes of thought, occurring in ontogenetic development, were believed to exhibit resemblances to those of primitive and early historic peoples. In educational circles at the end of the last century attempts were being made to correlate the succession of subjects taught in the curriculum with the "culture epoch" theory of ontogenetic development.[4]

15

The analogical reasoning utilized to support this extension of the recapitulation hypothesis should not be overlooked. Just as the theory of cultural stages was based upon an analogy to the biological development of life forms, the idea that the child, in the course of its *postnatal behavioral development,* recapitulates to some degree the major *cultural* periods of the race, rests ultimately upon an analogy with prenatal structural development upon which the original biogenetic law was formulated. The implication was that the behavior of the individual at different maturational stages was primarily, if not solely, a function of his innate biological endowment, just as the culture of savages was thought basically to reflect, if not to be completely determined by, their innate racial capacities.

Although it is possible, if the biogenetic law is accepted, to account for rather simple patterns of postnatal behavior in the individual without assuming the inheritance of acquired characteristics, it is difficult to see how more complex types of behavior, including the mental, can be explained without resorting to this second auxiliary hypothesis. For if the reputed parallelism between the course of behavior and thought in children and the cultural history of man is to be given genuine significance, the simplest biological nexus that can be assumed is that acquired modes of thought and behavior become assimilated to the biological ancestry of succeeding generations of individuals. Since the extension and development of the theory of recapitulation took place at the end of the nineteenth century prior to the development of modern genetics[5] it is easy to see how such an implicit assumption could be made.

It is clearly implied, for example, in many passages in the work of G. Stanley Hall, the most representative exponent of the recapitulation theory as applied to the early phases of child development. Hall wrote,

. . . we are influenced in our deeper more temperamental dispositions by the life-habits and codes of conduct of we know not what unnumbered hosts of ancestors, which like a cloud of witnesses are present throughout our lives, and . . . our souls are echo-chambers in which their whispers reverberate. [Consequently] we have to deal with the archeology of mind, with zones or strata which precede consciousness as we know it, compared to which even it, and especially cultured intellect, is an upstart novelty.[6]

To those familiar with psychoanalytic modes of thought there is a familiar ring in the overtones of Hall's rhetorical prose. This is not strange since the recapitulation doctrine, explicitly supported by the hypothesis of the inheritance of acquired characteristics, is intrinsic to certain aspects of psychoanalytic theory.[7] It is no historic accident that it was G. Stanley Hall who invited Freud and Jung to America in 1909.[8]

Before discussing the focal position of the recapitulation theory in orthodox psychoanalytic doctrine, I wish to mention a related aspect of Hall's work, which, in principle, likewise parallels psychoanalytic theory. I refer to the emphasis upon stages of development and the explanation of the characteristic thought and behavior of individuals as functions of these stages. Hall, in fact, was the first student of child psychology to give such stages of development as infancy, childhood, and particularly adolescence, an explicit psychological content.

These stages Hall envisaged as primarily a function of maturation and racial inheritance. "Adolescence," he writes, "is a new birth, for the higher and more completely human traits are now born. The qualities of body and soul that now emerge are far newer. The child comes from and harks back to a remoter past; the adolescent is neo-atavistic, and in him the later acquisitions of the race slowly become prepotent. Development is less gradual and more saltatory, suggestive of some ancient period of storm and stress when old moorings were broken and a higher level attained."[9]

There is no evidence here that Hall gave any weight to *concurrent* social and cultural variables as *external* factors of importance in the formation of adolescent personality. The individual is what he is because of past events in the history of the race and the level of maturity that he has reached. Moreover, "the normal growth of the mind necessitates the passing through of each stage, because the development of any one level is the normal stimulus to the next." This principle, indeed, is the guiding thread of Hall's whole theory of child development.[10] It is this feature of his theory in particular that finds its analogy in psychoanalysis.

The infant, according to Freud, develops through a number of stages, the main aspects of which are predetermined biologically. In psychoanalysis, too, developmental stages are linked with a recapitulation hypothesis. "It seems to be phylogenetically established," says Freud, "in what sequence the individual impulsive feelings become active and how long they can manifest themselves before they succumb to the influence of a newly appearing impulse or to a typical repression."[11]

Fortunately, we have a number of explicit statements by Freud himself with respect to both the recapitulation theory and the doctrine of the inheritance of acquired characteristics which is utilized to support it.

In his *General Introduction to Psychoanalysis* Freud mentions the recapitulation theory in connection with his discussion of dreams. He says, "The era to which the dream-work takes us back is 'primitive' in a two-fold sense: in the first place, it means the early days of the *individual*—his childhood—and, secondly, in so far as each individual repeats in some abbreviated fashion during childhood the whole course of the development of the human race, the reference is phylogenetic."[12] Applying this hypothesis to the formation of the superego Freud asserts that "all the traces left behind in the id by biological developments and by the vicissitudes gone through by the human race are taken over by the ego and lived through again by it in each individual. Owing to the way in which it is formed, the ego-ideal has a great many points of contact with the phylogenetic endowment of each individual—his archaic heritage."[13] The idea of recapitulation is, in fact, so deeply intrenched in

17

Freud's thinking[14] that in *Beyond the Pleasure Principle*[15] he broaches the hypothesis that one of the characteristics of instinct, "perhaps of all organic life," is a "repetition-compulsion," the "most imposing proofs" of which we find in the phenomena of heredity and in the facts of embryology. "We see that the germ cell of a living animal is obliged to repeat in its development—although in a fleeting and curtailed fashion—the structures of all the forms from which the animal is descended, instead of hastening along the shortest path to its own final shape." As a matter of fact, Freud expands the repetition idea far beyond what is ordinarily understood by the formula "ontogeny repeats phylogeny." For while he views the earlier stages of ontogenetic development as a condensed repetition of man's animal and prehistoric ancestry, the later history of the individual, in turn, is a repetition with variations of the major patterns laid down in childhood.[16]

Freud is equally explicit with regard to the inheritance of acquired characteristics. In *The Ego and The Id* he writes: "The experiences of the ego seem at first to be lost to posterity; when they have been repeated often enough and with sufficient intensity, however, in the successive individuals of after generations, they transform themselves, so to say, into the experiences of the id, the impress of which is preserved by inheritance. Thus in the id, which is capable of being inherited, are stored up vestiges of the existences led by countless former egos; and, when the ego forms its super-ego out of the id, it may perhaps only be reviving images of egos that have passed away and be securing them a resurrection."[17] Consequently, we find that Freud interprets what he calls the "restricting forces" of sexual evolution—disgust, shame, morality— "as historic precipitates of the outer inhibitions which the sexual impulse experienced in the psychogenesis of humanity. One can observe that they appear in their time during the development of the individual almost spontaneously at the call of education and influence."[18] "We gain the impression," Freud says, "that the erection of these dams in the civilized child is the work of education; and surely education contributes much to it. In reality, however, this development is organically determined and can occasionally be produced without the help of education. Indeed education remains properly within its assigned realm only if it strictly follows the path of the organic determinant and impresses it somewhat clearer and deeper."[19] These two statements expose with the utmost clarity the emphasis placed by Freud upon purely biological factors in human development. Such influences are naturally enhanced if one believes, as he does, that acquired experience can be organically incorporated and exercise a biological influence in the future.

Consequently, we are not surprised to find Freud asserts in his latest book that "the archaic heritage of mankind includes not only dispositions but also ideational contents, memory traces of the experiences of former generations."[20] And in another place, that ". . . when a child reacts to the first great instinctual deprivation with an excessive aggressiveness and a corresponding strictness of its super-ego, it is thereby following a phylogenetic prototype, unheedful of what reaction would in reality be justified; for the father of primitive times was certainly terrifying, and we may safely attribute the utmost degree of aggressiveness to him."[21]

Freud and Ferenczi have even advanced the view that the Ice Age of the Pleistocene geological epoch may have been the determining factor in the establishment of the latency stage in the development of the individual.[22] This hypothesis seems to have been motivated by the fact that "nothing analagous is demonstrable in man's animal kin," so that Freud thought "the origin of this human peculiarity would have to be sought in the primal history of the human species."[23] But it must be evident by now that the logic of Freudian thinking demanded that the source of the original stimulus, even though nonbiological, had to be found in the distant past because otherwise it could not have been assimilated to the organic heritage of mankind as a whole and thus become an inevitable stage of individual development.

The explanation advanced by Freud for the Oedipus phase and its reputed universality in the development of the individual arose from a similar logical demand.[24] The ultimate determinants of ontogenetic development must be sought in some phase of phylogenetic development. At the same time, it is assumed that events in the past history of the race may be reconstructed from events taking place in the early phases of the life cycle of the individual. Ferenczi has been particularly emphatic in regard to this aspect of psychoanalytic theory.

In his discussion of E. Mach's *Kultur und Mechanik,* published in 1883, Ferenczi says: "The plan of inquiring for the primitive history of mechanism by methodical genealogical researches into the individual psychic life, instead of by excavations, merely repeats the psychoanalytic thesis, according to which not only the psychic tendencies and contents of their own childhood, but also those of their racial ancestors, can be demonstrated in the unconscious of adults. Mach's idea of searching for the culture history of mankind—on the basis of the fundamental law of biogenesis—in the psychology of the individual is a commonplace in psychoanalysis. I merely mention Freud's epoch-making book, *Totem and Taboo* (1913), in which the nature of these, as yet unexplained, social institutions is brought nearer an understanding by means of individual psychic analyses reaching back into childhood."[25]

Although Freud explicitly recognizes the speculative character of the events which he assumes to have taken place in the primal horde, he does not hesitate to make other assumptions as well—namely, that the "fortunes of this horde have left indestructible traces upon the history of human descent," and that totemism "comprises in itself the beginnings of religion, morality and social organization."[26] It scarcely need be pointed out that without independent evidence, historical deductions based on the biogenetic law are only acceptable if we assume such a law to be true.

However, if one does assume the biogenetic law, it is not only possible to make deductions about past historical events; it is also possible to deduce a chronology of events. Ferenczi is explicit in regard to this point[27] and Freud likewise asserts a parallelism between cultural history and ontogeny in *Civilization and its Discontents*.[28] He says that "we . . . have recognized the evolution of culture as a special process, comparable to the normal growth of an individual to maturity. . . ." One of his disciples, Marie Bonaparte, has taken a further step by correlating the "narcissistic" stage of ontogenetic development with an "animistic" cultural stage, the "Oedipus" phase in the individual with a "totemistic" cultural stage, and the genital phase presumably with Western civilization, in so far as it is permeated with genuine scientific concepts.[29]

The logic of this procedure is plain. Cultural stages are reconstructed by analogy from ontogenetic development and then used to explain ontogeny through the hypothesis of the inheritance of acquired characteristics. A fundamental question remains unanswered, however. Do such cultural stages, either in their succession or in their reputed characterizations, correspond with the known data of human culture history independently arrived at by archeologists and ethnologists? Without this check the reasoning of psychoanalysis seems open to the charge of circularity and accounts of events in the past history of the race assume the nature of "Just So" stories.[30]

At any rate I hope that I have clearly exposed the theoretical framework upon the basis of which phychoanalysts and other exponents of the recapitulation doctrine have instituted comparisons between child mentality and primitive mentality. I should also like to draw attention to the fact that a theory of mind is implied in this recapitulation doctrine.

Thus, mind, whether viewed individually or racially, is primarily, if not solely, a function of organic structure, of inherited dispositions and tendencies.[31] Consequently, experience counts for very little as an important constituent of mind. This view of mind, however, is just what one might expect to be precipitated from the mechanistic-evolutionary intellectual climate of the late nineteenth century reinforced by a preoccupation with such purely biological concepts as instinct, race, and maturation, and with analogies drawn from the realm of biological observation. On the basis of such a theory of mind there is no demand for a closer and more detailed examination of the situational and cultural matrix of human behavior, nor even a serious evaluation of such influences except in a most general way. Environmental forces are primarily stimuli which evoke, or only modify immaterially, developmental trends and patterns that unfold from within the organism itself. They are not basic constituents of mind or behavior.[32]

We can now observe that the theoretical structure of the recapitulation doctrine involves the following points:

1. Thought and behavior in the race and in the individual are primarily a function of biological make-up.

2. Mankind has gone through a succession of cultural stages which are a function of an evolving mentality, biologically based. Therefore, differences in the mentality of human groups are implied. Occidental man represents the apex—biologically, mentally, culturally—of evolutionary development.

3. The occidental child condenses in its early prenatal development a succession of structures originating in remote phylogenetic stages of its prehuman ancestry; in its postnatal development it recapitulates in its thought and behavior patterns characteristic phases of early cultural stages in the history of mankind.

4. The inheritance of acquired characteristics is the means whereby the experience of past generations of individuals is to some degree assimilated to the biological heritage of succeeding generations of individuals.

If this theoretical structure is considered established, we not only have a logical basis for comparing child mentality and savage mentality, we also have an explanation of them. In a sense, no further investigation is needed, except to document the thesis in more detail. In effect this amounts to a purely deductive procedure.

On the other hand, if the theory does not bear examination and is not supported by independent evidence, then any comparison between primitive mentality and child mentality must be undertaken upon some other basis and any similarities that exist need some other explanation. Furthermore, if the theory of recapitulation is fallacious, then deductions with respect to the prehistory of man or the succession of cultural stages in the past cannot be inferred from the thought and behavior of children in occidental culture.

As an illustration of the influence of the recapitulation theory in non-psychoanalytic circles, as well as the manner in which it has been concretely applied to the interpretation of the developmental behavior of children and the culture history of mankind, I wish to discuss the comparisons often made between children's drawings and those of primitive peoples. The reputed parallelisms that have been observed have evoked the interest not only of psychologists and psychoanalysts, but of art historians, anthropologists, educators, and laymen. It is as good an index as can be found to the widespread influence which the recapitulation theory has exerted upon modern thought.

The prehistoric cave art of the Old Stone Age in particular has frequently been selected for comparison with children's drawings. The following quotation from the book of Hilda Eng, *The Psychology of Children's Drawings* (1931), will illustrate the kind of comparison made and the conclusion drawn. The author writes: "Paleolithic art gradually

21

develops from scribbling and formula until it reaches its highest point in the beautiful naturalistic polychrome paintings of the Madeline period. There can be no question that its development is a parallel to the development of children's drawing, such as we see in the typical series of Margaret's drawings which have been given as examples; these also show the development from scribbling and formula to many-colored, comparatively naturalistic drawings. That paleolithic art was more naturalistic from the beginning than children's drawing has nothing to do with the fact of this parallelism. The comparison between children's drawing and paleolithic thus confirms the biogenetic law that the development of the species is reproduced in the child." (Pp. 212-13.)

An examination of the recapitulation theory in the light of such an explicit statement will afford an opportunity to appraise its validity by raising the question whether it does afford a satisfactory explanation of the facts or whether alternative hypotheses do not need consideration.

In making any comparison between the drawings of children and savages on the basis of the biogenetic law, two questions arise:

1. Are there invariant stages of evolutionary development that we can recognize in the graphic art of any particular people or in the art of mankind as a whole?

2. Are there invariant stages in the development of drawing in the untrained child?

To the first question, anthropologists give No as an unequivocal answer. Unilinear evolutionary stages in art have been swept away along with all the other evolutionary stages of cultural development[33] postulated in the theories of the late nineteenth century. Furthermore, the figurative art of the late Paleolithic period, although it is the first art that we have knowledge of in human history, does not appear until the close of the Pleistocene. It cannot be more than 15,000 years old and is probably less, whereas human prehistory goes back to the beginning of the Pleistocene and possibly earlier. In temporal terms this means one-half million to a million years. Consequently the art which has been compared with the drawings of children does not even date from the actual "childhood of the race." Besides this, late Paleolithic art is a highly localized art. There is no reason to believe that even at the period when it appeared it was a style characteristic of humanity at large. Any comparison, therefore, of children's drawings with the art of late Paleolithic man simply narrows down to what is in effect a comparison of children's drawings with the art of one cultural group selected from dozens of other possibilities. Even demonstrable parallelisms can have nothing to do with a biogenetic law and consequently can neither prove nor disprove it.

But what about invariant stages in the drawing behavior of children themselves? It has been repeated again and again that this is an established fact.[34] If it were it would suggest that such behavior is primarily a function of maturation.[35] Cultural background ought to have very little to do with it. The reputed stages of development should hold good under any conditions and we could then speak of the evolution of drawing behavior in *The Child,* and make predictions with respect to the content, technique, and other features of the drawing behavior of any particular child, of known chronological age.

As a matter of fact, predictions on the basis of a purely maturational hypothesis are more than dubious. It has been stated, for example, that in the drawings of children at the younger age levels the human figure predominates. While this holds for American children, Anastasi points out that it is far from being a universal tendency. The generalization only appears to have validity under certain stimulational conditions. "In a study of Swiss children, for example, the human figure occupied a relatively insignificant position, miscellaneous objects and houses heading the list. Representations of people are likewise infrequent or almost completely absent in the drawings by children from several countries."[36] In this connection I might mention the fact that in Paleolithic figure art the human figure is almost totally absent at all stages; animals are everywhere predominant. Eng does not consider this significant, possibly because she recognizes the importance of environmental stimuli despite her assertion that a biogenetic law is operative. But the recognition of social and cultural variables as factors in both Paleolithic art and the drawings of children is just what casts doubt upon the theory that ontogeny necessarily repeats phylogeny.

In the art of contemporary children the occurrence of such wide variations in subject matter even within the sphere of occidental culture itself suggests that there is no sound basis at all for prediction on a maturational hypothesis. We can only conclude, in fact, that in so far as subject matter is concerned, it is more nearly a function of social and cultural conditions than of any determining factors within the organism.

It may be argued, however, that the manner of execution—the stylistic features of drawing, rather than the subject matter, may be a better index to stages of drawing behavior. But according to Anastasi and Foley there seems to be just as much variability in this respect.

If, on the other hand, we abandon the idea that drawing behavior is primarily a function of innate development or is connected in any way with the operation of a biogenetic law, and consider it as a function of observation, experience, and the traditional art style of the cultural group in which the child is raised, I think that we will have a much sounder basis for prediction.

In this way, for example, it would have been possible to predict the results obtained in an investigation of the drawings of a group of 159 Indian children of British Columbia, ages 5-18.[37] They were simply instructed to draw an animal. The animals they drew were (1) those familiar to them by direct observation, (2) those they had seen in books, (3) mythical animals typical of their cultural group. Animals of the last

23

mentioned category were drawn in the highly stylized manner of the adult art of this area. And these stylized drawings were done more frequently by boys than girls. This is culturally correlated with the fact that the characteristic art of this area is only executed by men. The familiar animals chosen were drawn naturalistically.

Anastasi and Foley conclude that "the results of the present investigation corroborate the conclusions reached in the writers' earlier analysis of drawings by children in different cultures. Both the subject matter and the technique of the drawings reflect specific cultural and experimental factors rather than age differences or developmental stages. Any attempt to employ specific features of the child's drawing as an index of developmental level independently of the child's experiential background is doomed to failure. An Indian child of the North Pacific coast, when directed to draw an animal, may produce a symbolical representation rich in stylized details which it would be futile to evaluate in terms of the norms established elsewhere. The fact that in response to the request to draw an animal, some of the children drew mythical creatures is itself significant and quite unlike results which would be obtained under similar conditions with children in our own culture."

On the hypothesis that children's drawings as well as those of primitive peoples are, in part, a function of experiential conditions, it is possible to explain certain *negative* similarities that undoubtedly exist. Lack of perspective is an excellent example.[38] In fact years ago Ernst Grosse,[39] one of the earliest students of the art of primitive peoples, wrote that: "The only real similarity between the art of children and the art of primitive peoples lies in the fact that the latter seem to know as little of perspective as the former."

In Western culture, of course, we know a great deal about the fumbling efforts at perspective that were made in the early Renaissance and the results finally achieved by a serious study of the problem. In the history of painting the absence of perspective is even one of the characteristic features of the so-called "primitives." Consequently, we do not expect children to draw in perspective unless trained to do so. Like primitive peoples they would never learn to do so unless the technical points necessary to this achievement were part of our cultural tradition. The same interpretation applies to the later work of the Paleolithic artists which is undoubtedly the result of an established art tradition and not simply the "expression" of individuals. So far as this phase of Paleolithic art is concerned, it is not comparable with the art of the average child of any age, or with that of the untrained adult of today.[40]

In the light of these facts it is amazing to read in a widely circulated work of the eminent psychologist Karl Bühler[41] (1930) that he believes one of the best sources for investigating prehistory has not been sufficiently recognized. He writes: "This source, I feel convinced, is the mental

24

development of *our* children. We are beginning to see, e.g., in the language and drawing of children, certain fundamental laws of mental progress manifesting themselves quite independently of external influences, laws which, as they govern the evolution of childhood, in like manner presumably governed that of prehistory. Whoever formulates them correctly will be able to render very valuable service to prehistory, or at least to put forward fruitful questions."

Such an inference can only be drawn on the assumption that drawing is primarily a function of innate factors of some sort. Even the emphasis by Bühler upon *our* children, meaning those of Western civilization, is naïve in view of the entirely different results obtained from Northwest Coast Indian children. On the basis of his suggestion which style are we to project upon prehistoric man?

Two recent articles in the *International Journal of Psychoanalysis* are also relevant to our discussion of the recapitulation theory in relation to art.[42] Melanie Klein and others have referred to the "combined parental imago" in early infancy. In Paleolithic art Heilbronner interprets certain forms as representations of the male and female sex organs. Despite the fact that even Heilbronner's interpretation may be questioned, Ernest Jones comments: "It is at all events highly interesting to learn that similar forces were at work among men of the Old Stone Age to those among our young children of the present day—one more example of the resemblance between primeval mentality in phylogenesis and ontogenesis."

Our examination of the recapitulation hypothesis as applied to the drawings of children and savages has exposed two fallacies upon which the theory has been built. First, invariant stages of cultural evolution, denied by the anthropologist, and secondly, reputed stages in children's drawings about which there is more than a serious question. It appears that the comparison of the drawings of children with those of savages has been based upon false assumptions. One conclusion inevitably follows: We have no reason to infer that anything about prehistoric art can be learned from the art of children.

However, the conclusions reached have not been altogether negative. An important positive point has been established: Drawing behavior is to some extent a function of observation, experience, and cultural tradition. This does not mean that it is *solely* a function of these, but it can be positively stated that it cannot be *solely* a function of biological determinants whether in the individual or in the race.[43] This, I think, is the basic fallacy of the recapitulation theory. By stressing organic determinants, either explicitly or implicitly, it has oversimplified a complex problem and even set up barriers to actual investigation by offering a facile explanation.

As a matter of fact, the search for characteristic and invariant stages of development, whether in terms of the history of culture or of the life history of the individual does not offer an approach to genuine dynamic problems at all. For even if there is such a succession, the problem is not solved. What is important throughout is to discover the *conditions* under which, and the *processes* by which, any succession of events takes place. The analogical reasoning of the recapitulation theory does not increase our understanding of actual processes of development in the slightest.

Paradoxically enough, the recapitulation theory itself has by no means proved to be fully acceptable to biologists, especially in its crude form. In fact it is still being debated.[44] One outstanding authority on human embryology and evolution says, for example, "this theory, which, at its inception, was even called a law, can not be taken literally, and is to be applied with great caution. Theoretically, it should be regarded as a working hypothesis and thus as a constant challenge for a possible other, and perhaps more satisfactory, explanation. . . . In the search for causes of ontogenetic changes the writer has always endeavored to look first of all for possible explanations other than those involving any phylogenetic speculations. However, if no direct causation offers itself, one is simply compelled to interpret the change as a phyletic contraction and by this is meant the inherited passing (or sometimes even permanent) reappearance of a condition having existed in ancestral forms at some period of their growth. A great many phenomena of growth could not be understood today without at least this conservative version of the recapitulation theory."[45]

Those who have attempted to extend the recapitulation theory to postnatal periods of human development have proved themselves to be less cautious than the biologists from whom they derived the theory.[46]

If we had time to extend our survey we would find that besides parallelisms between the drawings of children and savages, many other analogies have been pointed out, sometimes without particular stress upon the recapitulation theory. In respect to thinking, for instance, Werner[47] maintains that the child and the primitive, like the psychotic, fail to differentiate clearly between the real world and the world of imagination and fantasy. Werner and others also call attention to magical practices among children[48] that are said to parallel those among savages:[49] Nothing is interpreted as due to "chance,"[50] and so on.

Without going into a detailed discussion of these reputed parallelisms, a preliminary question, crucial to the comparison made, may be asked: Are such generalizations as those cited valid characterizations of the thinking of either of the two groups compared? It is obvious that if we wish to make any fruitful comparison between primitive mentality and child mentality it is necessary that we agree upon the characteristics of primitive mentality, on the one hand, and child mentality, on the other. So far as I am aware, no such agreement has yet been reached.

Outside of anthropological circles, for example, Lévy-Brühl's characterization of primitive mentality[51] has been widely accepted at its face value and analogies found in child mentality. Wallon[52] follows this procedure and so have Ernest Jones[53] and other psychoanalysts. Piaget borrows one of Lévy-Brühl's terms ("participations") and, in general, places child thought on the same level as that of savages.[54]

Among anthropologists generally, however, and particularly among those who have had long and intimate contacts with savage peoples, Lévy-Brühl's generalizations have not been found acceptable. What the French savant calls "pre-logical" or mystical thinking is by no means peculiar to primitives (as Lévy-Brühl himself has admitted[55]), and in so far as this type of thinking does occur it only appears under certain restricted conditions.[56] Furthermore, anthropologists are wont to stress the enormous variability in the cultures of primitive peoples. To group all the aboriginal peoples of the globe together in respect to *any* single category, whether it be the form of their religion, art, economic life, or social organization, is manifestly impossible. How fallacious, then, is the attempt to find a single formula that accurately describes their mode of thought.

If now we turn to the literature of child psychology we discover in the first place that all investigators do not agree with Piaget that children's thinking can be so sharply distinguished from adult modes of thought.[57]

In the second place, the characteristics of child thought that have been compared with those of savages are not accepted as valid by all observers. Susan Issacs, for instance, denies outright what Werner and others have asserted in respect to any confusion of fantasy and reality. She says that beyond the first three years the child very rarely confuses them. "He is almost as well aware as we ourselves of the difference between feeling and wishing, on the one hand, and thought on the other, between imagining the fulfillment of a wish, and actually gaining it. Phantasy may lead him to create a make-believe situation, but he continues to feel reality limiting him in that situation just as clearly as we do. Even while he gives himself up to the complete dramatic realization of a make-believe steamer, he *knows* it is make-believe. He does not believe himself to be 'on a ship' in the same sense in which he *knows* himself to be sitting on a chair."[58] A similar statement, of course, could be made about any flesh and blood savage.

Mrs. Issacs' statement about magical behavior is illuminating also because she is not willing to exploit a facile analogy by the glib use of a term without weighing relevant factors. Consequently she strikes at the very heart of an important qualitative difference between the so-called magical behavior of children and savages in the following passage: "The magic and omnipotence of the child are never crystallized out into organized systems of thought and custom, as the magic and omnipotence of the savage and the peasant are. If the child grows up in a community where magic and 'participations' and 'belief without proof' and 'com-

27

mand without limit' are to a greater or lesser extent fixed and systematized into *beliefs*, then we can say that his *thought* becomes by so much, egocentric and syncretistic. But in the young developing child, we have as yet only egocentric *impulses*, and syncretistic phantasies, which under favorable conditions, become progressively disciplined into relational thought through the impact of actual experience. In the psychoses, again, magical and syncretistic forms of phantasy have become fixed and systematized, and destroyed relational thought. But the young child as such is no more a psychotic than he is a savage. At no point of his mental history is he either of these, any more than he is ever a worm or a fish in the womb."⁵⁹

So far as animatistic thinking is concerned, a point made by Nathan Issacs, and quoted by Mrs. Isaacs, applies equally to savages. He says that we must not confuse the child's belief and his ignorance. "The child doesn't *believe*, for example, that 'everything is alive'; he simply doesn't *know* that everything isn't alive. He simply turns to all kinds of things with the expectations, or the habitual modes of behavior, which he has in fact drawn from his experience of living things. He does not *know* that locomotives don't want biscuits—how should he? He doesn't know this until he offers a biscuit to a locomotive (or things like it), and the locomotive takes no notice whatever, behaving quite differently from his brother or his dog. Then he learns from the breakdown of this habit that there are limits to its applicability; that things like locomotives have to be treated differently from his brother and the dog. It is by an accumulation of experiences of this kind that he learns to distinguish between what is alive and what isn't, what is human and what isn't. They give meaning, at once specifying and limiting, to the notion of aliveness. . . ." Issacs goes on to say that the distinction may remain a blurred one, if it is not explored in actual experience, but that sooner or later the child in a civilized community arrives at a clear-cut distinction between the living and the nonliving. "In a savage community, no such well-defined demarcation may be reached. It is simply a matter of the social interest and social knowledge attached to the distinction, and to the two sides of it."⁶⁰ This is quite true and it is also the point where traditional belief among savages enters the picture. Among the Saulteaux, individuals have been known to talk to stones as if they were alive. But these stones are sacred objects that have been sought out under supernatural guidance. One cannot assume then that to the Saulteaux stones of all kinds are "animate" in the sense that they possess "souls." I once asked an old man whether all stones were alive. He thought a moment and then answered, "No, but some are."

This incident shows very clearly that we must be just as careful not to overgeneralize the animatistic beliefs of the savage as of the child. It is not strange, then, that Piaget's generalizations about magical and "animatistic" explanations of phenomena by the child have not received complete support in the investigations of others. Zeininger, for example, found that "magical thought appears where the evidence of observation and experience is lacking." Within the sphere of their knowledge, observation, and experience, realistic explanations were always given;[61] this may occur at six years, but even at eleven or twelve years children may not give realistic explanations if the subject matter is outside their experience.

I think that it should be clear from this brief discussion that a great deal of preliminary investigation and analysis needs to be done before we shall be in a position to make any fruitful comparisons between child mentality and primitive mentality, to say nothing of explaining them. Analogies, of course, explain nothing unless, as has been pointed out, we simply fall back upon a recapitulation theory, as the psychoanalysts have done.

It also seems evident that the role of experience and the cultural constituents of mentality must be given more weight as contrasted with a view of mind and mental development that evaluates thought and behavior as primarily functions of organically determined factors. "If we stress maturation in mental growth too strongly," writes Mrs. Issacs, "and treat it too readily as a literal organic fact (of the same order as the facts of embryology) we are likely both to overemphasize the difference between children and ourselves, and to underestimate the part played by experience in their development. . . . It would in fact . . . be well if maturation were looked upon as a *limiting concept* . . . and strictly confined to those aspects of growth which *cannot be shown to be a function of experience*. We should be extremely chary of attributing to it any particular ways of behavior which characterize any given children at particular ages, except upon the basis of searching comparative studies of children in the most widely varying circumstances."[62]

It is in connection with controlled observations of this sort that I should like to draw attention to an enormous gap in our knowledge which, if filled, should contribute in the most positive way *both* to our knowledge of child mentality *and* primitive mentality. I refer, of course, to the fact that we know practically nothing about the *children* of savages. If we did have more extensive observations I have no doubt that many of the generalizations in regard to developmental stages, based solely upon observations of children in occidental culture and often interpreted as if such stages were solely a function of maturation, would have to be revised.[63] Mead's data on Samoan girls has already shaken our provincialism with respect to the syndrome of adolescent psychology, once taken to be universal,[64] and it was Mead also who, on the basis of observations made on the children of savage Melanesians, challenged the spontaneous development of animistic thought in children postulated by Piaget.[65] Even Roheim, a psychoanalytical anthropologist, failed to find evidence of a latency period among the natives of Central Australia that he studied.[66]

Investigations such as these, if extended to other problems, should offer genuine control data with reference to observations made upon children in occidental culture alone. And in the second place, the more we find out about the mental development of savage children the better we will be able to understand the conditions which mold the adult mentality of primitive peoples. But in both cases we need as a working hypothesis a theory of mind that gives weight to social and cultural, as well as possible biological variables.

There seems to be little doubt that, in our occidental culture, a contributing factor to the characteristic features of "child mentality" that we have discovered is the positive efforts we make to keep our children childish. In consequence there is a discontinuity in the transition from childhood to responsible adulthood which the individual must overcome and which is a result of cultural conditioning, not ripening maturity. In many primitive societies we find patterns of child training that are more continuous and that do not emphasize so sharply the distinction between child and adult.[67] The psychological effects arising from such differences in cultural emphasis are extremely important for the study of child mentality as well as for an understanding of the conditions under which the mentality of adults is molded.

In the Melanesian society where Margaret Mead made her observations, for example, children are never told that they are "too little." or "too weak" or "not old enough" to do anything. "Each child is encouraged to put forth its maximum efforts, in terms of its individual capacity. . . ."[68] Neither is the child given any but matter-of-fact answers to its inquiries. No Manus mother would tell a child who had spent hours exploring the internal structure of a piano that the sounds were made by little fairies who stood on the wires and sang, as an English mother did. Children likewise acquire sexual knowledge, and even experience, much earlier than they do in our society, so it is not strange to find that Roheim recognizes that in certain respects savages are more grown up than we. In particular he finds the sexual life of the Australians he observed more adequately genital.[69] Among the Saulteaux Indians stork stories such as were once current in our culture would be laughed at by many youngsters as too "childish" for comment.

The popular idea in our culture that folk-tales and myths are somehow a "natural" intellectual fare for young children, and that consequently the savages among whom they originated must be of childlike mentality, is in part due to the lack of a first-hand acquaintance with some of this folk literature. I doubt whether most occidental parents would permit their children to read the unbowdlerized versions of some of the stories that Saulteaux children have been hearing for generations. And I am certain that these myths could not be printed in any magazines or books designed for circulation among children in our culture. For these Saulteaux stories are extremely Rabelaisian, to say the least. Yet they are uncensored for the children. It was not so long ago that it was the custom of some anthropologists when they published the folklore of savages to reproduce the bawdy sections in Latin. Consequently, when these tales were made available to occidental readers, the adult hoi polloi among ourselves were denied ready access to passages a savage child could hear from infancy.

We are thus faced with a paradox. The children of savages are often less childlike in some respects than children in occidental society. Yet when these same children mature, their adult mentality often has been equated with the mentality of occidental children at the earliest levels of development. Perhaps we, too, need to make sure that we are not confusing fantasy and reality!

Chapter 3 - The Rorschach Test in Personality and Culture Studies*

THE USE OF THE RORSCHACH TEST BY ANTHROPOLOGISTS EMERGED IN the course of the development and expansion of a new research area initiated by American anthropologists in the present century. Although initially focused upon investigations of the relations between culture patterns and personality organization among nonliterate peoples, within the past decade essentially the same approach has been used in inquiries concerned with differences in "national character," as represented in the more populous, literate, and complex political units of our contemporary world. Personality and culture studies open up wide vistas of inquiry, once the facts of cultural variability and patterning are linked with our knowledge of the conditions necessary for the development of a personality structure in man, and the determinants relevant to its variability in form and functioning.

Group Membership and Personality Structure.—The link between the psychological data and the cultural data lies in the processes by which, and the specific conditions under which, the human neonate is groomed for adult life and activity. Physical maturation, learning, and the psychological integration of experience through symbolic mediation are processes essential to the acquisition, transmission, and maintenance of what the anthropologist refers to as the culture patterns of a people. The same processes are just as essential for the acquisition of a personality structure by an individual. No individual, whether anthropologically or psychologically viewed, is only human in the generic sense, unless we are content with a level of abstraction that merely emphasizes the lowest common denominator in each case. Every human being undergoes a socialization process that has reference to the beliefs, concepts, values, technological devices, skills, etc. which, in their totality, characterize a distinctive mode of life—a culture. The individual is an integral part of an ongoing sociocultural system that defines his relations to a physical and cosmic environment, as well as patterns and motivates his interpersonal relations with other members of his society. The socialization process, therefore,

*A more extended version of this paper will appear in Bruno Klopfer, and others, *Developments in the Rorschach Technique,* Vol. II: *Fields of Application* (Yonkers-on-Hudson: World Book Co., 1955). The World Book Company has kindly permitted the publication of this paper.

defines the content of the learning process and limits the conditions under which personal adjustments must take place. Whatever degree of individuation or idiosyncracy occurs can emerge only out of the matrix set by the traditional culture. Empirically and concretely, therefore, the question arises whether human beings differ not only as individuals and in sex and age, but likewise with respect to characteristics that are related to their membership in different sociocultural systems, and their position in that system.[1]

Once we view the human situation concretely and in its integral aspects, what we discern is a highly complex network of relations which, however labeled categorically, do not lend themselves to simple abstractions nor to easy manipulation as independent variables. Men live in societies and these groups always have a structure that is definable in terms of the differential roles of participant members; there is undoubtedly a sociological dimension to the human situation. But the participating members of any society would not be prepared to play their typical roles had they not undergone a learning process which, at the same time, was the necessary condition for their characteristic psychological structuralization. Personality structure is a psychological dimension of human societies that is directly relevant to the functioning of a human social order. But we cannot fully understand the motivational patterning and the roles played by individuals without examining the beliefs, goals, and values of their society. This implies another dimension: the meaningful content of the cultural heritage. Consequently, such concepts as culture, personality, and society are not significant with respect to any connotation they may imply as completely independent variables, but rather as convenient constructs, which, for particular types of conceptualization and analysis are useful in making certain kinds of distinctions.[2]

There are, indeed, a few contemporary anthropologists who conceptualize culture as a kind of supra-individual or supra-psychic phenomenon which has a life of its own, as it were, obeys its own laws, and in relation to which the human individual becomes essentially a "carrier" or a "creature" of culture. Culture is given the characteristic attributes of a phenomenal level that is, in effect, sui generis and to this extent extrinsic to the individual.[3] This conception of the nature of culture must be sharply distinguished from the viewpoint of those who have been responsible for the development of personality and culture studies.[4] The latter insist that culture is intrinsic to the psychological functioning of the human being and that the reality of culture must be understood as an aspect of psychological reality and by no means a phenomenon sui generis. This psychological reality of culture is rooted in the fact that, while the attributes of a sociocultural system can be abstracted, described and analyzed in terms that may have no reference to individuals as such, nevertheless, the system itself cannot function, or attain any phenomenal reality whatsoever, except through the social interaction of individuals who have become psychologically structured in a certain way. The concrete locus of the psychological dimension of a culture lies, therefore, in the personality structure of its individuals, and in the organized web of their interpersonal relations which makes a characteristic mode of life a social reality as well. Since, among other things, beliefs and concepts that define a world view—along with notions of the self that orient the individual "subjectively" as well as "objectively" in his actions in a world of values—are inherent in all sociocultural systems, perceptions, motivations, goals, attitudes, and modes of gratification must be organized in terms that are personally meaningful. The human individual would not be prepared for appropriate action unless his culture were actually a part of himself. It is through the learning process, symbolic mediation, and the integration of experience in the course of ontogenetic development that aspects of culture which, from a purely descriptive point of view, may be considered to be "outside" the infant become "interiorized" as an integral part of the personality structure of the adult.[5] It is because of this fact that culture may be said to have psychological reality.

So long as anthropologists were content to handle cultural data in terms of descriptive generalizations and abstractions (or as reducible to traits and complexes whose spatial and temporal relations were of major concern), the psychological reality of culture could be kept in the background, or ignored. Nor could the psychological dimensions of culture emerge as a special problem for investigation. So long as psychologists, too, were content to formulate their problems only in terms of abstracted attributes of the human mind—perception, learning, motivation, etc.— and investigate these segments in the individual without reference to the integrated whole that constitutes the personality, the psychological significance of the fact that human beings are always groomed for action within particular sociocultural systems could not be fully appreciated or investigated. A further consequence was that the psychological field of the individual was oversimplified. Certain determinants of psychological reality were overevaluated since, broadly speaking, only three major categories of determinants were clearly differentiated: (1) the inherent attributes of the human mind responding to (2) arrays of stimuli arising from an outer physical or geographic environment and other human beings, modified to some degree by (3) determinants mediated through learning that gave rise to a limited range of individual differences. The determinants traceable to *group membership* in one sociocultural system, as compared with another, and the differential consequences of this fact, were left out of the picture. Consequently, the psychological depth of determinants of this order, explored at the level of personality structure and personality dynamics, could not emerge as a matter for serious consideration.

Confusion of Culture and Race in Rorschach Testing.—Again it is easy to see how such an oversimplified paradigm could lead directly to an overweighting of reputed biological determinants. If cultural factors as a source of *group* differences are ignored, it is possible to interpret the latter as functions of differential components of the organism itself, since they cannot be accounted for by reference to the generic attributes of the human mind, or to outer stimuli. Thus group differences of a psychological nature may come to be taken as expressions of innate "racial" factors. This kind of interpretation is illustrated in the history of the Rorschach Test. Rorschach himself was apparently convinced that *Erlebnistypen* were, to some extent, if not entirely, determined by biological components.[6]

In 1935 the Bleulers, reporting their Moroccan data, which differed markedly in the psychological picture presented from that familiar in European protocols, invoked a "racial" factor as the ultimate determinant. Although they gave some weight to cultural factors, to them such determinants likewise had an underlying "racial" basis.[7]

While subsequent work with the Rorschach has included subjects of different racial groups in many parts of the world, the chief selective emphasis has been upon cultural rather than racial affiliation. This fact in itself reflects the growing interest in the relation between personality and culture, rather than in factors of a biological nature assumed a priori to be relevant to the study of personality. Nevertheless, there have been a few investigations undertaken where it appears that the choice of subjects was dictated by their "racial" affiliation and the desire to find out whether psychological differences would manifest themselves. Perhaps it will suffice here to raise the question whether, despite the exercise of methodological sophistication and restraint in drawing conclusions, such investigations have demonstrated conclusively that the differential results obtained can be attributed to "racial" factors at all.[8] Either someone should undertake systematic and well-designed investigations in order to demonstrate that the Rorschach Test is, in fact, an instrument capable of differentiating genuine racial components of the personality, or "race" as a possible determinant should be altogether eliminated from Rorschach interpretation as a misleading and confusing artifact.

As early as 1935 F. L. Wells specifically commented upon the inevitability of cultural components in the Rorschach. He says: "Before the age of 'intelligence' tests, Jung perceived the influence on association responses of intellectual background, and at every turn the meaning of Rorschach response is modified by imponderable factors of culture."[9] Instead of being a test that is in any way suited for the exploration of "racial psychology" it now appears, on the contrary, that there is good reason to believe that the Rorschach technique is particularly adapted for the investigation of psychological differences that are *culturally,* as well as personally, constituted. We already have a considerable body of Rorschach data on quite a number of American Indian groups. What is notable are the different personality profiles we get and the fact that these seem to vary regularly with culturally distinctive modes of life.

35

Since the American Indians have been shown to represent a racial unity in so far as the presence of certain genotypical characteristics is concerned,[10] even without going into the issue any further, it would appear to be demonstrated in this case that the kind of group Rorschach results obtained cannot possibly be attributed to any racial factor on a genotypical level. In other words, there is good negative evidence in support of the hypothesis that cultural rather than racial factors may be significant with respect to the observable group differences in Rorschach results.[11]

Behavioral Environment and Personality Structure.—If we adopt the hypothesis that the participation of human beings in different sociocultural systems has consequences that are psychologically significant, then new lines of investigation and new techniques are necessary in order that determinants derived from this variable may be taken into account, along with other components of behavior. Another way to state the problem is in terms of field theory: cultural differences must be taken into account because they are constitutive factors in the total behavioral, or functional, environment of the members of any sociocultural system. Without recognition of this fact, the actual psychological field of the individuals of such a group cannot be adequately defined or understood. (See Chap. 4, "The Self and Its Behavioral Environment.")

The culturally constituted behavioral environment of man is relevant both to the formative stages of personality development as well as to the organization of the total psychological field in which the mature personality functions. If this is so, it follows that the responses of any individual in *any* situation must, in some measure, be relevant to this total field. Even though the individual may manifest what can be recognized as common human traits, on the one hand, or highly idiosyncratic ones, on the other, nevertheless, if membership in a particular sociocultural system has any psychological significance, this fact should be demonstrable in terms of the psychological characteristics that are shared by, and distinctive of, one society or social group as compared with another. These common traits must, in turn, maintain their characteristic stability because they are a function of the "modal" personality structure[12] which underlies the continuity of a sociocultural system in its typical form.[13] Personality is never completely reducible to individuality. A common culture implies, therefore, a common psychological reality, a common way of perceiving and understanding the world, and being motivated to act in it with relation to commonly sensed goals, values, and satisfactions. It is in this sense that culture is intrinsic to the human personality as well as a variable but ubiquitous feature of all the societies of mankind. What we need to investigate, then, are the relations of psychological processes (perceiving, learning, thinking, motivation, etc.) to the differential conditions (cultural, situational) of man's existence in particular times and places, considered with reference to the psychological organization and integration of individuals (personality structure) and personality dynamics.

The constant principles underlying human behavior can only be discovered and thoroughly understood by taking account at the same time of the varying modes of human adjustment and their psychological significance as manifested in different human societies.

Criteria for Personality Tests Useful in Anthropological Research.—
But how are we to go about securing reliable information of a psychological nature that will enable us to compare one group of people with another? Is it satisfactory to rely upon deductions from descriptive cultural facts for information on personality dynamics? How is it possible to make sound generalizations about the personality organization of a whole group of people without adequate samples of the personality structure of a representative number of individuals? Can we obtain a representative sampling by interview methods and autobiographies? How are central tendencies or typical personality constellations to be understood without an empirically established range of variability? And what about patterns of ontogenetic development? Is it possible to use personality tests among primitive peoples that will give valid results? And what kind of tests are available?

Some of these questions, and others, are still under discussion. There is no reason to assume that, from a general methodological point of view, field techniques other than projective techniques are not appropriate to culture and personality studies. Other techniques have been used, but I am not concerned with them here. Once we raise the question, however, of the use of tests it is necessary to recognize that if they are to be employed at all, certain requirements must be met that are not necessarily equivalent to those upon which primary emphasis would be put by specialists in the testing field. Pragmatic considerations alone limit the range of choice. (And I have deliberately omitted any reference to the perennial question of validity and reliability, since debate ranges so hotly on this matter. However, the fact that the clinical validity and pragmatic values of projective tests insure their everyday use in our society makes it seem perfectionistic on the part of any anthropological field worker to insist upon even higher standards before a test is considered appropriate for his purposes.) The following points, I think, sum up the basic requirements of a test that is appropriate for use in culture and personality studies cross-culturally:[14]

It must be a test which is (1) both on theoretical and practical grounds not "culture-bound," and (2) practically adaptable for use among nonliterate peoples. This latter criterion means that the field conditions under which it has to be administered can seldom, if ever, be as rigidly controlled as in a psychological laboratory, or even to the extent that is possible in a clinic. Besides this, it must be possible easily to motivate the responses of any individual and it must be borne in mind that interpreters may have to be used. Yet, at the same time, it must be possible to maintain a sufficiently high level of standardization in administration to make the results obtained from different groups of subjects comparable. In addition, (3) it should be a test that is applicable to children as well as adults, so that information about developmental patterns in the group can be investigated and compared with other groups, and (4) the results must lend themselves to group characterization, as well as provide data on intragroup variation in personality patterns, including the possible identification of psychopathological syndromes. It was such considerations that initially led to experimentation with the Rorschach Test among nonliterate peoples and, since subsequent use appears to have substantiated so many of its assumed potentialities, it is intelligible not only why it was the first projective technique to be tried among such people, but why it has been used more widely than any other.

Cultural Variables, Perception, and the Rorschach.—The rationale of the use of the Rorschach Test in culture and personality studies is likewise becoming clarified on theoretical grounds. Rorschach theory, as well as that underlying other projective tests, has been based on the general assumption, as Macfarlane and Tuddenham have stated it,[15] that "every subject's responses are not the consequence of sheer accident, but are determined by psychological attributes of that subject." On the basis of this assumption no new principle need be introduced if we say that *among* the selective determinants are those derived from the subject's *group-membership* relations, and that such determinants may be thought of as varying from one group to another. Group-membership relations are those which link the subject with other individuals of the same sociocultural system (or subsystem) and, at the same time, distinguish him from individuals of other groups. Components of the personality derived from this source are integral to the responses of the individual in the same way as those that may characterize him at one age level as compared with another, or those that are derived from the influence of unconscious conflicts and repressive mechanisms. It is only by initiating group comparisons, however, that the nature and character of similarities and differences of this order can be identified or defined. Exclusive preoccupation with questions of individual variability within any one sociocultural system can never lead to the formulation of problems that focus attention upon the range and variation of man's psychological adjustment in a comprehensive *human* perspective. Although only a small beginning has been made, this is the basic orientation of personality and culture studies. Historically, it is interesting to note that, despite the fact that the Rorschach Test was originally devised as a clinical instrument for individual diagnosis, the potentialities it appeared to offer for the investigation and comparison of group differences in modal personality structure were among the reasons it attracted the attention of anthropologists.[16]

Furthermore, evidence indicating the extent to which the expression of group membership characteristics is actually *implicit* in Rorschach protocols became apparent in a few scattered comparisons of subjects from different nationality groups in Europe made quite independently of the investigations of anthropologists. Once the fallacious identification of "race" and "nationality" is put aside, such studies can be seen to belong in the same general frame of reference as the personality and culture studies of anthropologists. National differences imply subcultural differences, defined by political affiliation within the larger whole that we speak of as Western culture. The question then is whether there are not psychological correlates that can be formulated as differences in "national character." One example is the comparison of Spanish and English refugee children published by Tulchin and Levy.[17] One of the most striking points stressed by these authors is the *continuity* in the differential patterns that distinguish two groups of children they observed, when compared with previous studies made before the war, by others, of *non*-refugee children of the same national groups. What is the explanation of this continuity? While the authors attribute it to "national and temperamental difference," in the terminology employed here, the observed differences may be a function of cultural variables, being an expression of group membership differences in personality structure.

In other words, *if* it be assumed that personality structure is, in large part, a product of training, experience, and psychological integration that is directly related to the cultural variables that constitute the individual's group-membership situation; and *if* it be assumed that reliable information on personality structure can be inferred from the manner in which the subject responds to the stimuli presented by the Rorschach figures,[18] *then* it must be granted that the data obtained in this way are psychologically significant in relation to the individual's group-membership status and cultural background, as well as to age or sexual differences and whatever peculiar or distinctive idiosyncratic traits may be manifest. For, in terms of personality and culture theory, it is assumed that a human being always thinks, feels, perceives, and acts as a socialized *person* who must inevitably share psychological characteristics with his fellows in order to be capable of interacting *predictably* in interpersonal relations with them in an ongoing sociocultural system. The perceptions of the individual, then, must be anchored in the same meaningful world as theirs or else perception could not function effectively in relation to action. It is in relation to this fundamental fact that Rorschach theory and personality and culture theory approach a common focus. Besides this, the revived interest in the investigation of perception in a more inclusive frame of reference[19] enables us to appraise with greater clarity the psychological consequences of cultural differences and suggests why it is that responses to the ambiguous stimuli of the Rorschach figures, obtained from people with varying cultural backgrounds, are both comparable and diagnostic. Bruner, in fact, has pointed out that "the case can be made that Rorschach implicitly provided the axiom around which the first chapter of a dynamic theory of perception must be built. It is a simple one: 'the principle that every performance of a person is an expression of his whole personality'—perception included."[20]

Recent studies of perception have dealt with the determinative importance of those variables "which derive primarily from the needs, moods, past experience, and memory of the individual," in contrast with "autochthonous" or "structural" factors "derived solely from the nature of the physical stimuli and the neural effects they evoke in the nervous system."[21] The former category of "nonsensory," "functional" or "directive" variables in perception are, of course, precisely those which, in addition to having idiosyncratic aspects, are commonly structured and shared by individuals who have been prepared for action in a psychological field that is rooted in the same culturally constituted behavioral environment. Intervening variables of this common order of experience cannot be completely dissociated from the behavioral environment on the one hand, or, from the modal personality structure of individuals who belong to a particular sociocultural system, on the other. As I have pointed out elsewhere (1951a) we may thus speak of cultural factors in the structuralization of perception, i.e., those that are derived from the fact of group-membership. For if perception be considered in relation to action, the generic function of perception needs to be construed with reference to how the individual is prepared to behave in a world that is ordered, stable and meaningful for him.[22] It can scarcely be maintained that the human being undergoes perceptual adjustment to an abstract world-at-large, or without being influenced in any way by the experience of others. On the contrary, the objects of his world and their properties are those which become ordered and meaningfully defined for him by the kind of discriminations, classifications, concepts, qualities and values that are emphasized by his culture. (See Chap. 4.)

The kind of perceptual problem we have presented to us in the human species, then, is a complex one; but it does not involve a choice between purely psychophysical determinants, on the one hand, and personal or cultural relativism, on the other.[23] Recognition of the influence of cultural factors in perception does not imply that the *human* world of one people is psychologically disparate from and therefore absolutely incomparable with that of another, any more than deeply rooted individualistic factors in perception imply any absolute psychological disparity between one person and another. But what is implied is a system of interdependent relations between learning, the structure and functioning of the human personality and the dynamics of perceiving.[24] Thus perception as a psychological process has a generic aim or function related to what Bartlett long ago referred to as an "effort after meaning"[25] which is integral with the functioning of the human personality everywhere, however the latter may be structurally varied in relation to the meanings defined by different behavioral environments or to personal adjustment.[26]

One of the general propositions we can deduce from these assumptions is that in those instances where stimuli are in any sense ambiguous, the ambiguity will be perceptually resolved in meaningful terms that are related to the object content of the behavioral environment and personal needs of the individual in the situation. In actual life situations this means that individuals with different cultural backgrounds (1) will tend to structure ambiguous stimuli with the same objective properties differently; (2) that the meaningful character of their responses will give us information about the objects of their behavioral environment, and (3) attitudes towards such objects may be revealed. I have illustrated this point elsewhere. (See 1951a.) In one case, marks on a beach, interpreted as the tracks of the Giant Frog, caused a party of Ojibwa Indians to depart at once, although they had expected to camp there for the night. The Giant Frog was a threatening figure in their behavioral environment. In the other instance, an Indian structured auditory stimuli heard when he was alone in the bush as indicating the presence of a cannibal monster (*windigo*), the most threatening figure of all for the Ojibwa. In both cases perceptual cues were the sensible source of the definition of a situation whose meaningful character was a function of the behavioral environment of these Indians, and in terms of which there was a pressing need for flight. Responses in such ambiguous situations serve to highlight concretely the integral relations between perceiving, thinking, feeling, and acting that characterize individuals within the framework of the cultural factors that constitute their behavioral environment.

In the case of the Indian who gave ambiguous auditory stimuli the meaning "windigo," I pointed out, however, that it would be an error to assume any inevitable relationships of a deterministic order between beliefs about the existence of cannibal monsters shared by Adam with other Indians of his culture, and the attribution by him of a meaningful content to a set of ambiguous stimuli in the concrete situation described. All that can be predicted on the basis of a knowledge of the culture is that, given a belief in cannibal monsters as fearful objects in the behavioral environment, *some* Indians will, on particular occasions, respond to ambiguous stimuli as *windigowak* rather than Jabberwock. That is to say, in addition to cultural factors that may enter the situation as selective determinants, idiosyncratic factors must be recognized as well. In the case of Adam I suggested what these probably were, and also pointed to his test performance:

[In] Adam's Rorschach record . . . out of a total of thirteen responses he gave a whole answer to each card. This was always his first answer and he responded with considerable rapidity. Furthermore, in this immediate interpretation of each successive blot as a whole Adam was almost unique in my series. And when I add that his wholes were not particularly good ones, I believe that the relevance of his Rorschach performance to his responses in the situation narrated is even more fully evident. His rapid but not too accurate structuralization of an ambiguous situation gave free play to the influence of traditional belief as well as personal determinants.

41

Consequently, there appears to be clear evidence in this case of a direct analogy between the subject's response to a life situation and his performance in the Rorschach situation. As Fearing emphatically states it,

. . . organizing and structuring processes correlated with the attitude and need structure of the individual operate in *all* stimulus situations. In the case of those situations which are designedly ambiguous (the Rorschach cards might be an example) these factors have a maximal effect. At the other extreme, there would be situations, the objective properties of which would be such as to minimize, but not wholly obliterate their effect . . . it is necessary to postulate some system of needs with which the cognitive processes of the individual in the group may be correlated. *The need for meaning* is a basic construct in this connection. It refers to the need to structure cognitively a given situation so that the individual may come to terms with it.[27]

It is this "need for meaning" when considered integrally with the functioning of perception as an "instrumental activity" that is taken for granted when the assumption is made that subjects presented with a series of ink-blots can, rather simply, be motivated to resolve ambiguous forms into perceptually meaningful objects and relations. Rorschach himself noted that often subjects were astonished to find that other persons did not "see" the same thing they did. In the same way my Indian friends would have been astonished if anyone had not identified the marks on the beach as the tracks of the Great Frog, and no other animal. It seems to me that it has not been sufficiently emphasized that in the thousands of responses now on record from subjects with varying cultural backgrounds that we have empirical support for the theory that perception always involves an "effort after meaning," as well as a demonstration that the Rorschach Test is based upon a perceptual principle that is in no way culture-bound. Personally, I can recall a time when many of my anthropological colleagues expressed skepticism on just this point without, of course, taking perceptual theory into account: Could responses be obtained from people with *any* cultural background and experience?

The Universal Applicability of the Rorschach.—A specific illustration of the kind of question that arose in the minds of anthropologists was whether the production of responses to the ink-blots would not be greatly limited, or facilitated, according to the degree to which the subjects were familiar with some pictorial form of art either in their own culture or through contact with some other culture. Thus, one colleague who gave the Rorschach a trial, but without success, wrote me (1938), "They have no graphic art; a picture doesn't mean a thing to them," but then added the dubious psychological statement, "[They] just seem to be without imagination." Jules Henry, one of the pioneers in the use of the Rorschach among nonliterate peoples, was much concerned about the same problem. "Since ink-blots and even pictures were strange to the Pilaga," he writes, "they had to be prepared for the test over a period of months by being shown as many pictures as possible. They were also given the opportunity to see trial blots and experiment with interpreting them."[28] The assumption that the best orientation to the blots is by a picture analogy is illustrated in a recent investigation of a group of Canadian preschool children.[29] The instructions given followed those of the Brush Foundation except for the fact that the word *picture* was substituted for *design,* as it was thought that it would be more intelligible to most of the children. In other words, since most children in our culture are deluged with pictures, the picture analogy appears obvious, or even necessary, as a means of orientation to the blots.

Although the northern Ojibwa subjects that I began to test in the summer of 1938 were adults, and I knew that most of them were at least superficially familiar with pictures, I determined to make use of a trial blot as a matter of standard procedure. My initial instructions included the statement: "I am going to show you some cards, one after another. These cards have *marks* on them, something like you see on this paper." The Ojibwa term that I have translated "marks" was deliberately chosen because it *did not* have the connotation "picture." I thought it might confuse the subjects if they thought the blots were some new-fangled, strange, and confusing "pictures" of the white man, and what they were expected to do was to figure out what was "there." But I soon found that the trial blot was unnecessary and abandoned it. And I have not heard of anyone who has made a systematic use of a trial blot in collecting the hundreds of protocols from nonliterate subjects that have accumulated in subsequent years. On the other hand, I later found a trial blot useful in testing children, especially those at the youngest age levels. If I had used it more systematically from the first, I feel sure that the high percentage of rejections of Card I by children 6-9 years of age would not have occurred.[30]

Thus, while there are many problems that may arise in the use of the Rorschach in the field among nonliterate groups, I believe that most of them are of an administrative nature. We may assume that the task can be performed if it is understood and sufficiently motivated. But problems of this order must not be confused with the nature and potentialities of the Rorschach technique itself. The possibilities of the latter cannot be fully realized or appraised unless problems of administration are solved. But we must be aware, of course, of what these problems are. Strangely enough, there are no discussions of administrative problems in print by anthropologists who have used the test nor, to my knowledge, have such individuals ever met in conference to compare notes on this score.[31] Nevertheless, the futility of a priori judgments on points such as those referred to above is illustrated by the experience of Melford Spiro in Micronesia (1947). Despite the fact that the people of the tiny coral atoll of Ifaluk have no pictorial art in their own culture, and were besides unfamiliar with pictures in the Euro-American sense, his subjects had no difficulty whatever in giving meaning to the Rorschach blots. On the other hand, when the same subjects were presented with a series of *actual* pictures, paralleling the standard TAT set, but rendered in the form of line drawings and specially prepared for use among the peoples of Micronesia, certain problems did arise.[32]

Thus the Rorschach blots do not have to be seen as *analogous* to "pictures." If this were true, in a literal sense, then the presence or absence of a pictorial graphic art in the previous experience of the subjects might be relevant. But this is not a prerequisite. People can see the blots or parts of them as "like" something, or they can see something "there," once they are oriented to the task and sufficiently motivated to make an "effort after meaning" in response to the kind of stimuli confronting them. Anna Hartoch Schachtel and the Henrys make the acute observation that

Pilaga children see in the Rorschach plates an immediate picture of their objective world. They look for an exact copy of reality, as if they were looking through the wrong end of a telescope; they look for actual forms, and for the positions which the forms of animals or the body assumes. *What they see is real to them.* With us, both children and adults say of the plates, "This looks *like*," or "this looks *as if*." For the most part we are aware of the fact that we are interpreting the picture and are abstracted from the object perceived. Pilaga children do not have this feeling about the plates. They say "it *is*."[33]

The situation that confronts the subject when presented with the standard TAT cards, or their equivalent, is perceptually distinct. In our culture we are so familiar with various kinds of graphic symbolization that we can usually identify objects without hesitation, even though color may be completely abstracted and other natural perceptual qualities only represented in a highly conventionalized form. Certainly line drawings involve a fairly high degree of abstraction and conventionalization. In using the TAT it is ordinarily assumed that the subject is able to identify various classes of objects which are represented in a graphic form. Most of them are not intended to be ambiguous. The subject makes his identifications and goes ahead with his story. In contrast to the Rorschach situation, therefore, one might suppose that familiarity with pictures would be a sine qua non for the interpretation of TAT cards. What is of particular interest then is that most Ifaluk subjects, despite their lack of experience with pictures, were able to identify *correctly* almost all of the object content of the line drawings of the TAT cards.[34]

The special difficulties they encountered are particularly instructive because they point to basic aspects of the functioning of human perception in relation to experience as well as man's generic potentialities for responding to symbolic forms. Concretely, the perceptual difficulties these subjects experienced may be exemplified as follows: (a) In two cards (6 and 18) they could not identify any of the objects represented; these pictures were completely unmeaningful; (b) in certain other cards they failed to identify certain objects, e.g., the depiction of a fire by a few lines indicating pieces of wood and ascending smoke (card 8), and simple lines with no shading representing the trunks of trees; (c) human figures, on the other hand, were identified easily but clues to sexual differences seemed to depend on clothing; (d) perspective was not grasped by the subjects in all instances. Objects drawn above one another were seen as being above one another and not in spatially receding planes. A canoe, represented by the artist as being *in* a native canoe house, was seen as being *carried* by men standing in the foreground *outside* the house. In short, the difficulties that had to be overcome in interpreting these pictures appear to be precisely those which would offer *no* difficulties to subjects familiar with the conventions of graphic symbolization in our Western art tradition. This deduction is empirically supported by the fact that in parts of Micronesia where considerable acculturation has taken place, including acquaintance with pictures, subjects exhibited very few of the special perceptual difficulties of the people of Ifaluk. This is illustrated by an examination, for instance, of seventeen protocols collected by James L. Lewis[35] during his stay in Kusaie. Here the natives had been converted by American missionaries in the nineteenth century; they had even become Sabbatarians and celebrated the fourth of July. These subjects gave responses to Cards 6 and 18, although a few vocalized their initial difficulty with the latter. The fire was identified in Card 8, and in only a single instance were the men seen carrying the canoe in Card 3. On the other hand, although the people on Card 15 were identified and talked about, the trees were omitted in practically all instances. What is so remarkable then is the actual success with which the Ifaluk subjects in their "effort after meaning" transcend their culturally rooted limitations. This fact, along with the relative ease with which they informed the Rorschach blots with meaning, disposes, I think, of any a priori judgments in regard to the use of projective techniques among nonliterate peoples deduced from the presence or absence of particular culture traits, such as some form of graphic art. So far as the Rorschach is concerned, the raw data necessary for interpretation can be elicited because a universal function of human perception is exploited.

Comparative Productivity in Different Cultures.—This hypothesis receives support from the empirical data on the actual productivity of subjects drawn from peoples with varying cultural backgrounds from many parts of the world. Such data were not available even a few years ago. When I referred to this matter in 1945 I had to rely exclusively on the figures available for a few Alorese subjects[36] and the Ojibwa Indians. Turning to published and unpublished information, we find that our data have increased many fold. As a sample of the material now extant from additional American Indian groups and peoples in the Pacific, I have compiled the figures found in Table 1, in which 1676 subjects are represented. By way of comparison with American whites, for whom we likewise have some fresh information, I have included the Spiegel sample of adults, Gardner's nurses, and a calculation based on the Ames sample of American children. The figure refers only to subjects 6-10 years of age for purposes of a better comparison with the means for child subjects in other than white American groups.

TABLE 1.—MEAN PRODUCTIVITY OF SELECTED GROUPS

PLACE	GROUPS*	SOURCE	NUMBER OF SUBJECTS	MEAN RESPONSES
United States	Spiegel Sample: Adult whites	Beck, Rabin, et al	157	32.65 (SD. 14.05)
	Gardner Nurses: Adult whites	Gardner	100	22.0
	Ames Sample: White children (6-10)	Ames, et al	235	16.9
	White children (Chicago)	Thetford, Molish, Beck	155	27.16 (SD. 14.05)
	Tuscarora Indians (Iroquois): Adults	Wallace	69	27.9
Canada	Ojibwa (Berens River): Adults	Hallowell	102	27.0
	Children		49	18.3
	Kaska (B.C., Yukon Territory): Adults	Honigmann	19	22.15
	Children		9	15.5
	Micmac (Cape Breton Island): Adults	Steen	72	14.6
Mexico	Tepoztlan: Adults	Lewis	42	16.2
	Adolescents		25	16.8
	Children (5-12)		39	18.7
Guatemala	San Luis Jilotepeque:	Billig, Gillis, Davidson		
	Male Ladinos (11-75)		31	12.5
	Male Mayan Indians (10-78)		36	11.0
Polynesia	Samoan Males (16-27)	Cook	50	29.0
	Cook Is. (Aitutaki) Children (7-15)	Beaglehole	88	23.0
Micronesia	Saipan:			
	Chamorro: Adults	Joseph and Murray	30	23.1
	Children		100	13.6
	Carolinian Children		100	12.7
	Ifaluk: Adults	Spiro	110	14.1
	Children		41	13.9
Dutch East Indies	Alor: Adult Males	Dubois	17	29.1

*Unless otherwise specified both male and female subjects are included.

If Table 1 be examined with Beck's criteria[37] of *Medium* (20-30 responses), *High* (35 and up), and *Low* (15 or less) productivity in mind, it will be seen at once that not even American adult subjects *average High*. It is likewise interesting that in only four of the non-American groups do adult subjects produce an average of less than 15 *R*. And it seems quite likely that the productivity of the adult subjects in widely separated regions of the world and with diverse cultural backgrounds is in the *Medium* category for the most part. It will be noted, furthermore, that most of the mean figures for the groups represented fall within the range defined for American adults by the Spiegel sample, on the one hand, and Gardner's nurses, on the other.

How far variations in productivity may be a function of test administration, or of cultural values related to motivation in the test situation, or of personal adjustment at different acculturation levels, remains to be investigated. While the Ladinos and the Guatemalans of San Jilotepeque rate low, the Mexican Indians of Tepoztlan were more productive. "Among our adults," write Abel and Calabresi,[38] ". . . 15 out of 42, or roughly one-third, gave 20 or more responses . . . ." And in connection with this comparison, it is interesting to note that the subjects of Ifaluk, an isolated group of Micronesians almost completely unacculturated, were more productive than the Guatemalans. In the case of the Ojibwa, the average *R* for 115 adult subjects of both sexes at Lac du Flambeau (Wisconsin) was 17, as compared with 27 in the less acculturated Berens River Ojibwa, reported in Table 1. (See chap. 18.) Since the Ojibwa represent an instance in which there is evidence that the acculturation process, as shown in the Lac du Flambeau sample, has resulted in a great deal of psychological maladjustment, the correlation of relatively low productivity with this known fact suggests a relation between productivity, considered as a group phenomena, and a general level of sociopsychological adjustment. This hypothesis needs testing, of course, but Spindler's study of the Menomini Indians is extremely pertinent in this connection. He used objective criteria as a means of systematically discriminating the acculturational status of five different groups of individuals and then obtained a Rorschach sample of each group.[39] The most highly acculturated group of Indians on the reservation—the elite in socio-economic terms—were the most productive (average 27 *R*). They were also the best adjusted group of Indians. On the other hand, the least acculturated Menomini were the least productive (average 16.5 *R*). The other groups ranged in between. Although it would be a misleading oversimplification to assert that all these Indians except the elite group are as disturbed as the Flambeau Ojibwa, it is my impression, nevertheless, that the general level of psychological functioning they represent *is* lower than that of the Berens River Ojibwa. It is this Northern Ojibwa group, moreover, which was as productive as the elite Menomini. Why? Possibly because in both cases despite differences in acculturation level, the social-cultural conditions requisite for the emergence of a relatively healthy level of personality functioning were present. I only mention these facts in order to pose a problem, not to offer a solution. But it does seem that the average number of R for various groups may be psychologically significant and that they may offer clues that deserve more careful investigation.

Despite the low mean productivity in a few groups we now have unequivocal evidence that lack of productivity is no bar to the cross-cultural use of the RorschachTest. What is equally impressive is the fact that this statement needs no qualification with respect to child subjects even at lower age levels. I found, for instance, that despite the fact that my series of 25 Berens River children (6-10 years) showed a much higher percentage of card rejection than the American children of comparable age in the Ames sample, nevertheless the mean R for the Ojibwa children was 17.7 as compared to 16.9 in the latter group.

A special point of general interest is brought to a new focus in the tabulation. As Ames and her collaborators point out in their review of the Rorschach literature on children's responses: "Despite wide variation in reported N for the different studies, the general trend with increasing age is definitely an upward one.."[40] This implies, of course, that the productivity of adults may be expected to be greater than that of children. The samples of American adults and children published by Beck and his associates offer a specific illustration. This differential productivity is precisely what we also find in four out of the five groups in Table 1 where this information is recorded for people with other cultural patterns. Since these groups include two samples from Micronesia, on the one hand, and two American Indian groups with different cultural backgrounds, on the other, a much broader base is established for the general hypothesis derived from Rorschach data on children in Western culture only, that productivity increases with maturation. On the other hand, the Tepoztlan figures provide an outstanding exception.

Content Categories in Cross-cultural Perspective.—The more crucial questions that arise in any cross-cultural use of the Rorschach Test turn on the comparability of *what* is seen and *how* it is seen by different peoples, whether the responses have the same psychological significance everywhere, and especially, the validity of group differences as an index to culturally determined differences in "modal" personality structure— the "communal" aspects of personality, or however it be phrased.

It seems to me that it is not only possible for human beings to "see" the blots as meaningful objects but that *what* is seen is comparable in a *human* as well as a cultural and idiosyncratic sense. In the first place, the variations in the responses obtained are customarily ordered for analysis and comparison relative to the limits set by the objective attributes of the figures, on the one hand, and general content categories, on the other. The objects named are seen on the Rorschach cards in a particular locality, with reference to qualitative features of the blots, and so on, and, at the same time, they can be classified in a limited range of categories. Since the content categories now in use are at a fairly high level of generality—human beings, animals, nature, objects, etc.—with some possible elaboration they can be adapted for transcultural coverage. A much more important point, however, regarding the comparability of content categories is suggested by certain empirical data that have emerged from the cross-cultural application of the Rorschach. It has long been emphasized that most responses of both children and adults fall into only two major categories[41]—Animal $(A+Ad)$ and Human $(H+Hd)$. Klopfer says,[42] e.g., that "at least three-fourths of the responses of most subjects deal with human beings and animals, the number of categories in which the other responses could be designated is small." It has been observed, furthermore, that the proportionate number of R within these two categories, in the case of normal subjects, has a characteristic range: 10-15 H per cent, 35-50 A per cent.[43] A limited amount of cross-cultural data on the mean incidence of these two categories in different groups of subjects naturally raises some interesting questions: Do such categories maintain any constancy when such comparisons are made? What kind of variations occur?

In Table 2 information is tabulated from two widely separated geographical regions of the world—North American and Micronesia—where data are available on six groups of native peoples. Fortunately, we have some information on children, as well as the adults, in both regions. For this reason, I have included a calculation made from the Ames sample of American children, limited, however, to subjects 6-10 years of age.

TABLE 2.—MEAN PROPORTION OF HUMAN AND ANIMAL RESPONSES
IN SELECTED GROUPS

PLACE	GROUPS*	SOURCE	% H + Hd	% A + Ad	% TOTAL
Micronesia	Saipan:				
	Chamorro: Adults	Joseph and Murray	23.7	48.1	71.8
	Children		19.7	49.3	69.0
	Carolinian children		20.7	45.2	65.9
	Ifaluk: Adults	Spiro	9.0	18.7	27.7
	Children		8.0	17.3	25.3
North America (Canada)	Ojibwa (Berens River): Adults	Hallowell	29.0	48.0	77.0
	Children		24.0	52.0	76.0
	Micmac (Cape Breton Is.): Adults	Steen	12.0	74.0	86.0
	Kaska (B.C., Yukon Territory): Adults	Honigmann	16.0	62.0	78.0
	Children		18.0	50.0	68.0
United States	American children (6-10 years)	Ames, et al	14.8	46.4	61.2
	American children (6-17 years)	Thetford, Molish, Beck	...	47.95	...

*Both male and female subjects included in all cases.

It will be seen at once, that in all groups except the Ifaluk: (1) a large majority of all responses fall into the $H + A$ category; (2) that this holds for children as well as adults; (3) that the proportion $H : A$ shows some constancy, despite variations from group to group, such as the very high A per cent in the American Indian groups reported and what appears to be a higher proportion of $H + Hd$ responses in some groups, than is expected of subjects in our culture.

The constancy of such predominant content categories not only lends empirical support to the comparability of Rorschach responses cross-culturally; at the same time one cannot escape the implication that this must reflect some common psychological characteristic of the dynamics of human adjustment. And, if we ask: What are the most significant classes of objects with which human beings everywhere interact, I believe it must be replied: human or human-like, or animal or animal-like beings. Certainly the most active and vital orders of being in the behavioral environment of man are of the human-animal order, even though the line between the two may not be drawn on the same grounds in all cultures, as in those, for instance, where metamorphosis is considered a possibility. However this may be, it seems to me that the predominance of the $H+A$ category can be no accident. If it can be assumed that the major content of the Rorschach Test reflects the modes of responses to the most vital objects of the human behavioral environment everywhere, this in itself is a psychological fact of importance in relation to which variations, patterns, and qualitative differences in such responses should be of interpretative significance on a comparative basis.

Variability in object content involves selective factors, of course, which are assumed to be psychologically significant with reference to the personal experience and psychological structure of the subject. But it is taken for granted in using the Rorschach in our society that the concrete objects, relations, and events perceived by the subject are drawn from a large pool of objects and events that are more or less familiar in the experience or imagination of everyone. Consequently, it need hardly be argued that when we move from one people to another the responses of individuals with different cultural backgrounds may be expected to refer to the specific object content of their behavioral environment considered as a whole, aside from individual peculiarities. Of greater importance is the fact that the qualities attributed to objects, their utilitarian or esthetic values and their culturally defined association, must be thoroughly understood. A number of years ago Jules Henry, in preparation for the interpretation of Rorschach protocols obtained from the Pilaga, prepared a tabulation of the flora and fauna known to these people. He annotated each item according to its utility value in the culture, e.g., as food—whether if eaten it was thought to cause harm, or was considered a delicacy, etc. Other annotations referred to the attitude of the people toward animals—whether an animal was feared or thought

51

ridiculous, whether it played a prominent role in mythology, or whether its name could be used as an insulting epithet, and whether it had strong associations with sexual activity.[44]

In human perspective, therefore, (1) object content in the Rorschach will vary with group-membership as well as individually, and (2) the limits of any individual's choice will necessarily bear some relation to the range, nature, valence, and qualities of the objects defined by his culture. In other words, the behavioral environment of the subject must be understood in detail if the full psychological relevance of selective factors of a cultural order are to be appraised. The negative aspects of the problem are relatively simple: animals unknown in the behavioral environment cannot be represented in the responses; neither can unfamiliar reified beings. And without the presence of x-ray photographs or topographical maps in a culture, Klopfer's k response cannot be given in terms of these particular contents. If the intellectualization of anxiety is to be inferred from a record the cue must be derived from some other content that is meaningful to the subject. While no dogmatic conclusions should be drawn, the remarkably low A per cent of the people of Ifaluk requires comment here. In this case, it may very well be that the complete absence of any wild mammalian fauna on the atoll is of determinative importance. The only mammals known to them are the domestic dog and the pig. The predominant fauna known are fish, some insects, many kinds of lizards and a few birds. It is important to note, however, that their largest content category is "nature," comprised of natural objects other than animals.

The positive side of the matter is much more complex. Klopfer points out,[45] for example, that " . . . it happens surprisingly rarely that the professional background determines the choice of content to any extent, and when it does happen it usually indicates that the subject is clinging to his professional interests as a support for his personal insecurity." There are selective factors at work in the choice of object content that do not permit us to infer a simple one-to-one correspondence between perceptual experience in life activities and the content of responses to the Rorschach figures. It is the inferred presence of these personable variables, in other words, that makes the occurrence of anatomy responses of psychological significance, rather than professional training or experience. The same principle, I think, can be applied to the cultural aspects of the behavioral environment of groups of individuals. When I was planning my initial use of the Rorschach among the Northern Ojibwa I drew up a prospectus (1941c). At that time I thought that their A per cent might turn out to be a function of the fact that they were "professionally" a hunting people. Actual investigation proved that this was not the case, and we now know that nonhunting peoples, like ourselves or the people of Saipan, have a comparable A per cent in relation to H per cent. In effect, this is the question that Dennis raises, without offering any solution. Referring to my own material, he writes: "The recognition, on the part of the Saulteaux [Ojibwa], of Rorschach cards as figures previously seen only in dreams is in line with the importance given to dream experiences among these people . . . in other words, it seems probable that many of the Rorschach peculiarities of a given group could be accounted for in terms of the usual experiences common to that group."[46] Although I did not give the actual figures in the published articles to which he refers, the fact is that only 2 per cent of the 3684 responses (adults and children) can be thus classified. Dream experiences, even though so highly evaluated and reflected upon by these Indians, did not result in the *reporting* of dream images "seen" in the blots by most subjects. The Ojibwa do not ordinarily talk about their dreams. Such events are considered by them to be actual experiences of the self in interaction with superhuman beings (*pawáganak*) in the behavioral environment who bestow power, which may be lost if referred to lightly, or casually, or in a "profane" situation. Consequently, I did not expect to find dream images elicited by the Rorschach figures. Although one man did remark that he saw "some things" that he could not mention, I have no way of knowing, in general, to what extent dream images were perceived, but not verbally reported. This situation, however, serves to illustrate the importance of giving consideration to any cultural factors related to motivations that lead to the suppression of perceived content in a verbalized form. A broad analogy in our culture would be the perception of, but hesitancy in verbalizing, sexual content. The mean number of sexual responses in the Spiegel sample was 0.03.[47] Among the Ojibwa I originally expected a much freer verbalization of sexual content than actually occurred. This opinion was based on impressionistic observations of conversational freedom in so far as sexual matters were concerned, and certain episodes in mythology and folklore. But anatomy and sexual responses together only amounted to 0.01 per cent of the responses of adults. Without attempting any overall explanation, further reflection on this point leads me to believe that a more detailed and systematic analysis would show that sexual references among the Ojibwa are, in fact, highly channeled in conversation. Only when the individuals involved are in certain definable kinship relations (i.e., cross-cousins of opposite sex) is any freedom permitted. Theoretically, at least, the person administering the Rorschach in this society would have to be in the proper relationship to the subject in order that any sexual references might be freely expressed. It is no simple matter to relate the behavioral facts of daily life to Rorschach responses in a manner that has genuine psychological meaning.

On the whole, I believe it is reasonable to assume that the full significance of *what* is "seen" and reported by any subject cannot be accounted for without taking into consideration the total psychological field that is constituted for him and his fellows as members of an ongoing sociocultural system. At the same time, knowledge of and experience in any behavioral environment, or a segment of it, does not fully account for, or alone determine, the content of an individual protocol. In principle, such considerations are in harmony with Rorschach theory, in so far as the assumption is made that *all* responses involve selective factors that must have reference to the personality viewed as a functioning whole. If personality is conceived as a product of a socialization process in which differential cultural factors are an inherent and necessary part, there can be no conflict between Rorschach theory and personality and culture theory. In fact, the considerations mentioned above only serve to emphasize the paramount importance of personality structure as the focus of selective factors that involve integral relations between culture and personality in all perceptual experience.

To ignore the influence of these complex intervening variables is to oversimplify the relation between experience and perception, not only with reference to what is "seen" in the ink-blots, but to the interdependence in life situations of culturally constituted values, perceptions, motivations, and affective responses of the individual. Thus, even at a superficial level of analysis, inhibited verbalization of any kind of content in the Rorschach may be taken as a direct clue to certain aspects of the relations between the value system of a culture and the circumstances under which anxiety or other affective responses may be aroused in the individuals of that culture.

M Responses and Affective Values.—It has become increasingly apparent in the use of the Rorschach Test that the affective value, as well as the cognitive aspects, of the content, offers interpretative possibilities, although Rorschach himself did not develop this feature of the test.[48] While it is true that when hesitancy or avoidance in naming content becomes apparent we have direct behavioral clues to the affective value of particular kinds of content, it is "on the assumption," as DeVos phrases it, "that underlying tensions in the affective structure of an individual determine the affective value of a percept as well as its more formal characteristics,"[49] that a wider, deeper, and more systematic basis for interpretation is possible. And it seems to me that the psychological implications of this aspect of content may be fruitfully explored in inter-group as well as inter-individual differences. Abel and Hsu in their study of Chinese in America point out, for example, that "the ways in which human beings are imagined and perceived in the blots, that is, the kinds of human beings they are and, more particularly, the ways in which they appear to be acting or behaving, especially when two figures are seen opposite each other, give us some insight into the ways in which the subject taking the test conceives of other people in relation to himself, how he feels towards others and or how he considers other people's reaction to him. Attitudes of hostility, friendliness, wariness, fear, dependency, may be expressed by projecting such attitudes into perceived blot figures."[50] Their subjects were (1) China-born males, (2) China-born females, (3) American-born (Chinese) males and (4) females of the same category. It was found that "it is in the kinds of human beings perceived and in the manner in which these people are described that we obtain the clearest picture of differences in our four groups." There was a particultrly striking contrast between China-born and American-born females. In the M responses of the former there is not a single instance of two human beings "attacking or moving aggressively against one another." In the latter groups there are 25 per cent of the M responses "where aggression or fear of aggression is expressed or at least indicated, either through attack, implied threat, or through an authoritarian evil figure." The authors point out that,

The aberrant position in Chinese culture is to express hostility, while in the United States it is deviant for a male, and to some extent for a female, at least an adolescent one, not to show some outwardly aggressive behavior. "Acting polite," "to think and look" fit into rules of proper conduct as envisaged by Chinese culture. Thus, it is the American-born Chinese girls who approach to a greater degree the accepted American pattern than do the American-born Chinese males. But in so doing they seem to have conflict. . . .

A preliminary analysis of the M responses of my Northern Ojibwa (Berens River Saulteaux) subjects indicate an overwhelming incidence of people sitting, standing, lying down, watching, for the most part without reference to any kind of social interaction whatsoever. In the Inland group (the most aboriginal in culture) 82.3 per cent of the M's of adult subjects exhibit this characteristic content, the figure for the people of the Lakeside band (the more acculturated group) being somewhat less, 72.5 per cent. For the children, it is the same, the response given by one child—"two men trying to rob each other"—being unique. If one were to venture the prediction from these Rorschach data that the typical personality structure of these Ojibwa is one which involved the suppression of aggressive impulses and that to express them probably leads to considerable anxiety, this would be quite correct. Any expression of overt hostility is not only discouraged by their culture but does not in fact occur, except in cases of drunkenness. (See chapters 6 and 15.) On the surface, these people present a picture of amiability and placidity. None the less, aggressive impulses do find expression—covertly. One mode of expression is malicious gossip. The other major mode is sorcery. There is a latent wariness, therefore, that lurks behind their sitting, lying, standing, and watching. Anxiety tends to color interpersonal relations—especially between men—since some overt act may be *interpreted* as hostile and lead to retaliation through sorcery. It can hardly be expected, then, that these people would give a human content to the ink-blots characterized by highly active or aggressive human figures in any involved relations with each other. But what is "seen" reflects quite accurately qualitative and affective aspects of interpersonal relations, not just as observed, but as sensed.

These examples are sufficient to indicate in a preliminary way some interesting possibilities that suggest themselves when the content of Rorschach responses is pressed beyond the purely cognitive level and when group characteristics are made the focal point of inquiry. It may be added that any direct symbolic interpretation along Freudian lines, without detailed reference to the cultural setting, would be hazardous at this point even though it seems likely that there may be universal symbols that are functionally related to recurrent interpersonal situations and the operation of the same unconscious mechanisms in all mankind. Since Klopfer has advised caution in the interpretation of the content of the protocols of individuals in our culture in these terms, this caution should be redoubled when the records of persons with a different culture background are under consideration.[51]

Popular Responses in Cross-cultural Perspective.—An aspect of the content of responses that comes into immediate prominence in any cross-cultural application of the test is the scoring of P and O answers. Unlike M and C responses, "Populars" and "Originals" cannot have comparable significance for interpretation unless they actually represent what their symbolization implies—recurrence, on the one hand, and unusualness of responses to certain areas of the cards, on the other; a criterion of frequency is necessary, no matter what other criteria may be used.[52] Although it is an elementary point, the possibility of distinguishing P and O responses is based upon the expectation that in *any* group of subjects responses essentially similar in content will be given to the same parts of the blots by many subjects, whereas other responses, even if recurrent, will be much less frequently given and still others will be so very unusual that they will occur not more than one in a hundred times (the usual frequency definition of O). Thus, we can expect the same kind of distribution in other cultures as in our own, although the empirical data have only been worked out in detail in one instance.[53]

The diagnostic significance of P has been characterized in various ways: "intellectual adaptation to collective thinking," "the subject's participation in 'collective thought,' " "cooperativeness," "the ability to participate in common thinking or wish, hence adaptability," "intellectual rapport with the world," "the ability and need to think and feel as part of a group," "the ability to adjust to the practical requirements of life, to a sufficient participation in collective or common thinking."[54] What this means in generalized sociopsychological terms is that a normal human being is expected to manifest indications of a level of functioning that involves social and psychological participation with others in a common sociocultural system. In terms of variability in personal adjustment, however, some individuals may be over-conformed or pseudo-conformed while others may tend to deviate very far in the opposite direction. Too few P's, therefore, may be one index to a schizophrenic adjustment, where the private world of the individual tends to overwhelm him and separate him from his fellows. Excessive P's may likewise be diagnostic.[55] Since these general considerations apply to all societies P and O responses so scored have an actual reference to frequencies established for the group. Consequently, I should suppose that schizophrenics in any society would give fewer P's than normal subjects.

The central question is, then, *what* are the P frequencies for particular groups? The corollary questions are: Do we have to assume a unique and characteristic P frequency for subjects that differ in age, educational background, and national affiliation, within the gamut of the western European and American cultural tradition itself, as well as for the various peoples who do not belong to this tradition at all? Or, are there some P's of "universal" frequency that transcend particular groups in our culture, and are even found among some nonliterate peoples?[56] While at present we do not have available the range of empirical or quantitative data that would be necessary in order to give a definite answer to such questions, nevertheless they can hardly be ignored considering the widely extended use of the Rorschach beyond the confines of our own culture. The issues that have arisen within the more limited social framework of our own society are only compounded in this larger perspective. Besides this, such questions have implications beyond those directly related to practical and diagnostic problems: the nature of the test itself and the comparability of results that emerge from cross-cultural usage are involved.

We can, however, get some ideas of the problem from one example. In my Ojibwa sample the 4 P forms with the top frequencies among *both* children and adults ("animals" VIII; "animals" II; "rabbit" X; "winged creature" V) are among the best-known P forms in general Rorschach experience. They are among the P's which Hertz found three or more experts agreed upon, and Schneider,[57] on the basis of his wide German experience, likewise recognized them (using a criterion of 1 in 4). In other words, these 4 P forms are in a category that transcends age differences, national differences, and cultural differences in so far as they are now known to occur among children and adults in more than one nationality group in Western culture and in comparable subgroups of the Ojibwa Indians.

A series of comparisons among American Indian groups[58] (see Table 3) with varying cultural backgrounds not only indicates that "animals" VIII and "winged creature" V are Populars, but that they are among the Populars which occur with the highest frequencies in all these groups, the former never falling below second place. "Animals" II, while ranking between 2 and 4 in frequency in all but the Shoshone group, never occurs as the most frequent P. "Rabbit" X is about equal in rank with "human figures" III; in both cases there are two groups in which neither response falls among the 5 most frequent P's, and in the groups where these responses are high in frequency, neither one rises to higher than

TABLE 3.—*P* FORMS OF HIGHEST FREQUENCY IN SIX AMERICAN INDIAN GROUPS
WITH DIVERSE CULTURES

P FORM	ORDER OF FREQUENCY					
	OJIBWA (Hallowell)	MENOMINI (Spindler)	TUSCARORA (Wallace)	WIND RIVER SHOSHONE (Shimkin)	ZUNI (Leighton)	NAVAHO (Leighton)
Animals VIII	1	2	—	2 (bears)	1	1
Animals II	2	3	4	—	2	4
Rabbit X	3	—	—	3	5	5
Winged Creature V	4	1	1	1 (bat)	3	2
Human Figures III	5	4	3	—	—	3

third place. Furthermore, of the 15 *P* forms having a frequency of 1 in 6 or more in my total Ojibwa sample 11, or possibly 12, of them correspond to those quantitatively established by Hertz (1951) and 9 of them to those defined in a similar manner by Beck (1944) for American subjects.

At the same time it should be noted that the adult Ojibwa, considered as a unit, have a total of 23 *P* forms. This can hardly be without psychological significance. Both in winter and summer these people live in small face-to-face groups that are characterized by the limited range of social roles that are defined by the traditional kinship pattern. Besides this, the Ojibwa are hunters and, especially in winter, a band comprising only a few families at most will be isolated on their hunting grounds for months at a time. The high number of *P*'s may be an index to the correlation that exists between manner of living and the conformity to a highly homogeneous pattern in psychological outlook. From a developmental point of view this hypothesis receives support from the fact that 10 of the *P* forms of highest frequency among adults are already established in children at the 8–11-year-old level.

All of these data do not permit us to assume that as we move from one people to another we should expect to find a totally distinct series of *P* forms in each case. On the other hand, our present empirical knowledge does not enable us to define the actual extent, or the transcultural limits, of "universal" *P*'s. We can only determine these limits by assembling more data on group frequencies of all kinds. By accumulating such data on a much larger scale we will be able to view all the types of variation that may emerge in a more comprehensive human perspective, and better judge both the psychological significance and the determinants of such phenomena. It may very well turn out in

58

the case of the P responses to the Rorschach figures that we are presented with a problem that has analogies to the functioning of perception generally. The "universal" P forms may involve determinants that are a function of objective characteristics of the figures themselves and past experience with certain "universal" classes of objects. The four "universal" P forms referred to above, for example, all have an animal content. On the other hand, less universal P forms may be more predominately subject to the control of determinants of the "nonsensory" or "directive" category. On the basis of such an hypothesis it might be expected that the responses of children in different cultures may very well include "universal" P's, and that group differences in P forms may be more apparent among adults.

Integration of Culture, Perception, and Personality Structure and Rorschach Validity.—The nature of the cross-cultural data on P forms just discussed, the recurrent proportions of H and A responses, the range in productivity of subjects with culturally diverse backgrounds, to say nothing of other types of evidence that might be assembled, all seem to point in one common direction. Rorschach protocols wherever collected with care exhibit constant, as well as variable features which, considered as group phenomena, appear to be of the same order as the protocols of individuals within any particular group. Thus, in the light of what we now know about the psycho-dynamics of perception, and in view of the support which the general working hypotheses adopted in personality and culture studies have received, the comparability and psychological intelligibility of Rorschach protocols at both group and individual levels need no longer rest upon a priori considerations, but rather upon empirical evidence that is rapidly accumulating. It seems reasonable to conclude, therefore, that *if* the meaningful resolution of ambiguous stimuli is a valid means of obtaining data of psychological significance for an understanding of personality structure in one culture, the same technique is probably valid for subjects with any cultural background. So far as practical use is concerned, there is no reason whatever to believe that the Rorschach Test is "culture-bound," even if special administrative problems may arise from time to time. As Spindler and Goldschmidt have pointed out, it is meaningless to ask: Are Rorschach responses "culture free"? For as they say: ". . . we do not know what this concept could mean as applied to individual action. It is precisely because the individual's responses are cast in their particular form by his culture that we use such a tool. The ink-blots themselves are, or approach being, culture free (i.e., 'unstructured') stimuli. The subjects' responses are never culture-free. The protocol is therefore a *personal variant* of a *culturally patterned* response to a *relatively open* situation."[59]

This is what had to be assumed, of course, by all those who pioneered in experimenting with the test in cultures other than our own. But at this earlier period, the Rorschach Test was peculiarly novel, since other projective techniques had not yet been developed, nor had the principles underlying their use been clearly articulated. It now seems more obvious, perhaps, how Rorschach data fit into the general theoretical framework that is emerging from the investigation of perception in relation to personality, culture and personality studies, and a deeper understanding of the psychodynamics of personality. It also seems to me that the assumption that common principles of Rorschach interpretation can be applied to the protocols of subjects with any cultural background is thoroughly intelligible.

It is unnecessary to review here in full detail one of the most striking types of evidence in support of this assumption. This is the well-documented fact that a fair number of protocols have been interpreted "blind" in a *double* sense. Not only has this been accomplished without personal contacts with the subject, or a knowledge of his life history or clinical data; it has been done without explicit or detailed knowledge of the cultural background of the subject. A pioneer and classical instance of this is the interpretations made by Ann Hartoch Schachtel of the protocols of six Pilaga Indian children. Two of the three boys were only 6 years of age; the other was only 4 years old; the ages of the girls were 6, 8, and 9 years. Besides this, the records showed a high degree of constriction; there were no M or C responses. Nevertheless, when "compared with material taken from the notes of the ethnologists on the day-to-day behavior of the same children in their own village" and doll-play results a ". . . close correspondence between the Rorschach findings and the ethnological facts" were found despite "occasional differences in emphasis."[60]

Another instance of blind analysis is of unique interest because of the independent participation of Theodora M. Abel, Molly R. Harrower, Florence R. Miale, Bruno Klopfer and Martha Wolfenstein in the interpretation of a single record.[61] This was the protocol of Unabelin, an Arapesh (New Guinea) man about twenty years old obtained by Margaret Mead in 1932. Dr. Mead writes[62]

Thus a detailed study of his individual personality, by Rorschach methods, presents a way of specifying the type of personality who appears to me as an ethnological observer to be closest to the expected type for that particular culture. Seen from this point of view, Unabelin is not only a cultural sample, in the sense that any Arapesh is a sample of his culture, but he is further a particular type of sample. Ideally, such a record would be complemented by Rorschach records of those individuals considered most deviant in temperament from the culturally expected personality.

Oberholzer's blind interpretation of the Alorese material collected by Cora DuBois is an outstanding instance because Oberholzer himself was so skeptical of the cross-cultural applicability of Rorschach principles. He explicitly points out that he could rely upon the norms he was accustomed to work with when interpreting the protocols of European subjects. And he comments further that,

There are no more than thirty-seven [Alorese] Rorschachs and they are not likely to be increased in number. To work out norms we need at least some hundred or more tests, perhaps more than there are Atimelangers. There is little hope that standards will ever be established. [Nevertheless] the psychological meaning and significance of Rorschach's experimental factors have proved true for Europeans and Americans [so that it may be possible to apply them still more widely] . . . many hours were spent assigning rank order to subjects for personality traits. The ethnographer worked from her knowledge of the individuals; I worked blind from the Rorschach materials. The degree of coincidence between our ranking was so high that it left no doubt that the principles of the test could be applied cross-culturally.[63]

Other examples could be cited, such as the chapter contributed by Theodora M. Abel and Renata A. Calabresi to Oscar Lewis' study of the Mexican village of Tepoztlan[64] and the detailed interpretation of twelve male and eleven female Trukese records by Seymour B. Sarason. In the latter case the Rorschach records, life history information, and TAT records were obtained by Thomas Gladwin on Truk.[65] Although done informally, the interpretation of psychograms of Zuni and Navaho Rorschach groups results by Dr. Klopfer many years ago clearly indicated the possibility of blind interpretation at this level, too. Despite the fact that he was completely unfamiliar with either Indian group he put his finger upon characteristic differences that those who know these Indians at first hand recognized as valid.[66]

A recent example of the use of blind Rorschach analysis (and TAT) is reported by Kluckhohn and Rosenzweig. The subjects were two Navaho children who had been followed since birth; one was a boy, the other a girl. Four independent interpretations were obtained, three of them blind, and the results which are tabulated show a high degree of conformity. The authors comment:

The picture obtained of these two personalities by different testers and interpreters using a variety of projective techniques is, on the whole, remarkably consistent. Much of the work was done independently. In no case did any tester or interpreter have full access to all the materials which have been assembled for the writing of this paper. At most, each student was familiar with some fragment of the total data. Mr. Kaplan, e.g., had seen the interpretations of the 1942 Rorschach before he did his re-take in 1947. But this was all. The personality diagnoses made on the basis of projective tests also check well with the impressions of another set of workers who used ordinary interview and observation methods. In short, the present paper constitutes a partial validation of projective tests in another culture, with the caution that significant results are peculiarly dependent upon the relationship between tester and subject.[67]

While "blind" interpretation as a means of testing the validity of Rorschach principles is, of course, relevant to the cross-cultural applicability of the test, nevertheless I believe it belongs to a pioneer period. In this respect it parallels similar experiments made by those interested in its clinical application. So far as any serious and systematic use of

61

the Rorschach technique in personality and culture studies is concerned, it hardly can be argued that the interpretation of the record of a single individual, of a few children, or a handful of adults done blind and apart from a representative sample of the population as a whole including, of course, age and sex differences, is to be recommended as an ideal procedure for obtaining the most reliable and useful Rorschach data. Individual protocols, even if psychologically intelligible, do not give us reliable information about the common features that characterize a group and thus enable us to appraise the typicality or atypicality of the individual in reference to his group. The use of black and white as color and the proportions of the various categories of C answers in Alorese records would be quite as striking and intelligible in a single record, if that were all that was available. But it could not be known to be typical and related to their culture without further sampling. What struck Oberholzer so forcibly was the discovery that a Rorschach pattern, aberrant in our culture, could be so characteristic of the Alorese records as a whole. Standing alone such a record would inevitably suggest psychopathy. Thus Oberholzer comments:

I have mentioned more than once the similarity between the Rorschachs of the Alorese and the pathological findings of traumatics, some neurotics, and some schizophrenics. The Alorese, of course, are none of these; nor are they epileptics, although their color reactions are comparable. No one of these diagnoses can hold its ground when we know everything about their tests; it is only a more or less remote analogy. The Alorese Rorschachs are something *sui generis*.[63]

However, in the last analysis the psychological characterization of the Alorese as "sui generis" depends on more than knowing "everything about their tests," in the sense of having a group sample. Such an appraisal depends equally upon knowing everything about their culture. Important as blind analyses of a few individuals may be for certain purposes, these experiments must be clearly distinguished from investigations that are less concerned with methodological questions as such and more concerned with discovering and exploiting the full potentialities that appear to be inherent in the test results. One of the most striking and important theoretical implications of experiments in "blind" analysis has been overlooked. In so far as life history data, direct observations of behavior, information from other tests, *and* cultural facts have proved to be in accord with "blind" interpretations, we have much more than a validation of Rorschach principles—we have a most enlightening concrete demonstration in more than a single human society of the integral relations that exist between the variables that are abstractly expressed by perception, personality structure, and culture and which have so often been investigated separately. This is a discovery of major importance. It reflects the complexities of the human behavioral situation, the need for a comprehensive conceptual framework, and the usefulness of techniques that have already provided extremely important data.

62

Complementary Nature of Psychological and Anthropological Frames of Reference.—Information derived from the Rorschach and other projective techniques, therefore, cannot be ignored by the anthropologist if he is interested in joining forces with the psychologist in the pursuit of a common goal—a thorough understanding of *all* the factors that enter into the determination of the behavior of man and the functioning of human societies through cultural instrumentalities. From this point of view, the information obtainable from Rorschach data may be just as significant, at the personality level, in validating the anthropologist's interpretation of the functioning of cultures, as a consideration of cultural data has proved of value to the psychologist in gaining a more comprehensive knowledge of the determinants relevant to the functioning of individuals.

One of the major accomplishments of anthropology has been to record, describe, and analyze in great detail the many and varied cultures of mankind, particularly those of the nonliterate peoples of the world and to work out the historical relations among them. Consequently, if the cultural anthropologist asks what information about *culture* is provided by Rorschach data, the answer is little or none,[69] *if* what is meant is specific information about technology, kinship terms, religious beliefs and practices, economic organization, and so on. In other words, if culture is conceived exclusively or primarily in formal categorical, descriptive, or analytic terms and principally dealt with as phenomenally sui generis, psychological data of any kind are irrelevant.[70] On the other hand, if the psychologist asks what information cultural anthropology can offer about *how* we learn or the psychophysiology of perception, the obvious answer is nothing.

Nevertheless, men typically adjust themselves to modes of group living which affect their psychological structuralization and behavior, and cultural phenomena depend upon their activities. Consequently, the approach of cultural anthropology on the one hand, and psychology, on the other, supplement each other. In so far as the former is interested in the functioning of human societies through cultural means and not only in the descriptive content and patterning of cultures, and psychologists are interested in *what* is learned, and the relation between dependent behavioral variables and the traditional mode of life to which individuals become adjusted, a common area of interest emerges.

The focus of this area rests upon the assumption that personality structure emerges in the course of a socialization process beginning in infancy that prepares the individuals for action in a given culture, and that cultures only function and persist through the personality organization of the individuals whose activities are responsible for the group attributes that distinguish one mode of human life from another. Thus predictions about a great deal of overt behavior can be made on the basis of a thorough knowledge of culture in its traditional and local aspects. But such inferences have their limits; the psychodynamics of behavior and the structural basis of it in *depth* is more difficult to arrive at from such cultural data alone. Conversely, some predictions about behavior that have significance in cultural terms may be made from the data of projective tests. But information of this kind must remain at a high level of abstraction from the standpoint of cultural anthropology. From Alorese Rorschachs alone, for instance, one could say that highly elaborate and imaginative art forms could not be characteristic of the culture. Thus the anthropologist, if he is interested in how a culture functions at the "grass roots" level, must work with psychological blinders on unless he checks his inferences from independently derived psychological data. In the same way, the psychologist working with personality data in the narrow sense will be handicapped by cultural blinders, if he extrapolates his conclusions beyond a certain point. Working blind, in either case, does not seem to be the most desirable procedure where complementary data may prove enriching. There is a general analogy to the clinician who does not hesitate to use all the data at his disposal in his effort to understand thoroughly the psychodynamics of his patient. The anthropologist who wishes to understand the functioning of a culture must of necessity use description and historical information; but he can complement this by data derived from projective techniques. By using maximum information of both a cultural and psychological kind, our knowledge of the dynamics of culture and behavior may be considerably deepened and extended. It may be possible in the future to do more than compare and analyze cultures and culture change at the formal cultural level, or to describe and catalogue variations in personality type associated with different cultures and link them with early childhood experiences. Already it seems possible to compare different human populations with respect to the level of integral psychological functioning that is found in the typical life adjustment of the individuals in each group under the conditions imposed by varying historical circumstances.

The Rorschach in the Study of Cultural Change.—Investigations along these lines have been undertaken by the writer, several of his students, and the Spindlers, through using the Rorschach technique in studies of acculturation. (See Part IV.) I compared Rorschach data from *several groups* of Ojibwa Indians at progressive levels of acculturation in order to discover what has happened to the modal personality structure of these Indians, whose whole manner of life has undergone radical changes as compared with aboriginal days, or even the late nineteenth century. The Spindlers have studied *one* reservation group, the Menomini Indians of Wisconsin,[71] in order to discover "the degree to which evidences of personality structure vary in relation to the observed variances in the more external and social aspects of the personnel of the group undergoing the acculturative process." Criteria were devised that made it possible to rate individuals on the basis of a sociological variable in terms of which the population was found to be divisible into five subgroups, "four of them along a continuum of acculturation, and one differentiated on the basis of socio-economic status." Rorschach samples from all these groups were obtained, as well as from a white control group, so that a psychological variable pertaining to personality structure could be compared with the independently derived sociological variable.

All of these investigations have involved systematic sampling procedures. And it has been assumed that reliable psychological data, at the level of personality organization, could be obtained for the same kind of population units which the anthropologist has made the basis of cultural description and analysis. For it seems obvious that unless a sample be obtained from which psychological generalizations may be made, the psychological data cannot actually be considered relevant to the cultural data nor any significant relations discovered. Since it has been demonstrated that Rorschach data can be collected from population units for which we have the relevant cultural or sociological information and the results manipulated statistically, the methodological possibilities of projective techniques at this level offer interesting potentialities.

What is particularly significant in the Spindlers' Menomini study is not the emergence of an overall psychological picture of the Menomini as a whole—but rather the discrimination made possible by the analysis and interpretation of Rorschach data of different personality constellations representative of groups of Indians on the same reservation who have adjusted during the period of contact with the white man's culture in a variety of ways. Moreover, hypotheses were developed from sociocultural observations that could be tested through the use of Rorschach data at the level of personality structure and functioning. One level of acculturation, for example, "is represented in the membership of the Peyote Cult, as a special variant of a transitional acculturation type."[72] It was found possible to define the sociopsychological function of the Peyote Cult in the acculturation process, and, at the same time, to demonstrate a correspondence between cult membership and a characteristic personality organization of the Indians belonging to it.

The personality pattern of the adult male members differs dramatically from that exhibited in other acculturationally defined Menomini groups, according to Rorschach protocols. . . . Most of the women show the same symptoms and characteristics as the men, but they do not reach the same degree of pathological self-involvements as do some of the men. Even by Menomini standards, the deviant withdrawal type reactions of the men and the women find support in the group; for the cult sanctions schizoid-like behavior by the emphasis placed upon vision-seeking and autism. . . .[73] The inferences to be drawn from this for the understanding of the specifics of the role of cults of this sort in social and cultural change are important; but even more significant are the implications of this for the relationship between what have been called personality and culture, for here the two seem practically identical.[74]

Psychological Characterization and Comparison of Groups.—In making overall psychological comparisons between groups, even though it is assumed that the Rorschach data collected constitute a representative sample, there are problems in handling the data in a manner best suited to express their significance.[75] But such problems are by no means peculiar to group Rorschach data as such—they are inherent in making reliable statements about group phenomena of any sort. If the data are quantifiable and averages are used as the basis of characterization and comparison, the question always arises: How many individuals actually represent the integral combination of features that are expressed by mean frequencies? Here we should recall certain facts: (1) that group differences in the qualitative aspects of Rorschach data, as well as mean frequencies, have been shown to exist; (2) that this empirical fact is in accord with the hypothesis that cultural variability implies psychological differences (3) that the Rorschach constellations represented do make psychological sense when interpreted in accordance with established principles, and (4) that the psychological interpretations already made of such group results have been found consonant with the known cultural information collected by the anthropologist in a number of instances.[76] Consequently, it seems fair to ask: What are these group psychological differences a function of, if not of differences in the personality structure of individuals who, however they may vary in idiosyncratic fashion from one another, share certain common psychological characteristics because of the fact that they share common modes of behavioral adjustment as members of one sociocultural system rather than another? The only alternative, it seems, is to argue that the results obtained must be an artifact of those who have interpreted the protocols, to say nothing of those who have found some accord between the test data and the cultural facts. Since this hardly seems reasonable, the real core of the problem may lie in the technical and methodological difficulties imposed by the nature of the data to be handled, rather than in the data themselves.

One of the questions that arises in any statistical handling of Rorschach data for purposes of group characterization and comparison is some possible alternative to using a profile based on mean frequencies alone. An experiment in the use of such an alternative is in a study of the Tuscarora Indians by Anthony Wallace, who worked out some suggestions made by psychologists Malcolm C. Preston and Julius Wischner. On the assumption that "the characteristics under investigation have their locus in the individual, where they do not exist as independent traits, but in integral relationships to one another," Wallace does not seek to answer the question: "What are the traits most frequently observed in the Tuscarora population?" but rather, "What are the most frequently associated traits?" and "What is the form of association?" For the purposes of his study, therefore, he adopts an operational definition of "modal personality" as "that type of personality structure, formulated in terms of the Rorschach Test, from which the obtained Rorschach records of more individuals are indistinguishable in certain chosen dimensions than are indistinguishable in these dimensions from any other definable type."[77] The frequency of the modal class in a total sample of 36 men and 34 women (between the ages of 16 and 71) turned out to be 37.2 per cent (16 men and 10 women). Wallace tabulates the Rorschach attributes of this class and provides a composite psychogram, along with a detailed discussion that includes what he calls "sub-modal" and "deviant" types of Tuscarora personality.[78] For purposes of comparison, Wallace applied the same statistical analysis to the 102 adults in my sample of Northern Ojibwa (Berens River) Indians. In this case 28.4 per cent fell within the modal class (16 men and 13 women).[79]

It is obvious, then, that once we have a representative sample of Rorschach protocols from any group sufficient for statistical manipulation, overall comparisons with other groups can be handled with varying degrees of refinement not otherwise possible, or the basic data used for various other detailed comparisons and analyses. These comparisons likewise may be made the basis of psychological inferences that have significance at the group level. This latter type of procedure will be illustrated by the comparison of selected responses obtained from two groups of Ojibwa subjects with those produced by subjects in the Spiegel sample. Such a comparison offers another angle of approach to the validation of Rorschach principles of interpretation used cross-culturally. In this case, however, group frequencies of discrete Rorschach items are the primary data, rather than the total configuration of the responses of a single individual, or the composite profile of a group of subjects as represented by mean frequencies (or some alternative) for every type of response.

Beck and his associates, for example, have discussed the psychological significance of H and Hd responses of the subjects in the Spiegel sample. But they have gone beyond this. They raise the question[80] whether their findings may not be "representative of the national personality." Generalization at this level invites comparison with groups of subjects with a cultural background different from the American. Suppose, then, we compare H and Hd responses of "normal" adult American subjects in the Spiegel sample with those of two different groups of Ojibwa subjects, fairly similar in size and sexual composition. Comparative frequencies for these responses will be found in Table 4.

In the first place, a glance at these frequencies indicates that there is a valid basis for comparison. The general distributional pattern is the same and four-fifths of the responses in both categories fall within the

TABLE 4.—COMPARATIVE FREQUENCIES OF H AND Hd:
AMERICAN AND OJIBWA SUBJECTS

NUMBER OF H OR Hd	NUMBER OF SUBJECTS					
	Spiegel Sample		Berens River Ojibwa		Flambeau Ojibwa	
	H	Hd	H	Hd	H	Hd
42			1			
....			0			
30-31			1	0		
28-29			0	0		
26-27		1	0	0		
24-25	1	0	0	0		
22-23	0	0	0	0		
20-21	1	0	0	1		
18-19	0	0	0	0		
16-17	1	0	1	1		
14-15	2	0	3	4		1
12-13	0	2	8	1		1
10-11	4	0	2	1	1	2
8-9	8	5	4	7	0	2
6-7	20	10	10	7	3	2
4-5	38	18	22	8	8	11
2-3	46	41	23	30	24	21
0-1	36	80	28	41	79	75
Total	157	157	102	102	115	115
Mean	4.50 (N,157)	1.78 (N,156)	4.5 (N,101)	3.4 (N,101)	1.3 (N,115)	1.6 (N,115)
SD	3.62	1.95	4.07	4.16	1.43	1.78

range 0–7 in the three groups. Observable differences occur within this overall pattern. From these empirical facts, I believe it is legitimate to proceed on the hypothesis that we are dealing with phenomena of the same order in each case. If this is so, then the application of common interpretative principles is by no means an arbitrary procedure. As Beck has recently stated it:

The whole human form was noted by Rorschach, and identified by other students, as going with healthier, mature intelligence. Its absence, or low quantity in an otherwise intelligent individual, is likely to indicate repression of this theme. Hysterics produce fewer humans than others; the inference is that they are repressing painful or conflictual thoughts concerning their relations with others.[81] [The ratio between H and Hd] is a measure of the individual's mental freedom or his inhibition.[82]

In the interpretation of the frequency of H responses of the subjects of the Spiegel sample Beck and his associates stress the fact that 67 per cent of them "concentrated in the 2–7 range" and 37 per cent in the 4–7 range.

The off-hand interpretation [they write] would be that 67 per cent show moderate to much interest in other humans; and 37 per cent definitely much. On the other hand, there are 36 individuals, or 22.8 per cent whose H range is 0–1. This percentage may be the proportion in which, in the population generally, we find men and women not caring much about their fellows: not too allocentric. [these findings] are of fresh import in the light of the findings in the C nuances. [mean C 3.11; CF 1.44; FC 1.18]. The indication in the affective sphere is for a composite personality more self-gratifying than social, but with relatively little infantilism. The self-gratifying trait still includes an urge for human contact; even though this contact is on the "what's in it for me" level. In addition, it will be noted from the C figures that a sympathetic, helpful readiness also forms one considerable sector of this composite whole personality. One may speculate, in so far as these findings are representative of the national personality, that the Americans can be well disposed, easy-going; but with a low threshhold of irritability toward their fellows. . . . Since the mean H is so noticeably higher than mean $Hd,$ the inference would be for a relatively uninhibited state of mind; a relaxed attitude.[83]

TABLE 5.—THE RANGE OF H RESPONSES IN SAMPLES OF
AMERICAN AND OJIBWA SUBJECTS

RANGE OF H RESPONSES	GROUPS OF SUBJECTS					
	Americans Spiegel Sample (157)		Ojibwa Bereno River (102)		Ojibwa Flambeau (115)	
	N	%	N	%	N	%
2-7	104	67	55	53.9	35	30.4
4-7	58	37	32	31.3	11	9.5
0-1	36	22.8	28	27.4	79	68.6

For a further comparison of the American sample with the two groups of Ojibwa subjects, Table 5 shows the number and percentage of subjects whose H responses fall within the three ranges stressed by Beck and his association in their interpretation of American subjects.

The most striking difference is between the Flambeau Ojibwa and the Chicagoans, with whom they are essentially in polar contrast. The percentage of subjects in the 2–7 range is less than half that of the Spiegel sample, the proportion in the 4–7 range is only a fourth as great, and the percentage of individuals who only gave 0–1 H responses is three times that of the Americans. Besides this, as Table 4 shows, the ratio between H and Hd responses tends towards reversal. While the mean figures barely suggest this, the fact is that 33.1 per cent of the Flambeau subjects produced more Hd than H. But a concomitant fact has psychological implications. The striking contrast between the two groups is not exemplified in the frequency of mean Hd responses, these are approximately the same; it is the paucity of H responses in the Indian group that is striking. When we likewise consider that these

Flambeau Ojibwa subjects have a mean ΣC of only 1, whereas the American mean is 3.11, it not only appears that these Indians are very different from "normal" American subjects, the question arises: "Is there not an indication of some personality dysfunctioning here? The Flambeau subjects would appear to be far from enjoying an "easy-going" relationship to their fellows, or manifesting a "relaxed attitude." On the contrary, they would seem to be suffering from severe and deep-seated inhibitions in their interpersonal relations as compared with the Chicago-Americans. One might ask then: Is this psychological characteristic a function of the cultural differences between the two groups? Do we have evidence here that supports a relativistic conception of normality? Are we confronted with a peculiarity of Ojibwa personality? We might not be able to discuss this question at all, or even go very far astray, were it not for the fact that data from another Ojibwa group, the Berens River Ojibwa, are available.

While the cultural and linguistic background of both groups is the same—in this regard, they may be said to constitute a unit in contrast to the Spiegel sample—nevertheless situational differences in their recent history have led to social and economic readjustments that have had influential psychological effects. I have set forth the full range of detailed factual material in Part IV, but the crux of the matter is that the Flambeau Ojibwa of Wisconsin have been subjected to much more contact with Western culture than have the Berens River Ojibwa of Manitoba. In anthropological terminology the former are more acculturated than the latter. The northern group is much closer to an aboriginal mode of life despite their contacts with white men. What is particularly interesting to observe, then, is that the H and Hd responses of the Berens River Ojibwa, while assuming a somewhat *different* pattern than that of the Chicago-Americans, do not suggest dysfunction any more than do those of the normal white subjects. Mean H is not only greater than Hd in both cases—it turns out to be the same as in the American sample if one highly deviant subject be omitted in calculating the average. Mean Hd, however, is more than twice as high. An inspection of Table 5 indicates two things quite clearly: in the first place, the lower percentages of the Berens River subjects, as compared with those in the Spiegel sample, in the 2–7 and 4–7 range, and the higher percentage in the 0–1 range suggests that these Northern Ojibwa are not in such easy rapport with their fellow men as are the Americans. What is of special significance is the paradoxical fact that, while the mean for all human responses $(H + Hd)$ is even greater than in the American sample showing a preoccupation with human relations, at the same time the high Hd suggests that an inhibitory factor is likewise functioning that qualifies and limits this human interest. The affective aspect of this situation is indicated by the very low mean ΣC in the Ojibwa group (1.2) which is less than half that of the American subjects. Thus, while the Indian pattern is distinctive, it is certainly no less healthy than the American one. It is thoroughly consistent, moreover, with the total psychological picture we obtain when all the Rorschach determinants are taken into account—a highly introversive adjustment.

The social life of the Ojibwa has often been characterized as "atomistic"; the individual is brought up in a manner that encourages a high degree of reliance upon himself rather than upon other human beings. In this culture, in fact, individuals are highly motivated to place reliance upon the superhuman beings of their behavioral environment; each man has his personal tutelaries or "guardian spirits." (See Chaps. 15 and 20.) As I have already pointed out in the discussion of M content, suspicion bred of belief in sorcery, along with the anonymity of sorcerers, makes the individual wary of his fellow men. It is from this source, rather than from superhuman beings, that the greatest threats to life and health may come. Consequently, it is not strange to find evidence of a preoccupation with human beings, accompanied by inhibitions in free and easy affective ties with them. In the second place, an examination of both Table 4 and Table 5, without reference to the common background of the Ojibwa groups, would not suggest any connection between them. The $H\text{-}Hd$ patterns they manifest appear to be quite distinct from one another. If the Berens River group seems to be concerned with human relations, the Flambeau group with a mean $H + Hd$ of only 2.9 are in the opposite category. Why is this?

The explanation, I believe, is to be found in the psychological changes which the Flambeau Ojibwa have undergone under the pressures and frustrations of accelerated acculturation. Their $H\text{-}Hd$ pattern, which even may be interpreted as indicating hostility in human relations, is but one indication of this. These are the same subjects that I have dealt with in greater detail in my study of the psychological effects of acculturation among the Ojibwa. (Chap. 19.) My hypothesis has been based on evidence that indicates the persistence of an aboriginal personality structure that has surmounted earlier stages of acculturation but which appears to be breaking down at Flambeau. In a comparison of the Rorschach data of this group with that of the Northern Ojibwa I used "signs" of adjustment as an index to personality functioning. In the Flambeau sample 56 per cent of the subjects averaged less than 7 signs, i.e., more than half of them fell into the groups I called *Poorly* or *Badly* adjusted. Consequently, I should like to point out in the comparison made above that a tabulation of mean H responses with references to the five levels of adjustment I used shows a progressive decline associated with a decreasing number of signs. The subjects with less than 7 signs produced average H responses that amounted to less than 1 whereas the subjects with 7 or more signs averaged more than 1. The subjects with less than 7 signs were those who also tended to produce more Hd than H responses. It was only in this group of subjects, moreover, that the A per cent averaged over 50 per cent (52.5 per cent in the case of those with 4–6 signs and 68.9 per cent in those with 0–3 signs). Thus evidence from all directions points to the dysfunctioning of a large proportion of the subjects in the Flambeau group as compared with their culturally related kinsmen in Canada.

The comparison of the Flambeau sample with the normal subjects of the Spiegel sample, on the one hand, and the less acculturated Ojibwa sample, on the other, demonstrates the effectiveness of interpretative principles used cross-culturally. The Flambeau Indians are as badly adjusted psychologically when compared with their Canadian cultural relatives, as they are when compared with the subjects of the Spiegel sample. (Chap. 20.) Thus, I believe that a general conclusion of first importance can be drawn. It does not seem necessary to reinterpret our standard of mental health, when we move from one group to another, if we take as our criterion an *optimum level* of psychological functioning. In other words, what has been interpreted as evidence of psychological dysfunctioning in one group of subjects is based upon the same principles which in the other groups point to a level of psychological functioning that may be characterized as approximating mental health. For our present-day knowledge, imperfect as it may be in some respects, makes it necessary to differentiate a positive, higher, or optimum level of psychological functioning or psychodynamic adjustment (call it what you will) from a lower or less positive one. Mowrer has suggested *integrative* as contrasted with *non-integrative* behavior. Whereas the former is more psychologically rewarding than punishing, the latter is balanced in the opposite direction since adjustment is achieved "only at the expense of partial psychic self-destruction."[84] If we accept any such distinction, on the assumption that it is scientifically grounded and empirically verifiable, then it would seem to follow that mental health, or an equivalent concept, is not culture-bound but has universal significance both as a concept and a value. If this be so, then it may be possible to emerge from the chrysalis of an elementary cultural relativism. We should not close our minds to the possibility that, from the standpoint of the psychodynamics of human adjustment, different cultures may vary significantly as more or less efficient instruments in the molding of personalities that are fully capable of functioning at a level of mental health. If we adopt this as a hypothesis we have indicated to us another angle of approach to the investigation of human societies in cross-cultural perspective and the psychological effects of culture change and acculturation. Here the Rorschach and other projective techniques appear to provide the most useful psychological tools.

The results of the Spindlers' investigation of the Menomini are again in point here because the contact of these Indians with whites has led to the emergence of psychological characteristics in the most highly acculturated group that indicates a sharp break with the past and a level of personality integration which, in terms of mental health, is in marked contrast with what was found among the Flambeau Ojibwa. It is particularly significant that the personality structures of the least acculturated Menomini and the less acculturated Ojibwa are quite similar. According to my own hypothesis this is to be explained by the fact that both these tribal groups have their historic roots in the same culture area of North America (the Eastern Woodlands) and spoke languages which, although quite distinct, belonged to the same linguistic stock (Algonkian). But the Menomini, living on a reservation 400 square miles in area, "are unique among Wisconsin Indians in that they own and operate a saw mill and logging industry cutting 25,000,000 cubic feet of lumber each year, that affords them an annual income of over one million dollars."[85] In other words, it has been possible for them to become positively adapted to the American economic system, while remaining in control of their own affairs. At the same time, the acculturation process has not completely transformed every aspect of their lives. There is a cultural continuity with the past, exemplified, for instance, by a group that maintains the old Medicine Lodge. It is a striking fact, therefore, that the psychological data assembled by the Spindlers demonstrate personality types that somewhat parallel those found among the Flambeau Ojibwa but these can be said to be "transitional" among the Menomini; for, at the most acculturated level among the Menomini, where the values of the old culture are forgotten, and the goals and drives of white, middle-class [American] society find their fullest acceptance, a reformulation of personality structure occurs:

This emergent personality is characterized by effective emotional control, but a responsiveness to the impact of affective stimuli that is rarely present at the constrained nativistic level. They are more "outgoing" in their orientation towards life. But where the outgoingness of response and drive is accompanied, in the transition levels, by various forms of anxiety, here, its signs are absent. The greater affectivity and outward goal-striving, as compared to the native groups, is *not* a function of breakdown, as it is for the transitionals, but of integration. At the same time, all cases in the elite acculturated group express a certain kind of tension. It is probably not an indication of anxiety, in the forms and amounts present in each record. It seems to be, rather, a reflection of their struggle for achievement on white, middle-class terms.

One might expect that in this group *H-Hd* responses would not manifest the same pattern as at Flambeau and that the general level of personality functioning is at a higher level. Thus, we may likewise conclude that the acculturation process, with all of the personal readjustments to life that it implies, does not ultimately carry the seeds of psychological dysfunction within itself. The specific historic conditions, local circumstances, and other variables are of determinative importance. While at Flambeau there appears to be a psychological impasse and outward manifestations of acculturation conceal a psychological skeleton, on the Menomini reservation a transcendence of this situation is manifested in the case of the elite group.

73

It is difficult to think of any other psychological technique which would have implemented the kind of personality differentiation essential to investigations of this sort. Thus studies of the psychological aspects of acculturation have added a new dimension to the investigation of culture change. Since large-scale culture changes and personality readjustments are a prime characteristic of our contemporary world, the implications of such small-scale studies as those undertaken by anthropologists are not unrelated to the problem of mental health in general and the necessary conditions for its achievement.

Future Prospects.—Finally, it seems to me that a pioneer period in the use of the Rorschach Test by anthropologists, or other social scientists, is now over. I can recall occasions in the past when an archeologist, a physical anthropologist, and several cultural anthropologists, having no technical training in psychology, or in the use of the Rorschach technique, asked me whether I would not be interested in some records that they might manage to collect casually, and quite incidentally to some other specialized inquiries they planned to make. They sincerely believed that such protocols might be of some value and that with a little instruction on my part they could no doubt obtain them. It is now more generally recognized that, if used at all, the Rorschach should be chosen as a technique that has its own potentialities, as well as limitations, and that these should be carefully weighed in relation to the aims of any particular investigation. This means that the Rorschach technique, no more than another, cannot be expected to yield positive results unless such questions are carefully considered and unless the test is made an integral part of a systematically planned and well-designed inquiry. Furthermore, those who administer, score, and interpret the test results must have a training equivalent to that of psychologists who use it. While administrative problems, including the relations between tester and testee, should be given special attention, when the test is used outside our culture, these matters, like many investigations now concerned with questions of validity and reliability, lie mainly within the province of psychologists who can approach them with special professional skills. If it be thought that the data yielded by the Rorschach cannot be taken at its face value, there is no reason why the anthropologist should make use of the test. However, if the test is used, then the presentation of results obtained should conform to the same requirements demanded of those who use the Rorschach in clinical practice and the results should be subjected to the same standard of evaluation. It is only in this way that the limitations, as well as the potentialities, of the Rorschach Test as a tool in personality and culture studies can be finally appraised.

Chapter 4 - The Self and
Its Behavioral Environment*

INTRODUCTION

Self-awareness as a Generic Human Trait.—One of the distinguishing features of human adjustment, as compared with that of animals lower in the evolutionary scale, rests upon the fact that the human adult, in the course of ontogenetic development, has learned to discriminate himself as an object in a world of objects other than himself. Self-awareness is a psychological constant, one basic facet of human nature and of human personality.[1] As one psychologist has said, ". . . everyone, with the possible exception of infants, some philosophers, and some psychopaths, is aware of one's self.[2]

Self-awareness in man cannot be taken as an isolated psychological phenomena, however, if we are to understand the full range and depth of its human significance. For it is becoming increasingly apparent that this peculiarly human phenomena is the focus of complex, and functionally dependent, sets of linguistic and cultural variables that enter into the personal adjustment of human beings as members of particular societies. At the same time, it seems necessary to assume self-awareness as one of the prerequisite psychological conditions for the functioning of any human social order, no matter what linguistic and culture patterns prevail. If such be the case, the phenomena of self-awareness in our species is as integral a part of a human sociocultural mode of adaptation as it is of a distinctive human level of psychological structuralization.

It is likewise evident that, as one of the consequences of self-awareness, man has reflected upon his own nature as well as the nature of the world perceived as other than self. He has been able, moreover, to articulate and express through symbolic means explicit notions that embrace this polarity. Thus ideas of this order in concrete and conceptual form have become an intrinsic part of the cultural heritage of all human societies. It is possible, therefore, to investigate concepts of the self and its nature, as well as those linguistic and cultural variables that facilitate the emergence of the self as a perceptible object. In addition to investigations that are oriented in a traditional psychological or psychiatric

---

*Originally published as the first section of "The Self and Its Behavioural Environment," *Explorations*, II (April 1954).

frame of reference, concomitant inquiries oriented cross-culturally should widen as well as deepen our understanding of a distinctive human attribute.[3]

The nature of the self, considered in its conceptual content, is a culturally identifiable variable. Just as different peoples entertain various beliefs about the nature of the universe, they likewise differ in their ideas about the nature of the self. And, just as we have discovered that notions about the nature of the beings and powers existent in the universe involve assumptions that are directly relevant to an understanding of the behavior of the individual in a given society, we must likewise assume that the individual's self-image and his interpretation of his own experience cannot be divorced from the concept of the self that is characteristic of his society. For such concepts are the major means by which different cultures promote self-orientation in the kind of meaningful terms that make self-awareness of functional importance in the maintenance of a human social order. In so far as the needs and goals of the individual are at the level of self-awareness, they are structured with reference to the kind of self-image that is consonant with other basic orientations that prepare the self for action in a culturally constituted world. In his discussion of "The Primitive World View," Redfield points out that the concept of "world view" differs from culture, ethos, mode of thought, and national character. It implies "certain human universals." Among other things, it assumes "that in every society all men are conscious of self. Self is the axis of world view. Everyone distinguishes himself from all else. . . ."

It is the picture [he says] the members of a society have of the properties and characters upon their stage of action. While "national character" refers to the way these people look to the outsider looking in on them, "world view" refers to the way the world looks to that people, looking out. Of all that is connoted by "culture," "world view" attends especially to the way a man, in a particular society, sees himself in relation to all else. It is the properties of existence as distinguishd from and related to the self. It is, in short, a man's idea of the universe. It is that organization of ideas which answers to a man the questions: Where am I? Among whom do I move? What are my relations to things?[4]

As I have pointed out elsewhere (Chap. 1), "As a result of self-objectification human societies become social orders of conscious selves"; and from this standpoint cultures are "elaborate systems of meaning which . . . implement a type of adaptation which makes the role of the human being intelligible to himself with reference to an articulated universe and to his fellow men."

Historical Perspective.—Although man's self-awareness has long provided philosophers with an intriguing problem for speculation and psychologists have played fast and loose with it over several generations, anthropologists have paid comparatively little attention to the relevant ethnographic facts. It was recognized, of course, that concepts of the "soul" manifested considerable variability in content from one culture to another and a considerable body of data was put on record.[5] But concepts of the soul were seen primarily in their relation to religion and magic rather than in a psychological frame of reference, relevant to the generic fact of man's self-awareness on the one hand, and the content of a culturally constituted self-image, on the other.[6] When Wissler[7] set forth what he called the "universal pattern of culture" the absence of any concept of self in this pattern was not an oversight but a historically significant omission. Art, social organization, even war, were included, and, of course, religion. The implication is plain: Whereas concepts of the deity, or other spiritual beings, are assumed without any question to be an integral part of man's characteristic cultural adjustment to life, the concepts that man entertains about his *own* nature, exemplified in concepts of self, appear not to deserve any emphasis at all, to say nothing of an equal ranking with the other cultural categories included.[8] Subsequently, Murdock[9] listed a more specific series of items which he described as "common denominators of culture,"[10] saying, "they occur in every culture known to history or ethnology." It is interesting to note that while "soul concepts" are to be found in this list, self concepts are not. Traditional concepts of self, however, play the same kind of pragmatic role in the psychological adjustment of the individual to his world as do other classes of concepts and culturally derived means. Just as concepts of spiritual beings, for example, help to structuralize the vital part of the universe that is other than self and orient the individual in cosmic perspective, in the same way a concept of self not only facilitates self-orientation but enables the individual to comprehend the nature of his own being and, by inference, the nature of other selves with whom he interacts. Since concepts of this category define the most typical and permanent attributes of a phenomenal class of objects among which the personal self is included, their importance in any culture is obvious.

It is only within the last few decades, however, that anthropologists have manifested any vital interest in the relation between cultural variability, the psychological structure of the individual, and his differential behavior. There were also other obstacles which interfered with the development of any serious interest in questions focused upon such a topic as the concept of self. One of these was the fact that at various times self-awareness has been minimized or even denied as an observable phenomena among primitive peoples. This idea dates back half a century or more to the period when the concept of evolution was the guiding line for all thinking that concerned primitive peoples. At this period all sorts of attempts were made to differentiate the mind, the thinking, or the mentality of "early" man or "primitive" peoples from "civilized" (European) peoples. One point of differentiation was made to turn upon the status of self-awareness in the evolution of the human mind. Self-awareness was undeveloped in primitive man as compared with civilized man.[11] This interpretation of certain ethnographic facts still crops up, as for instance in the statement of H. Kelsen that "Hand in hand with the predominance of the emotional over the rational tendency in the soul of primitive man goes a remarkable lack of ego-consciousness, a lack of any developed experience of his self."[12]

Paul Radin in *Primitive Man as Philosopher* takes quite the opposite point of view. He raises the question: "How does primitive man regard the ego?" But he goes on to say, "Few ethnologists have ever attempted to obtain from a native any systematized account of their own theory. It has, in fact, been generally contended that they have none. As a result our material consists of isolated statements on different aspects of the Ego and we are perforce compelled to weld them into a consistent or inconsistent whole—as the case may be—in order to see their complete bearings. This unfortunately cannot be helped."

In 1938 Marcel Mauss took as the subject of his Huxley lecture "Une categorie de l'esprit humain: la notion de personne, celle de 'moi.' "[14] He points out that, while we have here "une de ces idées que nous croyons innées," an investigation is needed of how it was "lentement née et grandie au cours de longs siècles et à travers de nombreuses vicissitudes, tellement qu'elle est encore, aujourd'hui même, flottante, délicate, précieuse, et à élaborer davantage." While everyone finds "l'idée de 'personne,' l'idée du 'moi' " natural enough and, besides this, "au fond de sa conscience, toute equipée au fond de la morale qui s'en deduit," at the same time "il s'agit de substituer à cette naïve vue de son histoire, et de son actuelle valeur, une vue plus précise."

While Mauss excludes a psychological approach as irrelevant to his immediate concern, he assumes that "il est évident, surtout pour nous, qu'il n'y a jamais en d'être humain qui n'ait eu le sens, non seulement de son corps, mais aussi de son individualité spirituelle et corporelle à la fois." What interests Mauss is the concept of the self as "un sujet d'histoire sociale. Comment, au cours des siécles, a travers de nombreuses sociétés, s'est lentement élaboré, non pas le sens du 'moi,' mais la notion, le concept que les hommes des divers temps s'en sont crées? Ce que le veux vous montrer, c'est la série des formes que ce concept a revetues dans la vie des hommes des sociétés, d'après leurs droits, leurs religions, leurs coutumes, leurs structures sociales et leurs mentalités." Mauss characterizes his lecture as "un plan de travail." His discussion remains fragamentary, but nevertheless suggestive, especially in regard to the need for further historical elucidation of the concept of the self in Western culture.

More recently, a few anthropologists have become interested in the self as a topic. Dorothy Lee has published the most sophisticated analysis of the concept of self among a nonliterate people yet to appear. Her approach, however, is essentially a linguistic analysis.[15] At the meetings of the American Association for the Advancement of Science (1949)

Marian W. Smith read a paper on "Varying Concepts of Ego Extension," later published in *Psychiatry*.[16] And now, in contrast with earlier editions, the *Outline of Cultural Materials* includes an item called "Ethnopsychology"[17] under which we find "concepts of the self, of human nature, of motivation, of personality," so that, in the future, we should have more detailed inquiries into such topics.

There is an additional reason anthropologists of an earlier generation could hardly have been expected to concern themselves with concepts of the self, except at a purely descriptive cross-cultural level. If they had turned to their psychological colleagues for enlightenment, the latter would probably have discouraged, rather than encouraged, them. Despite the fact that William James had dealt with the "empirical self," and there had emerged from the work of J. M. Baldwin, C. H. Cooley, and particularly G. H. Mead, the hypothesis that the self is a social product, Sargent remarks that "between about 1910 and 1940 most psychologists preferred not to mention 'ego' or 'self' in their writings."[18] But following C. W. Allport's address to the Eastern Psychological Association in 1943 on "The Ego in Contemporary Psychology" this subject once again emerged as completely reputable and has proved to be a topic of expanding interest in psychological circles. It is in some of the current textbooks in social psychology as well as elsewhere that we find the most systematic discussions of the self.[19]

So far as psychoanalytic theories are concerned, it is of some historic interest that it was only in the early 1920's that "Freud finally formulated a theory of the total personality, and the ego with its function of reality testing became the Ego of the Ego, Superego and Id."[20] This shift in interest from the libido to the activities of the ego was signalized by the publication of *The Ego and the Id*. This occurred during the period when psychologists were still uninterested in questions relating to the self but when, on the other hand, some anthropologists were becoming vitally interested in personality structure and its dynamics in relation to variability in cultural patterns.[21]

Since the major purpose of this paper is to clear the ground for a more effective handling of cross-cultural data that seem relevant to a deeper understanding of the role of self-awareness in man as *culturally constituted* in different societies, I am not directly concerned with questions of personality dynamics as such. The discussion is deliberately couched at another level which, for want of a better term but without implying too many theoretical implications, might best be called "phenomenological." What I wish to develop is a frame of reference by means of which it may be possible to view the individual in another society in terms of the psychological perspective which his culture constitutes for him and which is the integral focus of his activities, rather than to content ourselves with the perspective of an outside observer

79

who may even pride himself on his "objectivity." In this way I believe we can also discern more clearly than otherwise some of the common functions that all cultures play in building up and reinforcing self-awareness in the individual through certain basic orientations, despite wide differences in actual culture patterns.

Terminology.—Before going on to a discussion of the assumptions and hypotheses that underlie the frame of reference I have in mind, it will be necessary to say a few words about terminology. It is impossible at the present time to escape entirely from the dilemma presented by the absence of any standardized usage. The only way to cut this Gordian knot is constantly to bear in mind the actual data that can be described on a phenomenological level (as, e.g., self-awareness, self-perception, self-reference by means of language, self-conception). While some writers use the terms "self" and "ego" as synonymous, others do not. I have chosen the term "self" as more convenient for several reasons. In psychoanalytic usage "ego" is used to refer to one aspect of the total personality as construed in terms of an explicit theory of personality development and functioning. To use this term in cross-cultural perspective would be confusing since it could not possibly carry the same connotation. I believe it is best to reserve this term as well as "superego" for technical use in a psychodynamic context. Besides this, where both the terms "ego" and "self" are used by some writers, "self" is the more inclusive term. At the same time, "self" is not ordinarily used as a synonym for "the total personality." This latter term, furthermore, has now assumed a more or less sophisticated usage as part of a technical psychological vocabulary, however it may still be used in common speech. From the standpoint of cross-cultural inquiry it seems to me much better to make the concepts of "self" a point of departure, rather than concepts of "ego" or "personality." The term "self," in short, does seem to connote a concept that remains closer to the phenomenological facts that reflect man's self-awareness as a generic psychological attribute. It retains the reflexive connotation that is indicated when we say that a human individual becomes an object to himself, that he identifies himself as an object among other objects in his world, that he can conceive himself not only as a whole but in terms of different parts, that he can converse with himself, and so on. Murphy's definition of the self as "the individual as known to the individual" exemplifies this essential emphasis upon the "reflexive mood." It is quite true, of course, that the self known to the individual may not represent a "true" picture from an objective point of view. But this assumes another perspective and indicates the point at which technical constructs such as ego or superego are necessary in order to help make analysis intelligible in *psychodynamic* terms. In cross-cultural perspective, on the other hand, and at the level of phenomenological description, the fact remains that human beings do function in terms of concepts of self which, in part, are culturally derived.

In this perspective we can seek answers to such questions as: By what cultural means is self-awareness built up in different societies? How do individuals view themselves in terms of the self that they know? What are the cultural as well as the idiosyncratic factors in their self image? What is the time-span involved in the continuity of the self as culturally defined? What relation is there between varying self concepts and differential behavior? What is the relation of the self as culturally constituted to the needs and goals of the individual as culturally defined?

If it is possible to view the self as culturally constituted and known to the individual in the same frame of reference as we view the culturally constituted world in which the individual must act, this preliminary step may enable us to apprehend with greater clarity both the essential role of culture in relation to a generic human attribute and to define with more precision some of the constant and variable factors that structuralize the psychological field of behavior for the individual in different societies.

GENERAL ASSUMPTIONS AND HYPOTHESES

Self-awareness a Cultural as well as Social Product.—Awareness of self is not given at birth. "Like all other objects of experience, the self grows out of the matrix of indefiniteness which exists at the first perceptual level. It comes gradually into being as the process of differentiation goes on within the perceptual field. . . . There is also considerable evidence to show that the body in all its forms is at first as strange, as unfamiliar, as unorganized as are any other perceived objects. For many months, much of it is not recognized as self."[22] But in the course of the socialization process self-awareness does eventually emerge so that, as Murphy says, "one of the most important things the child ever learns as a result of social contacts is that he is a person, a self."[23] Consequently, there is a conceptual as well as a perceptual aspect of self-awareness to be taken account of in the mature individual. Self-conceptualization in a significant meaningful form undoubtedly comes later[24] when, through mastery of speech and other aspects of his culture, the nature of the self as culturally defined becomes an integral part of the implicit assumptions that become the basis for the activities of the individual and the interpretation of his experience.

The foregoing aspects of ontogenetic development in man are, of course, universal. And, since human experience occurs in a social milieu, in the sense that intimate and continuing contacts with other human beings are the major sources which mediate the influences that mold the development of the child, the self has often been referred to as a "social product." It might be more accurately characterized as, also, a *cultural product.* For the acquistion and use of a particular language, the specific content that is given to an articulated world of objects that is

81

built up *pari passu* with self-awareness, and the integration of personal experience with a concept of the nature of the self as traditionally viewed, are among the necessary conditions that make possible the emergence and functioning of human awareness as a generic aspect of human personality structure. At the same time, such cultural constituents give various colorings to this unique psychological attribute of man.

Furthermore, the preeminent role which cultural factors play in the experience of self-awareness in man highlights a corollary problem which only needs mention in passing. The cultural factors referred to are dependent, in turn, upon a mode of social living that requires the functioning of complicated representative processes and the existence of symbolic systems. (See Chap. 1.) These mediate social and personal adjustment in a way that is only characteristic of man. Consequently, it seems reasonable to infer that, among other primates and the lower animals, not only the conditions that make self-conceptualization possible are lacking but, in some animals, even those conditions which in the child (and possibly in some of the anthropoid apes) permit the rudiments of a body image to develop out of perceptual experience. As Parr has pointed out,

An animal without appendages cannot touch himself and thus cannot through feeling become acquainted with his own body. Though long, sinuous creatures such as snakes or eels—or long-necked ostriches and giraffes—can turn around and see a large proportion of their bodies, a more rigid animal, like the mackeral, cannot see itself at all. There are, of course, mirrors in nature and an animal may occasionally chance upon his reflection; yet he lacks the powers of deduction to realize that the reflection is a counterpart of himself. This relative ignorance of self has its social implications. Having no adequate concept of his own body, an animal can have no clear conviction that his associates are of his kind. He does not consciously recognize his companions or even his offspring as being "birds of a feather"; his mate may be only a foreign object that has a special allure.[25]

For a differentiated sense of self-awareness to emerge it must be possible for the individual to react to himself as an empirical object, to identify himself and refer to himself in contradistinction to other selves and things, to represent himself to himself, to appraise himself, and so on. Such reflexive processes imply a concept and the use of symbolic means of representation and reference. Unlike some of the lower vertebrates referred to by Parr, the human individual through language and reflective thought is able to integrate perceptions of his own body and his personal experiences with a meaningful concept of self that is the common property of other members of his society.

While common roots of a rudimentary sense of self-awareness that lie at an unconscious level in man may be paralleled in some of the higher apes it is only under the conditions characteristic of human adjustment that self-awareness becomes differentiated and assumes a functional importance in the maintenance of a social mode of life. For

I believe that we must assume that the functioning of any human society is inconceivable without self-awareness, reinforced and constituted by traditional beliefs about the nature of the self.

This hypothesis receives support from the universal fact that, as compared with the societies of animals lower in the scale of organic evolution, any human society is not only a social order but a moral order as well. A moral order being one that is characterized by the fact that not only norms of conduct exist but organized or unorganized social sanctions to reinforce them, an inevitable conclusion must be drawn: the members of such an order are expected to assume moral responsibility for their conduct. Such an assumption, in turn, implies self-awareness of one's own conduct, self-appraisal of one's conduct with reference to socially recognized standards of value, some volitional control of one's own behavior, a possible choice of alternative lines of conduct, etc. Assumptions like these, of course, cannot be made in the case of insect societies, or the societies of infrahuman primates. Without the development of self-awareness as an intrinsic part of the socialization process, without a concept of self that permits attitudes directed towards the self as an object to emerge and crystallize, we would not have some of the essential conditions necessary for the functioning of a human society.

Self-awareness is also basic to the discrimination and learning of the multiple roles which are required of the individual in human societies. He must have some awareness of his statuses in the social structure with reference to sex, age, etc., in order to fit into the total patterns of social interaction that maintains the socio-economic system as a going concern. If he were not aware of his roles he would not be in a position to appraise his own conduct in terms of traditional values and social sanctions.

Cultural Definition of Subjective-Objective Dichotomy.—The psychological implications of the development of self-awareness cannot be fully appreciated, however, without reference to a corollary fact of equal importance. This is the concomitant emergence in the socialization process of the awareness of a contrasting world of articulated objects, experienced as "other-than-self." If this were not so, the human individual would be destined to remain at an infantile stage of psychological development. For this level is precisely one in which objects of an external world have not yet become clearly articulated in experience and where the beginnings of ego-centered processes have not yet developed to the point where the subject is able to perceive himself as an object in a universe that likewise contains objects other than himself. And, just as cultural factors are constitutive in the development of self-awareness, the structuralization of a world of objects other than self becomes organized, in part, in cultural terms. This is due to the fact that perception in man, as is now more evident than ever before, does not present the human being with a "picture" of an "objective" world which, in all its attributes, is "there" only waiting to be perceived, completely unaffected by the experience, concepts, attitudes, needs, and purposes of the perceiver. Perception is "never an absolute revelation of 'what is.' "[26] On the other hand, this does not imply any denial of the existence of an objectively definable order of phenomena existentially extraneous to the human individual or even the human species. It has been stated, e.g., that "there is some perceptual level at which exists absolute objectivity; that is, a one-to-one correspondence between experience and reality."[27] But a satisfactory definition of this level for man as a whole is obscured by the fact that the psychological field in which human behavior takes place *is* always culturally constituted, in part, and human responses are never reducible in their *entirety* to stimuli derived from an "objective" or surrounding world of objects in the physical or geographical sense. For the world of human awareness is mediated by various symbolic devices which, through the learning and experience of individuals, establish the concepts, discriminations, classificatory patterns, and attitudes by means of which perceptual experience is personally integrated. In this way assumptions about the nature of the universe become, as it were, a priori constituents in the perceptual process itself. Language, of course, plays a major role both in terms of its structural characteristics as well as of the potentialities inherent in narrative discourse (myths, tales, anecdotes) for the symbolic presentation of events. The graphic and plastic arts may likewise reinforce the same order through visual representation.[28]

If we accept the hypothesis that awareness of self as an empirical object and awareness of objects other than self are a coordinate result of maturation and socialization in man and that both involve cultural constitutents, then we can go a step farther. This categorical distinction, and the polarity it implies, becomes one of the fundamental axes along which the psychological field of the human individual is structured for action in every culture. This phenomenon may be thought of as generic. Where differential cultural factors enter the picture is in the varied patterns which the environmental field may take when viewed from the standpoint of the self. Since the self is also partly a cultural product, the field of behavior that is appropriate for the activities of *particular* selves in *their* world of culturally defined objects is not by any means precisely coordinate with any absolute polarity of subjectivity—objectivity that is definable.

Failure to recognize this fact appears to be the main reason some of the descriptive data on nonliterate peoples have, from the time of Tylor on, frequently been interpreted as an indication that they were unable to distinguish clearly between the "subjective" and the "objective." In the *Early History of Mankind,* Tylor, for example, spoke of the life of primitive man as resembling "a long dream."[29] And in his *Primitive Culture*[30] he generalizes,

84

Even in healthy waking life, the savage or barbarian has never learned to make that *rigid distinction* [italics ours] between imagination and reality, to enforce which is one of the main results of scientific education. Still less, when disordered in body and mind he sees around him phantom human forms, can he distrust the evidence of his very senses. Thus it comes to pass that throughout the lower civilization men believe, with the most vivid and intense belief, in the objective reality of the human spectres which they see in sickness, exhaustion, or excitement.

While even some early critics of Tylor, for instance Crawley,[31] found themselves unable fully to accept his statement, the major ground for the objection rested on common sense. Man's very existence depends on making *some* distinction between "objective" and "subjective." He cannot nourish himself in a dream world. While this is true enough, the issue remains oversimplified if we leave it there. For this common-sense answer itself assumes that there must of necessity be some easily recognized, if not sharply definable, "line" that differentiates the polar categories at issue. But it is the precise locus of this "line" that presents a problem that has not even been satisfactorily settled by philosophers or psychologists.[32]

If we take a fresh look at the ethnographic data it is quite true that the line between what *we* call objectivity-subjectivity may appear somewhat blurred. This is partly due to the fact that subjectivity-objectivity cannot be adequately conceived in simple "linear" terms, but only with reference to the total pattern of the psychological field. The "line" that we think should always be drawn precisely "here" may not be drawn sharply at all, although it may appear somewhere else as a recognizable boundary. I believe that the basic principle involved has been stated by MacLeod. He points out that "subjectivity and objectivity are properties of an organized perceptual field in which points of reference are selves (subjects) and objects, and the degree of articulation in this dimension may vary greatly." In our discussion here the "degree of articulation" in self-object relations may be construed in terms of a structure and content definable by reference to the cultural factors directly relevant to the psychological field of the individual. By thus approaching the matter we can apprehend the actual behavioral environment of the self. Instead of making any a priori distinction between "subjectivity" and "objectivity" a matter of primary concern, on the assumption that data assignable to such categories are readily separable in the experience of individuals in other cultures, it will be assumed that, in so far as such a distinction has a meaningful character, it will receive a varying emphasis that is only intelligible in terms of the total patterning of the behavioral field of the individual. For it must not be forgotten that the empirical self and the empirical world of surrounding objects have both emerged out of a common process of maturation, socialization, and personal experience. An intelligible behavioral environment has been constituted for the individual that bears an intimate relation to the

85

kind of being he knows himself to be and it is in this behavioral environment that he is motivated to act.

The Behavioral Environment of Man.—The concept of behavioral environment must be clearly distinguished from a concept of environment construed as being "external" to the individual, with properties that are definable independently of the selectively determined responses that the socialization process in man always imposes. The "objective," "geographical," or "physical" environment as thus conceived stands in contrast to the behavioral environment.[33] It has a limited usefulness even in the observation of animals at the subhuman level. On the other hand, the concept of behavioral environment takes account of the properties and adaptational needs of the organism in interaction with the external world as constituting the actual behavioral field in terms of which the activities of the animal are more thoroughly intelligible. Capacity or incapacity for color vision, for instance, defines an aspect of the behavioral environment that may radically differentiate one species from another irrespective of the properties of an external world described "objectively." The order of psychological reality in which the animal acts is, in the first instance, a function of its organic properties as much as it is a function of the properties of the objective environment as they impinge on the organism. This is why G. H. Mead[34] insisted long ago that the organism "determines the invironment . . . the organism, then, is in a sense responsible for its environment."

This is eminently true both of man in his unique potentialities as an organic species, and of the differential behavioral environments that are created for human individuals reared in different cultural settings. Human adjustment, on the whole, cannot be simply explained as responses engendered by factors attributable to a physical environment constituted for the individual in the socialization process. It may even be argued that human potentialities and a cultural mode of life *preclude* any reductive interpretations focused upon the outside physical world alone. Even the "natural resources" of any human society become constituted as "resources" only when, in a particular culture, the knowledge and technology necessary for their exploitation is developed. The same principle applies to classes of objects such as the "heavenly bodies" that we label as "natural" and which, following scientific procedures of observation, we find located in physical space and subject to mechanical laws. But the sun, moon, thunder, wind are not "natural" phenomena in this sense in the culturally constituted behavioral environment of all peoples. Our contemporary categorization is derived from highly specialized scientific investigations and a mode of reasoning that is typical *only* of recent phases of Western culture. It is sometimes forgotten in comparing other cultures with our own that, "From the time of Thales down through the period we broadly call 'the Renaissance,' a majority of philosophers taught and most men believed that the world was *animate*. It lived and flourished as did man, and like man, was susceptible of decay, even of death." It was only during the seventeenth century that "this conception gave way to the idea of the world as *mechanism—* a world machine, no longer animate, but mechanically responsive to the 'laws of Nature.' "[35] Consequently, while the "objective" properties of "natural" objects upon which we are accustomed to center our scientific attention may be equally perceptible in certain respects to individuals whose behavioral environment is structured differently from ours, at the same time such properties may be much less salient for them.

Evidence from human cultures everywhere also indicates that man typically responds to objects in his behavioral environment that to the sophisticated mind are symbolically constituted, i.e., spiritual beings of various classes. Such objects, in some way experienced, clearly conceptualized and reified, may occupy a high rank in the behavioral environment although from a sophisticated Western point of view they are sharply distinguishable from the natural objects of the physical environment. However, the nature of such objects is no more fictitious, in a psychological sense, than the concept of the self. Consequently, culturally reified objects in the behavioral environment may have functions that can be shown to be directly related to the needs, motivations, and goals of the self. Symbolically represented, such objects are integral parts of the psychological field of the individual and must be considered as relevant variables because they can be shown to affect actual behavior.[36]

Consequently, I believe it both preferable and clarifying for us to speak of the environment in which man lives as a "culturally constituted behavioral environment," rather than to say that man lives in a "social" or "cultural" environment, without further analysis. This is particularly the case if we seek for deeper behavioral understanding. It is of considerable importance in this connection to note that the same assumptions that have invalidated the usefulness of the concept of "objective" or "physical" environment find their logical parallels in the naïve use of such terms as "social" or "cultural" environment. For it is likewise assumed that a social or cultural environment can be defined in terms of properties or structures that are, in the first instance, conceived independently of the individuals they are said to environ. Without further analysis it is implied, if not explicitly stated, that this environment, as described by some objective observer, is the actual environment to which the individual responds. This leads to what MacLeod has called the "sociological bias" which, he points out, is somewhat analagous to the "stimulus-receptor bias" that once prevailed widely in the study of perception:

This bias in its most common form involves the acceptance of the structures and processes of society as defined by the sociologist as the true coordinates for the specification of behavior and experience. From this point of view, e.g., the church or the political party in which the individual possesses membership, is regarded as an institution of society, possessing the manifold properties and functions which a many-sided sociological investigation reveals, rather than as the church or political party as it is apprehended and reacted to by the individual. The process of social adjustment, of socialization or of attitude formation thus becomes defined in terms of a set of norms which have reality for the scientific observer, but not necessarily for the individual concerned.[37]

The traditional approach of cultural anthropology, having as one of its primary goals a reliable account of differential modes of life found among the peoples of the world, has not been directly concerned with the behavior of individuals. It has been culture-centered, rather than behavior-centered. In consequence, it has been found convenient to organize the presentation of the descriptive ethnographic data collected in terms of a more or less conventional series of topics (language, religion, technology, social organization, etc.). No matter how reliable such data are, or whatever their value for comparative and analytic studies of *culture,* of necessity the material is presented from the standpoint of an outside observer. Presented to us in this form, these cultural data do not easily permit us to apprehend, in an integral fashion, the most significant and meaningful aspects of the world of the individual as experienced by him and in terms of which he thinks, is motivated to act, and satisfies his needs. The language of a people, as objectively described and analyzed in terms of its formal categories, is not the language that exists for the individual who uses it as a means of communication, in reflective thought, as a mode of verbal self-expression. He may, indeed, be quite unconscious of its objective characteristics. It is an integral part of himself and his world. It is neither "objective" nor "subjective." The same holds true, in principle, for other cultural phenomena when viewed from the standpoint of the individual within his cultural setting. Because culture can be objectively described and for certain purposes treated as if it were a sui generis phenomenon, it is sometimes implied, or even argued, that it is in fact phenomenologically autonomous.[38] To do so is to misunderstand totally the basic conditions of human psychological adjustment. Any inner-outer dichotomy, with the human skin as a boundary, is psychologically irrelevant. As Murray points out, with reference to this problem considered ontogenetically—"much of what is now *inside* the organism was once *outside.* For these reasons, the organism and its milieu must be considered together, a single creature—environment interaction being a convenient short unit for psychology."[39]

The concept of behavioral environment enables us to take cognizance of this fact, to appraise and reorder culturally given data to bring into focus the actual structure of the psychological field of the individual. At the same time it enables us to approximate more closely to an "inside" view of a culture, the kind of naïve orientation we unconsciously assume towards our own culture, but which is so difficult to achieve in the case of another. More specifically, viewing a culture from the "inside" can best be achieved if we organize our data in a manner that permits us, as far as possible, to assume the outlook of the self in its behavioral environment.

BASIC ORIENTATIONS PROVIDED BY CULTURE

From this standpoint culture may be said to play a constitutive role in the psychological adjustment of the individual to his world. The human individual must be provided with certain basic orientations in order to act intelligibly in the world he apprehends. Such orientations are basic in the sense that they are peculiar to a human level of adjustment. They all appear to revolve around man's capacity for self-awareness. If it be assumed that the functioning of *human* societies depends in some way upon this psychological fact, it is not difficult to understand why all human cultures must provide the individual with basic orientations that are among the necessary conditions for the development, reinforcement, and effective functioning of self-awareness. It is these orientations that may be said to structure the core of the behavioral environment of the self in any culture. Whereas cultural means and content may vary widely, common instrumental functions can be discerned.

Self-Orientation.—Animals below man, for instance, even though they may be highly capable of acting in a complex behavioral environment that includes many classes of objects other than themselves, including other animals of their species, do not have to become self-oriented in order to function adequately in a social group. On the other hand, one of the common functions of culture is to provide various means of self-orientation for the human being.

It is quite generally recognized that language plays an essential role in this self-orientation. But only certain features of language have been emphasized, to the exclusion of others, while the generic function of all languages in providing linguistic means of self-orientation has not been sufficiently stressed.

Despite wide variations in linguistic structure Boas called attention years ago to the fact that "the three personal pronouns—I, thou, and he—occur in all human languages" and emphasized that "the underlying idea of these pronouns is the clear distinction between the self as speaker, the person or object spoken to, and that spoken of."[40] If this be accepted, we have an unequivocal indication that languages all have a common sociopsychological function. They provide the human individual with a linguistic means of self-other orientation in all contexts of interpersonal verbal communication. A personal existence and sphere of action is defined as a fundamental reference point.

Although we do not have parallel investigations in other societies, in Western culture we have had a number of studies which indicate the mastery of our system of personal and possessive pronouns at a very early age. According to Gesell, for example, the child begins to use self-reference words—mine, me, you, and I, in that order—at two years, whereas at eighteen-months self and "not self" are not clearly differentiated.[41]

As compared with the mastery of a pronominal system we know very little about the acquisition and use of kinship terms in ontogenetic perspective. In many nonliterate societies such terms are among the major linguistic means that orient the individual in a self-other dimension in relation to his roles in the social order.

Then there is the universal phenomenon of personal names. These are related to self-orientation in so far as they are personal and serve as a linguistic device for self-identification and unequivocal indentification of the self by others. The fact that in some cultures the individual knows his name although it may not be customary for him to use it freely for self-identification indicates the need for more detailed studies of the variable aspect of personal naming in relation to self-orientation. But the ubiquitous fact of personal naming must be considered to be in the same functional category as the pronominal pattern.[42]

In this connection it would also be interesting to know more about the role which personal names play in the sexual orientation of the self. Certainly in many cultures—although how widespread the custom is I do not know—the panel of names available for boys is not the same as for girls. Names are sex-linked. Under these circumstances, knowing one's own name is equivalent to knowing one's own sex. Awareness of one's sexual status is likewise implied in the use of certain kinship terms in many cultures, so that, in acquiring the proper use of kinship terms, the child likewise becomes sexually oriented. There are other aspects of language that should be considered in relation to self-orientation, but these illustrations must suffice.[43]

Whatever the idiosyncratic content of the self-image may be and whatever weight it may be given in psychodynamic analysis, the content of the self-image is, in part, a culturally constituted variable.[44] While one of the constant functions of all cultures therefore is to provide a concept of self along with other means that promote self-orientation, the individuals of a given society are self-oriented in terms of a provincial content of the self-image.

This by no means implies that we should expect to find a single linguistic term or a concept even roughly equivalent to "self," "ego," or "soul" in all cultures. The absence of any such single term and the correlative fact that the self-image may present subtleties foreign to our mode of thinking is one of the reasons such a topic, approached from outside a culture, poses inherent difficulties. On the other hand, there are analogies familiar to the anthropologist. Art, religion, and law, for example, have been investigated in societies in which abstract terms for such phenomena do not exist. It also has been found that too rigid a priori definitions and concepts, consciously or unconsciously modeled after those of our own intellectual tradition, may even lead to a denial that comparable phenomena exist in other cultures, only because the phenomena observed fail to meet all the requirements of the definitions and concepts employed by the observer. In any case, we must not expect to find concepts of the self among nonliterate peoples clearly articulated for us. To a certain extent it is necessary to approach the whole subject naïvely, to pursue it obliquely from different angles, to attack the conceptual core of the problem in terms of its pragmatic implications and in the full light of related concepts in a single cultural matrix. We already know from available data, for instance, that such concepts as reincarnation, metamorphosis, and the notion that under certain circumstances the "soul" may leave the body, must be relevant to variations in the self-image which different peoples have. But we know much less about the way in which such concepts become psychologically significant for the individual in relation to his motivations, goals, and life adjustment.

Object Orientation.—A *second* function of all cultures is the orientation of the self to a diversified world of objects in its behavioral environment, discriminated, classified, and conceptualized with respect to attributes which are culturally constituted and symbolically mediated through language. The role of language in object-orientation is as vital as in self-orientation. The late Ernst Cassirer laid special emphasis upon this point. "Language," he said, "does not enter a world of completed objective perceptions only to add to individually given and clearly delimited objects, one in relation to the other, 'names' which will be purely external and arbitrary signs; rather, it is itself a mediator in the formation of objects. It is, in a sense, the mediator par excellence, the most important and most precise instrument for the conquest and the construction of a true world of objects."[45] It is this objectifying function of speech that enables man to live and act in an articulated world of objects that is psychologically incomparable with that of any other creature.

Object orientation likewise provides the ground for an intelligible interpretation of events in the behavioral environment on the basis of traditional assumptions regarding the nature and attributes of the objects involved, and implicit or explicit dogmas regarding the "causes" of events. A cosmic and metaphysical orientation of the self supplies a conceptual framework for action in an orderly rather than a chaotic universe. It is not necessary, of course, that the individual be aware of the underlying metaphysical principles involved, any more than it is necessary that he be aware of the grammatical principles of the language that he speaks. But the former are as open to investigation as the latter. It is for this reason that considerable confusion has been

91

created by the application of the natural-supernatural category to non-literate peoples in approaching their religion or world view.[46] This dichotomy simply reflects the outcome of metaphysical speculation in latter-day thought in Western culture. Instead of assuming a priori that this dichotomy is really meaningful in other cultures, it might be more profitable to discover the metaphysical principles that actually exist. At any rate, if we assume the outlook of the self as culturally oriented in a behavioral environment with cosmic dimensions and implicit metaphysical principles, a great deal of what is ordinarily described as "religion" is seen to involve the attitudes, needs, goals, and affective experience of the self in interaction with certain classes of objects in the behavioral environment. These classes of objects are typically *other* selves—spiritual beings, deities, ancestors. The relation of the self to them may, indeed, be characterized by the same patterns that apply to interpersonal relations with other human beings. In any case, the individual must be quite as aware of his status in relation to other-than-human beings, as he is in relation to his human associates. He must learn to play his proper role in response to their roles as culturally defined.

In other words, the "social" relations of the self when considered in its total behavioral environment may be far more inclusive than ordinarily conceived. The self in its relations with other selves may transcend the boundaries of social life as objectively defined.[47] This is a fact of some psychological importance since it is relevant to the needs, motivations, and goals of individuals under certain circumstances. At the same time, the social relations of the self in this more inclusive sense may not be directly relevant in a sociological frame of reference where the aim of the observer is to define the lineaments of "social structure" in the usual sense. That is, the social structure, defined as a result of such an investigation, may not be the phenomenon apprehended by the self, nor represent the most salient aspects, for the individual, of the greater society of selves apprehended in the behavioral environment. In some cultures the social orientation of the self may be so constituted that relations with deceased ancestors or other-than-human selves become much more crucial for an understanding of the most vital needs and goals of the individual than do interpersonal relations with other human beings.

Spatiotemporal Orientation.—Since the self must be prepared for action, a *third* basic orientation that all cultures must provide is some kind of spatiotemporal[48] frame of reference. (For an extended discussion of spatial and temporal orientation see Chaps. 9, 10, 11.) Animals have to find their way about in space, but they do not have to be oriented in an acquired schema that involves the conscious use of culturally constituted reference points and the awareness of one's position in space.[49] Just as a culture provides the means that enable the individual

92

to identify himself and to define his position with reference to his behavior in a scheme of social relations, it likewise provides him with the means for defining his position in a spatial frame of reference that transcends immediate perceptual experience.[50] Getting lost or becoming spatially disoriented is apt to be an emotionally distressing situation for an individual in any culture. The capacity to move freely and intelligently from place to place, to conceptualize the spatial location of one's destination, and to be able to reach it, as well as to be able to return back home, is a commonplace of everyday human living.

Just as personal names mediate self-identification and personal reference, in the same way names for places and significant topographical features are a universal linguistic means for discriminating and representing stabilized points in space which enable the self to achieve spatial orientation. Place names become focal points in the organized directional schema made available to the individual through knowledge and experience. Such stable points of reference are not only a guide to action, once known they can be mentally manipulated in relational terms at a more abstract level, as in maps for example. Place names likewise become integrated with the temporal orientation of the self. For self-awareness implies that the individual not only knows where he *is*, but where he *was* at some previous moment in time, or where he expects to be in the *future*. The identification of the self with a given locus—be it a dwelling, a camp, a village, or what not—also depends upon the linguistic discrimination of place. Other selves, living or dead, and selves of an other-than-human category likewise can be assigned a characteristic spatial locale through the device of place-naming. Place-naming is another common denominator of cultures.

Orientation in time is coordinate with spatial orientation and, however simple the means or crude the temporal intervals discriminated may be, the self is temporally as well as spatially oriented in all cultures.[51] Temporal disorientation is abnormal in any culture if judged in relation to the traditional temporal schema. Of course, in a culture without names for days of the week self-orientation in time is not possible in terms of this particular schema. On the other hand, if "moons" are named it is assumed that the individual knows his "moons."

What we know all too little about are the earliest phases of temporal orientation in the child—a sensed relationship of experienced events in time—at a period before traditional cultural concepts are learned and consciously employed, and even before a concept of self is fully developed. L. K. Frank directed attention to this problem many years ago, indicating how what we have called motivational and normative orientations became integrated with the beginnings of temporal orientation and a growing sense of self at an early age:

Here then begins the characteristically human career of man who, not content to be ruled by hunger and other physiological functions, transforms them so that

93

hunger becomes appetite, bladder and rectal pressures become occasions for modesty, cleanliness, etc. and later sex becomes love. This transformation of naive behavior into conduct involves the acceptance of values, or, more specifically, necessitates value behavior and time perspectives wherein we see the individual responding to present, immediate situation-events (intra-organic or environmental) as point-events in a sequence the later or more remote components of which are the focus of that conduct. . . . If we let A represent one of the immediately impinging situation-events facing an individual, either within his organism or in the environment, it is clear that A is the first of a sequence A, B, C, D. . . N. When the infant responds naively to A (physiological need) by a physiological process (evacuation) he behaves organically and directly. As training in toilet habits proceeds, he learns to recognize A (the internal pressure) as a preparatory signal or behavior cue, not a stimulus to immediate releasing behavior; the bladder pressure A now becomes the first term in a sequence A, B, C, D. . . N, leading to the appropriate later term N which may be the household toilet. This response to A in terms of its consequences then becomes the prototype of value behavior with an almost infinite regression toward the future, for again we see that N (voiding at a specified place, in privacy, and keeping the clothes dry) is itself a first term or A in another sequence of holding or earning the much needed security of parental approval and love and a wider social approval and acceptance by teachers, schoolmates, and so on. What looks like a simple, childish achievement of control and elimination assumes, upon reflection, a large significance for understanding human conduct and the question of values within a time perspective. As will be realized the various time perspectives of a culture give the dimensions of the values that are operating in the lives of those living in that culture by specifying the conduct that must be observed in response to each situation, wherein that immediate situation is to be seen as instrumental to a more remote or deferred situation.[52]

The deeper psychological implications of the relation between temporal orientation and the emergence and functioning of self-awareness in the human being are nowhere more clearly apparent than in the integral connections between memory processes and the development of a feeling of self-identity. This integral relation is one of the necessary conditions required if any sense of *self-continuity* is to become salient. Human beings maintain awareness of self-continuity and personal identity in time through the recall of past experiences that are identified with the self-image. If I cannot remember, or recall at will, experiences of an hour ago, or yesterday, or last year that I readily identify as *my* experiences, I cannot maintain an awareness of self-continuity in time. At the lowest functional level, however, recall neither implies volition nor any capacity to organize the memory images of past events in any temporal schema. Even if we should grant animals below man a very high capacity for recall, without some symbolically based and culturally derived means, it would be impossible to organize *what* is recalled in relation to a temporal schema, on the one hand, and a self-image, on the other. Consequently, in order for a sense of self-continuity to become a functionally significant factor in self-awareness, the human individual must be temporally oriented as well as self-oriented. If we wish to postulate a sense of self-continuity as a generic human trait, a culturally constituted temporal orientation must be assumed as a necessary condition. This seems to be a reasonable

94

hypothesis in view of the fact that self-identification would have no functional value in the operation of a human social order if, at the same time, it was not given a temporal dimension. *Who* I am, both to myself and others, would have no stability. It would make it impossible to assume that patterns of interpersonal relations could operate in terms of a continuing personnel. From this standpoint, I believe it can be deduced that psychopathological phenomena that affect the maintenance of personal identity and continuity must of necessity be considered abnormal in any society.[53] For in order to play my designated roles I not only have to be aware of who I am today, but be able to relate my past actions to both past and future behavior. If I am unable to do this there is no way I can assume moral responsibility for my conduct. I am not quite the same person today as I was yesterday if the continuity of my experience is constricted through the impairment of memory or, as in the case of some individuals with "multiple" personalities, different sets of memory images become functional as a "new" personality manifests itself. Fugue states, in some instances, are unconsciously motivated devices for breaking the sense of self-continuity, for disconnecting the self from past actions felt to be morally reprehensible.

There is still another important aspect of the relation between the temporal orientation of the self and the maintenance of self-continuity. This is the time-span of recalled experiences that become self-related. Cultural variables are involved here. What we find in certain instances is this: not only is a continuity of self assumed, self-related experiences are given a retrospective temporal span that far transcends the limits beyond which we know reliable accounts of personal experience can be recalled. The earliest experiences of the human being cannot become self-related and recalled as such because the infant has not yet become an object to himself, nor has he incorporated any working temporal schema which makes possible the differentiation of experiences of this period from later ones. Besides this, past experience as recalled implies a spatial as well as a temporal frame of reference. Dudycha and Dudycha, as a result of systematic investigation, state that the "average earliest memory is somewhere in the fourth year."[54] But one of my Ojibwa informants referred to memories in his mother's womb (spatial locale), and he knew *when* he would be born (consciousness of *future* time).[55]

From modern observation, we also are aware of the distortion of early memories that can occur through repressive amnesia[56] and the phenomena of pseudo-memory. One instance of the latter, in the form of *déja vue,* turned up while I was collecting Rorschach protocols among the Northern Ojibwa. Having been presented with Card I this subject hesitated a long while before he would say anything at all. Then he went into a long disquisition the main point of which involved the statement that when he was a baby and still on a cradle board (i.e., long before he was able to talk) he had once looked up through the smoke hole of the wigwam and seen exactly what he now saw before him on the Rorschach card.

Facts such as these indicate plainly enough that self-related experience as recalled need not be true in order to be psychologically significant for the individual or his associates. Since reliable knowledge regarding the vagaries of memory is such a recent acquisition in our own culture, it is easy to understand how, through the long span of human history, the door has been left wide open to varying emphases in different cultures upon the nature and the time span of past experiences that can be self-related.[57] Although less directly related to the self, there is the correlative problem of how far it is possible for any reliable knowledge of past historical events to exist in communities of nonliterate peoples. Events of the past, whether connected with the self or not, cannot assume conceptual reality unless they are incorporated in the psychological field of present awareness. This is only made possible through symbolic means; past events have to be represented in some fashion in order to become salient. Even though some temporal orientation that permits the ordering of past events in sequence may exist, with no written records or other checks, knowledge of such events can only be communicated through the recalled memories of individuals,[58] and the repetition of narratives that embody these. And, just as retrospective self-related experience may be culturally defined as reliable, even though it may date from the womb or earliest infancy, in the same way myth and legend may be accepted as "history." Thus a temporal dimension transcending the life-span of living individuals can be given to significant events that pertain to the life histories of mythological as well as human figures of importance in the traditional belief of a people.

One common type of past experience that may become particularly important when integrated with certain concepts of the nature of the self is dreaming. Once we recognize the fact that self-awareness is a generic human trait, that a self-related experience of the past depends upon a memory process (recall) and that the human individual is at the same time exposed to some culturally constituted self-image, there is nothing psychologically abstruse about the incorporation of dream experience into the category of self-related experiences. Self-awareness being as phenomenally real in dreams as in waking life there is no inherent discontinuity on this score. Assuming an autonomous soul separable from the body under certain conditions, as in sleep, it is possible to interpret dream experiences as personal experiences, even though in retrospect the experiences undergone by the self in this phase may far transcend the self-related experiences of waking life in unusual spatial mobility, or in other ways. This by no means implies, however, that the individual ignores or is unaware of any distinction between self-related experience when awake and when asleep.[59] A sense of self-continuity conceptually integrated with a self-image, provides the necessary connecting link.

Dream experiences become integrated through the same kind of memory process through which other experiences become self-related. But this integration of experience from both sources does mean that the content of self-related experiences may in different cultures assume qualitatively distinctive attributes.

A dream of one of my Ojibwa informants will serve to document several of the foregoing points in a concrete form.

As I was going about hunting, with my gun in my hand, I came to a lake. A steep rock rose from the lake shore. I climbed up this rock to have a look across the lake. I thought I might sight a moose or some ducks. When I glanced down towards the water's edge again, I saw a man standing by the rock. He was leaning on his paddle. A canoe was drawn up to the shore and in the stern sat a woman. In front of her rested a cradle board with a baby in it. Over the baby's face was a piece of green mosquito netting. The man was a stranger to me but I went up to him. I noticed that he hung his head in a strange way. He said, "You are the first man (human being) ever to see me. I want you to come and visit me." So I jumped into this canoe. When I looked down I noticed that it was all of one piece. There were no ribs or anything of the sort, and there was no bark covering. (I do not know what it was made of.)

On the northwest side of the lake there was a very high steep rock. The man headed directly for this rock. With one stroke of the paddle we were across the lake. The man threw his paddle down as we landed on a flat shelf of rock almost level with the water. Behind this the rest of the rock rose steeply before us. But when his paddle touched the rock this part opened up. He pulled the canoe in and we entered a room in the rock. It was not dark there, although I could see no holes to let in any light. Before I sat down the man said, "See, there is my father and my mother." The hair of those old people was as white as a rabbit skin. I could not see a single black hair on their heads. After I had seated myself I had a chance to look around. I was amazed at all the articles I saw in the room—guns, knives, pans and other trade goods. Even the clothing these people wore must have come from a store. Yet I never remembered having seen this man at a trading post. I thought I would ask him, so I said, "You told me that I was the first human being you had seen. Where, then, did you buy all of these articles I see?" To this he replied, "Have you never heard people talking about *pāgítcīgan* (sacrifices)? These articles were given to us. That is how we got them." Then he took me into another room and told me to look around. I saw the meat of all kinds of animals—moose, caribou, deer, ducks. I thought to myself, this man must be a wonderful hunter, if he has been able to store up all this meat. I thought it very strange that this man had never met any other Indians in all his travels. Of course, I did not know that I was dreaming. Everything was the same as I had seen it with my eyes open. When I was ready to go I got up and shook hands with the man. He said, "Anytime that you wish to see me, this is the place where you will find me." He did not offer to open the door for me so I knew that I had to try and do this myself. I threw all the power of my mind into opening it and the rock lifted up. Then I woke up and knew that it was a dream. It was one of the first I ever had. (The narrator added that later he discovered a rocky eminence on one of the branches of the Berens River that corresponded exactly to the place he had visited in his dream.)

My informant W. B. narrated this dream as the equivalent of many other personal experiences he had told me about that were not dream experiences. The phenomenal reality of self-awareness is as evident here as in his other narratives, but he distinguishes this narrative as a dream. It is noteworthy, too, that the behavioral environment of the dreamer is spatially continuous with that of waking life. This is unequivocal, not only because the narrator starts off by saying he was out hunting and because the topographical features of the county conform to ordinary experience, but particularly because of the comment in parentheses at the very end. He recognized later when awake the *exact spot* he had visited in the dream. He could go back there at anytime in *the future* and obtain the special kind of medicine that the *mèmengwécĩwak,* the beings he met, are famous for. Had he been a pagan, this is what he would have done, he told me. For he received a special blessing—this is the implication of what they told him on parting, and of the fact that he was able to "will himself out" of their rocky abode. The fact that W.B. thought he could act in the future with reference to a dream experience of the past shows an implied temporal continuity of the self in a behavioral environment with a unified spatiotemporal frame of reference for *all* self-related experience. The anthropomorphic characters that appear in the dream are of particular interest because they are not human (*änicinábek*), yet they are well-known inhabitants of the behavioral environment of the Northern Ojibwa.

What is of special theoretical importance for our discussion is that whereas most nonhuman beings of the behavioral environment of the Ojibwa can *only* be met in dreams, it is otherwise with *mèmengwécĩwak.* These beings reputedly have been seen or heard singing in ordinary life by a number of Indians. This "equivocal" status also demonstrates the unified structure of the behavioral environment of the Ojibwa. It is impossible to dichotomize it in our terms and make psychological sense from the anecdotal accounts of the Ojibwa themselves. *Mèmengwécĩwak* are not human beings (Indians); nor are they "spiritual" entities in the sense of being perceptually intangible beings dwelling in a spatial region remote from man. From the Ojibwa point of view they are inhabitants of the same terrestial region as men and belong to the same class of perceptually apprehensible objects as a moose, a tree, or a man. And, like them, they may be "perceived" in dreams as well as in ordinary daily life.

Consonant with this conception of these beings anecdotes are told about Indians who sometimes have met *mèmengwécĩwak* while out hunting. One of these stories has an interesting climax. After following some *mèmengwécĩwak* to one of their rocky dwellings an Indian, according to his own account, attempted to follow them in. But the rocks closed as soon as *mèmengwécĩwak* had gone through. As the prow of his canoe bumped hard against the rocks, the Indian heard *mèmengwécĩwak* laughing inside. On the other hand, an old man once told me that he had seen his father enter the rocks. What the Ojibwa say is that it is necessary to receive a blessing from *mèmengwécĩwak* in a dream first. This is the significance that W.B. attributed to his dream experience, although, being a Christian, he never took advantage of it to become a *manao* (i.e., an Indian doctor who uses medicine obtained from *mèmengwéciwak*).

It would be possible to demonstrate from other dream material how the horizon of self-related experience is enormously broadened through the integration of this kind of experience with that of waking life. The range of mobility of the self in space and time may likewise be extended throughout the limits of the behavioral environment. In the case of the Ojibwa, human beings share such mobility with the non-human selves of their behavioral environment. (This will be illustrated in a later chapter, "The Ojibwa Self and Its Behavioral Environment.") Furthermore, the psychological fact that the individual actually does experience such phenomena (in dreams) is one of the main reasons the events of mythological narrative can assume reality in the context of the same behavioral environment. Experientially, the world of the self and the world of myth are continuous. How far this is actually the case in any culture is, I believe, open to empirical investigation.

In the past decade or so the "personal document" approach in anthropology has begun to yield a new dimension to ethnography.[60] A number of autobiographies of individuals in nonliterate societies have appeared. But one point has been overlooked. If concepts of the self and the kind of experiences that become self-related are culturally constituted, then the content of autobiographical data must likewise be considered in a variable framework. This content in some cultures will not be in accord with the kind of self-related experience that we consider autobiographical in Western culture. It may contain a great deal of the fantasy material that we exclude from autobiography and relegate to dreams or visions. The anthropologist may collect dreams, it is true; but such data may be separated from autobiographical data on an a priori basis and never considered as integrally related to a self-image. In recent years, the aim of collecting dreams has been principally inspired by their value for the analysis of personality dynamics.[61] At another level, however, dreams or other fantasy data may be relevant to autobiography, if we consider that autobiography involves a retrospective account of the experiences of the self. It would be interesting to know what a systematic phrasing of autobiography with relation to the self-image of a culture might bring forth. One thing the investigator would then encourage would be the searching of the subject's memory and the recall of *all* experiences that were interpreted by him as self-related. (I have used this approach in Chapter 8.)

Temporal orientation is not only an important means through which past experience can be organized in a self-related manner; a temporal schema is directly related to future conduct, to contemplated action, to the destiny of the self. This implies the notion of self-continuity as one of the ubiquitous aspects of self-awareness. The self not only has a past and a present, but a long future existence. Murdock lists eschatology as a common denominator of culture. The self may be conceived to be immortal, indestructible, or eternal. Such grandiose attributes of the self-image necessitate a spatiotemporal frame of reference since deceased selves, if they continue to exist, must exist somewhere. Frank says that

It has been the great office of culture, and specifically of religion to provide the major time perspective of conduct by insisting upon the relative dimensions of the immediate present as seen in the focus of eternity. Culture, as transmitted by parents and other cultural agents, prevents man from acting impulsively and naively, as his needs, urges, and desires might dictate, and so compels him to regulate his conduct towards the opportunities around him, which he sees in the time perspective of life after death or other forward reference. The Hindu belief in reincarnation and endless striving toward perfection is probably the most attenuated and compelling time perspective that sets every event and human action in this ever-receding perspective from which there is no escape. Each culture and each religion presents its own time perspective and emphasizes the necessity of patterning human conduct in its focus, so that one culture will repress and another foster sexual functioning, one will favor and another repress aquisitiveness, and so on. Thus asceticism, continence, and all other virtues may be viewed as responses to the dimensions imposed upon the presently religious, ethical time perspectives, many of which reduce the present to insignificance except as a preparation for the future in which this asceticism will be rewarded. To insist then upon time perspectives in human conduct is to recognize the ages-old significance given to the future, but to bring that future into the manageable present and give it an operational meaning by showing that *the future is that name we give to the altered dimensions of the present.*[62]

To understand the orientation of the self in its culturally constituted behavioral environment, future time and a cosmographic dimension cannot be ignored.

Motivational Orientation.—A *fourth* orientation with which a culture must provide the self may be characterized as motivational.[63] Motivational orientation is orientation of the self towards the objects of its behavioral environment with reference to the satisfaction of its needs. This is why the self must be groomed for action. The satisfaction of needs requires some kind of activity. A world of objects is not only discriminated; objects of different classes have specific attributes that must be taken into account in interaction with them; even the valence they have for the self is culturally constituted. Some classes of objects may have highly positive attributes; others may, on occasion, or even characteristically, be threatening to the security of the self. Consequently, any sort of activity must be given purposeful direction in order that the pursuit of appropriate goals may contribute to the needs of the self.[64] Since the motivational structure of individuals includes the entire range of needs, interests, wants, and attitudes that underlie the functioning of a human social order, a motivational orientation is as necessary for the

100

maintenance and the persistence of traditional culture patterns as it is for the psychological adjustment of the individual.

Motives at the human level are peculiarly complex because they are essentially acquired rather than innately determined.[65] In consequence, their range and variety is very great. Many attempts to reduce human motives to constant biological attributes of the organism, or physiological determinants, have proved inadequate. By this means we can, at best, only speak in terms of a common denominator of needs. In doing so we not only ignore the most characteristic feature of human motives, but also the relation of needs to the self as culturally constituted.

Referring to Cannon's theory of homeostasis, MacLeod writes:

The studies of homeostasis show how, when a deficiency cannot be met readily by means of the resources of the body, a craving is generated which persists until, through behavior, the optimum condition is restored. Here we have the basis for an understanding of some of our most elementary forms of motivation. But we have also the basis for a redefinition of the concept of need. A need is generated when a self-regulating system is disrupted. Its strength and the character of its directedness are determined by the character of the system and by the nature of the disruption. A self-sufficient system will generate no needs. If we take this argument seriously, we may discard as artifacts the conventional lists of primary organismic needs, and possibly all other inventories of fundamental needs as well.

Physiological homeostasis can account for the generation of some needs, but it does not follow that it will account for the generation of all needs. It would be pushing the physiological hypothesis to a ridiculous extreme if we were to insist that there must be a biochemical deficiency initiating every wish, ambition, hope, and inclination. Yet they are the stuff of which the motivation of real life is constituted. Under some circumstances I need friendship or need to catch a train just as truly as under other circumstances I may need water or calcium. Whence do these needs come, if not from the disruption of a physiological system? It has always been clear to everyone but the psychologist that these are needs of the self. And even the psychologist, goaded and shamed by the psychoanalyst, is beginning to concede reluctantly that whatever is denoted by the word "self" may have some reality. Once we free ourselves of the compulsion to explain away the facts of direct experience by reducing them to atoms or tracing them back to non-observable origins we realize that the self is just as compelling, just as inescapable a datum, as is the perceptual object. When "I need friendship" it is the "I" that has the need. If we analyze away the "I" we lose the meaning of the motivation, just as when we analyze away the perceptual object we lose the meaning of perception.[66]

If in approaching the problem of human needs we take into account the needs of the self, then it would seem necessary to investigate variant needs of the self in its behavioral environment. In this way we may be able to identify and discriminate motivational patterns in the psychological field of the individual that may escape us entirely if we rely exclusively upon any reductionistic approach.

It has been frequently pointed out that in the process of self-objectification the self becomes an object of value for the human individual. Sherif and Cantril, e.g., write, "A characteristic fact that holds for any individual in *any culture* [italics ours] is that experience related to ego-attitudes, ego-experiences, are felt by the individual with a peculiar warmth and familiarity."[67] Accepting this generalization, I believe that a further point needs special emphasis. This positive evaluation of the self represents the keystone of the characteristic motivational structure that we find in man. This is due to the fact that cultures not only share a common function in mediating self-objectification, it is one of their concomitant functions to constitute the self as a primary object of value in a world of other objects. While self-love when considered in terms of the psychodynamics of the individual may have its own idiosyncratic patterns and while there are undoubtedly cultural variables to be considered, it seems difficult to escape the conclusion that some *positive* rather than negative evaluation of self is one of the conditions necessary for a human level of normal psychological adjustment. Neither the principle of homeostasis nor an "instinct of self-preservation" accounts for the needs of the human individual at this level of adjustment. Motivations that are related to the needs of the self as an object of primary value in its behavioral environment are not in the same category as the needs of animals whose behavior is motivated in a psychological field in which any form of self-reference is lacking.

With this fact in mind, concepts such as self-enhancement, self-defense, aspiration level[68] become more meaningful in cross-cultural perspective. The same is true for a deeper psychological understanding of concepts such as selfishness, self-love, self-interest. That there are important cultural variables involved and that an examination of them is pertinent to motivation is implied by Fromm.[69] From the standpoint of motivational orientation the phenomena characterized as "ego-involvement," the identification of the self with things, individuals, and groups of individuals, is likewise of great importance. The range and character of "ego-involvements"[70] as constituted by variations in the structure of different behavioral environments need detailed examination.

By way of illustration, a brief consideration of some of the foregoing concepts in relation to the interpretation of the motives of individuals in a nonliterate culture may serve to highlight some of the essential problems.

Among the Ojibwa Indians, a hunting people, food-sharing beyond the immediate family circle might appear to suggest unselfishness, generosity, affection, kindness, and love. Without denying altogether motives that such terms may suggest, I believe that any immediate interpretation of this sort is misleading. Nor can it be assumed that food-sharing is an indication that the individual has become so closely identified with other members of his group that there is an inseparable coalescence of interests. It is demonstrable that one of the most potent motivations in food-sharing and hospitality is apprehension or fear of sorcery. Food-sharing is an act of self-defense against possible aggression, for sorcery is a potential danger that is always present, it is necessary to be continually on the alert. (See Chap. 15.) Conequently, food-sharing cannot be interpreted motivationally without further knowledge of relevant cultural facts.

Even from an economic point of view, food-sharing may be interpreted as a defense against a very realistic threat—starvation. In the aboriginal period and even in this century, there are vicissitudes inherent in Ojibwa economy and ecology that are potent with anxiety. While I may be very lucky in my hunting or fishing today, I am also likely to be periodically faced with starvation. For try as hard as I may, I cannot secure enough to feed my family. Thus a system of mutual sharing of food bridges lean periods for everyone. When considered in relation to sorcery it is not difficult to see how malevolent motives may be attributed to any individual who refuses to share food, or who fails to be hospitable. If I don't share what I have with you, when you need it, I must be hostile to you. At any rate, you may in turn become angry and attack me by means of sorcery. On the other hand, if I always share what I have no one will have reason to sorcerize me on that score, and I will suffer from much less anxiety. At the same time, by playing my expected role, any anxiety that I may have about what may happen to me in lean periods is allayed. The psychological reality of this motivational picture is supported by a case in which an Indian overlooked another man when he was passing around a bottle of whiskey. Later when this Indian became ill, he was certain that the man he overlooked got angry and sorcerized him. His illness was a revengeful act in retaliation for not sharing the whiskey. This pattern of sharing is so deep-seated that I have seen very small children, when given a stick of candy, immediately share it with their playmates.

If we consider motives to be intervening variables which, since they cannot be directly observed,[71] must always be inferred, it is even more apparent why the self must be given some motivational orientation. As observers of the behavior of people in another cultural setting, it is almost inevitable that we go astray unless we have some understanding of this orientation. While the positive evaluation given the self implies the basic importance of self-defense in relation to motivation, the discrimination of the actual motives that have self-defense as their goal requires some understanding of culturally constituted threats to the self. The fact that the Ojibwa live in a behavioral environment where the threat of sorcery exists inevitably gives a characteristic coloring to their motivational patterns related to self-defense. The need for some means of defense against sorcery becomes highly salient for them so that activities such as food-sharing, hospitality, and lending, which in another culture might be placed in another motivational category, must here be considered in relation to self-defense.

There is another side to this picture, however, which requires parallel emphasis. A more ultimate goal than self-defense is what the Ojibwa call *pīmằdazīwin:* Life in the most inclusive sense. One hears them utter this word in ceremonies over and over again. It means a long life and a life free from illness or other misfortune. To them it is far from a banal or commonplace ideal. Their daily existence is not an easy one and there are many things that threaten life. Motivational orientation toward this central goal involves a consideration of culturally constituted means that assist the individual in reaching it. Among these, the help of other selves—entities that are willing to share their power with men—is the most important. These are the *pawáganak.* They exist in the behavioral environment and they become primary goal-objects of the self in achieving *pīmằdazīwin.* An essential aspect of the motivational orientation of the self involves an attitude of dependence upon these *pawáganak.* Human beings are conceived of as intrinsically weak and helpless, so far as what we would call "natural" abilities are concerned. Consequently, it is essential that assistance be secured from other-than-human selves. This assistance is concretely conceived in the form of special blessings from the *pawáganak* that confer power upon human beings to do many things that would be otherwise impossible for them to do. The desire for such power thus constitutes the primary need of every Ojibwa man. For it is only by securing such power that he can be a successful hunter, practice curing, resist sorcery or retaliate in kind, and so on. It makes him feel that he can achieve Life.

The existence of such goal-objects as the *pawáganak,* towards which they are so highly motivated, influences much of the conduct of the Ojibwa. The fact that from the standpoint of the outside observer such objects are not in the geographical environment makes no psychological difference. Goal-objects, through symbolic representation, can mediate the satisfaction of certain needs as well as material objects can. If we wish to translate the need that is satisfied into psychological terminology we can say that the *pawáganak* are the major means of self-enhancement in the behavioral environment of the Ojibwa. They are the mainstay of a feeling of psychological security. This is why their native religion meant so much to the Ojibwa. Largely because of the way in which sorcery was conceived to operate, and for other reasons, the self could not achieve a basic sense of security through interpersonal relations with other human beings alone. Relations with and dependence upon the *pawáganak* were more vital. The crucial nature of this focus of Ojibwa needs, goals, and motivations for an understanding of the dynamics of personal adjustment is heightened by knowledge of what has happened to them in the course of their contacts with white men and Western culture. Under these conditions the structure of their behavioral environment has been radically modified and the primary needs of the self can no longer be met in the traditional way. Nor has any substitute been found. Acculturation in certain groups of Ojibwa has pushed their personality structure to the farthest limits of its functional adequacy under these newer conditions, with dire results.[72]

I have tried to indicate that the motivational orientation that Ojibwa culture structures for the self includes dynamic relations with other-than-human beings. This must be the case in other cultures, too, although the psychological significance of the nature of these relationships requires examination. But once we assume the standpoint of the self rather than the viewpoint of an outside observer, the motivational orientation of the self throughout the entire range of its behavioral environment must be considered. This is why I have emphasized the importance of the *pawáganak* as goal-objects in relation to the satisfaction of needs of the self that cannot, in *this* behavioral environment, be met through human contacts. Once this fact is recognized, we can deduce the "isolation" of the Ojibwa self which, in turn, is consonant with the "atomistic" character of their society. Especially among males, there is a latent suspicion based on the potential threat of magical attack that operates as a barrier to genuine affective ties, even among blood relatives. This barrier does not exist in relations with the *pawáganak*. For even though superhuman in power, they are not the sources of hostility or punishment. The only real danger from them is when they are in the service of some human being who may invoke their aid against *me* because they have conferred power on *him*. On the other hand, I am in the same position in relation to him, through my own blessings. My *pawáganak* are my best and most loyal "friends." Who they are and how much power I have is my secret, as it is every other man's, until matters are put to a pragmatic test. Women do not customarily acquire power in the same way as men, although stories are told of what women have been able to do when the occasion has arisen.

Normative Orientation.—A normative orientation is the *fifth* orientation with which a culture provides the self. Values, ideals, standards are intrinsic components of all cultures. Some of these may be implicit, others explicit. In any case, neither the psychological nor the sociological importance of this orientation of the self can be minimized.[73] On the one hand, motivational orientation in man cannot be fully understood without normative orientation, since values are an integral aspect of needs and goals. On the other hand, without normative orientation, self-awareness in man could not function in one of its most characteristic forms—self-appraisal of conduct. For the individual would have no standard by which to judge his own acts or those of others, nor any ideals to which he might aspire.

As pointed out earlier one of the most typical features of a human social order is that it is likewise a moral order. There is always the presumption that an individual is not only aware of his own personal identity and conduct in a spatiotemporal frame of reference, but that he is capable of judging his own conduct by the standards of his culture. Thus normative orientation is a necessary corollary of self-orientation. Among other things the individual must be motivated to consider whether his acts are right or wrong, good or bad. The outcome of this appraisal is, in turn, related to attitudes of self-esteem or self-respect and to the appraisal of others.

Implicit in moral appraisal is the concomitant assumption that the individual has volitional control over his own acts. This leads directly to the affective aspects of self-judgment—"In man," as Hilgard says, "anxiety becomes intermingled with *guilt-feelings*. The Mowrer and Miller experiments with animals carry the natural history of anxiety through the stages of fear and apprehension, but not to the stage of guilt-feelings. In many cases which come to the clinic, the apprehension includes the fear lest some past offense will be brought to light, or lest some act will be committed which deserves pain and punishment. It is such apprehensions which go by the name of guilt-feelings, because they imply the responsibility of the individual for his past or future misbehavior. To feel guilty is to conceive of the self as an agent capable of good or bad choices. It thus appears that at the point that anxiety becomes infused with guilt-feelings, self-reference enters."[74]

The fact that the human individual not only is motivated to become the moral judge of self-related acts, but reacts emotionally to this judgment is peculiarly human. At the conscious level, what the self feels guilty about or what particular acts arouse apprehension is one of the consequences of normative orientation. (As for the unconscious aspects of this same orientation and the processes through which values incorporated in a superego become an integral part of the self, any discussion of this problem would divert us into an aspect of the psychodynamics of human adjustment that is not our primary concern here.[75]) It is now clear that, in relation to this adjustment process, differential value systems are one important variable and that the orientation of the self in relation to these is of great importance. One broad conclusion seems inescapable. If the self were not motivated towards *conscious* self-appraisal, rationalization, repression, and other unconscious mechanisms of self-defense would have no ostensible purpose. On the one hand, the individual is self-oriented through cultural means in a manner which leads to the evaluation of the self as an object of primary value. Any kind of self-depreciation, loss of self-esteem, or threat to the self impairs the complex motivational systems that focus upon the self and its needs. At the same time, self-evaluation through culturally recognized norms is inescapable. Awareness of these is necessary because the individual has to take account of explicitly formulated or institutionalized social sanctions. This imposes a characteristic psychological burden upon the human being, since it is not always possible to reconcile, at the level of self-awareness, idiosyncratic needs with the demands imposed by the normative orientation of the self. For animals without the capacity for self-awareness no such situation can arise. In man, therefore, unconscious mechanisms that operate at a psychological level that does not involve self-awareness may be viewed as an adaptive means that permits some measure of compromise between conflicting forces.[76] They may relieve the individual of part of the burden forced upon him by the requirements of the morally responsible existence that human society demands. Hilgard points out that in addition to the role which such mechanisms may play as defenses against anxieties experienced by the self, they likewise permit the "bolstering [of] self-esteem through self-deception."[77] "The need for self-deception arises because of a more fundamental need to maintain or to restore self-esteem. Anything belittling to the self is to be avoided. That is why the memories lost in amnesia are usually those with a self-reference, concealing episodes which are anxiety- or guilt-producing. What is feared is loss of status, loss of security of the self. That is why aspects of the self which are disapproved are disguised." There seems to be little question that one of the crucial areas of human adjustment of necessity turns upon the tolerance with which the self views its own moral status and the sensitivity of the self to feelings of anxiety and guilt. A comprehensive understanding of this whole matter requires a better cross-cultural knowledge of the self-image and of the manner in which the self is normatively oriented with reference to the values, ideals, and standards of different cultures.

If we view normative orientation as one of the major orientations of the self in its behavioral environment, there are some novel areas of inquiry that suggest themselves. Just as, in terms of a given self-image, naturalistic time and space may be transcended in self-related experience and the self may interact socially with other-than-human selves, so in the moral world of the self the acts for which the self may feel morally responsible may not all be attributed to waking life, nor to a single mundane existence, nor to interpersonal relations with human beings alone. For the selves of this latter category may be only a single class of beings that exist in the total behavioral environment as constituted for the self. Consequently, one fundamental question that arises is the actual dimensions of the area within the behavioral environment to which the normative orientation of the self is directed and the consequences of this in the observable behavior of the individual. What does a consideration of the normative orientation of the self in its *total* behavioral environment contribute to our understanding of the role of values, ideals, and recognized standards to the needs and motivations of the self?

We have some reports in the literature, for example, where the moral responsibility of the self in dreams is viewed as continuous with waking life. Lincoln[78] refers to Ashanti dreams of adultery which subject the individual to a fine, and to the Kai where adultery dreams likewise are punishable. But much more detailed inquiry into these phenomena would be desirable.

A case of suttee that occurred in India at the beginning of the nineteenth century and was reported by Sleeman[79] is of particular interest because it brings to a concrete focus all the orientations of the self that have been discussed here.

The essential facts are these: A married man, a Brahman, died and his widow was persuaded not to join her husband on the funeral pyre. But on hearing of the death of this man a married woman of about sixty years of age, of lower caste, who lived with her husband in a village about two miles away, presented herself to members of the Brahman's family. She said she wished to burn on the pyre with the deceased man. This was because she had been his wife in three previous births and "had already burnt herself with him three times, and had to burn with him four times more." The Brahman's family were surprised to hear this and said there must be some mistake, particularly in view of the difference in caste. The old woman had no difficulty in explaining this. She said that in her last birth, at which time she resided in Benares with the Brahman, she had by mistake given a holy man who applied for charity salt instead of sugar in his food. He told her that, in consequence, "she should, in the next birth, be separated from her husband, and be of inferior caste, but that, if she did her duty well in that state, she should be reunited to him in the following birth." The Brahman's family would not, however, accede to her request. Among other things, the widow insisted that "if she were not allowed to burn herself, the other should not be allowed to take her place." What happened was this. Despite the fact that the Brahman's family at this time was not fully convinced of the old woman's claims and denied her plea, she carried out her intentions nonetheless. She stole a handful of ashes from the pyre of her "former" husband and prevailed upon her present husband and her mother to prepare the pyre upon which she immolated herself.

This had all happened twenty years before the youngest brother of the Brahman told the story to Sleeman. The latter requested his frank opinion. It turned out that, partly in view of a prophecy the old woman made at the pyre and other circumstances, the family of her "former" husband were, in the end, absolutely convinced that her claim was true. They defrayed all her funeral expense and the rites were carried out in accordance with her "real" social status. They also built her a tomb which Sleeman later visited. He found that everyone in her village and all the people in the town where her "former" husband had lived were thoroughly convinced of her claims.

It is perfectly clear that the motivation of the old woman of lower caste cannot be separated from a culturally constituted self-image which involves the conviction of reincarnation. Consequently, she could appeal to experiences in a former existence, through recall, to make her plea intelligible. From the standpoint of normative orientation her motives were of the highest in terms of the values of her culture. Suttee is a noble and divinely sanctioned act on the part of a wife. Although suttee, if viewed from outside this behavioral environment, may be considered as suicide in the sense of self-destruction, from the standpoint of the self-related motivational structure of the old woman, any self-destruction was literally impossible. She had already lived with her "former" husband during three births; she had only been separated from him during her present birth because of an error for which she had now paid the penalty; she had still other births ahead of her. The time had now come to rejoin her "husband." What suttee offered was an occasion for *self-enhancement* and self-continuity in thorough harmony with the continued maintenance of self-respect reinforced by the deeply rooted approval of her fellows.[80] Their behavioral environment was psychologically structured like hers so that their motivations and behavior could be very easily coordinated with hers in terms that were meaningful to them.

The role that normative orientation may play in giving moral unity to the relations of the self with *all* classes of animate beings throughout its behavioral environment is illustrated by the Ojibwa. In the case of certain central values, considered them from the standpoint of the Ojibwa self, it is completely arbitrary to isolate the relations of human beings with each other from the relations of the self to other-than-human selves. And from the standpoint of psychological understanding it is likewise unrealistic to ignore the significance of the dimensions of the normative orientation of the self.

It has been said that the grammatical distinction between animate and inanimate gender in Ojibwa speech is arbitrary and hard to master. It only appears so to the outsider. Actually, it is precisely these distinctions which give the Ojibwa individual the necessary linguistic cues to the various classes of other selves that he must take account of in his behavioral environment. It is also significant that he is not an "animist" in the classical sense. There are objects—an axe, a mountain, a canoe, a rainbow—that fall within the inanimate class. In addition to human beings and *pawáganak* all animals and most plants are classified as animate. So are Thunder, the Winds, Snow, Sun-Moon (*gizis,* luminary), certain shells, stones, etc. I once asked an old man whether all stones were alive. His reply was, "Some are." Another old man is said to have addressed a stone; another thought that a Thunder Bird spoke to him.

Many examples could be cited to show that on the assumption that animals have a body and a soul like man they are treated as if they had self-awareness and volition. Bears may be spoken to and are expected to respond intelligently; the bones of animals that are killed have to be disposed of with care. Although the Ojibwa are hunters and depend upon the killing of wild game, nevertheless cruelty is not only frowned upon but may be penalized by subsequent sickness.[81] Gigantic cannibal monsters exist in the behavioral environment of the Ojibwa. They have been seen and even fought with. To kill a *windĭgo* is a feat of the utmost heroism; it is a sure sign of greatness because it is impossible to accomplish without superhuman help. But cruelty to a *windĭgo* is not permitted, and in one case I have recorded this was the reputed source of a man's illness.

Greed is not only disapproved of in human relations. There is a story told of a boy who in his puberty fast wanted to dream of "all the leaves on all the trees." He was not satisfied with the blessing that had already been given him by the *pawáganak,* but insisted on more power. He did not live to enjoy the blessings he had been given.[82]

The psychological significance of considering the normative orientation of the Ojibwa throughout its total range rests upon the fact that in relations with animals or "spiritual" beings *departure* from traditional standards is subject to the same sanctions that apply in human relations. Any serious illness is believed to be a penalty for wrongdoing. The individual is encouraged to confess anything wrong he may have done in the past in order to facilitate recovery.[83] Consequently, it is possible to find out what the individual actually feels guilty about. It is demonstrable that, in addition to guilt based upon interpersonal relations with human beings, self-related experiences that transcend these and involve relations with nonhuman selves may likewise be the source of guilt.

CONCLUSION

In this chapter I have advanced the hypothesis that by giving primary consideration to the self and its behavioral environment all cultures will be seen to share certain central functions. In order for self-awareness to emerge and function in human societies, the individual must be given basic orientations that structure the psychological field in which the self is prepared to act. Thus, while the content of the behavioral environment of man may differ greatly and intermesh with the geographical environment in various ways, there are common functions that different cultural means must serve in order for a human level of psychodynamic adjustment to be maintained. At this level self-awareness is a major component of the personality structure of man. If we assume the point of view of the self in its behavioral environment, it is likewise possible to gain a more direct insight into the psychological field of the individual as *he* experiences it than a purely objective cultural description affords.

PART II

World View, Personality Structure, and the Self: The Ojibwa Indians

Chapter 5 - The Northern Ojibwa

A T APPROXIMATELY FIFTY-TWO DEGREES NORTH LATITUDE A SMALL river that has its source almost three hundred miles to the east flows into Lake Winnipeg. To the Indians who live in this region it is still *omīmīsīpī,* Pigeon River. The reference is to the passenger pigeon (*Ectopistes migratorius*), now extinct, but formerly one of the most familiar and distinctive avian species of North America. This bird once was a source of food to the native population at the season when huge migrating flocks numbering in the thousands were said to darken the sun. On maps, however, this is the Berens River, probably named after a factor in charge of one of the trading posts of the Hudson Bay Company more than a century ago. Another small stream to the south now bears the name of Pigeon River. (See Fig. 1.)

It is the nine hundred or more Indians of the Berens River among whom I did field work during the decade 1930-40 who are referred to in many of the papers collected in this volume. Locally known as *Saulteaux,* in the patterns of their speech and manner of life they belong to a much larger and geographically widespread ethnic and linguistic group—the Ojibwa. But this larger whole, although readily identifiable, was never at any time unified in any political sense, so that it cannot properly be called a nation or, except by traditional usage, even a tribe. The Berens River Saulteaux represent a local variant of this larger unit. Furthermore, the lineal ancestors of these Indians, and of other closely related neighboring people, only a few generations ago did not occupy the area east of Lake Winnipeg—they migrated into it. It is partly due to this migration into more remote regions that these groups of Ojibwa Indians were able to conserve a great deal of their aboriginal culture during a period when armed conflicts with an expanding white population, the effects of the fur trade, and Christianization led to more rapid culture changes among the Ojibwa elsewhere.

We can be fairly certain that there were no local trading posts in the country bordering on eastern Lake Winnipeg until quite late in the eighteenth century. The Northwest Company post at the mouth of the Winnipeg River, for example, was not established until 1792. While

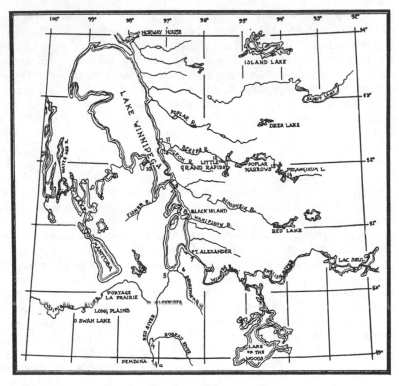

Fig. 1.—The Lake Winnipeg Region

two other posts to the north (at the mouth of the Bloodvein and the Popular River) appear on maps of 1817 and 1818, it is not likely that they were in operation prior to the last decade of the eighteenth century at the earliest. On the Berens River itself the present post of the Hudson Bay Company dates from the early nineteenth century.[1] It is traditional among the Indians, however, that the Northwest Company operated a small post in the same locality prior to this, as well as one about forty miles up the river at Old Fort Rapids. Thus, while the Ojibwa of the country east of Lake Winnipeg had local facilities for trade from the late eighteenth century onward, the presence of a few isolated trading posts did not change the major culture patterns of their lives.

Efforts to Christianize the Indians of this area were extremely tardy. As late as 1854 when the Reverend J. Ryerson made an inspection tour of the Wesleyan missions on Lake Superior and in the Northwest, there was no mission of any kind on the eastern shores of Lake Winnipeg between Fort Alexander at the southern end of the lake and Norway

113

House.[2] The latter was in Cree territory, north of Lake Winnipeg, where the Reverend James Evans had opened a mission in 1840. Ryerson stopped at Berens River en route to Norway House and, although the Hudson Bay Company factor informed him that the local Indians wished a missionary, Ryerson's conversations with them were far less encouraging. Consequently, during the early childhood of my mentor, Chief Berens, who was in his late sixties when I first met him, there was no missionary in residence on the Berens River. It was his father, Jacob Berens, who was active in recruiting the first missionary, but this effort did not bear fruit until 1873.[3] It is not surprising, therefore, that while every member of the band at the mouth of the Berens River was reported as a convert by 1892, during the entire period of my investigations un-christianized Ojibwa were still to be found inland. In the Lake Pekangikum band, which I visited in 1932, there was not a single Christian reported before 1924. A decade later the Dominion Census (1934) reports 130 Indians still adhering to "Aboriginal Beliefs" out of a total population of 891, a proportion of 14 per cent.

While it is impossible to say exactly when the Berens River—a relatively tiny waterway in a labyrinthine network of greater and smaller rivers and innumerable lakes of all sizes—first became known to white men, the Lake Winnipeg area was one of the last in North America to be explored. Lake Winnipeg itself, one of the lesser great lakes of the continent, was not discovered until the explorations of Sieur de la Verendrye and his associates (1731-44). It immediately became the pivotal point in the exploration of northwestern North America, the extension of the fur trade, and the eventual discovery of the long sought "Western Sea."[4] Before the end of the eighteenth century, Lake Winnipeg had become the crossroads of a continent, traversed by the canoes of explorers, fur traders, and missionaries, whereas before there had been only those of native Indian hunters and fishermen. Its northern end was crossed by white men who either had come all the way from Hudson Bay, or had followed the route from Lake Superior that led to Lake Winnipeg through its most southerly tributary on the east, the Winnipeg River, or had entered the lake from the Red River that flowed into it directly from the south. Most of them hurried on to ascend the main water highway that led to the greater Northwest, the Saskatchewan River.

Of the Indians who lived on the rivers and lakes directly east of Lake Winnipeg before the middle of the eighteenth century, we know nothing directly. There is some evidence that in the late seventeenth or early eighteenth century some Assiniboine, a branch of the Siouan-speaking peoples whose territory once extended as far as the Lake of the Woods, were living east of Lake Winnipeg as far north as the narrows. (At least this is what some of my Indian informants told me.) But there is no doubt that up until the eighteenth century the Woods and Swampy

114

Cree were the predominant people surrounding not only Hudson Bay but also Lake Winnipeg. Their neighbors in the prairie and wooded region to the west and south were the Assiniboine. As late as 1775 when Alexander Henry (the elder) reached the mouth of the Winnipeg River, he found a Cree village there.[5] By the beginning of the nineteenth century, however, a decided change had taken place. The Cree were no longer to be found to the east, south, and west of Lake Winnipeg. Bands of Ojibwa had displaced them and the locus of the Cree had shifted to the north. In the whole area east of Lake Winnipeg, Ojibwa—the direct ancestors of the Berens River population and of other Ojibwa now occupying the small eastern tributaries of Lake Winnipeg—had settled.

All these Indians represent migrant branches of an ethnic group which had occupied a comparatively restricted region in the seventeenth century. The Ojibwa were first reported near the Sault Ste. Marie, at the eastern end of Lake Superior, and in the Upper Peninsula of Michigan in the *Jesuit Relations* (1640).[6] This early association with the Sault is the source of one of their major ethnic appellations for over a century—*Saulteurs,* given to them by the French traders. It persists today in the Anglicized form *Saulteaux.* One of the earliest forms of the name given to them was *Baouichitigouian,* the equivalent of the modern Ojibwa *bawáᶜtigowininiwak,* literally "Rapids People" or "People of the Falls or Rapids." In some other Indian languages a similar designation for them was employed, while in others they were called "Leapers" or "Jumpers," probably an incorrect rendering of *Saulteurs. Outchibouec,* the source of the later English *Ojibwa,* is also an early name for them. It appears as a synonym in the seventeenth century, its meaning usually being rendered as "to roast until puckered up." This refers to the puckered seam of their moccasins. *Chippewa* is actually a corruption of Ojibwa and was officially adopted in the publications of the Bureau of American Ethnology many years ago. A further synonym *Bungi* was current at the beginning of the nineteenth century and probably did not originate much earlier. In 1808, the younger Alexander Henry, who was trading near Pembina writes: "The Ogeebois are commonly called by the English Algonquins, by the Canadians Saulteurs and by the Hudson Bay Company servants Bungees."[7] And one of the early settlers of Lord Selkirk's Red River Colony (Manitoba) says: "In the early days of the writer the Ojibeways living in the vicinity of the Red River and Portage [La Prairie, Manitoba] Settlements were usually called Bungees, for the reason that when they asked or begged for anything, they invariably commenced their petition with the word Pungee, a little. The settlers noticed this and so dubbed them Bungees."[8] When referring to themselves, Ojibwa use the term *änicinábek,* men (singular, *änicinábe*). This carries a highly provincial connotation since Frenchmen, Englishmen, and Americans received generic appellations of their own—they were not *änicinábek.* Thus the Ojibwa of the Berens River, and linguistically

115

and culturally related groups in the Province of Manitoba and elsewhere in Canada, retain a derivative of one of the old French forms of their name that still carries overtones of the rapids of the St. Mary's River, now so far away. On the other hand, Indians speaking the same language and with the same aboriginal cultural background are known in the United States as Chippewa or Ojibwa, although this designation for them is not entirely unknown in some parts of Canada.

In the United States the Ojibwa constitute one of the largest remnants of our aboriginal population, only exceeded in numbers by the Navaho and possibly the Sioux. They occupy reservations in Minnesota (10), in Wisconsin (5), in North Dakota (1), and in Montana (1); in Michigan there are to be found several thousand non-reservation Ojibwa. In all, they possibly number 30,000 persons, although all estimates are approximate and include mixed-bloods. Across the border in the Dominion of Canada, there are perhaps only 20,000 of these Indians, although the number of reservations in the provinces of Ontario, Manitoba, and Saskatchewan on which they now live outnumber those in the United States five or six to one.

An interesting sidelight on the Ojibwa is their special relation to American culture. Owing to the immense popularity of Longfellow's poem, *The Song of Hiawatha,* published in 1855, the Ojibwa have received a vicarious distinction, unique among aboriginal American tribal groups. They have achieved an enduring fame, not through wars or conquests, not because of any monuments of native art, but through the projection of an artistic image of them that has become an integral part of American literary tradition. The creation of this image came about through a peculiar combination of circumstances.

In 1839, Henry R. Schoolcraft, who took up his residence at Sault Sainte Marie in 1822 as agent of Indian Affairs and later married an Ojibwa woman, published *Algic Researches.* These little duodecimo volumes were not only the first extensive body of Indian myths and tales collected at first hand, they were published at a time when the term "folklore" was not even known to English usage, and they were mainly Ojibwa narratives. Despite the fact that Schoolcraft says that "the value of these traditionary stories appeared to depend, very much, upon their being left, as nearly as possible, in their original forms of thought and expression,"[9] he did not follow his own better judgment. He weeded out whatever he considered to be vulgar or indecent; some of the stories seemed too prolix, so he shortened and simplified them. And he could not escape the Romantic spirit of his age. The result was that despite his aim to be faithful to the spirit of the originals he reshaped the narratives in accordance with his own taste. As we know now from the comparative material that has since become available, some of the stories "are distorted almost beyond recognition."[10]

A few years later (1843) Schoolcraft published a long narrative

116

poem *Alhalla,* based on an Indian theme. But the theme was the Creek Indian wars and in no way reflected his personal knowledge of the Ojibwa. Like a number of other poems in the same category published before *Hiawatha,* it is known to none save literary specialists. What was primarily unique about Longfellow's poem was the fact that *"Hiawatha* was the first poem of its kind in America based on Indian legend rather than on Indian history."[11] Indeed, the legends Longfellow used were necessarily those of the Ojibwa because no other comparable collection was available. He derived his inspiration from *Algic Researches* and made use of other publications of Schoolcraft. Out of a total of fifty-eight myths and tales that I have listed in my *Concordance of Ojibwa Narratives in the Published Works of Henry R. Schoolcraft* Longfellow drew upon twenty-one for the material in his famous poem.[12] He himself actually knew nothing about the Ojibwa at first hand. But he had watched Black Hawk and his braves in a powwow on Boston Common in 1837, and he had seen the remnants of the northeastern Algonkian tribes who still lived in Maine. In 1849 *Ka-ge-ga-gah-bowh* (George Copway), a famous Ojibwa Christian convert, had lectured in Boston on "The Religion, Poetry, and Eloquence of the Indian," and Longfellow had entertained him in his home.

Four thousand copies of *Hiawatha* were sold the first day of publication; a year and a half later sales reached the 50,000 mark. Eventually, it became *the* poem of the American Indian. The picture of aboriginal life and values that emerged was shorn of a large measure of historical reality through the exercise of Schoolcraft's personal taste, in the first instance, and the subsequent refraction of the material through the poet's imagination. Nevertheless, despite some distortions of ethnographic fact, the background of the action is essentially Ojibwa.[13] Longfellow himself wrote in his notes, "The scene of the poem is among the Ojibways on the southern shore of Lake Superior." Besides, one of the special features on which the poem depends for effect is the liberal use of Ojibwa words and proper names. Even despite the choice of the name of an historic Iroquois for the hero—under the mistaken impression that it was a synonym for the quite distinct legendary *Manabozho* of Ojibwa mythology (the name Longfellow originally had in mind)[14]—and a Dakota name for the hero's mother, the Ojibwa flavor of the whole is not destroyed. In any case, the Ojibwa affiliations of the hero gradually were submerged in Hiawatha, *The Indian* of poetry,[15] a figure compounded of early nineteenth-century knowledge of the Ojibwa colored by the still persistent tradition of the Noble Savage and the Romantic spirit of the age.[16]

Prior to the conclusion of treaties with the Ojibwa and their assignment to reservations (in the United States not until after the War of 1812 and in Western Canada subsequently to the establishment of the Dominion Government in 1867), they had undergone an enormous ter-

117

ritorial expansion. This was roughly concomitant with the spread of the fur trade in the eighteenth and early nineteenth centuries. In what became the states of Wisconsin and Minnesota they had first displaced the Fox and then the Sioux by the middle of the eighteenth century. About the same time and later, many of the Canadian Ojibwa began to move closer to Hudson Bay and westward to the region of Lake Winnipeg and beyond. As early as 1794 Ojibwa were to be found near the Pas and even a considerable distance farther up the Saskatchewan River. Some of them, coming under the cultural influence of the Assiniboine with whom they came into contact on the northern Canadian prairie adjacent to the coniferous forest and poplar parkland, later became known as the Plains Ojibwa. Most of the Ojibwa, however, did not stray outside the northern coniferous forest belt, the region in which their aboriginal hunting, fishing, and gathering culture is so thoroughly rooted. In broad terms, their native culture is essentially a variant of that characteristic of other northern peoples of Algonkian lineage whose habitat in the aboriginal period, as now, was the Eastern Sub-Arctic and the Northern Great Lakes.[17]

The ancestors of the Berens River Indians were, then, among the western Ojibwa migrants, a fact for which I have abundant evidence in extensive genealogical data. By following back the various patrilineal family lines in the contemporary population to specific ancestors it was possible in most cases to discover something about the reputed birthplace of these individuals or the localities where they spent most, or all, of their lives, their movements from one locality to another, and similar information about their descendants. Thus, instead of finding that the family lines of the contemporary native population merged with other family lines of individuals who had formerly lived on the Berens River, it was discovered that the progenitors of almost every traceable patrilineal line came *to* the Berens River from some locality outside. Indeed, all the information collected turned out to be so consistent in this respect and so completely in harmony with the known facts of Ojibwa migrations that it became more and more apparent that it shed genuine light upon a local phase of the larger movement.

Since the small tributaries of eastern Lake Winnipeg north of the Winnipeg River do not connect with important lines of water travel to either Hudson Bay or Lake Superior, the Ojibwa who repopulated this region remained relatively remote from the traffic that passed through Lake Winnipeg by way of the well-known canoe routes. They were thus enabled to maintain their existence in a sheltered enclave until the seventies of the nineteenth century. Consequently, there was little intermarriage with whites, as compared with many Ojibwa elsewhere, since their only direct contacts were with the personnel of a few scattered trading posts. This probably accounts for the relatively few mixed bloods in my genealogies. The racial picture, in fact, is the inverse of that presented by Ojibwa in the United States where it has been estimated that only 18.7 per cent are *full bloods*.[18] Among the Berens River Ojibwa, on the other hand, probably less than this number are *mixed bloods*.

These Indians were thus able to maintain a high degree of cultural conservatism. The basic factor operative from the beginning in producing this result, and still influential in their lives (as well as in those of other northern hunting peoples), is somewhat paradoxical. While fur-trading posts were the original focal points for the mediation of changes in the technology of these Indians through their acquisition of firearms, kettles, awls, traps, etc., and in their consumptive habits by the introduction of flour, tea, tobacco, and liquor in the early days, nevertheless the demand for furs supported and encouraged the perpetuation of their aboriginal ecological adaptation—hunting.[19] In consequence, not only was their subsistence economy retained, but the seasonal movements, institutions, attitudes, and beliefs that were closely integrated with it.

Fundamental to the Northern Ojibwa mode of hunting, for example, was the hunting-territory system. Since sons usually hunted with fathers or fathers-in-law, or brothers with brothers, rights to the usufruct of tracts of land by successive generations of male hunters was institutionalized.

Furthermore, since the trapping of furbearing animals is a pursuit carried on when snow covers the ground and the lakes and rivers are frozen, the operation of the hunting-territory system involves a biseasonal movement of the population. In the late fall there is a centrifugal movement of families that have been camping together during the summer to their winter hunting grounds (average size, 93 sq. miles), and when the ice breaks up in the spring a centripetal movement to the summer fishing settlements again. These latter settlements vary in size from less than 50 to 200 persons. They are always larger than the winter hunting groups, which run, on the average, from 12 to 18 persons, with one active hunter to 3.5 other persons (1949a). Typically, they consist of a nuclear group of at least two married couples and their children. In composition we find most frequently a man hunting with a married son, or, if he has no sons, a son-in-law. Brothers, whose father is dead, may also be found together in the same winter hunting group. These patterns of seasonal movement have deep roots in the past and they largely persist today except for the fact that certain settlements, instead of being seasonal, are occupied all the year round, such as the one at the mouth of the Berens River. There the men visit their hunting grounds periodically during the winter, while their wives and children remain in the settlement.

But it is not merely the objective aspects of hunting that have persisted among these Indians; attitudes and beliefs about the nature of

119

animals and man's relation to them are equally involved. For, to these Northern Obijwa, hunting in the aboriginal period of their culture was not a secular occupation as it is among white men. Success depended as much upon a man's satisfactory relations with the superhuman "masters" of the different species of game and furbearing animals, as upon his technical skill as a hunter and trapper. In psychological terms these entities were among the great "givers," who bestowed extraordinary powers upon men, who acted as their "guardian spirits," and without whose "blessings" and assistance a satisfactory human life was thought to be impossible. (See Chap. 4 and the following chapters in Part II.)

Thus, since the persistence of hunting cannot be separated in Ojibwa culture from beliefs about the nature of the world, the dynamic entities that function in the cosmos, and man's relation to them, it was a factor in the perpetuation of the concomitant institutions, attitudes, and beliefs with which hunting was integrated. Much of this whole complex has persisted up until the present day, and it seems reasonable to infer that despite whatever acculturation may have occurred during the fur-trade era, the integrity of the aboriginal culture must have remained essentially intact until two events, occurring after 1870, gave an impetus to the more radical modifications which reshaped the cultural picture and gave it its modern form.[20] These two events were the establishment of a resident missionary at the mouth of the Berens River in 1873 and the Treaty of the Dominion Government with all the Indians of the Lake Winnipeg area in 1875, to which the Berens River Ojibwa were a party.

The mission was established when my friend, Chief William Berens, was a boy of eight or nine years, so that within his lifetime he saw the whole process of Christianization take place. But this process is still not complete, some of the Indians in the up-river region are only now being converted. On the other hand, the Indians living at the mouth of the river, where there has been the most continuous contact with whites, have been Christians for sixty years. By the Treaty of 1875 the Indians in almost all of the area surrounding Lake Winnipeg (100,000 sq. miles) were, for the first time, brought into formal relations with the young Canadian government. It was following this treaty that reservations were assigned to different groups, and that local bands, with chiefs and councillors, were constituted. Prior to this time there were no chiefs in the modern sense, nor any formal band or tribal organization. Of institutionalized penal sanctions there were none, nor were there any juridical procedures provided in the aboriginal culture. No one, in short, was responsible for punishing crime or settling disputes. The major social sanction was the fear of misfortune and disease, an inescapable penalty for wrongdoing and one that functioned through the internal psychological mechanisms of guilt and fear, rather than shame or any kind of direct punishment that could be instituted by one's fellows (see Chap.

14). Effective leadership rested in the so-called "medicine men," those who were reputed to have gained the most power, through their dreams, from superhuman entities (*pawáganak*, dream visitors). It is significant that such individuals were frequently the first "chiefs" elected to represent the newly constituted "bands" in their dealings with the Dominion Government. Today there are three of these bands on the Berens River.

Of the two inland bands, the one whose reservation is located on Lake Pekangikum (Ontario) at a distance of some 260 miles east of Lake Winnipeg is known by that name. Approximately midway between this group and the Berens River Band, at the mouth of the river on Lake Winnipeg, is the Little Grand Rapids Band. The reservation of this inland band is about a hundred miles from the mouth of the river and, if approached by canoe, there are some fifty portages to be managed. When I first made the trip from Lake Winnipeg to Lake Pekangikum in the summer of 1932, I was much impressed with the cultural gradient as one proceeded inland. The Indians of the Berens River Band were the most acculturated while those at Lake Pekangikum were the least acculturated. The latter band was still the stronghold of those Indians who clung to their native beliefs. During the past decade the situation has radically changed. Mining operations near Red Lake, not far to the south of Lake Pekangikum, have opened up a new channel of communication with the outside world; acculturation processes have been greatly accelerated. A secular school has been built by the government, and a small Catholic church has been erected on the reservation, services being held by an itinerant priest. In the summer of 1953 some Mennonites from the Chippewa country in Minnesota (Red Lake) arrived with the intention of spreading their version of the Gospel among these Indians.[21]

Because they have remained hunters and fishermen, even after Christianization and other changes in their culture, none of the Ojibwa on the Berens River live continuously within the confines of their reservations. Such confinement would make it impossible for them to make a living at all, since the nature of the country itself does not permit the raising of any crops, with the exception of a few potatoes and other garden produce. For physiographically this is a region that lies on the southwestern border of the Laurentian area (or Canadian Shield) surrounding Hudson Bay like an arc from Labrador to the Arctic Coast. It is low, with many swamps besides its myriad lakes; there is only the meagerest of soil cover for the great outcroppings of rocks striated by the glaciers that long ago scoured the surface of the whole Laurentian area. The winters are severe and the summers short. The average annual temperature ranges between a maximum of 76° and a minimum of 21° below zero (mean 31°). The lakes and rivers are frozen six months during the year; the normal snowfall averages highest in November (11.1 in.), but even in March a heavy fall may be expected (av. 7.2 in.) and the annual average is 47.4 inches. As there is little to encourage white settlement the region still remains a sheltered enclave; no highways or railroads have ever been built. In summer the only means of transportation, other than a few small passenger and freight vessels that ply Lake Winnipeg, is the canoe. In winter, travel is only possible on snowshoes or by dog train. The only alternative at either season is the airplane.

The population of the region, too, remains predominantly Indian. The only whites are the fur-traders, a few trappers, a lonely member of the Canadian Mounted Police, a handful of missionaries (Protestant and Catholic) and, before the last war, an increasing number of prospectors, always eager to wrest new mineral secrets from the depths of the Canadian Shield. It is even likely that the density of population remains fairly close to what it was in aboriginal times. In the area covered by the Winnipeg Treaty of 1875, I estimated it to be .028 persons per square mile, a figure that coincides with the estimate Kroeber made for the Eastern Sub-Arctic area in the aboriginal period.[22]

On the Berens River itself, however, the population has been steadily increasing, especially in the up-river bands. From 1892, when the first official census figures were published, until 1934 it had almost doubled and there is reason to believe that the acceleration had started before the earlier date. This conclusion is based upon figures obtained by calculating the average number of offspring per married woman and per fruitful woman as recorded in my genealogies for three generations.[23] The women of the youngest generation, when still living, were past the child-bearing age for the most part, the women of the next ascending generation were all past menopause, when living, and those of the oldest generation were dead. In temporal terms, the oldest women of the youngest generation selected represent those whose reproductive life began within the last quarter of the nineteenth century—in the period, that is, immediately subsequent to the treaty; the child-bearing period of their grandmothers began a century ago or more. In these three generations the average number of offspring per fruitful woman was 3.8, 4.2, and 4.9, respectively, and the average number of offspring for all three generations was 4.5. It thus seems apparent that, whatever the rate of infant mortality has been, the Berens River population, in gross biological terms, is a healthy one.[24] This is also indicated by the fact that in the up-river bands during the period of my observations in the thirties the percentage of children under sixteen years averaged almost 50 per cent of the total population of these bands. Up until that time there had never been a resident physician anywhere on the river and when, a couple of years before the war, a small hospital was opened by the Catholic mission at the mouth of the river, it was put in charge of nuns who were trained nurses. Aside from this, the Indians have been dependent entirely upon their own native remedies, except for the lay medical aid rendered by the local missionaries, both Protestant and Catholic.

So far as schools are concerned, these have been conducted primarily in connection with the missions, although a purely secular school, attended almost exclusively by Protestant children, has existed on the reservation of the Berens River Band for many years. Because of the seasonal dispersions of the Indians to their hunting grounds in winter, especially in the case of the inland people, education has been very sporadic in the case of most individuals. Consequently, very little English is spoken, even by the Indians of the Berens River Band who are the most acculturated.

On the Berens River Reservation there are few ostensible signs of the old culture. The Indians live in log houses all the year round; no native dances or ceremonies persist and one never hears the sound of an Indian drum. But during the period when I visited the settlements of the Little Grand Rapids Band and those farther inland, even in the groups officially listed as Christians, some flavor of old Indian life remained. In the summer months particularly, when one first caught sight of the birch-bark-covered tipis of an encampment of these inland Indians, sharply defined against a background of the dark and stately spruces that line all horizons, it was easy to imagine oneself to be approaching a summer settlement of a century or more ago. But a closer view soon revealed the more ostensible results of acculturation. An iron kettle would be swinging over an open fire while in an adjoining camp a woman would be chopping wood with an iron axe, and a frying pan would be in the hands of another. All such tools and utensils, obtained from the "company" store, have been taken for granted for several generations, as have woven dress goods. Sweaters, woolen underwear, stockings, overalls are more recent, and now candy bars and chewing gum are obtainable. Flour, too, out of which bannocks are made, comes from the store as does tobacco and the inevitable tea which is as integral a part of daily consumption today as it was completely exotic in the aboriginal past.

Nevertheless, men might be beaching a canoe containing the carcass of a deer or moose, evidence of a successful hunt, and out over the lake possibly other figures bending from canoes to obtain fish from set nets that scarcely were out of the water day or night. For fish, rather than flour, is actually the "daily bread" of these Indians during the summer months. Fish drying on scaffolds in the sun, or fish being smoked, or fish being "ponasked" by the fire, is everywhere. In another part of such an encampment the women were likely to be tanning skins, making moccasins, mending nets, or stitching with spruce roots the bark covers for the tipis. And it was still their duty to chop and haul wood. Babies, snugly strapped in their cradleboards were being carried on their mothers' backs while the raw sphagnum moss—the natural absorbent and deoderant in which they nestle—was sunning in almost every camp.

For a few days in midsummer the *wabanówīwīn*—a ceremonial "dance"—often was to be seen or, if someone was ill, the beating of a drum resounded in one's ear night after night. A "sucking" doctor might be at work, trying to remove a material object projected by sorcery into the body of the patient. And if the patient failed to recover, the cause of the disease might be sought through conjuring. Then, after nightfall, the barrel-shaped conjuring lodge, with the medicine man inside, swayed from side to side amidst an encircling group of Indians as the moon rose and the spruces became silhouetted against the sky. All ears would be keyed to hear the voices of the spirits that the conjurer had summoned to secure hidden knowledge of the patient's illness that no human being alone could discover. Or the conjurer might be asked to consult his spirit helpers about the health or whereabouts of some absent person, or the location of some lost object.[25] In this atmosphere one could not help but feel that, despite many outward appearances, much of the core of the aboriginal thought and belief still remained.

Chapter 6 - Some Psychological Characteristics of the Northeastern Indians*

In THE HISTORY OF ANTHROPOLOGY THE BIOLOGICAL AND CULTURAL attributes of human populations in their group aspects have been the major focus of attention. The questions which anthropologists most frequently have set out to answer have been of the following kinds: What are the physical characteristics of the population of a given region? What languages are spoken? What are the beliefs and customs? What kind of artifacts are used?

Questions of quite a different order arise if one approaches a human population as people; that is, as personalities in social interaction with one another. From this point of view such questions arise as: At what level of intelligence do these individuals function? What are the characteristic attitudes they display? What characteristic patterns of emotional expression are found? What are the personality traits exhibited by individuals? Which of these appear to be typical for the entire population? What is the range of idiosyncratic variation in personality? More searching questions lead to an investigation of the conditions that have given rise to specific constellations of personality traits, and, in terms of the deeper layers of the personality, the kind of character structure that underlies the behavior of individuals.

In short, the study of people as functioning personalities inevitably leads to a consideration of sociopsychological problems, central to which is the relation between personality organization and the cultural matrix in which it is formed. Instead of high-lighting the folkways, the mores, and institutions of a given population, and subordinating individuals as undifferentiated *bearers* of a culture, we accent human beings as differentiated personalities for whom the culture specifies the values of life, defines situations in a meaningful way, and provides patterns of social interaction for achieving traditional goals. Furthermore, if we assume that there are intimate connections between personality and culture, it follows that individuals in societies with different cultural backgrounds

*Reprinted from Frederick Johnson (ed.), *Man in Northeastern North America* (Papers of the R. S. Peabody Foundation for Archeology, III [1946], 195-225).

will reflect this fact and that changes in culture will be accompanied by changes in personality organization.

So far as the Woodland Indians are concerned this latter point was demonstrated in an investigation I made of the Berens River Saulteaux, which was based upon data obtained by the Rorschach method. A comparison was made between two groups of Indians with the same cultural background, and living on the same river, but acculturated to different degrees at the present time. While all these Indians exhibited tendencies towards the same basic type of character structure, the sample representing those who had come into closest contacts with whites departed significantly from the sample whose culture was most heavily weighted in the aboriginal direction. (See Part IV.)

The results of this investigation suggest a general inference. Since none of the Northeastern Indians have entirely escaped the impact of Western culture we cannot assume that their psychological characteristics today, any more than their culture patterns, are equivalent to those of the aborigines who inhabited this area in the seventeenth century. We cannot expect the remnants of the Micmac living in the Maritime Provinces today to manifest the psychological characteristics of their forebears described by Biard, Le Clercq, and Denys. Nor can we expect the highly acculturated Iroquois flourishing in New York State to exhibit the personality traits of those described by the Jesuits since, unlike the Algonkians among whom acculturation has been stimulated chiefly from without, the Iroquois have in addition been subjected to the influence of their native reformer, Handsome Lake, and his followers.[1] On the other hand, Algonkian groups like the Montagnais-Naskapi and, farther west, the Cree and Saulteaux-Ojibwa-speaking peoples, who have remained culturally conservative even under modern conditions, might be expected to approximate in some respects the psychological characteristics of their cogeners of earlier times. And since the Iroquois on the Six Nations Reserve in Ontario are not only very numerous, but retain certain aboriginal institutions, it is possible that a systematic investigation might expose some differences in personality organization if they were compared with the Iroquois of certain reservations in New York State. Whatever the answer may be to such questions, the fact remains that whereas we know a great deal about the culture of the Indians of the Northeast, we know very little about the Iroquois and Algonkians as people.[2]

Since the native population of the entire Eastern Woodland area, as compared with other regions of North America, had a certain community of culture traits in aboriginal times we might expect the people of the Northeast to share *some* basic psychological features in common. On the other hand, the differences between Algonkian and Iroquois cultures possibly imply some psychological differences.

Instead of initiating our discussion with the living peoples who have all been influenced to a greater or less extent by contact with whites, I should like to raise the question whether it is possible to secure any data of psychological value from our earliest sources of information on the Northeastern Indians. Although this way of attacking the problem has never been systematically exploited, and I do not intend to do more than sample the possibilities here, these old sources do offer some interesting data for investigation. Besides, if any conclusions of positive value can be established, we shall then have a base line from which to chart later developments.

While the early missionaries, traders, and explorers were neither trained anthropologists nor psychologists, they had one decided advantage over later investigators. They were able to observe the Indians under purely aboriginal conditions. Consequently, in building up a picture of native culture in the seventeenth and eighteenth centuries we have profited greatly by their observations. Is it not possible that their statements about the Indians as people also are worth considering? Missionaries and traders, we should remember, unlike modern anthropologists, were not primarily interested in the Indians as informants from whom a generalized picture of the culture was to be built up, nor as subjects in a sample of a population whose physical traits were to be measured. These early observers were forced to deal with the Indians much more as differentiated personalities. Part of their task was to obtain insight into the character of the Indians in order to devise ways and means for influencing them toward certain ends. It is not surprising, then, that the missionary, the trader, and the explorer reflected upon what we would now call the psychological characteristics of the Indians. Consequently, we find statements here and there that refer to the character of particular individuals or to whole tribal groups. While many of these observations are crudely stated generalizations that lack the psychological sophistication to which we have become accustomed in the present century, nevertheless one often wishes that such remarks had received further elaboration and documentation.

Of course it is true that if one takes some of these generalizations at their face value, without evaluating the relation of the particular observer to the natives he was describing, all we may have is a prejudiced view. As Kinietz has said, "In considering all of their characterizations of the Indians, it should be borne in mind that most of the Europeans wanted something: the missionaries sought converts, the traders were after furs, and the military men wanted warriors. To those who got what they desired, the Indians were sensible, brave, and upright people; but if the overtures of the Europeans were not favorably received, the tribe was composed of thieves, liars, dissemblers, and even traitors."[3] The margin of error involved can be controlled, however, in several ways: (1) In most cases we have the observations of more than one person, in which case we may have corroborative testimony by independent witnesses at our disposal; (2) we can ask ourselves whether the observations make psychological sense when put side by side with other remarks and with any concrete behavioral data cited; (3) we can evaluate the older observations in terms of our knowledge of contemporary peoples who are culturally the most conservative.

What I propose to do is to examine some of the early accounts of the Northeastern Indians in the light of our contemporary knowledge of the psychodynamics of human behavior to see whether the psychological characteristics depicted for an earlier period present an intelligible picture. The two major topics I have selected for discussion are (1) the general level of intelligence and (2) the emotional structure of the Indians.

Intelligence Level.—In view of the heated debate in modern times about the differential mental capacities of the various races of Man, the almost complete unanimity with which seventeenth-century observers equate the Indians with Europeans is striking. Apparently the idea never arose in the minds of those who had first-hand knowledge of them that the Indians were in any way mentally inferior to whites. Bressani, for example, who had been a missionary in Huronia from 1645 until 1649, and later wrote a general account of the New World natives, points out that they "are hardly Barbarians, save in name. There is no occasion to think of them as half beasts, shaggy, black and hideous." (*The Jesuit Relations,* XXXVIII, 257 ff., hereafter cited as J. R.)[4] He goes on to remark the acuteness of their senses and their tenacious memory. He is particularly impressed by their "marvellous faculty for remembering places, and for describing them to one another," for finding their way about and for recalling details that whites "could not rehearse without writing." Bressani even goes so far as to say that, "they have often persuaded us in affairs of importance, and made us change the resolution which, after mature deliberation, we had taken for the weal of the country. I doubt not that they are capable of the sciences. . . ."

Other Jesuits who, being intellectually trained men themselves, may be accepted as good common-sense judges of intellectual functioning, give similar reports. Du Peron (J. R., XV [1639], 157) writes of the Huron, and Ragueneau (J. R., XXIX, 281) corroborates him: "They nearly all show more intelligence in their business, speeches, courtesies, intercourse, tricks and subtleties, than do the shrewdest citizens and merchants in France." Jerome Lalemant writes, ". . . for I can say in truth that, as regards Intelligence, they are in no wise inferior to Europeans and to those who dwell in France. I would never have believed that, without instruction, nature could have supplied a most ready and vigorous eloquence, which I have admired in many Hurons; or more clear-sightedness in affairs, or a more discreet management in things to which they are accustomed." (J. R., XXVIII, 63)

The Micmac were said by Le Clercq not only to "have naturally a sound mind and a common sense beyond that which is supposed in France,"[5] but "they conduct their affairs cleverly." The editor of Le Clerq remarks, "indeed they were able to outwit the French captains in trade, as Denys makes very plain," for which there is likewise evidence in Father Biard's account.

It is worth noting, too, that Father Le Jeune, that sage Jesuit, appears to have sensed the importance of training in relation to the full exercise of native capacities. For he observes that, "Those who cross over here from your France are almost all mistaken on one point,—they have a very low opinion of our Savages, thinking them dull and slow-witted; but as soon as they have associated with them they confess that only education, and not intelligence, is lacking in these peoples." (J. R., XIX [1640], 39) In another *Relation,* after remarking that the "mind of the Savages" is of good quality, he goes on to write, "Education and instruction alone are lacking. . . . I naturally compare our Savages with certain villagers, because both are usually without education; though our Peasants are superior in this regard; and yet I have not seen any one thus far, of those who have come to this country, who does not confess and frankly admit that the Savages are more intelligent than our ordinary peasants." (J. R., VI, 231) Cadillac, referring to the Ottawa at Mackinac (1695), makes this general statement, "We may say without flattery, that all the Indians are naturally intelligent."[6]

These are extremely interesting appraisals and, so far as we know, as honest as could be desired. While other citations, supporting the high level of intelligence attributed to the Indians in their native state, could be given,[7] those referred to must suffice as an index of the general impression created upon the early observers.

Is this impression supported by the more refined methods and observational techniques we now have at our disposal? It is impossible to answer this question specifically for the Northeastern Indians since no attempt has ever been made to rate their level of intelligence in terms of the results of a systematic application of standard intelligence tests. When such studies have been made the same questions arise that have plagued all the investigators who have used such tests on other American Indians or native peoples on other continents. For example, a study was made of children of the Six Nations Reserve (Iroquois). They all spoke English, but on the whole their command of the language was not that of white children, a fact that adversely affected their scores in the verbal tests. In non-verbal tests they approximated white norms.[8] While test results, when taken at their face value, may show the subjects to be "retarded" in terms of the average I.Q. (the majority of I.Q.'s obtained from studies of Indians at large fall between 70 and 90),[9] sophisticated students are now aware that differences in language facility, schooling, speed in performance, motivation, and other factors related to the cultural background of the subject, all affect the results. Anne Anastasi writes,

Thus it would seem that intelligence tests measure only the ability to succeed in our particular culture. Each culture, partly through the physical conditions of its environment and partly through social tradition, "selects" certain activities as the most significant. These it encourages and stimulates; others it neglects or definitely suppresses. The relative standing of different cultural groups in "intelligence" is a function of the traits included under the concept of intelligence, or, to state the same point differently, it is a function of the particular culture in which the test was constructed.[10]

Consequently, until intra-cultural variables are properly weighed in inter-cultural comparisons, the results of intelligence tests may be highly misleading in the conclusions they suggest. Anastasi elaborates this point for primitive peoples:

Tests of abstract abilities, for example, are considered more diagnostic of "intelligence" than those dealing with the manipulation of concrete objects or with the perception of spatial relationships. The aptitude for dealing with symbolic materials, especially of a verbal or numerical nature, is regarded as the acme of intellectual attainment. The "primitive" man's skill in responding to very slight sensory cues, his talents in the construction of objects, or the powers of sustained attention and muscular control which he may display in his hunting behavior, are regarded as interesting anthropological curios which have, however, little or no intellectual worth. As a result, such activities have not usually been incorporated in intelligence scales but have been relegated to a relatively minor position in mental testing.[11]

The difference in the criteria used for evaluating superiority or inferiority of intelligence is strikingly brought out by the reports of the Indians' opinion of whites compared to themselves. They did not accept naïvely the white man's evaluation of himself as superior; actually, they considered themselves to be superior to whites. Europeans were sometimes perplexed by such an odd notion. Biard, for example, writes: "You will see these poor barbarians, notwithstanding their great lack of government, power, letters, art and riches, yet holding their heads so high that they greatly underrate us, regarding themselves as our superiors." (J. R., III, 73) Peter Grant, referring to the Saulteaux of a much later date, indicates quite clearly the nature of some of the criteria employed in judging the whites. After observing that, "Though they acknowledge the superiority of our arts and manufactures and their own incapacity to imitate us, yet, as a people, they think us far inferior to themselves," he adds, "They pity our want of skill in hunting and our incapacity for travelling through their immense forests without guides or food."[12] It is evident that the qualities of mind required for success in such pursuits are quite different from those exercised in abstract thinking or the manipulation of quantitative concepts.

The Standard Intelligence Tests, however, are not the only tool now at our disposal for gaining information about the intelligence level of nonliterate peoples. While designed as a technique for arriving at a more inclusive picture of personality structure and functioning, the Rorschach Test permits judgments of general intelligence level that the expert, also familiar with intelligence tests, can translate into I.Q. points with a fair degree of accuracy. "Form level rating," as a means of arriving at a more precise appraisal of the intellectual functioning of the subject, has been recently discussed by Bruno Klopfer.[13] The advantage of this technique is that the subject's intellectual approach to things is evaluated as only one facet of the personality picture the Rorschach protocol reveals. This means that the *qualitative* aspects of intelligence can be judged in relation to the functioning of the personality as a whole and not as something abstracted from it. The range of the individual's intellectual aptitudes can be evaluated, for the test material itself is not weighted in any particular direction. Thus, it is possible to discern whether the subject shows capacities for intellectual functioning on an abstract or concrete level; how far either type of functioning predominates, and the quality of such functioning. When the group results from an adequate sample of a population are considered it is possible to see how far the intellectual functioning of an individual is typical of the general trend of the group. Furthermore, since verbal facility, speed, and other factors that have complicated the interpretation of the results of intelligence tests among primitive peoples play quite a different role in the Rorschach, it can be used with very little difficulty among native peoples, and the results obtained are comparable with those obtained on white subjects. (See Chap. 3.)

The results of an analysis of the Rorschach records of 102 adult Saulteaux and 49 children, so far as general level of intelligence is concerned, are interesting to compare with the evaluation of the intelligence of the Northeastern Indians given by early observers, and the somewhat equivocal results obtained when Indians have been given intelligence tests. Of course, the contemporary Saulteaux cannot be fully equated with the Indians of the Northeast in the seventeenth century, yet there are basic cultural and linguistic connections and the inland Saulteaux of the Berens River still maintain today a modicum of their aboriginal life. Like the Indians of an earlier day the chief problems they have to solve are the practical ones that face them daily in order to make a living. There are no large ventures to be planned by anyone, nor has the individual any responsibilities that extend beyond the members of his family group. (Even a chief has very little more.) There was nothing in the aboriginal culture to stimulate abstract thinking and the very elementary schooling some individuals have received is not directed toward this end. Furthermore, there is nothing in the culture to call forth any imaginative powers of a highly creative sort. Myths and tales are *recounted,* not invented, and the same situation holds true for most of their music. The only art that seems to call out any inventiveness is beadwork. It is not strange to find, then, that the results of the Ror-

131

schach technique indicate that the intelligence of the Saulteaux functions at a concrete, practical, common-sense level and that their characteristic intellectual approach to things is very cautious and precise. Many of them add to this a capacity for observing acutely fine details that might escape other observers, but they show little interest in organizing such details into wholes with a significant meaning. The details are of interest for their own sake rather than as part of some larger pattern. Related to this concrete approach to things is the passive fantasy, a kind of idling imaginative activity, without boldness or genuine creativeness, which is also shown in the Rorschach protocols.

From this brief résumé we can readily see that the Saulteaux, on the average, could hardly be expected to rate as high as educated whites on any intelligence test which stressed a qualitatively different type of intellectual functioning. They are not an intellectual people; abstract concepts of the order of those developed in Western culture are tools that are lacking for the development of their theoretical or artistic thinking. Saulteaux culture has encouraged intelligence to concentrate on such capacities as sharpness of perception and detailed memory. A few individuals do show tendencies toward more abstract and combinatorial thinking. One of these men is a conjurer whose personal history shows him to be ill-adapted to the practical exigencies that the life of a hunter and trapper demands. His Rorschach record shows him to have superior intelligence and a genuine capacity for abstract thought. His lack of social adjustment may be due to the fact that he has found no adequate scope for the exercise of his abilities in Saulteaux society.

Turning again to the statements of the early observers, we see that their estimates of the intelligence of the Indians were based on some of the same intellectual qualities that emerge from the picture which the Rorschach presents of Saulteaux intelligence. They were highly appreciative of the "practical intelligence" of the Indian as evinced in judgment about everyday affairs, a detailed knowledge of place and events, and so on. It was probably for this reason, too, that the Indians were compared to the peasantry of Europe rather than to the educated classes. The comparison was an apt one, since it is not unlikely that the qualitative aspects of the intelligence of both groups is rooted in comparable modes of meeting the problems of life.

Emotional Structure.—The structure of the emotional life of human beings has proved to be of such major importance for an understanding of the foundations of personality development and functioning that I have sampled the statements of early observers for cues that provide some insight into the affective life of the Indians of the Northeast.

One thing which seems to have impressed all Europeans alike is what may be characterized as a multifaceted pattern of emotional restraint or inhibition. All observers do not document every aspect of this pattern but there is little doubt that it is all of a piece psychologically.

One receives the impression that it probably applied quite generally to all the Woodland peoples, irrespective of tribal or linguistic affiliation, and that it reflects an important aspect of their personality organization.

The most familiar facet of this pattern of emotional restraint is the basis for the stereotype of the Indian as a stoical type of human being. He is pictured as displaying the greatest fortitude and patience in the face of all the viscissitudes of life—hunger and hardships of all kinds, disease, losses in gambling, torture, childbirth, and so on. Jouvency, for example, in his general account of the Indians of Canada (1710) writes,

Whatever misfortune may befall them they never allow themselves to lose their calm composure of mind, in which they think that happiness especially consists. They endure many days fasting; also diseases and trials with the greatest cheerfulness and patience. Even the pangs of childbirth, although most bitter, are so concealed or conquered by the women that they do not even groan; and if a tear or a groan should escape any one of them, she would be stigmatized by everlasting disgrace, nor could she find a man thereafter who would marry her. (J. R., I, 277) [An exaggeration, no doubt, but the behavior expected of a woman is clearly indicated.]

During the winter Le Jeune camped with the Montagnais some of them said to him:

We shall be sometimes two days, sometimes three, without eating, for lack of food; take courage, *chichiné*, let thy soul be strong to endure suffering and hardship; keep thyself from being sad, otherwise thou wilt be sick; see how we do not cease to laugh, although we have little to eat. (J. R., VI, 231) [And later, generalizing, he says,] The Savages, although passionately fond of gambling, show themselves superior to our Europeans. They hardly ever evince either joy in winning or sadness in losing, playing with most remarkable external tranquility,—as honorably as possible, never cheating one another. (J. R., XVI, 201) [On the Micmac Le Clercq makes similar observations.] They have the fortitude and the resolution to bear bravely the misfortunes which are usual and common to all men. . . . They have patience enough in their sickness to put Christians to confusion. . . . .[14]

So far as torture is concerned, the fortitude of those subjected to this torment is almost too well known to need documentation. Jouvency says,

The prisoner who has beheld and endured stake, knives and wounds with an unchanging countenance, who has not groaned, who with laughter and song has ridiculed his tormenters, is praised; for they think that to sing amid so many deaths is great and noble. So they themselves compose songs long beforehand, in order that they may repeat them if they should by chance be captured. (J. R., I, 273)

A somewhat less celebrated aspect of the pattern of emotional restraint that seems to have characterized the Woodland Indians is the inhibition of any expression of anger in interpersonal relations. An amiable attitude was even maintained towards prisoners at the stake. According to the account of one eye-witness of the gruesome torture of an Iroquois captive by some Hurons,

Anger and rage did not appear upon the faces of those who were tormenting him, but rather gentleness and humanity, their words expressing only raillery or tokens of friendship and good will. There was no strife as to who should burn him—each one took his turn; thus they gave themselves leisure to meditate some new device to make him feel the fire more keenly. (J. R., XIII [1637], 67)

A cold-blooded affair, indeed, which the observer thought increased the victim's suffering, but nevertheless noteworthy because of the absence of any expression of anger.

The emotional structure of the situation just referred to becomes more intelligible when we consider the larger pattern with which it is connected. The early observers frequently comment on the amiability and mildness exhibited in all face-to-face relations in so far as these were *in-group* relations. This is merely a corollary of the fact that any overt expression of anger was characteristically inhibited. Of course, this impressed the missionaries in particular since it approximated a Christian ideal. Jouvency goes so far as to say that "they (the Indians) know nothing of anger" (J.R., I, 275), and Bruyas writing from the Oneida Mission observes, "I have never seen them become angry, even on occasions when our Frenchmen would have uttered a hundred oaths." (J. R., LI [1666-67], 129) Le Jeune, speaking in particular of the Montagnais, phrases the matter with greater psychological subtlety. He says,

They make a pretence of never getting angry, not because of the beauty of this virtue, for which they have not even a name, but for their own contentment and happiness; I mean, to avoid the bitterness caused by anger. The Sorcerer said to me one day, speaking of one of our Frenchmen, "He has no sense, he gets angry; as for me, nothing can disturb me; let hunger oppress me, let my nearest relation pass to the other life, let the Hiroquois, our enemies, massacre our people, I never get angry." What he says is not an article of faith; for, as he is more haughty than any other Savage, so I have seen him oftener out of humor than any of them; it is true also that he often restrains and governs himself by force, especially when I expose his foolishness. (J. R., VI, 231)[15]

This last statement leads us directly to another facet of the pattern since in dealing with such matters we must always take account of interpersonal relations. Le Jeune used to argue with the sorcerer about native beliefs in a provocative manner and evidently the old man did his best to hold his temper. But Le Jeune in this situation, as is clear from other evidence, was not following the Indian pattern. For the pattern of emotional restraint not only implies that the individual restrain his *own* anger, it also requires that he suppress open criticism of his fellows in face-to-face relations and avoid disputation of a personal kind in order to avoid arousing *their* anger. This is why Jouvency remarks,

[At first the Indians] were greatly surprised when the Fathers censured their faults before the assembly: they thought that the Fathers were madmen, because among peaceful hearers and friends they displayed such vehemence. . . . . [Later he goes on to say that] friends never indulge in complaint or expostulation to friends, wives to their husbands, or husbands to their wives. (J. R., I, 275, 277)

In other words, individuals avoid arousing emotions of displeasure or anger in others by the suppression of verbal criticism in face-to-face situations. (See Chap. 15 for details.)

All of this fits in with the reputed independence and individualism of the Indians, with the absence of much, if any, real political authority vested in so-called chiefs or leaders. Writing of the Micmac, Le Clercq says:

In a word, they hold it as a maxim that each one is free: that one can do whatever he wishes: and that it is not sensible to put constraint upon men. It is necessary, they say, to live without annoyance and disquiet, to be content with that which one has, and to endure with constancy the misfortunes of nature, because the sun, or he who has made and governs all, orders it thus.[16]

For the Delaware we have the statement of Loskiel:

[A *chief*] dare not venture to command, compel, or punish anyone, as in that case he would immediately be forsaken by the whole tribe. Every word that looks like a command is immediately rejected with contempt by an Indian, proud of his liberty. The chief must endeavour to rule over his people merely by calm reasoning and friendly exhortation.[17]

Zeisberger making the same point says: "They may not be prevailed on in any matter that does not please them, much less forced. If they cannot be persuaded with gentle words, further effort is in vain."[18] Even among the Huron, according to Baron de Lahontan, the leaders had no more power. Speaking through Adaric, the Huron chief, he remarks that our Generals and Presidents of the Council have not more Power than any other Huron; that Detraction and Quarrelling were never heard among us; and in fine, that everyone is his own Master, and does what he pleases, without being accountable to another, or censur'd by his Neighbour.[19]

In short, no one was in a position to order anyone else around. Tailhan, in an editorial footnote to Nicholas Perrot's elaboration of this same point ("the savage does not know what it is to obey . . .") extends the generalization to all "the savages of New France."[20] How even the semblance of what to us would be a very trivial kind of social pressure was avoided is illustrated by an anecdote related by Father Laure. Once he was descending the Saguenay River by night in a canoe. He had two Montagnais with him and when they both dropped off to sleep the father continued paddling. "Some time afterward, one of my men awoke, and took his paddle; and, as it is the custom of the Savages, who are exceedingly independent among themselves, never to say anything to one another about work, for fear of giving offense, he begged me to rouse the other." (J. R., LXVIII, 35)

This suppression of any impulse to tell someone else what to do if viewed as a generalized pattern of interpersonal relations partly accounts for the reputed lack of restraint exercised by parents upon their children. Le Clercq says that the Micmac "never contradict anyone, and that they let everyone do as he pleases, even to the extent that the fathers and the mothers do not dare correct their children, but permit their misbehavior for fear of vexing them by chastising them."[21] Jouvency comments on this same fact immediately following his reference to the restraint exercised between spouses and between friends: "They treat their children with wonderful affection, but they preserve no discipline, for they neither themselves correct them nor allow others to do so. Hence the impudence and savageness of the boys, which, after they have reached a vigorous age, breaks forth in all sorts of wickedness." (J. R., XLIII, 271)

These statements must be taken in a purely relative sense unless methods of child care observed among contemporary Indians are a revolutionary departure from those of aboriginal days. What early observers probably had in mind, although they did not say so, was the absence of the kind of *corporal* punishment known to Europeans. A more balanced statement is found in a passage of the *Relation* of 1656–57. Dablon, referring primarily to the Onondaga whom he knew best, says: "There is nothing for which these people have a greater horror than restraint. The very children cannot endure it, and live as they please in the houses of their parents, without fear of reprimand or of chastisement." But he also observes that they are sometimes punished "by having their lips and their tongues rubbed with a very bitter root." With reference to the general pattern we have been describing, it is of psychological interest that Dablon says this punishment is seldom administered for "fear that vexation might lead the children to cause their own death by eating certain noxious plants." In other words, parents are said to avoid certain disciplinary measures because their children may resent it and take retaliatory measures. Fenton, in his study of Iroquois suicide,[22] records only five cases in which the alleged motivation was rebellion against parental restraint, so that actually child suicide was scarcely a serious social problem among the Iroquois. What is psychologically significant is the anxiety-laden attitude of parents toward severe disciplinary measures and its persistence down to the present day. For Fenton says that even the modern Seneca have a stock excuse for not disciplining their children too much—they say that children might grow up to mistreat their parents! The anxiety that such a rationalization reveals points to the operation of the same underlying psychological pattern that we have been discussing. This pattern has its roots in the demand that individuals learn to suppress overt expression of aggression in interpersonal relations of all kinds. When any impulses which can be so interpreted are expressed, retaliation in some form is expected. This expectation, in turn, arouses anxiety. Thus the only way to avoid anxiety is to restrain *oneself* and to comply with the demands of others. The Iroquois seem to have been more self-conscious of the pattern as applied to the relations of parents and children than was the case in Algonkian groups.

Still another facet of the basic pattern we have described was the reluctance on the part of the Indians to refuse a favor outright. That is, they maintained a surface amiability in this respect, even though they did not wish to do what was asked. Biard, referring to the Micmac, says that "no one would dare refuse the request of another. . . . ." (J. R.,

III, 95) (But he gives a very neat instance of how some Indians avoided sharing *too much* on one occasion.) Peter Grant, writing of the Saulteaux, states the matter more fully: "Such is their notion of politeness that they seldom give a square refusal to any favor that is required from them; should they not be inclined to oblige, they know perfectly well how to give a plausible reason for their refusal."[23] Here again we can discern the obverse of the expression of displeasure, that is, a desire, motivated by anxiety, to avoid arousing displeasure or anger in others.

The same motivation undoubtedly was involved in what often seemed to be an intellectual assent to the teachings of the missionaries, when in fact this was not the case. Le Clercq[24] remarks that the Micmac "never contradict anyone." For the Montagnais we have the same observation recorded. Le Jeune says, "The Savages agree very readily with what you say, but do not, for all that, cease to act upon their own ideas" (J. R., V, 151), while Le Caron describing the people at Tadoussac, P.Q., remarks that one of the obstacles to their conversion "is the opinion they have that you must never contradict anyone, and that everyone must be left to his own way of thinking. They will believe all you please, or, at least will not contradict you, and they will let you, too, believe what you will."[25] All this was extremely disconcerting to the Jesuits, as Jouvency points out. "From the same desire for harmony," he says, "comes their ready assent to whatever one teaches them, nevertheless they hold tenaciously to their native beliefs or superstition, and on that account are the more difficult to instruct. For what can one do with those who in word give agreement and assent to everything, but in reality give none . . . ?" (J. R., I, 275) Undoubtedly this explains why the Indians sometimes were accused of deceit and dissimulation.

It can now readily be seen that with this strong weighting on the side of restraint not only in enduring the fortuitous circumstances of life, but in all the daily face-to-face relations with others that inevitably must have aroused emotions of annoyance, anger, or a desire to criticize or correct, all of which had to be suppressed for fear of arousing resentment in others, that individuals must have developed an extreme sensitivity to overtones of anger or the overt expression of it. The whole psychological picture is one that suggests underlying anxiety[26]—anxiety lest one fail to maintain the standard of fortitude required no matter what the hardship one must endure; anxiety lest one give way to one's hostile impulses; anxiety lest one provoke resentment or anger in others. As Willoughby says, "In the field of the aggressive impulses, there is little anxiety in groups accustomed to settling differences immediately and definitely, as by a passing exchange of blows; it arises most characteristically in individuals overtrained to a standard of forbearance which makes any expression of resentment impossible."[27] No wonder then that the Indians were taken aback by the openly expressed criticism of the Jesuits referred to by Jouvency, and no wonder that Le Jeune reports that only on one occasion did he hear an Indian say, "I am angry," and he adds that this man only said it once. "But I noticed," says Le Jeune, "that they kept their eyes on him, for when these Barbarians are angry, they are dangerous and unrestrained." (J. R., VI, 231) This is precisely what one would expect; it is the true psychological explanation of the apprehension felt both by the individual and his fellows. The suppression of all semblance of anger can be accompanied by a surface amiability in interpersonal relations, but at the same time open expressions of aggressive impulses become so markedly accented in this sort of affective balance that they become the symbols of the most violent intentions.

Of course, open fights and quarrels did sometimes occur, but it is interesting to note that after mentioning these Biard says they were usually adjusted easily. He then goes on to picture the same amity described by other observers:

. . . we have never seen anything except always great respect and love among them, which was a great grief to us when we turned our eyes upon our own shortcomings. For to see an assembly of French people without reproaches, slights, envy, and quarrels with each other, is as difficult as to see the sea without waves, except in Monasteries and Convents where grace triumphs over nature. (J. R., III, 93 [Micmac])

Assuming the actual operation of the characteristic pattern of emotional inhibition described, we can be quite sure that the affects generated in daily social life presented a genuine problem to the individual. How was he to deal with the emotions he experienced but could not always spontaneously express?

One procedure would be to maintain a certain emotional indifference to things, to avoid investing too much emotion in anything, and when deep feelings were aroused to put them consciously aside as quickly as possible. This attitude is well expressed by the sorcerer to Le Jeune. Perhaps it was a factor in the so-called haughtiness of the Indian. It represents an extension of the idea of fortitude to all aspects of the affective life. The whole philosophy of this manner of dealing with the emotions is beautifully expressed in a passage of Le Clercq:

If some one among them laments, grieves, or is angry, this is the only reasoning with which they console him. "Tell me, my brother, wilt thou always weep? Wilt thou always be angry? Wilt thou come nevermore to the dances and the feasts of the Gaspesians? Wilt thou die, indeed, in weeping and in the anger in which thou are at present?" If he who laments and grieves answers him no and says that after some days he will recover his good humor and his usual amiability,—"Well, my brother," will be said to him, "thou hast no sense; since thou hast no intention to weep nor to be angry always, why dost thou not commence immediately to banish all bitterness from thy heart, and rejoice thyself with thy fellow-countrymen?" This is enough to restore his usual repose and tranquility to the most affected of our Gaspesians. In a word, *they rely upon liking nothing, and upon not becoming attached to the goods of the earth, in order not to be grieved or sad when they lose them . . .*" [italics ours].[28]

Applied to one's relations with people such a philosophy would preclude any development of profound emotional ties.

If emotion could not be successfully handled by a stern indifference, and, particularly in cases of anger, face-to-face encounters were precluded, the individual had to discharge his affect in some less direct fashion. Jouvency clearly describes what happened. "If any person has injured another by means of a rude jest (for they are commonly very talkative and are ready jesters) the latter carefully conceals it, or lays it up, and in retaliation injures his detractor behind his back." (J. R., I, 277) In other words, the affect generated in such cases might be nursed and turned into a deep and burning resentment. This is one possible result of so deeply anchored and ramified a pattern of emotional restraint. The individual was compelled to be devious instead of direct and spontaneous. No wonder, then, that the Indians were sometimes characterized as incalculable, as "naturally fickle, mockers, slanderers and dissimulators,"[29] and why humorous sallies and often nicknames took the form of semidisguised attacks upon other persons. Biard, for example, says of the Micmac, " . . . they are droll fellows, and have a word and a nickname very readily at command, if they think they have any occasion to look down upon us." (J. R., III, 75 [1616]) Humor was one way of combining an amiable exterior with the necessity of expressing one's actual feelings. Besides, anything and everything that provoked laughter was thoroughly approved. Mirth seems to have been one expression of emotion that was relatively unrestrained. It provided a healthy psychological balance to all the other inhibitions demanded. Yet even laughter, as I have observed it, is muted among these people rather than boisterous.

Le Jeune gives the most vivid picture presented by any observer of the interplay of surface amiability and laughter combined with covert slander. While Le Jeune is referring to the Montagnais in particular, his remarks fit the general pattern analyzed so well that I believe his statement lends itself to a wider generalization.

I do not believe that there is a nation under heaven more given to sneering and bantering than that of the Montagnais. Their life is passed in eating, laughing, and making sport of each other, and of all the people they know. There is nothing serious about them, except occasionally when they make a pretense among us of being grave and dignified; but among themselves they are real buffoons and genuine children, who ask nothing only to laugh. . . . . (J. R., VI, 243) The Savages are slanderous beyond all belief; I say, also among themselves, for they do not even spare their nearest relations, and with it all they are deceitful. For, if on speaks ill of another, they all jeer with loud laughter; if the other appears upon the scene, the first one will show him as much affection and treat him with as much love, as if he had elevated him to the third heaven by his praise. (P. 247)

One day Le Jeune was left alone in the wigwam with the women after the hunters had departed. The women, unaware that he could understand what they were saying, began talking about a certain man who had failed to carry anything home to his wife from a feast he had attended.

[The women] spoke aloud and freely, tearing this poor apostate to pieces. . . . "Oh, the glutton," they said, "who gives his wife nothing to eat. If he could only kill something! He has no sense; he eats everything like a dog." [While all this was going on the man suddenly appeared.] They knew very well how to put a good face on the matter, showing countenances as smiling as usual, even to such an extent that the one who had said the worst things about him gave him a bit of tobacco, which was then a great present. (J. R., VII, 175)

Le Jeune goes on at this point to remark that "they are not troubled even if they are told that others are making sport of them, or have injured their reputation," because he believes "that their slanders and derisions do not come from malicious hearts or from infected mouths, but from a mind which says what it thinks in order to give itself free scope, and which seeks gratification from everything, even from slander and mockery." This interpretation does not coincide with that of other observers, for instance Raudot[30] who, referring to the Indians in general, says, "They are very polite and patient when one insults them, but they retain their resentment and do not lose any occasion to get vengeance." But it will be noted that Le Jeune himself stresses the fact that this raillery takes place behind a person's back and he says the Indians are "deceitful." Furthermore, he says that "at the first opportunity they will pay their slanderer in the same coin, returning him the like." It is to be presumed that this retaliation will also not be in a face-to-face situation. So we are bound to suspect that there is a more genuine aggressive component in all this raillery than Le Jeune says. He must have given considerable thought to this matter because in a later *Relation* (XII [1637], 13) he comes to the conclusion that there is a very real undercurrent of hostility involved despite all the surface amiability. "It is strange," he writes, "to see how these people agree so well outwardly, and how they hate each other within. They do not often get angry and fight with one another, but in the depths of their hearts they intend a great deal of harm. I do not understand how this can be consistent with the kindness and assistance they offer one another." This is an extremely astute psychological observation, thoroughly realistic and entirely consistent with the emotional structure I have tried to sketch. It highlights the psychological effects of suppressed affects and suggests that verbal raillery by no means disposed of all the animosity generated. It also suggests that the reputed indifference referred to by Le Jeune himself was not altogether genuine in all cases. Much undischarged hostility probably remained. In fact, Le Jeune himself in one of his early *Relations* (1632) had written: "So enraged are they against everyone who does them an injury, that they eat the lice and other vermin that they find upon themselves—not because they like them, but only, they say, to avenge themselves and to eat those that eat them." (J. R., V, 31) This remark is appended at the end of a description of the cruelty and torture meted out to enemies. In another place he again refers to this vindictiveness toward enemies (J. R., VI, 245) and says the women even surpass the men in this respect.

In connection with retaliation it may be recalled that there was a highly institutionalized means of *covert* aggression at the disposal of the Indians. This was sorcery. (See Chap. 15.) So far as the Montagnais are concerned, Le Jeune himself remarks that belief in sorcery was so prevalent among them that "I hardly ever see any of them die who does not think he has been bewitched." (J. R., XII, 7) This is sufficient evidence that from the standpoint of the Indians retaliation by this covert means was a stark reality. From a psychological point of view, of course, it can be said that this belief was supported by a large component of projection. Slander, backbiting, humor and witchcraft among the Indians all give evidence of the actual discharge of aggressively motivated affects that sought these indirect outlets because direct ones were not culturally approved. Because these other channels were approved the character traits of the Indians are found to be consistent with them. It could hardly be otherwise in view of what we know about the interplay of culture and personality.

Additional evidence is supplied by the data we have on what happened when the Indians got drunk. Liquor was supplied them from the beginning of their contact with Europeans and so even the earliest sources comment on how it affected them. Le Clercq was among the first to protest against its use in the fur trade because of its demoralizing effects.[31]

Alcohol, as we know, often releases inhibitions so that impulses are revealed which usually are kept in check when the individual is sober. Since there also appears to be a connection between personality organization, culture pattern and behavior under the influence of alcohol,[32] the conduct of the Indian when drunk was, in a sense, a natural experiment, a cue to his character.[33] If his basic emotional structure was one that led to the suppression of a great deal of affect, in particular aggressive impulses, then we would expect that these might be released in a notably violent form under the influence of alcohol. This seems to have been what happened. In fact, it is a commonplace that the Indians became exceedingly dangerous when drunk so that Europeans stood in great fear of them and traders who used alcohol in the fur trade barred the gates of their forts when the Indians were in their cups. MacKay says,

Precautions for the defense of themselves and the Company property were the only positive reactions of the English to the bestiality and murderous fury roused in the Indians by alcohol. The exclusion of Indians from the stockaded enclosures of the forts and the conduct of trading through a small wicket were practices which survived many years and arose from the necessity of protection from drunken natives.[34]

Here we are more concerned with the possible direction of aggression toward in-group, rather than out-group, members. No better testimony is available than a statement on this point by Le Clercq:

Injuries, quarrels, homicides, murders, parricides are to this day the sad consequences of the trade in brandy; and one sees with grief Indians dying in their drunkenness: strangling themselves: the brother cutting the throat of the sister: the husband breaking the head of his wife: a mother throwing her child into the fire or the river: and fathers cruelly choking little innocent children whom they cherish and love as much as, and more than, themselves when they are not deprived of their reason. They consider it sport to break and shatter everything in the wigwams, and to brawl for hours together, repeating always the same word. They beat themselves and tear themselves to pieces, something which happens never, or at least very rarely, when they are sober. The French themselves are not exempt from the drunken fury of these barbarians, who, through a manifestation of the anger of God justly irritated against a conduct so little Christian, sometimes rob, ravage, and burn the French houses and stores, and very often descend to the saddest extremes.[35]

The homicidal aspect of drunken behavior becomes still more significant when we recall that however implacable and cruel the Indian may have proved as a foe, in-group behavior was not only amicable, but, by and large, it was characterized by a remarkable absence of murder. This, of course, is a corollary to what has already been said. Thus, while individuals, projecting their own aggressive fantasies, often believed that they were the victims of witchcraft, in actual fact physical violence among in-group members was a rarity. Drunkenness, however, leading as it did to release from the pattern of emotional restraint, permitted the discharge of suppressed hostility in the form of overt physical aggression which in the sober state was inhibited and overlaid by an effective façade of amiability. Although he refers specifically to the Saulteaux of Ontario in the early nineteenth century, Duncan Cameron expresses the point I have been emphasizing with such precision that his statement lends itself to wider generalization:

When sober they are of very gentle and amiable disposition towards their friends, but as implacable in their enmity, their revenge being complete only by the entire destruction of those against whom they have a spite. They very seldom take that revenge when sober, as few people disguise their minds with more art than they do, but, when in the least inebriate all they have in their mind is revealed and the most bloody revenge taken.[36]

Duncan Cameron's statement that "few people disguise their minds with more art than they do," epitomizes to a large extent the impression which the Indian pattern of emotional restraint must have made on many white observers. Emotional expression provides the most direct cues to the inner life of other human beings and when the spontaneous play of emotion is concealed we are deprived of one of our chief guides to an understanding of others. Since the data assembled point very clearly to the fact that the emotional structure of the Indian was such that a great deal of emotional expression familiar to whites was inhibited, naturally it would appear to white observers that it was a matter of artful disguise rather than an integral part of the personality of the Indians. Their "persona" did seem to offer evidence of concealment, dissimulation, lack of candor, and deceit. In psychological terms, this inhibitory pattern suggests the characteristics of a defense mechanism against anxieties. And the inference would be that, since the manifestations of this psychic mechanism are typified' in the behavior of groups of individuals, the determining factors must lie in the culturally constituted world in which these individuals live. If this is true, and I believe it is, the emotional structure attributed to the Indians of the seventeenth and early eighteenth centuries should have persisted into later periods in so far as the cultural conditions that gave rise to it were not reconstituted through acculturation processes.

Evidence of the actual persistence of the old pattern is attested by the essential similarity between the psychological characterization reconstructed from the early sources and that written by Schoolcraft in the nineteenth century which, to a large extent, was based upon first-hand knowledge of the Indians of the Woodlands. Schoolcraft's characterization is also interesting because he phrases part of it with reference to certain conditions that he believes to be of determinative significance. These conditions, moreover, are those which are anxiety-provoking.

What are the facts that the Indian mind has had to guard against? Physical suffering of the intensest character! This has made him to exhibit the most hardened and stoical qualities. Sometimes deception of a deep dye. This made him eminently suspicious of everyone and everything, even things without life; for, being a believer in necromancy and witchcraft, he has had to suspect all forms of life and matter. It became a prime object, in all classes, to suppress the exhibition of the feeling of nervousness, susceptibility, and emotion. He was originally eminently a man of concealments. He always anticipated harm, never good. Fear and suspicion put double guards upon him. A look or a word might betray him, and he therefore often had not a look or a word to bestow. This severe mental discipline made him a stoic of the highest character to his enemies, and to all whom he had reason to fear or suspect. It is the aged, the sedate, the experienced, to whom these traits peculiarly apply. If such men are dignified and reserved before strangers and councils, it is the dignity of Indian philosophy. No wonder the French missionaries and officers of the crown admired such a man, and made strong efforts to convert him, and transmitted enthusiastic reports of him to the Court of France. Imperturbability, in all situations, is one of the most striking and general traits of the Indian character. To steel his muscles to resist the expression of all emotion, seems to be the point of attainment; and this is particularly observed on public occasions. Neither fear nor joy are permitted to break this trained equanimity. The newest and most ingenious contrivance placed before him, is not allowed to produce the least expression of wonder. And, although his language has provided him with many exclamations of surprise, he cannot, when placed in the gaze of public observation, be induced to utter any, even the slightest of them, to mark emotion. The mind and nerves are schooled to this from the earliest hours, and it is deemed to be a mark of timidity or cowardice to permit his countenance to denote surprise. [Even among

143

relatives] it is not customary to indulge in warm greetings. The pride and stoicism of the hunter and warrior forbid it. The pride of the wife, who has been made the creature of rough endurance, also forbids it.[37]

While it is true that this characterization of Schoolcraft's is discerning enough on the descriptive level, and while he does hint at links between emotional restraint and the culturally constituted world of the Indian (e.g., the suspicion and anxiety aroused by sorcery), nevertheless his statement is marred by over-generalization. For, to Schoolcraft, this "stern discipline of the mind and nerves," as he called it, was typical of the Indians as a whole, in South America as well as North America. This, of course, is not the case; the "stoical stereotype" is not applicable to the Indians as a race.[38] As a matter of fact, Schoolcraft himself was most familiar, by marriage and experience, with the Indians of the Eastern Woodlands. This enhances his character portrait of the Indians of this area while weakening it as a racial portrait of the Indian at large.

The same emotional structure remains characteristic of some of the Indians of the Eastern Woodlands at the present time. My own observations of the Berens River Saulteaux and the Rorschach records that I obtained from them corroborate the older descriptions. Among the less acculturated Indians of the upper reaches of the river in particular, the emotional structure to be observed is almost identical with that of the Northeastern Indians of an earlier period. Furthermore, the connection between this psychological pattern and the cultural conditions of which it is a function are fairly clear.

There are no parallels, of course, to some of the conditions which existed in earlier centuries. The modern Saulteaux have no tradition of the warpath, nor any experience of native war or torture. Native games have completely disappeared so that we have no direct knowledge of how individuals acted when gambling. Yet the hardiness which women display in childbirth conforms to the traditional pattern. And since the Saulteaux still depend mainly upon hunting and fishing for a living, hunger and the hardships accompanying a low standard of living must be faced. Chief Berens has commented more than once that Indians, as compared to whites, do not mind going hungry. They do not worry about it; in fact they continue to laugh and joke even when hunger is gnawing at their vitals. I believe that this attitude is typical, but I also believe that we must interpret it as an excellent defense against the real anxiety which the threat of hunger, or the experience of it, actually imposes upon the Saulteaux. As a matter of fact, the latent anxiety aroused is much more serious than is apparent and for this reason requires more suppression or emotional displacement than is obvious on the surface. What I have in mind is the belief among the Saulteaux that one may fail to find animals because some sorcerer is exerting a malevolent influence, or because one has offended the "masters" of the game animals or fish. In other words, according to native theory one *should* be able to make a living unless something goes wrong, and, if something does go wrong, it is *somebody's* fault. Since the aboriginal backgrounds of belief largely persists, it can only be concluded that fortitude in the face of hunger and hardship is a defense against latent anxiety derived from this source as well as from the objective conditions imposed by a food-gathering economy.

Illness among the present-day Saulteaux is also met with great patience, and this thoroughly coincides with what is reported for the Indians of earlier centuries. But here, again, while some anxiety naturally is intrinsic to such situations, there is a distinctive psychological attitude to be noted which is a function of the prevailing beliefs about the causes of sickness. Any kind of serious illness is a consequence of wrong-doing on the part of some individual or the result of sorcery. (Chap. 14 and 1939a.)

So far as interpersonal relations go, there is a great deal of restraint among the Saulteaux upon the expression in public of all categories of emotion—joy, irritation, anger, etc. The most outstanding exception is laughter. In fact, the very positive emphasis upon the expression of amusement, in contrast to the inhibitions imposed upon the expression of other forms of emotion is highly characteristic. What Gilfillan says about the Minnesota Ojibwa of the nineteenth century completely accords with my observation among the Manitoba Saulteaux in the twentieth century.

There is continual laughter, and jests flying all around the wigwam from the time they wake in the morning till the last one goes to sleep. As long as they have anything to eat, and if no one is very sick, they are as cheerful and happy as can be. The laughter and droll remarks pass from one to the other, a continual fusillade all round. The old woman says something funny; the children take it up, and laugh at it; all the others repeat it, each with some embellishment, or adding some ludicrous feature, and thus there is continual merriment all day and all evening long.[39]

Consequently anyone, Indian or white, who can tickle the risibilities of the Saulteaux is socially popular. The psychological importance of laughter among them is also evidenced by the institutionalization of humor. Despite the fact that their myths are sacred stories, many of them are characterized by a Rabelaisian humor that never fails to provoke a laugh. "Tear jerking" or tragic stories of any kind would, in fact, be unthinkable among the Saulteaux. Laughter seems to be the catharsis they need for their resolution of tensions. Then, too, there is the joking relationship between cross-cousins of opposite sex. The bawdy exchanges between persons of this category are not only permissible, they are actually demanded. Since cross-cousins are found in every camp and in practically all social situations, laughter may be said to be one of the psychological functions of Saulteaux social organization.

The characteristic balance maintained between the expression and inhibition of emotion among the Saulteaux and that which prevails among ourselves can be epitomized by a few concrete illustrations. Once when I was preparing to photograph an old man, several Indians gathered around. Among them was a very dignified old woman, a Christian and a pillar of the Church, the mother of a large family of grown children. The old man had assumed a position in which it happened that his legs were spread widely apart. Just before I was ready to snap the shutter of my camera, the old lady suddenly reached towards the old man's fly as if to unbutton it. Everyone went into peals of laughter. The old man was her cross-cousin. But on other occasions I have seen this same old woman watch the departure of her husband without a gesture or change of expression and accept his return home after weeks of absence with a similar nonchalance.[40] And once, when her favorite son returned from boarding school after three years' absence, I saw him step off the boat and walk past his mother with scarcely a greeting, while she stood there impassively. Since I was living with this family, however, I knew about the excited talk that anticipated that homecoming and continued long after we were all finally settled in the kitchen. Yet one would have gained no clue to the emotion that seethed beneath the surface from the behavior observed on the dock. In public the pattern is always one of severe restraint under such circumstances.[41] Peter Grant observed a similar pattern of restraint among the Saulteaux over a century ago. He says,

Their manner of salutation is most ridiculous: when strangers or long absent friends meet, they remain like statues for a considerable time, with their faces hid or inclined to one side and without exchanging one word. After a long pause, they smile or grin at each other, this is understood to be the prelude to asking news, and the conversation becomes general after they have smoken a pipe.[42]

I once witnessed the arrival of a group of inland Indians from Lake Pekangikum who had paddled two hundred and fifty miles to the mouth of the Berens River to receive their Treaty Money. They acted very much as the Saulteaux described by Peter Grant. After beaching their canoes they stood at the foot of the bank staring at the local Indians who had gathered at the top of the bank and were staring at them. Everyone seemed frozen by embarrassment. These Indians were not total strangers to each other, either. While there is not much social intercourse on account of the distance involved, there are blood connections and relationships through marriage. At the same time there are always latent suspicions between Indians of different communities, possibly very much greater in the past,[43] mainly due to the possibilities of sorcery, so that moving from one settlement to another even now stirs up a certain amount of anxiety. I found, for example, that some men of the Berens River Band at the mouth of the

146

river were very loath to have their hair cut when up the river for fear that someone might obtain strands of it and do them harm. They hardly thought of this when at home. Hence a cautious and restrained manner of approach is adopted.

But sorcery may also emanate from individuals of one's own community and even from one's own relatives. Even the Christianized Indians believe this. In the summer of 1940 I learned of the death during the previous winter of a man whom I knew fairly well. Later I heard a rumor that he had been killed by his father's brother. Consequently, I believe that it is reasonable to assert that the major factor which was at the root of the latent suspicion and distrust that colored the interpersonal relations of the Indians of earlier periods operates today. In the last analysis, almost every Saulteaux believes that it is possible for another person to harm him by covert means. This idea is supported by the fact that some individuals have confessed to killing dozens of persons by sorcery. From the viewpoint of the Indians no better proof is needed that such things do happen. Even today it is literally true, as Schoolcraft says, that harm rather than good is anticipated from others. The same is true in other Ojibwa communities. Jenness, for instance, speaking of the present day Indians of Parry Island says,

Every man suspects his neighbor of practicing the nefarious art to avenge some fancied grievance, and the older and more conservative the Indian, the more he is held in suspicion. Probably there is not a single adult on the island who has not been accused of sorcery at some time or other, and who has not himself suffered some misfortune which he attributes to the same cause.[44]

This is the psychological explanation, it seems to me, of the "atomism," or individualism, of Ojibwa society and of Indians with comparable cultures in the past. It is impossible for people to get together when their outlook is colored by the possibility of malevolence, particularly when there are no social institutions that demand a high degree of cooperation. Since covert malevolence is always potentially present in one's dealings with others and the only defense against it is one's own supernaturally augmented powers, psychological security can only be achieved by the enhancement of "confidence in one's power to stand alone. Close kin are important because identification with them is possible. Religion is a system of obtaining individual power for individual ends, originally dependent upon the individual's ability to attain it."[45] Consequently, the better part of wisdom is to avoid offending others. In practice this means that an amiable front, the suppression of one's own feelings or opinions, and even positive helpfulness, is the best policy to pursue. Naturally this policy leads to a certain amount of dissimulation and the inhibition of many spontaneous impulses because its foundation is anxiety. One is even led to mistrust the sincerity of those who *do* appear to be genuinely pleasant, amiable, and helpful people. When I heard that the old man mentioned above was reputed to have killed his nephew, I said to my informant, "But he was such a nice old man!" "That's just the reason I really believe he did it," was the reply. (See Chap. 15.)

Thus, the latent mistrust engendered by a belief in sorcery has the widest ramifications in Saulteaux society. I think it explains the suppression of criticism in face-to-face relations, also mentioned in the older sources, the hesitancy to command others, and the ready assent to requests even though the individual may not carry them out. Hospitality, lending, sharing, likewise may be motivated by anxiety, since a guest, a borrower or a neighbor may become piqued and seek retaliation by covert means. As Jenness says of the Parry Islanders, "He sets food before chance visitors of his own race, whatever the hour of the day or night, lest they resent any semblance of inhospitality and later cast a spell on himself and his household." A case is also cited in which a loan was refused. The man who requested it left in an angry mood. Later when the man who refused the loan was taken ill, he believed that he had been bewitched by the man he had turned down.[46] A Saulteaux whom I know sold some brown sugar, at a considerable loss, to one of the sons of the "nice" old man who was said to have killed his nephew. My friend, who really wanted to keep the sugar for his own use, was warned that it was best not to deny the old man's sons anything, so he let one of them have the sugar cheap. On the surface it looked like a very neighborly gesture; actually the loss that he took was a kind of "life insurance" for himself and his family. The whole transaction was carried out in what would have appeared to any outside observer as the friendliest spirit. But I know that it was not a generous act and that my friend suppressed his genuine feelings in the matter.

It can readily be understood that if such care is taken to avoid offending others in such small matters of daily life, that the Saulteaux are even more careful to avoid any open expression of anger in face-to-face relationships.[47] An overt expression of anger or aggression of any sort in this society is tantamount to a challenge to a duel by sorcery, since there is no institutionalized form for settling such matters in any other way. (Chap. 15.) Consequently, individuals maintain their taciturnity in face-to-face relations even though they may simmer with suppressed emotion. If retaliation is sought it is always by some covert means. It is obvious that the deflection of emotion that is demanded not only requires a great deal of restraint; anxiety is also generated because no one knows when, how, or even if, retaliation will take place. Hence, the amiable demeanor adopted by the Saulteaux cannot be separated from the suppressed aggression that is experienced. This means that there is a deep-seated ambivalence in their emotional structure.

148

Turning now to the Rorschach protocols, which furnish us with direct evidence of the manner in which the personality of individuals is functioning, we find corroboration for the inferences drawn from Saulteaux culture, firsthand observation of the behavior of individuals, and other case material. (For further details see Chaps. 3 and 19.)

The most prominent feature in the great majority of records is the emphasis on strong restraint and control. From the Rorschach evidence alone one would be bound to infer that the Saulteaux were a people whose personal lives were organized within the ambit of formalized habit patterns and that very little of their emotional and imaginative life escapes these bonds. Another inference would be that behind the façade represented by this severe control is wariness and caution. There is meager evidence of spontaneous emotional expression or testing other people's emotional reactions realistically in face-to-face relations. The sort of social roles the individual conceptualizes are on the whole very passive—standing, sitting, looking, sometimes talking. However, almost half of the individuals tested (over half of the inland women), in spite of their introverted personalities and their lack of spontaneous emotional reactions, were sensitive, in some cases hypersensitive, to outer emotional stimuli. Among the inland men who showed this sensitivity, only one showed a tendency to adjust to it and act upon it, but his protocol revealed that tension and fear restrained him. Not able to adjust in his extraversial way, neither has he been able to adopt in any great measure the general pattern of reactions, so that he is a very maladjusted person. Of the two inland women with a tendency to act upon their extraversial tendencies, one rigidly controls her hypersensitivity, and the other, not quite so rigidly controlled, has anxiety that interferes with her adjustment. In the group at the mouth of the river there are many evidences in the Rorschach records that changes are taking place in the basic personality structure. Many more of those who show sensitivity to outer emotional stimuli are attempting to adjust in an extraversial manner under the pressure of contacts with white people and their culture. These men and women, while on the whole less rigidly controlled and restrained, all show anxieties coming to the surface. The women, however, appear to be much more successful in their attempts at social adjustment. On the other hand the two persons who have broken most completely away from the old pattern are also women. One is a girl who has gone wild, losing all restraint, and the other is a very egocentric, hot-tempered individual by any Indian standards, who, however, retains a large measure of control.

The imaginative life also shows evidence of repression although this is less repressed than outward emotional reactions. Evidently, unless the individual feels strong enough through acquired magic powers, all fantasy is dangerous, more especially aggressive fantasy of which there is little evidence. Where aggression is mainly covert, hostile thoughts must be inhibited in the individual himself for fear of inviting the evil thoughts of others to attack him. The greater development, relatively speaking, of fantasy over social and emotional rapport exposes the individual to the development of convictions divorced from any testing of their objective reality. There is thus a danger that he will act upon some distorted idea of what another intends.

The typical Saulteaux character structure as revealed by the Rorschach is largely built upon the basis of defense mechanisms against anxieties. This is understandable in view of the great lack of other developed technics for mastering the economic and social environment. The best defense against all these threats is, as Mead has pointed out, a rigid self-discipline to stand alone and to acquire as much personal magic power as possible. For so rigidly patterned a personality it is not surprising that the missionaries found these Indians resistant to any change of beliefs. It is not stubbornness, nor obstinacy, but an incapacity for change in the habitual ways of thinking and feeling.

It should be understood that without a knowledge of the cultural background and actual behavior of individuals it would be impossible to infer from the Rorschach data alone the *specific conditions* which produced the typical personality picture. On the other hand, any deductions one makes about the personality of individuals from a knowledge of the cultural background of these people and their external behavior needs to be checked by some method of controlled observation on the individuals themselves. The Rorschach technique provides such a method since it offers an integral picture of the personality as it functions under given conditions. It enables us to approach people directly as people.

Chapter 7 - Spirits of the Dead in Saulteaux Life and Thought*

ABORIGINAL BELIEFS IN THE REALITY OF A LIFE BEYOND THE GRAVE cannot be viewed as simple dogmas that gain currency without any appeal to observation and experience.

In the case of the Berens River Saulteaux, they are supported by the testimony of individuals who are said to have traveled beyond the bourne and returned to tell their fellows about it; by the testimony of those who have approached the land of the dead in dreams; by the resurrection, or resuscitation, of persons reputed to be dead; by the invocation of the spirits of the dead in the conjuring lodge, and in other ways.

The individuals who are said to have visited *djíbaiàking,* the spirit (ghost) land,[1] are usually persons believed to be dead, or thought to be fatally ill. To the outsider it seems more likely, of course, that the former were not actually dead, and we would be inclined to say that in both types of cases the individuals *dreamed* that they made the journey to *djíbaiàking.* But the Saulteaux do not phrase things in this manner. Despite the fact that in native theory the soul (*òtcatcákwin*), detached from the body, makes the journey in any case, and that dream experiences are classified as "real" experiences, categorically continuous with those of the waking life, a purely empirical distinction is made. The experiences described by persons observed to be dead, or fatally ill, are not said to have been "dreamed," while the "experiences" described by healthy persons *are* said to have been dreamed. The distinction is based on the direct observation of the bodily condition of the persons involved. In the former cases it is coma, or illness, that lends support to their testimony. So far as I understand the matter, while healthy persons may *dream* of the dead, or even approach *djíbaiàking,* their souls do not ordinarily *visit* this land of the dead. To do so is very dangerous, if one wishes to return to the land of the living; so only persons with extraordinary spiritual powers could achieve the journey. One such case will be referred to below.

*Reprinted from *The Journal of the Royal Anthropological Institute,* LXX (1940), 29-51.

From the Saulteaux point of view, at any rate, Bevan[2] certainly errs when he unequivocally states that, with the exception of Saint Paul, "there is no single instance given us of a man visiting the spirit-world which is not either mythological or literary fiction" (p. 62). It is also curious that he does not mention Swedenborg. Of course, he is thinking primarily of classical antiquity, of Odysseus, of Plato's Er the Pamphylian and, in later times, of Dante. Apparently Bevan thinks that the "widely diffused idea amongst primitive peoples that a man might go or be carried into the spirit world and come back to tell what he had found" belongs to the same general category. Among the Saulteaux, at least, it is otherwise. Specific individuals are referred to, whose historicity is not in question, however one may choose to evaluate their testimony. When I made inquiries about life after death, it was the alleged experiences of these individuals that were first mentioned. I was not given generalized statements. Consequently, there is often no categorical distinction that can be drawn between alleged personal experiences and the more highly formalized narrative on the same theme, ordinarily classified as a myth.[3]

Once it is recognized that such reputed experiences need not be true, in any absolute sense, but may yet be accepted as genuine by those who share the cultural tradition which gives them reality, it is possible to penetrate beneath the surface of native beliefs, and to understand how they function in Saulteaux life.

Accounts by Travelers Returned from the Land of the Dead.—The following narrative of a human being's visit to *djíbaiàking* is said to have been repeated more than once by Nɑbagábek (Flat-Stone). One of his hearers gave me the account the first time I inquired about life after death. According to him, Nɑbagábek had said:

I saw a man who died and lay dead for two days. He told me what had happened to him. He never felt any pain. He thought he was going to sleep. Then, "all of a sudden," he said, "I found myself walking on a good road. I followed this road (*djíbai ikɑna,* spirit [ghost] road). On it I came to a wigwam. I saw an old man there. He spoke to me. 'Where are you going?' he asked me. I told him, 'I'm going this way.' 'You better stop and have something to eat.' he said. I told him I was not hungry, and started off again. He came along with me. 'I'll show you where your parents are staying,' he said. While we were walking we came in sight of lots of wigwams. As far as I could see, there were wigwams. The old man pointed one of them out to me. 'You go there,' he said, 'that's where your mother and father live.'

"So I went there. I found my father in the wigwam. He shook hands with me and kissed me. My mother was not there. Soon she came in, and greeted me in the same way. My father called out, 'Our son is here!' After that a lot of people came in to see me. They asked about people on this earth. They wanted to know whether their friends were well. I told them that they were not sick. Then I was offered something to eat. But I could not eat.[4] Some of these people that came to visit me had moss growing on their foreheads, they died so long ago.

"While I was talking, I heard three or four beats of a drumstick. They were very faint, I just barely heard them, they were so far away. All of a sudden I thought about coming back. I thought of my children I had left behind. I went outside the wigwam without telling my parents. I started back along the same road I had followed before. When I came to the old man's wigwam he was not there. I kept on walking along the road. Then I thought I heard someone calling me. I could hardly hear the voice and I could not recognize who it was. Finally the voice became plainer. I knew that I was getting nearer then. When I got still closer, I could hear my wife and children crying. Then I lost my senses. I could not hear anything more.

"When I opened my eyes and came to my senses it was daylight. But even daylight here is not so bright as it is in the country I had visited. I had been lying for two days. But I had traveled a long distance in that length of time. It is not right to cry too much for our friends, because they are in a good place. They are well off there. So I'm going to tell everybody not to be scared about dying."

Another man, Caúwɑnäs (One Who Travels with the South Wind), was once very ill, and was expected to die. But he recovered. Later he said to his brother's son: "I got pretty close to *djibaiàking*. I was on the road there." He said there were lots of strawberries on the way, and one enormous strawberry[5] just this side of the town (*ódena*[6]). He could see the chunks that had been scooped out of it by passers-by. As he approached the town he could hear the voices of people shouting and laughing. But someone met him on the road and ordered him back. "You're not wanted yet," he was told.

Caúwɑnäs said he got close enough to the town, however, to recognize one individual whom he knew. This was Pi'kotcīs (Sand-Fly) of the Poplar River Band, who had been talked about a great deal because he had once eaten human flesh.

Approach to the Land of the Dead in a Dream.—In the following account of a dream experience, the soul of the narrator traveled an even shorter distance towards the land of the dead.

I was sick. I dreamed that I saw a road—not a very good one—and I started to walk along it. I could see my body lying there as I left. When I had traveled along this road for some distance I came to a rocky hill. A voice said to me [indicating by a gesture that the voice came from near his head]: "Can you see beyond this hill?" "No," I said. "Well, I'll show you what is there." Then I could see a beautiful country beyond the hill with a road through it. The grass and trees were all green, there were lots of flowers and it seemed very bright there. Then the voice spoke to me again: "Can you go there?" I tried, but could not make it. The voice said: "You're not ready to go there yet. You must go back and prepare yourself" (that made me glad, I did not want to go yet). So the voice pointed out another road, that led back the way I had come, not the one I had traveled. I followed this road. Finally I reached the place where my body was. But in the place I lay was a big fire—I had to go through that.[7] Then I lost my senses, but woke up.

Since I obtained this account directly from the dreamer, and discussed it with no one else, I do not know how the other Indians would evaluate it; but I believe that the illness of the dreamer would be a substantial factor in its validation. However, this man did not actually reach *djibaiàking*.

Resurrection.—Although I have not obtained any personal accounts of the journey of the soul of a perfectly healthy man to the land of the dead while he was asleep, in the case of "resurrection," described below, this seems to be substantially what is supposed to have occurred.

Long ago, there was a man called Miskwádesíwískijik (Mud-Turtle's Eye). After being buried, he took up his earthly life again. His wife had visited his grave one day, and hearing a noise, had the grave dug up. She found her husband was alive. But he often acted strangely after this, as if he had not entirely detached himself from the spirit world. Sometimes in the summer, when it was getting dark, Mud-Turtle's Eye would say: "It's just coming daylight. There is going to be a game of lacrosse." Then, instead of preparing for bed, he would dress himself and make ready to play the ball-game. As the night wore on and it got still darker he would make the motions of playing lacrosse, although he still remained in his wigwam. And he fell backwards all of a sudden and shouted, "the ball struck my forehead." He grabbed something and, sure enough, there in his hands was a rock, shaped like a ball.

The implication is, of course, that this man was actually playing lacrosse with the spirits of the dead.[8] The latter sleep during the day, and dance and play all night.[9] There is likewise the well-known association of the Northern Lights with the playing and dancing of the deceased in *djíbaiàking*. This is what makes their land so bright.

Mud-Turtle's Eye is so well remembered, I may add, that a contemporary Indian bearing the same name is occasionally teased about being a lacrosse player, although this game itself has never been played on the Berens River in the memory of living individuals.

Resuscitation.—Closely allied to these cases are instances in which human intervention is said to have resulted in bringing the dead back to life. On account of the nature of the Saulteaux philosophy of the universe, and the acceptance of such testimony as that already cited, fetching the soul of a dead person from *djíbaiàking* is by no means an impossibility. The case cited below was narrated quite casually to me, at the same time as a number of other "cures," by the son of the "doctor" credited with the achievement, and no special emphasis was laid upon it at the time; yet it does fall in the miracle class. Tricks performed in the Midéwíwin, however, were equally celebrated. This is not to say, of course, that bringing a person back to life was a common occurrence. Only the most powerful doctors ever did it. The point is that it is *possible* to do so, according to the Saulteaux theory of the nature of things, and in this case the individual concerned was not a legendary figure.

Tcetcebú[10] was very ill. Otcíbámasís (Northern Barred Owl) was sent for. He found that it was too late to save her life. The day after he arrived where her father was encamped, she died. Otcíbámasís tied a piece of red yarn around the girl's wrist at once. Then she was dressed in her best clothes and laid out. "After this," said the narrator, "my father lay down alongside of her. He lay in this position for a long time. He kept very still; he did not move at all. Then he began to move ever so little. The girl began to move a little also. My father moved a little bit more. So did the girl. Finally my father raised himself into a sitting posture and at the same time the girl raised herself up in the same way."

The native explanation of this objectively simple procedure is this. In order to bring the girl back to life, it was necessary for Otcībámᴂsīs to follow her soul along the road to *djíbaiàking* and bring it back. Only a very powerful man would even attempt such a thing, but Otcībámᴂsīs was notable for his extraordinary powers. The yarn he tied about the girl's wrist was to enable him to identify her quickly, for no time could be lost. The journey to *djíbaiàking* does not take long. There are many, many people there, and if he had had to make a search for her, it might have been too late to bring her soul back. By lying down beside the girl, Otcībámᴂsīs symbolized the fact that he was making the journey with her. That is to say, his body lay there as hers did, but his òtcatcákwin traveled the road to *djíbaiàking,* too. Both returned to their "senses" together, since he found her soul easily and quickly in the land of the dead, thanks to the red yarn, and brought it back to animate her body. But, as the narrator commented, "he got her just in time."[11]

It can easily be seen, from such case material as this, how relatively unelaborated are Saulteaux conceptions of life after death. But there are a few additional details that should be mentioned.

The Location of the Land of the Dead.—The general location of *djíbaiàking* is said to be in the south,[12] and this may be the explanation of the north-south orientation of the body in the grave. The head is placed to the north, but the body is said to be "facing the south." One old man, in talking about his "Drum Dance," referred again and again to the "old people" (*keté änicinábek*) "down south," and how much they enjoyed hearing the Indians "up here" beating the drum. He did not refer, of course, to the people of the United States, but to the Indians of previous generations who had "gone away." A more sophisticated Indian once tried to explain that there were white people, and even "living" Indians, far to the south, but the old man did not find this account of things very intelligible.

According to the aboriginal view, at any rate, *djíbaiàking* was not conceived to be above the earth,[13] or below it, but in a distant region to the south. It was in this country that Indians whose souls left their bodies went on living, presumably forever; and it was a land presumably richer in game and bird-life than the northern country, a place where no one had any trouble in making a living, although life was in other respects a duplication of this one.[14]

The Road to the Land of the Dead.—The "spirit (ghost) road," *djíbai ïkana,* led to the land of the dead, but before one reached the great town in which the *djíbaiyɑk* dwelt, there was a river to be crossed. This river is not mentioned in the accounts given above, but it is a common feature of Ojibwa belief,[15] and is also encountered among the Berens River Saulteaux. The current of this river is said to be very

155

swift, and it has to be crossed on a bridge made of a single log. This log is very slippery, and sometimes people fall off. I was told by one man that the bones of such persons can be seen in the river.

I could find no one who knew about the dogs guarding the road near this river, or about the suspended line of shoulder blades that has to be passed, according to the beliefs of other Ojibwa-speaking peoples.[16] But the dog and shoulder blades do appear in the myth recounting the adventures of *Aásī*.

Because of the necessity of traveling the *djîbai ìkana* (a journey of which a very realistic concept prevails), some of the pagan Saulteaux have, from time to time, asked their relatives not to bury them in a coffin—a practice which began, of course, under the influence of the whites, but which is quite general now. These Indians believed that they would have to carry their coffin along the "spirit road" and across the river,[17] and they refused to be burdened with it. They were quite satisfied to be buried in their best clothes, so that they would not be ashamed of their appearance when they reached *djîbaiàking*, and to be provided (in their graves) with a small kettle, an axe, a knife, and perhaps a gun; for it was formerly the custom to wrap the body of the deceased in a new blanket, and also to leave a little food at the grave. These articles were all, they felt, that a person required.

God and the Devil in the After Life.—So far as I could discover, the Supreme Being is not associated in any way with *djîbaiàking* in the minds of the pagan Saulteaux. But there is a "boss" *djîbai*, regarding whom more will be said later. Moreover, though *mátci mánitu*[18] was attributed to the level of aboriginal beliefs by several individuals, there was no associated belief in a "hell." In fact, the notion that eternal happiness or misery in the life after death is in any way dependent upon the conduct of one's life "here " is derived from Christianity, even when held in a modified form.

Since all of these Indians, even when professed pagans, are superficially acquainted with the general outlines of Christian doctrine, it is extremely difficult to establish the complete *absence* of any particular concept in aboriginal theology. Even when a man of advanced years, whose own father was the headman of the Midéwiwin, maintains that, according to aboriginal beliefs, good people go to *k'tcī mánitu* after death, and have plenty to eat and are well off, whereas "bad" people go to *mátci mánitu,* where they are forever poor and miserable[19] (although they do not suffer torment as in the orthodox Christian hell), I think that one can hardly accept his testimony at its face value. It must be taken, rather, as evidence of the partial assimilation of Christian ideas, and the unconscious attribution of them to an aboriginal pattern of thought.[20] On the other hand, I believe that the genuine skepticism in regard to the Christian notion of hell, which many contemporary Indians show, is to be accounted for not only by the complete absence of this idea in their aboriginal culture, but by some persistence of the positive notion, traditional with them, that the life after death is a happy one for everybody.

Beliefs regarding the life after death, then, did not embody sanctions of any great importance with respect to man's daily conduct during life. Even today, fear of illness in this life is a controlling factor of much greater importance than any fear of unhappiness in the life after death. In former times, customs with a "disease-sanction" were undoubtedly those followed with maximum stringency.

With reference to the transitional character of the thought and customs of these Indians at the present day, I was told a "true" story which further documents aboriginal concepts, besides embodying the projection into the future life of the inferior social status the Indians occupy, with relation to the whites, in the present one, and their sensitiveness to it:

There was once an Indian boy, who lived at Lac Seul. He received a good education and became a teacher. After a while he became a preacher, a great preacher. Then he was taken ill. The doctors could not help him, and he died. He followed the "white man's road" to djibaiàking, and came to a house. He knocked. The door was opened, but only a crack, by the person inside. A man spoke to him and said, "You don't belong here on this road." So he found another road and followed that. He came to another house. The door was opened only a little. He could not see inside, but he was told that he had better go back. Now this Indian was feeling pretty bad by this time. So he retraced his steps by the way he had come. He came all the way back and regained his senses again. But he did not take back his job. Now all the Indians in that part of the country are turning to the old Indian ways again [the narrator concluded].

Offerings as a Means of Communication between the Living and the Dead.—It is apparent from the beliefs quoted above that those contemporary Indians who still adhere to the native concepts of life after death, or even approximate to them, must feel much less remote from the spirits of the dead than do those who have more completely capitulated to Christian notions. If human beings have visited *djibaiàking* and returned again, if a powerful doctor can follow the soul of a dead woman to the spirit world and bring it back to her dead body, and if Mud-Turtle's Eye could play lacrosse with the spirits of the dead, possible lines of communication are open, which more closely integrate the living with the dead than is conceivable from an orthodox Christian standpoint.

This more intimate communication is evidenced in a number of ways. Not only is food placed in the grave-house at the time of burial in order to provide the *djibai* with nourishment for his journey, but it was formerly the custom (and it sometimes happens up the River, even now) for relatives to place a little food at the grave from time to time, subsequent to burial. The graves of deceased Indians were much more scattered formerly than now, since when death occurred in the autumn and winter, individuals were buried wherever their relatives

157

happened to be. Today there are cemeteries near every summer settlement, and if the settlement includes resident missionaries, these burial grounds are under Christian control. But when an Indian paddling along some lake or river in the bush notices a grave, he will usually go ashore, especially if he knew the person buried there. If he finds some tea, tobacco, and food in the grave-house, he will help himself to just enough tea to make a cupful or two, enough tobacco for a couple of pipefuls, and enough food for a single meal. To drink tea, eat, and smoke at a grave is equivalent to having a visit with the dead. As one informant put it: "If the person had been alive and well, he would have offered these things to you, if you had come to his wigwam. Even after he is dead, it makes him glad that you should stop and visit him." Thus by leaving food in the grave-house from time to time the relatives of the deceased not only maintain a certain relationship with him, but they enable the spirit of the deceased to continue the tradition of hospitality and the sharing of food, drink, and tobacco with others that was customary to him during his life.

Communication with the dead through the medium of food and tobacco is also carried out in another way. A little of both may be offered to the spirits of the dead by throwing them in the fire. This is often done, up the River, at the present day. It is unnecessary even to think of any particular person, nor need there be any special occasion for the food-offering. One informant said:

Long ago there was an old man who went to *djibaiàking*. He found out that when a child died and its parents made a little birch-bark dish and put some food in it and placed it in the fire, the fire carried the gift to *djibaiàking*, and the child told the "boss"[21] about what had come from its parents. Something is sent back to the parents—perhaps they will live longer. But they are sure to receive some kind of "blessing." It is because of what this old man saw, that living people make offerings to *djibaiyak*.

Ghosts.—Since the spirits of the dead carry on their activities during the night, it is not surprising to find them occasionally wandering near their own graves, or in the bush. Sometimes one hears a whistle after dark, and it is most certainly a *djibai*. The Indians seldom whistle, except as a means of attracting the attention of a hunting partner to an animal, when the voice might frighten it away. This abstention seems to be connected with the association of whistling with the spirits of the dead. When Chief Berens was a boy he used to whistle, but his grandmother forbade him to do it after dark; and two of his children have been similarly cautioned by their mother. So far as tunes are concerned, such a practice would, indeed, be out of harmony with the way in which music functions in a conventional context, to say nothing of the personal property aspect of songs.

Since the Berens River Saulteaux live at a latitude where the days are relatively short during the autumn and winter months, thus necessitating the carrying on of some activities in darkness, an intense fear of moving about, because of the possible presence of some *djibai*, would be a severe handicap. (One informant specifically said: "There is no reason to fear the dead.") Graves and cemeteries are nevertheless avoided, if possible, after dark, but far out in the bush, it is not the spirits of the dead which occasion the most intense fear these Indians know, but possible encounters with *windīgowak*, cannibalistic monsters.

Possibly the fact that when *djibai* have been seen, it has usually been in the neighborhood of a grave, accounts for the avoidance of such spots. A man of the Berens River Band once saw a *djibai* near the graveyard of the Protestant church. It was years ago, when he was a boy, and he was with five other lads. They had left a prayer meeting, and were on their way down to the river to skate. It was moonlight, and as they passed the cemetery they all noticed the figure of a man lurking there. They wondered who it could be, and it was suggested that perhaps he was after a girl. "Let's head him off," someone said. They scattered and then closed in on him. They met no one, nor did they even find any tracks on the snow; yet there was no way for him to avoid meeting some of them. So it must have been a *djibai*.

Certain it is that whatever apprehension may be felt in meeting the dead in spectral form, the *djibaiyak* are conceived to be interested in human affairs and benevolently disposed towards the living, especially their kinsmen.

Metempsychosis of the Deceased.—Sometimes the spirits of the dead may visit their kinsmen in the form of a bird, according to one informant.

An Indian may be grieving over a child. The *djibai* knows its parents are very sad, and will turn itself into a bird, and come back to pay them a visit. Often a person is almost able to touch one of these little birds, it is so tame. A bird seen hopping close to a camp may be a deceased relative. [Usually, however, the approach of any wild animal is considered an ill omen.]

Once I lost a granddaughter. One day I went out to set my nets. I had a sail on the boat. While I was sailing, a bird came and sat on top of the sail. I said to my boys: "Don't bother that bird. It means something." The bird sat there a long time, as if it were visiting us while we were sailing. I told people about this, and the ones who had good sense believed me.

The Dead as Guardian Spirits.—Djibaiyak occasionally appear in dreams and even function as guardian spirits, that is, confer blessings. One instance is reputed to have occurred a long while ago, when native games were in full swing.

A moccasin game had been played, and on the losing side was a man named Kekekǫ́s (Little Duck Hawk). He had lost everything, even his shirt. Only his pants were left. He felt bad, he did not even move from the place where he was sitting after the game was over. He lay down there and finally dropped asleep. In his dream he heard some- one speaking to him. The voice asked him why he was so sad. He replied that he had been playing a game and lost. He did not know to whom he was talking, but the one that had spoken to him said: "I am *djïbai.* Now early tomorrow morning you must get the game started again"; and the *djïbai* told him exactly what to do.

So the next morning Kekekǫ́s got all the losers together to make up his side, and the game was started. Those who had been the winners before now became the losers. The men on the side of Kekekǫ́s got back all the goods they had lost, and more. This was because the *djïbai* had taught him what to do. People found out about it, and some of the old *midéwak* said they could beat him, because they had medicine that would help them win. But Kekekǫ́s played against them and beat them, too.

The point to be noted here is the lack of identification of the *djïbai* mentioned with any particular human being; and the fact of the matter is that the concept of "owners" or "bosses" of all phenomena likewise applies to the spirits of the dead. Consequently it is the *master* of the *djïbaiyak* that is believed to function here as a guardian spirit. The implication is that Kekekǫ́s must have been blessed by this spirit in his youth. The same notion is the key to the role which the *djïbaiyak* play in the Drum Dance of Kīwĭtc.[22] This dance, like other ceremonies of its class, was a dream gift, and its performance provocative of blessings from superhuman sources. Kīwĭtc was likewise the individual visited by a *djïbai* in bird-like form, and the one who told me the story about Kekekǫ́s, just related.

While I did not obtain full details of his dream revelation (which is strictly taboo), Kīwĭtc gave me sufficient information to permit certain conclusions:

One morning the old wife[23] spoke to me and said: "Do you know what I have been dreaming about?" "No," I replied. "I dreamed about a drum in *djïbaiàking.* It seemed as if this drum was offered to us," she said.

At the time I did not know what this dream of the old wife meant, but I was anxious to find out. Some time after this, I was lying on my bed when I heard someone speak to me. "Look!" the voice said. And right in front of me I saw two things. They were empty coffins. Then I heard the voice again. It seemed to come from somewhere between the earth and the sky. It commanded me to go to a certain point. "I will meet you there," it said. When I reached this place I saw four naked old men sitting there. (This place was between the earth and the sky.)

At this point in his narrative, Kīwĭtc unrolled a small piece of birch bark on which were drawn some animal figures, dots, and geometric devices, and indicated the point at which he had seen the empty coffins and met the old men. These were not drawn, however. "They came from the other end," he said, "through here"—pointing to the central line.

Who were these old men, and whose voice was it that Kīwĭtc heard? I think there can be no doubt that the latter was the voice of the Thun-

der Bird. The allusion to "between earth and sky" is in itself fairly con-
clusive, but even more so is the fact that, during part of the ceremony,
two eagle skins are attached to the south posts of the dancing ground.
These represent *pinési*, the Thunder Bird, and other allusions to this
pawágan (guardian spirit, literally "dream visitor") are usually made
during the course of the ceremony. Thus the dream revelation is, in part,
a blessing from *pinési*.

But what of the old men? These, as I understand it, were representatives of what Kīwitc termed *keté änicinábek,* "old Indians"
("Ancients"). They are equivalent to *djibaiyak.* With this identification
in mind, we are brought back to his wife's dream of a drum in *djibaiàking,*
and the coffins in his own dream. The connection of the Thunder Bird
and the spirits of the dead in a dream is not altogether an arbitrary one,
since in the Saulteaux universe *pinési* comes from the south and the
country of the dead lies in the same direction. This emphasis on the
south is objectified, to a certain extent, on the dance ground itself,
which is delimited by a series of stakes laid out in a square, with openings ("doors") left on the northern and southern sides. People enter
the dance ground by the north "door," and thus must face south as
they do so; moreover, the exit after the ceremony is through the south
"door." This orientation is in contrast to the east-and-west orientation of
the Wabano pavilions and, in former times, of the Midéwīwin.

The importance of the "old people down south," as Kīwitc sometimes called them, of the *keté änicinábek,* and of the *djibaiyak,* becomes
clearer by further reference to the bark. Pointing to the dots, Kīwitc said:

These are the dwellings of human beings, but not those living today or yesterday.
They lived long ago, when *wisakedjak* was living here, too. In those days these
Indians did not use the articles you see them using today. They made everything
themselves. They got nothing from the white man. They lived just like the
ätsokának.[24]

On the bark the dwellings of these ancients lay in the direction
from which the old men came. One may infer, therefore, that these
old men, whom Kīwitc saw in his dream, were actually the spirits of
deceased Indians—*djibaiyak.* He also saw the drum, which is likewise
represented on the bark, and he said: "All the animals that you see
drawn there spoke to me, even the flies."

Now it has already been mentioned that the drumming of human
beings can be heard in *djibaiàking,* and that the spirits of the dead themselves sing, dance, and drum. There is, then, a correspondence between
human activities and those of the *djibaiyak.* It is also believed that the
latter are extremely pleased when they hear human beings drumming.
Consequently the general setting, as well as the derivation and significance, of the Drum Dance of Kīwitc is intelligible. *Djibaiyak* were
among its spiritual sponsors; therefore, as Kīwitc remarked on another
occasion about the drum he uses, "in a way the drum *belongs* to the

old people down south." A line in one of the songs used in the ceremony may also be noted:[25] *djibai igamegong kanimīting,* "spirits of the dead wigwam where dancing is held."

Finally, I believe that the importance of the spirits of the dead in the dream revelation of Kīwitc is supported by a conversation subsequent to his description of part of the revelation. He said:

I went south in my dream. I was almost dead at the time I was telling you about. I saw all those people who died long ago and some that I knew myself. It was only when I came to my senses that I knew I was living in this part of the world. It was also at this time that I was told I would have gray hair. As long as I live, I'll hold to what those old men told me.

The drum used in the ceremony is called *kīmicómisanän,* meaning "our grandfather," a term which Kīwitc himself explained as due to the fact that it is one of the "oldest" things known to the Indians. But since "grandfather" is commonly used, not only as a term of respect for any old man, but also in addressing, or referring to, spiritual helpers of all types, it has probably a deeper significance in this context.

It is very striking that the *djibaiyak,* as conceived of in connection with this Drum Dance of Kīwitc, function as *pawáganak.* In the first place, they played an important role in his dream revelation; in the second place, there is the evidence of his own statement: "I ask in the wigwam [i.e., the ceremony] for blessings from our grandfathers down south for those of us here."

In 1934, when I first saw this ceremony, such a reference occurred in one of the first speeches that Kīwitc made. After the drum had been carried in and placed in the center of the dance ground, the singers had taken their places north, south, east, and west of it, and Kīwitc had circled the dance ground with his pipe, ceremonially pointing it in all the directions of the compass, he stopped southeast of the drum, and spoke. He referred to the beginning of the earth (*a'kī*) and the Indians (*änicinábek*). He said: "God (*mänitu*) was the creator and owner of everything, of all that we see growing. We must thank him for life (*pīmadaziwin*). He loves us and he will help us."

Kīwitc also spoke of children as "the gift of God" (*mänitu omigiwewin*).[26] Then he went on to say:

I'm thinking of the Ancients who sat in your places [referring to the singers] long, long ago, before any of us were born. Now I'm speaking to them, the old people down south, who gave this (the drum and the dance) to us to use. We expect blessings from them, and from all the *ätsokának* [= *pawáganak*] in the north, south, east, and west. No one knew the names of all these until the old people named them for us.[27] *Pinési* up there is watching us.[28] We were told how to name him. I open my hand for a blessing. We are pitiable. God knows what we need. He will bless us with Life.

After this speech, Kīwitc circled the dance ground once, and went to his seat on the east side. Later an equally definite grouping of the *djïbaiyak* and the *pawáganak* occurred. Taking a beaded tobacco pouch in his hand, Kïwitc said:

This tobacco was handed to me, but it is not for my own use.[29] It is for those old people down south, *keté änicinábek,* and the *ätsokának.* After I fill my pipe, one of them will circle around in the sky above to bless us, and he will also do some smoking.

This latter reference, of course, is to the Thunder Bird. But "the Ancients" and the *pawáganak,* as already observed, are expected to reciprocate, and Kïwitc went on to say:

Some of the people here are not feeling well. But we have this great tree,[30] and we shall take this tobacco as medicine[31] and smoke it. Now you can go on and darce.

The allusion here is to curative powers validated by the nature of the ceremony itself, and mediated to the human beings participating in it.

It would thus appear that, in connection with this ceremony at least, any sharp distinction between human beings long since dead and the superhuman *pawáganak* has been obliterated. Both are objectives of sacrifice, and are looked upon as potential sources of blessings. Although the emphasis noted here might be the product of individual interpretation on the part of Kïwitc, I doubt whether this was the case. Here and there among Algonkian-speaking peoples elsewhere, the *djïbaiyak* are found occasionally playing a comparable role.[32] Perhaps the most striking generic parallel among an Ojibwa people is that reported by Alexander Henry[33] in a description of a "feast to the dead," at which the leader "called upon the names of his deceased relatives and friends, beseeching them to be present *to assist him in the chase* [my italics] and to partake of the food which he had prepared for them."

Invocation of Deceased Persons in the Conjuring Lodge.—It is not so surprising, then, to find that, in the course of a conjuring performance, not only the master of the *djïbaiyak* may appear, but the spirits of deceased relatives of persons present may be invoked. While I was told that this was exceptional, Arthur Felix, an eye-witness of one such séance, gave me the following account:

In the early fall (October) of the year when the War started [1914], I was camping at Sandy Bar. There were several other families from Berens River, and a Poplar River man, William Franklin. We were fishing. One evening, when some of us were sitting in his tent, William said: "I'd like to try something. I want to conjure before the snow falls, but the kind of trees I need for the lodge don't grow here."

"What kind of sticks do you want?" I asked. "I'm going to take my fish to Berens River tomorrow."

"I want seven *cingubïwátigok* [generic term for evergreens], and one or two green birch sticks, straight ones," said William. So I agreed to cut the kind of trees he needed and bring them back with me.

After I had returned the next day, two other men and myself put up the conjuring lodge. We started before dark, and it took us an hour or a little more. The same day another man and his family arrived from the Berens River Reserve. This man, Jacob Berens, was sickly, and when he found that William was going

163

to conjure, he went to his tent and asked him to try and find out why the medicine he had taken did him no good.[34]

After sunset William came out of his dwelling. He had his coat on, and carried a blanket and pillow. He used the pillow to sit on while in the conjuring lodge. He went into the conjuring tent, and at once it began to shake. All the people, of course, were seated around it. Before he went in William called me to him and handed me some tobacco wrapped in a handkerchief.[35] He said: "Give this to the people, give everyone a pipeful." I did as he told me, and after he was inside I called to him and said I had some left. At this William replied: "That tobacco does not belong to me. It belongs to our grandfathers. Pass it to anyone that wants a smoke."

By this time the tent was shaking harder, and the *pawáganak* had started to come in. They named themselves and sang their songs. All the winds were there and, of course, *mikinák* [the Great Turtle]. There were also present *memengwéciwak* [semi-human creatures living in the rocks], *pijiu* [Lynx], and many others.

After a couple of hours someone came in singing very, very strongly. I heard William saying to it: "One thing I was asked and I don't know the answer. You are one of those that sees many things. You can look around and tell me what I don't know."

Then this *pawágan* sang again, a very long song. It was the boss *djíbai*. Then this *pawágan* spoke: "I saw something a long, long way back. It's the old people's fault this man here is sick." Then the boss *djíbai* talked to Jacob Berens. D.: "How long have you been sick?" J. B.: "Quite a long while." D.: "Where are you sick?" J. B.: "I'm always feeling pain around my waist. It is as if there were something drawing me together there." D.: "Your father has something to do with this. If you like, I'll call him, and ask him to come in here." J. B. (half to himself): "I wonder if it can be so." [The narrator commented here that it seemed as if Berens did not believe it could be true.] Then someone whispered to Jacob Berens: "It's all right. Go ahead." So Berens said: "I'd like to hear my father."

The boss *djíbai* sang again. All at once, while this was going on, someone else came into the conjuring lodge. The singing stopped, and everyone sat very quiet. Then William spoke: "Here is the one you asked for. You can talk to him," he said to Berens. The tent was shaking very gently now.

J. B.: "Is that you, father?" D.[1]: "Yes, my son." J. B.: "Who are you with?" D.[1] "I'm with my grandchild. Ever since I left, I've always been happy. I've never been hungry. I've never been thirsty. I've never suffered any pain. It is a beautiful country where I am living. When I was alive, I always tried to do what was right. Try to do the same thing, my son; don't do any wrong to anyone. If there is ever anyone who says something bad to you, don't answer. That's the way I tried to act. If you act this way you will be glad. You'll see me someday, too. I see some people I know sitting outside. I see my oldest daughter."

Suddenly another voice, that of a child, came from the conjuring lodge. D.[2]: "I see my mother sitting there. Don't do that, Mother! I don't like to see you do that" (the woman whose father and adopted daughter had appeared in the conjuring tent was crying). "You hear my voice here. Well, I'll tell you something. I'm living in a good place. I'm happy. It is always bright like day where I live. It is never dark. I was very sick that time, but now I'm not sick any longer. There are pretty flowers where I live, it's like a great garden. And there are lots of us. There are great singers there too. Don't forget what I am telling you. Live right and some day you'll find me."

Then the father of Jacob Berens spoke again. D.[1]: "Have you taken much medicine for your sickness, my son?" J. B.: "Yes, but it has not helped me." D.[1]: "There was one time, my son, that I made a mistake. A man died and I dressed him for burial. I pulled his belt too tight.

I pulled as hard as I could. That is what makes you sick now. That is the reason the medicine you have taken has not helped you. The medicine cannot work itself down into your body." J. B.: "I hope I will get well now." D.': "My son, I hope you will. It's my fault that you have been so sick around your waist."

Then William Franklin spoke again: "I don't know what kind of medicine to give this man tomorrow morning. Is there anyone here inside that has some medicine I can give this man?"

At this point, the *memengwéci* spoke up: "I'll give him a little," he said. W. F.: "You can give it to him tomorrow morning." M.: "No, I'll go and get it now." So he went out.

J. B.: "I wonder how far he has to go." A *pawágan* answered: "There is only one place to go." Someone in the audience: "Where is that?" *Pawágan:* "*Memengwéciwak* live at *kickábiskan* [high rock]."

Soon the *memengweci* was back in the conjuring tent, and said to W. F.: "When morning comes, you give that Indian this medicine of mine I have brought you, and tell him how to use it."

Drum Divination and the Spirits of the Dead.—Another method of communication between the living and the dead, one which has sprung up in recent years among the Berens River Saulteaux at the Pauingessi settlement, is apparently unique. I know of no specific analogies to it anywhere among Algonkian peoples.

Despite the emphasis given to the role of the *djíbaiyak* in the Drum Dance described above, when I mentioned to Kiwitc the ceremony I had witnessed at Pauingessi (in 1933), he said: "I have not gone *that* far." In the Pauingessi dance, the *drum* has become the medium of communication between the living and the spirits of the dead.

This dance was a dream revelation to Námawin (Fair Wind), now blind, and one of the oldest men on the river. For many years he has dominated a sector of the Grand Rapids Band, which has its summer fishing settlement and winter houses about twelve miles north of the other Grand Rapids settlement. Fair Wind has four married sons and one married daughter living there, and all his sons assist their father in carrying on both the Wabanówiwin and the dance in question. He is the ostensible leader of both of these ceremonies.

The dance, like the one owned by Kiwitc, has no specific name; but my interpreter said that it might be called, simply, *Djíbaisímowin,* "Ghost (or Spirit of the Dead) Dance." It differs from the dance of Kiwitc in that allusions to *pawáganak* are absent.

It is held within a pavilion, consisting of a circular structure made of poles,[36] which has four doors, facing north, south, east, and west. The northern door is used as entrance.

On the occasion when I witnessed it, the dance followed a three-day Wabanowiwin. It was cloudy and windy, and a little rain fell in the morning. Preparatory to the performance, the ground inside the pavilion was swept out, some broken poles were repaired, and spruce boughs were cut by the women and placed both around the periphery of the interior, and in the middle, where the drummers sit. There was a flagpole in the center, from which a British flag flapped in the wind.

The drum was brought in about noon, and a windbreak of canvas erected to one side of it. A fire was kindled outside the pavilion, to which the drum was later taken from time to time to stretch the drumskin. The drum was called "our grandfather."

The dance was opened by old Fair Wind, who with lighted pipe in hand (the stem pointing towards the drum), and his hat off, made some opening remarks. Then he circled the pavilion, took his place, and smoked for a while.

Before the actual drumming started, he made a speech, in a voice which expressed deep feeling, and was punctuated by many gestures. The gist of it was an explanation of how he had obtained the dance. He spoke about one of his grandsons, who grew up to be a good-sized boy, and then fell sick. He said:

I tried to cure him, but I found I was unable to help him. Others tried, too, but they also failed. Finally, he was so weak that he had to be fed with a spoon. Then one day he slept away. After that, even in the daytime it was dark to me. I was full of grief.

One day I was away in the bush by myself. The tears were running down my cheeks all the time, thinking about this boy. I put down my gun and my mittens. I made up my mind to die. I lay down on the point of a rock, where I could be found. When I closed my eyes, towards the sky I saw something like a nest.[37] When I looked towards the east, I heard something saying: "This is something that will stop you from crying. You'll not die. For this is one of the finest things to play with."

All this, of course, is typical of the situations in which many Eastern Woodland Indians have received a "blessing" from the superhuman powers. They provoked pity, and they were given something to "amuse" themselves with.

Fair Wind then went on to a homely human analogy in his speech. He said:

If any of you heard one of your children crying, you would run to the child at once to find out what made him cry. He might have hurt himself, and you would try to give him something to amuse him, so he would stop crying.

After a few more remarks that are irrelevant here, the drumming started. There were four drummers, two of them[38] sons of Fair Wind, and one of them his brother's son. Angus was the head drummer and sat on the south side of the drum. Not being aware at this time of the association of the djibaiyak with this dance, neither Chief Berens nor I paid any special attention to Angus, as he lightly tapped on the edge of the drum before they began to sing, and uttered a few words in a very low tone at the same time. We later discovered that these words were addressed to the djibaiyak, whose medium of communication was the drum.

After the drumming and dancing had been going on for some time, a new song was started, and a number of people, most of them women, appeared with dishes in their hands. These dishes were each covered with a handkerchief or small piece of cloth, and the women carried them into the pavilion, circled round the drum, and then deposited them beside the drum. Presently Fair Wind got up, and after some remarks about God as the creator, who had delegated a little of his power to the àtsokának, said:

I'm going to explain to the great visiting Chief the meaning of those dishes that have just been brought in here, and are lying there with a little food in them.[39] When a person has lost a brother, a child, or some other relative, we call upon them to look down upon us.[40] They have been on this earth once, and before that they were sent from above to come on this earth. Jesus, too, came from above to be the boss of the earth.

The food in the dishes, then, was offered to the djibaiyak, and it is noteworthy that it was not "the Ancients" that the participants had in mind on this occasion, but the more recent dead, those that were still being mourned.

Towards the close of the dance, the dishes of food were placed on the ground, arranged roughly in a ring around the drum; then the persons who had brought them in, while dancing around the drum took their respective dishes, and after circling around the dance path once or twice, placed them on top of the drum. The dishes were now unwrapped by the drummers, and every person in the pavilion stepped forward and helped himself to the bannock.

At this point, Angus made a speech. He said:

My beloved friends, when I was a boy, I never expected to be sitting here beating this drum. Even when I was a young man, I never thought of it. Later, when I was a full-grown man, I worked hard on the York boats, just like my father had done. Yet I knew nothing. Even when I got married, I was still ignorant. Recently one of my brother's sons slept away. He is sleeping over there [pointing in the direction of the grave]. I did not like to see his grave like that of an animal, all covered with snow. I went there and put my tent over the grave.[41]

A few months later, I went north to hunt. I was crying, even while I was hunting. Finally, I made up my mind that I would rather sleep than live.[42] Then I heard a voice saying to me: "I'll give you something to ease your mind and that of others. But you must take care and carry things through as you are told."

Even a minister's name was mentioned. But the minister did not tell me half of what he should have told me. He did not even know what pinési was. He is one of those that tries to make us believe that stones striking together makes the noise that we hear (thunder). I do not believe this. I mention it today because I know something different on account of what I have dreamed.

Shortly after this, during one of the intervals between songs, Angus talked to the djibaiyak that were reputed to be speaking through the drum. This episode was not dramatized in any way. It seemed to occur quite spontaneously. Because of its unexpectedness, as well as its unique character, my interpreter, Chief Berens, did not at first understand to whom Angus was talking, or even what he was talking about. The words were uttered by Angus in a low tone, with his head partly bent over the drum, which he gave slowly timed blows with his drumstick at fairly regular intervals.

167

It appears that Angus, while listening carefully to the drum, was at the same time repeating certain questions which were being asked, and then answering them. One of the questions he heard, for example, was repeated by him as: "The master (*kadabéndang*) wants to know how we are getting along." The answer was given: "Just the same as before. We are very poor." The reply to another question was: "You're merciful to the Indians. You know what they want—more Life, and the things we need for our bodies on this earth."

Once Angus called to his father and asked: "Did you understand what was said?" "No," replied Fair Wind, "I was not listening closely enough."

Then Angus began to sing another song, but suddenly stopped. He evidently had heard something more, but did not quite catch it. At any rate he said: "I missed it. I didn't finish it." He asked his wife for some tobacco. She did not have any, so he told her to run and get some, and to be quick about it. This tobacco was then immediately thrown into the fire outside the pavilion, evidently as a sacrifice because of a mistake Angus had made. He said: "I've started singing now and I'll have to go on"; and he talked no more to the *djibaiyak*.

Soon there was the last dance, led by the wife of Angus. After going clockwise, the direction was reversed and the participants went counterclockwise to the end of the dance. During this movement, Pīkwákīgan (Lump Breast), walking clockwise, wove in and out of the line of dancers. Then the drummers stood up, Fair Wind came forward, and the whole group sang a Christian hymn. Finally, Fair Wind lifted his hand in benediction, in the Christian manner, and Jesus was mentioned again. The exit was through the west door, where Fair Wind stood and shook hands with everyone as they went out. To some he said, "Good night," in English; to others, the women in particular, he said, *nīpá* (sleep well).

When I later inquired whether the dance was a gift of the *djibaiyak*, or of some *pawágan*, I was answered in the negative. It came directly from God. In this it contradicts, of course, one of the fundamental principles of even contemporary Saulteaux dream revelation. But the mixed character of the elements of the ceremony is obvious even in a superficial description. Moreover, the songs used are similar to, if not identical with, those employed in the ordinary *potáte* dances, and these songs came from the Plains. Nevertheless this dance also illustrates extremely well how diverse strands of belief and practice can be welded together under the influence of a strong personality, and yet still kept within the framework of the Saulteaux interpretation of the universe. To my mind, the dance indicates the dynamic character of syncretic processes, and the fact that it is of fairly recent origin shows that there is still some religious vitality left in the non-Christian beliefs of the Indian population along the river. The unique features it embodies stamp it as a creative, rather than a decadent, product.

There was one other practice, said to be associated with this Drum Dance, that should be mentioned. When a person dies, if his clothes or other belongings are sent to Pauingessi it can be determined, by consulting the drum, to whom they should go. This custom is certainly derived from an older one, which consisted in sending the clothes of the deceased to some other settlement in exchange for similar articles, in order to avoid being reminded of the loved one. But Fair Wind and his sons send nothing in exchange; the articles are reputed to go to those who loved the deceased most. The drum is the medium of this information; and only Fair Wind and Angus, I may add, understand the messages which come through the drum.

The fact should further be stressed that the curative function, associated with all the principal ceremonics of the Berens River people since the Midéwíwin has died out, is a feature of the Drum Dance also. This is the aspect of it which I heard about at the Poplar Narrows settlement. Their drum was made for them under the direction of Fair Wind and his sons, and by the purchase of it[43] they have been able to share the benefits of the dream blessings of Fair Wind and Angus.

Other Ceremonial Invocations of the Dead.—The only emphasis upon the spirits of the dead comparable to that in the two dances described above occurred in two ceremonies now extinct.

One was formerly held farther north on the Poplar River. This dance was once described to Chief Berens by his grandmother; he was unable to recall all the details, but she called it Djibaisimowin, and stated that it was held once a year. It began after nightfall, and continued until daybreak. Eight or more carved wooden figures, painted black, and looking like human beings, were attached to a string and hung up in a row inside the wigwam. When the old man who was the owner of the dance drummed and sang, these figures would dance. They represented *djibaiyak*. During the course of the dance a whistling noise would be heard outside the wigwam, and it was the *djibaiyak* who were in this way characteristically indicating their presence.

The second ceremony, held at Jack Head across the Lake, had become associated with the Wabanówiwin. It was called Djibai Wabano, and was said to have continued during ten nights. On the last night, the *cábandawan*, the multiple family dwelling of former days in which the ceremony was being held, was closed up tight. Only those who had dreamed of *djibaiyak*[44] were allowed in. As the drumming and singing went on, *djibaiyak* were seen to pass through the *cábandawan* from end to end and then disappear. They did not walk on the ground, but "floated" along some little distance above it. After passing through, they were heard calling outside. Their call sounded like that of gulls.

The Djíbaimídéwíwin Ceremony.—There was, of course, formerly the Djĭbaīmidéwīwin on the Berens River itself, but this was of a character entirely distinct from that of the ceremonies already described. A living person was conducted through the ceremony, in place of a deceased relative who had already accumulated goods, and for whom all arrangements had been made with the leaders, but who had died before the spring came and the Midéwīwin proper was given. Obviously these special circumstances in no way changed, indeed rather maintained, the emphasis of the fundamental ideology of the Midéwīwin as ordinarily held; it was merely believed that the soul of the deceased person would be present.

Reincarnation.—Finally, a few words may be said about the belief in reincarnation. In this connection it will be necessary to return to Kīwĭtc once more. When he was telling me about his early life, he said:

Some people say that a child knows nothing when it is born. Four nights before I was born I knew that I would be born. My mind was clear when I was born as it is now. I saw my father and my mother, and I knew who they were. I knew the things an Indian uses, their names and what they were good for—an axe, a gun, a knife, and even an ice-chisel. I used to tell this to my father and he replied: "Long ago the Indians used to be like that, but the ones that came after them were different." I have asked my own children about this, but there is only one of them that remembers when he was in his mother's womb. People said to me: "You are one of those old people who died long ago and were born a second time."

This last statement is certainly sufficient to indicate that a belief in the possibility of reincarnation is extant; but it remains almost wholly unelaborated. In the case of Kīwĭtc, it merges with the idea of *precognition,* the belief in which is stressed by making it one of the tokens of the possession of magical powers. It is this aspect of his account which is really significant. In terms of Saulteaux thought, the idea of reincarnation is in the nature of a secondary explanation of something remarkable. Thus Kīwĭtc, no doubt unconsciously, has invested himself with what, in Saulteaux opinion, is a sign of great spiritual power.

Reincarnation is also cited when a child is found to have a few gray hairs. People will say that it is some old man or woman who has been born again (*keté ànicinábe èändjīnictáuwige*). But no identification is made with any particular individual, and the linkage with the spirit of the dead therefore remains extremely vague.[45]

Conclusions.—Despite the emphasis given to the spirits of the dead in the ceremonies described, and the intimate relations which they are supposed to have with the living in many other respects, it is obvious that there is nothing that can be specifically characterized as ancestor-worship, or a cult of the dead. However, Saulteaux conceptions of the universe are of such a nature, and permit of so much flexibility in their concrete application as explanatory principles, that it is quite conceivable that discrete elements, now typically unelaborated, might, in the hands of some influential personality, be developed in that direction.

As it is, the spirits of the dead, instead of being central in the ideology of the Indians, are actually peripheral to other spiritual beings who are conceptually the dynamic forces of the universe, helping men to achieve the ends for which they strive. This relationship is demonstrated by the fact that the spirits of the dead tend to coalesce, in certain instances, with the *pawáganak,* conceptually and functionally. The gap is easily bridged, indeed, if for no other reason than the presence in mythology of anthropomorphic characters who themselves function as spiritual helpers; typical of such is *wîsɑkedjak.* These anthropomorphic beings, while now immortal like the dead, once lived on earth like the Indians, so that they too are among the *keté änicinábek.*

Nor must it be forgotten how shadowy is the line, in Saulteaux thought, between "humanness" and the essentially animate qualities of other orders of being. No wonder, then, that the spirits of the dead are such an integral part of the Saulteaux universe, and that they merge so intimately with other aspects of Saulteaux life and thought.

Chapter 8 - The Ojibwa Self and Its Behavioral Environment*

ALTHOUGH THERE IS NO SINGLE TERM IN OJIBWA SPEECH THAT CAN BE satisfactorily rendered into English as "self," nevertheless, by means of personal and possessive pronouns, the use of kinship terms, and so on, the Ojibwa Indian constantly identifies himself as a person. Every individual knows who he is, where he is, and what kind of being he is; he entertains definite beliefs and concepts that relate to his own nature. Besides this, his language enables him to express such concepts as self-defense, self-glorification, self-deceit, self-command. Large areas of his most characteristic thinking, his affective experience, his needs, motivations, and goals are not thoroughly intelligible unless we take the content of his self-image into account.

I believe that the essential features of the self-image of the Ojibwa, in their full psychological reality, can best be communicated by indicating how they function as an integral part of the experience of an individual. To present the material in this form I have let an Indian, long deceased, speak in the first person, rather than attempt an abstract exposition. In order to cover as many aspects of the topic as possible and yet remain as close as possible to data collected in the field, I have attributed to my Indian speaker knowledge and experience derived from the statements of a number of different informants. Furthermore, the statements of my Indian speaker, which all appear between quotation marks, may be taken as a free translation of a possible Ojibwa text, since I have not used any English words that do not have a fairly good equivalent in Ojibwa. Beside this, Ojibwa terms for key concepts are cited. In brackets I have added my comments on particular points in order to highlight significant concepts and have sometimes gone into further elaboration. In the footnotes are references to published articles or books where fuller data or case material highly abbreviated in the account given by my Indian speaker will be found.

"When I was born I had a body, *mīyóᶜ*, and I had a soul, *òtcatcák-win*. My body came out of my mother's womb and when I was an old man it was buried in the earth [the body has a definitive existence in

---

*Originally published as the second section of "The Self and Its Behavioural Environment," *Explorations,* II (April 1954).

time]. I was not one of those people who knew what was happening before he was born. But my father did. (See Chap. 7, *Reincarnation*.)

"I have heard some other old people say that they had heard babies crying constantly until someone recognized the name they were trying to say. When they were given this name they stopped crying. This shows that someone who had once lived on the earth came back to live again. [Reincarnation is possible, even if occasional. There are special cues in such cases: the recall of prenatal memories; crying and babbling that only stops when the name of a deceased person is mentioned,[2] which indicates the importance of the personal name in self-identification. Another cue is the presence of a few gray hairs on the infant's head. In cases like this no personal identification may be made. Certain inferences are clear: the soul is independent of a particular body; it transcends the body in time; an implicit concept of the self is intimately connected with the idea of the soul. Self-objectification is clearly implied since self-awareness is even attributed to the foetus. The informant says that his father knew when he was going to be born. To the Ojibwa to know what is going to happen ahead of time is one of the signs of a "great" man, i.e., a man with unusual powers.]

"When I was living on the earth I had to be careful that nobody got hold of any part of my body. When my hair was cut I always burnt the part that was cut off. I was afraid that someone with power [magic] might get hold of it. If he wanted to, such a person could make me sick or even kill me. I didn't want to die before I had to. I wanted life, *pimãdaziwin*. But someone did manage to kill me by sending something towards me that penetrated my body. That's when you need a *nibakiwinini* [an Indian doctor who tries to remove the object by sucking as part of his ritual]. Sometimes he will suck out a shell, a piece of metal, or a dog's tooth and show it to you. Then you can live. But he couldn't cure me. He didn't have enough power. The person who killed me had more. [The body is intimately connected with the self, so intimately that physical possession of even a part of it is considered as endangering the self. The self can also be attacked by magically potent material substances projected into the body. In general, it may be said that bodily illness of any kind arouses great anxiety. The Ojibwa tend to be hypocondriacal. There are two points of interpretation that are relevant in this connection: Since serious illness, in many instances, is thought to be due to sorcery, it becomes a direct personal attack upon the self by an enemy. At the same time since illness, viewed from the standpoint of experience, involves the dysfunctioning of bodily processes, the bodily aspect of the self assumes great importance. The further implication is that an attack on the body destroys the balance that should exist between soul and body in order to realize the Good Life, that is, life in terms of longevity, health, and absence of misfortune. Since self-awareness is given content in terms of a self-image defined by this dichotomy, anxiety may be aroused if either soul or body is endangered. In a positive sense this is why *pimādazīwin* expresses a very central goal for the self—a level of aspiration towards which the self is motivated.[3]

"When I died and my body was buried that was not the end of me. I still exist[4] in *djibaiaking*, Ghost land or the Land of the Dead. [Existence of self is not coordinate with bodily existence in the ordinary human sense.] When I was dead people called me a *djibai*, ghost. Some Indians have seen *djibaiak* (plural) or heard them whistle. [In other words, a dead person has a form, a ghostly appearance that can be seen by the living and, without being visually perceived, may occasionally be heard by the living. Death involves metamorphosis because the body formerly associated with the soul has become detached from it and lies in the ground. On the other hand "I" *know* when "I" am a *djibai;* self-awareness, personal identity, personal memories persist; there is a continuity of the self maintained.]

"It is a long hard journey to the Land of the Dead. To reach it you travel south.[5] [There are cases known in the past in which pagan Indians begged their Christianized relatives not to bury them in a coffin. They believed that they would have to carry it with them on the journey to the Land of the Dead, and they did not wish to be burdened with it. This journey is not conceived in "spiritual" terms at all; the "living" self can become emotionally disturbed by the anticipation of difficulties to be encountered by the "dead" self. It is plain that, psychologically, the behavioral environment of the self is all of one piece.]

"When I got there I found it to be a very fine place. The Indians who had died before me were glad to see me. Some of them had moss growing on their foreheads [like old rocks], they had died so long ago. I sang and danced with them. A few Indians have reached the Land of the Dead and then gone back to tell those who were alive what they saw there. [The dead in appearance are thought of anthropomorphically, not as disembodied spirits. They live in wigwams. But there are differences. In one account a youth visiting the land of of dead was offered food by his grandmother. It was decayed (i.e., phosphorescent) wood. When he refused, she said: "Naturally you are not truly dead. . . ." An essential point for emphasis is the continuation of a fundamental duality of essence. *Djibaiak* like *ănicinábek* have souls, and some kind of *form.* As will become more apparent later, this duality holds for *all* orders of animate beings.]

"If an Indian dies and a good medicine man starts after him quickly enough he may be brought back [i.e., his soul may be captured and returned to his body]. Then he can go on living as before. Once I saw Owl do this.[6] Tcètcebú was very ill. By the time Owl arrived where her father was encamped, she died. Owl tied a piece of red yarn around the girl's wrist at once [to enable him to identify her quickly in a crowd] and lay down beside her body. He lay in this position a long, long time.

He was still; he did not move at all. Then I saw him move ever so little. The girl began to move a little also. Owl moved more. So did the girl. Owl raised himself up into a sitting posture. At the same moment the girl did the same. He had followed her to the Land of the Dead and caught her soul just in time. Everything has to have a soul in order to exist (as an animate being). I'm in the Land of the Dead now but I have a soul just as I had one before I came here. [Death involves the departure of the soul from the body; the soul takes up its residence in a new locale. There is metamorphosis. The body becomes inanimate and "selfless." The persistence of the self in conjunction with the soul in its new form is implied in the self-awareness attributed to ghosts.]

"If a conjurer, *djisakiwinini,* has power enough he can bring a soul back from the Land of the Dead into his 'shaking tent.'. I was called by a conjurer once because my son was ill and this man was trying to cure him. My grandchild went with me. When her mother, who was sitting with the other Indians outside the conjuring tent, heard her speak, she cried.[7] I had to tell about something wrong I had done when I was living. This helped my son to get well.[8] [Under these circumstances the ghost has no usually perceptible form; only the soul is there. But functionally, a self continuous with a "living" existence is implied because personal memories of an earlier period in life are recalled.]

"When a person is sleeping anyone can see where his body is, but you can't tell whether his soul is there or not. Some conjurer may have enough power to draw your soul into his shaking tent while you are asleep. If he has the power you can't resist. Perhaps he only wants to have you talk to the people in his camp and tell them the latest news. But he may want to kill you. If your soul doesn't get back to your body then you'll be a *djibai* by the next morning and have to start off to the Land of the Dead. I had a lucky escape once. I was only sixteen years old. A conjurer drew my soul into his conjuring lodge and I knew at once that he wanted to kill me, because I had made fun of his son who was a 'humpy' [hunchback]. I said 'I'm going out.' But the old man said, 'No! You can't go.' Then I saw my own head rolling about and the 'people in the lodge were trying to catch it. [The "people" were the guardian spirits, *pawáganak,* of the conjurer —superhuman entities.] I thought to myself that if only I could catch my head everything would be all right. So I tried to grab it when it rolled near me and finally I caught it.[9] As soon as I got hold of it I could see my way out and I left. Then I woke up but I could not move my legs or arms. Only my fingers I could move. But finally I managed to speak. I called out to my mother. I told her I was sick. I was sick for a couple of days. No one saw my sould go to and fro but I knew where I had been. I told my father about it and he agreed with me.

[It is quite clear from all this that the soul is detachable from the

175

body and may occupy a different position in space. This is true both with respect to a dead person and a person asleep. It is also possible to infer with reasonable certainty that the soul cannot be conceptually dissociated from the self. Where a functioning self exists, there must be a soul. Where a soul exists there must be a self. In terms of an assumed dependent relationship the self-soul relation in Ojibwa thought logically parallels the self-body relation in our sophisticated thinking. We emphasize a certain kind of *physical* body or form as a necessary substratum for a functioning self. We are skeptics so far as any other kind of a structural substratum is concerned. On the other hand, the Ojibwa take it for granted that the soul is the only necessary substratum. Any particular form or appearance is incidental. Thus, various kinds of metamorphosis can be accepted so long as it is assumed that a soul continues to exist. What is particularly interesting to note, it seems to me, is that once we accept this assumption, it becomes more and more apparent that *functionally* the same generic attributes of the self as we understand it—and that we assume can only be manifested where a human bodily structure is present—are constant functions of the soul as thought of by the Ojibwa. The soul of the living or the dead knows who it is, what it is, where it is in space and time; it is conscious of past experiences, it has a capacity for volition, etc., irrespective of the form or appearance it may present to others at the moment. This interpretation is further illustrated by what follows.]

"There was a *djibai* here who paid a visit to her grandfather. He was so very sad after she died. She visited him one day when he had put a mast up in his canoe and with a blanket for a sail was crossing a lake. She appeared to him as a little bird that alighted on the top of the mast. She didn't say anything but he knew who it was because he was a wise old man.[10] [The deceased—one of the very old people, *ketéänicinábek*—may be seen by a living person, not as a ghost but in the form of a bird. Metamorphosis is possible for a *djibai;* in this case from ghost to bird.]

"The soul of a living person, too, after it leaves the body can look like an animal. A powerful medicine man can do a lot of harm because he can go about secretly at night. But you can see his body lying there in his wigwam all the time. A long time ago a friend of mine told me what he had seen.[11] He and his wife were living with an old man suspected of being a sorcerer. One night he thought the sorcerer was up to something. The latter lit his pipe and covered himself up completely with his blanket. My friend kept watch. After a long, long time had gone by, all of a sudden the sorcerer threw off the blanket and fell over towards the fire. Blood was running from his mouth; he was dead. My friend found out what killed him. At the very same time that the sorcerer was lying under his blanket so quietly, in another part of the camp Pindándakwan was waiting with a gun in the dark beside the body of his son who had been killed by sorcery. A kind of 'fire' had appeared around the camp several times before the boy died. This night Pindándakwan saw the 'fire' coming again. It[12] made a circle around the corpse, which was covered by birch bark. He heard a voice saying, 'This is finished.' Then he saw a bear trying to lift the bark near the head of his son; he was going to take what he wanted.[13] Pindándakwan shot the bear and he heard a man's voice crying out. Both the sorcerer and the boy were buried the next day. Everyone thought the old man was a bad one. No one blamed Pindándakwan.

[This anecdote requires some lengthy comment, since it will enable us to penetrate further into Ojibwa thought and the basic premises involved. (a) It is obvious that there is not metamorphosis of the body of the sorcerer. The *miyó*ᶜ remains in the wigwam in its usual form. (b) Unlike the previous case where the soul was drawn from the body by the power of another person, here the soul leaves the body behind through a volitional act of the conjurer himself. In fact the Ojibwa would say that *he* left his body and point out that this was not the first time, since his reputation for wickedness implies this kind of behavior. And the "fire" had been seen at Pindándakwan's camp before. (c) It is likewise obvious that, in this case, the conjurer was not understood to be prowling around *dressed up* in a bear skin. This was John Tanner's interpretation, over a century ago, of similar stories. He writes: ". . . by some composition of gunpowder, or other means [they] contrive to give the appearance of fire to the mouth and eyes of the bear skin, in which they go about the village late at night, bent on deeds of mischief, oftentimes of blood."[14] This is simply Tanner's effort at an explanation intelligible to him. (d) I believe that all we need to say is that the self of the sorcerer was in Pindándakwan's camp. To say that *he* was there is the meaningful core of the whole situation; it was Pindándakwan's assumption that *he* would be there and he acted on this premise. In these terms the situation is as humanly intelligible to us as it is to the Objbwa. What is always difficult for them is to explain what we would call the *mechanism* of events, exactly *how* they occur. To them, this line of thought seems "pedantic." Explanation is never pursued in much detail at this level (which is actually the level of science). But to say that *he* (the sorcerer) had visited Pindándakwan's camp on several occasions, that *he* had killed Pindándakwan's son, that he was caught there on a particular night and killed by Pindándakwan in revenge is thoroughly meaningful to them. All they take for granted (as an implicit metaphysical principle) is that *multiform appearance* is an inherent potential of *all* animate beings. What is uniform, constant, visually imperceptible and vital is the soul. A sorcerer being a person of unusual power is able to leave his human body in one place and appear in another perceptible manifestation elsewhere. (e) There is an additional point to be noted. Inquiry revealed that Pindándakwan was known to have considerable power himself. Since he assumed it was a sorcerer prowling around and not an ordinary bear, he did not load his gun with an ordinary bullet. He mixed "medicine," *máckíkí* (having magical potency), with his gunpowder. Just as it is thought possible to attack a person's ordinary body with intent to kill by projecting a material object with magical properties into it, in the same way the sorcerer, in the bodily appearance of a bear, could be directly attacked through his body, although something more than an ordinary bullet was required. (Under the circumstances there was no way of focusing the attack on his soul). In both instances the body is assumed to be a vulnerable point of attack. Since it is fairly clear that what death implies for the Ojibwa is the *separation* of the soul from its humanly-formed body, I believe they would agree that the soul of the sorcerer did not succeed in getting back to his human body. This explains why his body was seen to collapse. It could not resume its normal functioning without a soul. This is why Owl was in such a hurry to capture the soul of Tcètcebú. Not being able to reach his body in time to resume living (which was, no doubt, part of the magic employed by Pindánadakwan), the sorcerer's soul was compelled to assume the form of a *ghost*. In a brief account of his puberty fast, to which our Indian speaker now refers, the reàder will note another situation in which the *temporary* separation of the soul from the body occurs. To the Ojibwa there is nothing particularly unusual in such a personal experience. We lack autobiographical anecdotes, however, because there is a traditional taboo upon references to personal experiences during the puberty fast.]

"Long ago, when every boy used to go out alone into the woods to obtain his helpers his body remained in the *wazísán* (nest) his father built for him.[15] If you had been there you could have seen his body for yourself. But his soul might have been elsewhere. One of his helpers might have taken him somewhere. That is what happened to me.

When I was a boy I went out to an island to fast. My father paddled me there. For several nights I dreamed of an *ógímä* (chief, superior person). Finally he said to me, "Grandson, I think you are now ready to go with me." Then *ógímä* began dancing around me as I sat there on a rock and when I happened to glance down at my body I noticed that I had grown feathers. Soon I felt just like a bird, a golden eagle (*kíníu*). *Ógímä* had turned into an eagle also and off he flew towards the south. I spread my wings and flew after him in the same direction. After a while we arrived at a place where there were lots of tents and lots of "people." It was the home of the Summer Birds. . . .[After returning north again the boy was left at their starting point after his guardian spirit had promised help whenever he wanted it. The boy's father came for him and took him home again].[16]

From this account it can be inferred that in addition to living Indians and deceased Indians, there are other classes of animate beings in the behavioral environment of the Ojibwa self with whom the individual comes into direct contact under certain circumstances. For it is apparent that the dreams of the puberty fast are interpreted as experiences of the self. The being that first appears as a human being and then is transformed into a bird is representative of a large class of other-than-human entities that maintain an existence independently of *änicinábek* and are more powerful than man. The eagle-man is not the bird one ordinarily perceives but belongs to the class of "owners" or "bosses." All animal species, such as the golden eagle, are thought to have a *kàdabenīmíkuwat*. These "owners" are only perceived, however, in dreams or visions.

If we assume that dream experiences are interpreted by the Ojibwa as experiences of the self we then arrive at a very important deduction. The *pawáganak* are experienced as appearing in a specific form, that is, as having a bodily aspect, whether human or animal. Years ago I wrote in my notebook that Chief Berens, my most intelligent informant, said flatly that the *pawáganak* had "bodies" and "souls," but no "ghosts." Since *my* natural bias was to think of these *pawáganak* as "spiritual beings," I did not at first see the implications of the statement he had made. In our present discussion its full import is clarifying. The soul is the essential and persisting attribute of *all* classes of animate beings, human or nonhuman. But the soul is never a direct object of *visual* perception under any conditions. What can be perceived visually is only the aspect of being that has some form or structure. Consequently, it is not surprising to find that when the *pawáganak* appear in dreams they are identifiable in a tangible visual form. This *experiential* fact taken at its face value indicates, of course, that they, too, have a body as well as a soul. Structurally, they are the counterpart of man. On the other hand, it is *not* assumed that they have a uniform or stable appearance. Metamorphosis is always possible, as in the dream reported. It may be inferred, therefore, that there are inherent attributes which remain constant for different classes of beings. In the dream referred to the *being* that appeared was a *pawagan* of a certain kind and not a human being, even though he first appeared in a human form. This is just the reverse of the bad old sorcerer who was essentially human even though he appeared as a bear on certain occasions. This means, of course, that in the behavioral world of the Ojibwa, no sharp line can be drawn between animals, *pawáganak,* men, or the spirits of the dead on the basis of outward bodily aspect or appearance alone. Myths illustrate this, too, and unless we are aware of the point I have just made it is utterly impossible to apprehend their verdical nature from the Ojibwa point of view. Myths are sacred stories because they rehearse actual events in which the superhuman *pawáganak* are the main characters. These *pawáganak* are specially adept at metamorphosis. This is part of the dramatic interest of the myths. The Ojibwa are quite prepared to have the *pawáganak* manifest the same characteristic attribute in dreams. It is one of their essential attributes because

179

metamorphosis, especially when volitionally induced, has the implication of "power." It is thought that the human being who is capable of metamorphosis has derived his power through the help of *pawáganak*. This is the only source of it. When he possesses it he, therefore, becomes superior to his fellow-men in this regard. They have to respect him even though they fear him. The only metamorphosis of *all änicinábek* is brought about by death. The dead, however, have more power than the living; consequently they are more like *pawáganak*, including the power of metamorphosis. But the *pawáganak*, who are eternal, do not die; they never become *djibaiak*.

The only sensory mode under which it is possible for human beings to directly perceive the presence of souls of *any* category, and then under certain conditions only, is the auditory one. The chief context of this kind of experience is the conjuring tent where, as I have already pointed out, the souls of *djibaiak* may be present and speak.[17] It is only infrequently that ghosts may be heard to whistle, perhaps in the neighborhood of a grave, where it is sometimes said they have been seen. It is from the conjuring tent, too, that the voices of *pawáganak* may be heard to issue. They cannot be seen. Thus from the standpoint of our central problem it is difficult not to draw the conclusion that, while according to Ojibwa dogma it is a soul that is present, even to them it is always an identifiable self—*pawáganak* or ghost—that speaks. For them *òtcatcákwin* defines the conceptual substratum of beings with self-awareness and other related attributes (speech, memory, volition, etc.) that we associate only with a stabilized anthropomorphic structure. When Ojibwa speak of their own dream experiences or those of others, when they refer to what has been heard in conjuring performances, it is assumed that one's own soul or that of some other being was present and not the body. But this fact does not have to be explicitly stated any more than we have to be explicit about the presence of the body in referring to self-related experience or to social interaction with other selves. What is implied by the Ojibwa and by ourselves is an indication of the differences between their self-orientation and ours. What is held in common is a self-concept that assumes certain generic human attributes, despite conceptual differences in the nature of the substratum of a functioning self.

Returning once again to the puberty dream I should like to stress the fact that once dreams, on this occasion or any other, are construed as experiences of the self, we can only conclude that metamorphosis can be *personally* experienced. It follows from this, too, that to anyone who has had such a dream, episodes in myth, or anecdotes like those in which the sorcerer figured, cannot appear as strange or fantastic occurrences. In a dream, too, the self may experience the separation of the soul from the body and mobility over large distances. Accounts of such mobility also occur in myth and in anecdotes connected with conjuring. I was told by one informant that he once attended a conjuring performance to which another conjurer, from two hundred miles away, was called. He said, "I was sleeping, but I heard you calling me." People in the audience asked for news and received replies to questions. Then the soul of the visiting conjurer sang a song and departed for home.[18]

In addition to metamorphosis and spatial mobility, the self may likewise experience events in its dream phase that transcend the temporal schema of waking existence. Our autobiographer, for instance, not only made the long journey to the Land of the Summer Birds during his puberty fast; he stayed there all winter and flew north with the other birds under the guidance of his ógīmä in the spring. It is self-related experiences of this nature that coordinate the world as dramatized in myth with the world as experienced by the self in certain phases of its existence. Myths are understood as past experiences of superhuman selves—the pawáganak. Dreams are among the past experiences of the self. Thus the world of the self is not essentially different from the world of the pawáganak. The cultural emphasis given to dream experience helps to unify the world of the self through experience. For anthropomorphic entities such as wisakedjak may appear in both myth and dream as may the Winds, Snow, Thunder Birds, and so on, in personified form. No wonder that certain "natural" objects belong to an animate rather than an inanimate gender in linguistic expression. Furthermore, all classes of pawáganak are linguistically integrated in the kinship terminology since, collectively, they are spoken of as "our grandfathers." And in the dream reported by our autobiographer the pawágan calls him nózis, "grandson."

The Ojibwa self is not oriented to a behavioral environment in which a distinction between human beings and supernatural beings is stressed. The fundamental differentiation of primary concern to the self is how other selves rank in order of power. "Is he more powerful than I, or am I more powerful than he?" This is a crucial question applying to all human beings as well as to the pawáganak. But the fundamental distinction is that while other Indians may be more powerful than I, any pawágan is more powerful than any Indian. The power ranking of different classes of entities is so important because events only become intelligible in terms of their activities. All the effective agents of events throughout the entire behavioral environment of the Ojibwa are selves—my own self or other selves. Impersonal forces are never the causes of events. Somebody is always responsible. This is just as true for past events as the myths demonstrate. For example, Wiskadjak, the "culture hero" was responsible for certain events in the past that led, among other things, to the distinguishing characteristics of certain animals as known today.

A further assumption is this: While power may be used for good or evil ends, most of the pawáganak, but not all, are beneficent.

Human beings, too, for the most part use their power for beneficent ends. This is exemplified by all those who specialize in curative functions. They have received their power to cure from the *pawáganak* and, in turn, they help their fellow men. At the same time superhumanly acquired power may be used for malevolent ends.

Since "magic" power, as we have seen, is the ultimate source of successful adaptation in every sphere of life—from hunting to defense against sorcery—and the ultimate source of this power rests in the hands of the *pawáganak*, the fundamental relationship of the Ojibwa self to the *pawáganak* is clearly defined. It is one of dependence and is the root of their deep motivational orientation toward these powerful beings. But there is a normative aspect of this relationship as well. I must fulfill certain obligations that my guardian spirits impose upon me. I may have to make certain sacrifices, perhaps material ones (*pagitcígan*). In the dream visit of W.B. to the *memengwéciwak* these were mentioned. There is a story told about a man who, after he was married, went off hunting all winter. He never spoke to his wife or had sexual intercourse with her. She left him in the spring. It turned out that he had been observing taboos imposed upon him in his puberty fast as a condition of a long and healthy life. "If she could only have held out three more moons," he said, "it would have been all right." He married again but did not follow the taboos. One of his children died, then his wife. A third wife died, too. This was all the result of his failure to live up to his side of the bargain with his *pawáganak*. Since all the relations between an individual and his *pawáganak* are based on dreams, their psychological reality is fundamental. It is what makes the puberty fast so important. The conceptual reality of all these beings the Ojibwa boy has been acquainted with from babyhood by listening to the myths recited on long winter nights becomes in the course of the fast a *personal* experience. If the puberty fast of the Ojibwa is crucial to them for living in their world, this same experience, viewed psychologically, is equally crucial for making their world a reality for the self.

PART III

The Cultural Patterning of Personal Experience and Behavior: The Ojibwa Indians

Chapter 9 - Cultural Factors
in Spatial Orientation

SPATIALLY, LIKE TEMPORALLY, COORDINATED PATTERNS OF BEHAVIOR are basic to the personal adjustment of all human beings. They involve fundamental dimensions of experience and are a necessary condition of psychological maturity and social living. Without the capacity for space perception, spatial orientation and the manipulation of spatial concepts, the human being would be incapable of effective locomotion, to say nothing of being unable to coordinate other aspects of his behavior with that of his fellows in a common social life.[1] In addition to the psychophysical and psychophysiological conditions of human space perception, we know that variations occur, between one culture and another, with respect to the selective emphasis given to the spatial relations and attributes of things, the degree of refinement that occurs in the concepts employed, and the reference points that are selected for spatial orientation. The human individual is always provided with some culturally constituted means that are among the conditions which enable him to participate with his fellows in a world whose spatial attributes are, in part, conceptualized and expressed in common terms. Ontogenetically, self-orientation, object-orientation, and spatio-temporal orientation are concomitantly developed during the process of socialization.

Long ago Poincaré pointed out that the notion of space must be understood as a function of objects and all their relations. There is no such thing as space independent of objects. Relations among objects and the movements of objects are a necessary condition of space perception. More recently, James J. Gibson, approaching the problem from the standpoint of psychophysics, has developed the hypothesis "that space is constituted of the same variables as things . . . that surfaces and margins are what we see, not air. Space must be filled to be visible; empty space is an abstraction."[2] This author distinguishes problems concerned with (a) "the perception of the substantial or spatial world," "the world of colors, textures, surfaces, edges, slopes, shapes, and interspaces," what he calls *literal* perception, from (b) "the perception of the world of useful and significant things to which we ordinarily attend." He calls the latter *schematic* perception.[3]

While it remains an open question how far the purely psychophysical dimensions of perception may be influenced by culturally constituted experiential factors, schematic perception, involving the meaningful aspects of experience, can hardly be understood without reference to an articulated world of objects whose relations and attributes become meaningful for the individual, not simply through the innate psychological potentialities he brings to experience but, above all, through the significance for experience that the development, patterning, transmission, and accumulation of past experience, in the form of a cultural heritage, have come to imply. The question: Is space perception native or acquired? though once hotly debated, is in actuality a pseudo-problem.[4] What Gibson argues against is an extreme form of perceptual relativism: "that perception is inevitably a constructive process which creates the world to suit the perceiver; that we see things not as they are but as we are." While "it is perfectly true," he says, "that perception can be fluid, subjective, creative, and inexact . . . it can also be literal . . . the student of human nature and society needs to remember this when he is in danger of assuming that men are the passive victims of their stereotypes and perceptual customs."[5]

Psychologists repeatedly have emphasized that unlike other aspects of experience (e.g., color and sound), which are mediated through highly specialized sense organs, perception of space requires the participation of several sense modalities including, for instance, tactual-kinesthetic components. There is no "spatial sense," equivalent to vision and hearing, by means of which we perceive such attributes of space as extension, shape, size, direction, locality, and distance. Such experience is "intersensory" by its very nature; yet is as primary as experience mediated by specialized sensory modalities.[6] Furthermore, the role that differential linguistic and cultural factors play in the processes through which the spatial attributes of things become abstracted, conceptualized, expressed in traditional forms of speech, and made the basis of action cannot be overlooked in this case any more than it can be in the functioning of perception mediated through specialized sense modalities.

There is an additional factor, however, that has been neglected in discussions of space perception and spatial orientation. This is the peculiarly human capacity of achieving a level of psychological organization that makes possible the perception of the self as an object in a world of objects other than self. In addition to reference points anchored in the objective world, the human being constantly makes use of himself as a reference point. "Perceiving the world has an obverse aspect, perceiving oneself."[7] While we may, perhaps, assume this, it should not be forgotten that self-awareness as a universal psychological attribute of man is no more given at birth than the traditional schema of refer-

185

ences points to be found in a culture or the vocabulary of spatial reference. Self-identification and the perception of self as an object in relation to other objects is the result of a long socialization process, just as the skills underlying the achievement of a "sense of direction" only emerge from a complicated learning process. (See Chap. 4.)

Furthermore, in order to be spatially oriented in the widest sense, that is, beyond the field of immediate perception, the individual must not only be aware of himself but of his own position in some *spatial schema*. At the same time he must be capable of maintaining awareness of his own changes in position, and be able to assume the position of others in the schema with reference to himself. What spatial orientation in man actually involves is a constant awareness of varying relations between the self and other objects in a spatial schema of traditionally defined reference points. If I have a destination, beyond my limited field of vision, for example, I not only have to know where I am going but I have to know where I am now in relation to my goal and, as I move toward it, I have to be aware of the changing relations involved. In order to reach my goal and return to my starting point, I have to make use of formal or informal reference points. I may be guided, in part, by a "mental" map. But, in any case, I have to maintain some kind of topographical or astronomical,[8] if not directional, orientation, in which my own changing position must be appraised. Gibson points out that this type of locomotion—that is, "the act of going to an object or place beyond the range of vision—represents a much higher and more complicated level of mobility than that confined to a spatial field where optical stimulation yields all the necessary cues because the goal-object lies within it.[9] What we take for granted, without a close analysis of all the necessary conditions involved, is that the human individual will necessarily advance from the simpler to the more complicated level of finding his way about during the course of ontogenetic development. Yet this is certainly one of the vital points where the cultural factors that are an integral part of the spatialization of the world of man play an outstanding role. The human being not only advances from a rudimentary to a more complex level of spatial orientation and mobility; the possibility is opened to him through various kinds of symbolic means to become oriented in a spatial world that transcends his personal experience. Place naming, star naming, maps, myth and tale, the orientation of buildings, the spatial implications in dances and ceremonies, all facilitate the construction and maintenance of the spatial patterns of the world in which the individual must live and act.

While striking cultural variations occur, possible universals should be looked for. Is there any culture, for instance, in which there are *no* names for places and topographical features in the environment of the people? From the standpoint of human mobility and spatial orientation this practice would appear to have a generic human function. When integrated with individual knowledge and experience of the terrain it affords a schema of reference points for topographical orientation. Such points are not only a guide to action but, once known, can be mentally manipulated and organized in the form of "mental maps," and the spatial schema inherent in them communicated.[10] Maps among nonliterate peoples are, of course, the projection in the form of graphic symbols of space relations abstracted from knowledge already available in these "mental maps" rather than the outcome of such sophisticated techniques as surveying, serial photography, etc.[11] It is amazing how accurate such maps can be.[12] While maps are of limited occurrence among nonliterate peoples, names of topographical features and places appear to be universal.

Perhaps the most striking feature of man's spatialization of his world is the fact that it never appears to be exclusively limited to the pragmatic level of action and perceptual experience.[13] Places and objects of various classes are conceptualized as having a real existence in distant regions. Even though the individual never experiences any direct perceptual knowledge of them—since information must be mediated through some symbolic means (the spoken or written word, graphic representation) such regions are, nevertheless, an integral part of the total spatial world to which he is oriented by his culture. For man everywhere has cosmic concepts; he is oriented in a universe that has spatial dimensions. The individual not only has heard about other groups of human beings he may not have seen; they are given a *locale*. He knows *where* the land of the dead is and something about it even though he has not yet visited it. Gods and spirits are given an abode and mobility in space; they not only exist but they exist *somewhere;* they may be "here" now and later "there." Likewise in Western culture world explorations and science have accustomed us to accept as reliable all sorts of information about the location of distant peoples, about natural phenomena of various kinds, the location and contours of the land masses of the earth, and so on, all beyond our direct perceptual experience. Astronomers, too, tell us about the spatial relations of bodies in the far-flung stellar universe. We assume, of course, that our knowledge of distant regions is more dependable than that of the primitive peoples we study, and this is undoubtedly true. At the same time it should not be forgotten that it is acquired by most individuals through symbolic mediation and that the qualitative differences of this knowledge are extremely recent in our own culture. We need only to compare the spatial orientation and knowledge of medieval man in Europe with our modern outlook to appreciate this. In *The Other World,* Howard R. Patch devotes a chapter to "Journeys to Paradise," many descriptive accounts of which are to be found in medieval literature. This author points out that "The Garden of Eden was universally believed to exist, and, although cut off from ordinary approach, was supposed still to be waiting for the saints before their ascent to Heaven. Medieval maps often showed its location."[14] In other words, it was a *place* located on the earth that might be visited by travelers, "even if they had to have recourse to supernatural means."[15] Even subsequent to medieval times there are references to such journeys and the author notes that, "when Christopher Columbus discovered the New World, he thought he was close to the Garden of Eden. . . ."[16] Today the Garden of Eden has disappeared from our universe; it has no spatial existence. Similarly, Dante could present to his readers an intelligible image of hell "pictured as a huge funnel-shaped pit, situated beneath the Northern Hemisphere and running down to the centre of the earth."[17] If we now ask, *where* is hell, what answer can we give if the cosmographic picture of our universe, defined on the basis of scientific knowledge, is accepted? As *places* heaven and hell in this universe are "nowhere."

What appears to be particularly significant in our human adjustment to the world is that over and above pragmatic needs for orientation and without any pretense to reliable knowledge of regions of space outside their personal experience, human beings in all cultures have built up a frame of spatial reference that has included the farther as well as the more proximal, the spiritual as well as the mundane, regions of their universe. What the recent history of Western culture demonstrates is the revolutionary challenge offered to the spatial orientation embedded in an older tradition when more reliable knowledge of distant regions, combined with the development of abstract mathematical concepts of space, established the foundations of the qualitatively different type of spatial orientation that is now possible for us.

The unique combination of factors that account for the distinctive mode of human spatial orientation has not always been clearly recognized. For a long period, dating back to the late eighteenth century when the idea of the Noble Savage had such a vogue, the problem was obscured because of the widespread notion that savages, as compared with civilized man, had an innate sense of direction. This notion was based to some extent on the exaggeration, if not misrepresentation, of the observations of early travelers and missionaries. Pierre Jaccard, in a book which should be better known,[18] calls attention to the excellent observations of Père Lafitau (1724) on the Iroquois. Their later distortion by Charlevoix, he thinks, gave rise to "la legende de l'instinct d'orientation des sauvages." In the nineteenth century, after the concept of biological evolution took hold, one of the prevailing ideas was that the "senses" of primitive man were more acute than those of civilized man, even though he might be intellectually inferior. Indeed, "savages" and the lower animals were thought by some to be alike in many respects. Haeckel (1868) in his *Natural History of Creation* observed that if one compared African Negroes, Bushmen, and the Andamanese with apes, dogs, and elephants, on the one hand, and with civilized man, on the other, one would be compelled to make a distinction, not between man and animal, but between civilized peoples on the one side, and savages and animals on the other. The question then of an innate, or special, sense of direction in primitive peoples became entangled with the more general question whether "primitive" mind and "civilized" mind represented psychological categories that had an evolutionary significance. Jaccard concludes:

Si tous les sauvages possédaient des facultés de direction, inconnues de nous, on pourrait peut-être accepter provisoirement l'hypothèse d'une différence de nature entre leur psychologie et la nôtre. Mais cette supposition n'est plus même permise aujourd'hui : il est en effet démontré que la plupart des non-civilisés sont tout aussi embarrassés que nous lorsqu'ils se trouvent dans une région dépourvue de repères, loin des horizons familiers de leur pays natal . . . loin de montrer la bestialité des sauvages, les faits d'orientation lointaine témoignent de l'excellence des pouvoirs d'attention, de mémoire et d'observation des plus intelligents d'entre eux. . . c'est de reconnaitre que les sauvages et les civilisés possèdent à des degrés divers une même aptitude, plus ou moins développée chez les différents individus, selon les circonstances. . . l'hypothèse d'un sens particulier de la direction, affiné chez le sauvage et émoussé chez le civilisé, par suite des conditions d'existence, n'est pas plus soutenable que les interprétations basées sur une opposition entre l'intelligence et l'instinct. Aucune différence appréciable n'apparait entre les capacités sensorielles et les fonctions mentales élémentaires des diverses races humaines: ce fait seul suffit à démontrer l'erreur de toutes les théories attribuant aux sauvages des facultés d'orientation inconnues des civilisés.[19]

We now know, of course, that even in studying animal behavior, the concept of "instinct" is too categorical and affords us no help at all in explaining how animals find their way about. Despite the fact that we are still in the dark on many frontiers of this area of investigation, great progress has been made in our detailed knowledge of some of these determinants in vertebrates and insects.[20] Astonishing as the performance of some of these creatures is with respect to their mobility, we can be certain that the crucial determinants are of a different order than those in human spatial orientation. Consequently, although at a very rudimentary perceptual level, there certainly is some overlapping in the spatial world of ourselves and other animals, the phenomenological differences must be very great indeed no matter what local cultural variables are among the human factors involved.[21]

THE SPATIAL ORIENTATION OF THE SAULTEAUX

Directional Orientation.—From an abstract point of view it might appear that the basic directional orientation of the Saulteaux is equivalent to that of occidental culture, since they recognize four cardinal directions as fundamental reference points which can be roughly equated with north, south, east, and west. Actually, the equivalence is not only historically fortuitous, it differs from our own directional orientation qualitatively and functionally in important respects.

The occidental directional schema is based on scientific knowledge that the Saulteaux do not possess. In our schema "true" north is taken as an absolute reference point; it is determined precisely by mechanical means, and instrumental correction for possible error is made under certain circumstances. Furthermore, the possession of a magnetic compass and the knowledge of how to use it enables us to check our directional orientation exactly at any time.

The Saulteaux, on the other hand, rely exclusively upon the direct observation of natural phenomena in order to maintain their directional orientation. Their most inclusive reference points are the North Star, the movements of the sun, and the "homes" of the four winds. Sometimes to these are added "straight up" (zenith), and "down" (nadir). The standardized and linguistically formulated cardinal directions of their culture, however, refer only to the four winds. It is through the traditional emphasis upon these that the wider aspects of their spatial universe are defined.

In their mythology the winds are anthropomorphic beings each associated with a complementary direction. The winds are brothers who at birth enunciate their personal relations to humanity. The first-born was East Wind, who said, "I shall be fairly kind to human beings." The next was South Wind, who said, "I'll be very good and treat human beings well, as long as any exist on this earth." The third child born spoke and said, "Human beings shall call me West Wind. I'll be a little rough on them but I'll never be wicked." "Be easy on our mother," he went on as another boy popped out. This one said, "Human beings shall call me North Wind. I'll have no mercy on any human being. I'll treat him just the same as the animals." At this remark his brothers asked, "How do you expect human beings to exist if you are going to treat them like that?" (But no answer is given in the myth.) Shortly after this the brothers decided that they could not remain together any longer. The East Wind said, "I'll go to live in the east." The West Wind said, "I'll sit opposite you at the other end of the earth." The South Wind said, "I'll go to the southern end of the earth," and the North Wind said, "I'll go to the northern end."

In another myth North Wind invites his brother South Wind to a trial of strength, but is unable to worst him. Then the South Wind invites his brother North Wind to come south for a return contest. All the South Wind did was to blow on him. After the first couple of days North Wind could hardly hold his head up. One of his eyes drooped and then the other. Finally, on the sixth day he had to give up; he was beaten. The South Wind said, "Now you know you're not the boss of everything." "And we know he is not the boss," added the narrator, "for, if he were, we would never have any summer."

For the Saulteaux, direction is only partially abstracted from *place*. That is, their conception has more the meaning "in the direction of such and such a place," "toward *x*." What we refer to abstractly as the cardinal directions are to them the *homes* of the winds, the places they come from. Similarly, east is thought of as the place where the sun rises; west, the place where it sets; south is the place to which the souls of the dead travel, and the place from which the summer birds come. In a myth summer is stolen from a place in the south. Indeed, the Saulteaux equivalents for north, south, east, and west are *place names* in a very real sense, rather than abstract terms for direction. They are far, distant, it is true, but in myths at least, people have been there. They define the periphery of the Saulteaux world, being the "farthest" places, although not different except in generality of direction, from places in the immediate environment. Such a connotation exists in Western civilization side by side with the highly abstract one expressed in terms of angles and their measurement used in science. We say, "He lives in the West," or "The South grows cotton." The terms "Occident" and "Orient" are also used as nouns denoting places or regions. The latter arose at a period when, like the Saulteaux, the people employing them thought that the earth was flat.

I do not mean to imply that the Saulteaux terms are never used abstractly. But the degree to which this occurs is a function of the social situation. Abstraction is at its highest level when directional terms are employed in finding one's way about or in constructing a ceremonial pavilion. This may happen similarly with direction toward any place: a place, *x*, may be defined as "on the way to" *y*.

Thus it is inevitable that the directional orientation of these Indians is more flexible and less exact than our own, and that they must rely upon cues from several different classes of natural phenomena. Such limitations are intrinsic to the traditional means with which their culture provides them for ascertaining directional orientation. There are many instances of these limitations. I have heard Indians refer to the Milky Way, which is considered the path the Summer Birds follow flying north, as running north and south. This is not the case, but the approximate direction satisfies them. Another example is to be found on a map of Eagle Lake drawn by Adam Keeper, an Indian at Grand Rapids. On it he marked the four directions, but he was not aware of the discrepancy between his directional orientation and the measured directions of our schema. This is demonstrated by the fact that while he included a neatly ruled line representing the boundary between the provinces of Manitoba and Ontario, he made no use of it as one of his directional coordinates. Every Indian knows this line because it is actually cut out through the woods for miles and miles, and it runs exactly north and south. The fact that Adam ignored this cue shows the extent to which he has clung to his culturally constituted orientation in drawing the map, and the extent to which the local spatial interrelations of landmarks and contours predominated for him.

We can be certain, then, that the north of the Saulteaux is not our exact north and that the other directions they recognize are likewise approximate, more inclusive, than ours. For example, east means "in the general direction of east" and is closer to our everyday usage when exact reckoning is unnecessary. If an Indian is asked where the east is he will point to where the sun rises. From his point of view it is unnecessary to take into account the variations in the sun's positions at different seasons of the year and to arrive at a measured point on the horizon designated "due" east. What the range of their margin of error may be I do not know; but it is obvious that for the Saulteaux directions, unlike our own, are not fixed coordinates.

Qualitatively and functionally, therefore, the existence of a four-directional schema in Western culture, on the one hand, and in Saulteaux culture, on the other, presents only a superficial resemblance. The behavioral implications in the two societies are quite different. Western man has been freed from the direct observation of nature in so far as he depends upon mechanical instruments for the determination of direction, or does not need to maintain his orientation with respect to compass points at all so far as the pursuit of daily life is concerned. The latter is particularly true of urban populations where such directional orientation may be almost completely ignored.[22]

The Saulteaux, however, constantly maintain a directional orientation. Traveling in the open as they do at all seasons of the year, across lakes and through a network of waterways in the summer and over snowclad wastes in winter, the direction of the wind in particular is always noticed and their practical activities adjusted accordingly.

Knowledge of Terrain.—This culturally defined framework of directional orientation, with its customary reference points in certain natural phenomena, exposes the basic and most inclusive schema through which the Saulteaux orient themselves in a world of space. Closely integrated with it, and overshadowing it in importance, is the direct knowledge through experience of the topography of the country and the relations in space of one locality to another.

This direct experiential knowledge, however, varies greatly among individuals. Most of the Berens River Indians have never traveled any considerable distance from the locality in which they were born. There is also a marked sexual dichotomy in direct knowledge of the country. Women travel far less than men. There are certainly few, if any, women of the Pekangikum Band who have been to the mouth of the river and most of them have not been as far as Grand Rapids, halfway there. In contrast to this, most of the men of the Pekangikum Band have been both to the mouth of the river and Grand Rapids.[23] At any rate, it would be erroneous to assume that a first-hand, detailed knowledge of all parts of the river and its environs is possessed by any single individual. The terrain which is most familiar to these Indians is their winter hunting ground and the region surrounding the fishing settlement in which they live during the summer months. They are, in short, bound in their direct knowledge and experience to the areas with which their major economic activities are connected, a narrowly circumscribed spatial world which, even under modern conditions, has expanded very little. But within these limits the individual often possesses a phenomenally rich knowledge of the details of the terrain that contrasts sharply with his ignorance of parts of the country about which he has no direct knowledge[24] and of the still wider spatial world regarding which he sometimes entertains fantastic ideas.

In functional terms, it is not only the direct experience of the terrain which assists the individual in building up his spatial world; language crystallizes this knowledge through the customary use of place names. These in turn act as geographical reference points by means of which localities of various classes may be organized in spatial terms. This is not to imply that in Saulteaux culture the range of their application is coextensive with the total number of lakes, islands, points, rivers, and streams that might be named. Place names function integrally with the geographical knowledge and experience of the individual. Consequently, the local place names referring to topographical features within the radius of a particular summer settlement[25] are not known to the Indians of other settlements and the same applies to those attached to the geographical features of the winter hunting grounds. On the other hand, the place names of the major lakes, rivers, etc., and a general knowledge of their directions from their home and vague distances such as "long journey," of the environs of the Berens River as a whole are known to every Indian, regardless of whether he has ever traveled them or not. Correlated with the directions, these reference points define the wider limits of the geographical environment in which these Indians think and act, just as the place names for more circumscribed localities serve to organize the space relations of their local environment.

Beyond the Berens River itself, and peripheral to it, only a few geographical localities are at all familiar to the average Indian. On the west side of Lake Winnipeg the names of the larger lakes are known and a few Indian reserves and trading posts. To the north, trading posts such as Norway House, Oxford, God's Lake, stand out, and such geographical points as Deer Lake and Island Lake. Of course, every Berens River Indian has heard of Hudson Bay and the rivers that flow into it. To the southeast Lake Seul is well known because long ago a number of Berens River families came from there. To the south there are a number of rivers that are familiar, particularly the Red River which flows north to Lake Winnipeg. Cities like Selkirk and Winnipeg are known, and Ottawa because the government is there. But no Indian has been to all these places, and I am sure that their location with respect to one another and to the Berens River district is not understood.

193

If any of these places is thought of spatially I am certain that it is only as the context of the reference requires it. Any idea of its relation to other places in a spatial schema that is conceived as a geographical continuation of the Berens River region itself is totally foreign to the minds of these people. This seems to indicate that without some graphic means as an aid, place names are only effective in organizing one's spatial knowledge within the limits of one's direct experience or through a limited extension to regions immediately peripheral to such experience. Outside of this they tend to become disparate and unorganized, verbally known places.

Native Maps.—Within a familiar terrain, however, such as the part of the country which he has known since childhood, or his hunting ground, an individual clearly grasps the precise location and has some idea of the relative distances of every significant detail of the topography in relation to every other. When integrated with some inclusive directional orientation such knowledge needs only graphic projection, and we have a rudimentary *map*. It is significant, nevertheless, that this organization of the spatial perceptions of the individual into a coordinated whole, a "mental map,"[26] applies only within the narrow limits indicated. It is deeply imbedded in the "active" experience of the individual.

That such a well-integrated organization of the spatial relations of certain parts of their geographical environment exists in some terms in the minds of some individuals may be inferred in several ways. I had in my possession maps of the National Topographical Series which are based on airplane photographs and on which the smallest lakes, rivers, and creeks are represented. In the first place, a number of Indians who had never seen a detailed map of the part of the country with which they were most familiar almost immediately grasped the geographical relations on these once a few landmarks had been identified. But it was necessary to orient the map in relation to the observer. The Indians could not adapt themselves to looking at it in the conventional manner familiar to us with north at the top. They always had to have north on the map matched with north as it actually was from their point of view at the moment. Once they were fully oriented, it appeared as if they rediscovered on the map what was already organized in their minds. Some of them felt so much at home that often when I was trying to get them to delineate their trap lines or the boundaries of their hunting territories on the map, they would delay the process by side conversations with other Indians present, pointing to the outlet of some little creek where a moose had been killed or where some other event of interest to them had taken place.

Still more convincing evidence of the organization of the details of geographical relations in the mind of the individual was demonstrated by the objectification of such information in the form of maps which

194

certain individuals drew for me. I secured five of these from three different men. That there is considerable individual variation in the ability to project such knowledge in graphic form is suggested by the admiration of other Indians for these maps. They said that it would have been impossible for them to perform such a task. The making of maps, however, was known in aboriginal days.

These aboriginal maps were intended to guide the individual using them through territory unknown to him. Their purpose was not to delineate a section of the country as such, but to indicate a route to be followed, and the emphasis was upon a succession of landmarks roughly indicated in their relations to one another and with only such other details of the topography as were necessary for the identification of the landmarks of primary interest. This is a very rudimentary form of map which does not require the refined abstract coordination of place, direction, distance, area, and contour that we expect. Areas and distances might be only relatively proportional, for instance, and yet such a crude delineation would serve its purpose.[27] The graphic emphasis upon a succession of landmarks is worth noting because it bears a close correspondence to the actual method of traveling about, just as the very limited geographical region for which detailed special knowledge is organized in the minds of individuals [28] As might be expected, the narrow geographical limits of such organized positive knowledge bears an inverse relation to the ignorance of the terrain outside of the experience of the individual.[29] In this connection it is well to remind ourselves that without maps it would likewise be impossible for us to obtain any exact comprehension of geographical relations outside our experience.[30]

A startling illustration of this intrinsic limitation upon realistic spatial concepts of an unknown region is illustrated by the following episode. All the Indians were interested in a series of photographs I had taken of them, and some of them also were intrigued by the large-scale maps of their country, to which I have already referred. So, when one old man asked me to send him a *photograph* of the United States, I thought my interpreter had misunderstood him and that what he referred to was a map. But no! What he wanted was a photograph of the United States. Evidently the United States was to him a place regarding which he had only the vaguest idea and no notion whatsoever of its spatial extensity.

Travel.—There still remains the practical question: How *do* the Saulteaux find their way about and what cues do they employ? The answer is a simple one: by means of the directional cues already described, combined with the constant use of all the relevant knowledge of the topography of the country they possess.

In addition to standardized reference points, i.e., named places and named directions, this includes a mass of impressions undiscriminated in speech but immensely important nevertheless. The characteristic man-

195

ner of their procedure at all seasons, and whether traveling on land or water, can be reduced to a common principle. They always move from one point to another, rather than in a given direction toward a goal.[31] Directional orientation usually functions as the wider frame of reference to facilitate the step by step procedure.

In principle, this step by step procedure emerges in certain mythological narratives where it takes the following form: The protagonist is directed from point to point in a strange country by a series of old women. The first old woman he encounters not only directs him on his way, she tells him what to look out for, how to avoid obstacles to his progress, and so on. And finally, she tells him that he will come upon another old woman on whom he can depend for directional advice for the next stage of his journey. Of course, events occur as anticipated; the second old woman is reached who directs him to a third. The analogy to actual travel should be clear. Familiar landmarks in a journey correspond to the old women; they mark the nodal points in a geographical progression in space and while they fail to give advice in a literal sense, they are anticipatory signs of the particular features of the country in the ensuing segment of the journey that must be mentally prepared for before they are encountered.

A commonplace illustration of ordinary procedure is illustrated by the ascent of the Berens River from its mouth to Grand Rapids, a hundred miles inland from Lake Winnipeg. The river is not in its entire length the natural road we usually think a river to be, for in places it opens into lakes. On this portion of it there are approximately fifty rapids, all named, which function as the nodal points in the journey. It is these geographical items which are checked off, as it were, in traveling up and down the stream, and one's position on the river at any time, particularly when eating and sleeping, is always talked about with reference to this schema of rapids. They also function as anticipatory signs of the features of the country to be encountered between them. No wonder then that the local Indians thought it curious and even hazardous when some white men a few years ago ascended the river without a guide. They were probably equipped with the excellent maps that are available. To the Indians they would have no anticipatory signs to guide them; they would not know what to expect.

A journey I once made across Lake Winnipeg in a skiff with an improvised sail illustrates the step by step principle in terms of another mode of travel. It also happened that the early part of the trip was made in a heavy fog which obscured the ordinary visual cues. My guides were, of course, very familiar with the directions of landmarks. Leaving the reserve early in the morning we rowed along the shore to Flathead Point where we disembarked to eat breakfast. Pigeon Point was not visible, but we headed in that direction rowing all the way. The wind was from the northwest. We set sail for Commissioner's Island which we reached

196

about two and a half hours later. The fog having lifted somewhat in the meantime, we were able to sight the island some distance away and adjust our course accordingly.[32] From there we made for Sandhill Island which we reached in an hour and a half. We spent the night there. The next morning it was easy to reach Stony Point and then to follow the shore south to Jack Head.

An analogous principle of travel in winter is set up under quite different circumstances when an Indian lays his trap line and makes his rounds periodically. The relation of the traps to each other, to certain topographical features of the country, and to his camp define a spatial order in which he regularly moves from point to point.

In winter, however, during long journeys on snowshoes or with a dogsled, when darkness obscures familiar landmarks and a storm makes even the stars invisible, then directional orientation inferred from the wind must be depended upon as the main cue. Under these conditions one has no choice but to proceed in a given direction; it is impossible to follow the visible cues provided by a series of landmarks, and it is possible to lose one's way badly. If directional orientation by means of the wind fails, there is nothing to do but make camp and wait until weather conditions change and the usual cues can be picked up again.

Topographical cues are, in fact, so important that if masked by snow an individual may lose his way even on familiar ground. An Indian once told me of such an experience which he considered very humorous because the trail was one frequently traveled by everyone—I had often used it myself in summer. But my friend missed his way one winter night when the drifted snow had radically distorted cues familiar even at that season of the year. On the other hand, there are well-known general patterns in the topography of their country which are used by the Indians as cues. The rocky ridges as well as the muskegs east of Lake Winnipeg, for instance, run east to west like the rivers so that whether it is cloudy or misty, night or day, a general orientation is possible. This pattern also can be used as a cue in winter when snow is on the ground. A Berens River Indian once went to fight a forest fire on the west side of the lake. He got lost because he was not familiar with local topographical landmarks and the muskegs had a different directional pattern. Not being aware of this latter fact, he relied on the muskegs and became disoriented. To an outsider general topographical patterns would not be obvious so that without any explanation of the actual clues being used it might appear somewhat mysterious how the Indians familiar with the country did find their way about in stormy or snowy weather and without a compass.

In connection with this dependence upon topographical cues it is interesting to recall the predicament of Wisakedjak, the culture hero of the Saulteaux, told in a myth. Wisakedjak had been temporarily deprived of his sight by getting his head encased in a bear skull and the

197

method he employed to find his way about was to ask each tree he bumped into what its name was. Wisakedjak wished to reach a lake since he thought he might find some people there, and he accomplished this by differentiating between trees that grew near the water and those that did not, adjusting his course accordingly.

If, as sometimes is the case in winter, there is a well-marked trail in the snow to be followed, then travel is greatly simplified. Under such conditions the Indian participates in one of the amenities of Western culture, the road, which we take for granted and which so enormously facilitates our movements from place to place. Neither directional orientation nor the use of such cues as the Saulteaux are compelled to employ are necessary in following a modern road. The contrast between this method of getting about and the other procedures described brings into sharp relief a basic difference in the pragmatic aspects of spatial orientation as demanded by Saulteaux culture on the one hand and Western culture, on the other.

Fear of Disorientation.—The sharp contrast between the extremely intimate knowledge of a familiar terrain and the very hazy ideas which are entertained about other regions is sufficient, I believe, to account for a certain timidity on the part of these Indians in venturing into unknown territory unless accompanied by someone who is already acquainted with the region. While directional orientation can be maintained in unknown regions, the lack of all the well-known landmarks inevitably must lead to a certain amount of spatial disorientation. And there is always the possibility that one may really become lost. Hence, there is rational ground for apprehension.

A feeling of satisfactory spatial orientation, then, probably is one of the basic ties that bind the individual to familiar territory. The Indian would not analyze or express his feelings in such terms, but I think that it is a legitimate inference we are enabled to make from the very nature and character of his spatial orientation. It is likewise consistent with the basic role played by spatial orientation in all human behavior. For we, too, feel some sense of spatial disorientation in a strange city or country even when such orientation is less vital to our activities than to those of the Saulteaux and under cultural conditions which offer an opportunity for a more immediate and adequate reorientation. Furthermore, the feeling of the Saulteaux themselves about the loss of an adequate spatial orientation was illustrated in their concern when on one occasion I had difficulty in finding my way back to our camp, and their admonitions on others to be careful and not to lose my way when I went about by myself. Since I never was lost and their concern at times seemed a bit silly to me, I think that their attitude in these situations is quite revealing.[33]

The same apprehension on their part can be demonstrated in another way by the story of the Indian who found his way back home from a strange part of the country. Early in the nineteenth century, when the Hudson's Bay Company reigned supreme in western Canada, some Indians raided a post at Sandy Narrows in order to obtain knives, powder, etc. The leader of the party was a man called Brimmed Hat. After he was apprehended it was planned to send him to England where he could observe for himself the power and magnitude of the white man's civilization. On the way to York Factory where he was to be put on a ship, Brimmed Hat escaped. This was near White Mud Falls on the Hayes River. Later he showed up again at Sandy Narrows, a distance of approximately three hundred miles as the crow flies. To the Indians such a journey was miraculous, and they believe he must have had the aid of supernatural helpers. First of all, he could not proceed in the usual way from one known point to another in a strange country. From our standpoint a correct directional orientation might have been a sufficient guide to him, combined, perhaps, with some general knowledge of the watersheds since Hayes River drains into Hudson Bay and the Berens River is on a shed from which the rivers empty into Lake Winnipeg. Besides this, he had no gun, not even a knife, and no way to secure skins to make new moccasins.

Cosmic Space.—The apprehension with which the Saulteaux individual views excursions into strange regions, combined with his lack of experience in any but a circumscribed environment, and the limitations imposed by his culture upon the acquisition of accurate knowledge of distant regions, offers him no critical basis for an evaluation of what is beyond his experience. It is no wonder, then, that the traditional dogmas of his native culture in regard to the wider reaches of the universe are so thoroughly reified and uncritically accepted as part of his spatial world.

There is the Land of the Dead, for instance, far to the south. There is a road which leads directly to it which deceased souls follow, and a few individuals are known to have visited the Land of the Dead and afterwards returned to their homes. They have given accounts of their journey and of what they saw there. (See Chap. 7.) I remember that my interpreter once told an old Indian that I came from the south and that the United States lay in that direction. The old man simply laughed in a wise way and made no comment.

The earth itself, according to Saulteaux belief, is flat, a notion that is, of course, supported rather than contradicted by the naïve observation and experience of all human beings. No Indian can be convinced that the earth is spherical. According to Saulteaux dogma the earth is also an island, and there is an account in mythology (the earth-diver motif) of how this island came into existence. Contacts with the whites and, in certain cases, acquaintance with maps in the geography texts of their children have strengthened rather than undermined this dogma. For many Indians have been told, and others have seen it indicated on the maps of the world, that the western hemisphere is surrounded by water.

A stratification of worlds within the cosmos is another item of Saulteaux dogma that defines certain space relations in their conceptual universe. Since the earth is flat, it is easy to understand how this additional feature fits the general scheme. While this idea of the stratification of worlds is developed in considerable detail in other parts of America and even among related Algonkian peoples,[34] the Saulteaux emphasize only the lower world immediately below this one, although they assert that there are other worlds farther down as well as one or two above "the central plane" on which they live.

The world that lies just below is called *pitawákamik*. It is also peopled by *ănicinábek, Indians*. These lower world people only differ from those living on this earth by being immortal. When they grow old, they then become young again. This underworld was once visited by some Berens River Indians. They went out hunting and saw some strangers whom they followed to the lower world. At first the people living there wanted to kill them. But when the lower world people found that the Berens River Indians were so much like themselves, their lives were spared. The same species of animals and plants are found in *pitawákamik* as up here, but when it is night there it is day here and vice versa.

I have never heard of a corresponding upper world inhabited by human beings. However, the idea of strata in the universe is exemplified in the account in one of the myths in which the youngest brother of *matcikiwis* climbs up a tree to Thunder Bird Land. Here the Thunder Birds appear in human guise. When the daughters of the "boss" of these creatures come to earth they appear as women and marry human beings.

Within this cosmic scheme certain spiritual entities are given a specific location. To some extent such cosmic positions are correlated with observable natural phenomena. Since thunder is heard only in the summer and usually towards the south, the Thunder Birds are associated with the south as the spiritual controllers of the summer birds and are believed to inhabit one of the upper strata of the universe. On the other hand, the controllers of the fur-bearing animals are given a northern position in the cosmic space. In other cases the cosmic position of certain entities seems arbitrary, and some have no determinate location.

From the standpoint of the Saulteaux themselves, these concepts of cosmic space and the position of the various spiritual entities and other inhabitants within it, all are articulated as parts of an integral whole. It is in terms of the full sweep of this schema that we must endeavor to comprehend the qualitative characteristics of the farther reaches of their spatial world, as well as the relevant features of the proximate geographical environment in which they live.

Directional Orientation in Ceremonialism.—Directional orientation, however, is not altogether confined to situations in which individuals are moving from place to place. The lodge erected for the Midewiwin, rectangular in ground plan, was always built on an east-west axis, as are the Wabano pavilions seen today. The entrance to both types of structure is at the east although two or more doors are made. The "place of honor" where the leader or leaders sit in both cases is on the south side near the east entrance. Another ceremony I witnessed, which had no superstructure, took place within a square bounded by stakes. The sides of the square were deliberately oriented in the four directions. In this case the entrance used was on the north side and at the close of the ceremony everyone left by the south "door." Graves are likewise oriented north and south as a rule; the deceased faces the south which is the Land of the Dead. Elsie Clews Parsons reported that the Pueblo Indians usually avoid sleeping with the head in the orientation given the dead in burial. It never occurred to me to make inquiry on this point.[35]

Dancing always has a conventional direction. It is what we call "clockwise," but the Indians think of it in directional terms, i.e., from east to south to west to north to east. This is likewise the order of birth of the four winds in the myth cited. In the smoking of a ceremonial pipe the leader turns the stem in a clockwise direction and sometimes pauses when the stem has faced in each direction. The symbolism of this act lies in the fact that by including all the directions all of the spiritual entities in the entire universe are the recipients of the smoke offering.[36]

The pavilion is a structural representation, in one sense, of the directions so that the *opposites,* north-south, east-west, and the *order* about the horizon may be recognized, but no further use is made of this.

The directional ordering of the Saulteaux spatial universe, therefore, is one that penetrates religious as well as secular life. And it is obvious that it has psychological implications qualitatively different from directional orientation in Western culture. The build-up of associations of north, south, east, and west with symbolic and mythological meanings makes the directions meaningful places. It further integrates other aspects of the culture and behavior so that a "living in" the world is experienced which has its own peculiar character. In other cultures directional orientation may deeply penetrate still other spheres of life and give the spatial orientation of the people a distinctive psychological caste.[37]

CONCLUSIONS

The development of man's mastery of space and the abstract concepts that have evolved along with it cannot be explained in any psychological terms which ignore the cultural factors involved. Human space perception is biologically rooted, but the level at which it functions in the individual is not reducible to innate capacities or maturational development. The process of socialization contributes experiential components that must be considered. Some of these acquired components of space perception are a function of the cultural milieu in which the individual has been reared. The cultural patterns of different societies offer different means by which spatial perceptions are developed, refined, and ordered. The spatial concepts of different societies also vary with respect to the degree of abstraction attained. There is also inter- and intra-societal variation in the utilization of different degrees of refinement of spatial perception in connection with different life activities. The variability is correlated with the fact that one set of conditions may demand very little in the way of spatial discriminations of a certain order (e.g., measurement), but considerable refinement in other respects (e.g., directional orientation).

Such considerations point to a wider historical question: "How have the cultural means themselves developed? This is a matter for actual investigation, but our analysis of Saulteaux culture is suggestive in a negative respect. The point was stressed that the Saulteaux culture provided no incentive that would lead to the development of an abstract concept of area. On the other hand, they did draw crude maps in aboriginal days. The motive here was a very simple one: to provide a guide for the traveler in a strange country. There was a demand for maps for this purpose.

If we could illuminate the conditions and purposes in any given society which are relevant to the refinement and development of space perception, we would approach an answer to the historical question.

202

Chapter 10 - Some Psychological Aspects of Measurement Among the Saulteaux*

W E CANNOT INVESTIGATE MEASUREMENT AMONG ABORIGINAL PEOPLES upon the assumption that they explicitly recognize and fully abstract those attributes of things which we think of in quantitative terms. Nor can we assume that differences in magnitude, expressed in numerical terms, are particularly interesting to them. The problem, rather, is to discover what attributes of things are measured, how the operation of measurement is carried out, the purposes for which it is used, and the extent to which the results are expressed in numerical terms.

An attempt will be made here to show how such spatial attributes as distance, length, and area are handled by the Saulteaux and the extent to which their culture implements, but at the same time limits, the measurement of these attributes.

In the first place, observation and experience are sufficient to enable any adult human being to make crude estimates of distance, length, and area. Among the Saulteaux, as among us, such perceptual discriminations as "far" and "near," "long" and "short," "large" and "small" are made constantly and receive linguistic expression in connection with all sorts of activities in daily life. This is what may be characterized as the level of "contrast-comparison." Functionally, it is grounded in acquaintance with the qualities and relations of things derived from direct experience. This level of discrimination is undoubtedly a generic human trait. And for many purposes it is all that is needed. Such crude discriminations are useful enough for making comparisons within a given class of objects, but their scope is practically limited to such comparisons. A "big" tree, a "big" man, and a "big" lake simply are not commensurable in such terms. There is no translatability between such groups or kinds. There is no standard against which just the height of a man and the height of a tree can be measured. Any intercomparisons must be expressed as similes or metaphors such as, "a *windigo* (cannibal giant) is as tall as, or taller than, the trees."

It is out of this crude phase of perceptual discrimination, however, that the measurement of spatial magnitude has arisen. Measurement in

*Reprinted from *American Anthropologist*, XLIV (January-March 1942), 62-77.

this sense[1] is a refinement of such naïve comparisons. It cannot be viewed as categorically distinct because in its most elementary form it remains qualitative rather than numerical; only in its developed phases does measurement carried to the point of numerical determination become equivalent to quantitative statement. What measurement implies is simply this: For estimates of magnitude based upon naïve discrimination it substitutes the operation of *matching* as a determinative technique.[2]

The simplest form of this operation occurs when we determine by *direct matching* that string *x* is longer, shorter, or equal in length to string *y* by the juxtaposition of the two. Or we can determine (i.e., measure) the length of an object of another class by matching it against string *x*. But since direct matching necessarily has such a limited scope as a means of measurement, it being impossible to use it when two objects cannot be juxtaposed, another procedure must be adopted. By using string *x* we can match *indirectly* two logs of wood that are not easily manipulable. String *x* then becomes an informal standard of measure in such a procedure. If we standardize its length, it becomes a *unit of measure* by means of which we determine the length of a variety of objects and express their magnitudes in terms of the standard unit chosen.

Of course the units chosen as standards of measure may be extremely varied in character. They may be concrete or abstract, dynamic or static. They may be customarily employed without being highly formalized or part of an integrated system of measures. And they may vary from culture to culture. Their fundamental significance lies in the nature of the operation that is performed by means of them, not in their intrinsic character. For this reason it is more important to investigate the circumstances under which primitive people perform the operation of genuine measurement and the extent to which they use it, than it is to determine the fact that they employ this or that customary unit of measurement.

Furthermore, measurement as a particular kind of operation is more widely prevalent than the use of conventional units of measure. In a given society we can no more infer the actual extent and character of measurement as an operation from the use of standardized measures alone than we can infer the extent of numerical operations from a minimum vocabulary of number words. In certain circumstances empirically derived units of measure or a process of direct matching are adequate means for the ends to be achieved. In so far as this is the case, they are no less important for an understanding of measurement than the use of the more conventional units of measure.

It is the fundamental principle involved in the process of measurement that also enables us to gain further insight into the conditions under which differential units of measure must have arisen. For it would appear that under the cultural conditions found in most primitive societies there could have been no demand for the refined operational techniques of a culture like our own and the accompanying units of measure that they require. The technique of direct matching was sufficient for many purposes, and in many spheres of activity measurement was not demanded at all. Since there was no cultural motivation to this end, there was no incentive for the invention of new operational techniques in the measuring process. Even in occidental culture today there is no need under many circumstances for the measurement of spatial attributes in terms of the most refined units of measurement that are part of our heritage. In everyday life we, too, resort to naïve discriminations and often employ the simpler matching operations in so far as these are sufficient to the ends we have in view. But the psychological implications are quite different for ourselves, on the one hand, and the Saulteaux, on the other. We are able to choose from a variety of means provided by our culture and adapt them to our ends; the Saulteaux are limited to very simple means. Differential cultural factors, then, connected with the operation of measuring, have refined our perceptions of spatial magnitude, whereas individuals in Saulteaux society have been confined to a stage of spatial perception in which such refinements play only a minor role.

Distance.—Among the Saulteaux, as among ourselves, it is possible to answer the question "how far" in a purely relative way. The Saulteaux employ two contrasting terms for this purpose, one meaning "near" or "close by," the other "a great way off." Actual measurement is not involved here; the question is answered by indicating the relative position in space of the object or place referred to with reference to the speaker.[3]

In linear measurement, however, it is necessary to emphasize a basic difference between the Saulteaux and ourselves that penetrates to the very roots of both cultures. For us, distance-away, distance-apart, length, are all brought under the same conceptual system of measures. A linear dimension of any kind can be quantitatively expressed in terms of a single scale of graduated standardized units, the smallest and largest of which can only be arrived at by complicated instrumental means. The very existence of such a scale in occidental culture is, of course, a unique as well as a recent development. It likewise typifies the means which our culture provides for dealing with spatial attributes and the level of objectivity, refinement, and organization which our spatial concepts have attained.

Primitive peoples like the Saulteaux not only lack such refinements; they do not even have any common units which are applicable to *all* classes of linear measurement, to say nothing of a graduated scale of such units. This means that such measures as they employ for different kinds of linear distances are not comparable, nor is it possible to convert measures of a lower order into those of a higher order and vice versa. Consequently distance-away, or distance-apart, when thought of in terms of places or objects in space, is an entirely different thing from the length of a manipulable object of some sort like a canoe or a piece of string. There is no means of bringing linear concepts of all kinds into a single unified category of spatial attributes because the units of measure expressing the distance traveled on a journey, for example, are categorically d'stinct from those applied to the length of a piece of string.

Although some of the Berens River Indians today estimate distances in terms of miles, this is simply one of the results of acculturation processes which have been occurring for about a generation. An incident which occurred in July 1817 when Lord Selkirk made his treaty with the Cree and Saulteaux in the neighborhood of what is now the city of Winnipeg illustrates the culturally constituted barriers faced by the natives in situations where some comprehension of distance magnitudes was required. In this case the problem was solved on the spot by one of the chiefs who, not being able to fall back upon any units of measurement provided by his own culture, devised nevertheless a means whereby the miles of the white man were translated into a concrete and immediately perceptible datum that was comprehensible to his fellow Indians.

The settlers were to possess the land for two miles back from the western bank of the Red River according to the terms of the treaty, but the Indians wanted to know how far two miles was. Even though Mr. Fidler, the surveyor, produced his chains and measured off the mileage this did not quite satisfy the Indians. Then one of the chiefs is said to have had an inspiration. There happened to be some horses grazing out on the plain close to the spot the surveyor's man had reached with his measuring chains. Noticing these horses the chief announced that two miles was as far as a man could see daylight under the belly of a horse. All the Indians "puckered their eyes to the western glare, the setting sun" and were satisfied that they knew what two miles meant.[4]

Natively, distance is measured in units of activity.[5] In respect to a journey, for example, this is customarily expressed by saying how many times one has slept or will sleep en route. Such a unit is concrete and qualitative. It is processual in character in contrast to an abstract static unit like a mile. A concrete, recurring process within the larger activity, the journey, is abstracted and matched against the latter, instead of an abstract linear measure, the mile. Similarly, instead of "sleeps" the linear distance to a place may be measured by "nights" on the road. In this case the concrete recurring event utilized is darkness. Since all measurement involves some kind of matching operation, the underlying principle is the same despite the choice of categorically distinct units. The same principle is applied by the Saulteaux to the "length" of a journey that may take less than a day. The question "how far" is answered by reference to the position of the sun in the sky, i.e., the process of walking from one point to another is measured by matching it against a natural process, the course of the sun through the heavens.

For the life economy of the Saulteaux *when* one returns, *when* we shall expect to meet are more important than the distance traveled. For provisioning, too, the number of days consumed in the journey is the important thing. Such judgments can never depend upon linear distance predominantly: weather conditions, high or low water, the number of individuals paddling a canoe, or the size of the load, all are contributing factors to the rate of travel in summer. In winter the roughness of the going, the quality of the snow, or the flatness of the country must be considered. Thus the qualitative units employed by the Saulteaux as a measure of distance are extremely crude and variable. In terms of their system of calculation the distance between points traveled by water has been considerably reduced in recent years with the introduction of the outboard motor among them. And in effect this is quite true because the actual linear distance is inconsequential for them. Their terms of measurement, crude as they are, prove eminently satisfactory under the conditions of life which their culture imposes.

The intrinsic limitations of such units for accurately measuring distance are equally obvious. They are a contributing factor to the vague concepts of space beyond the experience of individuals. Their qualitative character makes It Impossible for the Indians to conceptualize distance in abstract numerical terms.

Unable, for example, to communicate the idea of distance in quantitative terms to the people up the river (particularly the Pekangikum Indians who are the least acculturated of any group), I do not believe that I ever succeeded in conveying to them any realistic notion of the distance I had traveled to reach their country. Matters were further complicated by the fact that my *rate* of travel in different kinds of conveyances was not the sort of knowledge that could be taken for granted. Consequently, my attempt to convert distance into the concrete qualitative units intelligible to them (i.e., sleeps) made my home only twice the distance the mouth of the river lay from Lake Pekangikum, about 260 miles. Actually it was more than six times that distance. The difficulty lay in the fact that I spent the same number of nights on the train and the boat between Philadelphia and the mouth of the Berens River as I spent ascending the river. The differential factor, of course, was the speed of the train. This mode of conveyance was known to them only by hearsay. The only mode of travel within their observation that could be used analogically to give them an idea of the speed of the train was the airplane, familiar through use in the Forestry Service and by prospectors who fly over the country to many inland points.

Manipulable Length.—As I have already said, measuring always makes use of the principle of matching. Consequently, in measuring what may be called "manipulable lengths," this principle may be applied without the use of any standardized units of measure. The following are illustrations:

One man told me, for instance, that in constructing a deadfall for bear, his father made the preliminary measurements in the following manner: After the bedlog[6] of the trap was in place he knelt upon it, bent forward and, keeping his back horizontal with the ground, extended his hands forward as far as they would reach. Where they touched the ground defined the limits of the "pen." The fall-log would then be sure to strike the right part of the bear's spine. To judge the height of the notch in the upright post where the outer end of the lever rests, he would elevate a knee.

In this case the matching of the trap to fit the bear is mediated through the close correspondence in size between the bears of the country and a man.

Matching is also used in making moccasins[7] where the length of the foot is measured by a piece of string, or nowadays by drawing the outline of the foot on a piece of paper.[8] The same principle sometimes was used in the manufacture of a birch-bark canoe. An old canoe was set upright and stakes driven into the ground at intervals around the outside of it in order to outline the size and shape of the new canoe to be built.

In dealing with manipulable length the Saulteaux likewise make use of various parts of the body as semistandardized units. The right forearm with the elbow as a base is one extremely convenient "yardstick" and variable lengths may be marked off on it by the side of the left hand, or the distance between the elbow and the tip of the forefinger may be used as a unit.[9] A man may say, for example, that he tracked a bear with footprints "as long as this," indicating the length by putting the right elbow on the ground, extending his arm, and marking the limit with his left hand placed across wrist or knuckles. The same kind of measure is used when reporting the size of the footprints reputedly made by a *windīgo*. In making a birchbark canoe the two crossbars fore and aft were made equivalent in height to the distance between a man's elbow and wrist, while the middle bars were of a height corresponding to the distance between the elbow and the tip of the forefinger or this dimension plus one thumb-first-finger-spread.

In addition to the use of the full spread of these, the thumb and forefinger may be used to indicate smaller dimensions. I recall a discussion of how much the water had risen at Little Grand Rapids. One man spread his thumb and first finger apart to indicate this. All the other men agreed that he was right. In our scale it was about three inches.

Another unit of length in which the fingers are employed is the spread of the thumb and middle finger (*pejiwákwagan,* one finger stretch). The width of three or four fingers, or even of all five digits (hand), was another type of unit used. Canoe ribs almost always were three fingers in width, whether used in small or large canoes.

To measure greater lengths the fist with outstretched thumb is used. Both hands are laid on the object with the tips of the thumbs touching. Together they cover two units. If the left fist with the thumb extended is now crossed over the right, a third unit is covered, and if the right fist is now withdrawn from under the left and the extended thumb touched to the left thumb, a fourth unit is measured, and so on.

The dimensions between the tips of the fingers when both arms are stretched out (fathom) constitute another unit (*pejigonik,* one arm-stretch); half of this is equal to the distance from the breastbone to the fingertips of one hand. When birch-bark canoes were manufactured, they were spoken of as two or three "stretches" in length, half a "stretch," and so on.

"Steps" or paces as units of length likewise are known to the Saulteaux. The length of a log house may be thought of in terms of "steps" and the logs measured off accordingly. The wabano pavilion of John Duck at Little Grand Rapids was said to be fourteen steps long and six steps wide. When measured this pavilion was approximately forty feet by fifteen feet. This makes the Saulteaux "step" about two and a half feet which is very close to our "pace," usually set at three feet.

All these units of measure are completely independent of one another. They are not part of a system of measures and cannot be expressed in terms of each other. But in contrast to the traditional inadequacies which beset them in dealing with linear dimensions of any considerable magnitude, the Saulteaux by the use of direct matching and of conventional units of measure are able to deal more accurately with the linear dimensions of the objects whose manipulation is important in their daily lives.

They have no measuring tools in the more literal sense, i.e., detached objects like a foot-rule, which embody standardized units of measure that are the same for any and every operation of measuring no matter who performs it. The integration of these more accurate forms of measurement with industrial processes is not accidental. The possession and use of such devices is also of inestimable importance from a psychological point of view. In dealing with space relations they refine perceptions to a degree impossible without them. In recent years the more sophisticated Saulteaux at the mouth of the Berens River have learned to use our measuring tools, especially in building houses. When using a foot-rule they also employ English terms for numerical values, as "three and a half" or "two and a quarter inches."

Area.—The limitations imposed upon the Saulteaux with respect to the measurement of non-manipulable length naturally restrict the accurate measurement of non-manipulable areas. Their judgments of differences in areas of any considerable magnitude can only be based upon the most elementary kinds of perceptual discrimination.

Since their country is studded with innumerable lakes of different sizes, the Saulteaux recognize proportional difference in the areas covered by these bodies of water. But in the absence of any means of measurement, area, as an abstract spatial attribute, cannot be mentally manipulated in an accurate fashion. Instead of being abstracted, area to the Saulteaux mind is only comprehended as a concept that remains closely linked with "region" or "place"; it retains all the character of a particular locality. If a region has natural boundaries, a lake for instance, that set it off from the surrounding country, it is easily comprehended in semi-abstract areal terms, and belongs more to the category of "thing" or "object" having shape and size and perceptible surface extensity. Otherwise it may never even be thought of in this way at all.

An interesting question arises here. The Saulteaux, like other Algonkian peoples, break up during the winter into hunting groups. The average number of persons per group is 14.9. Each hunting group is associated with a different locality. Related individuals in a paternal family line frequently occupy the same hunting ground for more than a generation. Hunting rights in such regions are socially sanctioned in native law and trespass resented.

In the course of collecting information in regard to the geographical aspects of this native economic system, Indians have been asked by the investigator to delineate the boundaries of their hunting terrtiories on a map; or the investigator has done it himself under their supervision. Although I have used the same procedure in securing data on the geographical locale of Saulteaux hunting territories, I believe, nevertheless, that a false impression is created if the inference is drawn that the natives themselves conceptualize their hunting grounds in abstract areal terms.[10] It is my impression that the contrary is the case, despite the fact that these hunting territories may vary greatly in size, from 13 to 212 square miles. (See 1949a.)

I believe that the reason why the Saulteaux do not make areal abstractions and comparisons of their hunting territories is not due simply to the lack of any accurate measures; it is, rather, explained by the absence of cultural values that would motivate such an abstraction on their part. If we consider for a moment how deeply the concrete details of the terrain over which they hunt must be embedded in their personal experience and their lack of knowledge of other districts than their own, it is difficult to see why judgments in abstract spatial terms should occur without an extremely forceful motivation as a leverage. And it is just this sort of motivation that we search for in vain.

In the first place, there is nothing in Saulteaux culture that motivates the possession of land for land's sake. Usufruct, rather than the land itself, is an economic value and land is never rented or sold. The use of the land and its products are a source of wealth rather than land ownership itself. There is no prestige whatsoever that accrues to the man who hunts over a large area. Nor is there any direct correlation between the size of the winter hunting group and the area of the hunting ground they occupy.[11] This is to be explained, perhaps, by the sectional variability in the incidence of the fur-bearing animals, differences in hunting skill, and maybe other variables. Finally, what is even more important is the fact that a smaller hunting territory may afford a living equal to, or even better than, a larger one. Consequently, it is impossible for the Saulteaux to measure areas in units of productivity (e.g., skins of animals trapped) as we find to be the case among some agricultural peoples (e.g., how much barley or rice can be grown).[12]

Under these conditions, why should an abstract concept of area arise, or comparisons of hunting territories in terms of size be made? Such a concept has no functional value for the Saulteaux, no more than has abstract distance.

In actual life, then, the Saulteaux simply employ such generic terms as "large," "small," "big enough." But in a myth that accounts for the origin of the "island" (that is, the earth) on which man now dwells, it is interesting to find the area *measured* in a unique fashion. Wisαkedjak and a few animals have survived a flood by building a raft. They are floating about and do not know what to do. Finally Wisαkedjak sets his animal companions diving for earth. They fail. But at last muskrat secures a tiny quantity. This is magically expanded when Wisαkedjak blows upon it. They land on the island created and then Wisαkedjak calls a caribou to him. He tells the animal to run around the newly formed island. The caribou soon comes back and says, "It's pretty small yet." So Wisαkedjak keeps blowing upon the earth. After a bit he says to another young caribou, "You run around now." So this caribou runs around. When he gets back he is old, he has lost some of his teeth. Wisαkedjak is not yet satisfied with the size of the earth, so he blows some more. Then he directs a third caribou to run around the "island." This one never comes back. So Wisαkedjak says, "It is big enough." (That is, "big enough for people to live on.")

Measurement in this case is based on the principle already described. Two kinds of processual units are employed: (1) the maturational changes in an animal, (2) the procedure of running around the island. It is impossible, of course, to obtain any idea of area in absolute spatial terms from the application of such units. Under the conditions described in the myth, a comparison of the differences in the area of the earth at subsequent periods was inferred from the relative time occupied by the animals in making the circuit. But any comparisons outside these conditions would be impossible unless the units employed were standardized in some way.

Manipulable Area.—If we now turn to manipulable areas, we find that the Saulteaux deal with them more effectively. But their approach is pragmatic rather than abstract. There are several reasons for this.

In the first place, elementary processes of perception are more adequate as a basis for making discriminations in the size of manipulable areas than in the case of those of greater magnitude. And through experience in handling materials and objects of various kinds excellent quantitative judgments can be made. In the second place, the Saulteaux are compelled to deal with simple problems of proportion in order to convert raw materials such as hides and bark into objects of domestic use. In making a bark container, for example, its proportions must be adequately controlled from start to finish. But in these relatively simple manufacturing processes area never has to be handled in a purely quantitative, abstract way. The size, shape, and proportions of the object being produced are all inseparable. Initially, of course, the question "is this piece of skin 'big enough' to make a pair of moccasins" or "is this piece of bark 'big enough' to make a rogan," does arise. But it can be answered in terms of an estimate based on experience, how it "looks," without resort to actual measurement. Once the process of manufacture itself is started further judgments become chiefly relevant to the interrelations of size, shape, and proportions which the finished product will have. Measurement is not in terms of any standardized unit; the basic unit chosen is some part of the object itself or a series of them.

Of course, in the past the flat patterns for such manufactured objects were developed through cutting and fitting directly. Perhaps when a

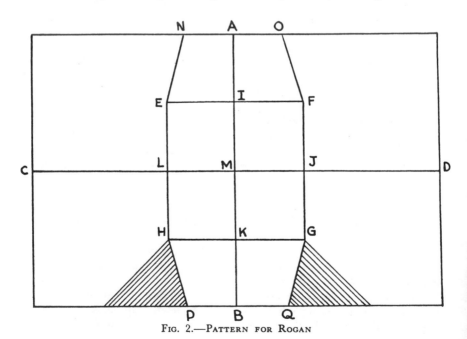

Fig. 2.—Pattern for Rogan

new one was needed, the old one was taken apart and thus the flat pattern shape exposed. With this as guide the outline of a new one could be traced on the material. Today these patterns may mediate the judgments of whether the material is "enough." The "key unit" will be judged against the actual object (for example the length of the foot in the case of a moccasin) and the rest of the pattern adjusted to keep the shape and proportions constant.

The manufacture of a bark container, a rogan, may be taken as an example. (Fig. 2) In this case the bottom is the basic unit, although of course, the total overall size of the finished product is the initial guiding judgment. (In this account I am paraphrasing the observations of my colleague, Dr. Dorothy M. Spencer, who collected the information under my direction.)

1. To begin with, a rectangular piece of bark is chosen; it must be roughly shaped by a crooked knife and rough spots are smoothed off. Its size is a matter of judgment based on the experience of the woman undertaking the task. (See diagram.)

2. The median point (A, B, C, D) on each edge of the rectangle is determined by folding the bark upon itself.

3. The median points on opposite edges of the rectangle are now joined by lines made lightly with a knife.

4. The next step is to measure off the area that will form the bottom of the container (E, F, G, H). This area may be square or rectangular. In the example given it is square. Its size is not measured by any conventional quantitative unit but is arrived at by a process of proportional measurement in the following way:

A small strip of bark, judged to be half the length of the bottom of the rogan is prepared (the worker usually experiments a little first before adopting a length). With this piece of bark the distance from the center M to points I, J, K, L are measured and marked on the bark; then the distance from L to E, L to H and so on. In this way the corners of the bottom, E, F, G, H, are defined. Small holes are punched in the bark at these points with an awl.

5. The points N, O, P, Q are not determined by measurement; they are a matter of "shape judgment." When marked, a line is drawn from the corners of the bottom of the rogan to them.

6. The lines referred to above serve as guides for cutting. This is now done and the pieces left free are folded up along the lines EF and HG.

7. The remainder of the bark sheet is now folded to form the sides of the container in such a way that the shaded parts appear on the outside of the bottom. The corners of these are temporarily tied together with string and where the other pieces of bark overlap at the sides, they are held together with wooden pins until the sewing is complete. (This step and the treatment of the rim need not concern us here.)

8. The lid is made of two pieces of bark, one circular, the other a long rectangular strip. These are sewn together so that the edge of the strip is perpendicular to the surface of the circular piece and fits into the container. The area of the circular piece is determined by direct matching with the top of the container after its completion: it is cut round more or less the right size, tried against the top, and trimmed to fit.[13]

Conclusions.—In this paper I have pointed out that measurement, as such, is a refinement of naïve discrimination mediated by some sort of matching process and I have described the kind of measurements that the Saulteaux use in dealing with such spatial attributes as distance, length, and area. Among these Indians there is relatively little interest in or use of measurement on a fully developed quantitative level. Yet their possession of certain conventional units of measure permits simple quantification, as in the estimation of distance in terms of a certain number of "sleeps." By and large, however, measurement among the Saulteaux remains on the most elementary level except in those instances where white influences are apparent. But this is thoroughly consonant with the type of culture they possess and the kind of life they lead. In such a simply organized and individualistic society, where articles are manufactured only for domestic use and not for sale, there is no demand for the application of *standard* measurements to any article produced. The variableness of units of measure (as e.g., body parts) consequently does not matter. Each person constructs for himself and measures for himself or other members of his immediate household group. No truly objective standard is necessary. In each situation the individual solves in his own terms problems of measurement that may arise.

The low level of abstraction that we find in respect to distance, length, and area is connected both with the relative absence of quantification and with general cultural conditions. There is no need to develop any traditional devices for rising to a higher level of abstraction because the processes of measurement already known are adequate to meet the simple problems to be solved. Consequently, we cannot point to any socially derived incentives that might lead to progressive changes in the methods of measurement. In fact, the traditional press of the culture fosters conservatism. This is illustrated specifically by the factors which would seem to discourage the emergence of any abstract notions of area in connection with the use of hunting territories. The only influences which are now at work in the opposite direction are those which come from increasing contacts with white people and new educational opportunities.

Comparative data from other primitive societies would, I believe, lend support to the conclusion that the level of abstraction utilized in dealing with certain spatial attributes is not a simple function of maturation or intellectual capacity on the part of individuals. It is a function of the status of the cultural heritage as well. For the cultural heritage of a people limits or promotes the manner in which and the terms in which the individual deals with the spatial attributes of the world about him. If a culture does not provide the terms and concepts, spatial attributes cannot even be talked about with precision. Individuals are left to fend for themselves, as it were, on the level of elementary discriminatory reactions. This limits the possibilities for the mental manipulation of more refined and developed concepts that require symbolic representation in some form. Without such instruments in the cultural heritage certain areas of action are excluded and the solution of many practical problems impossible.

Thus, an analysis of processes of measurement is one angle of approach to the problem of how individuals deal with the spatial attributes of things under different cultural conditions. It is also possible to throw some light on the concepts of space that are held. The relation of these questions to wider and more fundamental problems is evident—problems in which both psychologists and anthropologists find a common field of interest. A great deal more needs to be known about how the spatialization of the world arises in the experience of a human being; the kinds of discriminations that are made; the degree of refinement to which they are carried; how these are related to motility, the manipulation of objects, and the concepts of space that are held. It seems to me that anthropologists can contribute a great deal to the solution of such problems by analyzing the cultural constituents of the spatially coordinated behavior of individuals in different human societies.

Chapter 11 - Temporal Orientation
in Western Civilization
and in a Preliterate Society*

CULTURAL FACTORS IN TEMPORAL EXPERIENCE

In all human societies we find that certain classes of events have become established as formalized reference points[1] to which it is customary to relate past, present, and future occurrences, or in terms of which temporal intervals of greater or less duration may be expressed. Calendars, of course, immediately come to mind. Yet unsystematized, but no less customary, points of reference such as "a sleep"[2] are employed by many preliterate peoples as units in estimations of temporal length. Events in the life history of individuals—birth, marriage, or other significant occurrences—are constantly evoked to which other events may be related. Even in Western civilization, despite the fact that our cultural heritage provides us with the alternative of employing exact dates for all such events, similar unformalized reference points are in use.

Whether formalized or not, the characteristic reference points employed by the individuals of different human societies are relevant to a full understanding of the functioning of temporal concepts. They are basic cultural phenomena of the utmost importance in the ordering and coordination of human activities. It is impossible to picture any human society without them. In terms of individual experience, they are orientational. The individual's temporal concepts are built up in terms of them; he gets his temporal bearings by means of them, and his temporal perceptions function under their influence. It is impossible to assume that man is born with any innate "temporal sense." His temporal concepts are always culturally constituted.

Like other cultural phenomena, temporal frames of reference vary profoundly from society to society. This fact is as important psychologically as it is culturally. Thus Dagobert Fry[3] in a study of spatial and temporal concepts of the Middle Ages and the Renaissance asserts that no two peoples live conceptually in precisely the same kind of space and time. For those of us reared in contemporary Western civilization:

*Reprinted from *American Anthropologist*, XXXIX (1937), 647-70.

the dazzled but hospitable mind of twentieth-century man is offered a vast array of new discoveries, new theories, new intuitions having to do with the temporal in all its aspects, [for] not until the present era does there seem to have converged upon the problem in all its ramifications such varied and intense interest—philosophical, psychological, logical, and scientific.[4]

This paramount interest in Time is explicable on cultural-historical grounds. We moderns are habituated to a uniquely elaborated scheme of temporal norms that impinge upon our lives at every point. We not only possess a scientifically adjusted calendar, subdivided into months, weeks, days, and hours;[5] since the middle of the fourteenth century the hours of the day have been subdivided into sixty units of equal length and these units again subdivided, a development which became of more and more practical importance as clocks and watches became common.[6] By means of these devices, as well as a highly systematized calendrical scheme, individuals are enabled to maintain as exact a temporal orientation as is desired. And because it has become customary to "time" so many human activities and events with precision, a high level of *conscious* temporal orientation is inescapable. Consequently, as Parkhurst states:

That experience, that increased pervasive awareness of time as a super-sensible medium or container, as a stream, or an infinitely extended warp upon which the woof of human happenings is woven, is without question a notable characteristic of present-day consciousness.[7]

Time extends beyond the range of our personal observation and experience, or that of the life span of any one generation of human beings. Through the device of successively numbering the years that have elapsed before and since the assumed birth of Christ, it is possible to "date" events in the remote past and to conceptualize the past history of humanity in units of comparable length (years, centuries, millennia) and likewise the history of the earth and the solar system. Not only the past, the future is likewise part of the same temporal continuum. This structuralization of future time permits the exercise of foresight by individuals, or even nations, in planning and coordinating all kinds of future activities in detail, a possibility excluded for societies with time systems of a less developed order. Intervals on this time-scale can be measured and quantitatively expressed in orders of any magnitude.

This modern notion of time is also the matrix of derivative concepts that characterize Western civilization:

When one thinks of time, not as a sequence of experiences, but as a collection of hours, minutes and seconds, the habits of adding time and saving time come into existence. Time took on the character of an enclosed space: it could be divided, it could be filled up, it could even be expanded by the invention of labor-saving instruments.[8]

Time, in short, became reified to a considerable degree. It came to assume a commodity value.[9] To "waste time" is still almost a heinous sin unless confined to sacred days, holidays, vacations, or other formally defined periods.[10]

The use of a graduated scale of *small* temporal units, moreover, and the quantitative measurement of temporal intervals made other characteristic developments possible. Human activities could be accurately rated in terms of *speed*. Thus speed itself has risen into prominence as a value of Western society and functions as an important factor in the motivation of individuals. The cultural matrix, and hence the psychical relativity, of speed as an incentive in behavior is not always recognized as a derivative of our own temporal concepts. Psychological tests, standardized with respect to speed in performance, have been given to native peoples without due regard for the simple fact that speed does not have the same value for them.[11] No wonder, then, that their scores rate lower than those of individuals reared in Western culture. Yet the results of such tests have been interpreted as an indication of *racial* rather than cultural differences.

In Western civilization, too, we find an approach to an apotheosis of Time typified by its elevation to a position of supreme importance in certain philosophical systems. Bergson, for example, who took issue with the Newtonian idea of time, has been celebrated as the first philosopher of our day "to take Time seriously,"[12] as one "who finds in Time conceived as *durée* [i.e., as a process, rather than as a mechanical succession of separate instants] in distinction from Time as measured by the clock, *the animating principle of the universe.*"[13] Time has even been called the "Mind of Space."[14] It is hardly surprising then to find a *tour de force* written by Wyndham Lewis[15] in which he links such philosophers with Spengler and with literary figures such as Gertrude Stein and James Joyce, and characterizes them as typical representatives of a twentieth-century Time Cult.

The psychological significance of time-consciousness in Western civilization also emerges with great clarity when we consider pathological cases of temporal disorientation. A person so disoriented as to be unable to give the year, month, or day of the week is almost sure to be a case of amentia, senility, or some psychotic disorder. Thus temporal orientation is of diagnostic value in mental disorders,[16] although the cultural nature and consequently the relativity of the reference points used as a standard are not always recognized as such. In other societies the disorientation of individuals would have to be judged by different temporal norms.

From personal experience I can say that "regression" to temporal norms less elaborate than our own is an entirely painless and not unpleasant process. During the summer of 1932 when I spent most of my time up the Berens River with the Pekangikum Indians, I lost track of the days of the month, since I did not have a calendar with me; the days of the week became meaningless, since, in two settlements, there were no missionaries and hence no Sunday observance or other activities that differentiated one day from another, and, as my watch stopped running, I had no way of keeping track of the hours of the day. My "disorientation," of course, was only such relative to the reference points of Western civilization to which I was habituated. Once the usual mechanical and institutional aids to these were removed, the relativity and provinciality of Western time concepts became obvious. But the significant fact is that since I remained associated with human beings it was a very simple matter to make their temporal reference points my own. My re-orientation simply involved the substitution of new, less elaborate but no less culturally determined, reference points for the old.

Ella Winter[17] gives an example of the relative ease with which it is possible to adapt oneself to a new frame of temporal reference. On her second day in Russia she was invited to a party "on the sixth." She asked what *day* of the week it was but the reply was, "I don't know. They've abolished the week and we never think about the names of days any more." The author insisted that since she was not a Russian she must know. "No American," she comments, "could forget the names of the days of the week[18] just because the Russians had introduced the five-day week and abolished Sunday." But a month later when the author was asked to tea by an American friend—"next Wednesday"— almost unthinkingly she inquired, "What date is that?" The Russians have simplified our scheme of temporal references by omitting one item.

Individuals, of course, ultimately acquire the temporal frames of reference characteristic of their society along with the rest of their cultural heritage. But this acquisition is a process, not a mechanical transference of temporal concepts from one generation to another. Binet noted this many years ago, and Sturt carried out an investigation designed to throw light upon the genetic development of some temporal concepts of children in different age groups.[19] Detailed studies of individual children, such as those made by the Sterns, and Decroly and Degand, indicate how gradually the time-concepts of Western civilization are acquired. A summary quotation based on the work of the observers mentioned illustrates this.

Recognition that *yesterday, today,* and *tomorrow* had reference to certain days was gradually developed during the fourth year by both Hilde and Suzanne, but a clear grasp of the relationship symbolized by these terms was still confused and *only became established in the fifth year.* The correct use of *yesterday, today,* and *tomorrow* as names of days, and a fixed order of seven days making a week, involves abstract chronological schemata which first become fixed late in the pre-school period or in the early school grades. These words, to be sure, appear in the vocabulary much earlier, but they are used indiscriminately or with reference to continuous undefined past as such, continuous present, or continuous future.[20]

In some American Indian languages the terms for day-before-yesterday and day-after-tomorrow are the same.[21] It would be interesting to know how children in these societies learn to employ these words with different temporal meaning.

219

Once we step outside of our own society and examine the frames of reference that are relevant to the temporal orientation of other peoples, the cultural constituents of human temporal experience are thrown into even greater relief. Astronomical events, as Sherif points out,

furnish us with very convenient and stable frames of reference for a calendar. Nevertheless, we must not think that there is absolute necessity for using astronomical events as reference points for time-reckoning.[22]

Other objects, events, and activities can be and have been used. The Andamanese furnish a striking example of this:

In the jungles of Adamans [writes Radcliffe-Brown] it is possible to recognize a distinct succession of odours during a considerable part of the year as one after another the commoner trees and leaves come into flower. . . . The Andamanese have therefore adopted an original method of marking the different periods of the year by means of the odoriferous flowers that are in bloom at different times. Their calendar is a calendar of scents.[23]

In certain parts of the Pacific torches have been utilized as time-reckoning devices.[24] In some places market days or sacred days which occur at regular intervals have defined temporal periods similar in principle to our "week."[25] Various other human activities, the appearance of certain animals at regular seasons of the year, or meterological changes,[26] have elsewhere been used as traditional reference points for temporal orientation. Beyond the immediate observation and experience of individuals mythology may express chronological relations between past events or even outline a definite evolutionary sequence in the development of natural objects and man.[27]

THE TEMPORAL ORIENTATION OF THE SAULTEAUX

In what follows it is my purpose to examine in some detail the cultural constituents of temporal orientation among the Berens River Saulteaux.

Movements of the Sun.—According to Saulteaux belief the earth is flat and each day the sun travels from east to west above it. This is the period of daylight constituting a temporal unit for which the native term is *pezagógijik,* "one day." When the sun disappears behind the western edge of the earth, it travels eastward beneath the land, to reappear at dawn. It is during this part of the sun's journey that darkness reigns. This period is recognized as another temporal unit, *pezagwátabik,* "one night."

Strictly speaking, there are no standardized *durational* units of these alternating periods of light and darkness which, at the latitude 52° N., vary greatly in length at different seasons of the year. For the period of daylight a success of discrete moments are recognized. These are crystallized in more or less standardized phrases that indicate the position of the sun,[28] or refer to the relation of its light to discernible objects. At the beginning of the day some very fine distinctions are drawn. The intervals between the discrete points recognized vary enormously in temporal length as measured on our absolute time scale. But this is irrelevant to the Saulteaux and, of course, it is possible to employ the intervals between any two of the points recognized as a crude measure of temporal length.

When streaks of light, distinguishable in the east, announce the first signs of coming day, although darkness still reigns on the earth, this is *pītában*, "dawn." When darkness is dispelled so that one can discern terrestrial objects at some distance, but the sun has not yet risen above the tree tops, it is *tcībwaságàtik*, "before coming out from the trees (the sun)." Soon the light from the rising sun reddens the treetops. This point of time in the new day is called *miskwanagáte*, "red shining (reflected) light." In addition, there are two other expressions that refer to the position of the sun before it emerges into full view. One of these connotes the point in time when the sun is still behind the tree-tops, literally, "beneath trees when hangs (the) sun," *ánámatikèpi ágotcinggizis;* the other, when it reaches the tops of the trees, "tops of trees when hangs (the) sun," *ékwanákak épī'ágotcinggizis.*

Once above the trees but still low enough in the eastern sky for its position to be judged with reference to them, there are two further expressions used that involve rudimentary units of *spatial* measurement. The first refers to the fact that the sun "hangs" in the sky "the breadth of my hand" above the trees, *nīonindjèpīápi'tagotcing.* The second, that it hangs *pezagwákwagan èpīápi'tagotcing,* a thumb-middle-finger-stretch above the tree-tops, a distance of about twice that of a hand-breadth.

The position of the sun in the sky during the remainder of the day is differentiated with respect to much larger temporal intervals and in a less refined fashion. The following expressions are used: *eánikketcī skīobakwit,* "as high as it goes up"; *eàptagizigak,* "half-day (midday)"; *eàptawínazit,* "half way to setting"; *pangiciman gīzis,* "falling (out of sight) (the) sun" [sunset]; *poni'animīgijigan,* "disappearing underneath day." The last term applies when a band of light still rims the horizon, after the sun itself has disappeared. For dusk, which in summer is especially prolonged at this latitude, the term *nänitaga* is used.

Movements of the Stars.—While the Saulteaux do not have a highly elaborated star-lore they have names for a number of the constellations and they have observed the movements of these during the night. The appearance of the morning star, *wábanänang,* is also noticed. They know Polaris and they have noticed the rotation of the circumpolar stars, particularly Ursa Major, which they call *k'tcīotcíganang,* Great Fisher. They have also observed that from December to May the Belt of Orion (*odádawaämok,* three young men) comes up from the horizon, mounts in the sky, and disappears before dawn. From the position of the former constellation in summer and the latter in winter a rough temporal orientation is obtained, but the only term that I know of which expresses any particular point during the night is *kegáeapi'tatabíkak,* "nearly half (the) night" [midnight]. Night, therefore, lacks the *formalized* points of reference established for the daylight period,[29] but direct observation of stellar movements makes possible unformalized nocturnal orientation.

Night and day, then, are distinct temporal units,[30] formally subdivided by traditionally established discrete points of reference, but not reckoned in standardized units of duration. "Nights" or "sleeps," rather than days, are customarily used as measures of temporal length and of *distance*. A man leaving camp will tell his wife that he will return after a certain number of "sleeps" or he may express the distance to a certain point in terms of "sleeps" or "nights." This rendering of distance in temporal units reminds us of the astronomer who finds it convenient to make the vast distances beyond experience intelligible by translating them into the language of time, i.e., light-years.

Timed Daily Activities and Special Events.—It seems likely that sleep has proved a convenient point of reference because of its periodic and regular recurrence. In summer, the camps quiet down at dusk, unless there is some unusual event in progress, and the relatively short period of darkness is equivalent to the period of sleep. If any of the women or girls have been visiting, one sees them making for their own dwellings as darkness approaches and the men and boys soon follow them. This pattern of returning to one's own camp before nightfall is so well established even among the Indians at the mouth of the river that, on several occasions, the family with whom I lived thought that I must be lost in the bush when I did not show up at the expected time. In winter, of course, different conditions prevail. The men are out on their trap lines or hunting long before daybreak and often do not return until after darkness has fallen.

In Western urban culture, eating at regular intervals has come to be an established pattern that in itself provides unformalized reference points in our temporal orientation. Being hunters and fishermen, the sources of food supply among the Saulteaux are precarious and meals are irregular. Hence eating cannot function, like sleeping, as a relatively stable reference point in daily activities. Since my own day in the field was organized on a routine three-meal basis, I sometimes arranged to have one informant come to my tent in the "morning" and another in the "afternoon." But it happened more than once that an informant would come so late in the morning that it was almost time for the noon meal and on one occasion the man expected in the afternoon showed up a few minutes after the one scheduled for the morning session arrived. Neither informant, of course, had any sense of being "late" or "early," and I could not have said to either one, "come to see me as soon as you have eaten." The lack of common reference points made it difficult to coordinate our activities efficiently.

Since almost all the Indians in the upriver settlements set their nets at night and lift them in the morning, what I did say to the informants expected in the forenoon was, "Come over as soon as you have lifted your nets."

On the whole, however, there are no set times for daily activities. Their rhythm is elastic in the extreme and except when motivated by hunger or necessity they are dictated to a large degree by external circumstances and by whim.

With respect to such activities as conjuring, dances, and ceremonies, however, there is a definite temporal patterning. Conjuring, for example, is always done after dark. The Wabanówīwin, too, was formerly held at night but nowadays it takes place only during the day. As soon as night falls the dancing stops, to begin again the following morning. The giveaway dance (mändáitīwin), no longer performed, was also held at night. Today the only dance held after dark is the potáte; it is the most purely social affair that the Indians up the river have. The Midéwiwin was the ceremony with the most exactly defined temporal limits. The lodge was entered at sunrise as a song with the words, "the one that's going to rise, I'll travel with him," was chanted. And it closed at sunset with a salute to the sun.

The day set for the Midéwīwin was, of course, decided beforehand by the leader and word sent to his assistants. This likewise occurs today in the case of the Wabanówīwin which may be held on one to four successive "days." But the time of day when it starts is not set. When the leader is ready he starts to sing and drum. Those wishing to attend come whenever they are inclined. Even the singers that the leader has asked to help him do not all come at once. They dribble in one by one. If the leader has begun in the morning all of them may not have arrived until afternoon.

In the case of the Potáte dance, which is "owned" by several different men of the Grand Rapids settlement, and may be started by any one of them with the help of four singer-drummers, the signal for attendance is the drumming itself, begun at dusk. The songs are recognized and so everyone knows what is going on. If only a few people come the dance may cease. I was present once when this occurred.

Acculturation of Timepieces, Named Days, and the Week.—Contact with traders for a hundred years and the advent of missionaries at the mouth of the river in 1873 have been the chief sources of profound changes in certain aspects of the life of the Berens River Indians. But so far as time reckoning is concerned these influences have had little effect on daily life, except at the mouth of the river. On the reserve in this locality, e.g., there are both Protestant and Catholic missions, both of which include day schools in their program. The bell of the Catholic mission rings regularly at six A.M., noon, and six P.M., so that the Indians have come to recognize these hours as punctuating certain divisions of the day. School bells also summon the children to their lessons and adults to church services on Sunday. (But Mr. C. D. Street, the Protestant

223

schoolmaster, told me that even in the coldest weather a dozen or more pupils are on hand an hour before school starts. They are not guided by the bell, or by time-pieces, but set out for school as soon as they have had breakfast.) A similar situation obtains, however, in only one of the five settlements up the river. There are no other occasions when the collective attendance of any group of individuals is demanded at a certain hour. For, as we have already pointed out, the attendance at native ceremonies is much more flexible in this regard.

While clocks are not a novelty at the mouth of the river, where the children are taught to tell time in school, by no means every household owns one and up the river I remember seeing only two or three. At Lake Pekangikum one family had recently purchased an alarm clock, the deferred ting-a-ling of which seemed to fascinate them, rather than its utility as a time-reckoning mechanism. There are perhaps a dozen men at the mouth of the river who own watches. But they seldom carry them about, to say nothing of using them in the regulation of daily activities. I remember, too, the pride with which a young fellow of the pagan Duck Lake settlement showed me his recently-acquired gold-filled watch that contrasted more than favorably with my Ingersoll. And in 1936 I found that a young girl at Grand Rapids had acquired a wrist watch. The chief of the Berens River Band, however, constantly carries a watch and frequently consults it.

In the aboriginal cultural pattern, "days" and "nights" are not grouped in any temporal unit of a higher order. There is no "week." Nor are there any named "days," although there are special terms for yesterday, day before yesterday, tomorrow, and day after tomorrow. Under missionary influence, however, the emphasis upon the Sabbath as a day of rest and religious observance (*aiyamayegîjigan,* praying day) made it necessary to instruct the Indians in the calculation of its periodic recurrence. Consequently, the week is now recognized as a unit of time among the Christianized natives and there is a term for it. It is interesting to observe, however, that this temporal unit was assimilated as part of a new *religious* orientation, rather than as a secular temporal concept as such. Sabbath observance is such a tangible and fundamental tenet of Protestant Christianity that it was one of the first things taught to the Indians by the missionaries. Egerton R. Young, the first resident missionary on the Berens River, tells of a visit he once received in the summer from an Indian woman who lived some distance inland. She had heard of the "Great Book" and had come for information.

Before she left [says Rev. Young],[31] I gave her a sheet of foolscap paper, and a long pencil, and showed her how to keep her reckoning as to the Sabbath day, I had, among many other lessons, described the Sabbath as one day in seven for rest and worship; and she had become very much interested and promised to try to keep it. [The following winter he visited the woman's camp. During the course of a meal which he took in her wigwam, the old woman] inserting one of her greasy hands in the bosom of her dress . . . pulled out a large piece of soiled paper, and unfolding it before me, she began in excited tones to tell me how she had kept the tally of the "praying days," for thus they style the Sabbath. . . . Imagine my delight to find that through the long months which had passed since I had given her that paper and pencil, she had not once missed her record. This day was Thursday and thus she had marked it. Her plan had been to make six short marks, and then a longer one for Sunday. [Then the woman spoke] "Missionary, sometimes it seemed as though I would fail. There were many times when the ducks or geese came near, and I felt like taking my gun and firing. Then I remembered that it was the praying day, and so I only put down the long mark and rested. I have not set a net, or caught a fish, or fired a gun, on the praying day since I heard about it at your house so far away." [Nowadays nets are lifted if people are short of food; otherwise not.]

An Indian family I once visited in the Pauingessi settlement were keeping a similar record of the days of the week and their account was likewise accurate. But I fear that I did not exhibit the enthusiasm of Reverend Young when I verified it for them. Today, no one ever sets out on a journey from the mouth of the river on Sunday and even the Christian Indians at Grand Rapids have become so completely acculturated to this periodic holy day that on one occasion when a gold strike was reported nearby and on a Sunday the missionary made a visit to the spot to look it over with a view to staking a claim, he was subjected to open criticism on this account.

The spread of Christianity, then, has been responsible for creating the basis for a new temporal unit in the minds of the Indians. But even so the concept of the week as such does not seem to function very significantly in their life and thought. It is the periodicity of the Sabbath, signalized by going to church and abstaining from certain secular activities, that is the important reference point in their lives.

Following the establishment of this reference point, the day-naming pattern, with which we are so familiar, developed. But the Indians did not attempt a rendering of English names for the days of the week. Consequently their series of names has a quality all its own. Monday is literally "cease praying day" (*póniaiyàmɑyegíjigɑn*), Tuesday is two days "after" (*níjogíjigɑn*), Wednesday is "half (week) gone" (*apiꞌtaúwɑse*), Thursday, the "great half gone" (*kꞌtciapiꞌtaúwɑse*), Friday, "approaching day" (*eníogíjigɑn*), and Saturday, *pakwéjigɑngíjigan*, "flour (bread) day." This last designation, so I was told, arose from the fact that it was the custom of the Hudson's Bay Company to pay their employees in kind on Saturday.

These terms have been in use at least fifty years at the mouth of the river. At Grand Rapids they are known but not commonly used. Farther up the river, especially in the pagan settlements where Sunday is not observed, they would, of course, have no meaning.

It seems to me that one can observe in the naming process that has accompanied the acculturation of new features, the fundamental pattern of native temporal orientation. I refer to the emphasis upon particular concrete events as basic reference points. Thus Sunday becomes characterized as "praying day" and Saturday as "ration day," while the other days relative to these are neutral in character, because they are signalized by no outstanding events. But the whole psychological focus of the day names is obviously Sunday. A religious event colors the whole series, with the exception of Saturday, in which case an event of economic importance overshadows it.

The same underlying principle is reflected in the native nomenclature of the next highest order of temporal unit—the "moon."

Lunar Changes.—As in the case of the day, a "moon" is not a division of continuous time, it is a recurring event. The period when the moon is visible, and its changing appearance as it waxes and wanes is a "moon." Twelve named lunations form a loosely coordinated succession with which no day count is integrated. The moons are differentiated by names which refer to such noncelestial phenomena as the appearance in the country of certain birds, the condition of plant life, the rutting of animals, human economic activities, etc. These are all seasonal periodicities, subject to considerable variation, that are loosely coordinated with particular lunations. There is an interesting episode in one of the myths in which an attempt to identify a moon by trying to catch sight of an eagle beguiles an old cannibal to his death. The latter is asked what moon it is and replies, "Midwinter moon." "No, you're wrong. This is Eagle Moon. Look! There is an eagle now passing behind you." (Eagle Moon is the one following Midwinter Moon.) When the old man turned to look, his throat was cut and his murderer remarks, "Did you expect to see an eagle at this season?"

This episode reflects both the chronological uncertainty connected with the aboriginal lunar calendar and the court of appeal in case of doubt. Since in any solar year there are more than twelve and less than thirteen lunations, a seasonal dislocation arises which the Saulteaux correct by adding an unnamed moon to the series.[32]

Thus the lunar calendar itself is intrinsically flexible because its real emphasis is less upon the successive waxing and waning of the moon, than upon noncelestial phenomena. The succession of events of the latter class provides the real temporal guide. But the correlation of noncelestial phenomena with lunar periodicities by means of a conventional nomenclature defines *limits* of elastic, yet standardized, divisions of time which the mere observation of the arrival of different species of birds in the spring, the ripening of berries, etc., would not in themselves be sufficient to establish.

Although a nuclear group of characteristic names for the lunations seems to typify the Ojibwa-speaking peoples, the other names employed show considerable variation.[33] The calendrical nomenclature, as might be expected, is closely connected with local conditions and varies accordingly. Of the nuclear group of names, one referring to the appearance of vegetation, usually the blossoming of flowers, is always to be found, one or more than have reference to the ripening or gathering of berries, others that indicate the appearance of certain birds, especially the wild goose, etc. On the Berens River, for example, three lunations are named for birds which make their local appearance at that time of year. Roughly, these lunations correspond to our months of March (*migaziwigizis*, Eagle Moon), April (*ni'kigizis*, Goose Moon), and May (*mángogizis*, Loon Moon). The periodic reappearance of the geese in April is attested by the records kept for a series of years by the Natural History Society of Manitoba.[34] They usually appear during the first week of this month and are to be seen only until the second week in May. They do not reappear until August, after which they are seen no more until the following April.

Most of the moon names, as might be expected, are identical among all the Berens River bands. But it is noteworthy that not all of them are. The following differ. For the sake of convenience they have been correlated with our series of month names to which they roughly correspond. The letters in parenthesis preceding each native name indicates the band in which its use is found: B. R., Berens River Band; G. R., Grand Rapids Band; P., Pekangikum Band. January: (B.R.) *kictcopabiwatakinam;* (G.R.) *kaginwasigetgizis*, Long Moon; February: (B.R.) *äpi'tapibungizis*, Half-winter Moon; (P.) *kijégizis*, Kind Moon (so-called because the winter is beginning to moderate); July: (B.R.) *ati'ktemini'kawigizis*, Ripe-berries-gathering Moon; (G.R.) *wabagwaniwigizis*, Blossom Moon; September: (B.R.) *mánómini'kawigizis*, Wild-rice-gathering Moon; (P.) *ämanozówigizis*, Rutting Moon; December: (B.R.) *opa'piwatcagenazis;* (G.R.) *pitcibabunwigizis*, Early Winter Moon.

It will be noted that although different names are used, the terms for both July moons refer to the condition of plant life which is likewise reflected in the name for the June moon (*sagibagauwigizis*, Leaves-coming-forth Moon). The reappearance of vegetation at this season of the year after the disappearance of snow and ice transforms the external aspects of the country so radically that it would seem to be an almost inescapable standard of reference in any scheme of temporal divisions based on the general pattern characteristic of the Saulteaux. July marks the peak of vegetation development.

On the other hand, there are marked local variations in the occurrence of wild rice in sufficient quantities to make it worth harvesting.[35] This is the explanation of the difference in nomenclature for the September moon at the mouth of the river and at Grand Rapids, as compared with Pekangikum. Within the habitat of the latter band wild rice is so scarce that it is never harvested. Hence, one would hardly expect to find it in their calendrical scheme since, as I have pointed out, the nomenclature of the lunations is intrinsically elastic, and like-

227

wise pragmatic. It may also be remarked in passing that there are no sugar maples in this country so that, as compared with other Ojibwa peoples in whose calendar a "sugar-making moon" is found, the Berens River Saulteaux lack a lunation of this name.

Ceremonies are not standardized with respect to performance in particular moons and while some individuals know the moon in which they were born, others do not. At the mouth of the river English month names are known and utilized to some extent so that the aboriginal calendar, as such, is being supplanted. Children in school are taught the English names of the months. Mr. Street said: "They always prize a calendar and follow it studiously at home. Some homes use our names altogether; others never."

Within each lunation discrete points are recognized, but these are not conceptualized as periods of temporal duration. In principle they parallel the points recognized in the changing position of the sun during the course of the day. But in the case of the moon, reference is made to differences in its size as it waxes and wanes. The following terminology is employed: *eoskagotcing,* newly hanging; *eanimitcapikizazit,* bigger; *eàptawábkizit,* half; *kegáewáwīezit,* nearly round; *èwáwīezit,* round; *epákwezit,* going; *eàptawábkizit,* half (-gone); *eagasabikizit,* getting small; *emetasīget,* it is going.

Seasonal Changes.—Observable changes in temperature, vegetation, and other natural phenomena define the seasons for the Saulteaux. Six are recognized. The names of these differ from those of the lunations in being nondescriptive terms. The Indians cannot translate them. But chosen natural phenomena define the limits of each season quite specifically and no intercalation is ever necessary. It is recognized, too, that the moons fall into seasonal units. This is quite possibly the chief conceptual mechanism by means of which they are kept adjusted to the solar year.

The passing of winter, for example, is signalized by the appearance of the migratory birds, the first of which are seen in March. Now the moons that correspond to our months of March, April, and May are those with bird names and these three lunations together constitute the season called *äsígwan,* the spring season of the Saulteaux. The following season, *nībín,* equivalent to our summer, does not begin until the ice has completely disappeared from the lakes and rivers and there is no more snow to be seen on the ground. Since slightly over one inch of snow is to be expected at this latitude in May, *nībín* normally begins in June and continues through August and into early September. It is significant that the June lunation, the first moon of the summer season, bears a name that refers to the reappearance of leaves on the deciduous trees and that up the river July is called the "moon of blossoms." It is in this latter month that the highest mean annual temperature occurs.

The next season recognized, *tagwágin,* begins when the leaves of the poplars and birches start to fall. It is a short season, never longer than a "moon." It is immediately followed by another short but named interval, *pigǐ'kánaαn,* defined by the fact that, although the trees have lost their leaves, the winter has not yet set in. This is also the period of so-called "Indian summer" after which "freeze up" occurs and the first heavy snows of the winter are due. These normally do not occur until November, the term for which, "freezing moon," indicates that the winter, *bǐbún,* has actually set in, to continue through three additional moons. Two sub-season winter units comprising two moons each are named. The first part of the winter season is called *askibibun,* "new, fresh, winter"; the latter and most severe half, when the temperature drops the lowest, is called *megwábǐbun.*

Ceremonies like the Midéwīwin, the Wabanówīwin, the "give-away" dance, etc., were always held during the summer season. This was the period when the Indians congregated in their summer fishing settlements. With the falling of the leaves began the dispersal to their hunting grounds.

Seasonal names occur in the mythology and, in the myth accounting for the origin of summer, it is explained how it came about that winter was reduced to only five moons (*sic*) in length. In one myth, too, the *passage of time* is conveyed not with reference to nights or moons but in terms of seasonal change. Mikinak (the Great Turtle) chases a moose and, although there is snow on the ground when he starts the pursuit, he does not catch up with the animal until open water. Length of time is of importance in this story because it is one of the contributing factors to the humor of the tale.

In conversation that has reference to past events, seasonal names, too, appear to be more frequently employed than "moon" names. Although less exact, these larger units are sufficiently precise and they function in much the same way among ourselves. Despite the instrumental value of our exact time scale, for certain purposes constant references to month, day, and hour of past events would appear pedantic even in our society.

Annual Cycle.—As Cope, speaking of the Indians in general, says,[36]

the year may be regarded as the *interval* between recurrent events, since no attempt is made to compute its length in days,[37] and since the number of moons is somewhat uncertain in the native mind.

In native Saulteaux thought the concept of such an interval, reckoned with reference to the recurrence of winter, but not conceived as the sum of a series of smaller divisions of time, is undoubtedly present. But this concept is by no means identical with our concept of the year as a temporal unit of continuous duration reducible to smaller measurable units which we conceive to have a precise beginning and ending reckoned from the stroke of midnight on December thirty-first. When asked to name the "moons," for example, the Saulteaux will begin almost anywhere in the series but usually with the current "moon." Consequently the question whether the Indians, in the absence of such a concept of temporal continuity, actually reckon a beginning or ending of their annual cycle is irrelevant.[38] What is significant is whether some recurring solar event, like a solstice, or some terrestrial occurrence, is traditionally recognized as a discrete point of reference with respect to some temporal interval that is of a higher order of magnitude than the lunation or the season. Such an interval was an integral part of the temporal concepts of the native Saulteaux but was of little practical importance. Yet its recognition explains why at present the Indians often employ the term "winter" in reckoning their ages or to place events in a supra-annual time scale. "Winter," as a recurrent annual event can be used to symbolize a "year," if reckoning in such terms becomes of interest. And if one wishes to say, as Cope does in interpreting the calendrical schemes of other northern peoples, that winter signalizes the "beginning" of the "year" such a statement is also intelligible since it is the recurrence of this season that has received formal emphasis with reference to an annual cycle.

Today the Saulteaux of the Berens River Band proper are familiar, as I have said, with the white man's mode of temporal reckoning. And they use the term *pezígoa'ki,* "one earth," for one year. But I think this is a new term, a judgment that receives correlary support from the fact that Baraga makes "year" and "winter" synonyms.

Although winter is the formalized reference for computing yearly intervals in the aboriginal conceptual scheme, the recurrence of the other seasons provides unformalized points of reference that punctuate equivalent intervals. And among human activities the annual performance of the Midéwīwin was once prominent. Today, the payment of annuities each year by the Dominion Government is another regular occurrence and at the mouth of the river the Indians know that there are legal holidays, like Dominion Day and Labor Day, that recur annually.

Reckoning of Past Events.—The recognition of a yearly interval by no means implies that the year as a temporal unit functions very actively in native life and thought. In terms of aboriginal life, in fact, there was little, if anything, that demanded calculation in annual units of time. Consequently I believe that Cope rightly emphasizes the fact that

although it is often loosely stated the Indian could tell his age by the expression "so many winters had passed over his head," or that he was so many winters old, this expression is no doubt developed through contact with civilized peoples. The expression more in keeping with the Indian calendric systems is that found in so many tribes: "I was so large when a certain event happened." This event may be a year of famine, a year of some epidemic, the growth of a particular tree or grove, or some remarkable exploit. . . . Such vague statements or references as these are probably as near as the Indian, of himself, ever came to considering his age.[39]

Among the Saulteaux, so far as age is concerned, instead of a chronological year count, the life cycle of individuals was divided into a number of terminologically distinguished age grades corresponding to maturation stages. The generic term for child, *apĭnondjĭ*, includes the viable foetus within its connotation, while the infant from birth until it begins to walk is called *ockapĭnondjĭ*, fresh (new, young) child. Sexual differentiation is expressed in the terms *iᶜkwézes*, little girl, and *kwĭwĭzes*, little boy, applied to children under puberty. The next age-grade terminologically recognized is what may be called youth. After puberty and before marriage a male is *ockĭnīge* and a female *ockĭnigiᶜkwe*. For mature individuals there are only terms for married man, *onabemĭmä*, and married woman, *wĭwĭmän*. Bachelors and spinsters are rare and it is interesting to note that the words used for such unmarried individuals are the youth terms with a prefix, *kete-*, meaning "old" (*ketèockĭnīga*, "old young man," and *ketèockĭnĭkwe*, "old young woman".) a kind of temporal paradox. For succeeding periods of maturation there are no terms with a chronological connotation used until old age is reached (*mintĭmoye*, "old woman," *ákīwezi*, "old man.") To indicate extreme old age the augmentative prefix *kᶜtcī-* may be added to these terms.

Such terms, correlated with references to occurrences extrinsic to the individual, such as the signing of the Treaty, the advent of the missionaries in different settlements, the tenure of Hudson's Bay Company post managers, and the Great War (because several Berens River Indians enlisted) or events in the life history of individuals—marriage, journeys, former hunting grounds, customary camping sites—are sufficiently exact, though unformalized, points of reference for purposes of native temporal orientation. They occur again and again in conversation and in the personal reminiscences I have collected. It is in the use of such unformalized reference points that the Saulteaux are most like ourselves,[40] the difference being, of course, that they lack the more exact frame of temporal reference that we possess which permits time measurement in precisely defined units and temporal comparisons of a more accurate order.

Events in the past are also frequently correlated with the life-span of certain deceased relatives of the living or other deceased persons. So long as the names, personal characteristics, and activities of deceased individuals are carried in the memories of living persons a useful, although non-quantitative and unformalized, frame of reference for past events is maintained. The collection of extensive genealogical information has convinced me of the accuracy of the knowledge that is the basis of this human frame of reference. Through the assimilation of a considerable portion of it myself, I found that I was able to use the information acquired in relation to the temporal sequence of certain events much as the Indians themselves do. But in quantitative temporal terms retrospective genealogical information of this sort completely fades out in less than two centuries. One hundred and fifty years is the outside limit of any genuine historic past so far as the Berens River Indians are concerned. Events attributed to so distant a past that they cannot be connected with any known generation of human individuals are simply described as having taken place "long ago." Consequently we are plunged into a bottomless mythological epoch that lacks temporal guide posts of any conventional sort. As a matter of fact, it would be more accurate to assert that once we enter the mythological world of Saulteaux belief, temporal concepts actually lose most, if not all, chronological significance.

One of the reasons for this is the fact that the most prominent anthropomorphic characters of mythology like Wísɑkedjak and Tcɑkábec are not only living beings, they are conceived as immortal. They were alive when the earth was young and they assisted the Indians then. They are still alive today and continue to aid mankind, this latter fact receiving empirical demonstration in dreams and by the manifestation of the presence of such beings in the conjuring lodge. The conventional pattern of dream revelation and the conjuring lodge are, then, institutional means of keeping mythological beings and spiritual entities of other classes constantly contemporary with each new generation of individuals, despite the passage of "time." Such spiritual entities, in fact, are actually more "real" than distant human ancestors no longer remembered. Mythology itself sometimes reflects this emphasis on the contemporaneity of such beings by incorporating episodes with modern trimmings in narratives that contain nuclear elements not only found among the Saulteaux but over wide areas in North America.

It is true, nevertheless, that certain episodes in the mythological narratives provide a basis for certain broad temporal inferences. And independently of immediate mythological references, I found that the Indians entertain similar chronological notions. It is noteworthy, for example, that in many of the mythological narratives, the form of the name given to familiar animals contains the augmentative prefix. There are references to the Great Snake, the Great Mosquito, the Great Beaver, the Great Trout, etc. This has a temporal significance. Formerly the earth was inhabited by many of these monster species now only represented by smaller varieties of their kind. In the myths there are likewise accounts of how certain of these great animals became extinct (the Great Mosquito) or how the familiar variety of the species came into being (as, e.g., small snakes). It was explained to me that the mythological characters had power enough to overcome the monster fauna but that ordinary human beings would be constantly harassed if they had to live on the earth with such creatures today. Nevertheless, a few such species still survive according to the firm conviction of the Indians. There are Indians now living, in fact, who have seen them. But the events in the myths which involve the monster animals are conceptualized as occurring in a far-distant past. They took place "long ago" in a period when the earth was "new." Consequently a temporal distinction is recognized between those days and the present.

Another temporal clue is afforded by the transformation in the appearance of certain animals by Wísakedjak. The latter made the kingfisher much prettier than he once was, shortened the tail of the muskrat, gave the weasel a white coat in winter, etc. Here again a temporal inference lies in the fact there was once an epoch far distant in the past when the familiar animals of today had not assumed their contemporary characteristics.

Human beings, too, were not always like they are now, either in appearance or knowledge. Until Tcakábec, after being in the belly of a fish, was scraped clean by his sister, all human beings were covered with hair. All women once had toothed vaginas. And until Wísakedjak by accident discovered the pleasure of sexual intercourse no one knew about it.

The myth of the theft of summer likewise contains the assertion that at one time winter lasted all the year round.

The flood episode in one of the narratives of the Wísakedjak cycle also has chronological implications since Wísakedjak and the animals previously inhabited an earlier land mass. But the Indians themselves do not appear to follow through such temporal implications with reference to their mythological corpus as a whole. I found that they were not willing to commit themselves to any chronological relationship of the "flood," for example, and the adventures of Tcakábec, although they agreed to the obvious fact that the birth of the winds must have preceded the contest between the North and South Wind that appears in another myth. As a rule, however, the temporal sequence intrinsic to the events of each narrative is accepted without reference to the temporal sequences of any other narrative. Even the narratives of the Wísakedjak cycle are not systematized chronologically. But I have received the impression that the narratives with anthropomorphic heroes like Kaíanwe and Aási are conceptualized as occurring on the earth in the post-fluvial epoch.

On the whole, then, events that are believed to have taken place "long ago" are not systematically correlated with each other in any well-defined temporal schema. They are discrete happenings, often unconnected and sometimes contradictory. Yet the past and the present are part of a whole because they are bound together by the persistence and contemporary reality of mythological characters not even now grown old.

CONCLUSION

For the Saulteaux, as we have seen, temporal orientation depends upon the recurrence and succession of concrete events in their qualitative aspects—events, moreover, which are indications, preparatory sym-

233

bols, and guides for those extremely vital activities through which the Saulteaux obtain a living from the country which they inhabit.

Durations, too, are interwoven with, and experienced as, events in all their individuality. Night is darkness, the stars and their movements, sleep, quietness. Day is the light, the journey of the sun across the sky, the round of domestic duties. A "moon" is the waxing and waning of the moon which occurs when, for instance, the wild rice is being gathered, when activities spanning a number of days are pursued. Any comparison of such durations must be by metaphors and not by exact measures.

Ideas of speed and magnitude necessarily belong to the same category. The Saulteaux are confined to gross time estimates and relatively simple qualitative judgments about speed based upon the observation and comparison of objects in their immediate environment. It would be impossible for them to measure the rate of moving objects at all. Any idea of length of time must be confined to extremely narrow limits. Just as they will reply to the query: How many children have you? by naming them, a direct request for the number of "moons" will result in the naming of them one after another. An answer to: How long ago? becomes: When I was a child; when my father was young, and so on.

All these means of temporal orientation are *local*, limited in their application to the immediate future, the recent past, immediate activities, phenomena known and dealt with in their own environment. Beyond these all is vague and loosely coordinated temporally.

In Western civilization similar undifferentiated experience of time remains, but it is also transcended by abstract quantitative measures which enable us to think far differently about it. We can think in terms of abstract units of temporal duration: of a day in terms of hours, detached from the phenomena themselves, or of a month as a variable unit of time made up of a certain number of days.

Time conceived in this abstract fashion, in continuous and quantitatively defined units, is the basis of an intellectual order of temporal concepts available for use as a standard of reference, or measurement, for all classes of events. Time assumes for us an autonomous character and we are free to manipulate temporal concepts instrumentally, without constant reference to specific events. Thus we can think of it as infinitely divisible, a means for coordinating activities of all sorts with great precision. It likewise makes possible the measurement of exact temporal intervals and the rate and speed of moving objects.

These contrasting differences in the temporal orientation of Saulteaux culture and of Western civilization undoubtedly imply profound differences in the psychological outlook which is constituted by them. Such differences are not functions of primitive mentality or racial makeup. They are a function of culturally constituted experience. In these

234

terms our temporal orientation in Western civilization is likewise a function of experience in a cultural tradition with radically distinct patterns and entirely different historical roots.

Chapter 12 - The Nature and Function of Property as a Social Institution*

ONE OF THE MOST IMPORTANT AND FAR-REACHING CONCLUSIONS THAT has emerged from twentieth-century anthropology is the relativity of culturally constituted values and the immense variability to be found in the specific cultural forms of different human societies. Today this is a commonplace in the social sciences. At the same time, however, it has become increasingly apparent that there are some basic categorical similarities in human culture the world over. Every human group possesses speech, for example, and it has been found that the languages of the world, no matter how they may differ in detail, may be analyzed in comparable terms. Marriage and the family, magic and religion, economic organization, are other examples that come to mind. The recurrence and persistence of such categories suggest that somehow they are fundamental to the organization and maintenance of human society. Some years ago Wissler called attention to this phenomenon and drew up a list of nine basic categories which he called the "universal pattern of culture."[1] Whether every one of his items is correct or not need not detain us here. The main point is that our knowledge of human societies does clearly indicate the recurrence of some typical categories of culturally constituted behavior despite the great variability in the details of their content.

Now one of the items in Wissler's "universal pattern of culture" is property. But he neither defines it nor analyzes its nature and functions as a human institution. It is difficult, therefore, to appraise the validity of property as a basic cultural category in terms of this bald assertion alone. It will be the major aim of this chapter to discuss the fundamental nature of property in relation to the question of its ubiquity as a human institution, and its basic functions. A correlative question which also will be discussed is whether property is a uniquely human institution. This problem is pertinent to the issue involved since property has been attributed to animals.

The Concept of Property.—One of the difficulties in discussing such questions is obvious: When we wish to make cross-cultural comparisons

*Originally published in the *Journal of Legal and Political Sociology,* I (1943), 115-38.

we face lexical and conceptual problems at the outset. For we are compelled to make use of abstract terms like religion, law, or property that not only carry the specific connotations of the institutions to which they refer in Western civilization, but sometimes have been given such precise definition by writers that, in terms of such conceptions, the institutions of primitive peoples are immediately excluded.[2] Thus Seagle maintains that ownership is a relatively late development in human history; that the property "sense" is little developed among primitive peoples and that the "concept of 'possession' rather than ownership is far more suitable in describing the primitive institution."[3] R. A. Dixon uses the existence of an economic surplus as the sine qua non of property. At the beginning of his chapter on the "Origin and Development of Property," he writes:

Far back in the dim recesses of prehistory, when the individual was but an insignificant member of the hunting pack, the products of his feeble efforts—the crude implements, the skins used as clothes, and the food gained in the hunt—were not property. . . . Property did not appear until a definite surplus over subsistence arose. The economic surplus was the phenomenon that gave rise not only to property but to many of the most enduring elements of western culture.

Since, according to Dixon's historic speculations, genuine property as an institution arose in what he calls the "temple-town cultures" (Babylonia, Egypt, Assyria, Greece, and Rome),[4] the obvious inference is that peoples of food-gathering cultures in modern times, and even some of the food producers, do not have property in terms of the criterion adopted.

In contrast to these narrow concepts of property, we find that Thurnwald[5] and Herskovits[6] give innumerable details in regard to the institution of property among primitive peoples, while Beaglehole[7] gives the term a meaning which embraces what he cites as comparable phenomena among animals.

Do the exclusive or inclusive connotations of the term property as used by these authors mean that, after all, the problem is simply one of definition? Must we necessarily be arbitrary in our conceptualization? I think not. Part of the difficulty lies in the fact that when the topic is approached *exclusively* from either a legal or an economic point of view it is almost inevitable that some scholars will reflect their professional bias. And, since the data with which they are most familiar is that of Western culture, it is natural to expect that the characteristic peculiarities of these data will also influence in some way their legal or economic concepts. Thus it seems to me that Seagle is narrowly legalistic in his conceptualization of property, while Dixon's selection of a single economic condition as the criterion of the very existence of property is to my knowledge unique.[8]

Nevertheless, it is lawyers and economists, rather than sociologists or anthropologists, who, in dealing with the institution of property in Western culture from a practical and theoretical point of view, have contributed most to our understanding of it. In the legal field especially a rich and varied vocabulary and a traditional framework of concepts, many derived from Roman law, have been developed. And it is noteworthy that the historians of law and students of jurisprudence are fully aware of the changes in the structure of property relations which have taken place in Western civilization. Even though unfamiliar with the wider reaches of ethnological data they have been forced to grapple with problems in comparative property law because of the national differences within Western culture and the facts of cultural change. For these reasons alone legal contributions to the analysis of property relations must be taken into full account by other social scientists in approaching the study of property in primitive societies.

The Social Aspect of Property.—At the same time, I believe that it is necessary to distinguish between the study of property in its *purely* economic or legal aspects and property considered as a *social institution*. For even in our culture there are aspects of property which ordinarily escape the net of either economist or lawyer. Examples would be the relation of property to political organization as it functions in the power structure of our society and in relation to the class structure and social attitudes. Social institutions are systems of relations which may be crystallized in various patterns depending upon the overall culture patterns and values of a particular society. They cannot be compressed easily into cut and dried definitions. The verbal tags that we use for them are mainly orientational. What we wish to discover when we investigate social institutions is their structure and how they work in relation to other institutions and to the society of which they are a part.

Moreover, when we approach the data of any primitive society, we can neither foresee the particular design of an institution nor all its functional relations. In the case of property, we know how widely and deeply it ramifies into all aspects of our lives in Western society. In dealing with problems of this order we need concepts that lend themselves to structural and functional analysis rather than definitions based upon the particular data of any one culture. Definitions, if purely legal or economic, may only serve to direct our attention to partial aspects of the institution of property in another society, or they may overemphasize specific structural features and thus blind us to important dynamic aspects of the institution as a functioning whole. From a comparative point of view, for instance, property, conceived as a social institution, does not necessarily imply legal relations in the narrow sense as part of its structure. But it may be discovered upon analysis that the social *function* performed by law in securing property interests in our culture may, in another society, be performed by a nonlegal institution. Such variables are of great importance to our understanding of the structure and functioning of property as a *human* institution.

Property as a social institution implies a system of relations among individuals. Like other social institutions it involves rights, duties, powers, privileges, forbearances, etc., of certain kinds. It differs essentially from other social institutions—familial, political, religious, and so on—because, in addition to the relations among the individuals involved, there are always relations of a certain kind to a wide range of objects of various categories (or infrequently, people who function as objects in a particular system of property relations). As Cairns formulates it, "the property relation is triadic: 'A owns B against C,' where C represents all other individuals . . . ."[9]

This triadic relation which characterizes the institution of property has not always been clearly recognized. An oversimplified and inadequate formulation of the property relation is to omit C and say that "A owns B." In terms of such a dyadic formulation the essentially social dimension of property is submerged and only the relation between people and objects thrust into view. But the conditions under which A is enabled to assert and maintain any claim to object B, and the kind of rights he exercises over it, are the most fundamental aspects of property as an institution. The relations of other persons to A and A's relations to them are involved. Property is a social institution because, like other institutions, it structuralizes human relations in order that certain ends may be achieved.

It seems likely that the oversimplified conceptualization of the property relation in dyadic rather than triadic terms is at the root of the essential ambiguity which has characterized the term property in common speech and sometimes in law. For property is a term commonly applied to both *objects* that are said to be owned as well as the *rights* exercised over such objects. While this ambiguity has been noted for decades[10] and is assumed to be clearly understood in legal parlance, at the same time it has repeatedly called for comment down to the present day.[11] Cairns, indeed, after noting the ambiguity goes on to say that ". . . it would seem from the point of view of both legal and economic analysis that the use of the term property to denote external objects is misleading and should be abandoned."[12]

Patterns of Rights, Duties, and Powers.—If we wish to understand property as an institution in any society our primary concern must be an analysis of the pattern of rights, duties, privileges, powers, etc., which control the behavior of individuals or groups in relation to one another and to the custody, possession, use, enjoyment, disposal, etc., of various classes of objects.[13] In such an undertaking we have to reckon with an exceedingly complex network of structural relations and a wide range of variables, the specific pattern or constellation of which constitutes the structure of property as a social institution in any particular case.

First of all it is necessary to consider the nature and the kinds of rights exercised and their correlative duties and obligations. What sometimes has been considered the essence of the property relation in Western

239

society, viz. exclusive use, enjoyment, and disposition of an object for an unlimited period of time,[14] is only one specific constellation of property rights, a limiting case,[15] as it were. As a matter of fact, absolute control of property by an owner is nonexistent in our society and according to Seagle "in no legal system have rights of property been absolute. There are always the rights of escheat and eminent domain, and numerous restrictions on the use of property, etc."[16] And Ely quotes R. von Jhering as once remarking that an absolute right of property "would result in the dissolution of society."[17] This absence of absolute property rights as a sociological fact thus emphasizes the importance of ownership as part of an organized scheme of social relations that gains its full significance only with reference to the values and institutions of a society considered as a whole.

In all societies, then, property comprises a "bundle of rights,"[18] not a single right, nor an absolute right. These rights may be of different kinds. It is necessary to determine, for instance, whether only the right of using is implied or also the right of using up (*jus abutendi*). Is there the right to destroy in the case of things which can be used without destroying them, as well as in the case of things destroyed in the using? Is the right of alienation included? Does this right likewise include bequest and if there is the right of bequest are there also special limitations imposed? All of these rights—and others—that make up a "bundle" of property rights may be found as more or less independent variables in different cultural contexts and appear in different combinations and with various restrictions when we move from one society to another. In many primitive societies there is a very tangled skein for us to unravel.

The problem of analysis is further complicated by another fact. The term "right" is replete with ambiguity even in the law itself.[19] This has been long recognized by jurists but it was Wesley Newcomb Hohfeld who, in his system of basic legal concepts, forged an analytical tool that has been recognized as of capital importance in clearly distinguishing between rights of various kinds, as well as other jural concepts.[20] Hohfeld demonstrated the utility of his scheme by many examples from the law of torts and contracts, as well as property. But his attempt to deal precisely and realistically with legal relations in this manner has a wider sociological importance. Hoebel recently has shown how illuminating the Hohfeldian analysis may prove when applied to data derived from primitive societies.[21] He points out that "Hohfeld's fundamental concepts are more universal than even their inventor himself realized. They fit not only the fundamental legal relations, but also the fundamentals of any complex of imperative social reciprocity." Certainly Hoebel has been extremely successful in clarifying several cases involving complex property rights by means of them.

Concrete rights, duties, etc., are, of course, inseparable from persons so that the second variable in any comparative analysis of property as a social institution concerns the individuals or groups of individuals in whom rights and privileges, powers, etc., are invested and those who play the correlative roles in the operation of the whole complex schema of relations. If one simply starts with some vaguely defined notion of "ownership" and inquires in verbal terms alone about it among primitive peoples, an investigation of property as an institution among them does not get very far. As Firth says,

A preliminary approach through language is less valuable than it seems at first. It is easy to get statements from natives in which possessive pronouns are applied to things, and which even the anthropologist may regard as expressions of ownership. In fact, they may indicate simply activity in connection with the object, or participation with others in a complicated scheme of activities.[22] [Furthermore while] primitive communities rarely have a simple linquistic expression for "ownership" which can be equated directly with our terms . . . they do have expressions which amount in effect to the same thing, if they be interpreted in terms of concrete behavior.[23]

In fact, Diamond has pointed out that the term "ownership" which is so familiar to us was not used in England until the sixteenth century. But this does not mean that property as an institution did not exist.[24] It does mean, however, as Malinowski insisted, that "the anthropologist who has to define native property rights must rely not on verbal usage alone, but on the series of acts in regard to the object which represent immediate and ultimate control over it."[25]

Property in Primitive Societies.—It is an extraordinary fact, and probably one of historical importance from the standpoint of the sociology of knowledge, that the question *who* owns property in primitive societies has not only received an undue amount of attention, as compared with the problem of the analysis of the nature and kinds of rights exercised, but that it has been conceived in terms of such simple alternatives as individual *versus* communistic ownership.[26] Despite the insistence of contemporary anthropologists[27] that the antithesis is a false one, that "communism" as applied to primitive peoples is a fuzzy term, that as ordinarily used communistic property rights are not typical of primitive societies and that plenty of evidence for individual ownership exists, there are those who, like Seagle, still remain unconvinced.[28]

While it is quite true that the controversy has been beset with verbal ambiguities, as Herskovits says, nevertheless it is also true that anthropologists themselves have not always been precise enough in either their analysis or their terminology. It is here that the Hohfeldian schema may provide a sharper intellectual tool. Malinowski is a beautiful case in point because he has been unusually explicit in exposing the difficulties he experienced in working through to a satisfactory exposition of ownership among the Trobrianders. In the first place, he found it necessary to reject the statements of an earlier observer, Rivers, that "one of the objects of Melanesian culture which is usually, if not always, the subject of common ownership is the canoe."[29] He then proceeded to analyze

241

the ownership of Trobriand canoes in terms of concrete rights, privileges, and duties,[30] and later undertook the analysis of the even more complex situation with respect to land tenure in similar terms.[31] His conclusion was that, "ownership, therefore, can be defined neither by such words as 'communism,' nor 'individualism,' nor by reference to 'joint-stock company' systems or 'personal enterprise,' but by the concrete facts and conditions of use. It is the sum of duties, privileges and mutualities which bind the joint owners to the object and to each other."[32] As Hoebel comments,

. . . in this he is very close to the Hohfeldian type of thinking and terminology. It seems likely that if his case had been put explicitly in Hohfeldian fundamental terms, his comprehensive grasp of the nature of property forms in primitive Melanesian society could not be grossly misconstrued, especially not by a student of law [Seagle]. For if a complex legal and social institution is reduced in clarity to its fundamental components, the vagary of gross catch-all concepts is banished. Confusion and useless argumentation go out with the catch-alls, for it is in the periphery of their fuzzy boundaries that all the fighting occurs.[33]

The third set of variables is the things, or objects, over which property rights are extended. From this angle of approach it is interesting to note that, from time to time, categorical differences have been asserted to exist between the kinds of objects which are the subject of rights among civilized as compared with primitive peoples, or at different stages of cultural evolution, or in different "culture circles."[34] Rights in land, for example, have been denied to hunting and pastoral peoples,[35] rights in incorporeal property have been considered the offspring of highly sophisticated legal notions, and wives have been equated with chattels in certain primitive societies, as compared with our own. Recent investigation and analysis, however, indicate that such clear-cut differences simply do not exist.

As Herskovits points out,[36] the denial of land ownership among hunters and pastoralists was linked with the pseudo-history of the social evolutionary theories of the nineteenth century. According to these, "allotment of land regularised in customary law" was reputed to have its origin in the agricultural stage of evolution. F. G. Speck was a pioneer in demonstrating that the Algonkian hunters of the North American forests *did* have property rights in hunting grounds[37] and, despite the expression of dissent in a few quarters as to the complete aboriginality of all the features of their property system as it now exists, Speck's contention has prevailed.[38] Land tenure among hunting peoples in other parts of the world as well as among pastoralists has been subsequently demonstrated.[39]

If the core of the institution of property is rights rather than material things, then any profound significance in the differentiation of corporeal property from incorporeal property breaks down. Rights may be exercised with respect to any valuable object of any conceivable kind. This was clearly seen by MacLeod[40] and also by Hohfeld.[41] Consequently, neither the existence of incorporeal property among primitives should surprise us, nor the extension of the term property by the courts of the United States to cover such intangible assets as "good will."[42]

Lowie has discussed what he calls "incorporeal" property in primitive societies,[43] although the items he discusses clearly fall in Commons' "intangible" class. That is to say, they are valuables which are assets in the sense that they may have exchange-value. They are not in the nature of "promises to pay" (incorporeal property in Commons' sense). Thus, we have such things as rights in songs, in magical formulae and legends. Despite the evidence presented by Lowie, Seagle makes a number of objections to equating these data with modern legal concepts and thinks "it is wrong to criticize modern legal historians[44] for regarding the distinction between corporeal and incorporeal rights as characteristic of mature law." Hoebel supports Lowie against Seagle by a careful analysis in Hohfeldian terms of the songs and mystic powers of a Plains Indian obtained in a dream revelation.[45] It seems to me that it is as difficult to deny the term ownership in this case as it would be to dispute the logic by which the courts in our society have come to include good will or other intangible assets as objects of property rights.

Despite an old tradition to the contrary, property rights in wives are not in any way typical of primitive peoples and it would seem that cases in which it is asserted that wives are bought and sold as chattels need fresh analysis. In Africa, at least, where a transfer of goods so frequently validates a marriage, careful modern observers have pointed out again and again that the so-called "bride-price" (bride wealth) does not indicate that the bride is purchased,[46] or that the rights of her husband are in the nature of property rights. That European institutions, superficially viewed, can be interpreted in the same way is illustrated by the fact that a sophisticated Dahomean inquired of Herskovits "whether or not the French institution of the dowry did not imply that the father gave a *dot* to purchase a husband for his daughter." A basic confusion seems to have arisen from a bias created by the economic structure of Western society. Because of the existence of our price system and the market, we are apt to assume that any transfer of valuables is indicative of a commercial deal of some sort. Consequently the transfer of a woman to a man accompanied by a transfer of goods from the family of the man to her family savors of commercialism. The woman is seen as property in the narrow sense. An analysis of the whole situation in terms of the complex rights and obligations involved produces a totally different picture. It seems to me that one of Seagle's objections to accepting incorporeal property in primitive societies as genuine property illustrates the same kind of argument in reverse. He says that the transactions under which rights in incorporeal property occur "do not have a commercial flavor."[47] Presumably, one of the tests of genuine property for him is its transfer in commercial transactions. This is obviously an outstanding feature of property in capitalistic society. But it can hardly be an absolute test in the noncommercial societies of primitive peoples. In the case of "wife-purchase" we have seen how the assumption of such a commercial context may obscure the actual facts.

On the whole, the kinds of objects which enter into the system of property rights in different human societies intergrade and overlap rather than exhibit sharp categorical distinctions. It would be more fruitful to inquire into the conditions that give rise to an emphasis upon this or that class of object (e.g., land) than to attempt to make such differences as exist a function of social evolution, of "culture circles," or of factors intrinsic to primitive man as compared with ourselves. The more precise our analysis the sooner we shall be able to make fruitful cross-cultural analyses and to isolate differential conditions of genuine significance to account for the facts observed.

Property Sanctions.—Property, considered as a social institution, not only implies the exercise of rights and duties with respect to objects of value by the individuals of a given society; it also embraces the specific social sanctions which reinforce the behavior that makes the institution a going concern. The nature of these sanctions and the way in which they work is the fourth variable to be considered in any comprehensive view of systems of property relations. If the dynamics of the institution of property is to be wholly understood its sanctions are of fundamental importance.

The positive sanctions of property rights are those which integrate the motivations of individuals with the basic economic processes of production, distribution, and consumption and with traditional beliefs and values that may be connected with ownership (e.g., property rights in certain classes of objects which symbolize rank, afford prestige, or provide a fulcrum for the exercise of political power). Negative sanctions, on the other hand, are those which threaten the individual with penalties if he infringes upon the rights and privileges of others. Negative sanctions usually command more attention than positive ones in discussions of property since the exclusion of others from the control of an object is a fundamental correlative of a property right.[48] Sanctions, in short, are culturally constituted means for motivating the individuals of a given society in such a way that they will play their roles in the total scheme of property relations in the most efficient manner.

The actual sanctions which operate in any particular society stem from traditional beliefs about the nature of the world, the relations of man to spiritual beings or other forces, ethical values, and the structuralization of society itself. Since all of these vary widely as we go from society to society, so do the particular sanctions that reinforce property rights. From the standpoint of a narrow definition of law, for instance, it is quite true that we find societies in which there are no courts to hear disputes nor any organized means of enforcing remedies, nor any centralized political authority that exercises sovereign powers. It is obvious that in such societies property rights cannot be secured "legally" in the sense in which this term is used in Western culture (i.e., by the same organized means). But this does not mean that property rights are not sanctioned at all in societies without legal institutions. It simply means that they are sanctioned differently. In Saulteaux society, for example, the prevailing sanction rests on a belief that disease will strike the offender or a member of his family, or that an offended party may retaliate by witchcraft.[49]

Property and law, however, are so closely associated in the Western mind that it is not strange to find that in the legal theory of property—attributed to Hobbes, Montesquieu, and Bentham[50]—they are considered historically inseparable. According to Commons, "the 'legal theory' asserts that property cannot exist without the state. Viewed externally, it is the coercive *power* of the state that creates and enforces the rights of property. Viewed internally, it is the *purpose* of the state with reference to the objects which it wishes to attain which leads it to create, define, and enforce these rights."[51] Since there are many human societies in which a politically organized state in this sense does not exist, and since there are comparable rights and duties in such societies which organize the relations of individuals to each other and to classes of valuable objects, all the legal theory of property can mean is that in such societies property rights are not "legally" created nor "legally" secured. From a cross-cultural standpoint, therefore, the greatest sociological interest lies in the fact that legal sanctions in the narrow sense are a function of a certain kind of social organization. Sanctions of this order are only one among many other variables.[52] The *existence* of property as a universal social institution, once the empirical facts are taken into account, is not actually challenged by the legal theory.

In fact, Bentham's often quoted statement that, "Property and law are born together and die together. Before laws were made there was no property; take away laws, and property ceases,"[53] is not without ambiguity. What does Bentham actually mean by *law?* In the very paragraph preceding this quotation there is evidence that to Bentham "law" was practically equivalent to what we would now call "social order." For he says: "If we suppose the least agreement among savages to respect the acquisitions of each other, *we see the introduction of a principle to which no name can be given but that of law.*" (Italics ours.) Since all human societies do embody such a principle it is possible to reinterpret Bentham's meaning by the phrase, "property and society are born together." Thus the statements of one representative of the legal theory of property, if correctly understood, support the view that property rights are universally recognized in human societies and socially (legally) sanctioned.

Variation in sanctions leads to the general conclusion that different means may be employed in different societies to achieve the same ends. But sanctions of some kind are as universal as property rights themselves. In fact, Westermarck, on the basis of his survey of penalties for theft and robbery in a wide gamut of human societies, concluded that "the universal condemnation of what we call theft or robbery proves that the right of property exists among all races of men known to us."[54] The relative efficacy of different kinds of sanctions is another interesting question. One gets the impression, for example, that theft is of less frequent incidence in many primitive societies than in our own. One might argue from this that property rights in these societies were reinforced with greater success than in Western culture, but such questions need more detailed study. At any rate, nonlegal (i.e., moral and religious) sanctions may not only serve the same purpose as legal sanctions; under certain conditions they even seem to be more effective.

If the core of property as a social institution lies in a complex system of recognized rights and duties with reference to the control of valuable objects, and if the roles of the participating individuals are linked by this means with basic economic processes, and if, besides, all these processes of social interaction are validated by traditional beliefs, attitudes, and values, and sanctioned in custom and law, it is apparent that we are dealing with an institution extremely fundamental to the structure of human societies as going concerns. For, considered from a functional point of view, property rights are institutionalized means of defining *who* may control various classes of valuable objects for a variety of present and future purposes and the *conditions* under which this power may be exercised. Since valuable objects in all human societies must include, at the minimum, some objects of material culture that are employed to transform the raw materials of the physical environment into consumable goods, there must be socially recognized provisions for handling the control of such elementary capital goods as well as the distribution and consumption of the goods that are produced. Consequently, property rights are not only an integral part of the economic organization of any society; they are likewise a coordinating factor in the functioning of the social order as a whole.[55] Bunzel displays penetrating insight when she draws an analogy between the "structural and dynamic significance" of a system of property relations as "a channeling of the relationships between men and things" and the role "that kinship has in the field of relationships between individuals."[56] Bunzel does not expand this point, but it may be rephrased slightly by saying that if kinship be regarded as the social instrument that structuralizes the fundamental roles which individuals play toward each other as persons, property as a social institution is the instrument that structuralizes the roles which individuals play in the complex system of human relations that prevail in regard to the ownership of valuable objects, whether material or not. What the objects of value may be depends upon beliefs about the nature of the world and man's relation to the forces that are at work in it, as well as upon such factors as scarcity, in the economic sphere. Hunting or garden magic, therefore, may be as valuable as any material object or some resources of limited quantity. Social recognition of values is integrally connected with ownership regulations and these in turn are supported by social sanctions. In any society human relations must be ordered so that basic interests are recognized and secured. Property as a social institution fulfills this task.

A Reinterpretation of the Natural Right Theory.—If property is a ubiquitous human institution it is easy to understand how it was that some eighteenth century thinkers came to include property rights in the general class of "natural rights." These thinkers did not mean that property rights were instinctive, that men were born with an "acquisitive instinct"; this was a much later doctrine which, along with other instinctivistic explanations of human conduct, scarcely merits serious consideration today.[57] What was meant by the eighteenth century thinkers was that the individual as a member of society needed protection against any infringement of what were considered to be his fundamental rights as a human being.[58]

The term "natural rights" [says Ritchie] is generally restricted to those of them that are conceived to be more fundamental than others, from which others may be deduced, or to which the others are only auxiliary . . . . with regard to certain rights, notably the right of property, there is a marked divergency among different believers in natural rights, some giving it a prominent place in their list of natural rights, others denying that it is a natural right at all, or limiting the objects to which such rights apply, or restricting it in various ways, excluding at least some property rights from their law of nature.[59]

Such limitations were guided by what was believed to have "already prevailed in some primitive state of nature," or by the opposition of "natural" to "that which is clearly due to human institutions." Elaborate political institutions or rules governing inheritance or bequest did not seem to fall into a "natural" category. "The law of nature, moreover (as with the Roman jurists), is something behind and independent of the variations of local usage: it is a universal code." From the standpoint of our contention that property rights of some kind are in fact not only universal but that they are a basic factor in the structuralization of the role of individuals in relation to basic economic processes, it is significant that eighteenth century thinkers sensed the fundamental importance of property rights, even though their reasoning was along different lines.

Property in Infrahuman Societies.—If property rights are indeed ubiquitous so far as human societies are concerned, a further question still remains. Are they *uniquely* human or do property rights also exist in *infra*-human societies? Sometimes the latter has been asserted to be the case. However, in view of the analysis that has been given, there are a number of reasons why we must conclude that, on the contrary,

247

property as an institution is a unique as well as a ubiquitous human institution.

Discussions of property among animals have centered around such phenomena as food-storing, the defense of the nest, prey, territorial domain, etc. There will be no need either to review the reported facts here,[60] or to question them in any way. The problem at issue is the interpretation of their significance. To put the matter baldly, neither the *de facto* control exercised by animals over certain objects, nor the aggressive defense of them, is itself evidence that property as an institution exists among them. The question is: In what sense are such phenomena comparable with *the socially recognized and sanctioned rights* in valuable objects that characterize property in human societies? The ambiguity in the use of the term property is no doubt partly responsible for the reputed human analogies found among animals. If one starts with the naïve idea that property is some kind of physical object that "belongs" to someone and it is then observed that animals store food or defend their nests or territory against aggressors, it is easy to say that the food, nest, or territory is the animal's "property" and then to generalize further, on the basis of wider observations, and say that animals as well as human beings have "property." To do so, however, ignores the fact that the reputed analogy stops short at a very crucial point. In human societies the basis of ownership is the correlative obligations others have to allow me to exercise my property rights. Property rights, in short, are *rights in rem.* Indeed, one universal indication of this is the fact that property rights are not only socially recognized, they are socially sanctioned. From the standpoint of individual motivation this means that the infringement of such rights is not avoided simply because of the physical force the owner may exert against me directly if I challenged his rights. My motivation is a function of the process of socialization that I have undergone. I have introcepted the fundamental values of my society. They have become part of me. Consequently, I also recognize the moral, religious, or legal penalties that may be released if I do not do my duty. And lastly, as an active participant in the social order, I am likewise an owner and take the same attitude toward my property rights as another individual takes toward his.[61]

Among animals we meet with entirely different conditions. All we observe is the utilization or possession (in the sense of physical custody) of certain objects which bear a relation to the biological needs of the organism or group of organisms.[62] There are no social sanctions in animal societies and no attitudes comparable to human attitudes because there are no rights to be sanctioned. For we cannot properly speak of rights, obligations, and privileges among animals. Such abstractions as these arise from the specific values established in a cultural tradition; they can be verbally formulated and they function in terms of culturally constituted statuses occupied by individuals and the social roles which such statuses demand. Animals, on the other hand, lack speech and culturally determined values, and the roles which individual animals play are primarily a function of innate biological equipment rather than the product of a socialization process, as in man. Thus, while rights, duties, powers, and privileges are of the very essence of the human social order, because it is an order based on *learned* roles, the opposite is true in the case of animals. Lacking social sanctions, therefore, the behavior of animals is motivated in quite different terms from that of human beings. The individual animal cannot take the attitude of other animals because he has not been socialized in terms of common traditional values. Consequently, an individual animal, or group of animals, must be prepared to meet any threat to food, nest, or territory by the exertion of physical force. A dog will fight any other dog who tries to take his bone.[63] No other remedy is possible, for this is the inevitable result in circumstances where there is no institutionalization of claims to objects of value. Writers of earlier centuries, like Thomas Hobbes, who pictured the primeval condition of man as one in which there was no "notion of right and wrong," "no arts," "no propriety" [property], no industry ("because the fruit thereof is uncertain"), where social interaction was dominated by "continual fear and danger of violent death" because the hand of every man was against every other man and individuals were "without other security than what their own strength and their own invention shall furnish them withal,"[64] were not actually depicting human societies at all. For human society, by definition, implies the existence of ordered relations and ordered relations mean that individuals *do* enjoy the security of socially sanctioned rights and obligations of various kinds. Among them we inevitably find socially recognized and sanctioned interests in valuable objects. The fact that in all human societies individuals are secured against the necessity of being constantly on the alert to defend such objects from others by physical force alone is one of the primary contributions of the institution of property to a *human* social order and the security of the individual.

Chapter 13 - Fear and Anxiety
as Cultural and Individual
Variables in a Primitive Society*

$\mathbf{M}$ANY YEARS AGO DEWEY POINTED OUT SOME OF THE INADEQUACIES OF a simple stimulus-response concept in psychology.

> That which is, or operates as, a stimulus, turns out to be a function, in a mathematical sense, of behavior in its serial character. Something, not yet a stimulus, breaks in upon an activity already going on and *becomes* a stimulus in virtue of the relations it sustains to what is going on in this continuing activity. . . . It *becomes* the stimulus in virtue of what the organism is already preoccupied with. To call it, to think of it, as a stimulus without taking into account the behavior that is already going on is so arbitrary as to be nonsensical. Even in the case of abrupt changes, such as a clap of thunder when one is engrossed in reading, the *particular* force of that noise, its property as stimulus, is determined by what the organism is already doing in interaction with a particular environment.[1]

The general principle implied in these remarks suggests a further inference. The *effects* of stimuli cannot be predicted solely from their intrinsic properties. This conclusion is borne out by some recent experiments.[2] These indicate that inferences in regard to the emotional experience of individuals cannot wholly be based upon an account of immediate stimuli and bodily responses. In addition, knowledge is required of what the individual actually experiences. In the experiments referred to

> the stimulus-situation was identical: adrenalin chloride was intra-muscularly injected. The physiological or bodily response was identical: certain phenomena of sweating, shivering, etc., were produced. But the individual mental processes were remarkably different. One person had no emotion—the emotion was "cold" and impersonal; another had a *pseudo* or *quasi emotion,* reminiscent of another occasion when he had experienced a similar set of symptoms, but not an emotion in the present; and a third individual really felt the complete emotion of fear.[3]

The differential factors in these cases must lie, of course, in the constitution or personal history of the individuals concerned. If we seek them in the latter sphere the problem is further complicated by the universal and primary importance of learned or acquired experience in the broadest sense of the term. In life situations in particular, as contrasted with the more highly controlled experimental setup of the laboratory, the relevance of factors of this order, while extremely complex and difficult to evaluate with precision, cannot be ignored. It is hardly

*Reprinted from *The Journal of Social Psychology,* IX (1938), 25-47.

surprising, then, to find that C. Landis, at the close of a recent survey of experimental data stresses the need for further investigation of the relation between learning processes and affective experience. He writes:

> The question of nature *versus* nurture is as marked in emotions as in any other type of human behavior. It is customary to speak of emotion as a natural reaction; one which is little varied by experience. Certainly this is a very inexact concept. What the natural emotional life of an individual might be like is an unknown territory. Emotional life is modified more rigorously in the growth and education of an individual than perhaps any other variety of human experience. The reason for the statement so frequently made that emotion is a natural reaction, unmodified by learning, is that emotional reactions occur in such large units of physiological disturbances that they frequently swamp the mental life of the individual. [Consequently] the most important line of future research is that of the nature of the relation existing between emotion and learning in the broadest sense of each term.[4]

If we consider this problem not only with respect to the affective experience of individuals in Western society, but from the standpoint of humanity as a whole, a fresh angle of attack is indicated. It is possible to investigate, analyze, and compare the factors that influence the typical or commonly experienced affects of individuals in human societies with widely different cultural traditions, as well as the factors that are involved in the affective experience of individuals who deviate from the collective norms of these societies. Factors of the former order I shall call *cultural variables.*

Since culture includes the content of socially transmitted experience, to which each new individual born into a society is exposed, it provides the primary frame of reference to which all varieties of learned behavior may be related. With respect to the emotions, culture defines: (*a*) the situations that will arouse certain emotional responses and not others; (*b*) the degree to which the response is supported by custom or inhibitions demanded; (*c*) the particular forms which emotional expression may take.[5] It is to these norms that the individual will learn to accommodate his behavior and in terms of which his affective experience will function.

The Saulteaux Indians whose fears and anxieties I wish to discuss live on the Berens River in Canada. I think that the relation between some of the characteristic fears experienced by these people and their traditional system of beliefs will become sufficiently clear if I discuss the former with reference to the situations in which they occur. Some of these situations, such as illness, are common to human life everywhere. Yet they do not give rise to equivalent affects. The psychological differentia, I believe, are to be sought in the content of the beliefs that are part of the cultural heritage of these Indians. These beliefs not only define each situation for the individual in a typical manner, they structuralize it emotionally. But at the same time it is interesting to note that there are usually traditional means available for the alleviation of culturally constituted fears. The individual is not altogether left at loose ends; he may obtain some relief and reassurance through the utilization of institutionalized defenses.

Encounters with Animals.—The traditional attitude of the Berens River Indians towards animal life must be distinguished from our own. Animals, like men, have a body and a soul. (See Chap. 11.) Each species is controlled by a spiritual boss or owner that is of the nature of a transcendental being. Guns and traps are of no avail if this spiritual boss of the species is offended and does not wish human beings to obtain his underlings. Consequently, wild animals as a whole must be treated with respect lest their bosses be offended.

While this general attitude is characteristic, the affective responses of the Indians to different animals is not uniform. It would be impossible, however, to make any a priori judgment, based upon our attitude towards wild life, as to which animals are feared and which are not. Wolves and bears, for instance, are common in this region, but the Indians are never afraid of them. The creatures they fear most are snakes, toads, and frogs, animals that are actually among the most harmless in their environment. Indeed, the only species of snake that occurs is a small variety of garter snake.

The attitude of these Indians towards snakes was brought home to me by a striking occurrence. Once when I was traveling with a small party, one of the Indians sighted a snake, perhaps eight inches long, swimming in the water near the rock where we were eating lunch. The Indian picked up his gun and took a shot at it, missed, and shot again, and missed. The snake started to swim towards the shore, and as it began to wriggle up the rock, another man picked up a paddle and with a few hard strokes, managed to kill it. But that was not enough. They built a small fire and burned the harmless creature to a crisp.

While this episode may appear to be a trivial one, it was no trifling matter to the Indians. Even objectively considered it suggests an exaggerated affective response to an animal of this sort. To say the least, there was nothing intrinsic to the situation as such that demanded the immolation of a harmless garter snake on a pyre. It is partially intelligible, however, if reference is made to mythology. Once the earth was inhabited by many monster snakes and some of these persist today. A few individuals claim to have seen them and they are much feared. It is the identification of actual snakes with the mythical variety that accounts in part for the attitude of the Indians toward the former. But on the occasion described there was more involved than this: The snake was burnt because its approach to our camp was interpreted as having a meaning that aroused apprehension and consequently demanded the treatment received.

Wild animals, of course, habitually avoid the dwellings of men so that we might suppose that the Indian would "naturally" be startled

252

to find a bear or snake near his wigwam, or to find a bird or squirrel inside of it. The fear that some people in our society experience when a bat flies in their bedroom at night might be thought to be comparable to the emotions which the Indians experience. But this is not the case. The beliefs of the Indians make the affect a qualitatively different thing. For to them the approach of a wild animal of any sort to their camp or habitation is an ill omen. It is a sign that someone is trying to bewitch them. The animal is thought to be the malevolent agent of a sorcerer.

In one case a man had been ill. He had taken lots of medicine but it seemed to do him no good. Then he noticed that a bear kept coming to his camp almost every night after dark. Once it would have gotten into his wigwam if he had not been warned in a dream. Since an evilly disposed medicine man may sometimes disguise himself as a bear, the sick man's anxiety rapidly increased. He became convinced that a certain man had bewitched him. Finally, when the bear appeared one night he got up, went outdoors, and shouted to the animal that he knew what it was trying to do. He also threatened to retaliate with dire results to the suspected witch, if the bear ever returned. The animal ran off and never came back. (See also Chap. 8.)

Even if birds alight on a dwelling, it is considered an evil omen. It is still more serious if wild animals actually enter a human habitation. On such occasions, the animal may not only be killed but burnt, as was the snake, since this is the appropriate institutionalized procedure. This act serves to dispel the fear engendered as it is thought to be the safest way of disposing of malevolent agents of this kind.

One night after settling down to sleep in our tent, my traveling companion, an Indian about sixty-five years of age, found a toad hopping towards him. He became so panic stricken that it was difficult for him to kill it. But he finally managed to do so. Then he went outside the tent with a flashlight in order to discover if there were any more toads about. He killed several with a stone. Then he collected a number of large stones and, after carefully examining all sides of the tent, weighted down the canvas here and there so that there was no possibility of any more of them crawling in. He slept hardly at all the rest of the night. After this experience, W. B. always took special pains to see that the front of the tent was closed at night and weighted snugly to the ground with a line of stones. We jokingly called this our "toad dam." It must be emphasized that this man had spent most of his life in the bush, was an excellent hunter and accustomed to handling all sorts of animals. What then were the determinants of his phobia? In the first place, toads are not simply "loathsome creatures" to these Indians. They are associated with evil forces, certain parts of the animal being used in malevolent magic. Hence they are to be avoided and even their presence bodes no good for the reason I have stated. But there were more complex determinants in the fear response of W. B. It is said that if the taboo upon narrating myths in summer is broken, toads will come and crawl up one's clothes. Now my friend W. B. had been telling me native stories from time to time so that the visits of the toads were good empirical evidence of the truth of the native belief. But since W. B. was a Christian and believed himself to be emancipated from native "superstition" (although, of course, this was not actually the case) it may be inferred that the conflict engendered was somewhat disturbing to him. There were then several etiological factors at work: (a) the generalized belief in the malevolent attributes of toads; (b) the notion that their presence in a dwelling was an ill omen; (c) the fact that a taboo had been broken, specifically indicated by the presence of the toads; and (d) the conflict engendered by the semiemancipated attitude of W. B. towards these notions.

In addition, however, there was another factor peculiar to the personal history of W. B. When a young boy, a toad had crawled up his pants and he had crushed it against his bare skin. This experience would appear to be an important differential factor which may account to some extent for the *exaggerated* fear reaction of W. B. to toads as compared with that of the other Indians. This difference was objectively proved on one occasion when I saw another Indian deliberately pick up a toad and put it near W. B. to tease him. Judged by strength of affect, W. B. was abnormal in comparison with the other Indians observed. But etiologically viewed, his phobia cannot be fully explained by reference to his personal history alone. It needs to be related to the native beliefs in regard to toads and the situational factors already mentioned.

The generalized fear of toads and frogs among these Indians is fostered by another fact. Monster species are reputed still to inhabit the country, the tracks of which are sometimes seen.

A few years ago several Indians were traveling across Lake Winnipeg in a sail boat. They pulled in at Birch Island. While a fire was being built and some food cooked, the man who told me this story took his gun and went off to shoot ducks. He came across some fresh tracks near the shore. They were about the size of a man's hand and formed exactly like the tracks of a frog. They indicated a jump of approximately six feet. The Indian who made this discovery hurried back to his companions. They went and examined the tracks, and agreed with him that they were those of the giant frog. The narrator said that he wanted to follow the tracks inland but his companions were so frightened that they insisted upon leaving the island at once.

The psychological significance of this anecdote can best be appreciated by emphasizing two points. First, these Indians are expert hunters and accustomed to recognizing the tracks of all the animals in their environment; second, they were armed. We can only conclude that their misidentification of the tracks was a result of the mental-set which their belief in the reality of monster frogs imposed and that their fears cannot be dissociated from the malevolent attributes reputed to creatures against whom even guns might not be adequate protection. If we take these factors into account, they evidenced a normal response to a danger situation as defined for them in cultural terms.

Disease Situations.—Since disease situations occur and recur among all peoples, they provide excellent material for the investigation of the cultural differentia that may influence the individual's attitude towards his own illness and the quality of the anxieties that his relatives and friends may experience. Different human groups have different traditional theories of disease causation and when an individual falls ill, his emotional attitudes and those of his associates are intimately related to the theories held.

Among the Berens River Indians, broken limbs, colds, constipation, toothache, and other minor ailments are considered fortuitous in origin and do not arouse any marked affective states. But a prolonged illness, which has not responded to ordinary methods of treatment, a sudden illness, or one that is characterized by symptoms that are considered in any way peculiar, arouses apprehension or even fear. Why? Because of the belief that the person may have been bewitched. The individual believes that some one is trying to kill him. He becomes more and more worried and begins to reflect on his past activities and associations in order to recollect who it is that may wish him out of the way. In such a situation institutionalized means of protection are readily available. A conjurer or seer may be hired to discover the person responsible and measures taken to counteract the evil influence. Jealousy is often the motive attributed to the witch, frequently arising out of rivalry situations.

In 1876 when the Treaty with the Dominion Government was signed and an elective chieftainship first established, J. B. and a powerful medicine man named Sag-α-tcīweäs were rivals for the new office. J. B. won. The next day he put on his new uniform and felt fine. But that night he was suddenly taken ill. It was inferred that Sag-α-tcīweäs was responsible. Later he developed a recurrent skin disease that did not respond to native drugs. This was likewise attributed to the powerful medicine man he defeated. In this case the usual apprehension typical in such a situation was balanced by the powerful ego of J. B. and the confidence he had in his ability to withstand the malevolent intention of his rival. J. B. asserted more than once that he would outlive Sag-α-tcīweäs, and he did.

The special form of sorcery that causes the most fear is based on the theory that material objects can be magically projected into the body of the victim. Sebaceous cysts, lumps of any kind, and other symptoms are evidence of the presence of such objects. They are removable by a pseudo-surgical technique in which certain medicine men specialize.

255

It involves the withdrawal of the object by sucking. These men, of course, produce actual objects that they claim to have removed from their patients' bodies. This serves to allay the latter's fears and in cases where a recovery is made, empirical support is given to the native theory of disease causation. Examples of such disease-causing objects are magic shells, dogs' teeth, bits of metal, and stones. One Indian showed me a series of such projectiles that had been "sent" him. His body was strong enough to resist them and they fell at his side where he found them.

Feelings of guilt for past moral transgressions are also the source of apprehension in a disease situation, since these Indians believe that sickness may be the result of such transgressions. Again, it is the fact that an individual does not respond to the usual drug remedies that precipitates apprehension. The transgressions that fall in the panel of traditional sins are murder, incest, deceit, and sexual practices such as masturbation, fellatio, the use of parts of animals as artificial phalli and bestiality. Confession is the necessary preliminary to cure when it is thought that sickness is connected with sin. An interesting aspect of their theory, however, is the belief that such sins on the part of parents may be the source of illness in their children. Consequently the anxieties aroused in disease situations where some transgression is believed to be back of the illness, are not confined to the patient. His parents are likewise suspected and they may confess sins committed in childhood or adolescence. In a series of fifteen cases illustrating the transgressions confessed, twelve were those in which sexual sins were involved (1939a).

Encounters with Cannibals.—The most intense fears the Berens River Indians experience are generated in situations that are emotionally structured by their beliefs concerning *windĭgowak*, cannibals. They believe that human beings may be transformed into cannibals by sorcery, that cannibal monsters can be created "out of a dream" by a sorcerer and sent into the world to perform malevolent acts and that cannibal giants roam the woods, particularly in the spring. Consequently, when some human individual is reputed to be turning into a cannibal, the Indians become terror stricken. They are similarly affected when it is reported that a cannibal, created by magic, is approaching their encampment, or when some individual traveling in the bush discovers traces of a cannibal or claims that he has seen one.

Gastric symptoms are among those that the Indians interpret as evidence of incipient cannibalism on the part of human beings. When a person refuses to eat ordinary food or is chronically nauseated or cannot retain the food he ingests, suspicion is at once aroused. Even the individual so affected will develop anxiety and make the same inference. He may even ask to be killed at once. For this is the inevitable fate of reputed cannibals according to native custom. Usually they are strangled and their bodies burnt, not buried.

The last case of this sort to occur on the Berens River was in 1876 when three men killed their mother, built a pyre, and burnt her body. Since that time similar cases have occurred farther north. In 1906 two men from Sandy Lake were arrested for murder by the Mounted Police, because they had participated in the disposal of a woman reputed to be a *windīgo*. From the standpoint of native customary law, the strangling of a cannibal obviously is not murder. It is a communally sanctioned defensive act, rationally justified in the circumstances.

Another type of situation is illustrated by the behavior of the Indians when it is reported that a cannibal monster is headed in their direction. One midwinter night at Poplar River, when a terrific gale was blowing, word got around that a *windīgo* would likely pass that way. All the Indians on the north side of the river left their homes at once and congregated in a house across the river. In order to protect themselves they engaged one of the leading shamans to conjure all through the night in order to divert the *windīgo* from his reputed path. The Indians firmly believed that the cannibal passed without harming them and part of the evidence they adduced was the fury of the wind, which was interpreted as a sign of his presence. Similar episodes are said to have occurred in the past and mythology recounts terrific fights between strong shamans and cannibal giants in which the former are always successful. To these Indians such monsters are quite as real, quite as much a part of the environment as the giant animals already mentioned, or, in our culture, God, angels, and the Devil.

It is not surprising then to discover individuals who claim to have seen the kind of cannibal that is reputed to roam the woods, or to have been pursued by one. Such illusions are particularly interesting in view of the fact that these Indians are expert woodsmen, who not only have spent all their lives in the bush, but are familiar with the detailed topography of their country to an amazing degree, as well as with all the various species of fauna and flora. Consequently it might be expected that the whole gamut of possible sights and sounds would be so well known to them that they would be insulated against false perception of any kind. I know from personal experience, at least, that many sounds that have startled me from time to time have always been explained by my Indian companions in the most naturalistic manner. It is all the more significant then to discover cases in which the perceptions of individuals have been so thoroughly molded by traditional dogma that the most intense fears are aroused by objectively innocuous stimuli. It is the culturally derived *Einstellung*, rather than the stimuli themselves, that explains their behavior.

One old man, for instance, narrated the following experience.

Once in the spring of the year I was hunting muskrats. The lake was still frozen, only the river was open, but there was lots of ice along the shore. When it began to get dark I put ashore and made a fire close to the water edge to cook my supper. While I was sitting there I heard someone passing across the river.

I could hear the branches cracking. I went to my canoe and jumped in. I paddled as hard as I could to get away from the noise. Where the river got a little wider I came to a point that has lots of poplars growing on it. I was paddling quite a distance from the shore when I came opposite to this point. Just then I heard a sound as if something was passing through the air. A big stick had been thrown out at me but it did not strike me. I kept on going and paddled towards the opposite side of the river. Before I got to that side he was across the river already and heading me off. I paddled towards the other side again. But he went back and headed me off in that direction. This was in the spring of the year when the nights are not so long. He kept after me all night. I was scared to go ashore. Towards morning I reached a place where there is a high rock. I camped there and when it was light I went to set a bear trap. Later that day I came back to the river again. I started out again in my canoe. Late in the evening, after the sun had set, there was a place where I had to portage my canoe over to a lake. I left my canoe and went to see whether the lake was open. There were some open places so I went back to get my canoe. Then I heard him again. I carried my canoe over to the lake—it was a big one—and paddled off as fast as I could. When I got to the other end of the lake it was almost daylight. I did not hear him while I was traveling. I went ashore and made a fire. After this I heard something again. I was scared. "How am I going to get away from him," I thought. I decided to make for the other side of an island in the lake. I was sitting by my canoe and I heard him coming closer. I was mad now. He had chased me long enough. I said to myself, "The number of my days has been given me already." So I picked up my axe and my gun and went in the direction of the sounds I had heard. As soon as I got closer to him he made a break for it. I could hear him crashing through the trees. Between the shore and the island there was a place where the water was not frozen. He was headed in this direction. I kept after him. I could hear him on the weak ice. Then he fell in and I heard a terrific yell. I turned back then and I can't say whether he managed to get out or not. I killed some ducks and went back to my canoe. I was getting pretty weak by this time so I made for a camp I thought was close by. But the people had left. I found out later that they had heard him and were so scared that they moved away.[6]

In the situations thus far passed in review I have attempted to indicate the cultural constituents of the fears of individuals and the institutionalized means available for their alleviation. In societies with different culture patterns the same situations would be emotionally structured in a different way, the affects of individuals would be qualitatively, if not quantitatively, different, and other traditional defenses would be invoked.

To an outsider the fears of the Berens River Indians, and those of other primitive peoples, appear to be "neurotic," in the sense that they occur in situations where no actual danger threatens and for the reason that the sources of some of these fears are of the nature of fantasies. Can we speak, then, of "cultural neuroses" that are characteristic of whole populations? I think not. If we do so, as Karen Horney[7] has pointed out, "we should be yielding to an impression based on a lack of understanding" as well as being guilty of a fallacy in reasoning.

In the first place, the Berens River Indian *is* responding to a *real* danger when he flees from a cannibal monster or murders a human being who is turning into a *wíndigo,* or when he becomes apprehensive in a certain disease situation. To act or feel otherwise would stamp an individual either as a fool or as a phenomenal example of intellectual emancipation. Furthermore, the Indians themselves are able to point out plenty of tangible empirical evidence that supports the interpretation of the realities that their culture imposes upon their minds (1934a). They are naïve empiricists but not naïvely irrational.

Once we relegate commonly motivated fears to their proper frame of reference—cultural tradition—a fundamental etiological distinction can be made between fears of this category and those which arise in individuals from conditions primarily relevant to the circumstances of their own personal history. The *genuine* neurotic, in addition to sharing the culturally constituted fears of his fellows, as Horney says, "has fears which in quantity or quality deviate from those of the cultural pattern." Any comparison, then, between the fears and defenses of such individuals and the culturally constituted fears and institutionalized defenses of whole human societies is not only superficial, it is actually misleading, since no account is taken of differences in etiological factors. Primitive peoples are sometimes accused of the logical fallacy that results from an inference that two phenomena are identical if one or more elements are shared in common. To seriously maintain that the culturally constituted fears and defenses of primitive peoples are evidence of "cultural neuroses" which are of the same order as the neurosis of individuals in Western civilization, is just such a fallacy. Manifest surface analogies are compared whereas the underlying differences in the dynamic factors that produced them are ignored.

A further differentiation between the genuine neurotic and the person experiencing the "normal" fears of his culture is important. The former is inevitably a suffering individual; the latter is not. "Thus the normal person," writes Horney,

though having to undergo the fears and defenses of his culture, will in general be quite capable of living up to his potentialities and of enjoying what life has to offer him. The normal person is capable of making the best of the possibilities given in his culture. Expressing it negatively, he does not suffer more than is unavoidable in his culture. The neurotic person, on the other hand, suffers invariably more than the average person. He invariably has to pay an exorbitant price for his defenses, consisting in an impairment in vitality and expansiveness, or more specifically, in an impairment of his capacities for achievement and enjoyment, resulting in the discrepancy I have mentioned. In fact, the neurotic is invariably a suffering person, . . . [8]

although he may not himself be aware of this fact.

This distinction, so clearly elucidated by Horney, is demonstrable among the Berens River Indians. There are individuals in this society who manifest phobias that are quantitatively or qualitatively deviant from those of the other Indians. These persons are among the genuine neurotics. I have already mentional W. B. whose toad phobia was quantitatively distinguishable from that of the other natives. Further differential factors in this case, as I have pointed out, have to be sought in his personal history. It is not without interest in the present connection to add that this old man, who is of mixed white and Indian blood and an outstanding leader among his people, also manifests a marked fear of thunder and lightning (which has no cultural sanction), a periodical stutter under emotional stress, a mild echolalia at times, and an identification with his father who was chief before him. He is far less provincial in his general outlook than the other Indians on account of his many intimate contacts with white people over a long period of years and the opportunities he has had to see a little of the "outside" world at first hand. Besides, he is a man of superior intelligence and mental alertness, with a rich sense of humor and fine physical vitality. Consequently his personality traits, considered as a whole, approach those of the white man more closely than most of the other Indians of the river and to the casual observer present an essentially "normal" picture. Yet were a deeper analysis of his personality possible, I dare say that W. B. would prove to be an example of a neurotic fairly well adapted to the conditions under which his life has been lived. I also suspect, as pointed out above and also in connection with one of his dreams (1936a), that an etiological factor of importance lies in a deep-seated conflict between W. B.'s ostensible acceptance of Christianity and the very profound importance which many native beliefs have had for him. The cogency of this hypothesis is suggested by the widely different attitudes taken by W. B.'s parents and grandparents towards Christianity during the early decades of missionary efforts. For W. B. was only a boy of ten years when the first resident missionary arrived on the Berens River. W. B.'s mother, being white, was a thorough-going advocate of Christianity, and his father, with some personal reservations, no doubt, reputedly was instrumental in obtaining a local missionary for his band. On the other hand, W. B.'s paternal grandfather with whom he was very intimately associated in his upbringing immersed him in native beliefs. That W. B. has been exposed to some inner conflict in consequences of these varying attitudes is evidenced by the fact that he has frequently remarked to me that as he has grown older, and as a result of discussions engendered by my ethnological investigations, during which he has served more as a collaborator than interpreter, the truth of native beliefs has more and more impressed him. He has contrasted this with the more "superior" and critical attitude he assumed when he was a young man. While it is true that all of the Indians of his generation were undoubtedly exposed to the same general conflicts in belief, the fact that W. B.'s mother was a white woman presents a unique circumstance which, combined with the extreme pagan views to which W. B. was subjected in the same family circle (household group) may have affected both the quantitative and qualitative aspects of his early identifications.

In contrast to W. B. other Berens River Indians exhibit such marked qualitative deviations from the established culture patterns of their society that there is no obvious connection between certain of their phobias and traditional beliefs. In addition to being afraid of witches, mythical animals, cannibals, etc., these individuals suffer from anxiety as distinguished from fear. (See Chap. 14.) Their phobias are personal and have no culturally phrased causes. Individuals subject to such phobias often rationalize them in terms of whatever beliefs seem appropriate. The most striking fact that characterizes phobias of this category is this: they occur in situations that easily can be distinguished from those that are emotionally structured by common beliefs.

One man, for example, who had hunted and trapped all his life, found himself beset by anxiety whenever he attempted to go any distance into the woods alone. He happened to be a conjuror and rationalized his anxiety by confessing that he had practiced his profession without the proper supernatural sanction (1936a).

Another man could go nowhere unaccompanied by one or more companions. When alone he would always keep within sight of human habitations or people. This was the rule even when he had to urinate or defecate. If he had to relieve himself at night his wife would always get up and go with him. Sometimes his companions would tease him by stealing out of sight. As soon as he discovered this he would start to call for them and run frantically in the direction where he thought they were. One winter when he was traveling with a party of men and found himself alone in the woods he threw off his hat and mits in his frenzy and yelled until his companions came back. Once when he was hired by the Hudson's Bay Company to cut wood he induced some small boys to go along for the ride and walk back with him while he ran ahead of the team of oxen. He rationalized his anxiety by saying that he once dreamed that a jackfish would swallow him, if this creature found him alone.[9]

A third man, whom I know personally, lives a hundred miles up the Berens River at Grand Rapids. The Indians of this band are only superficially Christianized and live much in the purely native fashion. J. D. has spent all his life here. His children are all married and he is now about sixty years of age. He is a tall, sparsely built individual, energetic in speech and movement and an exceptionally fine singer and drummer. But he has suffered from phobias all his life. Darkness disturbs him profoundly. "Ask J. D. to go and fetch a kettle of water for you some night," one of the Indians said to me, "you'll find that he will refuse, even if you offer to pay him well for it." Once when J. D. was traveling in winter with some other men they were attempting to reach their camp late at night because they had no blankets or bedding with them. Before darkness fell, J. D. insisted that they help him collect birch bark so that they could make torches to carry with them during the rest of their journey. They did this, but every now and then the wind would blow them out. When this happened and they were plunged in darkness J. D. would fall to the ground and writhe and scream like a "crazy" man. The situation described is one which may be contrasted with those referred to earlier in this paper. J. D.'s fears are unsupported culturally. They are unique and his behavior sharply deviates from that of other individuals in the same situation. When it is understood, moreover, that the winter months are those in which these Indians are most active, since this is the trapping season, and that at the latitude at which they live the days are shortest then, so that there is constant necessity for moving about when it is dark, the abnormality from which J. D. suffers is thrown into even greater relief.

J. D. also suffers from a kind of agoraphobia. He usually skirts the shore when he goes out alone in his canoe on the lake. In fact, he never will head directly across any extensive body of water if he can avoid doing so.

The case of J. D., however, transcends in interest the fact that he exhibits such obvious neurotic symptoms. He is a well-known conjurer (seer), doctor, and the "owner" of one of the four Wabano pavilions up the river, in which the most important native ceremony that still survives is held. According to Indian dogma the "ownership" and hence the leadership in this particular ceremony is a supernatural blessing, mediated in a dream. The details of the structure erected by different leaders thus differ in minor ways and so do the procedure followed and the content of the dream validation itself. But superficially there is adherence to a common pattern and the prophylactic and therapeutic purpose of the ceremony is common to all.

Since a man who is both a conjurer and Wabano leader is reputed to be an extremely powerful individual because he has been "blessed" by many supernatural guardian spirits, it would appear that the exhibition of such deviant fears as J. D. manifests would prove to be not only inconsistent but a definite liability. Consequently it was of some interest to discover that J. D. has long been the subject of comment for just this reason. "If he is such a strong man as he claims to be," one old Indian remarked to me, "and he has so many *pawáganak* (guardian spirits), why is he afraid to do so many things?" This commentator went on to say that while some of the people had faith in J. D. he himself had none. Because these Indians are extremely individualistic and pragmatic a wide range of judgments in respect to the abilities of any person who essays to conjure or cure is possible. Consequently the expression of a skeptical attitude towards J. D. is not in itself significant. These Indians are genuinely tolerant because they are always ready to have an individual demonstrate his professed abilities, while at the same time they never "pull their punches" if they find some flaws in his claims. In former days it is even possible that any expression of skepticism whatsoever was rarer. For the traditional attitude towards great medicine men was typically one of prodigious respect verging on fear. No one would have dared tease such a person nor challenge his authority unless he considered himself equally powerful.

In view of J. D.'s neurotic traits, which are not, of course, classified as pathological by his fellows, it is all the more interesting to note the expression of skepticism referred to above and also a lack of respect, which I found to be fairly widespread. But even this would be less significant were it not for the fact that no such attitude was manifest towards the three other Wabano leaders on the river. One of these even shared the distinction accorded the medicine man of a generation ago in being somewhat feared because he was reputed to have done away with several Indians by magical means. So far as J. D. is concerned, I was told that on one occasion when he was conjuring, members of the audience quietly stole away without his knowledge while the performance was in progress. Since seership is one of the functions of a conjurer this put J. D. on the spot. For, as people said, his guardian spirits could not be much good if they did not immediately tell him what had happened right in the neighborhood of the conjuring lodge itself. On two other occasions that I know of, some of the younger men deliberately stimulated J. D.'s fears in order to tease him. Once when he was making a speech in his Wabano pavilion during the course of a ceremony, a toy mechanical snake was released on the earthen path. It was headed for J. D. who stamped around in a panic when he saw it coming and finally ran out. Another time a young fellow obtained a firecracker and set it off at J. D.'s side while he was singing and drumming. On this occasion J. D. was so frightened that he not only ran away, he failed to come back for his drum (an extremely sacred object) until the next day. Amusing as they are, these episodes sufficiently indicate in themselves the profoundly personal character and depth of J. D.'s anxiety. They also document the attitude which many of the Indians hold towards J. D.

Although I know practically nothing about the details of J. D.'s personal life, I suspect that his conjuring, doctoring, and Wabano leadership are intimately bound up with his neurosis. They probably screen repressed aggression and somewhat compensate his deep feelings of insecurity. There is some evidence, at least, that this may be the case. J. D. assumes a domineering attitude towards others that is frequently a matter of comment. It was J. D., too, who showed me the magically projected objects that symbolized a half-dozen futile attempts to kill him. It is possible that the discovery and personal interpretation he attributed to those objects may represent the projection of his own repressed hostility towards others. At any rate, the culture of these Indians, containing as it does a theory of "disease-object" intrusion, provides an institutionalized background against which projective mechanisms in individuals can readily function. J. D.'s propensity to impress others is also so very evident that, together with the other features mentioned, it may be taken as evidence of a fundamental insecurity, connected with his anxiety. In recent years, for example, he has incorporated in his Wabanówĭwin certain features of the defunct Mĭdéwĭwin, the curative ceremony that once ranked highest in prestige not only among the Berens River Indians, but elsewhere among Algonkian peoples. He has even gone so far as to coin a new term, *wabano mĭdéwĭwin*, for his ceremony. To further enhance his prestige he has also borrowed features, originally found in some of the other Wabanówĭwin. Almost every year he makes some new innovation while the other Wabano leaders do not. He was the only Wabano owner, moreover, who tried to sell himself to me as an informant, when I first visited Grand Rapids. This made me mistrustful as I was aware that such information is traditionally sacred and esoteric. In fact, previously I had been able to obtain the information I wanted from a Wabano leader farther up the river only with the greatest difficulty. The last time I was at Grand Rapids J. D. said he had much more to tell me but I soon found out that all he was able to do was to repeat himself with minor variations. One summer he asked me to send him a flag with an eagle (associated with the mythical Thunder Bird) on it from the United States. He wished to fly it over his Wabano pavilion. I was told later that upon receiving the flag J. D. called a number of the old men together. Exhibiting it to them he baldly pointed out that whereas some of the Indians had no faith in him here was a token of the regard of a white man who had journeyed all the way from the United States to obtain medicine and information. As might be expected, J. D. is also extremely sensitive to real or fancied slights. Once when he had planned to hold his Wabanówĭwin for three days, I attended the first day but spent the whole of the second day with an informant a couple of miles across the Lake. J. D. was much annoyed, despite the fact that my contribution of tea, flour, and tobacco had practically subsidized his ceremony. On another occasion he got angry because only a few Indians attended the third day and he was forced to close the ceremony earlier than he intended. He once berated his sister, too, when he heard she had been giving me some personal reminiscences that included information about his father. J. D. evidently considered this his prerogative, a fact partially explained by the position of women among these Indians and the marked sexual dichotomy in social, economic, and religious life. But I doubt very much whether any other Indian would have become quite so emotionally upset over a matter of this sort. By and large, it would thus appear that, unfortunately for J. D., the institutions of his society that have offered compensatory defenses for his inner conflicts have not been sufficiently adequate to his needs. He remains not only a suffering individual but a deviant one, even from the standpoint of native culture itself.[10]

It would be highly desirable, of course, to know a great deal more about the four individuals discussed above. In order to demonstrate the *actual* etiological factors at work a psychiatric or psychoanalytic study of each case would have to be made. I have only attempted to indicate that the manifest behavior of these individuals suggests that the causes of their anxieties are of a different order than the culturally constituted fears of the general run of the population. In contrast with the latter, the situations that provoke the fears of these individuals are emotionally structured by highly subjective meanings that are personal and unconscious.

This differentiation, it seems to me, is of general significance. It indicates that a comprehensive account of the determining factors in the affective experience of individuals must include on the one hand an analysis of the influence of cultural patterns and, on the other, an investigation of the factors that determine quantitative or qualitative individual variations from a given cultural norm. In any particular society these two aspects of the problem are inseparable. But in Western civilization a great deal of attention has been paid to factors thought to be relevant to individual deviation without reference to the influence of the characteristic culture patterns that mold the ideologies and affects of individuals in a common manner.

In clinical practice, cases have turned up more than once that necessitate an evaluation of such factors. Some years ago a Negro committed to a mental hospital and thought to be suffering from private delusions was discovered by a psychiatrist to belong to a local religious cult of which his ideology was characteristic.[11]

It is only through the study of affective experience in a number of different human societies that the role of cultural variables can be thoroughly understood. Comparative data of this sort may also indicate that individual deviations themselves take on characteristic forms in different societies. But while the typical conflicts engendered by different cultures may vary and the symptomatology of individuals may reflect the traditions of their society, from an etiological standpoint genuine neurotics will remain comparable in so far as we can account for their behavior in terms of common dynamic processes.

Chapter 14 - The Social Function of Anxiety in a Primitive Society*

IN HIS DISCUSSION OF ANXIETY, FREUD EMPHASIZES THE FACT THAT it is essentially an affective reaction to danger.[1] The relationship of anxiety to danger is anticipatory, the affect is a signal: "one feels anxiety *lest* something occur."[2] Anxiety is not confined to the human species. Freud states that it "is a reaction characteristic of probably all organisms, certainly of all of the higher ones."[3] He further suggests that since it has an indispensable biological function, anxiety may have developed differently in different organisms.[4] Freud does not elaborate the point, but I think it follows from the biological role he assigns to anxiety that it must be conceived as a function of the particular danger situations that the organism faces. These vary from species to species. What is dangerous for one species of animal would not necessarily be equivalent for another species, and danger situations in the human species may differ again from those faced by infrahuman animals. For the human species itself, Freud stresses another variable. Danger situations vary ontogenetically[5] and the birth process is the "prototype of anxiety in man."[6]

What Freud does not explicitly recognize is that the occurrence of anxiety in the human species is further complicated by another variable that I shall call "cultural." However, his assumption that anxiety reactions in man are based on experience and are in that sense learned,[7] leaves the door open for an evaluation of such variables within the framework of psychoanalytic principles. These cultural variables operate through the socialization process that all human beings undergo and result in the definition of situations as dangerous in one society which, in another, may be viewed as less dangerous or not dangerous at all. This means that individuals may manifest anxiety reactions that are appropriate in a particular culture but not in another.

Such cultural variables are of importance with respect to two problems: first, the basic question in which Freud himself was particularly interested, viz., the relation between anxiety and neurosis; secondly, the *positive* role of anxiety. This social function of anxiety is definitely

*Originally published in *American Sociological Review*, VII (1941), 869-81.

linked, in principle, with the biological role which Freud stresses as a generic function of anxiety. I mean that an affective reaction to danger situations, as culturally defined, may motivate behavior on the part of individuals which is as significant in terms of societal values as comparable reactions are valuable in terms of biological utility. Anxiety-preparedness in the face of any danger is a very adaptive reaction.[8]

Before discussing this second problem, however, I wish to return to the first one, the relation between anxiety and neurosis. In this connection, Freud asks, "why it is that not all anxiety reactions are neurotic, why we recognize so many of them as normal," and he emphasizes the need for distinguishing between true anxiety (*Realangst*) and neurotic anxiety.[9] The conclusion to which he comes is this:

A *real* danger is a danger which we know, a true anxiety the anxiety in regard to such a known danger. Neurotic anxiety is anxiety in regard to a danger which we do not know. The neurotic danger must first be sought, therefore: Analysis has taught us that it is an instinctual danger [that is, fear of the intensity of one's own impulses].[10]

This differentiation led to the terminological distinction often made between fear, i.e., real or objective anxiety, and neurotic anxiety. I shall continue to use anxiety in its widest connotation, qualifying it with the adjectives "neurotic" or "objective" according to the meaning intended. In fact, I think there is a considerable conceptual advantage in considering fear-anxiety reactions as a broad affective continuum and not attempting to make categorical distinctions except in terms of known etiological factors, since what may seem to be instances of "pure" objective anxiety actually may have neurotic involvements when all the facts are known. On the other hand, as will appear later, there may be analogies to neurotic involvements in anxiety-laden situations which, in a particular culture, may present real objective dangers to the individual concerned.

Let us turn now to the second problem, the positive role of anxiety. I wish to show how anxiety is instigated and reduced among the Saulteaux through the operation of cultural factors (beliefs and institutionalized procedures) which define certain situations as dangerous, how the motivations of individuals are affected, and how the resulting behavior is related to the maintenance of the approved social code. The beliefs relevant to our discussion still flourish today and the more recent changes in their social system have not essentially affected their functioning.

One of the striking features of Saulteaux society is the anxiety with which certain disease situations are invested.[11] In order to understand *why* such situations are the focus of so much affect, we have to know something about native theories of disease. These theories reflect traditional notions. They represent an ideology which is culturally derived and they involve fundamental assumptions about the nature of the universe. From the standpoint of the Saulteaux themselves, such assumptions are taken a priori and are unchallengeable. They not only represent beliefs but are also a basis for action. The affect which arises in certain disease situations is a product of reflection upon the symptoms observed in the patient and the cause of the illness interpreted in terms of the native notions of disease causation. Thus, the anxiety aroused is intimately connected with a cultural variable.

There is a correlative fact, however, which gives *social* significance to the affect generated. Disease situations of any seriousness carry the implication that something wrong has been done. Illness is the penalty. Consequently, it is easy to see why illness tends to precipitate an affective reaction to a culturally defined danger situation. Furthermore, a closer examination of the dynamics of Saulteaux society reveals the fact that fear of disease is the major social sanction operative among these Indians. In this society, certain classes of sexual behavior[12] (incest, the so-called perversions in heterosexual intercourse, homosexuality, autoerotism, bestiality), various kinds of aggressive behavior (cruelty to animals, homicide, cruelty toward human beings, the use of bad medicine to cause suffering, rough or inconsiderate treatment of the dead, theft, and a number of ego injuries like insult and ridicule, failure to share freely, etc.), behavior prescribed by guardian spirits, the acquisition of power to render specialized services to others (i.e., curing or clairvoyance), all fall under a disease sanction.

This leads us directly to the heart of one of the basic problems in the social sciences, viz., the determination of the specific conditions under which social codes are maintained and the means by which they operate under different cultural frames of reference. For despite the widest cultural variability in *homo sapiens,* we observe that all human societies are characterized by norms of conduct which, in MacIver's words, "assure some regularity, uniformity and predictability of behavior on the part of the members of a community."[13] Sheer anarchy, or literal rampant individualism, is unknown.

But this problem is not wholly a sociological one. It has important and far-reaching psychological implications, particularly in view of the fact that in many nonliterate societies, the institutions we associate with the maintenance of "law and order" are unelaborated or even absent. In the case of the Saulteaux, e.g., there were no chiefs nor any kind of political organization in aboriginal days. Nor were there any institutionalized juridical procedures or jails.

The psychological aspects of social control become evident when we examine the relation between the social sanctions operative in a given society and the motivations of individuals instigated by the prevailing sanctions. As Radcliffe-Brown has pointed out[14] "the sanctions existing in a community constitute motives in the individual for the regulation of his conduct in conformity with usage." Hence, there is an integral, inextricable relationship between sociological and psychological factors.

In Saulteaux society, it is not fear of the gods or fear of punishment by the state that is the major sanction: it is the fear of disease.[15] Or, putting it in the terminology already employed, the motivating factor is the affect connected with certain disease situations. Individuals in Saulteaux society are highly sensitized to anxiety as an emotional reaction to a danger signal, the precipitating cause being illness interpreted as punishment. The manifest danger to which the anxiety is directed is the direct threat to someone's well-being or even life. But there is also a menace to the social code which is implied because some dissocial act has been committed. Insofar as individuals are motivated to avoid such acts through fear of disease, anxiety performs a distinct social function.

With this thesis in mind I should now like to analyze in more detail how disease operates as a social sanction in Saulteaux society in connection with anxiety-laden situations. (See also Chap. 13.)

In the first place, health and a long life are very positive values to the Saulteaux. *Pīmādazīwin,* life in the fullest sense, is stressed again and again in their ceremonies. The supernaturals are asked for it. It is a prime value. In psychological terms, it is a major goal response. Disease interferes with achieving this goal. Ordinary cases of illness, however, colds, headaches, etc., do not arouse anxiety among the Saulteaux any more than they do among ourselves. They are not danger situations. But the nature of disease is such that it may become a threat to life itself, may be a real danger to the human organism. Real or "normal" anxiety is appropriate in such circumstances.[16]

A comparable affect under equivalent circumstances is found among the Saulteaux and ourselves. In both cases, the danger threatened is met with what are thought to be appropriate measures. Most disease situations among the Saulteaux, however, do not conform to this type. They correspond either to the nondangerous variety or they rapidly pass from this type into situations where the anxiety level is not only high, but where the *quality* of the affect suggests neurotic anxiety without its actually being so. What are the conditions that bring this about? It is here that native beliefs about disease causation enter the picture.

In Saulteaux belief, one of the major causes of illness arises from what they term "bad conduct" *(madjīijiwé bazīwin).* "Because a person does bad things, that is where sickness *(ákwazīwin)* starts," is the way one informant phrased it. In other words, a person may fall ill because of some transgression he has committed in the past. It is also possible that an individual may be suffering because of the bad conduct of his parents. "When a man is young he may do something to cause his children trouble. They will suffer for this." Illness derived from this source is designated by a special native term *(odjīneaúwaso).* Consequently, if a child falls seriously ill, it is often attributed to the transgression of a parent. It is easy to see the anxiety-provoking possibilities in this theory of disease causation. In addition to the normal anxiety that the objective factors of the disease situation may stimulate, a sense of guilt may be aroused in one or both parents. They are bound to reflect upon what they may have done to cause their child's suffering, or even death. Their own acts are entangled with the disease situation.

Another cause of illness is witchcraft, the hostile action of some other human being. The significant fact to be observed in cases of this class is that the sick person almost always believes that his sickness is due to revenge. Some previous act of *his* has provoked retaliation in this form. Here the patient's own impulses, previously expressed in some form of dissocial behavior, are projected into the situation just as they are in those instances where disease is thought to have resulted from "bad conduct." In cases of witchcraft, the penalty that threatens has acted in a mediate fashion instead of automatically as in the instances where bad conduct is thought to be the source.

An illuminating clue to the psychological significance of disease situations interpreted as a result of the causes just cited is obtained if we follow Freud's differentiation of what he terms a *traumatic* situation from a simple *danger* situation. He introduces this distinction by asking what the kernel of the danger situation is.[17] He finds that it revolves about the estimation of our strength in relation to the danger. If we feel a sense of helplessness in the face of it, an inability to cope with it, then he calls the situation *traumatic*. This is precisely the differentiation that applies to those disease situations among the Saulteaux where the cause of the illness is uncertain and obscure. In these situations, the quality of the anxiety aroused is different from that where illness is faced in the same way any danger situation is faced. It is disease situations of this *traumatic* type that operate as a social sanction.

The qualitative aspects of the anxiety aroused emerge from the combination of two determinants. The first is purely objective: ordinary medical treatment of the sick person has failed to produce improvement. The symptoms persist or the person gets worse. It is at this point that the situation becomes serious. Prior to this, the illness may not even have been considered dangerous, but when the medicine does not work, the situation rapidly becomes traumatic. This is because the suspicion is aroused in the patient or his associates that the cause of the illness is hidden. It may be a penalty for something done in the past. It may be due to bad conduct or witchcraft. But who knows? Yet if this is so, his very life is in jeopardy. Consequently, a feeling of helplessness arises which can only be alleviated if the precise cause of the sickness is discovered. Otherwise, appropriate measures cannot be undertaken. Meanwhile, the source of the danger remains uncertain and obscure; further suffering, even death, menaces the patient.

Thus, while from an objective point of view we often may have displayed what seems to be a "disproportionality of affect" in disease situations, at the same time the definition of such situations in terms of Saulteaux beliefs presents dangers that are not comparable to those we would recognize in similar situations. This is an important qualitative difference. The affective reactions of the Saulteaux are a function of this difference.[18]

It would also appear that there are some analogies, although by no means an identity, between the anxiety created in some of these traumatic disease situations among the Saulteaux and neurotic anxiety. This is true, at least, in the cases where the danger that threatens is believed to have arisen out of the patient's own acts, so there is the closest integral relation between inner and outer danger as in neurotic anxiety, but there are no substitute formations in the individual which project the danger outwards, as in animal phobias, while the real source of danger remains unknown. Nevertheless, it is true that the impulses of the individual become the sine qua non of the external danger, just as in neurotic anxiety. Consequently, these impulses are the ultimate source of the danger itself. The disease is not considered to be impersonal and objective in origin and for this reason it cannot be faced in the same terms as other kinds of illness or other objective hazards of life. The real source of danger is from within and, like neurotic anxiety, it is connected with forbidden acts.

Take the case of an Indian who believes himself bewitched, for example. At the first appearance of his illness, he may not have been worried because he may have thought that there was some other cause of his trouble, but as soon as he believes he is the victim of a hostile attack, he gets anxious. Why? Because he believes his illness is in retaliation for some previous act of aggression he has perpetrated. The assertion of these aggressive impulses on his part has led to a feeling of guilt and the illness from which he is suffering has aroused anxiety because he senses danger. His very life may be threatened. What this man fears is that he had endangered his life by acting as he did. He is afraid of the consequences of his own impulses. The source of the outwardly sensed danger lies in his own hostile impulses.

So far I have tried to explain how anxiety is integrated in disease situations among the Saulteaux and why it is that the emotion generated has qualitative features which suggest neurotic anxiety. I hope that I have made it clear, however, that these features are only analogies deduced from the manner in which the belief system of the Saulteaux compels the individual to interpret the objective aspects of disease situations under certain conditions. What we actually appear to have exhibited in these cases is an affective reaction on a fear-anxiety continuum that lies somewhere between true objective anxiety and real neurotic anxiety.[19] That this is indeed the case is supported by the fact that, on the one hand, we can point to occurrences of real anxiety in danger situations among the Saulteaux and, on the other, to cases of neurotic anxiety. An instance of the latter is the behavior of a man I have described at some length in Chapter 13. Among other things he had severe phobic symptoms, a kind of agoraphobia and fear of the dark.

The point I wish to emphasize particularly is that at both extremes of the fear-anxiety continuum the main function of the affect has reference to the individual alone. This is true whether he runs away from some objective danger or develops phobias which are reaction formations in self-defense against some instinctual danger. The anxiety associated with disease situations among the Saulteaux, on the other hand, has a social function insofar as it motivates individuals to avoid the danger (disease) by conforming to the dictates of the social code. This is accomplished by forcing the individual to reflect upon disapproved acts under the stress of the anxiety aroused by a disease situation or to anticipate possible discomfort through a knowledge of the experience of others. In either case, the disease sanction encourages the individual to be responsible for his own conduct.

The full implications of the social function of anxiety in Saulteaux society can best be exposed, however, if we return to the traumatic disease situation and inquire what steps are taken to reduce anxiety in the individual. I have already pointed out that, in such situations, the cause of the disease is at first problematical though the suspicion is aroused that the patient himself or some other person is responsible for the illness. This means that the true cause of the trouble must be sought before the disease can be alleviated. Once the cause of the illness is discovered, the disease situation loses some of its traumatic quality because the danger can be squarely faced like any other danger and some action taken to meet it. The therapeutic measures employed can be looked upon as anxiety-reducing devices.

Now one of the distinctive features of the Saulteaux belief system is this: if one who is ill because of "bad conduct" *confesses* his transgression, the medicine will then do its work and the patient will recover. This notion is the most typical feature of the operation of the disease sanction in cases where the penalty threatened is automatically induced. In fact, it adds considerable force to the sanction so far as the individual is concerned. It means that deviant conduct may not only lead to subsequent illness but that in order to get well one has to suffer the shame of self-exposure involved in confession. This is part of the punishment. Since it is also believed that the medicine man's guardian spirits (*pawáganak*) will inform him of the cause of the trouble, there is no use withholding anything.[20] At the same time, confession provides the means of alleviating the guilt and anxiety of the individual, because, if a feeling of helplessness or being trapped is an intrinsic factor in these traumatic situations (or in any severe anxiety situation), confession provides a method of escape according to both Saulteaux belief and sound psychological principle.

From the standpoint of Saulteaux society as a whole, confession is also a means by which knowledge of confessed transgressions is put into social circulation. Confession among the Saulteaux is not equivalent to confession to a priest, a friend, or a psychoanalyst in Western culture. In our society, it is assumed that what is exposed will be held in absolute confidence,[21] but among these Indians the notion is held that the very secrecy of the transgressions is one of the things that makes them particularly bad. This explains why it is that when one person confesses a sexual transgression in which he or she has participated with a second person, the latter will not become ill subsequently or have to confess. Once the transgression has been publicized, it is washed away or, as the Saulteaux phrase it, "bad conduct will not follow you any more."

Perhaps this attitude towards what is secret is connected with the lack of privacy that is intrinsic to the manner in which these people live. Anything that smacks of secrecy is always suspect. There is even an aura of potential menace about such things, fortified no doubt by the covert practice of magic and sorcery. Consequently, in disease situations where any hidden transgression is thought to be the cause of the trouble what is in effect a public exposure is a necessary step to regaining health.

In actual practice, this works out in a very simple way. When anyone is sick, there is no isolation of the patient; on the contrary, the wigwam is always full of people. Any statement on the part of the patient, although it may be made to the doctor, is not only public but also very quickly may become a matter of common gossip. Where conjuring is resorted to, in cases where all other efforts have failed to reveal the hidden cause of the malady,[22] almost the whole community may be present en masse. Under these conditions, to confess a transgression is to reveal publicly a secret "sin." Consequently, the resistance to self-exposure is very great and the shame experienced by the individual extremely poignant. In terms of our own society it is as if the transgressions committed were exposed in open court or published in the newspapers so that everyone knew that Jerry had slept with his sister or that Kate had murdered her child. Among the Saulteaux, however, it is only after such a confession is made that the usual medicine can do its work and the patient can recover. In one case, three children of a married couple were all suffering from a discharge of mucous through the nose and mouth. They had been treated by a native doctor who was also a conjurer but his medicine had done no good. Finally, a conjuring performance was held. Despite the fact that the woman's husband, who was present, had threatened her with death if she ever told, she broke down in a flood of tears and confessed to everyone that he had forced fellatio upon her.

273

This public aspect of confession is one of the channels through which individuals growing up in Saulteaux society and overhearing the gossip of their elders *sense,* even though they may fail to understand fully, the general typology of disapproved patterns of behavior. Children do not have to be taught a concrete panel of transgressions in Saulteaux society any more than in our own. Nor does it have to be assumed that they have been present on numerous occasions when transgressions have been confessed. Even if they are present, they may not always understand what is meant. Yet some feeling is gained of the *kind* of conduct that is disapproved. The informant who told me about the case of fellatio was present at the conjuring performance when this was confessed. She was about ten years old at the time and did not understand what was meant until later when her stepmother enlightened her.

In actual operation, the disease sanction among the Saulteaux does not completely deter individuals from committing socially disapproved acts but it functions as a brake by arousing anxiety at the very thought of such conduct. Functionally viewed, a society can well tolerate a few breaches of the rules if, through some means such as confession, a knowledge of dissocial conduct is publicized with the result that a large majority of individuals follow the approved types of behavior.

These deductions are by no means theoretical. That individuals in Saulteaux society actually are deterred from acting in forbidden ways by the disease sanction is illustrated by the following story.[23] In this case, illness did not follow incestuous intercourse. Perhaps this was because it occurred only once. In fact, this may be the moral of the story from the point of view of the Saulteaux themselves. At any rate, it gives a very clear picture of the conscious conflict between the impulses of the individual and socially sanctioned modes of conduct.

An unmarried woman had "adopted" her brother's son, a boy who was already a fairly good hunter.[24] They were camping by themselves alone in the bush. The boy had shot some meat and they were drying it. One night after they both lay down to sleep, he began to think about his *kīsagwas.*[25] After awhile he spoke to her. "How's chances?" he said.[26] "Are you crazy," she replied, "to talk like that? You are my brother's son." "Nothing will happen to us," the boy said. "Yes, there will," said his aunt, "we might suffer." "No we won't. Nothing will happen," her nephew replied.

Then he got up, went over to where she was lying and managed to get what he wanted. After he had finished, he went back to his own place and lay down again. He could not go to sleep. He began to worry about what he had done to his father's sister.

In the morning he said to her, "I'm going now." "Where?" she asked. "I'm going to live somewhere else, I'm ashamed of what I did. I'm going away. If I starve to death, all right." "No! No! Don't go," said his aunt. "If you leave who is going to make a living for me? I'll starve to death. It's not the first time people did what we did. It has happened elsewhere."

But the young man was much worried and determined to go. "No, you can't leave me," said his aunt. "I've brought you up and you must stay here." "I'll go for awhile, anyway," the boy said. "All right," said his aunt, "just for a short time. No one knows and I'll never tell anyone. There might come a time to say it, but not now."

So the young fellow went off. He came to a high rock and sat down there. He thought over what he had done. He was sorry that he did it. He pulled out his penis and looked at it. He found a hair. He said to himself, "This is *nīsagwas,* her hair." He threw it away.

That night he camped by himself, half thinking all the time that he would go back to his aunt. In the morning, he did go back to where they had their camp. He arrived at sundown.

All during the night he was away his aunt had been crying. She was so very glad to see him now. He said to her, "I wonder if it would be all right if we lived together, just as if we were man and wife." "I don't think so," the woman said. "It would not look right if we did that. If you want a woman you better get one for yourself and if I want a man I better get one."

The trouble was this young man had tasted something new and he wanted more of it. He found a girl and got married in the spring. He and his wife lived with his aunt. Later his aunt got married, too.

The narrator commented that the boy's aunt was a sensible woman. They just made one slip and then stopped. This may explain why nothing happened to them, i.e., neither one got sick and had to confess.

Among the Saulteaux, then, desire for *pīmädazīwin* can be assumed to be a major goal response. Everyone wants to be healthy, to live long, and to enjoy life as much as possible. In order to achieve this aim, certain kinds of conduct should be avoided, not only for one's own sake, but for the sake of one's children. If one does commit transgressions and then falls ill, or if one's children become ill, it is better to suffer shame than more suffering or even death. This is the setting of confession and its individual motivation.[27] Confession, in turn, by making public the transgression committed permits the individual to recover. This is its ostensible purpose. But confession has a wider social function. It makes others aware of disapproved types of conduct which act as a warning to them. At the same time, since patients who confess usually recover, the publicity given to such cases supports both the native theory of disease causation on which the sanction rests, and the efficacy of confession itself. So while most individuals are motivated to avoid the risk of illness, there is consolation in the fact that even if one's sins find one out, there still is a means of regaining health.

In some traumatic disease situations where witchcraft is thought to be the cause of the illness, the anxiety of the patient and his associates is relieved by the removal of a material object from the patient's body by the doctor. This type of therapy is based upon the belief that it is possible to project material objects into the body of a person that will cause illness. Once the object is removed the patient is supposed to recover. The sociopsychological reverberations of cases diagnosed as due to witchcraft are much the same, however, as those in which confession has occurred. This follows because the same factors are involved: (a) a disease situation that requires explanation in terms of some previous behavior on the part of the patient; (b) the selection, perhaps with the help of the doctor, of some offensive act that is brought forward because the patient feels guilty about it; (c) the dissemination of the cause of the illness through gossip about the case; (d) the resulting publicity given to socially disapproved types of conduct that act as a warning to others.

We can see, then, how the therapeutic measures utilized by these Indians in traumatic disease situations have the social function of anxiety-reduction, although this is not their ostensible purpose from the standpoint of the Saulteaux themselves. We can likewise understand how it is that in a society where so much anxiety is associated with disease the persons who specialize in curative methods are individuals who enjoy the highest prestige. In psychological terms, this prestige accrues to those who are instrumental in reducing anxiety.

It is impossible to discuss here all the further ramifications of the functional aspects of anxiety, but we may point out that the whole magico-religious apparatus of the Saulteaux is a complex anxiety-reducing device.[28]

In summary, the thesis developed here is that, by its very nature, disease may arouse "normal" or objective anxiety, but among the Saulteaux, native theories of disease causation invest certain disease situations with a traumatic quality which is a function of the beliefs held rather than of the actual danger threatened by the illness itself. The quality of the anxiety precipitated in the individuals affected by such situations suggests neurotic rather than objective anxiety because the ultimate cause of the disease is attributed to the expression of dissocial impulses. The illness is viewed as a punishment for such acts and the anxiety is a danger signal that heralds the imminence of this penalty. Insofar as individuals are motivated to avoid dissocial acts because of the penalty anticipated, the pseudoneurotic anxiety aroused in disease situations has a positive social function. It is a psychic mechanism that acts as a reinforcing agent in upholding the social code. Thus, in a society with such a relatively simple culture and one in which formalized institutions and devices for penalizing the individual for dissocial conduct are absent, the utilization of anxiety in connection with disease is an extremely effective means for supporting the patterns of interpersonal behavior that make Saulteaux society a going concern.

Finally, I should like to point out that this role of anxiety in Saulteaux society is consonant with the results that are emerging from certain researches in contemporary experimental psychology.[29] It has been found possible, in Mowrer's view, to recast the Freudian theory of anxiety in stimulus-response terms and to set up hypotheses which can be tested. In this paper, I have attempted to show how such a hypothesis is useful in interpreting observations made in a primitive society.

Chapter 15 - Aggression
in Saulteaux Society*

THIS PAPER MIGHT HAVE BEEN GIVEN THE PARADOXICAL TITLE "aggression among a patient, placid, peace-loving preliterate people." For among the aborigines of North America the Algonkians of the northern woodlands, in contrast with Indians like the Iroquois or the Sioux, have long enjoyed the reputation of being as mild-mannered and overtly *unaggressive* a people as could be found anywhere among the native tribes of this continent. Indeed, the statement made by Speck that among the Montagnais-Naskapi of the Labrador peninsula, "strife is scarcely present; violence strenuously avoided; competition even courteously distained"[1] is just as outwardly true of that other branch of the Algonkians, the Saulteaux, whom I shall discuss.

Yet Father Le Jeune, a Jesuit missionary who lived among the Montagnais-Naskapi in the early part of the seventeenth century, qualifies this idyllic picture of outward harmony by an astute observation. "It is strange," he wrote, "to see how these people agree so well outwardly, and how they hate each other within. They do not often get angry and fight with one another, but in the depths of their hearts they intend a great deal of harm. I do not understand how this can be consistent with the kindness and assistance that they offer one another."[2]

What interested me when I stumbled across this characterization not long ago was the fact that it could be applied with equal validity to the Saulteaux. In my opinion, it goes to the very heart of the characterological problem presented by them. What I propose to do in this paper is to offer an explanation of what to Le Jeune was a psychological paradox, by examining the conditions under which ambivalent traits similar to those noted by him are molded. While my explanation applies primarily to the Berens River Saulteaux, there are many analogies to my observations in Le Jeune's account of seventeenth-century Montagnais society.

To the casual observer, cooperation, laughter, harmony, patience, and self-control appear to be the keynotes of Saulteaux interpersonal

*Originally published in *Psychiatry: Journal of the Biology and Pathology of Interpersonal Relations*, III (August 1940), 395-407.

relations. These people have never engaged in war with the whites or with other Indian tribes. There are no official records of murder; suicide is unknown; and theft is extremely rare. Open expressions of anger or quarrels ending in physical assault seldom occur. A spirit of mutual helpfulness is manifest in the sharing of economic goods and there is every evidence of cooperation in all sorts of economically productive tasks. No one, in fact, is much better off than his neighbor. Dependence upon hunting, fishing, trapping for a living is precarious at best and it is impossible to accumulate food for the inevitable rainy day. If I have more than I need I share it with you today because I know that you, in turn, will share your surplus with me tomorrow.

This is the superficial picture that the Saulteaux present to the observer and it could be reinforced by a detailed description of the functioning of their economic and social institutions. But it is not a complete or fully realistic portrait. It does not expose the deeper psychological realities of Saulteaux life. While at first glance there seems to be no manifest evidence of aggression and while I myself did not at first sense the undercurrents of hostility that actually exist, on more intimate acquaintance I was forced to correct my earlier impressions.[3] Furthermore, I came to the conclusion that in all probability the undercurrents of aggression that I shall describe were even stronger in the past when native beliefs flourished in full strength and acculturative influences had not set in.

I shall attempt to show how, under the cultural conditions imposed by Saulteaux society, aggressive impulses are both stimulated and channeled; what the range of behavior is that has agggressive meaning for them and the behavior considered appropriate to combat it; and what are the effective reinforcements of these patterns of behavior from other sources. I believe that the cultural molding of such impulses provides a definite clue to the psychological sources of certain personality traits which are typical of these Indians. These traits are, in part, a function of dealing with people in terms of certain culturally imposed modes of behavior. Saulteaux patterns of social behavior create a fundamental ambivalence in the interpersonal relations of individuals. My hypothesis is that the outwardly mild and placid traits of character which they exhibit and the patience and self-restraint they exercise in overt personal relations are a socially constituted façade that often masks the hostile feelings of the individual. If some of the basic beliefs and concepts of these people were changed their aggressive impulses would be reconstellated and the personality traits referred to would no longer assume their characteristic forms.

This absence of overt aggression in face-to-face situations is an outstanding feature of interpersonal relations in Saulteaux society. While in other preliterate societies unformalized or even formalized modes of open aggression frequently are found, among the Saulteaux behavior of this kind is not sanctioned, except in the mildest form.[4] The joking relationship between cross-cousins of opposite sex[5] and the exchange of belittling remarks between men of different sibs are the only formalized patterns of such behavior that I can think of. Aside from these, hostility in face-to-face situations seldom occurs. Consequently, when expressions of hostility *do* break through in the form of verbal threats, gestures, or physical assault, they are taken more seriously than is the case in societies where such modes of behavior are commoner because they are socially sanctioned. I have never observed boys or girls in exchange of blows. At the mouth of the river I know of a case where a man gave his brother a severe beating because he believed that the latter had attempted to seduce his wife. One couple is said to quarrel frequently and even to beat each other occasionally. Parents, I may add, seldom inflict corporal punishment upon their children.

Insulting remarks, direct rebuke or expressions of disapproval, open contradiction, sneering or calling a person names are avoided by the Saulteaux. Swearing, in the sense of blasphemy, is not a problem because their language is inadequate in this respect.[6] Gestures that suggest an approach to physical assault, like shaking one's fist in a person's face, are a deadly insult. It immediately suggests extreme hostility. Even pointing one's finger at a person, accompanied by an angry facial expression or insulting words, may be interpreted as a serious threat against one's life. Actual physical assault is only legitimate in self-defense. In the past, individuals who, according to native belief, were judged to be cannibals—*windigowak*—were killed. But since such individuals were thought to be a menace to the lives of others, public opinion sanctioned their execution. (See Chap. 13.)

Saulteaux society functions in terms of primary group relations and in certain respects the kinship structure buttresses the discouragement of open aggression, just as the struggle to make a living may be partly responsible for food sharing and outward cooperation in economic tasks. The Saulteaux kinship system is centripetal in tendency in the sense that everyone with whom one comes in social contact not only falls within the category of a relative, but a blood relative, through the extension in usage of a few primary terms. There are no distinct terms for persons that in English we classify as relatives-in-law. This means that from the standpoint of a man, for example, all other men will fall into the following categories: grandfather, father, step-father (father's brother), mother's brother (father-in-law), brother, cross-cousin (brother-in-law), son, step-son (brother's son), sister's son (son-in-law), grandson.[7] Thus open quarrels would be tantamount, in terms of the formal kinship structure, to the expression of hostility between relatives. But since there are many other societies in which the same situation exists, I do not believe that the kinship structure as such is the basic factor in the discouragement of open aggression. There is no intrinsic reason, moreover, why relatives should not quarrel.

However, certain specific attitudes and behavior patterns that characterize certain classes of relationship among the Saulteaux do tend to discourage *open* hostility and thereby fortify self-restraint. There is considerable emphasis laid, for instance, upon the solidarity of brothers and, in fact, of all relatives in the male line. This means that quarrels between brothers or other closely related males are more shocking than those between cross-cousins. And since the relation between a man and his mother's brother (=father-in-law) is a highly formalized one requiring at all times a display of respect and even continence of speech, this type of habitual attitude and conduct in itself inhibits open aggression.[8]

At any rate, in Saulteaux society the inhibition of openly expressed aggression in face-to-face situations is not only a socially sanctioned ideal, in actual fact it seldom breaks down. What Duncan Cameron said of the Lake Nipigon Saulteaux more than a century ago is true of the Berens River people. He remarked that ". . . Indians, in fact, seldom quarrel when sober, even if they happen to hate each other." It will be noticed that Cameron's last phrase echoes the note of aggression struck by Le Jeune. The Indians whom both these men knew were by no means devoid of aggressive impulses, but they were observed to exercise restraint in the open expression of them.

The same is true of the Berens River Saulteaux. The problem, therefore, is to discover how individuals in this society dispose of their aggressive impulses. For it must not be supposed that in situations where any open display of hostility has been suppressed that this is the end of the matter. In fact, complete inhibition of such hostile emotions is neither expected nor demanded.

Broadly speaking, the culturally sanctioned channels for hostility are of two kinds. The first is typified by all the unformalized ways and means that may be utilized in any human society for the *indirect* discharge of aggression. Gossip is as rife among the Saulteaux as among any other people and many unpleasant and even scandalous things are said behind a person's back that no one would utter in a face-to-face situation. Even serious threats are made that may never be carried out.

The chief of one of the Berens River bands has been in office for many years. Again and again some of the Indians of his band have used devious means to remove him from his office, principally by accusations in anonymous letters sent to Ottawa or circulated locally by word of mouth. But when the band has met formally no one has dared to accuse him openly of the things said behind his back. All sorts of accusations were made against a missionary up the river a few years ago and from what I could gather a great many of them were true. But when a meeting was held to air the whole matter it came to nothing because the Indians would not state their grievances to his face. This is typical. An example of another kind of covert unformalized aggression is the following:

Some years ago several Berens River Indians who were out hunting came upon the traps of an Indian of the Sandy Lake Band. There is no love lost between the people of the Berens River and the Sandy Lake Indians; in fact, no marriages occur between the two groups. One of the hunters, egged on by his companions, defecated on one of the traps. Then he sprung the trap so that a piece of feces was left sticking out. Such an act was an insult to the owner of the trap and a deterrent to any animal that might approach it. It was a doubly aggressive act because, in addition to insulting the owner, it interfered with the purpose for which the trap was set and consequently menaced his making a living. That the Indian who did it recognized the nature of his act is proved by the fact that he later dreamed that a conjurer of the Sandy Lake Band tried to kill him by sorcery.

This leads us to the second channel for the expression of aggression—sorcery and magic.[9] This society does not actually say, "Thou shalt love thy neighbor." What it does say is, if I hate my neighbor it is better that I should not openly quarrel with him. On the one hand, that is to say, the open display of aggression is not socially sanctioned while on the other, uniformalized types of *covert* aggression are tolerated and in *addition* institutionalized means of covert aggression are provided. The use of these not only enables me to injure my neighbor, but they permit the accomplishment of my ends without his knowledge. He can only suspect, but never be quite certain, that I am using sorcery and magic against him. It is this obverse side of the discouragement of open aggression that gives a potentially ambivalent aspect to all forms of cooperative effort and harmonious interpersonal relations among these people. For the availability of sorcery and magic in this society may just as truly be said to foster *covert* aggression as the cultural norms requiring self-control in face-to-face situations may be said to discourage overt aggression. With sorcery and magic at my disposal, in fact, I can vent my anger with greater effectiveness than would be possible by verbal insult or even a physical assault, short of murder. I can make a person suffer a lingering illness, interfere with his economically productive activities and thus menace his living; I can also make his children ill or lure his wife away by love magic; I can even kill him if I wish. But when I meet him face to face I will give no evidence of my hostility by gesture, word, or deed. I may even act with perfect suavity and kindness toward him and share the products of my hunt with him. Of course he may suspect that I hate him or am angry, but even if he goes so far as to accuse me openly of using sorcery and magic I will not admit it. To do so would be tantamount to an open threat. And since he suspects me it would do no good to deny hostile intentions because he probably would not believe me anyway. So I may not answer him at all, but just turn and walk away.

It can now be understood that, while there are no *official* records of murder among the Saulteaux, this does not correspond with the psychological realities of this society. Within their behavioral world, murder has occurred again and again but always as the result of sorcery, not of overt physical aggression.[10] These Indians will not only name individuals who have met their death by sorcery, they will also name their reputed murderers. And they will go on to mention an even larger number of cases in which illness or failure in hunting have been caused by the malevolent action of human beings.

But the use of sorcery and magic as instruments of covert aggression is two-edged: whether an individual himself uses them or not, the threat that other individuals may be using them against him constantly lurks in the background of his daily life. In addition to the personal friction and unconscious hostilities that arise in all human relations,[11] these people are dogged by anxieties and fears arising from the belief that human beings may do them positive harm in this covert way.

Such fears have very deep and wide ramifications in view of the fact that human viscissitudes of all sorts may be interpreted as due to magic or sorcery. Such emotions are precipitated under circumstances where the cultural definition of a situation weights the explanation of events in favor of sorcery or magic. Whereas we might attribute such inevitable hazards of life as illness, misfortune, or death to chance or impersonal causes of one sort or another, the individual in Saulteaux society is bound to consider magic or sorcery as a possible cause; in fact he is forced to do so because of the character and limits of the explanation of phenomena his culture offers him as alternatives. Consequently, it is inevitable that this explanation of events will be applied under appropriate circumstances and that these cases, in turn, will later be adduced as evidence of the reality of sorcery. This vicious circle cannot be broken without radical cultural changes. The type of knowledge accessible to the Saulteaux is primarily a function of their culturally constituted attitudes towards the nature of the phenomenal world. It is impossible for them to think in terms of our category of natural causation, without utilizing the premises which have been built up in occidental culture as the result of the accumulation of scientifically acquired knowledge.

At the present day, as a result of acculturation processes, the explanation of events in terms of sorcery and magic appears to have been somewhat relaxed and diminished in range, especially in the band of Indians at the mouth of the river. But it has by no means died out. Individuals, for example, still suffer from *änicinábewápine*, "Indian sickness." This is a modern term which shows that the contemporary Saulteaux clearly recognize a distinction between the diseases known to the whites and those which are peculiar to them. Indian sickness occupies an autonomous etiological category because it is "sent by someone," as they put it. More specifically, it is based upon the idea that some material object can be projected by sorcery into a person's body in order to cause illness. White doctors cannot cure this kind of disease, so native doctors still flourish who are prepared to treat it by removing the object. Illness or even death also may be caused by an attempt on the part of a conjurer to steal one's soul during sleep.

An examination of cases of illness attributed to both these types of sorcery indicates how this explanation extends the range of personal hostilities upon a thoroughly irrational and nonrealistic plane. For in such instances suspicion usually falls upon some particular person. In fact, if an aggressor is not immediately identified a conjurer may be employed to discover him by clairvoyant means. The reason for this is that countermeasures may have to be instituted in order to save the patient.[12] The chief point of psychological interest here is what determines the selection of an aggressor? In many cases I have found that the determining factor is the belief held by the victim that he has offended the suspected aggressor in some way. In other words, the sick person is apprehensive because he feels that he has aroused another person's hostility by some act of his and that the offended person has retaliated by making him sick. This measure-for-measure philosophy is very deep-seated among the Saulteaux, pervading many aspects of their social and economic life,[13] so that it is not strange to find it operating in connection with aggressive patterns of behavior. Le Jeune, referring to the Montagnais, gives an amusing application of it which is psychologically diagnostic as well. He says, "They eat the lice they find upon themselves, not that they like the taste of them, but because they want to bite those that bite them."[14] Once we understand that the Saulteaux always think and act in terms of this same principle it is not difficult to see why an individual who thinks he may have offended another is quite ready to believe that he has been bewitched by the person he has offended. One case already mentioned illustrates this. The Indian who defecated on a trap thought that the owner of the trap had identified him because he dreamed that a conjurer of the Sandy Lake Band was attempting to steal his soul.

I have another account of a dream experience which was interpreted by the dreamer in the same way. In this instance the dreamer was a boy who had made fun of a hunchback by imitating the way the cripple walked. The boy believed that the father of this cripple, a conjurer, attempted to retaliate by trying to steal his soul.[15] The next day he was ill. He soon recovered, but he considered it a close call. In other words, both these men were threatened with death because of what they had done. In another case a young man suffered from Indian disease. It was thought that the man who had sent it was angry because the victim had beaten him in a dog team race. In this instance the young fellow died despite the efforts of a native doctor who tried to "suck out" the malignant object. From a native point of view this was a clear case of murder.

In all these cases we would consider the reputed retaliation—attempted murder— entirely disproportionate to the offenses committed if we considered them to be serious at all. But within the context of Saulteaux society it is obvious that their evaluation is quite different. They were considered sufficient grounds for the counteraggressive actions that menaced the lives of their perpetrators. In this respect they are excellent psychological clues to the kind of behavioral world in which these people live and act. If individuals believe that such actions of theirs are sufficient to arouse such extreme forms of retaliation, we can only conclude that they, in turn, might be offended by acts of a similar nature. It seems reasonable to infer, therefore, that these Indians are extremely sensitive to the slightest trace of aggression.[16] There is also the concomitant inference that individuals must be constantly on their guard lest they give offense to others.

An informant once told me that his father had cautioned him thus: "Don't laugh at old people. Don't say to anyone that he is ugly. If that person is *mändáuwīzī*—has magic power—he will make you so." It is obvious from the phrasing of this statement that no abstract ethical ideal was involved. Avoidance of offense is clearly a matter of self-defense.

The cases cited also illustrate another point of psychological interest. It is apparent that it is the prevalent belief in sorcery that is of prime importance, not its actual practice. I do not mean to imply by this that no one really uses magic or sorcery to gain his ends. Quite the contrary is true. But from the standpoint of the individual who interprets his illness or misfortune as due to sorcery, it makes little difference whether in actual fact someone has gone through certain procedures or not. Such procedures in any case are secret and no one can be sure. The point is that the psychological effects are the same. This is why sorcery and magic are real to the Saulteaux. Everyone acts as if they were and they thus become effective constituents of thought and feeling. From an obejctive point of view, the belief system of the Saulteaux thus fosters fantasy situations in which aggressive impulses become easily entangled with interpersonal relations in ways that may engender deep and irrational consequences. I may be easily led to believe that you are hostile to me and have bewitched me when this is not true at all. Yet there is no way of coming to grips with the situation in a realistic fashion. The following story illustrates this point, and since I happen to know one of the participants well I can speak with some assurance about his feelings in the matter.

About fifteen years ago at Treaty time, representatives of a number of the Berens River bands and some men from Deer Lake were camped at the mouth of the river. Joe, a young man of the Berens River Band, and Wabadjesi, a man from Deer Lake were wrestling. They were having lots of fun and a crowd gathered about them. But Joe was getting the better of Wabadjesi. The latter became irritated at this. Since there was such a crowd of men present evidently his pride was hurt. "If you throw me to the ground," he said to Joe, "you will see sparks of fire." The narrator commented that he did this to scare Joe who knew Wabadjesi had the reputation of being a powerful shaman.

"There won't be any sparks from the ground," Joe retorted, "but when you hit the ground you'll see plenty," and with that he let Wabadjesi go. But Wabadjesi was really mad by this time and said, "Watch out for me the first part of the winter. Then you'll know something about a Crane [his totem]." To this Joe replied, "And you'll know something about a Cree." Parenthetically it is stated that Joe was joking. He was not a Cree but his mother was. People began to talk about this exchange of open threats between the two men. Some of them even felt sorry for Joe, because Wabadjesi had such a big reputation as a man who was known to use sorcery and magic. Joe, on the other hand, had been to boarding school, was a Christian, and was entirely innocent of any malevolent intent.

The following winter the man who told me this story went trapping with Joe. They left the settlement in October. The first night out, just at dusk, they made camp in the shelter of a tall white spruce. They had hardly gotten settled when they heard what appeared to be the voice of a bird coming from the tree. They could not catch sight of it; neither could they identify its cry which kept sounding almost every ten minutes until midnight. They thought it strange but were not disturbed. The next morning they started off and continuing from that day throughout the winter, no matter where they went a pygmy owl seemed to be accompanying them. This was an untoward sign because sorcerers sometimes use the birds to accomplish evil ends. But neither man was ill.

In the spring after returning to the mouth of the river, they received news that Wabadjesi was very sick, in fact, that he was not expected to live. This made some people think that perhaps Joe really "was something." One man who had been present at the exchange of threats the previous summer even went so far as to say to him, half jokingly, "You almost killed Wabadjesi." "I did not intend to kill him," Joe replied in the same mood; "I had pity on his two boys."

This anecdote shows how, under certain circumstances, it is possible for an individual to be accused of using sorcery when in fact he has not done so. In this case I know that Joe did not entertain hostile feelings of any sort against Wabadjesi. Yet if Wabadjesi had died as a result of his illness, I think there is no doubt that people would have believed that Joe killed him. It certainly would have been the interpretation of the Deer Lake Indians who are much less acculturated than those of the Berens River Band. For it must be noted, among other things, that Joe *did* return Wabadjesi's threat. At the same time it is interesting to observe that Joe on his part was a bit apprehensive during the winter. Had he been a pagan, however, he would no doubt have suffered more severely. Furthermore, I am convinced that if Joe *had* been taken ill he would have blamed Wabadjesi, and if he had then followed the native pattern of behavior he would have been fully justified in retaliating by some covert means. As it was, there is no doubt that Wabadjesi, on his side, believed that Joe had taken some aggressive action against him. He could hardly think otherwise since he openly threatened Joe in the first place.

Another explanation offered me was that Wabædjesi undoubtedly tried to injure Joe but that for some reason or other, as sometimes happens, his magic turned upon him and caused the same sickness in him that he tried to project toward his victim.

One has only to multiply such episodes imaginatively to gain an idea of the extent to which the fantasies arising out of such situations can insinuate themselves into the fabric of Saulteaux society, engendering antagonisms that affect the interpersonal relations of individuals in various ways.

It is possible to cite other cases in which it can be shown how repressed—unconscious—aggressions of individuals are caught up and put into social circulation, as it were, through mechanisms of projection, displacement, and rationalization. Some frustrating experience of mine may release repressed aggression toward an associate or some other person who is in no way the cause of my frustration nor even hostile to me. But the prevalent belief in magic and sorcery enables me to rationalize my own projected aggression as hostility directed toward myself emanating from the person I have unconsciously chosen. These are familiar dynamisms, but among the Saulteaux we can discern them operating in a cultural milieu that facilitates rather than nullifies or offsets the canalizing of unconscious hostilities through them.

In one instance that I know of G. accused two of his brothers-in-law (cross-cousins), with whom he was hunting, of using magic to attract animals to their traps. This is an aggressive act because magic should only be used when hunting alone. It is so powerful that there is no chance for my hunting partner to catch any fur if I use it. Consequently, the use of hunting magic by one man of a group is tantamount to depriving the others of part of their living. G. felt frustrated because for a month and a half no animals came to his traps. "Not even a weasel," he said. Yet often he saw tracks circling them. All during this time his brothers-in-law were quite successful in their catch. G. told me about the whole affair himself and in this case there was no mention of any offense he may have committed against them. He was simply infuriated and vowed that the next time he went hunting with them he would use plenty of medicine.

Why was G. so ready to accuse his brothers-in-law of hostility? I happen to know G. quite well and, without going into detail, I will merely state that I believe there is plenty of evidence in his personal history and behavior in general to suggest that he has constant difficulty in disposing of unconscious aggression. G. is often at swords points with his father and he is the man I mentioned previously who gave his brother a severe beating. This brother, moreover, is his mother's favorite among the sons so that the source of G.'s aggression probably is very old and deep. For another thing, I strongly suspect that G. has a considerable amount of repressed hostility toward his wife. The hunting episode I believe to be thoroughly symptomatic of G. and my guess is that it involves the displacement of some of his aggression toward his wife upon her relatives. He has given additional evidence of this and it is facilitated by the fact that whereas G. is a militant Protestant, his wife and her people are strong Catholics.

On the hunting trip referred to G. had not only accused his brothers-in-law of using magic, he had gone on to insult them as Catholics by hinting that the local priests had sexual intercourse with the local nuns. I do not believe that it is accidental either that he launched into a tirade against X, one of his brothers-in-law, and his father-in-law as well. G.'s sister is married to X and G. told me the way he got her was by love magic—that is, unfairly. Then he went on to say that he believed that his own wife had only had one child because her father had given her medicine to prevent her impregnation. G.'s wife is an attractive girl and had many suitors before her marriage, among them G.'s brother. It was a forced marriage following the girl's pregnancy. For some time G. has suffered from the suspicion that his wife has been unfaithful. While he has discovered no proof, I happen to know that his suspicions are by no means groundless and that G.'s brother is involved. G. feels disadvantaged in many other ways and seems unable to adjust himself. It is not surprising, therefore, to find G. utilizing the beliefs of his culture to screen his own repressed hostilities. This permits a plausible defense against their emergence into his conscious life.

In still another case, Kiwetin, an old man, told me about a dream he had had in which one of his spiritual helpers informed him that a neighbor of his, a middle-aged woman, was using sorcery against him. Kiwetin had been sick and this was the explanation he finally adopted when the medicine he took did no good. The woman was married, in fact she was notorious for her many husbands, her dynamic personality, and her reputed knowledge of sorcery. One of the interesting points about this case is the fact that Kiwetin emphasized the woman's outward display of kindness and amiability toward him. He was a widower and lived alone and he said she often invited him into her house to have something to eat. But he always refused. He also said that she smiled pleasantly at him, but he knew this was put on, "it was only on her face, not in her mind."[17] In other words, Kiwetin's suspicions made any genuine friendliness with this neighbor impossible. I suspect there were unconscious involvements here but I know nothing about this old man's personal history in any detail.

In this case, however, there was another psychological factor involved which I have not yet touched upon. It requires emphasis in order to round out the analysis of the strains and stresses to which a belief in magic and sorcery subjects individuals in Saulteaux society. Kiwetin was a man who, in his earlier days, was one of the leaders of the Midéwīwin, an institution which offered curative services for payment. The leaders of the Midéwīwin also possessed a great deal of information about magic of various kinds which they dispensed at a price. So in Kiwetin's account of the woman who he thought had bewitched him he made it quite clear that he felt secure against any measures she might take. In his dream he even turned down the offer of one of his spiritual helpers to injure her. Kiwetin was fully confident that he could protect himself. His sense of security sprang from his belief in the power of his *own* supernatural helpers. In this respect he was in a different situation than G. The latter was a much younger man who had been brought up during a period of fairly rapid acculturation. He did not claim to have any spiritual helpers. Consequently he lacked the inner security of members of the older generation who believed that they had powerful guardian spirits to help them. Hence, G.'s belief that magic was being used against him made him feel the full impact of the hostility of others because he was exposed to it without protection.

It is important to recognize, then, that native belief does provide a means for protection against the covert hostility of others even though from our point of view this is likewise on a fantasy level. Up until recent years every boy at the age of puberty or a little before was sent out to fast in the forest. It was then that he secured the blessings of supernaturals who were to be his guardian spirits through life. While there was no formalized fast of this kind for girls, they were not debarred in native theory from the acquisition of supernatural helpers. In Saulteaux society the belief in the power of one's guardian spirits provides the ultimate basis for a sense of security in the individual. Nevertheless, the supernatural protection thus afforded varies greatly from individual to individual. Some persons are thought to have a great deal of power derived from this source, others little. And, following the extremely individualistic patterns of this society, no one knows how strong an individual is until he exercises his power. A few individuals are known to have considerable power because they utilize it in connection with conjuring, curing, or in other professional ways. It is also possible to add to the power one acquires at puberty by purchasing a knowledge of magic from others. This is what the midé men did, thereby enhancing their prestige.

In the give and take of social life, therefore, the apprehension of aggression varied concomitantly with the reputed power of the aggressor. And the ambivalence I have referred to reached its apex in the attitude toward the midé men and conjurers whom everyone knew to be the most powerful men of all. They were greatly feared and highly respected at the same time. Outwardly they were treated with the utmost show of deference. Only an individual supremely confident of his own powers would run the risk of offending an individual of this class.[18] But one could be less certain about others because there might be no reason for a man to exhibit or exercise his powers until he was in a tight place. It is also true that the midé men and conjurers often took advantage of the reputation they enjoyed. They were the ones who were sometimes openly aggressive in situations where other men would fear to be.[19] In fact, the Indians say that formerly such individuals were constantly trying each other out.

An instance of this is the following story told to me by the son of the man called Owl.

Pazagwigabo, the one who provoked the duel by sorcery, was the arrogant leader of the Midéwiwin.[20] He is reputed to have killed many persons by sorcery, and one informant described him as "savage looking in the eyes." The father of this informant warned him as a child never to play near Pàzagwigabo's camp. Owl, on the other hand, was a quiet-mannered man, small in stature and said to be kind to everyone. He was not a midé, but he had the reputation of being an excellent doctor and he was a noted conjurer. These two men belonged to different local groups and seldom came into personal contact. But on the occasion to be described Pàzagwigabo had come down the river to the Hudson's Bay Co. post and found Owl sitting on the platform of the store with a lot of other Indians.

Pàzagwigabo went up to Owl and said, "You think you are a great man. But do you know that you are no good? When you want to save lives you always bring that stone along. I don't believe it's good for anything." To this Owl replied, "Pàzagwigabo, leave me alone. I have never bothered you."

"You are not worth leaving alone," the midé said, and with this he grabbed Owl by the front part of his hair and threw him down. Owl simply got up and said, "Leave me alone." But Pàzagwigabo grabbed his hair a second time and when Owl made no resistance, he did it for a third time. Then Owl said, "Are you looking for trouble?"

"That's what I want," said Pàzagwigabo, "I want you to get mad. That's why I did this." So Owl replied, "All right. I know you have been looking for it for a long time. I know you think you are a great midé. You are nothing. If I point my finger at you you will be a dead man. But now I'll tell you something. Don't you do anything to my wife or my child. Do it to me and I'll do the same."

"Ho! Ho! Thanks, thanks," said Pàzagwigabo. "Expect me at *kijegîzis* [kind moon, February]. I'll give you a chance to do what you like to me."

Sure enough, during *kijgîzis* Owl was taken sick. He got the shell[21] all right, but of course he brought it out. But Owl was not sick long; he easily recovered. Shortly after this, news came down the river that Pàzagwigabo was sick. He was unable to walk. News spread about that he was getting worse and worse. Every once in a while Owl was heard to say, "Huh! Huh! I guess I nearly killed him. I did not mean to, I was only playing with him." When the *ni'kîgîzis* (goose moon, April) appeared Pàzagwigabo was only barely able to walk about. At the beginning of the summer Pàzagwigabo came down the river again with some other members of his band. They camped near Little Grand Rapids where Owl lived. When Owl saw the old midé he walked right up to him and said, "You know who Owl is now! I was only playing with you this time. I did not intend to kill you. But I never want to hear again what you said in this place. And I don't expect you to do again, what you did here. Don't think you are such a great midé!"

Of course this story may be a biased version of the events that actually occurred. We do not know what Pàzagwigabo had to say. But as it stands it is a beautiful illustration of how overt aggression, even when it occurs, is almost immediately displaced to the level of sorcery (fantasy) for a showdown. It also exhibits in dramatic fashion the confidence of both men in their own powers. In a situation where their very lives were in imminent danger, this made each of them courageous. Although men of lesser power might have suffered greater apprehension in such a situation, yet every Saulteaux has a modicum of spiritual armor because of the blessings from the supernaturals that he has secured in his puberty fast. He is not completely at the mercy of hostile forces. A consciousness of this fact is the balancing factor in the total situation. One might even say that *some* confidence in one's ability to ward off possible aggression is in the nature of a psychological necessity. Otherwise, the apprehension and fears of individuals in this society might drift too easily into a paralyzing terror. In principle, confidence in one's ability to face the hostility of others, or to match hostility against hostility might be said to give a realistic, healthy tone to situations where the warp and woof are so frequently constructed of fantasies.

However, apprehension and fear cannot be totally eliminated. This is not due entirely to the fact that a belief in sorcery and magic fosters such emotions. There is always the possibility that another man's power *may* be greater than my own. To provoke him to exercise it by offending him is always a gamble. What may happen if I do suffer from delusions of grandeur is well illustrated by Pazagwigabo. And still another aspect of the use of sorcery and magic has been referred to that may make me hesitate to use them at all: the possibility that if they fail to work for any reason, or my victim is stronger than I, they may be retroactive in effect. Instead of accomplishing my ends I may fall ill or die by my own sorcery. But in such matters it is not possible to be wise before the event. One has to risk defeat in attempting to achieve the ends desired. Thus both for the man who is confident of his powers, as well as for the common man, the best defense is to avoid offense if one seeks what the Saulteaux call *pīmädaziwin*—life in the fullest sense.

Chapter 16 - Psychosexual Adjustment, Personality, and the Good Life in a Nonliterate Culture*

Introduction.—AN ADEQUATE UNDERSTANDING OF HUMAN PSYCHO-sexual adjustment calls for more than a taxonomic study of actual sexual behavior. For sexual adjustment in man, as compared with that of other animals, is psychologically unique, whatever his overt behavior may be. One primary key to the nature of man's peculiar adjustment arises from the fact that his sexual activity is everywhere drenched with moral evaluations. In addition to the biologically rooted and intrinsically rewarding values of sexual stimulation and gratification, human beings respond to culturally phrased negative sanctions if approved sexual objects are not chosen, and traditionally recognized patterns of expression are not followed. Fully rewarded sexual behavior involves an inevitable compromise between instinctual impulses and the moral appraisal of their expression that is characteristic of a particular society. This compromise is not conscious or rational. It is a necessary part of the socialization process, begun in infancy, by means of which the psychosexual development of the individual becomes an integral part of his total personality organization. Consequently man's sexual behavior cannot be fully explained as a function of purely biological factors such as zoological status or level of maturation, although such factors cannot, of course, be ignored. Neither can human sexual behavior be fully understood as the result of a relatively simple learning process in which the individual is more or less passively molded to the prevailing cultural norms and values of his society. An examination of actual behavior may reveal wide variations from the culturally phrased ideal. The Kinsey-Pomeroy-Martin report has made this clear, so far as American males are concerned.[1] Knowledge of individual adjustment and the resulting psychological structuralization of the personality is necessary to an adequate understanding of the dynamics of the process. Once we turn to this aspect of the problem, the psychological derivatives of the ubiquitous moral evaluation of human sexual behavior become apparent. Psychosexual adjustment is fraught with anxiety, guilt, shame,

*Originally published in Paul W. Koch and Joseph Zubin (eds.), *Psychosexual Development in Health and Disease* (New York: Grune and Stratton, 1949). Reprinted by permission of the publisher.

291

frustration, and other affects which influence and color it. As a social being, in constant interpersonal relations with his fellows and groomed to take account of the goals and values of his society, man is induced to contemplate his sexual fantasies[2] and his sexual acts, to react affectively toward them, and to evaluate them. Impulses, as well as overt behavior, may be felt, or judged, to be good or bad. At the same time, human beings are subject to the institutionalized rewards and punishments that overt human behavior provokes. Thus the process of psychosexual adjustment is fraught with all sorts of possibilities for conflict. But some resolution is also demanded. The actual balance that eventuates between biological determinants, cultural standards, and the effects of social sanctions is intimately related to societal organization and personality structure. The anthropologist can best contribute to an understanding of human psychosexual adjustment by taking account of *all* the relevant factors in the societies that he studies.

Here I shall try to give an integral picture, in outline form, of the factors relevant to psychosexual adjustment among a relatively unacculturated group of Indians, the Saulteaux. The primary data on which statements in this paper are based comprise: systematic ethnographic inquiry, personal interviews, participant observation, and a Rorschach sample of the population (adults and children of all age groups and both sexes). Space will permit only illustrative documentation.

Cultural Evaluation of Sex Behavior and Social Organization.— Among the Northern Ojibwa all sexual behavior is evaluated from two points of view: first, with respect to the persons who may properly become sexual objects, and second, with respect to the technics of sexual stimulation and gratification that may be used. The emphasis upon *both* these categories of moral evaluation is so fundamental that even if sexually appropriate partners are married an *improper mode* of gratification subjects them to the same negative sanction that applies in cases of incest. Evaluations of the first category are closely integrated with the structuralization of the social world of these Indians viewed in terms of personal interaction and, in particular, with their kinship system.[3] Kinship terms are used in a widely extended sense and are not indices to actual blood relationship, except in the case of father and mother. They function as direct guides to interpersonal relations, since customary attitudes and patterns of social behavior are implied in the use of them. So far as sexual activity is concerned, moral values are intrinsic to the system, since only a single term (*ninam*) indicates sexual potentialities between the persons who use it. All other terms carry the connotation of sexual avoidance.

Such avoidance is accentuated in the case of (a) persons in the class of siblings of opposite sex (classificatory or real), (b) persons in the relationship (classificatory or real) of "father's sister"—"brother's son" and "mother's brother"—"sister's daughter." In the Ojibwa social structure such persons are also in the potential, or actual, relationship of "mother-in-law"—"son-in-law" and "father-in-law"—"daughter-in-law" since there are no special terms for relatives by marriage. All social interaction between persons in these categories is hedged about with elaborated restrictions which makes them extremely self-conscious of the social distance that must be maintained between them. Among other things, all verbal references to sexual matters must be strictly avoided when such persons are in each other's presence. This pattern of avoidance is the antithesis of the verbal freedom that is permissible between individuals who use the term *ninam*.

Sexually approved behavior, then, is defined in terms of the position which individuals occupy in the social structure and between whom a certain term is used. These potential mates are of the same generation in the kinship system. They include one type of actual blood kin, cross-cousins. Since kinship terms are extended throughout the social world of the individual there are no equivocal cases. These Indians have patrilineal clans but the rule of clan exogamy automatically follows when a mate is selected from the proper kinship class.

Stated so abstractly, the culturally phrased evaluation of an approved class of sexual objects looks very simple. In order to bring into sharper relief the actual nature of the sexual values this society stresses, I wish to call specific attention to the categories of sexual objects that are logically excluded.

(a) Persons of the same sex do not use the term that defines permissible sex relations, so homosexuality is ruled out.

(b) All persons in the usual incestuous categories are also ruled out, as well as many individuals *not* related by blood. Since *ninam* is only applicable between people of the same kinship generation, this fact alone makes legitimate sex relations between persons of different generations impossible. The tabu on sexual relations between close blood relatives is actually a function of the operation of the social system as a whole.

(c) Bestiality is a priori ruled out.

Turning now to the evaluation of sexual stimulation and gratification we find (a) That kissing, manipulation of the breasts and oral contact with them, and coital variations involving genital contacts, are *neutrally* evaluated.

(b) That masturbation,[4] (self or mutual), oral-genital contacts, the use of artificial phalli of any kind, and anal intercourse are *negatively* evaluated, and subject to sanction.

It is quite apparent that among these categories of sexual behavior, genital gratification alone is positively evaluated. Consequently, in this society, sexual activity is only approved between persons of opposite sex, occupying a defined position in the social structure, who use a reciprocal kinship term, and only genital gratification receives full moral sanction.

Cultural Sanctions and the Good Life.—The social and psychological significance of these fundamental evaluations of erotic behavior cannot be fully understood unless a word is said about what constitutes the Good Life, the main sanction that is exploited to uphold it, and the responsibility that devolves upon the individual for the consequences of "bad conduct" (*madjī jīwebazīwin*).

The central concept of the good life and the highest value is *pimādazīwin,* life in the fullest sense; life in the sense of health, longevity, and well-being, not only for one's self, but one's family. *Pimādazīwin* is a word heard again and again in ceremonies, and the supernaturals are petitioned for it. It is made possible primarily only through supernatural help, by "blessings" from guardian spirits. Bad conduct interferes with achieving this desired goal. One of the principal categories of bad conduct is some kind of sexual transgression. (See Chaps. 14 and 15.) Illness may be a sign of bad conduct. Since there are no organized penal sanctions and, in fact, no adult has any authority to impose any sort of penalty upon another person, and since openly expressed moral disapproval is avoided because it may be taken as a sign of hostility, fear of disease is the major social sanction.

Consequently it is believed that any departure from culturally evaluated sex behavior provokes its own penalty—disease and sometimes death. The significant thing is that the supernaturals have nothing directly to do with this.[5] There are other obligations one owes them. The universe is simply constituted in such a way that disease automatically and inevitably follows sexual transgression. This means that ultimately no one can escape moral responsibility for his sexual conduct. He must contemplate it in that light. It is also possible that an individual may suffer illness because of the bad conduct of his parents. The latter may thus be responsible for the sickness or death of their children. When serious illness occurs and the life of the patient may even be threatened, there is only one thing to do—confess the bad conduct. The transgressions confessed are, of course, those that the individual feels most guilty about; at the same time they correspond to conduct that is culturally disapproved. (For further details and examples, see Chap. 14.)

Nature of Sexual Misconduct Confessed.—Under the first category (disapproved sexual objects) fall cases of homosexuality, incest, and bestiality. I have collected instances of all of these.[6] Women as well as men were partners in homosexual relations. It is perhaps worth noting that all of these individuals were unmarried.[7] All varieties of incest occur. Although I have no quantitative data for the society as a whole based on systematic interviews, in my sample of twenty-four cases, there are eight cases of parent-child incest (four mother-son; three father-daughter and one instance in which a marriage occurred between a man and his step-daughter)[8] and ten instances of brother-sister incest. Of these there was one actual marriage between a brother and a sister and three instances in which the persons were classificatory siblings (parallel cousins). In addition, there were three cases in which the severe tabu upon sex relations between individuals in the kinship category father's sister-brother's son was violated and one in which the parallel relationship between mother's brother-sister's daughter was breached. Only a single case of incest between a man and his mother's sister was recorded and one involving a grandfather and granddaughter. Bestiality includes reputed relations of men with the following animals: dog, moose, bear, beaver, caribou, and porcupine; and a woman with a dog.

Under the second category, forbidden types of technics of gratification, my cases include: masturbation (self and mutual), fellatio, the use of a sucker's bladder,[9] a caribou penis and a mink as artificial phalli, and anal intercourse. Mutual masturbation is found in homosexual context, fellatio in both heterosexual and homosexual context; the artificial phalli in both, but anal intercourse in a heterosexual context alone.

Modal Patterns of Sex Behavior.—A rather sharply defined sexual dichotomy is characteristic of Northern Ojibwa society. This is not only apparent in the division of labor in economic tasks; it applies to prerogatives of all kinds. Leadership of ceremonies and specialized services, like curing and conjuring, that require supernatural validation, all fall to the men. In aboriginal days boys were sent out in the woods to fast before they reached puberty in order to obtain blessings from supernatural spirits; girls were isolated at menarche but this isolation was not connected with the acquisition of guardian spirits. Men were the approved mediators between the supernatural world and mankind.

Male dominance is culturally supported in this society. This is made evident throughout a wide range of attitudes and behavior. Women are supposed to be self-effacing. Self-assertion and mastery are reputed to be male characteristics. Yet it should be noted that the women chop and haul wood the year round, take entire charge of the building of wigwams and carry infants, bound to heavy cradle boards, upon their backs, in addition to performing all other domestic tasks. Physically, they are as strong and robust as the men.

Yet, so far as sex is concerned, they play an almost completely passive role in the sexual act itself. As one Indian, who had had some experience with white women, expressed it to me, "An Indian woman never helps you." The passive role of women in sexual activity is likewise indicated by the fact that the verb applied to the hunting of animals is commonly used by men when speaking of the pursuit of a girl. And this association between animal and woman appears in one of the dreams I collected. A hunter dreamed of a beautiful girl approaching him. Waking up, he interpreted this dream as meaning that an animal had been caught in one of his deadfalls. He went to the trap and, sure enough, he found a female fisher.

With this preliminary characterization of the culturally defined relations of men and women in mind, I wish briefly to describe in more concrete detail the modal aspects of sex behavior.

Nothing of a sexual nature is systematically concealed from children as they grow up. The sexual side of life is an open book. Some of the myths and tales that are told over and over again have a decided Rabelaisian flavor. Indeed, it is impossible for children living in such close proximity to their parents, either in the old-fashioned wigwam or the more modern log cabin, to escape being aware of the "primal scene." While I do not have sufficient information from which to generalize about the incidence of sex play among prepubescent children, there is no doubt that it occurs. Nonetheless, some phases of it are considered wrong. This is clearly indicated by a case in which the old mother of a grown man, who was ill because he could not urinate freely, confessed that years before when she was a little girl,

we had made a little wigwam and we were playing that we were camping like the old folks. Of course I did not know that I was doing anything wrong. I had a little thimble belonging to my mother and I had been sewing. One of the little boys was lying down and I was lying down, too. His little penis was standing erect. I took the thimble and shoved it on the end of his penis. Then I told him to go and piss. He said, "I can't, I can't. It's too tight. It hurts." Then he started to cry a little. So I took the thimble off and we told him not to tell.[10]

Boys and girls soon learn to differentiate individuals of the *ninam* class from siblings of the opposite sex and to differentiate their behavior accordingly. The possibility of bawdy verbal exchange between *ninamak* is soon learned, too. There are no polite synonyms in Ojibwa, so sexual references always go unmasked. So far as these verbal references are concerned they are not merely permitted, but encouraged. And they continue throughout life, even if no sexual relations actually occur. On one occasion when old Chief Berens and I were making a trip together we had barely stepped out of the canoe at one encampment when he began bantering an old woman about sneaking into her tent at night. She was one of his *ninamak* whom he had not seen for perhaps twenty-five years. On another occasion, a married woman much younger than himself said to him, "Do you think you can make your way through?" The answer was, "The older you get the stiffer the horn." I have heard such talk again and again, by people of all ages. Between preadolescents of the *ninamak* category horse-play and practical jokes may occur that are discouraged between siblings of opposite sex. This continues between *ninamak* who are married. A man told me that very early one cold winter morning he arrived at a camp where everyone was asleep. He saw one of his *ninamak* lying under a rabbit skin blanket. Her husband lay nearby and there were other relatives in the same wigwam. My friend said he quietly stole in, threw himself at her side and put his arms around her. She woke up and began to laugh. So did her husband and everyone else. Later he used to joke about "being under the blankets" with her. She would deny it; he would insist and everyone would have a good laugh. (For another episode of this kind see Chap. 6.)

In former days, as I have said, all boys were sent out for a vigil. If the boy was not "pure" (*pékize*) in the sense of having avoided *all* contact with girls, he stood no chance of obtaining the blessings that were essential to every man's career. From all accounts, the older Indians were very strict about this and I believe that the motivation was strong enough to have reduced overt sexual behavior in the previgil period to a minimum.

Once puberty was reached marriage was in the offing, so that it is possible that, with a reduction in the length of the premarital period, there was actually less sexual activity between the unmarried than is true today. Nevertheless it occurred and, as now, the reputed "hunting" of girls by boys indicates that the girls did not run "to get away," but rather to be pursued—and caught! In the initiation of sexual activity Ojibwa girls and women often play anything but a passive role.

Old Josie Josie, who lived a generation ago, used to tease the girls by telling them how his grandmother proceeded to get her man. On a fine afternoon, she would put on clean clothes, comb her hair well, take her axe and walk past the wigwams of several girls of her own age declaring loudly she was going out to cut wood. Of course they were delighted to go, too. And immediately some of the boys, who overheard all this, would begin preparations to go out hunting small birds and mammals with their bows and arrows. The girls would then go off together and, as they were engaged in chopping wood, one of them would notice that an arrow hit a tree nearby or even whizzed close by her head. This made them all laugh because they knew the party of boys was not far away. But none of them would give any outward indication of this. The next thing that might happen would be the breaking of some branches as a boy or two appeared. Then the girls would "run for their lives" (each in a separate direction). If a boy managed to catch up with her she would brandish her axe, but in a moment the boy would grab it away from her. Then the girl would be likely to trip over a root or fallen tree and there she would lie on the ground. The boy would soon have his arms around her and he would not find her an unwilling partner in his desires. Chief Berens once said to me, "Don't let anyone ever tell you that an Indian girl is ever raped. There may be such a thing among the whites, but not among us."

On the other hand, if a particular young man was too avid in his pursuit of girls, they might get "mad." In one case it is said that after luring a young fellow into the bush, a half dozen of them set upon him. They tore off his clothes, threw him to the ground and one of them urinated on his naked belly, while the others held him. "You know what women are like now," they said. He became a laughing stock after this and for a long time none of the girls would have anything to do with him.

Rendezvous of the unmarried may take place on the outskirts of dances held at night, on the way home at dusk when everyone, in summer, begins to settle down for the night. Sexual contacts may be initiated in a very casual manner. As one informant put it, "If you feel like having it you may say, 'Let's go this way' (off the path). She will go if she wants you. If not, she won't. She knows what you are after." Sometimes a young man may be encouraged to seek a girl out in her wigwam during the night, leaving at dawn. But he must be careful to know just where she sleeps! In one case a boy entered the wrong side of the wigwam and his sweetheart's grandmother hit him with a frying pan. Another informant, recounting many of his youthful escapades, described all sorts of ruses which might be used. More than once he obtained entrance to a wigwam after a dance by donning a shawl, thus disguising himself as a "girl friend" of his sweetheart.

During the premarital period, in fact, secret rendezvous are practically the only means of social contact between boys and girls. No opportunity occurs for genuine companionship. Their economic activities segregate them, there are few games in which both sexes participate, in dances the sexes are separated and no boy openly walks with a girl, is seen in a canoe alone with a girl, or even talking to one. But *groups* of boys and girls are constantly seen together. Consequently any kind of isolation of a girl and a boy has an aura of sex about it.

No Indian girl is surprised if asked to make a rendezvous. But if it is somewhere in the bush or anywhere but in her wigwam, another girl usually goes along, even if no "double date" is in prospect. The friend sees to it that the lovers are not surprised because it is desired to keep such affairs as secret as possible. Yet just because a friend is taken along they often become open secrets. Foreplay is not elaborated in these affairs. In fact heterosexual petting, as defined by Kinsey, is practically nonexistent. In the first place, kissing and especially deep kissing, is not customary, although there is no tabu against it. Nor are female breasts an object of erotic interest to men. I can well imagine an Indian dismissing such an idea as mouth-breast contact in the same terms as those used by lower level American males, viz, "As something that only a baby does."[11] So far as manual manipulation of the genitalia is concerned there may be some by the boy, but seldom any by the girl. And I have already referred to the fact that oral-genital contacts can only be indulged in the face of the disease sanction. The idea of oral contact with a woman's genitalia is particularly disgusting to the Ojibwa. In this connection it is worthy of note that the verbal reference to a woman's genitals is the most obscene reference that can be made. All in all then, the culturally constituted incentives are all weighted in the direction of genital contacts rather than in the direction of elaborated petting. And, as Kinsey points out,[12] in American culture elaborated petting is *not* characteristic of lower level sex behavior where genital intercourse is accepted, but is "to some extent . . . the outcome of the upper level's attempt to *avoid* pre-marital intercourse" (Italics ours). If, as Kinsey says, lower level Americans are astonished at the elaborated petting technics of higher level Americans, I am sure that the Ojibwa would be amazed and shocked beyond measure. Among them genital intercourse is highly typical of premarital sexual behavior and it usually takes place with great dispatch.

A missionary friend of mine once characterized the premarital sexual conduct of these Indians as *amoral*. This, I think, is essentially correct. For if the partners are in the correct kinship category and no forbidden modes of stimulation or gratification occur, there is no negative sanction of any generalized sort that applies. Consequently, the missionaries have found such behavior hard to modify because no pangs of conscience are involved. At the same time it must be recognized that *verbal* disapproval is often expressed by parents, particularly with respect to their daughters' behavior. And the girls may be punished if caught. There is also the risk of pregnancy, but since a girl who bears an illegitimate child is in no way socially ostracized, this possibility is hardly an effective sanction. Perhaps this premarital sex behavior may best be characterized as tolerated, much in the same way as comparable behavior is accepted by lower level Americans.

Because of the cultural support of male dominance and the sexual accessibility of women, the male ego is peculiarly sensitive to *rejection*. To turn a man down too abruptly, for example, may be tantamount to a personal insult. This applies both to a request for a rendezvous and an offer of marriage. Aggression is easily aroused in men under such circumstances. Sometimes, there may be a resort to love magic which is reputed to make the victim infatuated with the person using it. Or, the girl may be made ill through sorcery as a means of retaliation. I have information on several cases where illness was thought to be due to sorcery, employed as retaliation for sexual frustration. In one of these the woman was able to use counter sorcery and worsted her former suitor. Her life had been threatened but she did not kill him, although she had the power to do so. This outcome is significant when considered in relation to the dominant role of men in this culture. What seems to be implied is the assumption that men have potential sexual *rights* over women that must always be respected. This is one of the less consciously articulated but, none the less, basic facets of male dominance. There is a myth which supports the same idea. A girl refused man after man. She was very proud. Finally, a handsome youth appeared in her camp. She wanted to marry him. But he was Dung-man. As she followed him he melted away in the sun. There is also an anecdote about some medicine men who considered a certain girl much too proud because she refused to marry anyone. They lured her out in the bush and had serial intercourse with her. Such narratives are fairly obvious warning to women of what men expect of them.

Since every woman and every man is expected to marry and rear a family, and because this expectation is closely approximated in fact, marital intercourse becomes the modal form of sexual outlet. It is so extremely unusual not to marry that cases of bachelorhood and spinsterhood that do occur receive an explanation that really transcends any personal choice in the matter. There is a belief that such persons have dreamed of *mīcīpījiu* (Great Lynx), one of the few superhuman entities that is given a purely malevolent character. This spirit may appear to the dreamer as a beautiful young woman or man and intercourse may take place. After this, the true character of the Great Lynx is revealed. This spirit is extremely jealous and if a person does later marry, misfortune, disease, and even death may follow. One man who dreamed of the Great Lynx did marry. Once when a child of his was sick he had a dream in which he fought the Great Lynx and won! His child recovered and he felt himself released from any further menace. Thus individuals who dream of the Great Lynx are fearful of marriage lest their spouses and children as well as themselves suffer misfortune. The only unmarried man of middle age that I have knowledge of was probably a suppressed homosexual.

Not long ago polygyny was still practiced. The range in number of wives was 2–6, the latter figure being unique. In the seventies and eighties of the last century the percentage of polygynous men in various bands in the region studied ranged from 5–24, the percentage of men with *more* than 2 wives from 0–6. One selective factor in polygyny was skill in hunting. Only very good hunters could support several wives and their children. Sometimes plural wives were sisters and occasionally a man married his deceased brother's wife.[13]

I found that neither impotence nor frigidity were understood by these Indians. I have no statistics, but my guess would be that impotence is less frequent than among us. At any rate it is expected that potency will continue until late in life. A tottering old man was once pointed out to me. Gossip had it that recently he had met a woman on a lonely path and that she had resisted his advances and had run away. I took this as a joke but the Indians took it seriously.

High frequency of intercourse is expected; nightly by the younger men. Since women are realistic about sex, if a man does not have intercourse with his wife she may suspect him of other affairs. The physiology of conception is not thoroughly understood. Most of these Indians do not appreciate the fact that a single act of intercourse may result in conception. Kinsey points out[14] that restraint of the wife constantly lowers the frequency of marital intercourse in all segments of our population, but chiefly among the educated groups. Despite the fact that I have no frequency figures it can be asserted that no such factor operates among the Northern Ojibwa. When he was a young man, my friend, Chief Berens, often had several climaxes in one night, particularly when he had been off hunting for a period, and had just returned home. Intercourse is avoided during the menses and then sometimes during the later phases of pregnancy. It is resumed a month or so after the birth of a child.

There is certainly no attempt on the part of the men to delay orgasm or any self-consciousness about achieving simultaneous climax. The women experience a relatively passive type of orgasm. Any tendency to bite, or any other sadistic manifestations, seemed strange to the men I talked to. Intercourse usually takes place at night. Since these people have no night clothes and seldom, if ever, completely undress for any purpose whatsoever, nudity in intercourse is almost unheard of. Nevertheless, I did record an anecdote about an orphan girl who was sent to live with her grandfather and became his mistress. In the story *she* takes the initiative, strips off her clothing, and offers herself to him. The initiative taken, the incest, and the nudity make this story a treble shocker. But the extremely deviant behavior of this girl highlights morally approved behavior at the same time.

Foreplay in marital intercourse is not elaborate for reasons already referred to in the discussion of premarital sex behavior. One of the cases of fellatio, however, involved a married couple as did the use of a mink as an artificial phallus. Two cases of anal intercourse involved married pairs. One of the women claimed that her husband forced it upon her and that once she fainted. All the women are "scared" of it, I was told. And one informant said, "If a girl bothers you, tell her you will do it that way and she will be sure to keep away from you."

Kinsey observes that "there has been an insistence under our English-American codes that the simpler and more direct a sexual relation, the more completely it is confined to genital coitus, and the less the variation which enters into the performance of the act, the more acceptable the relationship is morally." This corresponds to the Ojibwa ideal and also general practice. The further statement that "For most of the population, the satisfaction to be secured in orgasm is the goal of the sexual act, and the more quickly that satisfaction is attained, the more effective the performance is adjudged to be,"[15] can also be applied to these Indians.

Extramarital intercourse has a high incidence among the Northern Ojibwa, but I have no figures. Like premarital sexual activity it does not fall under the disease sanction that applies to the improper choice of a sexual partner or improper techniques in sex relations. One of my informants pointed out that it was too prevalent to be punished by illness.

Like premarital sex relations it is tolerated rather than culturally approved. For faithfulness in marriage is verbally upheld as an ideal and certain women are often cited as being good women and good wives, because they have been virtuous.

Extramarital affairs are carried on by secret rendezvous and, like premarital affairs, are usually casual. I know of only one case of a long continued liaison. This was between a married man with quite a large family of children, and a widow with two children. A married woman may take a companion with her to a rendezvous, as do unmarried girls. There is the same danger of being exposed, of the spreading of gossip, and in addition, the possibility that, if caught, a woman may be beaten by her husband.

The Reinforcement of Modal Patterns.—If a sufficient number of deviant cases were to set up an accumulative trend, changes might be anticipated in the social organization of a group like the Northern Ojibwa and some reorganization in their value system might be also expected. Personally, I see no evidence of this in my data. In fact I should like to emphasize that the publicity given cases of "bad conduct" through confession actually reinforces the basic sexual evaluations of their society. For the confessions made in disease situations are never kept secret. (See Chap. 14.) Functionally viewed, a society can well tolerate a few breeches of the rules if a knowledge of such cases is a constant reminder to live the Good Life and thereby avoid illness and possibly death. The only real danger to the social order would come from an accumulative trend, in a deviant direction, of actual conduct or, from a direct challenge to primary values that might influence actual conduct.

The one case of actual brother-sister marriage is particularly interesting in this connection. In the first place it obviously runs directly counter to the sanctioned rules of sex relationship in or out of marriage, and it was not a casual affair, as are all other cases of incest of which I have knowledge. But there was no action that could be taken about it. Sαgáskī went on living with his sister, had three children by her and, when she died, married again. Of course, it was said that the death of his first wife and one or two of his children was a penalty for bad conduct. But if we stopped here, the much deeper significance of this case for an understanding of the operation of Ojibwa society and the psychosexual adjustment of individuals in it, would be lost. In the first place, Sαgáskī was a well-known medicine man and therefore someone noted for his power and feared because of it. Since power in this society means supernaturally derived power Sαgáskī was in the strongest possible position to flout the mores. From one point of view this is exactly what he did. But this is not the whole story. While he flouted the mores he did not challenge their traditional validity in any way. What he actually did is extremely interesting. He claimed he had a dream, in which one of his guardian spirits, the "master of the beaver," *commanded* him to do as the beaver did, that is, mate with his sister. Sαgáskī, in short, felt just as guilty about his incestous impulses as any one else, but he rationalized them in culturally approved terms by appealing to the highest authority in his society—the spirit helpers of mankind. And I have no doubt that he actually dreamed what he said he dreamed. However, a man who felt less confident of his own power might never have dared to do what Sαgáskī did, because of a fear, among other things, of the ubiquitous disease sanction. But in Sαgáskī's case we have a man who was undoubtedly involved in the deepest kind of libido struggle and the unconscious forces at work were scarcely under his control. This is indicated by two things. First, he is said to have urged his son to follow his incestuous example, but the son refused. Secondly, he always camped by himself—in summer on a little island—and would never allow any boys to court his daughters. Two of them never married, although one had an illegitimate child. The case of Sαgáskī, then, was not viewed by anyone, and certainly not by himself, as a challenge to the established sexual code. In fact, this case is still pointed to as an example of what *not* to do.

Sex Behavior, Myth and Tale.—Only incidental mention has been made of the treatment accorded sexual activities in myth, tale, and anecdote. If space permitted it would be interesting to examine more thoroughly the sexual interaction of the characters in myth and tale and the implicit values expressed in them with reference to actual behavior. For such traditional narratives, which are told and retold, constitute symbolic material of prime importance for a deeper psychological understanding of the people. In this society oral narratives are not regarded as fiction. They are believed to be true stories, accounts of actual events. In the myths, which are the sacred stories, the major characters are spiritual entities of one sort and another. Myth narration is equivalent to talking about these existent entities and invoking their presence. In the tales, the characters are human beings. The complex relations that exist between these traditional narratives, the kind of universe they depict, the values expressed in them and the characterological structure and behavior of the Indians, cannot be profitably discussed except in considerable detail. But a few indications of the nature of these relations may be given.

So far as the evaluation of sexual conduct is concerned, some of the narratives clearly support the established mores in the same way that confession on the part of individuals does. Characters who are guilty of sexual, or other bad conduct, instead of achieving *pīmădazīwin,* come to a bad end. Transvestitism, combined with overt homosexuality, for instance, is the theme of one naturalistic tale. A woman leaves her husband and children, disguises herself as a man and takes a "wife." In order to avoid the usual masculine role in intercourse she rubs the genitals of her partner with her fingers. The "wife" is dissatisfied with this,

303

whereupon the "husband" makes an insulting remark about her vulva as an excuse for not inserting "his" penis. Since masturbation is likewise disapproved, this tale is full of forbidden sexual conduct. Finally, the heroine is discovered and killed by her real husband. This denouement points a moral consistent with the values assumed in actual conduct. The heroine is bad not only because of her sexual transgressions; she had deceived her husband and other people and deserted her own children, so her fate is thoroughly deserved as a penalty for bad conduct.

The occurrence of anal intercourse in the myths presents a more complicated problem. In two instances, its occurrence is purely symbolic. Impregnation takes place by blowing upon the anus. In other cases, however, a transvestite-homosexual theme appears. But the hero is not a human being but Wísɑkedják, the trickster-culture hero. He is reputed to be always doing things backwards. In the narrative Wísɑkedják disguises himself as a woman, marries, and anal intercourse takes place. Wísɑkedják poses as a stranger and tells "her" husband that this mode of intercourse is customary in the locality from which "she" comes. The mythological dramatization of what is forbidden conduct in real life is thought uproariously funny. I am reminded, in this connection, of a long conversation I once had with an old Indian about sexual vagaries. At one point he remarked that it was best to laugh at all such things. The myth referred to affords just such an opportunity. Since anal humor of all kinds is quite characteristic of these Indians, the occurrence of anal intercourse in myth and the attitude towards it points to a strand in the personality structure of the Ojibwa that is deeply rooted. We also find in myth an account of how sexual intercourse itself was accidentally discovered by Wísɑkedják. And his extremely long penis is dramatized to humorous effect. But there are anecdotes from real life about men who had sex organs of unusual size that were instrumental in bringing grief to girls. It is also interesting to note the remarkable correlation between the kind of animal "wives" with whom men mate in myths and the animals with whom actual bestiality is reported. The porcupine is the most striking example.

Sexual themes in myth and tale and sexual behavior and attitudes in actual life are related. They are part of one culturally constituted behaviorial world. The many connections that exist are complex but their full psychological significance cannot be understood except by probing beneath the surface of overt behavior.

Personality Structure and Psychosexual Adjustment.—In this paper I have discussed the problem of psychosexual adjustment chiefly from the standpoint of the cultural evaluation of sexual conduct in relation to the social order and its sanctions. The actual dynamics of social organization is ill-conceived, however, if some account is not taken of the fact that the individuals who interact in particular ways, behave thus because they have been psychologically structured for living and acting

304

as they do. Thus personality organization and actual behavior in society are part of a basic continuum, an integration of personal adjustment and organized social living. In conclusion, I wish briefly to point out what seem to be the most significant items in the personality organization of the Northern Ojibwa that have a bearing upon their psychosexual adjustment.

The average Ojibwa is a highly controlled person. This is especially true of the men, for the women do not feel so vulnerable in their self-respect. All the early parental nurture and training of both boys and girls are in the direction of strengthening self-reliance, self-control, and developing skills. They are gradually weaned at an early age from parental help both literally and psychologically. But for the boy there is a further step: he is explicitly directed to seek the help of supernaturals. These actually become parent surrogates from puberty onward.

In this process of strengthening the individual to deal alone with the problems of survival, to rely upon his inner resources and "blessings," there is a general muting of any extensive development of emotional responsiveness, tender affective ties, or social relations. Nor do advantages accrue from any social position. For men, in particular, self-esteem rests mainly upon their own powers and achievements reinforced by the inner support obtained from supernaturally derived blessings. So too, feelings of guilt come from a highly internal conscience and often take the form of hypochondriacal fears of various kinds. There is no external rewarding and punishing agent to relieve one of such a strict conscience. As we might expect, such individuals are introverted, highly sensitive to others, are friendly only in a reserved way, for they are wary of others' powers that may be covertly exercised through sorcery. Any fancied rebuff may be taken as a slight. With so little real give and take, or learning to know each other on an openly confident and genuinely friendly basis, there is a high degree of projecttion in interpersonal relations.

Among the women, however, there is more outgoingness and, although they, too, do not develop extensive friendly relations and are shy, toward their children they are warm and affectionate. A woman's life being primarily domestic does not necessitate all the safeguards about her ego that men develop.

Between men and women whose personality structure is characterized by such an underdevelopment of deep and fully elaborated affective ties, sexuality functions primarily as a means of satisfying basic biological urges, rather than an enriching factor in a mutual integration of their emotional lives at a more complex level of psychosexual development.

PART IV

The Psychological
Dimension in Culture Change

Introduction: Problems

I N HIS BIBLIOGRAPHICAL SURVEY OF THE LITERATURE ON CULTURE
change, Keesing begins by remarking that "studies of culture in its time-
dimension aspects are as old as cultural anthropology itself." At the same
time "this field of theory and method is currently weak and not well
integrated. Only in the last handful of years has it been undergoing
the complete rescrutiny it deserves in the light of newer approaches to
the study of behavior which have been developing both within anthropology itself and in collateral behavioral science fields as well as in
certain aspects of study in the humanities."[1] Although the wider ramifications of the problem have been kept in mind, the three papers in
this section deal primarily with the psychological dimension of a single
aspect of culture change, acculturation. A recent survey of the anthropological literature by Beals[2] shows that very limited attention has been
paid to this factor in acculturation. The psychoanalysts, too, for example
Fromm[3] and Kardiner,[4] have not focused their interest primarily on
the acculturation situation in their studies of the relation between culture
change and personality structure. Again, Barnett in his treatise on *Innovation* is not concerned in explicit detail with psychological processes
and personality structure, although they are implied in his whole conceptual scheme. He recognizes that some distinction is necessary "between the acceptance of a new idea by people within the cultural sphere
of the innovator and acceptance by those of other ethnic groups." At
the same time he rightly points out that diffusion, acculturation, and
faddism are all "varied patternings of the process of acceptance. Each
has its own condition and so the final result is different; they come
about through the differential operation of acceptance and rejection
on the individual level."[5] This, of course, is the psychological level.
We know that if any people undergo changes in their mode of life
eventuating in new or varied culture patterns this implies some readjustment in the habits, attitudes, and goals of the individuals concerned,
that such processes of readjustment have to be motivated, and that learning is involved. These are the most obvious psychological events that
any process of acculturation implies; they must be assumed as an integral
part of the total conditions under which acceptance or rejection takes
place. The first paper in this section discusses the psychological aspects
of acculturation primarily on this level.

But there is a further question that invites inquiry. Instead of being
concerned with the goals and motivations of individuals which *lead*
to the acceptance of new cultural items, or the conditions under which
social learning takes place, we are now confronted with the question
of the psychological *depth* of the readjustments—with the cumulative
psychological effects which acceptance may bring about in a given

population over a period of time. Whatever may have been the situational and psychological determinants that motivated the selective acceptance of exotic cultural items, and however these latter may have been reinterpreted and integrated in an ongoing sociocultural system, a merely descriptive account of changes in technology, dress, food habits, kinship systems, beliefs, language, still leaves this further question unsolved. Specifically, we want to find out what kind of personality structure characterizes the individuals who are now the agents of a sociocultural system that has been modified through acculturation. We want to know whether the ostensible readjustments in cultural patterning that we observe have, or have not, led to any demonstrable changes in the psychological structuralization and functioning of the human beings involved. Obviously we are dealing with extremely complex variables: the time span over which the acculturation process has taken place, the rate of acculturation, factors involving the qualitative aspects of the whole process, and the way the relations between individuals of the two interacting groups are socially structured. All individuals, moreover, may not have responded to the situation in the same way. Women, for instance, may have been affected differently from men.

Confronted with such problems, the hypotheses, methods, and techniques adopted in any investigation assume great importance. This is particularly the case if we wish to measure in some way the psychological depth of acculturation: to discover, for example, whether there is, or is not, any basic change in the "modal" or group membership aspects of the personality in a given society.[6] Or to answer the further question whether it is possible to obtain any evidence regarding the degree to which the individuals of a selected population are functioning successfully or unsuccessfully, when measured by some reliable standard of personal adjustment, such as the level of psychological integration which they exhibit. If substantial evidence of this kind were available, it would be possible to examine and compare the range and variability of personal adjustment in acculturated groups.

So far as the extent of the psychological readjustments brought about by acculturation is concerned, I think one basic assumption we should make is suggested by the question: Why should the structural pattern of the modal personality of a group undergo any change at all so long as it is possible to get along without any radical change? Furthermore, if the psychological "set," or personality structure, is acquired and stabilized early in life and is not under conscious control, we can hardly adopt the hypothesis that changes in personality organization throughout a society would be among the *earliest* effects of acculturation. Indeed it is hard to imagine how a psychological change of this depth could be brought about in less than several generations. By its very nature a typical personality, once established as an integral part of a sociocultural system, would seem to be highly resistant to change. If this is so, then one of our fundamental hypotheses would be that the modal personality structure of a society may be expected to persist until conditions arise that *enforce* change.

Thus, while all acculturation involves psychological readjustments in the sense that new habits must be learned or new attitudes and goals acquired, there is no reason to assume that such readjustments in themselves involve the psychological core of the personality. Surely iron tools may be substituted for those made of stone, one style of dress replace another, or a new language be learned, without any radical effect upon the personality organization. Let us say, then, that the culture of one group of people may be influenced in many ways by that of another without the people of the borrowing group undergoing any necessary changes in their modal personality structure. Psychological changes of great depth are probably a consequence of qualitative and temporal factors of the acculturation process that as yet are little known and need special investigation. For instance, we would like to know how far one language can displace another, a new world view or religion be acquired, and sweeping technological changes occur *without* deep and penetrating psychological effects. And the related question: Exactly what happens to the modal personality organization of a group of people when it *is* affected by acculturation?

Chapter 17 - Sociopsychological
Aspects of Acculturation*

O NE OF THE MOST IMPRESSIVE EVENTS IN THE RECENT HISTORY OF mankind has been the global expansion of European peoples. The Greek and Roman expansion in the ancient Mediterranean world, the migration of the Arabs across North Africa and into the Iberian Peninsula, the Mohammedan expansion into Northern India, are hardly to be compared with it. For our time the subsequent economic, political, and military repercussions of this movement of European peoples and the influence of their culture have created the modern world as we know it and the world crisis in which we live.

Among other things, this invasion, conquest, and colonization of various parts of the world by Europeans stimulated an interest in the aboriginal peoples who were discovered in Africa, Asia, Australia, the islands of the Pacific, and the New World. Collections were made of native manufacturers, very strange at the time to European eyes, and ultimately the systematic study of the mode of life of these peoples was begun. Before the end of the nineteenth century cultural anthropology had been born.

At first, anthropologists were primarily interested in speculating upon possible stages of cultural evolution. They became engaged in salvaging all possible information about the life that aboriginal peoples had lived prior to the influence of European culture. There was also a tendency to identify nonliterate peoples with the different stages through which it was believed mankind as a whole had passed. The fact that various aboriginal peoples had been undergoing cultural changes and readaptation in mode of life ever since Europeans had come in contact with them aroused scarcely a casual interest. Even after the pseudohistorical theories of unilinear cultural evolution were given up, native peoples with a "living" or "functioning" culture were chosen for study in preference to those having a "broken down" or "disorganized" culture. When the latter were investigated at all it was with the intention of "reconstructing" the aboriginal culture of the

*Originally published in *The Science of Man in the World Crisis*, edited by Ralph Linton (New York: Columbia University Press, 1945). Reprinted by permission of the publisher.

past from the memories of individuals, rather than of obtaining information about the conditions which had promoted changes, the aspects of the native culture that had changed, the processes by which these changes had come about, or the results.

In recent years, however, the study of the influence of the culture of one people upon that of another has emerged as one of the major interests of anthropologists. There is no doubt that, to some extent, this interest has been stimulated by the inescapable magnitude of the problems created by racial and cultural contacts in the modern world and, in particular, by the practical administrative problems faced by all governments which now have to deal with aboriginal peoples who have come within the domain of their political control. But the scientific stimulus to the study of the contacts between peoples with different modes of life lies in the contribution it can make to our understanding of the dynamics of human behavior and adaptation. The more that is known about the actual dynamics of human adaptation and readaptation under observed conditions, the sounder will be the foundations for a study of the general principles involved in these processes.

One is reminded here of the doctrine of uniformitarianism enunciated by Lyell when he wrote his *Principles of Geology* over a century ago. Whereas earlier geologists had sometimes invoked specific explanations (for example, catastrophes) for certain past events, Lyell emphasized the fact that the same processes must be assumed to be operating in the past as at present. By carefully observing the effects of contemporary processes we will be in a better position, he said, to understand the events of past epochs. This principle has become well established in the natural sciences and is just as applicable in the scientific study of man.

There is no reason to assume, for instance, that the societies of nonliterate peoples whether past or present are intrinsically more static or conservative than the literate, historic, or so-called "advanced" peoples. Neither can we assume the operation of an automatic law of progressive unilinear stages in human adaptation or that there were some mysterious or "X" factors at work in the past. The scientific problem consists in the discovery of the actual factors that create stability in human culture, as well as the necessary and sufficient conditions under which modifications in the mode of life of a people take place.

So far as the distant past is concerned, it is obvious that we can never know very much about the actual processes and conditions of adaptation and readaptation that took place. We do know that there was a revolutionary change in man's subsistence economy, in more than one area, when a transition was made from a food-gathering to a food-producing economy. But the details escape us; we are only acquainted with the results produced. Archeologists have also supplied us with a great deal of information about the tools, weapons, utensils, and other objects that man used in the past and the changes that occurred in the forms of these. And while we assume that some of these changes must have been the results of indigenous inventions and discoveries in particular societies we can know nothing about the concrete events that led up to them. We do not even know whether such inventions and discoveries resulted from a conscious attempt to solve certain practical problems, or how far they were the result of fumbling trial and error methods, or the accumulative trend of small changes. Hence, it is practically impossible to deal with the dynamics of inventions and discoveries in early human societies except in a relatively few instances. We have to be satisfied with a knowledge of the end-products. We have some notion of *what* occurred but not *how* it occurred.

Some kind of contact of different peoples is as old in human history as differentiated modes of adaptation themselves. While it is true that, after man had reached his maximum expansion, peoples in certain parts of the world never knew of one another's existence, to say nothing of coming into contact with one another, yet it would be difficult to demonstrate a case in which any particular people has been completely isolated from all other peoples throughout its entire history. All our present knowledge of human migrations and racial mixture precludes this. Besides, how many culture traits of any human society can be demonstrated to be locally invented and completely unconnected with those of any other people whatsoever? Indeed, the resemblances between cultural items of peoples widely separated in space, and sometimes in time, has presented a major problem to the anthropologist. In the history of anthropology the interpretation of such data has resolved itself again and again into weighing the possibility of local or independent origin and development against the possibility of the diffusion or spread of such traits or complexes from one people to another.

Studies of cultural diffusion usually have begun, however, with an inventory of the geographical distribution of particular traits or assemblages of them, rather than with a study of the contact of specific peoples in a concrete historical setting. While the possible origin and presumed spread of such cultural items may be considered an historical question in the broadest sense of the term, it is history devoid of real knowledge of any specific events, conditions, or personalities. When considered at all, the actual processes that mediated diffusion and the conditions of cultural change have to be inferred. The consequence has been that in such studies culture traits and complexes often undergo a kind of reification, in so far as they are treated as if they had a life of their own, quite unconnected with human beings of flesh and blood. The most extreme example is typified by members of the German "historical" school. They have abstracted assemblages of culture traits which are asserted to be highly integrated and of great stability. These "culture circles" are then manipulated in time and space as reified units which meet, blend, or overlie each other so that certain new combinations are produced. There is no attempt to deal with the complex details of actual historical events or the processes of interaction that follow contacts between actual human beings.

While American anthropologists have been more cautious, on the whole, the conceptualization of culture as a "superorganic" or "sui generis" level of phenomena does lend itself to unconscious reification in unskilled hands. There are also difficulties encountered when the dynamics of culture are dealt with. For it is hard to see how culture —an abstract summation of the mode of life of a people—can exert an influence except as it is a definable constituent of the activities of human individuals in interaction with each other. In the last analysis it is individuals who respond to and influence one another. Culture, as Bidney[1] has pointed out, "is not an efficient cause and does not develop itself, hence it is not capable of interacting with any other entity." To argue otherwise leads to what he calls the "culturalistic fallacy" "which is based on the assumption that culture is a force that may make and develop itself and that individuals are but its passive vehicles or instruments."

Although anthropologists often speak of the "movements" of culture or the "meeting" of cultural traits or complexes, this manner of speaking must be understood as an economical mode of abstract speech. In a literal sense cultures never have met nor will ever meet. What is meant is that peoples meet and that, as a result of the processes of social interaction, acculturation[2]—modifications in the mode of life of one or both peoples—may take place. Individuals are the dynamic centers of this process of interaction. If perceptible differences in the mode of life of either people result it means that new ways of acting, thinking, and feeling have been learned by individuals.

By capitalizing on his capacity for invention and learning, by making the experience of the individual available to other individuals and the experience of others available to him, man created a new world, a human world, one that depended upon the character and efficiency of the cultural instrumentalities that man himself invented and learned to use. It was a world that functioned and possessed meaning in terms of cultural achievement. And because achievements could be added to, discarded or modified, as circumstances demanded, man found himself in the possession of an adaptive instrument of remarkable flexibility. On the one hand, it was possible to reap the security afforded by tested instruments of living by incorporating them into a mode of life that was transferable from one generation to another; while, on the other hand, should circumstances demand it, readjustment was always possible. As compared with adaptation dependent upon germinal changes where stability is overweighted and relatively rapid readaptation impossible, cultural adaptation has proved of high survival value in the human species.

In fact, adaptation mediated in cultural terms permitted so much latitude that, in time, man created many quite different worlds for himself. All of them had adaptive value under given conditions. Each of them was an experiment in social living, ecological adjustment, and psychological orientation, that is, a culture. The many and varied cultures of the nonliterate peoples of the world described by anthropologists may be considered arresting samples of the immense range in the cultural means employed by members of a single organic species in achieving adaptation. We can only conclude that it is possible for many widely different cultural forms to serve basic adaptive ends. The significance of acculturation as a process of readaptation lies in this fact.

The human individual, however, because of the spatial and temporal accident of birth is always faced with the necessity of learning to live his life in terms of the traditional cultural forms of his society, despite the fact that he is potentially capable of social and ecological adjustment in terms of any system of cultural instrumentalities. So far as our empirical data go, some set of cultural forms is always prior to the individual. Through a process of learning or socialization (motivated by biologically rooted as well as acquired drives which are reinforced by a system of rewards and punishments), specific beliefs, attitudes, and values are acquired, technological processes are mastered, roles are learned, and a personality structure is built up that prepares the individual for meeting the problems of life in the provincial terms characteristic of his society. The basic function of the socialization process, therefore, is to prepare individuals for participation in a specific behavioral world.

Such a process is also one of the fundamental stabilizing agencies in all human societies, since it tends to produce the regularities in patterns of behavior that lend themselves to abstract summarization as culture. But socialization does not produce robots. The persistence of cultural forms is only a function of the expected or predictable behavior of individuals in social interaction. Idiosyncratic or deviant behavior occurs in all societies. It may or may not become accumulative and take a socially significant trend. Imaginative and fantasy processes are also a constant factor in the psychic life of individuals so that new solutions to old problems may be found, or a novel situation may be met in a novel way. In short, readjustment on the part of individuals may influence the thinking, feeling, or behavior of other individuals and perhaps lead to readaptation in the mode of life of the group.

In other words, the analysis of cultural changes always leads us from our initial descriptive abstractions of stabilized cultural forms, through a series of processes involving conditions that have led to readjustments on the part of individuals, and then back again to the socially discernible effects of such readaptation which can once more be described as new or modified cultural forms. The problem of cultural change hinges, therefore, on the conditions and processes that bring about socially significant readjustments of the individual behavior.

One of the generic conditions of culture change lies in the fact that the specific cultural equipment of any single society does not provide its members with the means of adjusting themselves to all possible circumstances or for the solution of every possible problem that may arise. Every mode of cultural adaptation has its own peculiar limitations. Just as organic adaptation implies structured types of responses that have phylogenetic roots, so cultural adaptation implies structured responses with ontogenetic roots in the training and experience of individuals. This is the price that must be paid for any kind of stabilized form of adaptation, whether organic or cultural. Otherwise, new and untried means would have to be improvised by the individual to meet each situation. Difficulties may arise, however, when conditions occur which expose the inadequacy of traditional means. The bow and arrow may be a highly adaptive device in the food quest of a given people under certain conditions but utterly inadequate as a weapon against another people in possession of firearms.

We in Western civilization and people in nonliterate cultures alike must accept the intrinsic limitations of techniques or institutions until new ones can be invented. But we are aware of this fact. In the technological sphere we even encourage the invention of novel mechanical devices. We are less conscious of the instrumental nature of our social and economic institutions and their limitations. In times of crisis we, too, tend to solve our problems in traditional ways instead of devising novel means. Consider, for instance, the situation which arose in the depression when the market was glutted with certain commodities which it was unprofitable to sell. In Western society the market constitutes our established social mechanism for the distribution of goods. Commodities, that is, are produced for sale at a certain price. Consequently, when they cannot be sold profitably there is no way to distribute them to consumers. Thus some unsalable commodities were destroyed in the depression despite the fact that there were consumers who could have used them. In other societies where goods are not produced for sale in a market but are distributed in other ways, the destruction of consumable goods when potential consumers exist would be unthinkable.

To human beings whose whole behavioral world has been built up in culturally provincial terms, however, it only becomes apparent under special circumstances that their native language, social and economic institutions, their system of beliefs, or any other aspect of their traditional mode of life have any intrinsic limitations. This is because different cultural forms share basic instrumental functions, whatever their specific limitations may be. The Iroquois and English languages may be considered functionally equivalent as means of communication despite their differences as linguistic structures. Similarly, the polygynous family as well as the monogamous family may serve basic familial functions. If individuals never have to adjust to situations they are not fully prepared to meet in terms of their own traditional beliefs and institutions, if they never feel frustrated in their conventional roles, if there is no intellectual awareness of any other than their own scheme of values or technological equipment, if there is never any external threat to the continuance of established cultural forms, or any internal conflicts that suggest modifications in them, conditions that might serve as a fulcrum for cultural changes would seemingly be reduced to a minimum. Consequently, it is true, as has often been pointed out, that relatively isolated or marginal societies incline to conservatism and stability in their cultural forms. So long as cultural change is dependent upon some impetus from within, such changes may be relatively insignificant and the rate of change extremely slow. The problem in such cases is to define the conditions and to seek out the possible motivations which impel individuals to develop modifications of their institutions without any stimulus from outside their own group.

Our concern here, however, is with the antithetical case. How do changes result from the contact of peoples with different modes of life? The problem of central scientific importance here is not the *fact* of culture borrowing or the reality of the process of culture diffusion— there are hundreds of thousands of historically verifiable facts that could be marshaled—the problem is to understand the conditions and processes involved in borrowing and the effects upon the mode of life of the people concerned.

When peoples with different modes of life come into contact, this event does not necessarily precipitate any radical modifications in the culture of either group, even though they may remain in continuous social interaction with each other. That is, such contacts are a necessary but not a sufficient condition of acculturation. One should expect to find some instances, therefore, wherein, instead of leading to radical changes in the cultural mode of adaptation, social interaction between groups with different cultural systems is limited to securing the benefits of specialized goods or services which members of either group can offer.

Such a situation is concretely exemplified in the relationship that existed among four tribal groups, neighbors for years, in the Nilgiri Hills (India). Culturally and linguistically distinct, they "lived in economic and social symbiosis," says Mandelbaum.[3] The economic life of the Toda was centered on their sacred buffalo; the Badaga were agriculturalists; the Kota, smiths; while the Kurumba were food gatherers of the jungle and noted for their sorcerers. The latter were often called in by the Kota and Badaga. But on such occasions the transactions usually took place outside the village and the women and children always disappeared immediately into their houses. Kota musicians, on the other hand, were called upon to serve in all major Toda ceremonies, but were never allowed near the dairies for fear of pollution. The Badaga wore turbans, the Kota did not. Once when some Kotas took to wearing the prized headdress they were ambushed by Badagas and beaten up. The Kotas had borrowed a prestige symbol and the Badagas resented it.

"Although contact was frequent," says Mandelbaum, "social intercourse was confined to a fixed number of narrowly defined activities. Any intimate contact, of a kind which would allow members of one group to mingle freely with another, was stringently tabooed." Consequently, these people retained their cultural uniqueness until recent years when Hindu and European influences have intruded themselves with varied results.

Thus contact situations may sometimes produce negative responses so far as any fundamental readaptation is concerned. For why, indeed, should any people whose own way of life is satisfactory to them learn new skills or remodel their institutions if they can supplement the services that are lacking in their own society by hiring specialists from neighboring groups?

In principle, such a relationship may become the basis of mutual benefits, the social interaction of the two peoples much less channelized and more positively friendly than that of the Indian groups mentioned, with the result that only a minimum of acculturation occurs. This is essentially the situation pictured by Lindgren in her characterization of the relations that have persisted for almost a century between Russian Cossacks and Reindeer Tungus in northwestern Manchuria as "culture contact without conflict."[4] Markets, encounters in the woods, and sometimes even protracted residence of members of one group in the communities of the other group are the main channels of social interaction. There is practically no intermarriage, it may be added. Regular trade relations are the most active mode of contact mentioned and "when these brief meetings are over," she says, "the routine of their daily life proceeds quite independently." While the Cossacks enjoy a higher degree of literacy than the Tungus, "all Tungus men, the older boys, and most of the women understand Russian, often expressing themselves fluently in that language, which is used exclusively in trade." Although nominally Christian, shamans play an important role in Tungus society and the Cossacks, while they may feign skepticism, often give genuine credence to these shaman prophecies.

Lindgren stresses the friendly nature of the contacts between the two groups, the reciprocal benefits of trade, and the interchange of a few cultural traits. By and large any demand for readaptation in mode of life is absent and what readjustment has taken place is on a purely voluntary basis. Although Lindgren presents her data as an uncommon situation, Redfield[5] points out certain analogies with "the situation that prevails between the lower-class agricultural *ladinos* of the Lake Atitlan region of the midwestern highlands of Guatemala and the Indians of that region," although the cultural differences between these latter groups is less marked. The common factors in both situations which seem to be productive of "benign ethnic relations" says Redfield are:

The absence of recent attempts by one group to dominate the other; the fact that there is little or no economic competition along ethnic lines; the circumstance that natural resources are plentiful; the individualistic character of the economy and the social organization; and the fact that both groups carry on some of the same prevailing means of livelihood. It is also no doubt important that neither Cossack nor Spaniard brought into the area of the new contacts any very strong tradition of prejudice against people of other skin color or physical type.

Moreover, in Guatemala there is a "prevailing cultural pluralism" which, "combined with the widespread commercialism, tends to free differences in custom from depreciative sentiments and to make them clear of emotional attachments." Guatemalan communities, Tax points out,[6] may be viewed as "separate local societies, and it may be said that as such they merely recognize in each other groups which appropriately have different cultures."

A plant or technique or custom appears to be considered as belonging to a particular community, its people and its soil. Thus, there is a fairly strong belief in Panajachel that if a crop that grows well in one town is planted in another where it has not been grown, the "spirit" of the plant might shift its locale and the plant consequently prosper in its new habitat and fail in its old. (Hence the Indians are disturbed when Indians of another town begin to cultivate a local crop.)

Viewed in broad sociopsychological terms it can readily be seen that, in the situations just referred to, relatively little acculturation occurs because of the limited incentives on the part of the individuals of the groups in social interaction to learn the ways of their neighbors, for learning is the psychological crux of acculturation.

When peoples with different cultural systems come into contact with one another, an examination of the barriers to learning, on the one hand, and the incentives to learning on the other, afford us direct insight into the dynamics of acculturation, although this angle of approach has not yet been systematically explored. The essential questions are the specific conditions under which individuals of either group gain an opportunity to learn about the ways of the other group, how far such learning is promoted or discouraged, what is learned and the various incentives to learning, the kind of people who have taken the initiative in learning, and the results of the process with respect to the subsequent relations of both groups and their cultural systems.

For learning to take place at all there must be adequate motivation. That is to say, primary or secondary drives must be aroused that elicit responses (any activity of the organism—muscular, glandular, verbal, ideational) to certain cues which, in turn, determine when, where, and how we act. Hunger, thirst, and sex are primary drives. In human behavior it is the secondary drives that are of major concern. These are acquired drives that depend on the past experience of the individual and are themselves inculcated through social interaction with other individuals in the learning process. Fears and anxieties, desires for prestige, appetites for particular foods, are examples of acquired drives. And, since all secondary drives are built up as part of the training an individual receives in order to participate in a society dominated by a particular cultural system, the kinds of responses elicited and the cues responded to, as well as the rewards which serve to reduce the various drives, are all colored by this original adaptation. While a new mode of life may demand the same primary drives and perhaps some of the secondary ones also, acculturation on a major scale implies radically significant readaptation in an individual's behavior. New responses, new cues, and new drives are all involved. Obviously, the incentives to such readaptation must be well rewarded.[7]

All such processes offer an extremely important field for study. Food habits are a pertinent example. In human beings food habits have been overlaid with so many acquired drives that they are never a simple function of the primary hunger drive. There are definite food preferences in all human groups. This means that appetite is only rewarded by certain kinds of food and not by others. When a strange kind of food is presented to an individual or eaten by him, his reaction may be one of disgust or nausea. Instead of being rewarded, the food drive is punished, thereby prompting rejection on subsequent occasions so that the individual may never learn to eat the new food.

Once I offered an old Indian and his wife some oatmeal with milk on it. They refused it, although I know they were hungry. The Saulteaux Indians that I know do not like milk, but they will eat oatmeal without it. To adapt themselves to milk as a food would require a very strong incentive indeed. On the other hand, the same Indians love strawberry jam, but then they have always been very fond of wild strawberries. They are also very fond of fat, so it is no hardship for them to eat pure lard instead of butter with their bannock, a habit I could not adopt with relish. Another example which illustrates in a more subtle fashion the difficulties presented by readaptation in food habits comes from modern Hawaii.[8] The old Hawaiians preferred cool or even cold foods. It has been very difficult for them to learn to like hot foods, despite a long period of acculturation. One woman, for example, found it impossible to enjoy the cup of "nice hot tea" presented to her by her hostess. It was not the tea that was distasteful but the temperature of the drink. The American father of this same woman was accustomed to eat his meals separately from the other members of his family because he preferred his food hot.

The kind of social learning that is typical of the acculturation process is imitative learning in the technical sense of the term. This is because the behavior that occurs always involves some kind of model as a stimulus. Whether the newly learned responses only approximate the model or whether a close matching is achieved depends upon a number of variables which require technical distinctions that it will be unnecessary to go into here (they can be found in any detailed analysis of concrete situations). Imitation is not necessarily a conscious process, and inexactness in "copying" and its determinants provide some of the most interesting problems for analysis in the acculturation process. Then, too, copying may itself become a drive that is rewarded in some situations. So we are always brought back to the drives that have motivated individuals toward readaptation and how these drives are rewarded.[9]

It may be assumed that, if individuals with one cultural background are brought into social interaction with those of a different cultural heritage and are allowed to respond freely to the differences encountered, they will imitate only those food habits, skills, attitudes or other items that, for one reason or another, satisfy their own culturally acquired drives. There is also no demand for exactness of imitation if approximate imitation is rewarding. One old Indian I know used to wear a hat he obtained from the missionary box. It happened to be a woman's hat, but he did not know this. Neither did the other Indians. What was imitated was the wearing of a hat, not a particular style of hat. Thus in this case only part of our pattern of hat-wearing was copied. There was no incentive to great exactness. In fact, there was no one to teach him what the precise pattern among white men was. A contrary case is the one where missionaries have motivated natives to copy European forms of dress instead of letting them choose freely or modify the items of dress congenial to them.

The study of acculturation processes, then, involves not only an examination of drive and reward, but the details of the process of imitative learning in the transfer of habit patterns. In the social interaction of Cossacks and Tungus, for example, it undoubtedly was a rewarding experience for the Tungus to learn Russian for trading purposes. But it would be interesting to know how much Russian they learned and what the peculiarities were of the Russian they spoke. Another interesting aspect of this case is the fact, recorded by Lindgren, that the women as well as the men understood Russian. On the basis of our knowledge of trade relations between other groups where a language is learned without systematic instruction, one might have predicted that the Tungus men but not the women would have become bilingual. The question arises why the learning of a new language was a rewarding experience to Tungus women. One might also ask whether the Russian spoken by them differed at all from that spoken by the men and whether such differences might be linked to diverse motivations. A still broader problem would be an investigation of the conditions that have determined sexual differences in the acquisition of new languages when people meet.

The kind of foodstuffs obtained in trade by the Tungus (flour, tea, salt, sugar) indicate a change in their food habits; the same articles, incidentally, being primary trade commodities among the Indians of Canada today. The demand for them, in both cases, probably lies in the manner in which these foods supplement and enhance the native diet which consists mainly of fish and meat. Like the northern Algonkians, the Tungus obtain firearms, axes, iron pots and frying pans, copper kettles, enamel dishes, forks, knives, needles, thimbles, scissors, and so on, the utilitarian values of which to a people with no metallurgical techniques of their own is obvious. Nevertheless, the fact that the Tungus have learned to use such articles does not mean that they have imitated the complete pattern of their usage found among the Cossacks. Lindgren does not discuss this point, but among the northern Algonkian I have seen thimbles used decoratively and as jingles. Indians have also bought alarm clocks, not as timepieces but just to hear them ring, and one man whom I knew carried a watch, although it was doubtful whether he could tell time. In East Africa safety pins have been worn as hair ornaments.[10]

The fact that imitative learning can take place without exact copying enhances the reward values of trade objects far beyond their obvious utilitarian values. It means that various secondary drives may be satisfied in new ways. In terms of trait analysis it explains the latitude permitted in fitting borrowed items into the culture pattern of the borrowers and the necessity for considering the form, meaning, and function of traits as interrelated but independently variable attributes.[11]

Where there is freedom for imitative learning to take place in the social interaction between two peoples, it is hardly conceivable that acculturation can be in any sense a disruptive process, since the cultural features of one society that are imitated by members of another become functionally connected with established drives or with new ones that are in harmony with the cultural system of the borrowers. Learning a new linguistic medium of communication, learning to prepare and eat new types of food or condiments that have positive nutritional value but are only obtainable in trade, learning to use more efficient types of tools, or supplementing objects of local manufacture with trade objects that reward some drive, are no more disruptive than a new invention or discovery when considered from the standpoint of a cultural system as a whole. In other words, it is possible for acculturation to take place on a modest scale through selective processes of voluntary imitative learning without radical readaptation in the behavior of individuals or a reshaping of the total mode of life of the society in which they function.

In most of our case studies of acculturation, however, the situation is scarcely so simple as this. There are other complex variables that act as determinants. Instead of one group permitting the individuals of another to imitate freely any aspect of their culture, we encounter situations in which there is active discouragement of any such behavior. This may be expressed by some penalty meted out to individuals who attempt to adopt a certain habit or custom, or a similar result may be achieved by setting up barriers to imitative learning. The penalization of the Kota who started wearing the headdress of the Badaga has already been referred to. So far as the relations of these peoples of the Nilgiri Hills are concerned, it seems likely that the ubiquitous institution of caste in India may have had something to do with the maintenance of their cultural autonomy. For one of the distinctive features of caste is the nontransferable character of activities or services caste members everywhere perform. This might account for the barriers to acculturation and might explain why, for example, the Todas always hire Kota musicians for their ceremonies.

Another example is the attempt on the part of the Spaniards of the colonial period to prevent some of the Indians from possessing firearms or riding horseback.[12] The Dutch administration of the East Indies offers a large-scale and highly organized attempt to errect barriers against acculturation of the native peoples. Kennedy characterizes it as an anti-acculturation policy. The idea was to discourage acculturation by fostering the persistence of certain native institutions. Native forms of government were kept intact wherever possible, missionary zeal was rigidly controlled, and the communalistic system of landholding was upheld. Kennedy says that the effect of this has been "intact and flourishing native cultures, a just and comprehensible legal system, a basically sound native agricultural economy—and an Indonesia so far behind the times that it is helpless unless protected by some strong, modern, outside power."[13]

Aside from institutionalized attitudes or policies on the part of one group that offer barriers to members of another group who desire to imitate certain aspects of their way of life, there are also intrinsic barriers which may make it impossible for one people to adopt the cultural instrumentalities of another people even if they should desire to do so. While many aboriginal peoples with whom Europeans came into contact almost immediately appreciated the metal implements and utensils of the latter and soon learned to use them, there was no attempt to learn the processes of their manufacture. This was impossible because of the enormous gap between the level of knowledge and technology of these stone-age peoples and that of European peoples. The Japanse, on the other hand, who had previously drawn so heavily on the resources of Chinese culture, were prepared by the middle of the nineteenth century to assimilate and use for their autonomous ends the technology of Western culture, while rejecting certain other aspects of it.[14] The nonliterate peoples of the world, on the other hand, were merely drawn into the world market of a rapidly expanding capitalism as consumers of commodities which they never aspired to produce themselves.

This brings us to one of the most important, as well as characteristic, features of the process by which the expansion of European peoples came to exert such a profound influence upon the lives of the nonliterate peoples with whom they came into contact. From the very beginning of this movement two classes of European people, traders and missionaries, immediately began to play a promotional role in the contact situation. They made it their special business to persuade aboriginal peoples to adopt new tools, implements, skills, beliefs, and moral attitudes. The traders were essentially salesmen of material objects; the missionaries, salesmen of immaterial values. The presence of these two groups of peoples as agents in promoting the acculturation process must, therefore, be considered as one of the differential features of the contact of Europeans with non-Europeans, rather than as typical of acculturation wherever we find it in human history.

The role of the trader has been to offer the natives goods that quickly rewarded already existent primary and secondary drives (although he would not understand these terms) and to foster the acquisition of new secondary drives. It is no concern of his whether the natives accept or reject Christianity or in what ways learning the use of new objects or techniques may affect the traditional pattern of native life.

Primitive man [says Reed] was once believed to have so few needs that the only trade-articles he desired at first were those which gratified his love for ostentation. This has never been the case in New Guinea, where tribe after tribe of new, previously unknown peoples have been encountered, from the time of Finsch's explorations [1880-1882 and 1884] down to the present. Always they have first demanded iron tools; only after these most highly desired articles are in their hands will they show interest in beads, face paint, and calico. If one enters the uncontrolled area of the upper Sepik River today he is surrounded by natives who literally howl for iron knives, axes, and fishhooks. In all except the most remote regions, however, the simpler type of European tools and artifacts have almost entirely replaced aboriginal implements.[15]

In the Canadian north the process has gone much further. There is a steady demand for canvas canoes (the designs based, of course, on Indian models) in an area which is the home of the aboriginal birchbark canoe. The trade canoe, however, will stand much rougher usage, carries a bulkier and heavier load, lasts longer than the birch-bark canoe, and is equipped so that oarlocks may be attached for rowing. The Indian is no sentimentalist; it is not he who bemoans the passing of the more picturesque craft and the extinction in many places of the skills required for its manufacture. Thus the trader has been able to meet an old-established and continuing demand by marketing a variety of canoe that meets contemporary needs better than the aboriginal article. This is good business, and what has proved good business in the contact of nonliterate peoples with Europeans has promoted acculturation. In the north, too, the fur traders have promoted the use of the outboard motor, a distinct labor-saving device so long as gasoline is available. Unlike the canoe itself, the outboard motor is far from a necessity in this part of the world. It is also expensive and unless the individual running it knows something about machinery, it may delay rather than aid ease and speed of travel. The traders, however, have been willing to give the Indians some of the necessary instruction, and up until the outbreak of the war the number of sales was multiplying rapidly. A great deal of prestige satisfaction was involved in the possession of a motor: all the best hunters had them. A parallel situation is to be found in South Africa where "the art of iron work, formerly in the hands of special craftsmen, has completely disappeared. Iron goods are now obtained from the traders, while such work as repairs to wagons and plows is done exclusively by European blacksmiths."[16]

Missionaries were faced with a more complicated and difficult task than the traders. The system of beliefs and values they endeavored to "sell" were more intangible instruments of living than the commodities of the trader and, at first, had a less obvious appeal. The existence of gods or other supernatural powers was not unfamiliar to primitive peoples, nor were techniques for obtaining benefits from them. The discovery of certain analogies, not sensed at first by the missionaries, undoubtedly helped to bridge the gap between native beliefs and practices and Christianity. The northern Algonkian soon identified their own Supreme Being with the Christian God, despite the fact that some missionaries resisted this idea. Indians who have spoken to me about this cannot understand why the identification was not an obvious one. Beaglehole, referring to the Hawaiians, remarks that

a religion based on ten tapus was easily understandable by a mind nurtured in a way of life where the multitudinous observances of tapus gave one secular and religious satisfaction and success. The very dogmatism with which Calvinistic Puritanism was preached to the natives was without doubt a point in its favor. The native was used to gods that were all-powerful, and all-dreadful, sometimes benign, sometimes ruthless.[17]

Syncretisms, too, have arisen out of the awareness of analogous attributes of native gods and the saints of the Catholic Church.[18] Verbal techniques (prayers) for influencing supernaturals may become identified with verbal magic (spells) since both may be used for similar ends.[19]

Learning new religious beliefs and practices, however, had to be motivated. Man is essentially a pragmatist, and a belief in the existence of supernatural beings and powers cannot be dissociated from his drives. The reality of the supernatural realm must meet the test of experience. When conditions arose which seemed to indicate that activities carried out in accordance with the native belief system were unrewarding, an opportunity was presented that the missionary could exploit. That is to say, there was the possibility that the anxieties that had arisen could be reduced by encouraging individuals to learn new articles of faith. Some natives joined one of the Solomon Island missions, says Hogbin, "after a run of extraordinary bad luck. The *akalo* (ancestral spirits), they point out, did not live up to their part of the bargain and they determined in consequence to make no more sacrifices."[20] Eiselen points out that the success of the early missionaries in certain South African tribes probably can be explained by the synchronization of their arrival with "singular events."

Petty intertribal wars, with little bloodshed, had been common enough among the Bantu, but when the missionaries came to this country it was just one great battlefield. The tribes of the Free State and the Transvaal had been reduced to terrible straits by the wars of Tshaka and his emulators and by the ensuing years of famine. Starving remnants of once powerful tribes were wandering aimlessly about the country in constant fear of attack by some band of cannibals, or they were eking out a miserable existence in some mountain refuge. To these harassed people the missionaries came like so many Good Samaritans. Their faith in the ancestral gods had been badly shaken and they were ready to open their ears to the message of love and hope.[21]

On the other hand, "all those tribes which emerged with flying colours from the chaos of the Zulu wars of the early nineteenth century—the Zulus, the Swazi, and the Amandebele of Mapoch—did not in the beginning befriend the missionaries."

There were, of course, other rewards than a reduction in anxiety drives which missionaries could make use of, some of them being of a definitely material sort. A systematic study of the various methods the missionaries used and the measure of their successes and failures when viewed from the standpoint of learning theory would constitute a valuable study. The local conditions and events that they exploited, the kind of people they attempted to influence, the motives they appealed to, the acquired drives they fostered, the types of reward they emphasized, and the rewards that the natives themselves found in adopting Christianity, would all throw a great deal of important light on the acculturation process.

Although the activities of both traders and missionaries were aimed at introducing new objects, beliefs, or usages, they were in the vanguard of European expansion and, at first, were not in a position to force changes in the lives of the peoples with whom they came into contact. At times their lives were even endangered if the people among whom they lived and worked found their presence uncongenial, so that they were almost compelled to adopt persuasive methods. Their clientele could take or leave the objects or doctrines offered them.

As the expansion of European peoples continued to gain momentum, however, conditions were created that directly or indirectly forced native peoples to make all kinds of cultural readaptations for which they were totally unprepared. This was inevitable since the ultimate aim of European expansion was the colonization and economic exploitation of new regions, and the extension of sovereignty over the aboriginal peoples who lived in them. Furthermore, this expansionist movement was carried on by military conquests or the threat of force; it was prepared to meet and overcome all opposition. In short, it was a movement compounded of conflict and patterns of social interaction that always resulted in the subordination of native groups to the power exercised by the intruders. Whole populations were decimated or displaced in the process; new diseases were carried to regions where they had not existed before and were followed by epidemics of great destructiveness; and well-established ecological adjustments of native peoples were disturbed. Consequently, new problems were created which native peoples had to solve either in terms of their own cultural means or by learning some new mode of adaptation.

The culmination of enforced readaptation was reached with the establishment of more and more local settlements, the dispersal of native people beyond the frontiers occupied by Europeans, or the settlement of them upon reservations and the extension of sovereignty over them by formal means. In this way they were brought within the jurisdiction of various European nations and made subject to their penal sanctions. This resulted in the deliberate suppression in some regions of certain tribal usages (cannibalism, head-hunting, intertribal warfare, sorcery), the passage of new rules and regulations, and in some cases the presence of officials (native or otherwise) appointed by the government. As some natives of the Solomon Islands put it,

You white men give us orders; we no longer give orders to ourselves. . . . The white man has come and tells us we must behave like *his* father. Our own fathers, we must forget them. . . . In the olden days we did this thing, we did that thing. We did not stop and say to ourselves first, "This thing I want to do, is it right?" We always knew. Now we have to say, "This thing I want to do, will the white man tell me it is wrong and punish me?"[22]

The negative effects of the impact of Western culture upon that of the nonliterate peoples has frequently been described. In many cases their mode of life has been so completely transformed that they have become almost completely Europeanized and little of their old manner of life remains. While this result is negative in so far as it involves the disappearance of a once flourishing cultural system, nevertheless it is positive in so far as various peoples have met the challenge of new conditions through the acculturation process. Much less is known, however, of the detailed steps involved.

But the fact that European encroachment upon the domain of the nonliterate peoples everywhere created such a large variety of anxiety-arousing situations suggests that an examination of the role that anxiety drives of all kinds play as motivating factors in readaptation may be especially valuable. Of all acquired drives those keyed to what is probably a primary drive toward avoidance of pain or the threat of pain are among the strongest motivating forces in human behavior. This is the reason anxiety drives are important in the socialization process as well as in the operation of many social sanctions. Through a conditioning process and personal experience, the human being learns what is physically and psychically painful to him, and which events may bring threatening or punishing effects—sickness and death, for example, may be interpreted as punishments, mediated by supernatural beings or other persons, for wrong conduct. Thus certain anxieties may be inculcated in individuals in order to motivate them in the performance of patterns of behavior that are socially approved. In stabilized societies the range of socially acquired anxiety drives is limited; they are functionally important in the maintenance of the social order. There are characteristic dangers and threatening situations in the behavioral world of the individual—there is pain and trouble that he has to face—but traditional instrumentalities are provided for dealing with them. The individual has been taught how to get relief from the expected anxieties which may arise. In terms of learning theory this relief is rewarding. It helps provide the individual with a basic sense of security. If conditions arise, therefore, which threaten a people through death or disease, which compel them to seek new homes, which menace their livelihood or force them into new economic tasks, which compel them to give up old, traditional usages and ultimately threaten their whole manner of life, it is obvious that many new anxiety drives will arise that cannot be rewarded in their own cultural ways.

But anxiety drives of all kinds are very strong motives to action; they demand relief. How have the nonliterate peoples acted under such pressures, and how has their behavior affected the acculturation process? Only a few examples can be given here. The realistic way to meet any danger is to combat it as best one can. So the hostile reactions provoked by Europeans need no documentation. The fact that whole populations were in some cases soon wiped out (Haiti, Tasmania) is evidence of the reality of the dangers faced and is justification for the anxieties that must have been aroused. On the other hand, native peoples were given the strongest kind of incentives to acquire and learn to use firearms as quickly as possible in order to be able to defend themselves. This can be interpreted as rewarding their anxiety drives. In the United States some Indian tribes who became excellent fighters successfully resisted the further encroachment of the whites for a long period. But it should also be noted that in certain areas such drives must have been heightened rather than relieved by local governments, as, for instance, when the English High Commissioner for the Western Pacific forbade British subjects to supply guns to the natives under his control.[23] Where in the same area (Melanesia) guns were secured by some native peoples and not by others, intertribal tensions were greatly increased, because the former could more easily rout their enemies. How acute such a situation could become is vividly illustrated by a casual remark of Keesing's that "even up to a few years ago, for a native to be without a gun in some parts of Melanesia meant certain death.'[24] It is easily understandable why in New Guinea "two or three years work [at indentured labor] was not considered too high a price to pay for a weapon which would bring not only prestige to its possessor, but also great advantages to the clan or village in native warfare."[25]

Another source of anxiety created by European expansion was the spread of such disease as smallpox, scarlet fever, measles, and diphtheria, familiar enough to Europeans but unknown to the peoples of North America or the South Seas. There were no native remedies for these diseases, which frequently took a more virulent form in populations that had built up no resistance to them. Since there was no way for these people to learn to apply the medical techniques of Western culture, their anxieties could not be alleviated through acculturative means. The only resort was to apply their own remedies or to invent new ones. To this day the northern Indians are in great fear of syphilis, yet modern procedures known to us are still unavailable to them. Some of their own medicine men are said to have a cure. The Mohave in the old days had a "cure" for arrow wounds. "After the introduction of firearms," says Devereux, "they felt helpless, since arrow-wound magic could not cure gunshot wounds. The situation remained unsolved until a native shaman claimed to have received special power to cure gunshot wounds."[26] In other words, there was no more realistic means of relieving this anxiety than magic could provide. The introduction of new sources of disease, therefore, in view of the limitations of the native methods for combating them, may be considered a continuing cause of unrelieved anxiety, except as relieved by what Devereux calls "cultural bromides."

Any disturbances that influence traditional sources of food supply are a serious threat and are bound to result in anxieties. It is not merely a matter of hunger or deprivation, but of acquired appetites for the particular kinds of food which are an integral and satisfying part of existence. This is why the food habits of human groups or individuals have a deep psychological significance. Even though some new sources of food are discovered or the balance redressed by rations issued by some government agency, the food that may be nutritionally adequate may not be psychologically rewarding. Even under the stress of hunger, as I have already mentioned, certain foods may be refused. Disturbances in the food supply may also demand a change in occupation—new techniques for earning a living may have to be learned. The history of the Indians of the Plains subsequent to the disappearance of the buffalo is a classic illustration of the difficulties of enforced readaptation in food habits and occupation. Despite pressures of all kinds, men who had been hunters and warriors could not be motivated for a generation or more to find farming or cattle-raising rewarding occupations. Undoubtedly there is a deep conflict here between various drives, so that inhibitions to learning were at first operative despite what must have been a heavy burden of anxiety connected with food and status. The opportunities for readaptation, however, were not of a rewarding kind in the eyes of the Plains Indians. This is a striking example of the highly structured relations that can exist between acquired drives and their specific rewards in a culture.

Where social interaction involves marked differences in power between the members of two groups, one type of response that may result from anxieties arising from feelings of insecurity in members of the subordinate group is identification, in one way or another, with the dominant group. In this case anxiety may function as an important stimulus to learning. Easily adopted symbols of the powerful group— for example articles of clothing—may be sufficiently rewarding, or there may be deeper or more comprehensive imitation. Native opportunists who, for one reason or another, feel insecure in their own social hierarchy may hasten to embrace Christianity and then influence others in the same direction, thus gaining the support of the whites for the enhancement of their personal prestige. There have been several examples of this in the South Seas. (Pomare of Tahiti was a lesser chief who managed to have himself elevated over his native superiors.) Thus new leaders arose in some regions who were equipped with symbols of the white man's power—guns, clothing, household furnishings, and so on. But in turn this threat to the status and power of traditional leaders causes further tensions and anxieties in other quarters.[27]

Furthermore, to the natives the power of the white man sometimes seems explicable only in magical terms. Reading books may furnish the key, and thus learning to read becomes the chief desire. A Solomon Island lad said to Hogbin, "You white men are like us. You have only two eyes, two hands, two feet. How are you different? Because you can read books. That is why you can buy axes, knives, clothing, ships and motorcars. . . . If we could read your books we would have money and possessions."[28]

For those in a social or power hierarchy to seek reassurance consciously or unconsciously for their insecurities by imitating those higher in the same social scale is not an unknown phenomenon in Western culture, where it is also a factor in learning.[29] Possibly, therefore, the tendency of the younger generation in many nonliterate societies to imitate the more powerful whites instead of their elders belongs in a comparable category. But this leads to a decline in the authority of their elders over them, a fact that has been commented upon in almost every region where there has been more or less continuous social contact between whites and natives. This behavior may be interpreted as an unconscious search for a new basis of personal security which, since it is not always found, may give rise to further anxieties. Imitation of the dominant group may offer only temporary rewards. An extremely important factor in the outcome is the total configuration of relations that crystallize between Europeans and native peoples. Where a caste structure has developed or is developing, the limited nature of the participation in Western culture to which individuals may aspire naturally creates problems of sociopsychological adjustment different from those where such a structure is absent. In New Guinea, says Reed,

so long as European domination avowedly rested upon armed guards and European weapons of war, there could be no threat to the white man's position. But now that rights have been freely parceled out to the natives and the use of armed force is condemned, the white man resorts to caste rules—taboos, prescription, and juridical sanctions—to assure his continuing superiority.[30]

Even where no well-defined caste lines have crystallized, native peoples who continue to speak their own language, wear their own traditional dress, or observe certain customs, may discover that the retention of these is punishing rather than rewarding in social intercourse with whites. They may be made the subject of ridicule or invidious comparisons, or they may find themselves underprivileged in certain situations as compared with the dominant group. Gillen has called this "status anxiety."[31] Although the subject needs further study in other areas, on the basis of Tsimshian material from the Northwest Coast, Barnett maintains the thesis that the "socially unadjusted or maladjusted, the suppressed and frustrated and those who have suffered a social displacement" in their own society, more especially "half-breeds, widows, orphans, invalids, rebels, and chronic trouble-makers have been in the vanguard of those accepting newly introduced patterns,"[32] rather than those persons of real eminence who have a vested interest in native institutions. From the standpoint of anxiety drives and the possible rewards that may accrue to such persons from readaptation in new cultural terms this seems entirely plausible.

In some cases, however, instead of turning toward acculturation as a way out, the confusions, frustrations, and social inequalities that have accompanied contacts with Europeans have created nativistic movements, consciously organized attempts to revive or perpetuate certain aspects of the aboriginal culture. Linton has presented a tentative typology of these[33] which distinguishes magical and rational forms. Both arise in times of stress, but in the magical varieties

moribund elements of culture are not revived for their own sake or in anticipation of practical advantages from the elements themselves. Their revival is part of a magical formula designed to modify the society's environment in ways which will be favorable to it. . . . The society's members feel that by behaving as their ancestors did they will, in some usually undefined way, help to recreate the total situation in which the ancestors lived.

In the more rationalistic movements, on the other hand, the "culture elements selected for symbolic use are chosen realistically and with regard to the possibility of perpetuating them under current conditions" in order to maintain social solidarity and to "help reëstablish and maintain the self respect of the group's members in the face of adverse conditions."

The literature on nativistic movements is extensive, but here it must suffice to point out that while those of the magical type may reward the anxiety drives of those that participate in them, there is no ultimate readaptation possible that will prove satisfactory in such terms. The old manner of life can never be revived. On the other hand, as Linton observes, rational revivalistic or perpetuative movements may provide a mechanism of adjustment that may compensate in a more positive way for the feelings of inferiority that have been aroused.

All these processes of readaptation are still going on and, so far as the nonliterate peoples are concerned, the global scale of the second World War will only serve to accentuate them, since the domain of such peoples is in some instances the actual theater of military operations. The revolutionary changes in their lives since the expansion of European peoples began cannot be viewed in adequate perspective, however, without considering the radical transformations that have occurred in Western culture itself during the same period. It is well within this period that our scientific tradition arose, that our technology has been revolutionized through all sorts of mechanical inventions, that a world economy has come into existence, that nationalism in its modern form has arisen, and that wars on a momentous and enormously destructive scale have been fought. As a result, the capacity of Western man to readapt has also been put to the test. Again and again in our society, too, there has been expressed a nostalgia for "the good old days," whether those of yesterday or many centuries ago. The question whether nonliterate peoples' assimilation of our culture, or certain aspects of it, has proved more satisfying to them than their native ways may be paralleled by the question how far we are fully satisfied with the mode of life that is our own traditional one. Furthermore, those of us in the democracies have recently experienced the anxiety of having our way of life disrupted by the threatened imposition of another manner of life. But we are in a better position than the nonliterate peoples to meet the challenge and to help mold our future.

If man's life is one of continual adaptation and readaptation through cultural instrumentalities, a large part of the efforts of students of man must be devoted to understanding as thoroughly as possible the nature of these instrumentalities and their relation to the healthy functioning of the human organism. When the application of our knowledge becomes possible, man in his role of the creator of cultural instrumentalities should be able to devise cultural forms that will bring to human beings the maximum rewards in living. Further study of the sociopsychological aspects of acculturation may contribute valuable knowledge to this end.

Chapter 18 - Background for a
Study of Acculturation and the
Personality of the Ojibwa

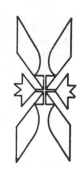

THE AMERICAN SETTING

IN AMERICA WE HAVE HAD A LONG HISTORY OF CONTACTS BETWEEN the native Indian population and peoples with a European cultural background. Today in a number of regions units of this aboriginal population still persist and have not yet been assimilated to Western culture, so that there are excellent opportunities for studying acculturation processes and their consequences. Moreover, not only are varying levels of acculturation discernible among tribal groups with entirely different cultural backgrounds, within the same ethnic unit people in different local or other groups manifest various stages in acculturation level. Although anthropologists have not developed precise indices for these stages, nevertheless it is possible to distinguish different acculturation levels in terms of the degree to which such cultural items as technological devices, house types, patterns of clothing, Christian beliefs, and the English language have been taken over by the Indians and made part of their lives.

My own initial aproach to the problem was tentatively formulated in a paper, "Acculturation Processes and Personality Changes as Indicated by the Rorschach Technique" (first read at the 1941 annual meeting of the American Anthropological Association; see Hallowell, 1942b). In that paper I reported certain findings obtained by the Rorschach technique which showed the effects of acculturation upon the Berens River Saulteaux. This same problem was made the subject of inquiry in a subsequent field study among the Lac du Flambeau Ojibwa in the summer of 1946. The major results of this investigation are summarized in the last two chapters of this section. (A briefer summary, without supporting evidence, was presented to the XXIXth International Congress of Americanists, 1949 [see 1952a].)

In Chapter 5, "The Northern Ojibwa," I referred to the cultural gradient which was apparent on the Berens River during the period I was making my investigations. I made no systematic study of these local differences at the time, but going over my material and applying such criteria as the prevalence of English as a secondary language, the adherence to native beliefs, the occurrence of native ceremonies involving the use of the drum and special songs, the methods of treating illness, and conjuring by means of the shaking tent, it was evident that the people of the two Inland bands offered a striking contrast to those of the Lakeside band. The Inland people were undoubtedly much less acculturated. Thus, two levels of acculturation were identified. Besides this, from information obtained at the same period from Indians who had come in contact with Ojibwa at more inaccessible inland points, such as Deer Lake and Sandy Lake, it was possible to infer that in these localities there was a still lower level of acculturation than that of the Inland bands. It was equally clear that in eastern Canada and certain parts of the United States there were Ojibwa groups much more acculturated than the band at the mouth of the Berens River. Thus the cultural gradient on the Berens River might be considered as part of a wider continuum of acculturation, the manifestation of an historical process which, under varying pressures and events and at different rates, has been transforming the lives of these American aborigines.

Consequently, I was interested to discover whether there were any demonstrable differences between the Lakeside and Inland groups of the Berens River that corresponded with the observed cultural gradient. With this objective in mind, I divided the Rorschach protocols I had secured into two series and discovered that there was not only evidence that suggested psychological differences between the two groups, but that the basic shift in psychological orientation that appeared to be taking place was intelligible in the light of the known facts of acculturation. This was what I somewhat cautiously reported in the 1942 article. I found that the Lakeside Indians showed signs of developing a more extraverted type of adjustment in contrast to the almost ubiquitous introverted adjustment of their Inland kinsmen. No radical shift, however, had occurred. There was an essential continuity in personality organization with some modifications. Particularly significant, however, was the nature of these modifications in certain individuals: some serious, if not actually neurotic, strains were developing within the personality structure. But what impressed me most was the sensitivity of the Rorschach technique as an instrument for collecting data that could be used both to demonstrate empirically an overall psychological picture of a modal personality and to appraise the life adjustment of individuals involved in the acculturation process. I was also struck by the fact that the generalized psychological picture that I had independently pieced together from seventeenth- and eighteenth-century accounts of the Indians of the Northeastern Woodlands (see Chap. 6), was fundamentally equivalent to the inferences I could make from the Rorschach protocols of the Ojibwa of the Berens River. This was particularly true of the Inland groups. Hence it seemed reasonable to take the personality characteristics of the Inland group as a psychological base line from which to measure any changes.

On the basis of the data available up to this point I assumed the following: (1) The personality structure of the Inland group of Berens River Indians approximated, if it was not identical with, an aboriginal type of modal personality structure which was not only characteristic of the Ojibwa, but of other Indians of the Eastern Woodlands. (This deduction later received support from the Rorschach data collected by Wallace in his investigation of the highly acculturated Tuscarora Iroquois,[1] and particularly from the results of the Spindlers' study of the relations between acculturation and psychological adjustment among the Menomini Indians.[2] The least acculturated group in this latter case presented a Rorschach picture almost identical with that of the least acculturated Ojibwa of the Berens River.) (2) A considerable degree of acculturation could occur without any radical change in this personality structure. (3) In the most highly acculturated group the readjustments demanded in the acculturation process produced stresses and strains that were leading to certain modifications in the modal personality structure. (4) While some few individuals, more especially women, were making an excellent social and psychological adjustment, the men, on the whole, were much less successful.

I was anxious, therefore, to secure a sample of Rorschach protocols from a more highly acculturated group of Ojibwa for comparison with those already obtained. This opportunity arose while I was at Northwestern University and led to the investigation conducted at Lac du Flambeau.

Prior to my own investigation at Lac du Flambeau, John Gillin and Victor Raimy had spent part of a summer on this reservation in 1938-39. Their published papers are: John Gillin and Victory Raimy, "Acculturation and Personality," *American Sociology Review,* V (1940), 371-80; John Gillin, "Acquired Drives in Culture Contact," *American Anthropologist,* XLIV (1942), 545-54. Subsequent to this, Victor Barnouw initiated an investigation of his own, the results of which are to be found in his monograph, *Acculturation and Personality Among the Wisconsin Chippewa* (Memoir 72, American Anthropological Association [1950]). He was kind enough to allow me to use the Rorschach records he collected independently at Flambeau as part of his study. In his monograph will be found relevant background material on the history and ethnography of the Ojibwa, as well as a discussion of their differential reactions to acculturation as contrasted with certain Plains tribes.

In addition to my wife, Maude F. Hallowell, and myself, five graduate students from Northwestern University (Blanche G. Watrous, Erika Eichhorn Bourguignon, Beatrice Mosner, Melford E. Spiro, Ruy Coelho) and one graduate student from the University of Chicago (William A. Caudill) participated in the Flambeau study. I am greatly indebted to them for the use of the material they collected, most of which remains in manuscript form Dr. Caudill's "Psychological Characteristics of Acculturated Wisconsin Ojibwa Children," *American Anthropologist*, LI (1949), 409-27, embodies an analysis of the TAT records he obtained from a sample of Flambeau children. Dr. Watrous made the extensive Rorschach data she collected for the same age groups, the subject of her doctoral dissertation (*A Personality Study of Ojibwa Children*, MSS, 264 pp.). A large series of children's drawings collected by Mr. Coelho was later analyzed by Michal Lowenfels Kane (*Free Drawing as a Projective Test in Cross-Cultural Investigations. An Interpretation Based on Spontaneous Drawings of 78 Ojibwa Children*. MSS, 100 pp., M.A. thesis, University of Pennsylvania, 1950).

Subsequent to this 1946 investigation, Mr. and Mrs. Stephen Boggs and Mr. and Mrs. Thomas Hay (Washington University, St. Louis) spent the winter of 1951-52 at Lac du Flambeau and the following summer on the Berens River. They concentrated upon intensive observations on parent-child interaction in selected family samples on both reservations in order to determine the earliest and most basic factors in social learning in infants and children. Stephen Boggs' Ph.D. thesis deals with "Ojibwa Acculturation and Personality Formation."

Since the articles in this section as originally printed offered no opportunity for the presentation of the ethnohistorical background of the Flambeau Ojibwa and other relevant material, the full significance of the psychological similarities and differences that emerged when the Lac du Flambeau results were compared with the data on the Canadian Ojibwa were, in a sense, obscured. In order to remedy this and to make the material from both regions more fully comparable, a short account of the Lac du Flambeau with certain unpublished material follows.

THE LAC DU FLAMBEAU OJIBWA

Just as the present-day Ojibwa population of the Berens River represents the outcome of a northwestward migratory movement of these peoples in Canada from the region of the Sault which they formerly inhabited, another such movement is represented by the Ojibwa found in Wisconsin and Minnesota. In these latter areas they came into conflict with the Sioux, some of whom they displaced. In Wisconsin the Ojibwa were the last Indians to arrive. At an earlier period other Algonkian peoples—the Menomini, Sauk and Fox, and the Siouan Winnebago—inhabited what later became the state of Wisconsin. Prior to this there were still other aboriginal peoples who have not been fully identified.[3]

In the state of Wisconsin today there are between three and four million white inhabitants. In 1800 there were not more than two hundred. Most of these lived at Green Bay. This was the period when the fur trade was still flourishing, before the movement of the white population of the United States into the "Old Northwest" subsequent to the War of 1812. While acculturation in its initial phases must have been under way by this time, mediated through the articles exchanged for fur (tea, tobacco, knives, needles, guns, etc.) and some missionary efforts, nevertheless, there is no reason to believe that the general manner of life of the Indians or their personality characteristics had been greatly modified. With the influx of whites into Wisconsin, the ensuing conflicts, and later the lumber boom, the whole situation was changed. A large part of the Indian population was moved west of the Mississippi, but many Indians remained and were settled on local reservations. Today there are over 12,000 Indians in the state, whereas in 1860 there were approximately 1,000. There are six groups of Ojibwa (Bad River, Lac Courte Oreilles, Lac du Flambeau, Red Cliff, Mole Lake, St. Croix).

The Indians on the Lac du Flambeau Reservation live in the High Lake District of the state.[4] Some of their ancestors lived in this locality long before the reservation was established. Warren, in his *History of the Ojibways,* says:

> The French early designated that portion of the tribe who occupied the headwaters of the Wisconsin as the Lac du Flambeau band, from the circumstance of their locating their central village, or summer residence, at the lake known by this name. The Ojibways term it Waus-wag-im-ing (Lake of Torches), from the custom of spearing fish by torch-light, early practised by the hunters of their tribe who first took possession of it.
>
> Before eventually permanently locating their village at this lake, the Ojibways, under their leader, Sha-da-wish, made protracted stands at Trout Lake and Turtle Portage, and it was not till the times of his successor and son, Keesh-ke-mun, that this band proceeded as far west as Lac du Flambeau, for a permanent residence.[5]

The two leaders mentioned are direct ascendants in the male line of one of the oldest men living on the Lac du Flambeau Reservation in 1946, Jim Gray (*waswewégíjik*). Keesh-ke-mun (Sharpened Stone) was his great-great paternal grandfather, who according to Warren died about 1820. It was this Indian who counseled the Ojibwa against affiliation with the British in the War of 1812, although he was subjected to considerable pressure.[6] "To his influence," says Warren, "may be chiefly attributed the fact that the Ojibway of Lake Superior and Mississippi remained neutral during the progress of the last war [1812]." It was in the time of this Indian's father, Sha-da-wish (Bad Pelican), after the final expulsion of the Fox from the Wisconsin River, that a group of Ojibwa first made Lac du Flambeau their permanent headquarters. This must have been around the middle of the eighteenth century, which was also the period of French hegemony in Wisconsin. The outlet of Lac du Flambeau is the Flambeau River which is a tributary of what is now known as the Chippewa River. At this time the latter was called the Sauteux River.

So far as historical circumstances are concerned, the sharp contrast between the Lac du Flambeau Ojibwa and the northern Ojibwa of the Berens River is illustrated by the history of the fur trade in these two regions. In the north, the fur trade still persists; the primary occupation of these Ojibwa is still hunting. In Wisconsin the situation is quite different. At Lac du Flambeau itself we know that the fur trade was still flourishing in 1820 since James D. Doty in his *Report on Indians, Communications and Trade* to Governor Lewis Cass says that "the Southwest Company have an establishment of five traders and twenty hands, the return from which last season was about fifty packs."[7] The principal articles of trade at this time were blankets, stroud, guns, balls and powder, beaver traps, tobacco, axes, hatchets, scalping knives, and beads.[8]

By 1843, however, the fur trade was on the decline in Wisconsin, and by 1845 "lumbering had completely overshadowed mining (lead) and agriculture was for the first time growing important. From then until nearly the end of the century the lumber output increased steadily."[9] The Indian population was soon drawn into the lumber industry. Ernestine Friedl has succinctly summarized the consequences:

> The Indians took to logging and became quite skilled in various phases of the work. In many ways the jobs in the lumber camp permitted the Chippewas to continue a life not essentially different from the hunting and fishing to which most of the men were still accustomed. They could derive satisfaction and prestige from the individual exercise of difficult skills in both types of activity, and they received immediate tangible rewards from both. Moreover they had to move frequently to follow the lumber camps, just as had been previously the case in following game. Hunting had permitted alternate periods of activity and rest. A relatively short period of work in the lumber camps enabled an Indian to collect enough wages to let him cease work while he spent the money. The advent of lumbering therefore permitted the Chippewa men to engage in non-sedentary skilled work with quick returns, a type of endeavor which was much more attractive to those accustomed to the economics of the fur trade and of hunting than was the settled life of the farmer, with its delayed returns.
>
> The tendency of the Chippewas to punctuate their periods of work with periods of idleness had other consequences for reservation life. It meant that they were not a reliable labor force for the lumber companies. In spite of the efforts made by the government to require the companies, when logging Indian lands, to use Indian labor (except in supervisory positions), non-Indian loggers worked on the reservations in considerable numbers. The prosperity on the reservations also brought large numbers of American store-keepers, innkeepers, and traders to the reservations. The penetration of these non-Indians resulted in a fairly large scale intermarriage between the Chippewa women and the American men. In the meantime, non-Indian farmers were permitted to buy some reservation lands, thus reducing the amount of land available to the Indians.[10]

In the annual Report of the Commissioner of Indian Affairs to the Secretary of the Interior in 1889 it is stated that 120 of the Indians at Flambeau could speak English and that 70 could read.[11] At the same time it is interesting to note that in the opinion of the Commissioner these Flambeau Ojibwa were far from being as progressive (acculturated) as those on the nearby Courte Oreilles Reservation. The latter Indians possessed 173 horses, 78 head of cattle, and 68 hogs. Besides this, farms were flourishing. The commissioner concluded that 65 per cent of the Ojibwa at Flambeau were still in a state of "savagery." Nevertheless, the Flambeau Indians were employed in the lumber industry and a sawmill was in operation there from 1894 until 1916,[12] so that many of the older men living in 1946 were in their youth employed in lumbering operations. As late as 1914 modern roads did not exist in this region. Once they were built the area became immensely popular with summer residents and tourists who now flock there in greater numbers than ever before by automobile and railway. As compared with this transient white population, many of whom own summer homes, the resident whites probably number under two hundred. These persons comprise employees of the Federal Government (i.e., employees of the Office of Indian Affairs, the teachers at the Government Indian School, the postmaster) and owners and operators of the stores and garages in the town of Flambeau. Consequently, the Lac du Flambeau Ojibwa have been subjected to an accelerating contact with whites from the middle of the nineteenth century onwards which has had no parallel among their distant cogeners on the Berens River.

Demography.—In order to secure a realistic demographic picture of the Lac du Flambeau Reservation, it is necessary to consider *both* the white population and the Indian population.

Although the original Lac du Flambeau Reservation comprised 73,600 acres, through alienation only 31,933 acres now remain in the hands of the Indians. Practically all the most valuable acreage along the lake shores is in the possession of white owners. This has been the inevitable outcome of the General Allotment Act of 1887 which provided for the allotment of Indian lands in severalty, without making any provision for allotment to families or tribal groups. In the course of time, Indians sold their land so that—as in other similar cases—the reservation became checkerboarded with alien holdings as vast acreages of allotted land passed into white ownership. The remaining Indian holdings are the cut-over and burnt-over timber lands and swampy tracts, the terrestrial residue of the lumbering which ceased about the beginning of World War I. Subdivision among heirs of lands originally allotted in severalty has also created insoluble legal tangles for which there is no practical solution, since a number of individuals may have equity in a very small acreage or one individual may have equity in a number of scattered holdings. Although the Wheeler-Howard Act of 1934 reversed the old allotment policy, the alienated land cannot be reacquired except at heavy cost, so that there is no escape from the influence of past events.[13] The contemporary juxtaposition of a white and Indian population at Flambeau is, then, a special element in the total local situation.

The Indian population does not present an altogether simple picture because of the following facts:

(1) All the Ojibwa who are enrolled members of the Lac du Flambeau Band do not reside on the reservation. Some have married Indians belonging to other groups and are living on other reservations; still

others may live in the cities and towns of Wisconsin, or even in Chicago. A few, especially men, live on the reservation during the summer, but work in the cities, or elsewhere, during the winter. According to the census figures of the Office of Indian Affairs as of January 1, 1946, there were 192 (93 males, 99 females) of these nonresident Ojibwa out of a total of 968 (464 males, 504 females) enrolled members of the band. This makes the resident Ojibwa number 776 (371 males, 405 females). Since there was no way of checking this figure, except by a census, it is assumed that there were at least this many Ojibwa of the Flambeau Band in residence during the summer of 1946. The local Indian population is always at its maximum at this season and among our acquaintances we found a number of individuals who were not resident all year round.

(2) In addition to enrolled members of the Lac du Flambeau band there are Ojibwa Indians who live on the reservation but who, officially, are enrolled members of some other Ojibwa band (e.g., Bad River or Red Cliff). Some of these individuals have lived at Flambeau for many years and have reared families there. For the purposes of our sample we made no distinction between Ojibwa of this category and enrolled members of the Flambeau band.

(3) Another category of the resident Indian population at Flambeau consists of the non-Ojibwa spouses of Ojibwa. These include Indians of Winnebago, Menomini, Potawatomi, Dakota, Oneida, or other tribal affiliations. Some of these persons also have been resident at Flambeau for many years.

It was estimated that persons of categories (2) and (3) numbered about 55. If this figure is added to the presumed number of resident Ojibwa who are also enrolled members of the band (776), the total number of Indian residents at Flambeau in the summer of 1946 would be *at least* 831 persons.

The Indian population is concentrated in two major centers. One is the village of Flambeau where the post office, stores, garages, the Indian Agency, the school, churches, and the factory are located. It is the center of the tourist trade in summer. Most of the Indians live in this neighborhood. It is frequently referred to as the New Village, in contrast to the second area where there is a concentration of Indian population, the Old Village, located on Lac du Flambeau itself and about three miles by road from the New Village. About a hundred Indians were resident here in the summer of 1946, their dwellings strung out along the road which skirts the lake. There are no stores, so that the Indians have to go to the New Village to make their purchases. Located here is a characteristic octagonal log dance hall, now seldom used. Back of the Old Village is a ceremonial dance ground in a beautiful grove of pines, where exhibition dances for tourists are held during the summer. Besides these there is also the characteristic structure of poles used when the Mïdéwïwin is performed. A second structure of the same type is in a wooded section of the New Village. A few of the houses in the Old Village also have the sacred lobsticks erected in front of them. These are commented upon in the account given of the Old Village in the *Wisconsin State Guide* which stimulates many tourists to make a detour through the village. They are inevitably disappointed by what they see. Broadly speaking, most of the Indians in this settlement are more conservative than those living in the New Village. This is partly due to the fact that a few of the oldest and most conservative men live here. They are the "last" leaders of the Mïdéwïwin and the only remaining reservoir of what remains in the way of aboriginal ideology and practice. The most highly acculturated families (with one exception) live in the New Village. The line, however, is by no means a sharp one, or easy to draw.

Outside of these two major concentrations of population, a few Indian families live at Sand Lake and several others near the Lac du Flambeau railway station, about two miles from the New Village. Another family lives isolated from other Indians on the main highway to Minocqua, perhaps six miles from the New Village.

Race Mixture.—As might be expected, the Flambeau Ojibwa show a very high proportion of racial mixture with whites. In this respect they are in striking contrast with the Northern Ojibwa. "Probably not more than 18.7 per cent (1930) of the present number of enrolled Ojibwa in the United States," says Lyford, "can be regarded as fullbloods since intermarriage with Europeans began with the first fur traders and has continued throughout the years. The French, Scots, and English intermarried with the Ojibwa during the fur trading period, extending through the eighteenth and the early part of the nineteenth century. Intermarriage with the Scandinavian and Irish began when lumbering was at its height, from 1850 through the eighties. Intermarriage with the Poles, Hollanders and various other nationalities followed. Intermarriage of the Ojibwa with Indians of other tribes has been increasingly common."[14]

TABLE 6.—DEGREE OF INDIAN BLOOD OF LAC DU FLAMBEAU SUBJECTS

INDIAN BLOOD	CHILDREN				ADULTS				TOTAL SUBJECTS			
	M	F	N	%	M	F	N	%	M	F	N	%
Full	12	15	27	18	20	21	41	35	32	36	68	25
¾	13	16	29	19	6	5	11	9	19	21	40	15
½	25	31	56	37	4	9	13	11	29	40	69	26
¼	16	10	26	18	3	0	3	3	19	10	29	11
< ¼	0	1	1	1	0	0	0	0	0	1	1	1
Unknown	7	3	10	7	18	31	49	42	25	34	59	22
TOTAL	73	76	149	100	51	66	117	100	124	142	266	100

Table 6 shows the degree of Indian blood of the 266 Flambeau subjects on whom data of various kinds were obtained. The information is derived from Federal Government records. Since our sample includes almost all of the oldest Indians, the proportion of Indian blood represented is probably a fair measure of the adults of the entire community. The proportion of full-bloods in the sample of children is less. This is no doubt indicative of a general trend. But even so, it is worth noting that for the Flambeau Ojibwa as a whole the total percentage of full-bloods (25), even with the degree of racial mixture in 22 per cent of the subjects unknown, is considerably higher than the average percentage of full-bloods (18.7) for the Ojibwa at large, estimated by Lyford.

Level of Acculturation.—It need hardly be argued, in the light of historical circumstances and the facts of racial mixture, that the Flambeau group of Ojibwa represent a more advanced level of acculturation than the most acculturated group on the Berens River. Nevertheless, reference to some additional facts will add depth and specificity to this appraisal.

In the first place, the prevalence of English speakers is one of the primary indices to this advanced level, as compared with the situation that prevails in the north. With two exceptions, there was no need for an interpreter at Flambeau, while even in the Berens River Band it was found necessary to use an interpreter for almost the entire series of Rorschach protocols obtained. Many middle-aged Indians at Flambeau confessed that they knew little Ojibwa. Some of them had attended the government boarding school at Hayward early in this century. At that time, we were told, children were punished for speaking Ojibwa. Many Flambeau children are no longer bilingual and in a large proportion of the homes English is spoken. Most of the children do not know Ojibwa myths at all. They are, however, quite familiar with *The Three Bears* and other stories they have heard or read in the excellent government day school on the reservation.

All the Flambeau Ojibwa live in frame houses all the year round and there are wood-burning or kerosene stoves in every house. Any kind of aboriginal dwelling is a thing of the far distant past. No cradle boards are to be found, but homemade swings for infants, frequently seen among the Northern Ojibwa, are still in use. The wearing of moccasins is unusual except at the exhibition dances given for tourists. Even the old men and women wear shoes in their houses. Although a trivial item in one sense, this fact alone is actually a highly significant index of acculturation. In the north the Indians of both Lakeside and Inland bands wear moccasins continually; they have no shoes. A white missionary, moreover, resident in the country for many years, not only wore moccasins habitually, he appeared with them in the pulpit.

The younger people at Flambeau seldom join in the Indian dances given as exhibitions, even for fun. Many of them do not know the Indian steps. But they do attend dances of a modern American type given at the school. This situation is paralleled in the Ojibwa band at the mouth of the Berens River where native dances never take place, but square dances are extremely popular.

So far as the Flambeau men are concerned, hunting and fishing have become incidental occupations, except where Indians act as guides for sportsmen and tourists. The system of hunting territories, so characteristic among Algonkian peoples, has long since disappeared, possibly with the rise of lumbering. During the summer months both men and women engage in various jobs made available in connection with the tourist trade. Women often make and sell beadwork. A small local factory for the manufacture of electric meters was opened in 1946 and Flambeau women and girls are employed there. In the *Handbook on Wisconsin Indians*, prepared by the Governor's Commission on Human Rights (1952), it is reported that

Today seventy-five percent of the employees are Indians and a majority of these are women. Some difficulties were encountered at first in the adjustment of the Indians to the wage-hour system of working. New work habits such as arriving punctually and regularly had to be learned. But these problems have been overcome. The labor turnover at Flambeau is about five percent per year as compared with seventy-five percent at a similar plant owned by the same company in Chicago. The present construction of a new addition to the Flambeau plant with plans to bring the number of employees up to 200 indicates that the firm is satisfied with the progress of the Wisconsin branch.

The impact of this industry on the Flambeau Indians has been considerable. It is the first time since lumbering days that a steady flow of income has appeared in the community and the first time that most of the workers have had regular wages. Clothing and grocery stores have reported a sharp spurt in their business from Indian patrons.

Another project that has also been successful is the amphitheater built in 1951 to serve as a place for civic gatherings and for the performance of Indian dances and ceremonials for the tourists. This has been an additional source of employment for the Indians during the summer.

In 1934 these Indians voted to accept the Indian Reorganization Act and adopted a constitution and by-laws. A tribal council of twelve members is elected annually.

Although most of the Flambeau Ojibwa maintain active church affiliations (Catholic or Protestant), a handful of individuals retain aboriginal beliefs. These center in the Midéwīwin which is still carried on, a somewhat paradoxical fact since it has altogether died out in the Lake Winnipeg region (see 1936b). Recently (1953) I heard that one of the chief leaders of this aboriginal rite has died, so that it may not persist much longer at Lac du Flambeau. Belief in sorcery has continued to persist along with corresponding remedies. A "sucking doctor" treated a patient in the summer of 1946, although this man came from another reservation. On this occasion the setting was indeed aboriginal. The rite was performed in a bark-covered native *wáginogan* (a dome-shaped

343

house) erected at the time the exhibition dances for tourists were put on. But now the dances were over and the tourists gone. Late at night, in the midst of a tall grove of pines bordering on the lake, the singing and rattling of the *nibakiwinini* could be plainly heard by those of us outside the *wáginogan* as the doctor bent over his patient exerting all his magic power to remove the material object that was believed to have made the man ill. Thus, while the aboriginal culture has not totally disappeared at Flambeau, its outward manifestations have been reduced to extremely narrow limits. As the psychological results show, however, the little that is ostensibly Indian is not a simple measure of a personality change in the direction of American patterns. Despite their relatively high level of acculturation the Flambeau Indians, too, are still Ojibwa.

Chapter 19 - Acculturation
and the Personality of the Ojibwa*

In THIS STUDY OF THE EFFECTS OF ACCULTURATION ON PERSONALITY the major questions to which I have sought answers are essentially the following:

1. What are the typical psychological characteristics of the Ojibwa, those which we may reasonably infer to be rooted in their aboriginal culture and which are an expression of their modal personality type? This is our psychological base line.

2. What has been the effect of the acculturation process upon these psychological characteristics?

a. From a purely descriptive point of view we may ask: Do we find continuity or discontinuity in the modal personality picture exhibited by the Ojibwa at different levels of acculturation? Are the people at Flambeau, e.g., psychologically identifiable as Ojibwa despite their high level of acculturation? Or, have they been psychologically transformed?

b. We may likewise ask questions that have functional implications. What about the personal and social adjustment of individuals at different levels of acculturation? Are the Indians at Flambeau, as compared with the Inland group on the Berens River, better integrated psychologically and functioning more adequately, or the reverse? Are sexual differentials to be noted? Before I proceed to a discussion of my data and the conclusions reached I must interpolate a brief resume of the methods and techniques employed to secure the data on which my conclusions rest.

Methodology and Techniques.—One of the intrinsic difficulties which, in the past, has made it almost useless to seek answers to such questions as I have just raised, is the fact that no means were available for obtaining the kind of personality data that would furnish the basis for any reliable conclusions. This is where projective techniques enter the picture. A series of Rorschach protocols, in particular, does make possible the construction of a modal personality picture of a group as well as provide information on intragroup variability.

*Reprinted from "The Use of Projective Techniques in the Study of the Socio-psychological Aspects of Acculturation," *Journal of Projective Techniques*, XV (No. 1, 1951), 27-44 (presidential address to the Society for Projective Techniques, 1950). The introductory section has been omitted.

My major conclusions have been drawn from Rorschach protocols of adults obtained from Indians of the Inland, Lakeside, and Flambeau groups. The total series numbers 217 subjects, 120 men and 97 women, in age from 16 to 80 years. In all samples the median age of the women is lower than that of the men. Subjects from the Inland group, the least acculturated, number 44; from the Lakeside group, 58; and from Lac du Flambeau, 115.

TABLE 7.—DESCRIPTION OF SAMPLES

Age Groups	Inland			Lakeside			Berens River Total			Lac du Flambeau			Total (All Groups)		
	M	F	Total	M	F	Total	M	F	Total	M	F	Total	M	F	Total
16-25	2	7	9	8	8	16	10	15	25	16	24	40	26	39	65
26-35	8	2	10	10	9	19	18	11	29	9	17	26	27	28	55
36-45	4	2	6	5	2	7	9	4	13	7	6	13	16	10	26
46-55	11	2	13	5	2	7	16	4	20	8	5	13	24	9	33
56-65	3	0	3	5	1	6	8	1	9	8	6	14	16	7	23
66 +	3	0	3	2	1	3	5	1	6	6	3	9	11	4	15
N	31	13	44	35	23	58	66	36	102	54	61	115	120	97	217
Mdn Age	46.4	24.8	40.5	33.0	29.4	32.3	41.2	28.2	34.5	38.4	29.3	32.2	39.9	28.7	33.4

By comparing the overall picture of the three groups it has been possible to distinguish certain basic similarities as well as significant differences. With the Rorschach data from the groups analyzed and well in hand it was found possible, on a descriptive psychological level, to draw conclusions with respect to what had happened to the personality organization of these Indians in the acculturation process. But I wanted to secure more substantial evidence of what was happening in functional terms. What kind of personal and social adjustments were these Indians actually making at these different levels of acculturation?

In order to obtain information that would provide an answer to this question, I decided to make use of Helen H. Davidson's signs of adjustment as a measure.[1] A set of such signs may be taken as discrete yet significantly related indices to a broadly conceived norm of personality integration which approaches an optimum level of psychobiological functioning. Without some such standard, whether made explicit or not, we cannot measure degrees or levels of personal adjustment at all. We can only analyze and describe; judgments on any scale of unsuccessful-successful *functioning* are excluded. It is not necessary to maintain a priori that the particular list of signs referred to have universal validity. But, since these signs are actually among the most important criteria in interpreting any Rorschach protocol, there is every reason to believe that their indicative value is of a high order. Besides this, since these signs have been tested for internal consistency, the always present danger of evaluating the psychodynamics of personality functioning by some arbitrary standard, or one that has little actual reference to the realities of psychological integration, is avoided. Consequently, although so far these signs have been applied primarily to selected groups of school children, *in principle* there is no reason why they cannot be extended to adults in our culture and even to subjects with a different cultural background. Davidson recognizes this possibility and the larger problems involved when she writes: "Is it possible and desirable to construct a universal set of signs independent of age, or of intelligence or even of cultural background, or is it more feasible to construct a generalized set of signs which may be modified to suit the particular group being studied?" (p. 35). Thus one way to test out the full potentialities of the sign approach is to extend the use of the set which already has been formulated as a measure of adjustment, to different and varied groups of subjects, including those with different cultural backgrounds, especially where other types of observation may be used as a check upon the results derived from the signs alone.

The Ojibwa Indian protocols presented one such possibility for the following reasons:

(a) Quite aside from the use of signs alone as a measure of adjustment, the Rorschach results obtained have been pragmatically validated in much the same way as in clinical experience. Historical information, ethnographic data, direct observation of the people, some knowledge of life histories, and the results of other projective techniques (TAT and drawings) have been found to be in essential accord with the group picture emerging from the Rorschach protocols. (See Chap. 14.)

(b) The systematic use of the "sign approach" simply involves the quantitative ordering of the same subjects according to a common measure of adjustment. Since our fundamental hypothesis has been that the process of acculturation involves psychological readjustment and the problem has been to discover the nature, depth, and extent of such readjustment in three groups rated independently on a continuum of acculturation, some differences were expected.

(c) The advantage of the sign approach for purposes of group studies is obvious. Each subject can be assigned a numerical value, the number of signs revealed by an examination of his Rorschach protocol. The group picture can be handled with respect to mean number of signs as well as in terms of the distribution of subjects with different numbers of signs. Davidson has listed seventeen signs. I have made use of only sixteen, because I have omitted any rating of the number of *Popular* answers. Since, as I have previously shown (1945c), there seem to be only a few "P" responses that remain constant from culture to culture and no quantitative analysis of the content of the Flambeau responses has yet been made, this seemed to be the most conservative course. Otherwise, some individuals might have been penalized for not giving the "P's" expected of persons rooted in Euro-American culture. Consequently, the figures I

347

obtained run slightly lower than would have been the case if I had used seventeen signs.

(d) Another advantage of the use of these signs for the comparative study of groups is that any semblance to psychiatric diagnosis or terminology can be avoided. The anthropologist, of course, is not prepared to make any such technical characterizations. In this respect he is in a worse position than the clinical psychologist, that is, from the standpoint of a severely conceived psychiatric orthodoxy. While subjects with a low number of signs may be poorly integrated for any number of reasons and even fall into quite distinct clinical groups, nevertheless, from a functional point of view they fall into a different category from those with a large number of signs. From the standpoint of group comparison, therefore, the discrimination made possible by the sign approach appears to be a positive asset.

In order to deal with the intragroup variability of subjects as objectively as possible, I divided them into five groups, i.e., those having 0-3 signs, 4-6, 7-9, 10-12, and 13-16. In effect, this gives us a 5-point scale which represents an ascending series of levels of adjustment (V, IV, III, II, I) and of psychological integration. In the terminology I have used these run from *Badly* integrated subjects with 0-3 signs, through levels characterized as *Poor, Fair,* and *Good,* to *Excellent,* i.e., subjects having 13-16 signs. On this scale subjects having 7-9 signs are the mean group, which I have taken as representing a *Fair* level of adjustment. These verbal translations of levels of adjustment, discriminated on the basis of quantitative data, are, of course, highly tentative and partly a matter of convenience for purposes of more meaningful psychological reference than levels I-V would be. Nevertheless, I should like to point out that my personal acquaintance with practically all of the Berens River subjects and many of those at Flambeau, does make the verbal characterization used meaningful, if any label of this kind is used at all. I should also like to emphasize a fact that will be apparent later. Any characterization of the social adjustment and psychological integration of these Indians must be viewed in terms of the limits set by their personality type, which happens to be of a highly introversive variety. I may add that composite profiles of Rorschach determinants were made for the subjects falling at each level of adjustment and that these reveal fairly consistent and distinguishable patterns at each level in the three locales. For, after all, quantitative statements and verbal characterization alike are only approximations of the psychological reality to which the Rorschach protocols provide the most direct cues. A few characteristic details will suffice, I think, to give substantive Rorschach content to the variation in the patterns found when we move from subjects having a high number of signs to those having a low number, as well as offering justification for the verbal characterization employed to designate different levels of adjustment.

Total R shows a progressive decline. In the total Berens River subjects (102), for instance, those classified as having an *Excellent* adjustment gave 3 times the average number of responses as compared with those exhibiting a *Bad* adjustment. The number of M and FM also show a progressive decline and the relation between these determinants tends towards equality or $FM > M$. Fc and c decrease as do FC and CF. In the total Berens River series the average sum C at the 5 adjustment levels runs: 3.5, 1.4, 1.2, 0.4, and 0.0. The percentage of responses to the last three cards likewise declines. On the other hand, there is a progressive increase in F per cent and A per cent. With regard to intellectual approach W's are always greatest in number in the case of the best adjusted subjects and lowest in the *Badly* adjusted group, with a regular decline in between. But the percentage of W's is always overemphasized to a slight degree in the *Badly* adjusted subjects. $Dd+S$ show an irregularity in both absolute numbers and percentages at the different levels of adjustment.

For the treatment of a portion of the data obtained by standard statistical methods, I am greatly indebted to my friends, Dr. George K. Bennett and Dr. Alexander G. Wesman of the Psychological Corporation, New York. They cannot be held responsible, of course, for any of the conclusions that I have drawn from the totality of the material.

The Psychological Consequences of Acculturation Among the Ojibwas.—A brief characterization of native Ojibwa culture and personality will, I think, be sufficiently intelligible for the purposes of this paper. (For details, see Parts II and III.)

In the first place, the culture of these Indians was relatively simple and homogeneous, as compared with many others in aboriginal America. The Ojibwa were food gatherers, hunters and fishermen; they had no agriculture or settled villages in the aboriginal period. From the standpoint of behavior one of the significant features of their culture was the absence of any institutionalized development which brought organized social sanctions to bear upon the individual. They were chiefless, courtless, jailless. Their society has been called "atomisitic." The type of personality structure that we find was highly introverted. It functioned in terms of internalized controls; the individual felt the full brunt of responsibility for his own acts. Sickness and misfortune were thought to be the penalty for wrongdoing and experiences of this sort provided the occasion for deep feelings of guilt. Ego support, especially in the men, was closely linked with a belief in the necessity for supernaturally derived assistance. This was the basis of psychological security and dreams were the prime medium of human contacts with supernatural beings. On the other hand, psychological security was never absolute since besides sickness and misfortune, even the strongest man might be menaced by sorcery. Therefore, it was necessary to be extremely cautious in interpersonal relations lest aggression be aroused and covert hostility released.

So a surface amiability and emotional restraint, tinged with latent suspicion and anxiety, were characteristic. With so little real give and take on an open and genuinely friendly basis, a high degree of projection colored interpersonal relations.

TABLE 8.—COMPOSITE RORSCHACH PROFILES

Locale	Inland		Lakeside		Berens River Total		Lac du Flambeau	
N	44		58		102		115	
Mean No. of Signs	7.4		7.9		7.7		6.2	
Rorschach Items	Mean No.	Mean %	Mean No.	Mean %	Mean No.	Mean %	Mean No.	Mean %
R	25		29		27		17	
W	5	24	5	22	5	23	5	36
D	12	52	14	52	13	52	8	47
d	2	9	3	9	3	9	1	6
$Dd+S$	5	15	6	16	6	16	3	11
M	4		3		3		1	
FM	3		3		3		3	
m	.02		0.3		0.2		0.2	
k	0		0		0		0.4	
K	0.2		0.4		0.4		0.2	
FK	0.1		0.6		0.4		0.2	
F	16	65	18	60	17	63	7	45
Fc	0.4		1.2		0.9		0.8	
c	0.2		0.7		0.5		0.8	
C'	0.1		0.1		0.1		0.4	
FC	0.4		0.9		0.7		0.6	
CF	0.3		0.9		0.7		0.7	
C	0.02		0.2		0.1		0	
ΣC	0.5		1.7		1.2		1	
% 8,9,10		38		40		39		33
H	6		4		5		1	
Hd	4		3		4		2	
A	9		10		10		7	
Ad	3		4		3		2	
$A\%$		49		47		50		53
$Anat$	0		0.5		0.3		1	

Now the Rorschach data of the Inland people are in substantial accord with this description. The ΣC average 0.5 while the achromatic score $(Fc+c+C')$ is greater (0.7) and the average percentage of responses to the last three cards is 38. On the other hand, the average M is 4. Accompanying this introversive picture is a very high F column, the average F per cent being 65. The average percentages for W, D, and d are all within the expected range but there is an overemphasis on the number of $Dd + S$ (15 per cent), $M > FM$, the A per cent average is 49 and total responses average 25.

This composite profile of the Inland group approximates very closely to the personality picture which, on other grounds, seems generic for the Algonkian peoples of the Eastern Woodlands of the earliest contact period. Consequently, I believe it is legitimate to conclude that in the case of the Ojibwa a considerable amount of acculturation actually has taken place without any major change in their modal personality structure. Thus the Inland group may be taken as a direct psychological link with the past. If this be true then psychological continuity, despite outward indications of acculturation, becomes an empirically established fact.

What has happened to this characteristic configuration of Ojibwa personality at the other two acculturation levels studied? The most striking fact is the continuity of the same basic psychological pattern through these stages of acculturation. There is a persistent core of generic traits which can be identified as Ojibwa. Thus even the highly acculturated Indians at Flambeau are still Ojibwa in a psychological sense whatever their clothes, their houses, or their occupations, whether they speak English or not, and regardless of race mixture. While culturally speaking they appear like "whites" in many respects, there is no evidence at all of a fundamental psychological transformation. On the other hand, the fact of psychological continuity must not be taken to imply that no modifications in the psychological structure of the Ojibwa have taken place. The nature of these modifications will direct attention to what is perhaps the most important conclusion that can be drawn from our data.

While the Rorschach picture at Flambeau retains certain generic features which we have noted in the Inland group such as the low percentage of answers to the last three cards, the very low ΣC and the fact that the achromatic score is greater, there are some interesting differences to be noted. The average percentage of responses to Cards VIII, IX, and X, for example, drops to 33, the lowest in all three groups; the average M's drop to 1, whereas the average FM's rise to 3. The F per cent drops to 45. It should be noted, however, that this latter change is not accompanied by either a higher color score or a greater number of M's. It indicated a weakening of the rigid control on which the Inland Ojibwa depends, without any compensating factors emerging. So the picture is one that reflects an apathy which is further substantiated by a tendency to respond with very simple W's.

While some of these trends are slightly perceptible in the Lakeside group, such as a tendency for FM to exceed M, in individual instances this is compensated by a gain in color. In the composite profile FM just equals M. The Lakeside group, in fact, exhibits a definite tendency towards a greater expansion in color score than any other group. (Av. ΣC 1.7 as compared with Inland, 0.5, and Flambeau, 1.) At Flambeau, this incipient tendency has been reversed. On the whole, however, the Lakeside picture differs little from that of their Inland kinsmen. It is at Flambeau where we can see reflected in the Rorschach data an introversive

351

personality structure being pushed to the limits of its functional adequacy. The whole trend is one that seems to be accelerating in a regressive direction. These people are being thrown back on their psychological heels, as it were. They are compelled to function with a great paucity of inner resources. There is a kind of frustration of maturity. This could be further demonstrated by an examination of the children's records. Those of adults are too much like them and the children are badly adjusted as well. (For a statistical evaluation of this significance of interlocal differences see Table 9, compiled by Dr. Solomon Diamond.)

TABLE 9.—PROBABILITY OF A CHANCE DIFFERENCE AS GREAT AS THAT OBSERVED, DETERMINED FROM CHI-SQUARE VALUES OF FOUR-FOLD TABLES, IN WHICH THE CRITERION OF DICHOTOMY IS AS CLOSE AS POSSIBLE TO THE MEDIAN FOR THE THREE GROUPS COMBINED

Category, and criterion for dichotomy		Flambeau Lakeside	Flambeau Inland	Lakeside Inland
R	< 19	.001	.001	* .2
W	< 5	.8	* .8	* .3
$W\%$	> 25.5	.01	.01	.8
D	< 10	.001	.001	* .4
$D\%$	< 50.5	.01	.1	* .5
d	< 1	.001	.001	.7
$d\%$	< 5.5	.001	.01	* .9
$dd+s$	< 2	.001	.1	* .2
$dd+s\%$	< 10.5	.3	.6	* .7
M	< 2	.001	.001	.1
FM	> 3	.5	.02	.2
FM	$\geqq M$	.001	.001	.1
m	< 1	.2	* .1	* .01
k	< 1	.001	.01	..
K	< 1	.02	.4	* .3
FK	< 1	.02	* .1	* .001
F	< 10	.001	.001	* .6
$F\%$	< 50.5	.001	.001	.02
Fc	< 1	.02	6 .05	* .001
c	> 1	.3	.001	.02
c	> 1	.01	.02	* .8
FC	> 1	.9	.02	.6
CF	< 1	.7	* .05	* .05
CF	$< FC$	.7	* .98	* .7
C	< 1	.001	..	* .1
$8,9,10\%$	< 35.5	.001	.001	.8
$A\%$	< 50.5	.6	.6	* .95

*The relationship stated as the criterion for dichotomy is more likely to occur in the first group named of each pair, except where an asterisk indicates reversal.

352

So much then for the generalized picture we get from a qualitative examination of the Rorschach protocols of the three Ojibwa groups. An analysis of the same body of data in terms of the signs of adjustment worked out by Helen Davidson, makes it possible to secure quantitative information which measures more precisely the trend towards a lower level of psychological integration that is taking place in the Flambeau population.

The number of signs for each subject being determined according to the criteria used by Davidson, the distribution of these values was made separately for each sex in the Inland, Lakeside, and Flambeau groups in order to discover whether sex differences were of significance. "The means, standard deviations, and standard errors of the means were computed. Differences were in each case divided by the standard errors of the differences to obtain the critical ratio, and the probability of chance occurrence of such differences was determined by reference to the Table of the Normal Probability Integral. The p values given are those corresponding to the areas under both tails of the distribution. Since the number of cases was small (particularly the Inland Female Group) N-2 was used in computing the standard deviation to allow for the restriction in degrees of freedom," Table 10 (from memorandum of George K. Bennett.). Since differences between sexes tend to be small and approach significance only in the case of the Inland group, as will be seen in Table 10 (compiled by Bennett and Wesman) the sexes were combined for

TABLE 10.—ADJUSTMENT SIGNS BY SEX AND TRIBAL GROUPS

No. of Signs	Inland M	Inland F	Lakeside M	Lakeside F	Flambeau M	Flambeau F
15	0	0	0	1	0	0
14	0	0	0	0	0	0
13	0	0	4	2	1	0
12	1	0	2	2	1	1
11	2	0	1	1	2	2
10	4	1	3	2	4	4
9	8	2	4	4	1	7
8	3	2	2	2	10	7
7	7	2	7	0	4	7
6	2	2	1	2	8	9
5	1	1	4	4	8	8
4	0	2	6	2	5	5
3	1	0	1	1	7	8
2	2	1	0	0	2	2
1	0	0	0	0	1	1
N	31	13	35	23	54	61
M	7.8	6.5	7.7	8.3	6.3	6.3
S.D.	2.52	2.35	3.14	3.31	2.61	2.59
S.D.(M)	.47	.72	.55	.72	.36	.34

subsequent statistical treatment. Table 11 (compiled by Bennett and Wesman) presents the basic data on mean sign differences and variability

353

TABLE 11.—ADJUSTMENT DISTRIBUTIONS BY LOCALE

No. of Signs	Inland	Lakeside	Flambeau
16	0	0	0
15	0	1	0
14	0	0	0
13	0	6	1
12	1	4	2
11	2	2	4
10	5	5	8
9	10	8	8
8	5	4	17
7	9	7	11
6	4	3	17
5	2	8	16
4	2	8	10
3	1	2	15
2	3	0	4
1	0	0	2
	—	—	—
N	44	58	115
M	7.4	7.9	6.3
S.D.	2.58	3.32	2.60
S.D.(M)	.40	.42	.24
S.D.(S.D.)	.27	.31	.18

as exhibited by the three groups of subjects. It will be noted that the mean number of signs for both the Inland and Lakeside Groups fall within the sign range that I have taken to represent a Fair level of general adjustment, whereas the Flambeau Indians fall below this. Despite the fact that, without further investigation, the comparison may be taken only as suggestive, it seems worth while to call attention to the fact that in the various groups of children reported by Davidson[2] the range in the mean number of signs runs from 6.85 in the case of a group of "Unsuccessful High School Boys" to 11.34 in the case of a few "Successful High School Girls." In the terminology I am using here the former would fall at the Poor integration level, the latter at the Good one even when we take into account the fact that Davidson used 17 signs while I used 16. Furthermore, considering the fact that Davidson subjects are drawn from school populations while mine are drawn from an essentially random sampling of the adults of a general population with an Ojibwa cultural background, it seems to me that the sign approach merits further exploration on a comparative basis.

This conclusion is further supported by the fact that, as the following tabulation shows, a statistical evaluation of the mean differences exhibited by the three Indian groups indicates that the fewer signs of the Flambeau group may be taken to be significant. On the other hand, the observed difference between the Inland and Lakeside Indians could readily have arisen by chance.

	D	S.D.	CR	2P*
Inland—Lakeside	− .5	.585	− .85	.39
Inland—Flambeau	+1.1	.466	+2.36	.02
Lakeside—Flambeau	+1.6	.488	+3.08	.002

*Compiled by Bennett and Wesman.

Turning now to intragroup differences in variability (Standard

TABLE 12.—PERCENTAGE OF SUBJECTS AT DIFFERENT LEVELS OF ADJUSTMENT IN OJIBWA ACCULTURATED GROUPS

No Signs	Characteri- zation	Inland	Lakeside	Berens River Total	Lac Du Flambeau
13-16	Excellent	0	12	7	1
10-12	Good	18	19	19	12
7- 9	Fair	55	33	42	31
4- 6	Poor	18	33	26	38
0- 3	Bad	9	3	6	18
		100	100	100	100

Deviation) the following tabulation indicates that the somewhat greater variability in the Lakeside group, as compared with the other two, approaches statistical significance.

	D	S.D.	CR	2P*
Inland—Lakeside	.74	.413	1.77	.08
Inland Flambeau	.02	.325	.06	..
Lakeside—Flambeau	.72	.355	2.03	.04

*Compiled by Bennett and Wesman.

From the standpoint of adjustment I think it can be maintained that in the Lakeside group, where the process of acculturation has proceeded rather slowly, it has been possible for individuals to become psychologically readapted to the exigencies of the situation within a wider range of possibilities than in the Inland group or at Flambeau. This is suggested by the variation in each of the three groups of the percentage of subjects at the five levels of adjustment discriminated. (Table 12.[3]) In the least acculturated Inland group the range is narrow, since 55 per cent of the subjects are in the median or Fair adjustment category, none are in the Excellent, and only 9 per cent at the Bad adjustment level. This is the group, too, it will be recalled, in which the typical features of the Ojibwa personality structure are most clearly apparent. The characteristic cultural pressures which defined social interaction no doubt limited the range of psychological integration as well. In this connection, it is a striking fact that the highest percentage of subjects (12 per cent) who show an Excellent level of psychological integration were found in the Lakeside group. At Flambeau, while the spread is great, the largest percentage of subjects (38 per cent) falls into the Poorly adjusted category. In contrast to the Lakeside group it would seem that there must be factors at work at Flambeau which set barriers to the

355

achievement of personal adjustment on higher levels. A simple quantitative comparison which dramatizes the situation at Flambeau can be derived from Table 12 by contrasting the percentage of subjects in each group who have 7 or more signs. In the Inland group this figure is 73 per cent, in the Lakeside group 64 per cent, while at Flambeau it is only 44 per cent.[4] In other words, Flambeau is the only one of the three groups in which more than half (56 per cent) of the subjects fall into the Poor and Bad adjustment category.

With some hesitation I should like to mention another contrasting fact with respect to intragroup variability which appears to differentiate the Berens River Ojibwa from those at Flambeau. When the subjects are classified into three ascending age levels (16 to 35 years, 36 to 55 years, and 56 years and upwards) and the percentage of individuals that have 7 or more signs of adjustment contrasted with the proportion having 6 signs or less in each age group, it appears that the pattern at Flambeau is almost the reverse of that found in the Canadian groups. For the combined Berens River subjects the percentage of those at each successive age level having 7 or more signs follows the sequence 54, 76, 100. In the Flambeau group there is no comparable tendency. In fact, the percentage of subjects with 7 or more signs is 45 per cent or less at *each* age level. Since these data have not been statistically tested they may not be significant. Nevertheless, from a psychological point of view, the relatively small percentage of subjects 36 years and upwards that do not even fall into the Fair adjustment category at Flambeau possibly provides a quantitative hint to what, on other grounds, I have referred to as a frustration of maturity. Nor can I dismiss the possibility that the quantitative fact noted likewise illuminates one of the conditions that may account for the disturbing picture presented by the Flambeau children. This has been documented by the Rorschach data collected and analyzed by Dr. Blanche Watrous, the conclusions drawn from TAT records of the same children by Dr. Wm. Caudill and, more recently, the inferences made from a blind analysis of the drawings of Flambeau children by Michal Lowenfels Kane. (See Chap. 18.)

It is obvious, I believe, from the foregoing data that, although three levels of acculturation can be discriminated among the Ojibwa studied and that while some minor qualitative differences in the overall Rorschach pattern can be discerned when we compare the Inland and Lakeside groups, on the whole the major psychological contrast, as clearly indicated by the signs of adjustment, lies between the Berens River Ojibwa considered as a whole and the Flambeau Ojibwa. It must be concluded, therefore, that the tendency towards a low level of psychological adjustment at Flambeau is not to be attributed to "acculturation" considered abstractly or as some inevitable force, but to a set of complex factors that we know too little about and which are extremely difficult to analyze.

Apparently there have been differential factors operative in the situation at Flambeau which have not been present on the Berens River.

I cannot, of course, go into an extended analysis here of all the various factors that may account for the breakdown of the old personality structure of the Ojibwa under the pressures of acculturation at Flambeau. But I can say that one of the most crucial factors involved seems to be the lack of any positive substitute for that aspect of the aboriginal value system that had its core in religious belief. As I have pointed out (Chap. 20) there was once an intimate connection between the content of Ojibwa beliefs, the source of their psychological security and the optimum functioning of inner controls in their psychic economy. While this inner control is still present at Flambeau it has been modified in a regressive direction so that it easily breaks down. In actual behavior, evidence of this is to be seen in the tremendous incidence of drunkenness and juvenile delinquency on the reservation and the fact that externally applied controls seem quite ineffective. The behavior of many Indians is also symptomatic of the terrific inner struggle which many individuals are experiencing in reaction to the present paucity of their inner resources. An apathy is created which they cannot overcome. They are attempting, as best they may, to survive under conditions which, as yet, offer no culturally defined values and goals that have become vitally significant for them and which might serve as the psychological means that would lead to a more positive readjustment.

Finally, I should like to emphasize the fact that the psychological consequences of acculturation among the Ojibwa that I have described must not be generalized to include all American Indians or aboriginal peoples elsewhere that have come into contact with Western civilization. While we do not have any precisely comparable data from other groups I can think of peoples where the contrary situation may exist.

The aim of this paper has been to call attention to the expanding usefulness of projective techniques and to demonstrate how the Rorschach, in particular, has been used to attack problems in an area of research far removed from the clinic and yet not entirely divorced from the values that are growing out of clinical work. For if we can measure the outcome of acculturation in concrete instances with respect to its effects upon the psychodynamics of personal integration, in the end we may learn a great deal about the instrumental values of *different* cultural systems in relation to human adjustment. And we may be on our way to discovering the essential elements that are necessary in any sociocultural system in order that man can most nearly achieve an optimum level of psychobiological functioning.

Chapter 20 - Values, Acculturation, and Mental Health*

Anthropologists, like many other social scientists, have fought shy of dealing with one of the most characteristic features of the life of man. This is the plain and simple fact that implicit as well as explicit values of various kinds are one of the central and inescapable phenomena of a human existence. Diversity in systems of value is a concomitant of cultural variability in the development and functioning of the human species.

Consciously striving to be objective, tolerant, and sophisticated in the study of our own species, anthropologists usually have considered various classes of values as phenomena that must be considered primarily in their cultural context and thus relativistic in nature. They have been content to leave generic problems—such questions as intrinsic or universal human values—in the hands of the philosopher, moralist, or theologian. Anthropologists have felt that their major contribution lay in reporting the variations in value systems which came under their observation. Most of us have not had the temerity to attempt an evaluation of the value systems of different cultures because it is said we have no supercultural standard that can be used as a yardstick in making any such judgment.

In addition to recognizing the relativity of different value systems and the inherent difficulty in making any appraisal of them with reference to any absolute ethical or other standard, we should not close our minds to the possibility that, from the standpoint of the psychodynamics of human adjustment, the value systems of different societies may vary significantly as more or less efficient instruments in the molding of personalities that are fully capable of functioning at a level of mental health. If we adopt this as a hypothesis, we have indicated to us another angle of approach to the value systems of different human societies. We may ask: What is the role of different systems of value with reference to the general level of personality adjustment which is found in different groups? Or, in the phraseology of Dr. Henry in a recent article: "What are the

---

*Reprinted from *The American Journal of Orthopsychiatry*, XX (October 1950), 732-43.

consequences in terms of the physical and spiritual well-being of the population of the culture's attempt to live out in daily life this particular value system?"[1] (Italics ours.)

The crucial question remains: Are there, or are there not, any significant differences in personal adjustment to be observed if, by using an optimum concept of integrative behavior[2] as a measure, we examine the consequences of one set of culturally embedded value systems as compared with another?

It is possible, I believe, that some light may be thrown on this question by the anthropologist: first, by studying systems of value in different societies from the standpoint of total personality integration and functioning viewed in the perspective of our knowledge of mental health; secondly, by studying more closely the psychological aspects of acculturation, particularly the effects of the social readjustment involved with reference to personality structure and value systems. One of the questions that arises here is how far, and under what conditions, the value system of one culture is transferable to individuals of another in the process of acculturation in order for it to become an integral part of their life adjustment.

The purpose of this paper is to show how the modifications of the personality structure of the Ojibwa Indians under the very acute pressures and frustrations of acculturation highlight the integrative role of the value system of their native culture in relation to the functioning of the total personality.

In the course of acculturation their personality structure has been skewed in a nonintegrative direction, instead of being reconstituted. One of the reasons for this seems to lie in the fact that, despite many outward manifestations of acculturation, no substitute for the value system of the old culture has become psychologically functional. Consequently these people exhibit a psychological impasse. Their characteristic personality structure can no longer function at its optimum level, so that there are many signs of regression, withdrawal, and aggression to be observed. Individuals can no longer depend upon culturally constituted group support, since the old mode of life has disintegrated for the most part. The only positive avenue open for psychological readjustment is for the individual to struggle through alone as best he can. This, in turn, places an enormous burden upon him with highly variable consequences. On the whole, an optimum of mental health has not been maintained.

First, I shall give a brief sketch of the central values of the old culture of the Ojibwa with primary reference to their psychological implications.

Secondly, I shall summarize the steps taken in a series of investigations designed to discover the psychological consequences of various levels of acculturation. At least four of these levels are distinguishable. They are concretely represented by the following groups of Ojibwa: Level 1,

The Ojibwa of certain parts of Western Ontario (Canada); level 2, The Inland Ojibwa (Saulteaux) of the Berens River (Manitoba); level 3, The Lakeside Indians of the Berens River; level 4, The Lac du Flambeau Ojibwa (Northern Wisconsin). (For extended description see Chaps. 18 and 19.)

Thirdly, I shall make some concluding comments on the psychological impasse that appears to have been reached in the case of the most highly acculturated group mentioned, the Lac du Flambeau Ojibwa.

The Value Systems of Old Ojibwa Culture and Modal Personality Structure.—The central value of aboriginal Ojibwa culture was expressed by the term *pīmädazīwin,* life in the fullest sense, life in the sense of health, longevity, and well-being, not only for oneself but for one's family. The goal of living was a good life and the Good Life involved *pīmädazīwin.*

How was it possible to achieve *pīmädazīwin?* The answer to this question leads directly to the core of the world view of these people. (See Chaps. 7 and 8.) In the first place, *pīmädazīwin* could only be achieved by individuals who sought and obtained the help of superhuman entities and who conducted themselves in a socially approved manner. In the second place, the functioning of sexual dichotomy in this culture was such that, while *pīmädazīwin* was a central value for both sexes, it was absolutely imperative that males, rather than females, seek out and obtain superhuman aid. Women might obtain such help; men could not get along without it. Thus we find the institutionalized expression of this culturally constituted imperative in the so-called "dream fast" for boys as they approach puberty. Thirdly, it is important to note that superhuman help was sought in solitude, that the "blessing" or "gift" could not be compelled, but was bestowed because the superhuman entities took "pity" upon the suppliant who, in effect, asked for Life (i.e., *pīmädazīwin*). In the fourth place, it should be understood that the solitary faster usually obtained "blessings" from many "helpers" or guardian spirits, but that the nature of the gifts depended upon his own interpretation of the dreams or visions he experienced. For example, one dream might be interpreted as meaning that the individual would be invulnerable to bullets; another that, in due course of time, he would be able to cure people with certain kinds of medicine or conjuring. From a cultural point of view, the fasting experience was a sacred experience since direct contact with superhuman entities had been made. This was why the individual never referred to this experience lightly. Unless he were willing to lose his blessings he could not recount his dream in whole or even in part except under extraordinary circumstances.

It is fully characteristic of the highly introverted personality organization of these people, and the rudimentary cast of their social organization, that this direct contact with superhuman entities was made by each individual alone, that it necessitated the interpretation of a highly subjective experience, the details of which were not usually revealed to anyone else, except perhaps the boy's father. Thus the dream fast was the most highly treasured experience of every man. It was a psychological talisman of *pīmädazīwin*, if he did his part by conducting himself properly throughout the rest of his life. It was the foundation of all he was to be in the future. Every special aptitude, all his successes and failures, hinged upon the blessings of his supernatural helpers, rather than upon his own native or acquired endowments, or even the help of his fellow human beings.

From a psychological point of view the Ojibwa boy in his dream fast met the personified forces of his own unconscious, reified in culturally constituted images. And this occurred at a crucial period in his psychological maturation. The fast marked the transition from the infant and child state to adulthood. Formerly the boy had been dependent upon older *human* beings, who, in addition to teaching him necessary skills, had trained him to rely upon himself to the extent of his capacity. Henceforth he was to rely primarily upon *superhuman beings,* that is, upon *inner* promptings, derived from further dreams or the memories of his fasting experience. Culturally phrased, his objective security depended largely upon his contact with superhuman entities, a conviction which was the basis of the sense of inner personal security he now felt. At the same time the dream fast introduced the boy to new obligations. He must respect his blessings and use them carefully. In effect, the basic principle involved might be stated as the obligation to preserve the equilibrium of nature. Nature's bounty depends on his using his powers skillfully, being self-reliant, ready to endure hardship, even starvation. He may be aggressive, predatory, in relation to the flora and fauna of his habitat, for his was a food-gathering and hunting economy. But he must only take what he actually needed to provide food, clothing and warmth for himself and his family. He must not be destructive or greedy, and he must never torture any animal. If he acts otherwise the animals will be withdrawn from him by the superhuman entities who directed them to him. In the end he will destroy himself since neither the material nor spiritual sources of life will be any longer available to him.

Thus the Ojibwa was far from considering himself the "lord of creation." He was only one of the "children" of nature, a suppliant *for pīmädazīwin*. Fundamentally, therefore, his relationship to nature expressed a passive attitude. He did not enter the creative process in order to control it for his own ends, as does the horticulturalist who plants seeds, tends them, and gathers in the harvest, thereby controlling his food supply.

From the standpoint of this characteristic attitude toward his place in the universe, it can be said that the main binding force of Ojibwa institutions was not so much to link individuals together through common cooperative aims as it was to permit individuals seeking a common central value to achieve it without too much human interference from without. Thus there was no institutionalized chieftainship in the old days

361

nor any organized penal sanctions. In his relations with his fellows the extended use of kinship terms throughout the social world of the individual defined accompanying roles in what was, in effect, an extended family group. Thus, highly individuated relationships with people were not required, since basic attitudes and behavior patterns learned in childhood prepared the individual for dealing with kin of every traditional category. Departure from approved behavior, especially in the sexual sphere, provoked its own penalty automatically—disease or sometimes death—that is, withdrawal of *pimädaziwin*. Thus no one could ultimately escape moral responsibility for his conduct. (Chaps. 14 and 16.) Other human beings, however, could interfere with the achievement of *pimädaziwin* through sorcery. They could mobilize their "helpers" against one and one's only recourse was to defend oneself in the same terms. This possibility was the source of much latent fear since no one, of course, could ever know the power of another person until it was demonstrated. Consequently, there was a general suppression of overt hostility accompanied by a surface amiability between people who were actually wary of one another. This was especially true among men, since women ordinarily did not practice sorcery. But covert hostility, especially in the form of gossip and slander, was rife (Chap. 15).

Thus, with so little real give and take on an open, confident, and genuine basis, and so few economic tasks where any but the very simplest kinds of cooperative efforts were necessary, there was no great emotional depth or security possible in personal relationships. Instead, all such relationships were fraught with a high degree of projection.

Although I have had to present the material in a highly condensed form, I hope that it has been possible to communicate the essential psychological characteristics of the Ojibwa viewed in relation to their central system of values. Theirs was a personality structure that was necessarily introverted and that functioned in terms of a highly internal conscience[3] that made the individual bear the full brunt of responsibility for his own acts. In the case of men in particular, ego support was intimately linked with a belief system and values that made it necessary for them to be firmly convinced of their own superhumanly derived power in order to feel psychologically secure. But this security was never absolute since they might fail to conduct themselves properly and their power could be challenged by other men. This latter possibility was a great source of potential anxiety. Women, on the other hand, were less sensitive in this respect since their life adjustment did not depend primarily upon direct contact with superhuman entities, so that their psychological security was more essentially a function of their human contacts.

Acculturation Levels and Psychological Consequences.—What have been the psychological effects of acculturation upon the Ojibwa? In what respects are they similar to, or different from, their aboriginal ancestors? Has there been a complete psychological break with the past at one of these levels of acculturation, or is there a demonstrable psychological continuity in personality structure? Is it possible that the psychological readjustments that the acculturation process implies, or certain stages of it, can take place without any radical change in the personality organization of the people involved? If there are modifications what is their nature? And how has the actual behavior of these people been affected?

Detailed studies of the Rorschach and TAT, along with the other data already cited, provided a body of evidence that all points in the same direction—a persistent core of psychological characteristics sufficient to identify an Ojibwa personality constellation, aboriginal in origin, that is clearly discernible through all levels of acculturation thus far studied. For this reason all the Ojibwa referred to, including the most highly acculturated group at Lac du Flambeau, are still Indians in a psychological sense, whatever the clothes they wear, whatever their occupation, whether they speak English or not, and regardless of race mixture. Although, culturally speaking, they appear more and more like whites at "higher" levels of acculturation, there is no evidence at all for a basic psychological shift in a parallel direction. Thus, familiar anthropological terms like "borrowing" and "diffusion," which are entirely appropriate to describe the acculturation process in a cultural frame of reference, are misleading and inappropriate if the acculturation process is viewed from the standpoint of a psychological frame of reference. At least in the situation described, no identifiable constellation of *psychological* "traits" has been "borrowed" by the Ojibwa or "diffused" to them as a result of their contacts with whites.

All the evidence points to far more complicated psychological processes than those which have led to the acquisition of the culture traits which I have used as objective empirical guides to different levels of acculturation. Consequently, descriptive facts of this order are no direct index to facts pertaining to personality adjustment and personality organization.

Perhaps I can best indicate the nature of this more complex psychological problem by clarifying another fundamental point in the data. While these show, as I have said, the persistence of an aboriginal character structure among the Ojibwa, this must not be interpreted to mean that no psychological modifications whatever have been produced in the acculturation process. Actually, quite the contrary is true. Personality structure is a dynamic construct, not a substantive one. When the data at hand are viewed in terms of the actual life adjustments which individuals have been making, the nature and dynamics of these modifications are fairly clear, although I have not yet assembled all the evidence. But it is a striking fact that all through the Rorschach data there are common trends. These are evident whether we compare the Lakeside Indians with the Inland Indians of the Berens River, or the Flambeau children as a whole with the Northern children, or the Flambeau adults with the Berens River adults. The impression one receives is of a personality structure which, under the varying pressures of acculturation in these localities, is being pushed to the limits of its functional adequacy at Lac du Flambeau. (See Chap. 19 for further details.)

What seems to have happened is that the acculturation process at Flambeau has reached a level which presents a situation in which we find the personality structure of the Ojibwa in the process of breaking down, rather than undergoing reintegration in any new or positive form. It is also at this level of acculturation that, along with the disappearance of language, old economic pursuits and customs, the native system of belief and values exhibits the most striking disintegration. Consequently there is little or nothing of genuine integrative value that the old culture can offer the individual.

The Psychological Impasse at Lac du Flambeau.—There is a real psychological impasse at Flambeau for three reasons: (a) The functional support, in the form of a system of values, which was one of the factors that enabled the personality structure of the Ojibwa to function at an optimum level under aboriginal conditions, is no longer available. (b) On the other hand, contact with the version of Western culture available to these Indians has provided no substitute. (c) Furthermore, the objective economic and other conditions are not conducive to any constructive resolution of the psychological impasse that exists.

In conclusion I should like to make a few interpretative comments: 1. The disintegration of the old belief system and the substitution of a superficially acquired Christianity as the basis of a new world view have been particularly serious in the case of the men. Their inner life has been emptied of the deep convictions, motivations, and goals that were all integrated in terms of the older belief system and its concomitant stabilized values. Besides this, the men have been cut off from their traditional economic occupation, except as guides for white men, while, at the same time, vocational opportunities are limited unless they leave the reservation. They have become apathetic, and drink all they can. Young men just out of the Armed Services in 1946 were sitting around idly, drawing their unemployment insurance until it became exhausted. The government had become the great provider. The old passive attitude of dependence on natural products and superhuman helpers which was so fruitful for their old adjustment has become a liability, like a dead weight that pushes them further into apathy. For it is unbalanced by the pressures of the old life in which daily efforts to wrest a living from a rigorous environment were a primary necessity. Many men are not even successful breadwinners, whereas in the old culture this task devolved almost entirely upon them. There has been an accompanying impairment of self-regard, of any feeling of real security. The women, on the other hand, are becoming more and more important as a potential source of cash income. Quite a few of them, almost all married women, have taken jobs in a small local factory. But their children are running wild.

An unconscious sense of the keen loss of vital central values to these peoples is indicated by an attempt on the part of a few of them to retain the Midéwiwin. This aboriginal rite might be said to symbolize the old belief system, and the values inherent in it. But the psychological weakness of this kind of withdrawal was exposed to me by the question one of the leaders once asked me. He was an old man with whom I had become quite friendly, partly because of the interest I had shown in the old religion and no doubt because he was interested in what I could tell him about the less acculturated Ojibwa in Canada. One day he sent for me and asked me whether I thought the Indian religion was really true. This question, of course, clearly indicated the doubts that beset him and demonstrated to me the lack of vitality which the old belief system now had as any sort of psychological resource.

2. As indicated in the sketch of the aboriginal value system and personality organization, there was a great deal of suppressed hostility in the interpersonal relations of these people even under optimum conditions. In the stage of acculturation represented at Lac du Flambeau overt aggression appears to have replaced the covert aggression that formerly existed in the form of sorcery.

While verbally expressed aggression remains, all white people getting a large share of it, in addition there has been a marked increase in crimes against property by boys and young men. Furthermore, overt hostility comes to the surface with remarkable rapidity as soon as these Indians start drinking, even though they may be otherwise very friendly. While inner control is still present, its threshold has been greatly lowered by the loosening of the psychological integration that has occurred under present conditions. And, of course, the only outer controls now are the institutionalized penal sanctions of the surrounding white community, since even in the old culture these were not developed among the Indians themselves. Aggression may also be interpreted as a sign of the terrific psychological struggle many individuals are experiencing in reacting to the apathy which the paucity of inner resources has produced. These Indians have been thrown back on their psychological heels, as it were. They are attempting to survive in a situation which offers them no culturally defined values and goals that they can really make their own, that have any vital psychological significance for them. Consequently, they lack the kind of cultural fulcrum which is necessary, it seems to me, for full psychological maturity and an optimum of mental health in any human society.

3. Finally, the inner core of their nonintegrative adjustment may be characterized as regression in the sense of a kind of primitivation.[4] That is to say, not literally falling back upon actual modes of earlier behavior, but what is perhaps even more serious, a *frustration of maturity*. From the Northern Rorschach data, for example, we can see what the

steps in the process of psychological maturation are. At Flambeau it is a striking fact that the protocols of adults are so much like those of the children. This means that these regressive trends in their personality structure make an optimum of mental health impossible under the conditions that now confront them. In this respect the Flambeau adults are the antithesis of the Berens River Ojibwa, who are quite well adjusted on the whole. Thus the Flambeau Indian represents what is, in effect, a *regressive version* of the personality structure of the Northern Ojibwa.

So far as I have been able to analyze the situation, it does not seem to me that there is any positive resolution of this psychological impasse in sight. While, externally viewed, these Indians are highly acculturated, their level of psychological adjustment falls far below the optimum that we know was possible with their type of personality structure, not only under aboriginal conditions but at lower levels of acculturation. At Flambeau, a high level of acculturation conceals a psychological skeleton. *Pīmädaziwin* has become an empty word for these Ojibwa. To give it a vital content a new set of values will have to emerge that will either implement a reintegration of their old personality structure or serve as a catalyst for a reconstitution of their whole psychological orientation.

In this paper I have analyzed the role of certain values in relation to the functioning of personality among the Ojibwa, both in the aboriginal culture and under the conditions created by contact with Western culture. If I have analyzed the data adequately it would appear that the role of values as a factor in an integrative level of adjustment has implications beyond this particular instance. Values have an important significance with reference to the whole problem of mental health and the conditions necessary for its fulfillment.

Notes

PART I. CULTURE, PERSONALITY, AND EXPERIENCE

Chapter 1

Personality Structure and the Evolution of Man

1 Leslie A. White drew attention to this problem a number of years ago in an article entitled "On the Use of Tools by Primates," *Journal of Comparative Psychology,* XXXIV (1942), 369-74. He wrote (p. 371), "Tool-using among men is a different kind of activity, fundamentally and qualitatively different in a psychological sense, from tool-using among apes. Among apes the use of tools is a sensory, neuro-muscular conceptual process. Among men it is a sensory neuro-muscular conceptual and symbolic process. It is the ability to use symbols which has transformed anthropoid tool behavior into human tool behavior."

2 St. George Mivart, *Man and Apes, An Exposition of Structural Resemblances and Differences bearing upon Questions of Affinity and Origin* (New York, 1874), p. 251. I am indebted to Dr. J. Gruber for calling my attention to this reference.

3 *Ibid.,* pp. 188-189; italics inserted. Mivart was a Roman Catholic and he and G. J. Romanes, a close follower of Darwin, locked horns in a famous controversy. See St. G. Mivart, *The Origin of Human Reason,* (London, 1889) and G. J. Romanes, *Mental Evolution in Man* (London, 1889).

4 More recently Leslie A. White discussed the mind-body question, from a behavioristic point of view, in a short article, "Mind is Minding," *Scientific Monthly,* XLVIII (1939), 169, and three phyletic levels of mental organization in "The Mentality of Primates," *Scientific Monthly,* XXXIV (1932), 69-72, in which he maintains that the difference between man and ape "is one of kind, not of degree." In 1935, John M. Cooper in "The Scientific Evidence Bearing upon Human Evolution," *Primitive Man,* VIII, 1-56, reviewed the problems of both organic and mental evolution. So far as the former is concerned, he says that the evidence is in favor of the theory, but he maintains paradoxically that evidence for the latter has weakened since the days of Darwin "with the progress of cultural and linguistic anthropology and seemingly with the progress of comparative psychology and of the experimental psychology of the higher human mental processes." So he concludes that "the chasm between the brute mind and the human mind is at present unspanned, and we can see no way in which it could have been spanned in the past" (p. 52). It should be noted that Cooper's *a priori* assumptions about the nature of the human mind are closely related to both his conceptualization of the problem and the conclusion to which he comes.

5 For a recent authoritative summation based on animal experimentation see T. C. Schneirla, "Levels in the Psychological Capacities of Animals," in R.

4—16

W. Sellars, V. J. McGill, M. Farber (eds.), *Philosophy for the Future* (New York, 1949).

6 See Wilton M. Krogman, "The Man Apes of South Africa," *Scientific American* (May, 1948), p. 18, quoting W. E. LeGros Clark.

7 K. S. Lashley, "Persistent Problems in the Evolution of Mind," *Quarterly Review of Biology*, XXIV (1949), 29-30.

8 Many years ago John Dewey emphasized this fundamental point ("The Need for a Social Psychology," *Psychological Review*, XXIV [1917]). Although it has become much more familiar since that time, his statement is worth repeating. He wrote that "What we call 'mind' means essentially the working of certain beliefs and desires, and that these in the concrete,—in the only sense in which mind may be said to *exist,*—are functions of associated behavior varying with the structure and operation of social groups." Thus instead of being viewed as "an antecedent and ready-made thing," mind "represents a reorganization of original activities through their operation in a given environment. It is a formation, not a datum, a product and a cause only after it has been produced. Now theoretically it is possible that the reorganization of native activities which constitute mind may occur through their exercise within a purely physical medium. Empirically, however, this is highly improbable. A consideration of the dependence in infancy of the organization of the native activities into intelligence upon the presence of others, upon sharing in joint activities and upon language, makes it obvious that the sort of mind capable of development through the operation of native endowment in a non-social environment is of the moron order, and is practically, if not theoretically, negligible." Cf. also George H. Mead, *Mind, Self and Society* (Chicago, 1934).

9 Quoted by Roger P. McCutcheon, *Eighteenth Century Literature* (New York, 1949), p. 34.

10 O. H. Mowrer and A. A. Ullman, "Time as a Determinant in Integrative Learning," *Psychological Review*, LII (1945), 79.

11 See, e.g., Susanne K. Langer, *Philosophy in a New Key* (Cambridge, 1942), Chaps. 2 and 3; Ernst Cassirer, *An Essay on Man* (New Haven, 1944), Chaps. 2 and 3.

12 Mowrer and Ullman, *op. cit.*, p. 78.

13 C. R. Carpenter, "Characteristics of Social Behavior in Non-Human Primates," *Transactions of the New York Academy of Sciences*, Series II, IV (No. 8, 1942) 256-57.

14 David Bidney ("Human Nature and the Cultural Process," *American Anthropologist*, XL [1947], p. 376) maintains that "all animals which are capable of learning and teaching one another are capable of acquiring culture. Hence *not culture in general but human culture,* as manifested in systems of artifacts, social institutions and symbolic forms of expression, *is peculiar to man.*" By conceptualizing culture from a broad "genetic and functional point of view," Bidney avoids drawing an absolute categorical distinction between the mode of adaptation in man and other animals. At the same time he stresses the distinctive character of "anthropoculture." In terms of Bidney's distinction I am concerned with the psychobiological structure that makes anthropoculture possible.

15 Sigmund Freud, *New Introductory Lectures on Psychoanalysis* (New York, 1933), p. 112.

16 O. H. Mowrer, "The Law of Effect and Ego Psychology," *Psychological Review*, LIII (1946), 321-22, is of the opinion that it is "desirable to speak

of ego processes rather than egos. By so doing one is in a much better position to set up operational criteria for determining the precise extent to which such processes may be said to be in operation in any given organism and at any given stage of development. My own understanding of what ego processes are suggests that they are gradually elaborated both as the human child develops and as one ascends the phylogenetic scale."

17 Sigmund Freud, *An Outline of Psychoanalysis* (New York, 1949), p. 16.

18 *Ibid.*, p. 17.

19 Cf. T. H. Huxley and Julian Huxley, *Touchstone for Ethics, 1893-1943* (London 1947). Julian Huxley maintains (p. 4), "that man is inevitably (and alone among all organisms) subject to mental conflict as a normal factor in his life, and that the existence of this conflict is the necessary basis or ground on which conscience, the moral sense, and our systems of ethics grow and develop."

20 Mowrer and Ullman, *op. cit.*, p. 81.

21 For explicit references, *see* Mowrer and Ullman, *op. cit.*

22 Quoted in George Devereux, "The Logical Foundations of Culture and Personality Studies," *Transactions of the New York Academy of Sciences*, Series II, VII (No. 5, 1945) p. 122.

CHAPTER 2
THE RECAPITULATION THEORY AND CULTURE

1 For a history of the recapitulation theory see A. W. Meyer, "Some Historical Aspects of the Recapitulation Idea," *Quarterly Review of Biology*, X (1935), 379-96; for an appraisal of it in biology today see G. R. de Beer, *Embryos and Ancestors* (Oxford, 1951).

2 For references see K. C. Pratt, "The Neonate," in C. Murchison (ed.), *Handbook of Child Psychology* (Worcester, 1931), pp. 197-98.

3 A. Hrdlicka, *Children Who Run on All Fours* (New York, 1931), p. 93. "It seems just to conclude that just as the human child before birth recapitulates, more or less, various phases of its physical ancestry, so the child after birth recapitulates and uses for a time various phases of its prehuman ancestral behavior."

4 See the *First* and *Second Year Books of the Herbart Society*, 1895, 1896, in particular C. C. Van Liew, "The Educational Theory of the Culture Epochs" (First Year Book, pp. 70-123), and John Dewey, "Interpretation of the Culture-Epoch Theory" (Second Year Book, pp. 89-95). See, also, Percy E. Davidson, *The Recapitulation Theory and Human Infancy* (Teachers College, Columbia University Contributions to Education, no. 65 [1914]).

5 See Thomas Hunt Morgan, *The Scientific Basis of Evolution* (1932), Chap. 9. Chap. 9.

6 G. Stanley Hall, *Adolescence* (New York, 1904), II, p. 61.

7 Cf. Cora Du Bois, "Some Anthropological Perspectives on Psychoanalysis," *The Psychoanalytic Review*, XXIV (1937), 246-73.

8 Jung has made less explicit and systematic use of the recapitulation idea than has Freud. But it is one of Jung's basic assumptions since it is invoked in support of the distinction he makes between *directed thinking* and *dream or fantasy thinking*. The latter is characteristic of primitive peoples, children, and, to some extent, modern civilized man. Jung says (*Psychology of the Unconscious* [New York, 1916], pp. 27-28): "All this experience suggests to us that we draw a parallel between the phantastical, mythological thinking of antiquity and the similar thinking of children, between the lower races and dreams. This train of thought is not a strange one for us, but quite familiar through our knowledge of comparative anatomy and the history of develop-

ment, which shows us how the structure and function of the human body are the results of a series of embryonic changes which correspond to similar changes in the history of the race. Therefore, the supposition is justified that ontogenesis corresponds in psychology to phylogenesis. Consequently, it would be true, as well, that the state of infantile thinking in the child's psychic life, as well as in dreams, is nothing but a re-echo of the pre-historic and the ancient." The inheritance of acquired characteristics is utilized by Jung in support of his theory of a "racial unconscious."

9 Hall, *op. cit.*, Preface, p. xiii.

10 Dorothy E. Bradbury, "The Contribution of the Child Study Movement to Child Psychology," *Psychological Bulletin,* XXXIV (1937), 27.

11 S. Freud, *Three Contributions to the Theory of Sex* (4th ed., New York, 1930), p. 96.

12 S. Freud, *A General Introduction to Psychoanalysis* (Trans. Joan Riviere, New York, 1938), p. 177.

13 S. Freud, *The Ego and the Id* (London, 1927), pp. 48ff.

14 In an article contributed to *Scientia* (XIV [1913], Part I, pp. 240-50; Part II, pp. 369-84) under the title, *Das Interesse an der Psychoanalyse,* Freud pointed out the significance of psychoanalysis for psychology, linguistics, philosophy, biology, evolution, culture history, etc. At the end of the section on "Das entwicklungs-geschichtliche Interesse" he writes (p. 378):

"In den allerletzten Jahren hat sich die psychoanalytische Arbeit darauf besonnen, dass der Satz: die Ontogenie sei eine Wiederholung der Phylogenie, auch auf das Seelenleben anwendbar sein müsse [note to Abraham, Spielrein, Jung], und daraus ist eine neue Erweiterung des psychoanalytischen Interesses hervorgegangen." And he continues in the next section ("Das kulturhistorische Interesse"), "Die Vergleichung der Kindheit des einzelnen Menschen mit der Frühgeschichte der Völker hat sich bereits nach mehreren Richtungen als fruchtbar erwiesen, trotzdem diese Arbeit kaum mehr als begonnen werden konnte. Die psychoanalytische Denkweise benimmt sich dabei wie ein neues Instrument der Forschung. Die Anwendung ihrer Voraussetzungen auf die Völkerpsychologie gestattet ebenso neue Probleme aufzuwerfen wie die bereits bearbeiteten in neuem Lichte zu sehen und zu deren Lösung beizutragen."

It is likewise interesting to note that J. S. Van Teslaar in an essay on "The Significance of Psychoanalysis in the History of Science," originally published in the *International Journal of Psychoanalysis* and later reprinted as the final chapter in *The Outline of Psychoanalysis,* edited by him for *The Modern Library* (New York, 1925), hails the recapitulation theory, as applied to the development of the human mind, as one of the outstanding scientific contributions of psychoanalysis. "For the first time since Darwin announced his discoveries, an important corollary of the theory of evolution— recapitulation—is thus proven to hold good of the psyche. . . . The recapitulation theory, so interesting in other fields of biology, becomes here of the utmost *practical* significance. It will be understood, of course, that the idea of recapitulation had been conceived as a principle of mental development and somewhat exploited long before Freud. Various attempts, some of them more ingenious than convincing, had been made to trace correspondents between the behavior of children and the life of primitive people on the supposition that children and so-called savages stand psychically close to each other. We have long been familiar with such expressions as 'the childhood of the human race' and by many comparisons we have been led to infer what is implied. The propensity of children for climbing, for instance, has been described as a vestigial tendency harking back, as it were, to the arboreal habits of man's ancestors. Children's games, peculiar choices, curious likes and dislikes, and many of their imageries have been similarly related. But all such observations were conjectural. *Proof was lacking. Freud has stumbled upon the proof* [italics ours]; and what is more, he has had the sagacity to recognize the importance of his discovery for science. He has disclosed the role of ontogenetic recapitulation in the growth and interplay of our psychic forces. *For the first time in the history of psychology we now have the key to the understanding of human behavior in the light of its biological history"* [italics ours].

15 *Beyond The Pleasure Principle* (London, 1920), pp. 44-45.

16 Cf. Karen Horney, *New Ways in Psychoanalysis* (New York, 1939), pp. 44-45, and her discussion of repetition-compulsion, p. 133 et seq.

17 P. 52. Cf. p. 46, "We see, then, that the differentiation of the super-ego from the ego is no matter of chance; it stands as the representative of the most important events in the development both of the individual and of the race; indeed, by giving permanent expression to the influence of the parents it perpetuates the existence of the factors to which it owes its origin."

18 *Three Contributions to the Theory of Sex*, p. 25, note.

19 *Ibid.*, p. 39.

20 S. Freud, *Moses and Monotheism* (New York, 1939), p. 157. The thesis of this book depends, of course, upon the inheritance of acquired experiences. Freud explicitly recognizes this and consequently devotes considerable space to an exposition of the archaic heritage. He writes (p. 154), "A new complication arises, however, when we become aware that there probably exists in the mental life of the individual not only what he has experienced himself, but also what he brought with him at birth, fragments of phylogenetic origin, an archaic heritage. Then the question arises, in what does this inheritance consist, what does it contain, and what evidence of it is there?"

21 *Civilization and Its Discontents* (New York, 1930), p. 64.

22 *The Ego and the Id,* p. 46. The latency period "which seems to be peculiar to man, is a heritage of the cultural development necessitated by the glacial epoch." S. Ferenczi in his "Stages in the Development of the Sense of Reality," *Contributions to Psychoanalysis* (Boston, 1916), made the original suggestion in connection with his discussion of the *phylogenesis* of the reality-sense. "According to a remark of Professor Freud's, racial character is the precipitate of racial history. Having ventured so far beyond the knowable, we have no reason to shrink before the last analogy and from bringing the great step in individual repression, the latency period, into connection with the last and greatest catastrophe that smote our primitive ancestors (at a time when there were certainly human beings on the earth), i.e., with the misery of the glacial period, which we still faithfully recapitulate in our individual life." Not all psychoanalysts have accepted this derivation. Cf. G. Roheim, *The Riddle of the Sphinx* (London, 1934), pp. 166-68. "But since the ice ages arrived by imperceptible degrees, it is difficult to imagine that they can have had any effect upon the lives of individuals. Moreover, these cold periods were interspaced by warm ones, so that their effects cannot be summated. . . . We must therefore question the social influence of measurable geological changes that have no influence upon the individual."

23 *Three Contributions to the Theory of Sex,* p. 90.

24 The theoretical structure which the analysts have used to support the Oedipus Complex must, of course, be separated from the *clinical facts* observed. But Horney, *op. cit.,* has not only challenged the biological determination of the Oedipus Complex; she denies that it is an inevitable stage of "normal" de-

velopment and hence universal. The whole problem is a matter of some moment since Ernest Jones says, "All other conclusions of psychoanalytical theory are grouped around this complex, and by the truth of this finding psychoanalysis stands or falls." *Psychoanalysis* (London, 1928), p. 36.

25 S. Ferenczi, *Further Contributions to Psychoanalysis* (London, 1926), p. 386. Cf. Freud, *Moses and Monotheism* (1939), p. 133 ". . . analytic study of the mental life of the child has yielded an unexpectedly rich return by filling up gaps in our knowledge of primeval times."

26 *Group Psychology and the Analysis of the Ego* (London, 1922), p. 90. Freud remained unshaken in his convictions on this point to the end of his life. In fact, the validity of his major thesis in *Moses and Monotheism* hinges on the assumption that experiences of the race in primeval times were repressed and millennia afterwards "reawakened" (p. 209).

27 Ferenczi, *Further Contributions to Psychoanalysis* (1926), p. 374. "In accordance with the fundamental law of biogenesis the racial history of the evolution of the mind is thus repeated in the psychical development of the individual; for the serial sequence here described is the same as that by which we must imagine the progressive evolution of psychical systems in organisms." (Cf. "Stages in the Development of the Sense of Reality.") "It is to be assumed that we shall some day succeed in bringing the individual stages in the development of the ego, and the neurotic regression-types of these, into a parallel with the stages in the racial history of mankind, just as, for instance, Freud found again in the mental life of the savage the character of the obsessional neurosis."

28 P. 64.

29 Marie Bonaparte, "Psychanalyse et Ethnographie," in *Essays Presented to C. G. Seligman* (London 1934), p. 24. This author explicitly affirms the "biogenetic law." She writes (p. 22): "L'enfant reproduit d'ailleurs en général, au cours de son évolution, les attitudes du primitif. La loi biogénétique se vérifie au psychique comme au physique; l'ontogénie y reproduit la phylogénie. L'importance de ce phénomène est très grande, car rien ne s'effaçant de l'enconscient au cours de la vie, chacun de nous est comparable à un document où se serait inscrite, certes en abrégé, toute l'histoire et la préhistoire de l'humanité. C'est ce qui permet au psychanalyste, au cours de son long, minutieux et difficile travail, de retrouver, au fond de l'inconscient du plus civilisé des hommes, ces vestiges des temps disparus, les modes de réaction archaïques de ses ancêtres primitifs. Ces vestiges, une fois mis au jour, rien n'est plus instructif que de les comparer à ce que nous pouvons observer des primitifs réels peuplant encore la terre, et c'est ici que l'ethnographie et la psychanalyse, comme nous l'avons déjà indiqué, peuvent réciproquement s'éclairer."

30 Cf. A. L. Kroeber, "Totem and Taboo: An Ethnographic Psychoanalysis," *American Anthropologist,* XXII (1920), 48-55; and "Totem and Taboo in Retrospect," *American Journal of Sociology,* XLV (1939), 446-51.

31 Cf. K. Horney's critique of the libido theory and note Freud's expressed anticipation that, "all our provisional ideas in psychology will some day be based on an organic substructure. This makes it probable that special substances and special chemical processes control the operation of sexuality and provide for the continuation of the individual life in that of the species. We take this probability into account when we substitute special forces in the mind for special chemical substances." ("On Narcissism: An Introduction," *Collected Papers IV.*)

32 Hence the charge of Francis H. Bartlett that despite Freud's emphasis upon

the relations of the child to its parents, in effect, psychoanalytic theory deals with the human individual *as if* he were socially isolated. "The Limitations of Freud," *Science and Society*, (1939).

Cf. J. F. Brown's discussion of psychoanalysis as "class theory" in contrast with "field theory." "Freud and the Scientific Method," *Philosophy of Science*, I(1934), 323-37.

33 The reasons for this rejection have been frequently discussed. See, e.g., C. Du Bois, *op. cit.*

34 See Anne Anastasi and John P. Foley, Jr., "An Analysis of Spontaneous Drawings by Children in Different Cultures," *Journal of Applied Psychology*, XX (1936), 690. The relevant literature concerning genetic stages in drawing is summarized by these authors. For the most detailed survey extant of the literature of children's drawings see H. Graewe, "Geschichtlicher Überlick über die Psychologie des kindlichen Zeichnens," *Arch. d. ges. Psychol.*, XCVI (1936).

35 Cf. Anastasi and Foley, *op. cit.*, p. 690.

36 Anne Anastasi, *Differential Psychology* (New York, 1947), p. 592.

37 Anne Anastasi and John P. Foley, Jr., "A Study of Animal Drawings by Indian Children of the North Pacific Coast," *Journal of Social Psychology*, IX (1938), 363-74.

38 Cf. H. Eng., *Psychology of Children's Drawings* (New York, 1931), p. 152, who points out this negative similarity and discusses perspective in children's drawings.

39 Ernst Grosse, *The Beginnings of Art* (New York, 1898), p. 194.

40 Cf. G. Rouma, *Le Langage Graphique de l'enfant* (Paris, 1913), who believes the best Paleolithic drawings to have been produced by individuals of special talents. In addition they attained this level because of practice and participation in a genuine art tradition. He also points out that the drawings that have been collecced by explorers like Koch-Grunberg from average persons in primitive communities are crude and formal, in short, comparable to those of children in Western society. Recently Norman Cameron attempted to answer the question, "Does normal adult thinking, uncomplicated by emotional distortion, exhibit features generally described as characteristically childish?" by inducing a group of adults (physicians on the staff of Johns Hopkins Hospital) scientifically trained but untrained in drawing, to execute a series of sketches (e.g., a "girl pushing a baby-carriage"). The results were amazing. They "show unmistakably most of the principal characteristics of functional immaturity, e.g., inadequate fusion, incongruities, arbitrary representations of functional relations such as are typical of children, grossly inadequate grasp of the needs of others for explicit links in functional units (asyndesis), and an uncritical attitude of self-satisfaction with the results." Objectively, the drawings obtained from these physicians are indistinguishable from those of children. The author comments that in Rouma's classification "they would be assigned, on the basis of the same characteristics we have stressed in the analysis, to the very immature groups." They have nothing to do with intelligence or maturity but represent "a functionally immature form of symbolization coexisting at least potentially with the socially mature forms." See "Functional Immaturity in the Symbolization of Scientifically Trained Adults," *Journal of Psychology*, VI (1938), 161-75.

41 Karl Bühler, *The Mental Development of the Child* (New York, 1930), p. 1. The English edition followed five German editions.

42 Heilbronner, "Some Remarks on the Treatment of the Sexes in Paleolithic

Art," and Ernest Jones, "A Psychoanalytical Note on Paleolithic Art," *International Journal of Psychoanalysis*, XIX (1938).

43. Cf. Norman Cameron, "Individual and Social Factors in the Development of Graphic Symbolization," *Journal of Psychology*, V (1938), 165-84. "We must diverge from Eng's view that in the child's drawing we are witnessing a natural process that is learned alone. Instead we see it as the outcome of a complex relationship in which the natural organismic activity develops within the social process in terms of social factors, and includes and embodies these as critique" (p. 171). In this author's view, "If children's graphic productions are looked upon only as the acquisition of another skill, or as indicators of intelligence levels, or even as simply the expression of antecedent mental pictures, something very fundamental to the growth of their peculiar characteristics will be missed. The early drawings of children, like their speech, are *patterns of action* in which eventually form emerges and becomes fixed through the same factors of social impact and self-stimulation that help in speech to build the early word-sentence out of babble. Drawing is always primarily organismic activity, a sort of graphic gesture. Its development in children takes the direction it does because of the social participation of others, which modifies and directs the operation of basic organismic tendencies" (pp. 165-66).

44 See, e.g., the following: T. H. Morgan, *op. cit.*, Chap. 8, and articles in *Biologia Generalis*, XIII (1937); J. J. Jezhikov, "Zur Rekapitulationslehre," pp. 67-100; S. Lebedkin, "The Recapitulation Problems," pp. 391-417, 561-94.

45 A. H. Schultz, "Fetal Growth of Man and Other Primates," *Quarterly Review of Biology*, I (1926).

46 Cf. the comments of W. D. Wallis, "Human Recapitulation," *Scientific Monthly*, XXXIX (1934), 443-48. Among other things, Wallis points out that "much of the resemblance between prenatal development in different genera is a sheer result of the laws of growth. Many of the 'facts' of recapitulation, then, resolve into analogy and homology rather than into genetic relationship." W. K. Gregory is quoted by Wallis to the effect that "the universality of the biogenetic law may not be taken for granted" and that to prove that a particular ontogenetic character is primitive "requires independent evidence." "If," says Gregory, "the biogenetic law were without exceptions, the marvelous processes of ontogenetic development would have only a historical or reminiscent aspect and not an anticipatory or adaptive one, since they would all be directed solely toward preserving a clear record of earlier adult states rather than toward the production of viable animals." Hrdlicka's recapitulatory explanation of running on all fours (*op. cit.*) is a case in point. N. L. Munn (*Psychological Development* [1938], p. 319) points out that it "could easily develop as a result of chance variation in creeping. Moreover, infants conceivably could copy it from the patterns set for them by adults (in play) or by animals."

47 H. Werner, *Comparative Psychology of Mental Development* (New York, 1940). Cf. J. F. Brown, *Psychology and the Social Order* (New York, 1936), pp. 301-2.

48 See S. Blachowski, "Magical Behavior of Children," *American Journal of Psychology* (Jubilee Number), I (1937), and the literature there cited.

49 J. Piaget, *The Child's Conception of Physical Causality* (New York, 1930). On the other hand, Piaget has pointed out ("Children's Philosophies," in *A Handbook of Child Psychology* [2nd ed. rev. 1933, C. Murchison, ed.], p. 538), that child animism must not be confused with animism in the Tylorian sense. Child animism simply involves a general anthropomorphic

tendency, "the attribution of life to objects which educated adults classify as inanimate." (Wayne Dennis, "Historical Notes on Child Animism," *Psychological Review*, XLV [1938], 257.) It has nothing to do with soul-concepts and, as Dennis says, it is somewhat unfortunate that Piaget selected a term made so familiar by Tylor in a different usage. R. R. Marrett (*The Threshold of Religion* [3rd ed., London, 1914], Preface, p. x) expresses this difference when he writes that children are "animatists without being at the same time animists."

50 J. Piaget, *The Language and Thought of the Child* (New York, 1926), p. 212. " . . . whatever may happen, it can always be accounted for, for behind the most fantastic events which he believes in, the child will always discover motives which are sufficient to justify them; just as the world of the primitive races is peopled with a wealth of arbitrary intentions, but is devoid of chance." Cf. Lucien Lévy-Brühl, *How Natives Think* (London, 1926), p. 23. K. Koffka, *The Growth of the Mind* (2nd ed. rev., New York, 1931), p. 361, says: "According to both Lévy-Brühl and Piaget, primitive mentality knows nothing of chance, a conclusion which is in perfect harmony with our own view of mental development." F. Lorimer points out, however, that the "child lacks a sense of chance because he lacks the sense of the expected against which 'chance' is recognized as such." (*The Growth of Reason* [New York, 1929], p. 188n.) The same explanation may be advanced in the case of savages, although Lévy-Brühl's generalization cannot be accepted without further inquiry.

51 L. Lévy-Brühl, *How Natives Think; Primitive Mentality* (New York, 1923).

52 H. Wallon, 'La Mentalité primitive et celle de l'enfant," *Revue Philosophique* (1928).

53 E. Jones, *Psychoanalysis* (3rd ed., New York, 1923), pp. 58-59.

54 J. Piaget, *Judgment and Reasoning in the Child* (New York, 1928) p. 256. "It is therefore our belief that the day will come when child thought will be placed on the same level in relation to adult, normal, and civilized thought, as 'primitive mentality' as defined by Lévy-Brühl, as autistic and symbolical thought as described by Freud and his disciples, and as 'morbid consciousness,' in the event of this last concept, which we owe to M. Ch. Blondel, being eventually identified with the former." In fairness to Piaget it must be added that he advises caution in proceeding to such an equation.

55 See *La Mentalité Primitive* (Herbert Spencer Lecture, Oxford, 1931), p. 26.

56 I.e., "Mystical thought is a function of particular situations." Lévy-Brühl failed to see this point as E. E. Evans-Prichard has pointed out in an admirable exposition and critique of his work. See "Lévy-Brühl's Theory of Primitive Mentality," *Bull. of the Faculty of Arts* (Univ. of Egypt, Cairo), II (May, 1934), 28.

57 E.g., V. Hazlitt, "Children's Thinking," *British Journal of Psychology*, XX (1930), 361. "Piaget's picture of a striking difference between adult and childish thinking, is, I believe, due to an overevaluation of verbal expression as a measure of thinking, and an exaggerated view of the logicality of adult thought." This latter charge may, in fact, be levelled against Lévy-Brühl who overevaluates "rational" civilized thinking, and, on the other hand, makes the thinking of the savage appear more "mystical" than it really is. See also Susan Isaacs, *Intellectual Growth in Young Children* (London, 1930), p. 57. "Taking these records as a whole, then, the first impression which the unsophisticated reader receives is that the cognitive behavior of little children, even in these early years, is often all very much like our own in general outline of movement. Allowing for the immense difference in knowledge and experi-

ence, they go about their business of understanding the world and what happens to them in it, very much as we do ourselves. And, contrary to some current opinions about them, they do show a lively and sustained interest in real physical events. . . ."

58 Issacs, *op. cit.*, pp. 106-7.
59 *Ibid.*, pp. 107-8.
60 *Ibid.*, pp. 108-9.
61 Karl Zeininger, "Magische Gesiteshaltung in Kinderalter und ihre Bedeutung für de religiose Entwicklung," *Zeit. Angew. Psychol. Berh.*, XLVII (1929), 70 et seq. Cf. I. Huang, *Children's Explanations of Strange Phenomena* (Smith College Studies in Psychology, I [1930]) and Jean M. Deutsche, *The Development of Children's Concepts of Causal Relations* (Univ. of Minnesota, The Institute of Child Welfare, Monograph Series XIII, 1937). A review of the relevant literature on children's thinking is to be found in the Introduction. Summarizing, the author writes (p. 13), "We find investigations supporting Piaget's stages of development—in which types of answers are found at rather specific ages. But the preponderance of the studies report great overlapping between age groups, and a scatter of different kinds of answers throughout this age range. Some investigators agree with Piaget in his classification of types of casual thinking and substantiate his findings, whereas others discover little evidence to support his age relationships and his claim as to the prevalence of precausal thinking in younger children. There is conflicting evidence as to the relative rôles of innate factors and experiential factors or direct training. We have evidence for and against (mainly against) real differences between the thinking of children and adults." This author's own investigations do not support Piaget. Among other things, Mrs. Deutsche not only found experience in general to be important but she was able, by quantified methods, to show a higher correlation between the answers given and school training than with intelligence or socio-economic status.
62 *Op. cit.*, p. 57.
63 Cf. Anne Anastasi, 1937 *op. cit.*, p. 588 et seq. "Theories of developmental *stages* furnish a good illustration of the tendency to overgeneralize from observations within a single (cultural) group. Child psychology is replete with such theories."
64 Margaret Mead, *Coming of Age in Samoa* (New York, 1928).
65 Margaret Mead, "An Investigation of the Thought of Primitive Children, with Special Reference to Animism," *Journal of the Royal Anthropological Institute,* LXII (1932), 173-90. For a summary statement of her conclusions see her "The Primitive Child," in *A Handbook of Child Psychology* (1931), p. 675. Cf. R. W. Russell and Wayne Dennis, "Studies in Animism: I. A Standardized Procedure for the Investigation of Animism," *Journ. of Genetic Psych.,* LV (1939), 389-400. According to the authors, this method makes "it possible to classify children into the four stages of animism which are outlined by Piaget and, by so doing, permits an objective study of factors associated with the development of animism."
66 G. Roheim, "Psychoanalysis and Anthropology," in *Psychoanalysis Today* (New York, 1933), S. Lorand (ed.), p. 309, "My field work in Central Australia led me to the conclusion that repression among the really primitive races of mankind has neither the depth nor the intensity of repression as we find it in Europe, a fact that is strikingly demonstrated by the absence of a latency period in Central Australia."
67 See Ruth Benedict, "Continuities and Discontinuities in Cultural Conditioning," *Psychiatry,* I (1938), 161-67. "From a comparative point of view our

culture goes to great extremes in emphasizing contrasts between the child and the adult. The child is sexless, the adult estimates his virility by his sexual activities; the child must be protected from the ugly facts of life, the adult must meet them without psychic catastrophe; the child must obey, the adult must command this obedience. These are all dogmas of our culture, dogmas which, in spite of the facts of nature, other cultures commonly do not share. In spite of the physiological contacts between child and adult these are cultural accretions." (p. 161)

68 Mead, *op. cit.*, p. 188.
69 G. Roheim, "Racial Differences in the Neuroses and Psychoses," *Psychiatry*, II (1939), 386.

Chapter 3

The Rorschach Test in Personality and Culture Studies

1 See R. Linton, in *Culture and Personality*, Sargent and Smith (eds.), (New York, 1949), on "status personality."

2 Kluckhohn and Murray, e.g., characterize "the bipolarity between 'personality and culture' as false or at least misleading in some important sense" (*Personality in Nature, Society and Culture* [New York, 1948], Chap. 9); G. Murphy inclines towards a "double aspect" theory, culture and personality are two aspects of one phenomena ("The Relationships of Culture and Personality," in S. Sargent and M. Smith, eds., *Culture and Personality* [New York, 1949]); M. Spiro considers "personality and culture" as a false dichotomy ("Culture and Personality, The Natural History of a False Dichotomy," *Psychiatry*, XIV [1951]). Nadel gives explicit references to the conceptual differences between "society" and "culture" that have been stressed by various anthropologists. "In recent anthropological literature," he observes, "the terms 'society' and 'culture' are accepted as referring to somewhat different things or, more precisely, to different ways of looking at the same thing." (*The Foundations of Social Anthropology* [Glencoe, Ill., 1951], pp. 79ff.) T. Parsons and E. A. Shils write: "Culture patterns when internalized become constitutive elements of personalities and of social systems. *All concrete systems of action, at the same time, have a system of culture and are a set of personalities* (or sectors of them) and a social system or sub-system. Yet all three are conceptually independent organizations of the elements of action." (*Toward a General Theory of Action* [Cambridge, 1951], p. 22.)

3 Leslie A. White is the most explicit exponent of this conception of culture. (See Chap. 4, Note 38.)

4 These divergent concepts of culture not only represent a contemporary dichotomy; they have historical roots. David Bidney, "The Concept of Meta-anthropology and Its Significance for Contemporary Anthropological Science," in F. S. C. Northrup (ed.), *Ideological Differences and World Order* (New Haven, 1949), p. 347, points out that: "In the development of modern cultural anthropology one may discern two major 'themes.' On the one hand, there is the theme derived from the naturalistic, positivistic, evolutionary tradition of the nineteenth century that cultural reality represents an autonomous, superorganic, superpsychic level of reality subject to its own laws and stages of development or evolution. On the other hand, there is the recurring theme, which dates back to the humanistic tradition of the Renaissance and the rationalism of the eighteenth century philosophers of the Enlightenment, that human culture is the product of human discovery and cre-

ativity and is subject to human regulation." Cf. Bidney, "Human Nature and the Cultural Process," *American Anthropologist,* XLIX (1947), 375-99.

5 See Chapter 4, Note 38. Spiro brings the whole problem to a focus in his 1951 (*op. cit.*) article. "What cultural realists have failed to realize," he says, "is that once something is learned it is no longer external to the organism, but is 'inside' the organism, and once it is 'inside' the organism becomes a bio-social organism determining its own behavior as a consequence of the modifications it has undergone in the process of learning. But the individual-culture dichotomy accepted by the realists prevents them from acknowledging this most elementary point and, as a consequence, they think in terms of a superorganic culture determining the behavior of an organic adult."

6 H. Rorschach, *Psychodiagnostics* (English translation by Lemkau and Kronenbury, New York, 1942), pp. 96-97; p. 92 in the 4th German edition (Bern, 1941).

7 M. Bleuler and R. Blueler, "Rorschach's Ink-Blot Test and Racial Psychology," *Character and Personality,* IV (1935), 97-114. In the first place, the Bleulers cannot avoid the conclusion that there is some correspondence between the Rorschach results and the national culture of the people. This is epitomized in the statement that "we are of the opinion that the Moroccans' responses in the Rorschach test show the essential characteristics of their national life, their literature, their art, and their science." If taken out of context, this statement might seem to indicate that the Bleulers had adopted the same point of view as that found in American personality and culture studies. However, they go on to say that ". . . it seems probable that both the inexperience in the interpretation of pictures and *some deep-seated racial characteristic* explain the responses in the Rorschach test, because this inexperience is due to some peculiarity of the *racial character.*" (Italics ours.) The emphasis of the authors on a racial factor becomes even more apparent when they express the opinion that the origin and perpetuation of the well-known Muslim taboo on the artistic representation of human beings can scarcely be due to anything less than a national character and culture that is "racially" determined. This interpretation, if generalized, amounts to no less than a "racial" theory of human culture. Nothing could be more antithetical to the findings of cultural anthropology. Yet Hertz ("The Normal Details in the Rorschach Ink-Blot Test," *Rorschach Research Exchange,* I [1937], 104-19) accepts this interpretation since she writes (p. 115): ". . . Bleuler *has demonstrated* that Moroccans do not react to the ink-blots as Europeans in every respect . . . and that these differences cannot be considered as indicative of mental inferiority *but due to peculiarities of their racial* history." (Italics ours.)

8 As, e.g., in the comparison of white and Negro subjects by M. Hunter (Sicha), (*A Study of the Rorschach "Erlebnistypus" of Comparable White and Negro Subjects* [privately published Ph.D. thesis, Columbia University, New York, n.d.]) and by E. J. Stainbrook and P. S. Siegel ("A Comparative Rorschach Study of Southern Negro and White High School and College Students," *Journal of Psychology,* XVII [1944], 107-16) to single out only two carefully conceived studies. I have not seen the development and comparative investigation of Negro and white school children made by Nel in South Africa and referred to by Theodora Abel ("The Rorschach Test in the Study of Culture," *Journal of Projective Techniques,* XII [1948], 1-15). But with respect to any inference from group differences to "racial" determination of such differences, it is extremely interesting that Abel in a footnote points out that: "The Negro children in the study of Nel were living in their native

villages." Under this circumstance it is quite obvious that cultural determinants, mediated by child training, cannot be left out of consideration.

9 F. L. Wells, "Rorschach and the Free Association Test," *Journal of General Psychology*, XIII (1935), 413-32.

10 See William C. Boyd, *Genetics and the Races of Man* (Boston, 1950), particularly Chap. 9. The American Indians as a group are characterized (p. 268) as "possessing varying (sometimes high, sometimes zero) incidence of gene A_1, no A_2, and probably no B or rh. Low incidence of gene N. Possessing Rh^z."

11 Parallel results may be forthcoming in the case of the African Negroes since, genotypically defined, they constitute a race. Personally, I should not expect Rorschach data from different African groups to show equivalent psychological pictures. And it may be that when we have such information for comparison, the *reputed* psychological characteristics attributed to the *American* Negro (a racially mixed group from any point of view) will fall to the ground of their own weight. There is an additional point of interest. There are Oceanic, as well as African and American, Negroes. The Alorese belong to this branch. If "racial psychology" is considered to be the fundamental question, then the Alorese Rorschach data should be examined primarily with reference to their "racial" status rather than to their culture. Oberholzer makes no reference to "race" in his analysis of the protocols and DuBois, of course, was interested in investigating culture and personality relations. (Cora DuBois, *The People of Alor* [Minneapolis, 1947])

12 Despite the fact that the terminology employed has varied, both in semantic content as well as linguistic expression, psychological phenomena of the same category have been brought to an explicit focus in what has been characterized, e.g., as "basic personality structure" by Abram Kardiner, *The Individual and His Society* (New York, 1939); "The Concept of Basic Personality Structure as an Operational Tool in the Social Sciences," in Ralph Linton (ed.), *The Science of Man in the World Crisis* (New York, 1945); "modal personality structure" (DuBois, *op. cit.*); the "communal aspects of personality" by Clyde Kluckhohn and O. H. Mowrer, "Culture and Personality: A Conceptual Scheme," *American Anthropologist*, XLV (1944), 1-29. Kluckhohn says in the Introduction to *Personality in Nature, Culture and Society* (p. 39), "The members of any organized enduring group tend to manifest certain personality traits more frequently than do members of other groups. How large or how small are the groupings one compares depends on the problem at hand. By and large, the motivational structures and action patterns of western Europeans seem similar when contrasted to those of the Near East or to eastern Asiatics. Most white citizens of the United States, in spite of regional, ethnic, and class differences, have features of personality which distinguish them from Englishmen, Australians, or New Zealanders. In distinguishing group-membership determinants, one must usually take account of a concentric order of social groups to which the individual belongs, ranging from large national or international groups down to small local units. One must also know the hierarchical class, political or social, to which he belongs within each of those groups. How inclusive a unit one considers in speaking of group-membership determinants is purely a function of the level of abstraction at which one is operating at a given time." E. Fromm uses the term "social character," and the concept of "national character" likewise belongs in this category. For a survey of the literature on "national character" see Otto Klineberg, *Tensions Affecting International Understanding, A Survey of Research* (Bulletin 62, Social Science Research Council

[New York, 1950]); and Margaret Mead, "National Character" in A. L. Kroeber (ed.), *Anthropology Today* (Chicago, 1953).

13 Fromm has pointed out ("Psychoanalytic Characterology and Its Application to the Understanding of Culture," in Sargent and Smith, *op. cit.*, pp. 4-6, 10) that "Modern industrial society, for instance, could not have attained its ends had it not harnessed the energy of free men for work in an unprecedented degree. He had to be molded into a person who was eager to spend most of his energy for the purpose of work, who acquired discipline, particularly orderliness and punctuality, to a degree unknown in most other cultures. It would not have sufficed if each individual had to make up his mind consciously every day that he wanted to work, to be on time, etc., since any such conscious deliberation would have led to many more exceptions than the smooth functioning of society can afford. Threat and force would not have sufficed either as motive for work since the highly differentiated work in modern industrial society can only be the work of free men and not of forced labor. The *necessity* for work, for punctuality and orderliness had to be transformed into a *drive* for these qualities. This means that society had to produce such a social character in which these strivings were inherent." Human beings, in other words, have to become psychologically structured in such a way that they *"want to act as they have to act* and at the same time find gratification in acting according to the requirements of the culture." According to Fromm there must be some nuclear character structure "shared by most members of the same culture," the functioning of which is essential to the culture as an on-going concern.

14 What follows is a restatement, with a slightly different emphasis, of the main points to be found in Hallowell, 1945b. This article was also a discussion of the use of the Rorschach technique in culture and personality studies up until that time. Another review and general discussion was published by Abel in 1948 (*op. cit.*); cf. Lantz, "Rorschach Testing in Preliterate Cultures," *American Journal of Orthopsychiatry*, XVIII (1948), 287-91. In 1952 Henry and Spiro prepared an inventory paper on psychological techniques in anthropological field work for the International Symposium on Anthropology. (See *Anthropology Today*.) They tabulated all the published Rorschach material under the categories of the purpose of the investigation, the size of sample, results claimed, etc. Besides the Rorschach, they list the following projective techniques as having been used among nonliterate peoples: TAT, Free Drawings, Doll Play, Bender Gestalt.

15 Jean W. MacFarlane and R. D. Tuddenham, "Problems in the Validation of Projective Techniques," in H. A. Anderson and G. L. Anderson (eds.), *An Introduction to Projective Techniques and Other Devices for Understanding the Dynamics of Human Behavior* (New York, 1951), p. 33.

16 The same potentiality of the test has been exploited simultaneously for studying various groups of subjects in our culture. In 1945, Ruth Munroe stressed the fact that this was a somewhat novel development, in "Considerations on the Place of the Rorschach in the Field of General Psychology," *Rorschach Research Exchange*, IX (1945), 30-40. She wrote (p. 31): "Until recently Rorschach examiners themselves have concentrated almost exclusively on individual clinical diagnoses. The rapidly increasing number of studies using the test as an instrument for the investigation of more general problems should soon awaken more interest in its potential resources for such purposes. Methodologies for group comparisons are still in a formative stage, but promising results have been obtained." It is significant that in citing, by way of illustration, Hertz's studies of personality development in adolescence, Ross's analysis of "the psychological components in migrane and neuro-circulatory asthenia,"

reference is made to Oberholzer's analysis of the psychological characteristics of the *People of Alor* (DuBois), and that Munroe likewise observes that "It is precisely in these wider applications that the Rorschach can *eventually* prove most useful to general psychology."

17 S. R. Tulchin and D. M. Levy, "Rorschach Test Differences in a Group of Spanish and English Refugee Children," *American Journal of Orthopsychiatry,* XV (1945), 361-68; p. 368.

18 I have in mind here the critical discussion of the three corollaries which MacFarlane and Tuddenham, *op. cit.,* maintain are implicit in the general assumption involved in the use of all projective techniques.

19 Bruner and Postman, e.g., contrast an older view in which a stimulus object was "merely something to be seen, heard, touched, smelled or sensed" with one that treats perception ". . . in a broader behavioral context. For its primary concern is with the manner in which perceptual functioning is imbedded in and interacts with other psychological functioning. Perception is viewed as an instrumental activity." ("Perceptions, Cognition and Behavior," *Journal of Personality,* XVIII [1949], 14-31.)

20 Bruner, "Perceptual Theory and the Rorschach Test," *Journal of Personality,* XVII (1948), 157-58. (The quotation in this passage is from Robert W. White, "Interpretation of Imaginative Productions," in J. McV. Hunt (ed.), *Personality and the Behavior Disorders* [New York, 1944], I, 228.) In concluding his article Bruner remarks (p. 167) that "It seems apparent that Rorschach methodology and the interpretation of Rorschach responses are closely linked to the development of perceptual theory. Perceptual theory, in the past so neglectful of personality dynamics, has on its part the task of contributing a fuller understanding of why such techniques as the Rorschach have been so successful. The future will perforce witness the coalescence of research on perception and research in diagnostics. The two belong together."

21 D. Krech and R. S. Crutchfield, *Theory and Problems of Social Psychology* (New York, 1948), pp. 81-82. See likewise the *Symposium* in the *Journal of Personality,* XVIII (1949), and R. R. Blake and Glenn Ramsey, *Perception, An Approach to Personality* (New York, 1951). The latter phrase the matter as follows: (p. 5n) ". . . perception refers to those interactions between an organism and its (necessary) environment in which the form of response is governed by the *signal* or *sign* significance as contrasted with the *energy strength* or *quality* or *pattern* of the stimulus configuration itself. In these cases the signal or sign significance of the stimulus comes to exist (either spontaneously or effortfully) as an emergent from certain specific previous organism-environment interactions of the individual. Responses in this restricted aspect of the total gamut of interactions, then, are always *indirect;* the reaction is not governed solely by the energy characteristics or pre-formed pattern of stimulus–neural configurations; it is determined by the meanings the individual's prior experience has 'given' to the stimulus configuration (i.e., the conceptual set, or assumption, or personality configuration, or schema defined as an emergent from prior perception). With explicit reference to projective tests see L. E. Abt, "A Theory of Projective Psychology," in L. E. Abt and L. Bellak, *Projective Psychology* (New York, 1950).

22 Postman and Bruner, *op. cit.*

23 Cf. the remarks of Else Frenkel-Brunswik (in Blake and Ramsey, *op. cit.*), pp. 373-75.

24 Bruner (Blake and Ramsey, *op. cit.,* p. 121) argues that "a theory of personality . . . cannot be complete without a complementary theory of perception, and, by the same logic, one cannot account for the full range of perceptual

theory to a point where it contains personality variables."

25 F. C. Bartlett, *Remembering* (Cambridge, England, 1932).

26 Cf. Hilgard (Blake and Ramsey, *op. cit.*, p. 103): "Perception is not a passive process of registration . . ." [but] "an active process of interaction between organism and environment. Perception is an achievement. As in the case of other achievements, it is regulated and given direction by what the organism is trying to do."

27 Franklin Fearing, "Group Behavior and the Concept of Emotion," in Reyment (ed.), *Feelings and Emotions* (1950), p. 453.

28 Anna H. Schachtel, Jules Henry and Zunia Henry, "Rorschach Analysis of Pilago Indian Children," *American Journal of Orthopsychiatry,* XII (1942), 679-712; p. 680.

29 Hugh McLeod, "A Rorschach Study with Pre-school Children," *Journal of Projective Techniques,* XIV (1950), 453-63.

30 See Hertz, "The Method of Administration of the Rorschach Ink-Blot Test," *Child Development,* VII (1936), 237-54; and Ford, *The Application of the Rorschach Test to Young Children* (University of Minnesota Institute of Child Welfare, Monograph Series No. 23 [1946]), on the trial blot.

31 Abel, *op. cit.,* does discuss some of these problems.

32 There were 18 plates in this series prepared by Dr. William E. Henry. The field work of Spiro and others was carried on under the auspices of *CIMA* (Coordinated Investigation of Micronesian Anthropology) organized by the Pacific Science Board of the National Research Council and carried out with the cooperation of the U. S. Navy.

33 Schachtel, Henry and Henry, *op. cit.,* p. 681.

34 Spiro also collected a large number of drawings despite the fact that most of his subjects had never handled a pencil before.

35 Lewis, now employed in the Trusteeship Division of the United Nations, participated in the CIMA project under the sponsorship of the University Museum and the Department of Anthropology at the University of Pennsylvania where he was a graduate student.

36 DuBois, *op. cit.,* p. 590, where Oberholzer gives the total number of *R* given by males. I have divided this figure by the number of male subjects (17). Unfortunately, no comparable figure is given for the 20 female subjects.

37 S. J. Beck, *Introduction to the Rorschach Method. A Manual of Personality Study,* American Orthopsychiatric Association, Monograph No. 1 (1937), p. 272.

38 Oscar Lewis, *Life in a Mexican Village: Tepoztlan Restudied* (Urbana, Ill., 1951), p. 310.

39 See Chap. 19.

40 Ames, and others, *Child Rorschach Responses. Developmental Trends from Two to Ten Years* (New York, 1952), p. 21.

41 S. J. Beck, *Rorschach's Test,*Vol. I, *Basic Processes*(NewYork, 1944), p. 196.

42 Bruno Klopfer and Douglas McG. Kelley, *The Rorschach Technique. A Manual for a Projective Method of Personality Diagnosis* (Yonkers-on-Hudson, 1942), p. 171.

43 See, e.g., Ames, *op. cit.,* p. 279, "Normal Expectancies of an Adult Rorschach Record."

44 See Jules Henry, "Rorschach Technique in Primitive Cultures," *American Journal of Orthopsychiatry,* XI (1941), p. 233, for a sample of the faunal tabulation.

45 Klopfer and Kelley, *op. cit.,* p. 215.

46 Dennis, in Blake and Ramsey, *op. cit.,* p. 156. The statement made in my 1941 article which was written before I had made a quantitative analysis of

content categories was that "in quite a few instances reference is made to dream material" (p. 241).

47 S. J. Beck, A. Rabin, and others, "The Normal Personality as Projected in the Rorschach Test," *Journal of Psychology*, XXX (1950), 241-98.

48 See John E. Bell, *Projective Technique. A Dynamic Approach to the Study of Personality* (New York, 1948), pp. 128-30; and in particular, Ernest Schachtel, "The Dynamic Perception and the Symbolism of Form," *Psychiatry*, IV (1941), 79-96; Robert Lindner, "The Content Analysis of the Rorschach Protocol," in L. E. Apt and L. Bellack, *op. cit.;* Abraham Elizur, "Content Analysis of the Rorschach with Regard to Anxiety and Hostility," *Journal of Projective Techniques*, XIII (1949), 247-84; and George DeVos, "A Quantitative Approach to Affective Symbolism in Rorschach Responses," *Journal of Projective Techniques*, XVI (1952), 133-50. Beck, "The Rorschach Test: A Multidimensional Test of Personality," in Anderson and Anderson, *op. cit.,* p. 118, lays particular emphasis upon the fact that "It is in the sphere of content, therefore, that important research in the Rorschach test still lies before us. The structural dimensions give us a measure that tells us what the person is. The content, when we know more about it, will tell us where he has been, and to what he has been exposed." It should also be noted that the dynamic character of cognition, generally speaking, has not been traditionally recognized by psychologists. See the article by Heidbreder, "Toward a Dynamic Psychology of Cognition," *Psychological Review*, LII (1945), 1-22.

49 DeVos, *op. cit.,* p. 133.

50 Theodora Abel and Francis L. K. Hsu, "Some Aspects of Personality of Chinese Revealed by the Rorschach Test," *Journal of Projective Techniques*, XIII (1949), 285-301, pp. 289-90.

51 Mary Salter, *The Rorschach Test Technique: Klopfer Method* (mimeographed, University of Toronto), referring to Klopfer.

52 For a discussion of the different frequency criteria used in scoring *P* in the history of the test see Hertz, "The 'Popular' Response Factor in the Rorschach Scoring," *Journal of Projective Techniques*, VI (1938), 104-19. Actual quantitatively established norms for the scoring of *P* responses for different groups of subjects in American culture is a recent development. For quantitative data on original forms see Hertz, *Frequency Tables for Scoring Responses to the Rorschach Ink-Blot Test* (3rd ed.; Cleveland, 1951).

53 See Hallowell (1945c) for the Ojibwa. In this article I was able to make use of a preliminary study along the same lines made by Dr. Dorothea Leighton for Navaho and Zuni children.

54 Quotations from the summarization by Hertz, *op. cit.,* p. 3.

55 Beck, *Rorschach's Test,* III (1952), pp. 24-25, writes: "The popular (P) response has been correctly evaluated as a measure of the ability to recognize the most common percepts of one's milieu. It points, therefore, to conformity in the thought content. . . . Schizophrenics score low P; they do not share their communities' thoughts. . . . Low P is found in some adult neurotics as a rebellion symptom at the conscious level. . . . [In some homosexuals P is low; in others very high. Beck interprets the latter as camouflage] a defensive effort to cover up the nonconventional sexuality by being very conventional in everything else."

56 Klopfer (Klopfer and Kelly, *op. cit.,* pp. 177-78) points out that "The value of establishing such a group frequency for any concept is undeniable. However, it does detract from the importance of the concept of *universal frequency.*

To every Rorschach expert who has seen records from many different groups it is rather surprising how many concepts even the most divergent groups have in common. Thus, it seems worthwhile at least to aim at the establishment of a universally representative frequency distribution of concepts."

57 Ernst Schneider, *Psychodiagnostisches Praktikum für Psychologen und Pädagogen* (Leipzig, 1936), p. 19.

58 Information on the Zuni and Navaho is based upon data collected as part of the Indian Education Research Project sponsored by the U. S. Office of Indian Affairs and the Committee on Human Development of the University of Chicago which has not yet been published in full. The frequencies based upon the records of 106 Navaho boys and girls ages 6–18, and 83 Zuni children of both sexes, 8–18 years old, were compiled by Dr. Dorothea Leighton. Although Dr. D. B. Shimkin's study of the Wind River Shoshone was a pioneer investigation, carried out in 1937, it has never been published. I have relied upon a personal communication for the figures tabulated.

59 George D. Spindler and Walter Goldschmidt, "Experimental Design in the Study of Culture Change," *Southwestern Journal of Anthropology*, VIII (1952), 68-82; p. 78.

60 A. H. Schachtel, J. and Z. Henry, *op. cit.*, p. 680.

61 For the nature and sequence of this participation, see Margaret Mead, *The Mountain Arapesh, V. The Record of Unabelin with Rorschach Analysis* (Anthropological Papers, American Museum of Natural History, XL, Part 3 [New York, 1949], p. 371).

62 Mead, *op. cit.*, p. 389.

63 DuBois, *op. cit.*, pp. 588-89.

64 O. Lewis, *op. cit.*, Chap. 13. This interpretation might be classified as semi-blind, if any such distinction seems necessary, since the author, in a footnote at the beginning of the chapter (p. 306), says that it was written by Abel and Calabresi "prior to their reading of an earlier chapter on the people. However, they had seen three short published articles of mine, one of which dealt with inter-personal relations. In addition, they had read an early version of one of my family studies."

65 Thomas Gladwin and Seymour B. Sarason, *Truk: Man in Paradise* (New York, 1953). Dr. Sarason contributed sections on Rorschach analyses and on TAT.

66 The data, unpublished, are collected as part of the Indian Educational Research Project sponsored by the U. S. Office of Indian Affairs and the Committee on Human Development of the University of Chicago.

67 Clyde Kluckhohn and Janine C. Rosenzweig, "Two Navaho Children Over a Five-Year Period," *American Journal of Orthopsychiatry*, XIX (1949), 266-78; p. 277.

68 DuBois, *op. cit.*

69 Cf. Mead, *op. cit.*, p. 318.

70 Kroeber, for example, has clearly expressed his personal preference for this frame of reference.

71 The experimental design of this study was set forth by Spindler and Goldschmidt, *op. cit.* The results are given in a monograph in the University of California Publications in Culture and Society, University of California Press (1955), *Sociocultural and Psychological Processes in Menomini Acculturation* by George Spindler.

72 George Spindler, *op. cit.; Psychiatry*, 1951, p. 151.

73 Louise Spindler, *American Anthropologist*, 1952, pp. 515-16.

74 George Spindler, 1951, *op. cit.*, p. 158.

75 See, e.g., Schafer's methodological strictures on the interpretation of the

psychological attributes of clinical groups. "Psychological Tests in Clinical Research," *Journal of Consulting Psychology,* XIII (1949), 328-34.

76 See Henry and Spiro, *op. cit.*

77 Wallace, *The Modal Personality Structure of the Tuscarora Indians as Revealed by the Rorschach Test* (Bureau of American Ethnology, Bulletin 150 [Washington, 1952]), p. 55.

78 See Wallace, *op. cit.,* p. 79, for a novel graphic representation of modal type, modal class, sub-modal class, deviant class. (Fig. 5, The "saucer" distribution of personality variables.)

79 The difference between the composite Ojibwa profile of the modal class as worked out by Wallace and the profile as represented by mean figures computed by myself can be seen by comparing Figure 7, p. 100, in Wallace with Table 8 in Chapter 19. The parallel comparison for the Tuscarora is to be found in Wallace, Fig. 8, p. 111.

80 Beck, Rabin, and others, *op. cit.,* p. 270.

81 Beck, *Rorschach's Test,* III, p. 28.

82 Beck, *ibid.,* p. 62.

83 Beck, Rabin, and others, *op. cit.*

84 O. H. Mowrer and A. D. Ullman, "Time as a Determinant in Integrative Learning," *Psychological Review,* LII (1945), 61-90; pp. 86, 84. Mental health as a functional concept does not necessarily find its antithesis in the concept "mental disease." S. S. Marzolf, "The Disease Concept in Psychology," *Psychological Review,* LIV (July 1947), 211-21, concludes (p. 219) that there is no need for the term "mental disease." "Disease is not an important concept in physiology; 'syndromes of dysfunction' is a fully adequate expression. 'Syndromes of dysfunction' is adequate for psychology too." In other words, the *optimum functioning* of a human being, considered as an integral psychological whole and in his sociocultural setting, is implied as a standard of judgment. Cf. Brewster Smith's, "Optima of Mental Health," *Psychiatry,* XIII (November 1950), 503-10, for discussion of "optima" of mental health.

85 This and subsequent quotations referring to the Menomini are from Spindler, *op. cit.,* 1955.

CHAPTER 4

THE SELF AND ITS BEHAVIORAL ENVIRONMENT

1 Cf. Erich Fromm, *Man for Himself* (New York, 1947), pp. 39-40. In the characterization of Patrick Mullahy, "The key problem of psychology for Fromm is the specific kind of relatedness of the individual towards the world and to himself." *Oedipus: Myth and Complex* (New York, 1945), p. 241.

2 I. Chien, p. 305. "The Awareness of Self and the Structure of the Ego," *Psychological Review,* LI (1944), 304-414.

3 In a recent discussion of basic problems of visual perception James J. Gibson, *The Perception of the Visual World* (Boston, 1950), p. 226, emphasizes the fact that "perceiving the environment includes the ego as part of the total process. In order to localize any object there must be a point of reference. An impression of 'there' implies an impression of 'here,' and neither could exist without the other." He then goes on to remark that although "the definition of the ego is a problem with which psychologists and philosophers have struggled without much success, the concept of a self, by whatever term

it is called, is necessary for any scientific theory of personality, of social behavior, of abnormal behavior, or of ethical behavior."

4 Robert Redfield, "The Primitive World View," *Proceedings of the American Philosophical Society*, XCVI (1952), p. 30. Cf. *The Primitive World* (Ithaca, 1953), pp. 86, 91.

5 An early survey by A. E. Crawley, *The Idea of the Soul* (London, 1909), now seems completely antiquated from a psychological point of view.

6 It is perhaps of some historical significance that an article published in 1916 which did concern itself with "Primitive Notions of the 'Self' " was written by Arthur J. Todd, a sociologist, and published in a psychological journal. A few years later (1921) Geza Roheim published a series of articles on "Das Selbst" in which he interpreted the material reported from a wide range of cultures according to psychoanalytic principles. These articles appeared in *Imago* and were among the contributions for which Roheim was awarded the Freud prize in 1921. But they did not affect the main stream of anthropological thought.

7 Clark Wissler, *Man and Culture* (New York, 1923).

8 It is worth noting, therefore, that as early as 1937 and thereafter Lawrence K. Frank repeatedly referred to concepts of the self as an intrinsic aspect of all cultures. In an article on "The Task of General Education" he wrote: "In any culture, we find that the basic conceptions that underlie the whole framework of man's life are concerned with the nature of the universe, man's place therein, his relations to his society or group life, and to other individuals, and finally his conception of human nature and of the self." See the collection of Frank's papers published under the title *Society as the Patient: Essays on Culture and Personality* (New Brunswick, 1948), p. 215, and pp. 152, 162, 226, 277, 290.

9 G. P. Murdock, "Common Denominators of Culture," in Ralph Linton (ed.), *The Science of Man in the World Crisis* (New York, 1945).

10 John Gillin, *The Ways of Men* (New York, 1948), p. 196, repeats Murdock's items without emendation.

11 See, e.g., C. J. Bittner, *The Development of the Concept of the Social Nature of the Self* (Iowa City, 1932), p. 10, who cites Durkheim, Baldwin, and Lévy-Brühl as among those "who assert that primitive man is devoid of self-consciousness, and that he fails to distinguish between subject and object, between things in consciousness and out of consciousness, between self and other." But Lévy-Brühl actually represents a more qualified view.

12 Hans Kelsen, *Society and Nature* (Chicago, 1943), p. 6. The ethnographic evidence adduced in support of this statement is not convincing, quite apart from any possible evolutionary implications.

13 Paul Radin, *Primitive Man as Philosopher* (New York, 1927), pp. 259-60. In his chapter on "The Nature of the Ego and of Human Personality" Radin deals with the Maori, Oglala Sioux, and the Batak. It is interesting to note that the Maori are cited by Kelsen (*op. cit.*, p. 11) to make the point that, since the pronominal use of "I" may have an extended use that includes the tribal group, they "lack ego-consciousness."

14 Marcel Mauss, "Une categorie de l'esprit humain: la notion de personne celle de 'moi,' " *Journal of the Royal Anthropological Institute*, LXVIII (1938), 263-81.

15 Dorothy Lee, "Notes on the Conception of the Self among the Wintu Indians," *Journal of Abnormal and Social Psychology*, XLV (No. 3, 1945).

16 Marian W. Smith, "Different Cultural Concepts of Past, Present, and Future. A Study of Ego Extension," *Psychiatry*, XV (1952), 395-400.

17 G. P. Murdock, C. S. Ford, and others, *Outline of Cultural Materials* (Behavior Science Outlines, I [3rd ed.; New Haven, 1950]). Item 828 in Section 82, "Ideas About Nature and Man."

18 S. Stansfeld Sargent, *Social Psychology* (New York, 1950), Chap. 8; P. M. Symonds, *Dynamic Psychology* (New York, 1949), Chap. 20. For additional material on Baldwin see Vahan D. Sewny, *The Social Theory of James Mark Baldwin* (New York, 1945), Chap. 2, "The Individual: Social Origin of the Self and Society." Some of the deeper historical roots of thinking about the social nature of the self have been reviewed in the doctoral dissertation of Bittner.

19 Since this paper was completed in the summer of 1951, with the expectation that it would appear in Volume IV of *Psychoanalysis and the Social Sciences*, under the editorship of the late Dr. Roheim, I have not attempted to include all relevant articles and books that have appeared since that date. But, as examples of a trend of interest in varying aspects of the subject dealt with by those outside of anthropology, the following items are cited here: Percival M. Symonds, *The Ego and the Self* (1951); Carl R. Rogers, *Client-centered Therapy* (1951); David P. Ausubel, *Ego Development and the Personality Disorders. A Developmental Approach to Psychopathology* (1952); Harold Palmer, *The Philosophy of Psychiatry* (1952); Solomon E. Asch, *Social Psychology* (1952), Chap. 10; Risieri Frondizi, *The Nature of the Self* (1953).

20 See Clyde Kluckhohn, "The Influence of Psychiatry on Anthropology in America during the Past One Hundred Years," in J. K. Hall, G. Zilboorg and H. A. Bunker (eds.), *One Hundred Years of American Psychiatry* (New York, 1944). He points out that up to 1920 "The dominant currents in American Anthropology . . . were descriptive and historical . . . indeed, most anthropologists of the period 1920 seem almost apologetic when they incidentally allude to individual variations. Anthropology was focused upon the standard, the average, the abstracted culture patterns. It is hardly too much to say that the prevalent trend of American anthropology was 'anti-psychological.' "

21 Clara Thompson, *Psychoanalysis: Evolution and Development* (New York, 1950), pp. 61, 63. The original publication date of *The Ego and the Id* was 1923; the English translation appeared in 1927.

22 Gardner Murphy, *Personality: A Biosocial Approach to Origins and Structure* (New York, 1947), p. 480.

23 G. Murphy, L B. Murphy and T. M. Newcomb, *Experimental Social Psychology* (rev. ed.; New York, 1937), p. 207.

24 Symonds, *op. cit.,* pp. 71-72.

25 A. E. Parr, "On Self-Recognition and Social Reaction in Relation to Biomechanics, with a Note on Terminology," *Ecology,* XVIII (1937), 321 ff.

26 W. H. Ittelson and F. P. Kilpatrick, "Experiments in Perception," *Scientific American,* CLXXXV (1951), 50-55.

27 *Ibid.*

28 See Chap. 1 and Hallowell, 1951a.

29 E. B. Tylor, *Researches into the Early History of Mankind* (New York, 1878), p. 137. (1st ed., 1865.)

30 E. B. Tylor, *Primitive Culture* (1st American ed ; New York, 1874), I, 445.

31 Crawley, *op. cit.,* pp. 15-16.

32 See, e.g., R. B. MacLeod, "The Phenomenological Approach to Social Psychology, *Psychological Review,* LIV (1947), 193-210. He introduces his dis-

cussion of "The Self as phenomenal datum" (p. 200) with a brief resume of the subjectivity-objectivity problem as viewed by philosophers and then goes on to remark: "In recent psychology, the problem has been more frequently stated in terms of degrees of dependence on the organism—with the same resultant confusion. It becomes speedily clear that any act or experience of an organism is dependent on the organism, and that any attempt to differentiate exactly between the contributions of the organism and those of the environment is doomed. Thus, in the traditional sense, all psychological data become 'subjective.' " Ernst Cassirer in *The Philosophy of Symbolic Forms: I. Language* (New Haven, 1953), touches upon the linguistic aspect of this problem in his discussion of "Personal and Possessive Expression" (pp. 259 ff.), Among other things, he points out (p. 262) that the "fusion of a nominal term with a possessive pronoun is not limited to parts of the human body but extends to other contents, in so far as they are conceived as standing in close relationship with the I and in a sense to form a part of its spiritual-natural substance." He cites kinship terms as one example and then generalizes to the effect that "Here language does not look upon objective reality as a single homogeneous mass, simply juxtaposed to the world of the I, but sees different strata of this reality: the relationship between object and subject is not universal and abstract; on the contrary, we can distinguish different degrees of objectivity, varying according to relative distance from the I."

33   While this distinction is, by now, familiar enough, there is no uniformity in the contrasting terms employed. With reference to the study of animal behavior the contrasting terms employed by J. von Uexküll appear in the English translation of his book as "world" and "surrounding world" (*Theoretical Biology* [London, 1926]); in Kurt Koffka, *Principles of Gestalt Psychology* (New York, 1935), the parallel terms are "geographical environment" and "behavioral environment"; in Andreas Angyal, *Foundations for a Science of Personality* (New York, 1941), "external world" and "environment" ("The external world can be called environment only when and in so far as it is in interaction with the organism." [p. 97]); in Lewin, "objective environment" or "foreign hull of the Life Space" and "psychological environment" or "environment." Kurt Goldstein in *Human Nature in the Light of Psychopathology* (Cambridge, 1940), p. 88, says: "Each organism has its own characteristic milieu. Only that, a certain segment of all that surrounds it, constitutes its world. We call this milieu the adequate milieu; that is, the milieu that is appropriate to the nature of the organism"; Ross Stagner uses the term "behavioral environment" (*The Psychology of Personality* [2nd ed.; New York, 1948], pp. 95, 136), and Murray makes reference to the problem (*op. cit.*, p. 166); D. Krech and R. S. Crutchfield write in *Theory and Problems of Social Psychology* (New York, 1948), p. 38: "The real environment of a person is that environment which would be described by an objective observer; the psychological environment is that which would be described by the experiencing person himself. . . . The very same physical environment can result in radically different psychological environments for two different persons." Philosophers have dealt with this problem, too. See, e.g., Grace A. DeLaguna's penetrating book, *Speech, Its Function and Development* (New Haven, 1927), and John Dewey and Arthur F. Bentley, *Knowing and the Known* (Boston, 1949), pp. 271-72, where they touch upon this question at a high level of abstraction.

34   G. H. Mead, *Mind, Self and Society* (Chicago, 1934), pp. 129, 130; "Nature —the external world—is objectively there, in opposition to our experience

of it, or in opposition to the individual thinker himself. Although external objects are there independent of the experiencing individual, nevertheless, they possess certain characteristics by virtue of their relation to his experiencing or to his mind, which they would not possess otherwise or apart from those relations. These characteristics are their meanings for him, or, in general, for us. The distinction between physical objects or physical reality and the mental or self-conscious experience of those objects or that reality—the distinction between external and internal experience—lies in the fact that the latter is concerned with or constituted by meanings . . . (p. 131*n*).

35 Marjorie Nicholson, *The Breaking of the Circle. Studies in the Effect of the "New Science" Upon Seventeenth Century Poetry* (Evanston, 1950), p. xviii. Cf. R. G. Collingwood, *Idea of Nature* (Oxford, 1945); and the remarks of J. H. Randall, "The Nature of Naturalism," in Y. H. Krickorian (ed.), *Naturalism and the Human Spirit* (New York, 1944), especially pp. 355-56.

36 It is unnecessary to invoke any novel principle to cover such data among "primitive" peoples. Referring to an even broader range of phenomena Mac-Leod (*op. cit.*) points out that, "Purely fictitious objects, events and relationships can be just as truly determinants of our behavior as are those which are anchored in physical reality."

37 *Ibid.,* pp. 198-99.

38 Leslie White, "Ethnological Theory," in R. W. Sellars, V. T. McGill, M. Faber (eds.), *Philosophy of the Future,* (New York, 1949), p. 368, says that culture is ", , , a specific and concrete mechanism employed by a particular animal organism in adjusting to its environment. It is the mechanism that articulates man with the earth and cosmos. It is therefore something describable in zoological, material, mechanical terms. Yet we have only to browse through the literature to discover how often it is conceived otherwise." And, "The Individual and the Culture Process," in *Centennial, American Association for the Advancement of Science* (1950), p. 75, "Culture is . . . a thermodynamic system in a mechanical sense. Culture grows in all its aspects—ideological, sociological, and technological—when and as the amount of energy harnessed per capita per year is increased, and as the means of expending this energy are improved. Culture is thus a dynamic system capable of growth." And (*ibid,* p. 80), "Relative to the culture process the individual is neither creator nor determinant; he is merely a catalyst and a vehicle of expression." For a contrary view see David Bidney, "Human Nature and the Cultural Process," *American Anthropologist,* XLIX (1947), 375-96, and Melford E. Spiro, "Culture and Personality: The Natural History of a False Dichotomy," *Psychiatry,* XIV (1951), 18-46.

39 Henry A. Murray, *Explorations in Personality* (New York, 1938), p. 40. More recently E. C. Tolman (see T. Parsons and E. A. Shils [eds.], *Toward a General Theory of Action* [Cambridge, 1951], p. 359) has remarked that "psychology is in large part a study of the internalization of society and of culture within the individual human actor." Cf. T. M. Newcomb, *Social Psychology* (New York, 1950), p. 6, with respect to the same point and the more elaborated exposition by Spiro (*op. cit.*).

40 Franz Boas, *The Mind of Primitive Man* (New York, 1911). Ernst Cassirer, *op. cit.,* p. 250, calls attention to Wilhelm von Humboldt's opposition to the view, current in his time, that since in the traditional classification of the parts of speech the pronoun was said to be a substitute for a noun, it could not be considered autonomous in development. According to Cassirer, Humboldt insisted "the pronoun cannot possibly be the latest part of speech: for the first element in the act of speech is the personality of the speaker himself,

who stands in constant contact with nature and in speaking must inevitably express the opposition between his I and nature. 'But in the I [says Humboldt], the thou is automatically given, and through a new opposition the third person arises, which, now that language has gone beyond the circle of those who feel and speak, is extended to dead things.' "

41 A. Gesell, *The Psychology of Early Growth* (New York, 1938). It is worth noting Cassirer, although he was not a psychologist, was well aware of the subtle relations between the development of self-feeling, on the one hand, and linguistic reference, on the other. Following his reference to Humboldt's theory (see footnote 40) he goes on to say (*op. cit.*, pp. 250-51), "The philosophy of language would indeed reduce itself to the narrow, logical grammatical view which it combats, if it strove to measure the form and configuration of the *I-consciousness* solely by the development of the pronoun. In the psychological analysis of children's language, the mistake has often been made of identifying the earliest phonetic expression of I with the earliest stage of I-feeling. Here it is overlooked that the psychological content and the linguistic expression never fully coincide and above all that unity of *content* need not be reflected in *simplicity* of expression. Language has many different means of expressing a specific fundamental intuition, and we must consider them as a whole in order to see clearly the direction to which they point. The formation of the I-concept is not bound up exclusively with the pronoun, but proceeds equally through other linguistic spheres, through the medium of the noun, the verb, etc." Cassirer's discussion of the role of possessive pronouns (p. 259 seq.) as mediating the self–not-self relation contains ideas for further cross-cultural exploration.

42 M. Sherif, *The Psychology of Social Norms* (New York, 1936), p. 174, quotes W. McDougall as saying that one's name "becomes a handle by the aid of which he gets hold of himself and acquires facility in thinking and speaking of himself as an agent, a striver, a desirer, a refuser."

43 G. A. Pettitt, *Primitive Education in North America* (University of California Publications in American Archeology and Ethnology, XIII [1946], 1-182), Chap. 6, has discussed other functions of names among the North American Indians, such as "stimulating self-development and achievement through ridicule, as a type of prestige reward for specific achievements or general good behavior and popularity; as the principal medium for transference of ready-made personalities."

44 D. Snygg and A. W. Combs, *Individual Behavior: A New Frame of Reference for Psychology* (New York, 1949), p. 82, appear to be among the few who have given this fact explicit recognition. They write, "To this point we have spoken of the development of the phenomenal self only in terms of the child's reactions to his physical surroundings. As a matter of fact, the culture into which the individual is born is a far more potent factor in the development of the phenomenal self. While the child is born into a world of physical objects, even these are subjected to the particular interpretations of the culture so that the phenomenal self becomes overwhelmingly the product of the culture. For most of us, the phenomenal self we develop is a direct outgrowth of the cultural matrix of our parents and early guardians."

45 E. Cassirer, "Le langage et la construction du monde des objets," *Journal de la psychologie normale et pathologique*, XXX (1932), p. 23.

46 David Bidney, *Theoretical Anthropology* (New York, 1953), emphasizes the point that the fact that "natives do differentiate between secular, everyday experience and sacred, superhuman tales and traditions about gods and spirits, since they have special terms to designate the different categories of narrative

and tradition . . . does not mean that they distinguish clearly between the sphere of the natural and that of the supernatural, since gods and spirits are just as much a part of the order of 'nature' as are men and animals." "The dichotomy of the natural and supernatural," he goes on to say, "implies a scientific epistemology and critical, metaphysical sophistication which must not be assumed without reliable evidence " (pp. 165-66).

47 From a psychological point of view this is by no means a peculiarity of primitive peoples. Krech and Crutchfield, *op. cit.*, p. 471, point out that "our social world does not consist only of 'real' people but also characters of literature, history and fable."

48 Gibson (*op. cit.*, p. 157) emphasizes the fact that "the abstractions which we call space and time are not as distinct as they have been assumed to be, for space cannot be apprehended except in time."

49 The remarkable spatial mobility and directional orientation of bees described by Von Frisch, for example, in no way depends upon the self-awareness and self-reference that we assume in man. The mechanics of their spatial orientation are of a completely different order. G. Revez, "The Problem of Space with Particular Emphasis on Specific Sensory Space," *American Journal of Psychology*, I (1937), 434 *n.*, has pointed out that "although the experience of space and perception of objects of animals seem to agree with that of our own, the theory of a general phenomenal agreement between animal and human perception is highly disputable from a logical and theoretical angle. . . . Because of lack of language and ideas, all animals must have a different space concept . . . their objects must be perceived in a fundamentally different configuration and order than ours. . . . This must be the case regardless of their particular stage of evolutionary development and their biological relationship to man." Sherif and Cantril (*op. cit.*, pp. 93-94), while accepting William Stern's emphasis upon the fact that "the personal world of every individual becomes centered around himself," and that "in making judgments of 'space' and 'time' the individual inevitably uses himself as a central point of reference," do not emphasize the dependence of the individual upon cultural means in order to achieve spatio-temporal orientation.

50 With reference to locomotion, Gibson (*op. cit.*, pp. 229-30) differentiates a simple type, which is "oriented directly toward the goal" and where "the body movement is a function of optical stimulation which yields the perception of a visual world with the goal-object in it" from a more advanced form which involves the "act of going to an object or place beyond the range of vision." In the latter case "one must know both where he is going and where he is now. It requires, over and above the visual world, a frame of reference or a topographical schema. The individual must perceive the space which surrounds him on all sides . . . and must also apprehend the world beyond the visible scene—the layout of the building, of the city and its streets, of the region, and of the country with its highways and cities. He is then said to be oriented in space—actually, in a series of more and more inclusive spaces of which the most general is the astronomical universe. The conception of an objective world, independent of the standpoint of any observer, rests upon this type of orientation." Thus, a culturally constituted orientation in a world of objects other than self must be integrated with a spatial orientation of the self that provides a frame of reference for activities in this world. Redfield, "The Primitive World View" (p. 31), remarks: "I suppose that every world view includes some spatial and temporal dimensions, some conceptions of place and past and future. Man is necessarily oriented to a universe of extension and duration."

51 Murdock, *op. cit.*, 1945, lists calendars among the common denominators of culture. Since the chapter on Ojibwa temporal orientation included in this volume was published (1937) E. E. Evans-Prichard, *The Nuer* (Oxford, 1940); Meyer Fortes, *The Dynamics of Clans-ship among the Tallensi* (London, 1945); and Paul Bohannon, "Concepts of Time among the Tiv of Nigeria," *Southwestern Journal of Anthropology*, IX (1953), 261-62, have dealt with the topic among African groups. S. N. Eisenstadt has analyzed the perception of time and space among oriental Jews in Jerusalem in "The Perception of Time and Space in a Situation of Culture-Contact," *Journal of the Royal Anthropological Institute*, LXXIX (1949), 63-68 (published 1951). See also P. Sorokin, *Socio-cultural Causality, Space, Time* (Durham, North Carolina, 1943).

52 L. K. Frank, *op. cit.*, p. 341.

53 See M. Abeles and P. Schilder, "Psychogenic Loss of Personal Identity: Amnesia," *Archives of Neurological Psychiatry*, XXXIV (1935), 587-604; G. W. Kisker and G. W. Knox, "The Psychopathology of the Ego System," *Journal of Nervous and Mental Diseases*, XLVI (1943), 66-71; M. Sherif and H. Cantril, *The Psychology of Ego-Involvement* (New York, 1947), Chap. 12, "Breakdown of the Ego"; D. Rappaport, *Emotions and Memory* (Baltimore, 1942), pp. 197 ff. According to Rappaport, Abeles and Schilder "were the first to recognize that the loss of personal identity is a specific disturbance."

54 G. J. Dudycha and M. M. Dudycha, "Childhood Memories: A Review of the Literature," *Psychological Bulletin*, XXXVIII (1941), 668-82; p. 681.

55 The emphasis laid upon the recall of prenatal memories, memories at conception, and even memories of deaths in previous incarnations by those practicing dianetics, is an interesting anomaly in American culture. In one case a patient reported what her mother said while she was still an unborn foetus. See J. A. Winter, *A Doctor's Report on Dianetics. Theory and Therapy,* Introduction by F. Perls, M. D. (New York, 1952).

56 Sometimes these may assume a symbolic form and be derived from actual events of a previous period even though the individual is not conscious of them as recalled memories. Freud discovered early in his investigations that what he first took to be authentic early memories were not so in fact.

57 Further inquiries are needed. How widely prevalent in nonliterate cultures is the idea that memories from early infancy or the prenatal period can be recalled? What is their content and under what conditions is the individual motivated to recall them? Where the notion of reincarnation is present, answers to the same questions might be sought.

58 Oscar Oppenheimer, " 'I' and Time: A Study in Memory," *Psychological Review*, LIV (1947), p. 223, points out that "we are able to experience the past in a symbolic way because past is passed present. It is exactly the same as our present moment with the one all-important qualification that it is not real. It could be real only if it was the present moment. There is no past as a reality, there is a past only as a hypothesis. Ah, to be sure, of high probability. The belief that things happen the way we visualized them in an act of memory is so strong in most cases that we do not consider the possibility of a mistake for a moment, and therefore we are shocked when in some cases we find out later that we were mistaken and things did not happen the way we 'remembered' them."

59 J. S. Lincoln, *The Dream in Primitive Culture* (London, n.d.), p. 28, e.g., remarks that "Tylor and early anthropologists used to speak of the primitives' inability to distinguish dream and reality. Although cases of such confusion do occur, the description is not altogether accurate as a universal generaliza-

tion. . . . Most cases show that in spite of regarding the experience of the dream as real, primitives do distinguish between dreams and the perceptions of waking experience, yet often the dream experience is rgarded as having a greater value than an actual experience."

60 Clyde Kluckhohn, "The Personal Document in Anthropological Science," in L. Gottsschalk, C. Kluckhohn, R. Angell, *The Use of Personal Documents in History, Anthropology and Sociology*, prepared for the Committee on Appraisal of Research, Social Science Research Council (New York, 1947); "Needed Refinements in the Biographical Approach," in S. S. Sargent and M. Smith, *Culture and Personality* (New York, 1949). Georg Misch remarks in *A History of Autobiography in Antiquity* (London, 1950) that "as a manifestation of man's knowledge of himself, autobiography has its basis in the fundamental—and enigmatical—psychological phenomena which we call consciousness of self or self-awareness. . . . In a certain sense the history of autobiography is a history of human self-awareness."

61 G. Roheim, "Dream Analysis and Field Work in Anthropology," in *Psychoanalysis and the Social Sciences*, I (New York, 1947).

62 L. K. Frank, *op. cit.*, p. 345; cf. Smith, *op. cit.*

63 Hadley Cantril, *The Psychology of Social Movements* (New York, 1941), pp. 45-46: "For only by understanding the development of the ego can motivation be put into its proper *social* context, and only by understanding the relation of needs, derived drives, frames of reference, and attitudes to the ego can motivation be placed in its proper *personal* context. If we leave the ego out of account, our picture is inadequate and we deal only with some abstract or incomplete man."

64 Krech and Crutchfield, *op. cit.*, p. 64, point out that "Since the nature of the preferred goals depends largely upon the pattern of past experiences to which the individual has been exposed, it is to be expected that typical goals will differ from individual to individual and from culture to culture. The physical and social environment of the person limits and shapes the goals he may develop." Stagner devotes a chapter to "A Cultural Interpretation of Motivation."

65 Cf. T. M. Newcomb, *op. cit.*, p. 131 et seq.

66 R. B. MacLeod, "Perceptual Constancy and the Problem of Motivation," *Canadian Journal of Psychology*, III (1949), 62-63.

67 Sherif and Cantril, *op. cit.*, p. 119; Newcomb, *op. cit.*, p. 327 says: "One's self is a value—a supreme value to most persons under most conditions"; Krech and Crutchfield, *op. cit.*, p. 52: "Among society's most pervasive effects on the individual is the development in him of self-regard. Self-regard, essentially, is the social in man. Self-regard is related to one's conception of himself; his proper role in life; his ideals, standards, and values. And in connection with self-regard some of the most potent demands and needs of the individual develop." E. R. Hilgard, "Human Motives and the Concept of the Self," *American Psychologist*, IV (1949), p. 378, likewise emphasizes the point that the "self of awareness is an object of value."

68 See Murphy, *op. cit.*, particularly Chap. 22; Snygg and Combs, *op. cit.*, p. 58, define "the basic human need as: the preservation and enhancement of the phenomenal self."

69 Fromm, *op. cit.*, pp. 119, 135-36.

70 Sherif and Cantril, *op. cit.* Krech and Crutchfield, *op. cit.*, p. 70, write: "The normal processes of growth and socialization of the individual is one of development and multiplication of various self-involvements with objects, people, groups, and social organization in the world about him. The involvements

of the self in these more and more complex social relationships give birth to new needs, new demands, and new goals as the horizons, interests and concerns of the individual continuously expand." Cf. Sherif, *Outline of Social Psychology* (New York, 1948), Chaps. 11 and 12.

71 See Newcomb, *op. cit.,* p. 31, for a paradigm of motives conceived as intervening variables.

72 See Chaps. 19, 20 and Hallowell, 1951a.

73 E.g., Sherif, 1936, *op. cit.,* pp. 185-86, writes: "Values are the chief constituents of the ego . . . these values are the social in man . . . the values set the standards for the ego . . . the violations of the standards of the ego and ego-misplacements are painful; they produce conflicts or feelings of guilt." Cf. Krech and Crutchfield, *op. cit.,* p. 68. See also Clyde Kluckhohn, "Values and Value-Orientations," in Talcott Parsons and Edward A. Shils (eds.), *Toward a General Theory of Action* (Cambridge, 1951).

74 Hilgard, *op. cit.*

75 See Chap. I and Spiro, *op. cit.,* p. 34 et seq.

76 The nature of this conflict stated in terms of personality structure may be construed differently. With reference to normative orientation as discussed in the context of this paper, it is worth noting that O. H. Mowrer, "Discipline and Mental Health," *Harvard Educational Review,* XVII (1947), pp. 289-90, contends "anxiety, guilt, depression, feelings of inferiority, and the other forces of neurosis stem, not from an id-ego conflict, but from an ego-super ego conflict. The trouble, in other words, is between the individual's conscious self and the values implanted in him by his social training, rather than between the conscious self, or ego, and the biologically given impulses, of lust and hostility." Cf. Mowrer, *Learning Theory and Personality Dynamics: Selected Papers* (New York, 1950), Chap. 18, "Learning Theory and the Neurotic Paradox." Furthermore, Mowrer (1950, *op. cit.,* p. 445) points out that "Freud has repeatedly remarked that repression of an impulse or memory characteristically occurs when it arouses affects which are so strong that they threaten to overwhelm the 'ego.' To this extent repression is definitely a 'defensive' mechanism, but the resulting advantages usually prove to be achieved at a great cost. Repression is effected by excluding the symbolic representative of certain impulses from consciousness, i.e., from the dominant integrative center of the personality. Although repression thus brings a temporary peace, the process is likely to be pathogenic for the reason that energies which formerly submitted themselves to the management of, and thereby strengthened, the 'ego' are now withdrawn and left free to seek—through those habits called 'symptoms'—their own irresponsible, nonintegrative paths to gratification. This is why Freud has characterized repression as a reversion from the 'reality principle' to the more primitive 'pleasure principle,' from the 'ego' (consciousness) to the 'id' (unconsciousness)."

77 I.e., "by *denial* of impulses, or of traits, or of memories . . .," or "through *disguise,* whereby the impulses, traits or memories are distorted, displaced or converted, so that we do not recognize them for what they are." Hilgard, *op. cit.* p. 376.

78 Lincoln, *op. cit.,* p. 29.

79 Sleeman was an Anglo-Indian administrator who had thirty-five years' experience when his book was first published in 1844. (Major General Sir W. H. Sleeman, *Rambles and Recollections of an Indian Official,* [2 vols., Westminster, 1918].) I am indebted to Dr. Dorothy Spencer for this reference.

80 If suicide is *only* viewed in an "objective" or "naturalistic" frame of reference, it seems to contradict the "instinct of self-preservation," and thus present a

paradox. On the other hand, if it be assumed that the constitution of the self in its behavioral environment may pattern the motivational system of the human individual in various ways, it does not seem paradoxical to say that the individual may come to view himself in terms of a self-image that makes it possible to transcend *bodily* destruction. A culturally constituted self-image makes it possible to make use of a conceptual dichotomy that not only permits the individual to maintain a positive attitude towards the self as an object of value but, at the same time, to rule out self-destruction as a consciously motivated act, since the self may be thought to be essentially indestructible. Consequently, it is possible to be highly motivated towards self-enhancement even if this involves bodily destruction. Where such an ideology prevails, any concept of "self-destruction" must be completely reduced to an unconscious level of motivation. In order for bodily destruction to involve self-destruction at the level of self-awareness, there must be a self-image that conceives the body as a necessary substratum of the self. The so-called "instinct of self-preservation" is really a misnomer. For the biological forces that operate to preserve the life of the individual organism are not equivalent to, nor do they explain, all of the acquired drives that may become self-related in man.

81 E.g., stretching a snake until it breaks in two; cutting off an animal's leg while alive and letting it go; pulling all the feathers from a live bird.

82 Radin, *op. cit.*, p. 177, has called attention to the fact that "throughout the area inhabited by the woodland tribes of Canada and the United States, over-fasting entails death." For the Winnebago he elaborates this point by analyzing three tales, showing in each case how one of the cardinal virtues of these Indians, a sense of proportion, is violated by over fasting. Other Ojibwa cases are found in the literature. In one of them the bones of a boy who had over fasted were found by his father.

83 Hallowell, 1939a; Chaps. 16 and 14.

PART II. WORLD VIEW,
PERSONALITY STRUCTURE, AND THE SELF:
THE OJIBWA INDIANS
CHAPTER 5
THE NORTHERN OJIBWA

1 For information on the dates and locations of Forts and Trading posts, see the compilation of Ernest Voorhis, *Historic Forts and Trading Posts of the French Regime and of the English Fur Trading Companies* (Department of the Interior, National Development Bureau, Ottawa, Canada [1930], mimeographed); Gordon Charles Davidson, *The North-west Company* (Berkeley, 1918).

2 John Ryerson, *Hudson's Bay, or A Missionary Tour in the Territory of Honorable Hudson's Bay Company* (Toronto, 1855).

3 A reference to Jacob Berens, and an excellent photograph of him and his wife, is to be found in John Maclean, *Vanguards of Canada* (Toronto: Missionary Society of the Methodist Church, 1918), p. 124.

4 See Lawrence J. Burpee, *The Search for the Western Sea* (London, 1908), pp. xxv-xxvi.

5 Elliott Coues (ed.), *New Light on the Early History of the Greater Northwest.*

115—128

The Manuscript Journals of Alexander Henry and David Thompson, 1799-1814 (3 vols.; New York, 1897),I, 35n.

6 See Atlas of the Historical Geography of the United States by Charles O. Paullin, John K. Wright (ed.), (Carnegie Institution of Washington and the American Geographical Society of New York [1932]). John R. Swanton, who prepared the map, "Indian Tribes and Linguistic Stocks, 1650," confines the Ojibwa of southern Canada to an area north of Lake Superior bounded by the Albany River. Immediately to the west are the Assiniboine who sweep up towards the eastern side of Lake Winnipeg as far as the Narrows and likewise appear west and south of it. Cf. Swanton, The Indian Tribes of North America (Bureau of American Ethnology Bulletin 145, [1952]).

7 Coues), op. cit., I, 533.

8 Reverend A. C. Garrioch, First Furrows: A History of the Earl Settlement of the Red River Country, including that of Portage la Prairie (Winnipeg, 1923). It is obvious from the testimony of the foregoing writers, and others that could be mentioned, that the name Bungi was used in a generic sense and did not refer exclusively to any particular group of Ojibwa. Hence, the later use of it by Alanson Skinner in a specific sense ("Political Organization, Cults and Ceremonies of the Plains-Ojibwa and Plains-Cree Indians," Anthropological Papers, American Museum of Natural History, XI [1914], Pt. 6, 477) was only confusing, especially in historic perspective. Skinner's use of Saulteaux (ibid., IX [1911], Pt. 1, "Notes on the Eastern Cree and Northern Saulteaux," p. 117) is scarcely clarifying either. He attempted to distinguish Ojibwa, Chippewa, Northern and Southern Saulteaux, and Plains Saulteaux. The latter was another synonym for "Long Plains Ojibwa" (=Plains Ojibwa =Bungi). The Southern Saulteaux are, in his terminology, the Ojibwa of the northern shore of Lake Superior and the Northern Saulteaux an offshoot of this group. The confusing if not meaningless identification to which Skinner's terminology gave rise is illustrated in the work of that most erudite scholar, Father W. Schmidt (Der Ursprung der Gottesidee, II [Münster in Westfalen, 1929]), p. 504), who writes: "In die Gruppe der Steppen-Ojibwa rechne ich auch die Nord-Saulteaux ein. . . ."

9 Henry R. Schoolcraft, Algic Researches, Comprising Inquiries Respecting the Mental Characteristics of the North American Indians. First Series, Indian Tales and Legends (New York, 1839), I, 43.

10 See Stith Thompson, Tales of the North American Indians (Cambridge, 1929), Introduction.

11 W. L. Schramm, "Hiawatha and its Predecessors," Philological Quarterly XI (1932), 321-43; Stith Thompson, "The Indian Legend of Hiawatha," Modern Language Association, XXXVIII (1922), 128-43.

12 The figure referred to was arrived at by collating the sources cited in Chase S. Osborn and Stellanova Osborn, "Hiawatha" with its Original Indian Legends (Great Lakes Edition of the Song of Hiawatha [Lancaster, Pa., 1944]) with the narratives listed in my Concordance (Hallowell, 1946b).

13 For the appraisal by two anthropologists see Herman F. C. Ten Kate, "The Indian in Literature," Report of the Smithsonian Institution for 1921 (Washington, 1923), pp. 511-12; Frank G. Speck (with Florence I. Speck), "The Ojibwa, Hiawatha's People," Home Geographic Monthly, II (no. 4, 1932), 7-12.

14 As Grace Lee Nute (Lake Superior [Indianapolis, 1944], p. 97) has said: "What a pity the poet substituted another name for the one first chosen! Nanabozhoo is known east, north, south, and west of Lake Superior: Hiawatha

is a minor Iroquois substitute." The same mythological character is known among the Berens River Ojibwa as *wisakedják*, possibly due to Cree influence.

15 Douglas Leechman, a Canadian anthropologist ("Longfellow's Hiawatha," *Queens Quarterly*, LI [1944], 307-12), writes: . . . no matter how confused in origin or how far from the truth Longfellow's hero may be, there is no doubt that he is *the* Indian of poetry, just as the Fenimore Cooper Indian, despite Mark Twain's strictures, is *the* Indian of fiction."

16 Cf. the comments on Schoolcraft and Longfellow in Roy Harvey Pearce, *The Savages of America. A Study of the Indian and the Idea of Civilization* (Baltimore, 1953).

17 See A. L. Kroeber, *Cultural and Natural Areas of Native North America* (*University of California Publications in American Archeology and Ethnology*, XXXVIII [1939]); Regina Flannery, "The Culture of the Northeastern Hunters: A Descriptive Survey," and John M. Cooper, "The Culture of the Northeastern Indian Hunters: A Reconstructive Interpretation," in Frederick Johnson (ed.), *Man in Northeastern North America* (Papers of the R. S. Peabody Foundation for Archeology, Phillips Academy [Andover, 1946]). For a bibliography of the Ojibwa see George P. Murdock, *Ethnographic Bibliography of North America* (2nd ed; New Haven, 1953).

18 Carrie A. Lyford, *The Crafts of the Ojibwa (Chippewa)* (Education Division, U. S. Office of Indian Affairs [1942]), p. 12.

20 For examples of two different types of cultural change that have occurred see my papers "The Incidence, Character, and Decline of Polygymy Among the Lake Winnipeg Cree and Saulteaux" (1930c) which is supported by quantitative information, and "The Passing of the Midewiwin in the Lake Winnipeg Region" (1936b). The former article contains a map indicating the boundaries of the area covered by the Winnipeg Treaty of 1875. For other cultural changes see Chapter 11 on temporal orientation and for samples of folktales of European derivation see 1939c.

21 Letter from R. William Dunning (August 1953). Mr. and Mrs. Dunning have been summer school teachers at Lake Pekangikum since 1950.

22 See Hallowell, 1938c, p. 238.

23 Unpublished data.

24 A comparable study by Hortense Powdermaker in Melanesia showed, for example, that the average number of offspring per fruitful woman was only 2.9. See "Vital Statistics of New Ireland as Revealed in Geneologies," *Human Biology*, III (1931).

25 See Hallowell, 1942a.

CHAPTER 6

SOME PSYCHOLOGICAL CHARACTERISTICS OF THE NORTHEASTERN INDIANS

1 Morris Wolf, *Iroquois Religion and Its Relation to Their Morals* (New York, 1919).

2 Since this paper was published Anthony F. C. Wallace has published *The Modal Personality Structure of the Tuscarora Indians* (Bureau of American Ethnology, Bulletin 150 [1952]).

3 W. Vernon Kinietz, *The Indians of the Western Great Lakes, 1615-1760* (Occasional Contributions from the Museum of Anthropology of the University of Michigan, No. 10 [1940]), p. 167.

4 Reuben Gold Thwaites (ed.), *The Jesuit Relations and Allied Documents* (73 vols.; Cleveland, 1896-1901).

129—148

5 Chretien Le Clercq, *New Relation of Gaspesia,* trans. and ed. with a reprint of the original by W. F. Ganong (Toronto, 1910), p. 241.

6 Kinietz, *op. cit.,* p. 232.

7 Cf. Duncan Cameron (on the Saulteaux) in R. L. Masson, *Les bourgeois de la compagnie de Nord Ouest* (2 vols.; Quebec, 1890), II, 238.

8 E. Jamieson and P. Sandiford, "The Mental Capacity of the Southern Ontario Indians," *Journal of Educational Psychology,* XIX (1929), 536-51. See also T. R. Garth, *Race Psychology: A Study of Racial Mental Differences* (New York, 1931); Beatrice Blackwood, *A Study of Mental Testing in Relation to Anthropology* (Mental Measurement Monographs, No. 4 [1927]); Otto Klineberg, *Race Differences* (New York, 1935), Chap. 8; Cecil Mann, "Mental Measurements in Primitive Communities," *Psychological Bulletin,* XXXVII (1940), 366-95; Ann Anastasi, *Differential Psychology* (New York, 1937), Chap. 7.

9 See Klineberg, *op. cit.,* p. 153.

10 Anastasi, *op. cit.,* p. 511.

11 *Ibid.,* pp. 510-11.

12 Masson, *op. cit.,* II, 325.

13 Bruno Klopfer, "Form Level Rating," *Rorschach Research Exchange,* VIII (1944), 164-77.

14 Le Clercq, *op. cit.,* p. 243.

15 *Ibid.,* p. 242. Le Clercq phrases a parallel statement in a manner which may indicate that he had Le Jeune's *Relation* of 1634 at hand. (See editor's remarks.) But he undoubtedly intended the observation to apply to the Micmac.

16 *Ibid.,* p. 243.

17 H. G. Loskiel, *History of the Mission of the United Brethren among the Indians in North America* (London, 1794), Part I, p. 132.

18 David Zeisberger, "History of the North American Indians, etc.," *Ohio Archeological and Historical Society Quarterly,* XIX (1910), Nos. 1 and 2, p. 90.

19 Louis Armand, Baron de Lahontan, *New Voyages in North America,* reprinted from the English edition of 1703, Reuben G. Thwaites (ed.), (2 vols.; Chicago, 1905), II, 579.

20 E. H. Blair, *Indian Tribes of the Upper Mississippi and Region of the Great Lakes* (2 vols.; Cleveland, 1911), I, 195.

21 Le Clercq, *op. cit.,* p. 242.

22 W. N. Fenton, "Iroquois Suicide: A Study in the Stability of a Culture Pattern," *Anthropological Papers, No. 14 (Bureau of American Ethnology Bulletin,* 129 [1941]), 80-137.

23 Masson, *op. cit.,* II, 327.

24 Le Clercq, *op. cit.,* p. 242.

25 Quoted by Chretien Le Clercq, *First Establishment of the New Faith in New France,* translated with notes by J. G. Shea (2 vols.; New York, 1881), II, p. 222. (First printing Paris, 1691.)

26 The original text read "a suffusion in anxiety," but since this suggests "free-floating anxiety" which is not at all the case, I have substituted "underlying anxiety."

27 Cf. R. R. Willoughby, "Magic and Cognate Phenomena: A Hypothesis," in C. Murchison (ed.), *Handbook of Social Psychology* (2nd ed.; Worcester, 1933), p. 504.

28 Le Clercq, 1910, *op. cit.,* p. 243.

29 *Ibid.,* p. 252.

30 Letter 25, p. 344, in Kinietz, *op. cit.*

31 For references to the sources and a general discussion see A. G. Bailey, *The Conflict of European and Eastern Algonkian Cultures, 1504-1700* (Monographic Series, No. 2, Publication of the New Brunswick Museum, St. John, New Brunswick, 1937), Chap. 6.

32 Cf. Ruth Bunzel, "The Role of Alcoholism in Two Central American Cultures," *Psychiatry,* III (1940), 361-87.

33 For an analysis of the interrelated psychological and cultural variables that characterize several distinctive patterns of drinking behavior in a sample of seventy-seven societies, see the significant pioneer study of Donald Horton, "The Function of Alcohol in Primitive Societies: A Cross-cultural Study," *Quarterly Journal of Studies on Alcohol,* IV (1943), 199-320.

34 Douglas MacKay, *The Honorable Company: A History of the Hudson's Bay Company* (New York, 1936), p. 220.

35 Le Clercq, 1910, *op. cit.,* p. 255. For nineteenth-century Ojibwa parallels see, for example, J. A. Gilfillan, *The Ojibways of Minnesota* (Minnesota Historical Society Collections, X [1901]); Peter Jones, *History of the Ojibway Indians; With Special Reference to Their Conversion to Christianity* (London, 1861), p. 167; John Tanner, *A Narrative of the Captivity and Adventures of John Tanner During Thirty Years Residence among the Indians in the Interrior of North America,* prepared for the press by Edwin James, M.D. (New York, 1830), pp. 163-65.

36 Masson, *op. cit.,* II, 248; also the statement of James, the editor of Tanner, 1830.

37 Henry R. Schoolcraft, *Information Respecting the History, Conditions and Prospects of the Indian Tribes of the United States* (Philadelphia, 1851-57), Part III, p. 58.

38 Klineberg, *op. cit.,* p. 280.

39 Gilfillan, *op. cit.,* p. 64; cf. p. 114.

40 *Ibid.,* p. 86. Gilfillan writes, "I have never seen the slightest endearment pass between husband and wife, not the slightest outward token of affection. Yet there is no doubt that they are as much attached to each other, especially in middle and later life, as those of our own race."

41 Egerton R. Young, *Stories from Indian Wigwams and Northern Camp-Fires* (New York, 1892). Young, who spent a long period as a missionary among the Cree and Saulteaux of the Lake Winnipeg region, comments (p. 19) on the emotional restraint in domestic life.

42 Masson, *op. cit.,* II, 328; cf. J. G. Kohl, *Kitchi-gami; Wanderings round Lake Superior* (London, 1860), p. 35.

43 This ever recurrent suspiciousness has been frequently commented upon. Cf. Ruth Landes, "The Ojibwa of Canada," in Margaret Mead (ed.), *Cooperation and Competition among Primitive Peoples* (New York, 1937), p. 102; and Gilfillan, *op. cit.,* p. 92.

44 Diamond Jenness, *The Ojibwa Indians of Parry Island, Their Social and Religious Life* (Canadian Department of Mines, Bulletin 78, Anthropological Series No. 17 [Ottawa, 1935]).

45 Cf. Mead's analysis of the Ojibwa, *op. cit.,* pp. 489, 491, 498.

46 Cf. Jenness, *op. cit.,* pp. 87, 88.

47 Jenness, *op. cit.,* p. 88, says that the Parry Islander "strives to avoid malice and ill-will by hiding his emotions, and by carefully weighing his words lest he give vent to some angry or ill-timed remark," Timolean Ducatel ("A Fortnight among the Chippewa," *United States Catholic Magazine,* V [1846]),

a casual observer of the La Pointe Ojibwa in 1846, writes (p. 28), "A very remarkable trait of character in the Indians is, that they never quarrel, nor address insulting epithets to each other."

CHAPTER 7

SPIRITS OF THE DEAD IN SAULTEAUX LIFE AND THOUGHT

1 See E. L. M. Conrad, "Les Idées des Indiens Algonquins relatives à la Vie d'Outre-Tombe," *Review of the History of Religion*, XLII (1900), 9-81, 220-74. Pp. 43 ff. where references to visits to the land of the dead, culled from the older sources, are given. See also William Jones, "The Youth Who Died and Came Back to Life," *Ojibwa Texts*, II (Publications of the American Ethnological Society [1919]).

2 Edwyn Bevan, *Sibyls and Seers: A Survey of Some Ancient Theories of Revelation and Inspiration* (London, 1928), pp. 42 ff.

3 A. H. Gayton ("The Orpheus Myth in North America," *Journal American Folk-Lore*, XLVIII [1935], 263-86) points out, for example, that such a journey is invariably described as an historic event among certain California tribes (p. 269), and that there, as elsewhere, versions of this myth, or related tales about visits to the after-world by human beings, form the basis of tribal beliefs concerning life after death. A Fox account, for example, is "given as a personal experience of the informant's grandfather" (p. 275); "supposed actual visits to the land of the dead are not uncommon or unnatural experiences in the Plains" (p. 277); and "on the Northwest Coast tales which deal with pursuit or resuscitation of the dead are common. Beside these there are experiences described by persons who believed that they had visited the land of the dead while unconscious or 'dead' " (p. 280). See Conrad, *op cit.*, pp. 48-49.

4 This point has a significance which I did not grasp at the time. In the Ojibwa account of a similar journey (Jones, *op. cit.*, p. 11), a youth visiting the land of the dead is offered their "supremely selected food"— decayed (i.e., phosphorescent) wood—by his grandmother. When he refused it she said: "Naturally you are not yet truly dead. . . . When the time is at hand for you also to come here, then will you also want to eat this food of ours."

5 See Conrad, *op. cit.*, p. 77.

6 A term used for a large unit of population, and applied to the settlement occupied by the dead by Ojibwa-speaking peoples generally. See Jones, *op. cit.*, p. 9.

7 A similar incident is found in the personal account of an Ojibwa (Gitchegausiné) who dreamed he was journeying to the Land of the Dead (T. L. Mckenney, *Sketches of a Tour to the Lakes, of the Character and Customs of the Chippeway Indians, and of Incidents Connected with the Treaty of Fond du Lac* (Baltimore, 1827), pp. 370-72.

8 Taking the account at its face value, one suspects a delusional state. That the man was suffering from some mental disorder is likewise suggested by another peculiarity in his behavior which was mentioned. When he had to evacuate his bowels, he would not always leave the place where he happened to be, but would throw the feces to one side with his hand. My interpreter commented that Mud-Turtle's Eye did not seem to have all his senses, after he "came back," but that half of his mind had remained in the spirit world.

9 See Jones, *op. cit.*, p. 11.

10 A nickname for which I could obtain no translation.

11 D. Jenness, *The Ojibwa Indians of Parry Island, Their Social and Religious Life* (Canada Department of Mines, Bulletin No. 78 [1935]), p. 110, records three *unsuccessful* attempts to bring back the souls of deceased persons. Two of these attempts were made by his informant; one by the latter's father.

12 Other Ojibwa peoples locate it in the West; see Conrad, *op. cit.*, p. 71.

13 The Christianized Indians use the term *k'tcigijik*, lit. "great sky," for heaven, and *k'tcigijikodenawan*, lit. "great sky town (city)," for kingdom of heaven (or heavenly city).

14 The Indian referred to above, however, maintained that there were no trees, and said that he supposed the *djibaiyak* needed no plants for medicine.

15 See Conrad, *op. cit.*, p. 77, and Jones, *op. cit.*, p. 7.

16 See Jones, *op. cit.*, p. 7. The word *odinigang*, translated as "wild cucumber," should, it seems to me, be translated "shoulder-blade."

17 Note the reference to the child who was buried in a cradle-board, and was laboriously making its way along the *djibai ikana*, in Jones, *op. cit.*, p. 5.

18 "Bad spirit," the contemporary term for the devil.

19 "Bad" deeds, according to this informant, were those which injured other people without just cause: e.g., murder (including infanticide), sorcery, theft, and wife-beating ("if the woman does not deserve it").

20 I suspect that this process has been underestimated, particularly with reference to the moral and religious notions of peoples undergoing acculturation. I have the highest regard for the character and veracity of the man in question, and the statement quoted was of particular psychological interest because of the many details of aboriginal life and thought concerning which his statements were undoubtedly authoritative.

21 *Kadabéndang*, "the master" (of the spirits of the dead), i.e., not the Supreme Being; see Conrad, *op. cit.*, p. 81.

22 A nickname for which I have no translation

23 A characteristic epithet, used regardless of age.

24 Anthropomorphic characters occurring in myths; of these *wisakedjak* is the most important.

25 A number of other songs allude to the Thunder Bird.

26 Just how much these statements owe to Christian influence it is hard to say; but I would not wish to assert their complete aboriginality.
   Kiwitc also referred to "our friends who have come from such a long distance," and expressed the hope that we would be taken care of and be given "Life."

27 In a private conversation, Kiwitc once expressed naïve amazement that all the plants, animals, etc., had names.

28 A specific illustration of the belief that the *pawáganak* are always imminent at such times.

29 That is, it was a sacrifice, and therefore must be shared among the participants in the ceremony, and be smoked to during the course of it.

30 This refers to an unpeeled, decorated birch tree, placed outside the southern boundary of the dance ground, on which sacrifices were hung. It is considered one of the "leading" trees, and it appeared in the dream of Kiwitc. It symbolizes, in this case, the medicinal properties of the plant world. There is a dreamed song, a gift of the birch tree, that is sung when the sacrifices are hung up.

31 In another speech, Kiwitc also referred to the "medicine" he had asked me for, "to help us with a few mouthfuls." This was flour, of which bannocks were made and consumed by the participants. These commonplace things were sacramentalized through their use in the dance.

163—180

32 See Jenness, *op. cit.*, for a reference to an annual Feast of the Dead, held in the autumn, before the Indians scattered to their hunting grounds; also Conrad, *op. cit.*, p. 64.

33 Alexander Henry, *Travels and Adventures in Canada and the Indian Territories, 1760-76* (New York, 1809), pp. 130-31.

34 The description of the conjuring performance is oriented with respect to this man's request, and is thus only a partial account of what took place.

35 The narrator was acting as *skabéwis* (usher).

36 I saw a similar pavilion in use at Poplar Narrows, farther up the river. The dance in this settlement was purchased from Fair Wind, but when I witnessed a performance there in 1932, no reference was made to *djibaiyak*.

37 The allusion here is to a drum.

38 A nickname for which I have no translation.

39 Sugared bannock.

40 This phraseology is significant because of subsequent references to Christian beliefs. Fair Wind was once a professing Christian, and had only obtained the revelation on which the dance is based a few years before this speech was made.

41 This indicates that no grave-house had been built, as was the custom in former times. Angus was unconsciously reviving this old custom.

42 This repetition of his father's experience not only repeats a cultural pattern but must have a personal significance. The same mode of identification was noted in another instance.

43 The price is reputed to have been so exorbitant that the payments are not yet finished.

44 This is further evidence, not only that the spirits of the dead functioned as guardian spirits, but that dream-visits from the *djibaiyak* were not exceptional.

45 Subsequent investigation (1940) has revealed the belief that infants who cry constantly are trying to utter the name they bore in a previous existence, and that if this name is given them, they stop crying.

CHAPTER 8

THE OJIBWA SELF AND ITS BEHAVIORAL ENVIRONMENT

1 Victor Barnouw ("The Phantasy World of a Chippewa Woman," *Psychiatry*, XII [1949], 67-76.) cites verbatim the intra-uterine reminiscences of a Wisconsin Chippewa (Ojibwa) man and refers to specific examples of memories from early infancy on the part of other individuals.

2 I discovered that the occurrences of identical personal names, sometimes more than a generation apart in my genealogies, could be explained in every case by reincarnation. None of these people were living at the time of my inquiries.

3 See Part IV, Chap. 20, where this goal is discussed with reference to what has happened to the Ojibwa as a consequence of acculturation.

4 There is a term for existence that is applicable to any class of animate beings.

5 For details about the Land of the Dead and stories of visits there, see Chap. 7.

6 For this case, and a reputed case of resurrection, see Chap. 7.

7 For details and a full account of this episode see 1942a.

8 For the role of confession in relation to illness see Chaps. 14 and 16, and 1939a.

9 Even in this "dream" a *bodily* part of himself—his head—assumes vital importance. The dreamer gives himself "form."

10 See Chap. 7.

11 What I have given here is a highly abbreviated version of a longer text (unpublished).

12 This reference to "fire" illustrates the allusive manner of Indian narration. The listener is supposed to know what is meant. What is referred to here is made explicit in another anecdote. "One night when I was asleep, I was suddenly awakened. My strength came to me and I managed to get on my feet and walk outside" [the narrator had been very ill and thought he knew who had sorcerized him]. "Right in front of me I saw something. It was a bear lying right outside the tent." [Wild animals do not ordinarily come so close to any human habitation]. "I saw the flame when he breathed. I said to my wife very quietly: 'Hand me the axe.' She could not find it. The bear started to go. I tried to follow but I could not walk fast enough. I spoke to the bear. I said, 'I know who you are and I want you to quit. I'm good natured but if you come here again I won't spare you.' He never came back and after that I gradually got better."

13 It is said that a sorcerer who kills a person in this way is bound to visit the grave. He cuts off the fingertips of the corpse, the tip of the tongue, and gouges out the eyes, and stores them in a little box for magical use. This is why Pindándakwan made a pseudo-grave for his son outside the wigwam. It was a deliberate "trap" for the sorcerer. Pindándakwan was an actual person who appears in my genealogies.

14 John Tanner, *Narrative of the Captivity and Adventures of John Tanner, etc.,* E. James (ed.), 1830, p. 343. Tanner was a white man captured by Indians as a boy. He lived with Ojibwa and Ottawa, learned their language and published his reminiscences in later life. For further information on bear walking and the attitude of contemporary Indians toward it, see R. M. Dorson, *Bloodstoppers and Bearwalkers. Folk Traditions of the Upper Peninsula* (Cambridge, 1952), pp. 26-29 and Notes, p. 278.

15 The Ojibwa boy, at puberty or before, sought tutelaries or guardian spirits: without their help no man could be expected to get much out of life or amount to anything. The "nest" referred to was a sort of stage constructed by laying poles across the branches of a tree about fifteen feet from the ground. The boy was expected to remain on this stage several days and nights without food or drink. He was only allowed to descend to the ground to urinate and defecate. This fast was the most crucial event in a man's life and to undertake it he has to be *pekize,* pure (without sexual experience). Failure to observe all preliminary conditions and the fasting regulations destroyed his chances of blessings from other-than-human entities—the *pawáganak* (literally, "dream visitors")—who were more powerful than human beings. The situation is often described by the Ojibwa by saying that the *pawáganak* took "pity" upon the *kigusámo,* the faster. It was through dreams or visions, while the body lay inert, that direct experience of these entities occurred.

16 This account was repeated to me by a man who said he had heard the dreamer narrate it when he was an old man.

17 The conjuring tent consists of a barrel-like structure, covered with bark or canvas, that conceals the conjurer who kneels within. Those who witness the performance are *outside* this structure. Since the *pawáganak* reputedly are *inside* they, like the conjurer himself, are invisible to the audience without.

181—187

On the other hand, it is said that the *pawáganak* do have a visible aspect from inside the tent. They look like tiny stars or minute sparks. It is only under very exceptional circumstances, however, that any person except the conjurer ever has an opportunity to even peep inside the structure during the performance. Consequently, the sensory manifestation of the spirits is typically auditory, not visual. See Hallowell, 1942a, pp. 50-51.

18 Hallowell, 1942a, p. 59, where other similar cases are given.

PART III. THE CULTURAL PATTERNING OF PERSONAL EXPERIENCE AND BEHAVIOR: THE OJIBWA INDIANS

CHAPTER 9

CULTURAL FACTORS IN SPATIAL ORIENTATION

1 In the Preface to his *Perception of the Visual World* (Boston, 1950), James J. Gibson remarks (p. vii) that, "The perception of what has been called space is the basic problem of all perception. We perceive a world whose fundamental variables are spatial and temporal—a world which extends and endures. Space perception (from which time is inseparable) is not, therefore, a division of the subject matter of perception but the first problem to be considered, without a solution for which other problems remain unclear. That a solution is lacking, most psychologists would agree. The existing theories to account for the spatial and temporal character of our perceptions are not very satisfactory."

2 *Op. cit.,* p. 228.

3 *Op. cit.,* p. 10.

4 See, e.g., M. D. Vernon, *Visual Perception* (Cambridge, England, 1937), who says (p. 64), "The problem, however, which today appears to us of greater importance is concerned with the relative importance of the various types of perceptual and ideational data which subserve spatial perception, and their mutual relationships and coordination."

5 Gibson, *op. cit.,* pp. 210, 211. Cf. Preface, p. viii, "For many years, experimental evidence has accumulated about the effect of the observers' attitude on perception, the influence of culture on perception, and the roles of past experience and of sensory organization in perception. All of these experiments, however revealing, leave out of account the simple question of the relation of the stimulus to perception. Until this question is settled the other evidence will be hard to evaluate."

6 See, e.g., William Stern, *General Psychology from the Personalistic Standpoint* (New York, 1938), who likewise points out (p. 99) that, "The fact that sense perception happens to be constituted under different 'modalities' has led to the practice of cutting up the investigation of dimensions and treating visual space, tactual space, auditory space, etc., as independent. These special forms of psychological space are artificial fictions; indeed, they are misrepresentations of the true nature of mind. In so far as the individual experiences space in general, this is the *one* space of his personal existence and world; specific sensory constituents of vision, touch, etc., contribute materially to this experiential structure of space, but they remain submerged and interdependent aspects."

404

7 Gibson, *op. cit.*, p. 225, ". . . perceiving the environment includes the ego as part of the total process. In order to localize any object there must be a point of reference. An impression of 'there' implies an impression of 'here,' and neither could exist without the other."

8 See, for example, Ward H. Goodenough, "Native Astronomy in the Central Carolines," *Museum Monographs* (Philadelphia, 1953).

9 Cf. Gibson, *op. cit.*, p. 229-30.

10 "The capacity of men for forming correct mental maps is very great," write the authors of *Psychology for the Armed Services* (E. G. Boring [ed.], The Infantry Journal [Washington, 1945], p. 158), "although most persons do not use their capacities to the limit. Roads and streets and signs are enough to get them around in civilized familiar regions, and they do not feel a constant need to put everything into precise spatial relation. If they had more need for constant orientation, they would practice more on the building of their mental maps, would more easily find new and better ways of getting to old familiar places, would learn more rapidly to find their way around in new regions." The stress laid here upon the absence of the need for orientation only serves to highlight the positive motivation that is found in many nonliterate cultures.

11 The most comprehensive work on such maps is in Russian: B. F. Adler, *Maps of Primitive Peoples* (Bulletin of the Imperial Society of Students of Natural History, Anthropology and Ethnography, CXIX [St. Petersburg, 1910] approx. 350 quarto pp.). An English resume by H. D. Hutorowicz is to be found in the *Bulletin of the American Geographical Society*, XLII (1911), 669-79. Adler's work is based on 55 maps from Asia, 15 from America, 3 from Africa, 40 from Australia and Oceania, and 2 from the East Indies. There is an earlier, but less significant work (a doctoral dissertation) by W. Drober, *Kartographie bei den Naturvölkern*, 1903 (90 pp.).

12 Dr. E. S. Carpenter has called my attention to the maps obtained from Ookpuktowk and Amaulik Audlanat, two Eskimo of Southampton Island, by George M. Sutton ("The Exploration of Southampton Island, Hudson Bay." *Memoirs of the Carnegie Museum*, XII [1936], 45-47). Sutton obtained these in 1929 when no accurate maps of the island were available. More than a decade later a modern map, prepared from aerial photographs, was made. It was then possible to make a comparison between the native maps and the one made with the use of modern facilities. Although I cannot reproduce the three maps here, the level of accuracy is certainly high in the Eskimo maps. Dr. Carpenter says: "Certain digressions, often shared, are immediately apparent, particularly in the shape of the Bell Peninsula. But the striking feature is certainly accuracy, especially in the details of the shoreline."

13 Ernst Cassirer in *The Philosophy of Symbolic Forms. I. Language* (New Haven, 1953) discusses the expression of space and spatial relations in language in brilliant fashion, and in *An Essay on Man* (New Haven, 1944) he devotes a chapter to "The Human World of Space and Time." In this chapter Cassirer differentiates (1) organic space, (2) perceptual space, (3) symbolic space, (4) abstract space. *Organic* space he conceives of as the "space of action," a level of spatial orientation that is nonideational and, in effect, is confined to animals who "seem to be led by bodily impulses of a special kind," creatures who "have no mental picture or idea of space, no prospectus of spatial relations (p. 43)." *Perceptual* space is more complex in nature; it involves "elements of all the different kinds of sense experience—optical, tactual, acoustic, and kinesthetic." (p. 43) When we reach the level of *symbolic* space, we are on the borderline between the human and animal

worlds. At a still higher level of human reflection and experience *abstract* space, i.e., mathematical or geometric space (p. 44) emerges, but only after many intermediate stages. "In primitive life and under the conditions of primitive society," Cassirer says, "we find scarcely any trace of the idea of an abstract space. Primitive space is a space of action; and the action is centered around immediate practical needs and interests. So far as we can speak of a primitive 'conception' of space, this conception is not of a purely theoretical character." While this latter point is true enough, the very fact that the cosmic aspects of the world views of primitive peoples involve spatial concepts, is sufficient to show that "practical needs and interests" are actually transcended.

14 Howard R. Patch, *The Other World According to Descriptions in Medieval Literature* (Cambridge, 1950), p. 134.

15 *Ibid.,* p. 153.

16 *Ibid.,* p. 173.

17 *The Divine Comedy I: Hell,* translated by Dorothy L. Sayres (Harmondsworth, 1949), p. 68 and diagram p. 70.

17 Pierre Jaccard, *Le sens de la direction et l'orientation lointaine chez l'homme* (Paris, 1932), a doctoral dissertation done under the direction of Edouard Claparède.

19 *Ibid.,* pp. 330-31.

20 See, e. g., William J. Beecher, "The Unexplained Direction Sense of Vertebrates," *Scientific Monthly* (July 1952); Albert Wolfson, "Day Length, Migration and Breeding Cycles in Birds," *Scientific Monthly* (April 1952); Charles M. Bogert, "Why the Homing Toad 'Comes Home,'" *Natural History* (September 1948); Karl Von Frisch, *Bees* (Ithaca, 1950).

21 G. Revez ("The Problem of Space with Particular Emphasis on Specific Sensory Space," *American Journal of Psychology,* I [1937]), p. 434n expresses the opinion that: "Although the experience of space and perception of objects of animals seem to agree with that of our own, the theory of a general phenomenal agreement between animal and human perception is highly disputable from a logical and theoretical angle. . . . Because of the lack of language and ideas, all animals must have a different space concept . . . their objects must be perceived in a fundamentally different configuration and order than ours. . . . This must be the case regardless of their particular stage of evolutionary development and their biological relationship to man."

22 Jaccard, *op. cit.,* pp. 224-25, refers to a Malagasy who, traveling in Europe, was profoundly impressed with the ignorance of directional orientation he found. In contrast, he himself constantly endeavored to maintain his orientation.

23 These remarks refer to the period of my investigations (1930-40).

24 Explorers frequently give excellent testimony on this point by their reference to the need for changing guides in the course of their journey. Cf. Jaccard, *op. cit.,* pp. 217-19. Foureau, for example, who made the first journey from North Africa to the Congo via the Saraha and Lake Chad, complained that his high-priced guides "ne connaissaient pas le pays au delà de quelques journées de marche. Les uns après les autres, arrivés à la limite, cherchaient des indigènes pour les remplacer."

25 I possess an outline map of the Poplar Narrows settlement made by a local Indian which gives all the place names in the environs of this settlement.

26 Cf. Jaccard, *op. cit.,* p. 213.

27 H. D. Hutorowicz says (*op. cit.,* p. 671), "Of course the fundamental purpose of all these primitive maps is to show routes to hunting grounds, fisheries, settlements, etc." The maps of primitive people are oriented in various ways.

The Tungus do not employ the cardinal points but use the prevailing direction of a major waterway. The Turkoman peoples use the main direction of the mountain ranges. The comments of V. Stefansson on Eskimo maps are pertinent here. "These Eskimo maps are likely to be good if you interpret them rightly. Here are some of the points. They are more likely to have the right number of curves in a river and the right shape of the curves than the proper distance scale. They are most likely to emphasize the things that are of more importance to themselves; for instance, portages they have to cross are of more significance to them than mountains that stand to one side. . . . Primitive men are likely to confuse the time scale with the mileage scale— after a ten-day journey of say six hours each day, they are likely to dot these camps at equal intervals, although, because of better going, they may have made twice the average distance one day and half the average another." See E. Raisz, *General Cartography* (New York, 1938), p. 9.

28 Hutorowicz, *op. cit.*, p. 672, "Like all maps of primitive or ancient peoples, a Tungus map is truest of the region best known to the map-maker, and this region is usually shown in the central part of his map, so that nearer the border, distances and surface features are likely to be less accurately shown." The comparison of an early Roman map (p. 677), made in the reign of Augustus (the *Tabula Pentigernana*) with the maps of primitive peoples is interesting. "They differ greatly in the fact that the Roman map attempts to show the whole world as then known, while primitive map-makers confine themselves to regions with which they are acquainted; but both are alike in having no degree nets, and in being little more than sketches of routes; and in both cases, the author tries to present the information of greatest importance to himself, other facts being almost ignored."

29 This may explain, perhaps, the geographical ignorance of the natives in certain parts of Malekula referred to by Tom Harrison, "Living with the People of Malekula," *Geographical Journal*, LXXX (1936), p. 100. "This difficulty of the natives not knowing a name or direction for any point a few miles away, this complete geographical ignorance of the Malekula (much less marked in Santo) is a handicap in travel, and particularly in taking a census. It means that one must cover all the ground oneself, and accept no negative statement as to the absence of villages."

30 Raisz, *op. cit.*, p. 1, quotes a neat analogy of the geographer P. E. James who, speaking of the individual's direct knowledge of the earth's surface, writes: "Like an ant upon a rug he may know very exactly the nature of the fabric nearby, but the general design is beyond his range of vision. In order to reduce the larger patterns of the face of the Earth to such proportions that they can be comprehended in a single view, the geographer makes use of a map." From a psychological as well as from an historical point of view the last sentence of this quotation is of particular significance. Maps, by abstracting and transforming such spatial attributes as distance, direction, area, and contour into symbolic forms that are easily perceptible in all their spatial relations, not only enable the individual to comprehend these relations more abstractly; they enable him to make measurements and calculations and plan his practical activities in a wider spatial sphere. And in travel he need have no fear of disorientation. The importance of maps as basic instruments for a realistic mastery of space by man cannot be exaggerated.

31 Cf. H. St. J. B. Philby, *The Empty Quarter* (London, 1933), p. 173, who describes the surprise of his Arab guides that he could march south on a compass course towards nothing, then turn due west and hit off the main camp that had been left the day before on a northeast course. Such a feat

197—208

implies, of course, a developed geometry and abstract space concepts.

32 Ordinarily the crossing between these two points would have been made without getting out of sight of land, and bearings would have been constantly taken. Wherever there has been little knowledge of the science of navigation sailors have depended upon landmarks. Cf. B. Malinowski, *Argonauts of the Western Pacific* (London, 1922), p. 224. ". . . In journeying across Pilolu," the enormous basin of the Lousancay Lagoon, the largest coral atoll in the world, "the natives never go out of sight of land, and in the event of mist or rain, they can always take sufficient bearings to enable them to make for the nearest sand bank or island. This is never more than some six miles off, a distance which, should the wind have dropped, may even be reached by paddling." Even the early Greeks proceeded in much the same manner. Cf. W. H. Heidel, *The Heroic Age of Science* (Carnegie Institution of Washington, Publication No. 442 [1933]), p. 123. "We also read of sailors guiding their course by the stars, though in general they skirted the shore line."

33 Jane Belo has emphasized the severe anxiety experienced by the Balinese when, for whatever reason, they became disoriented. They have a special term for the sensation of being spatially disoriented. "To be *paling,* they say, is 'not to know where North is'; in other words, he is *paling* who has lost his sense of direction, or who has lost the sense of his own position in relation to the geography of his world. One man whom I knew was taken for a trip in a motor car. He fell asleep during the ride. When the car stopped he awoke, and leaping out, looked about desperately, crying, 'Where's North, where's North? I'm *paling.'*" ("The Balinese Temper," *Character and Personality,* IV [1935], reprinted in *Personal Character and Cultural Milieu: A Collection of Readings,* compiled by Douglas G. Haring [Syracuse, 1949]).

34 Cf. H. B. Alexander, *Mythology of all Races,* X, *North America* (Boston, 1916), p. 275.

35 Elsie Clews Parsons, *Pueblo Indian Religion* (2 vols.; Chicago, 1939), I, 98-99.

36 Cf. H. B. Alexander, *op. cit.,* pp. 286-87, speaks of smoke offerings of this type as "constituting a kind of ritualistic definition of the Indians' cosmos."

37 Parsons, *op. cit.,* p. 99, states that "the order of the cardinal directions establishes the conventional circuit which is the countersunwise or sinistral, whether in coiling baskets (Hopi second mesa) or in pottery design or in dancing, although now and again the sunwise circuit is followed. A striking illustration of how the circuit may be read into life is the view, held at Zuni, that eagles nest successively in four places and then repeat their nesting round."

In China categorical-symbolical thinking as applied to space and time has deep implications for all sorts of actual behavior. (Cf. Marcel Granet, *La Pensée Chinoise* [Paris, 1934], pp. 86-114.) Derk Bodde states in "Types of Chinese Categorical Thinking," *Journal of the American Oriental Society,* LIX (1939), p. 201, that the Chinese are constantly made aware of directional orientation not only by the "layout of city streets along north-to-south and east-to-west axes," but by habitually thinking of the relations of household objects in terms of the directions. "When in China, for example, one wishes to have a table moved to a different part of one's room, one does not tell the servant to shift it to his right or his left, but to 'move it a little east' or west, or whatever the direction may be, even if it is a matter of only two or three inches."

Such a custom is so strange to Western thinking that some years ago when a twelve-year-old boy was discovered who appeared to possess an unusual sense of directional orientation, the question arose whether this might not be an innate ability. (H. R. deSilva, "A Case of a Boy Possessing an

Automatic Directional Orientation," *Science,* LXXIII [1931], 393-94.) Investigation of his personal history, however, gave the proper cue. The child's mother was left-handed and found it more convenient to substitute the cardinal directions for left and right in giving the boy directions about the locations of objects about the house. Consequently, he was brought up from babyhood to respond to such orders as, "Get me the brush on the north side of the dresser; go sit on the chair on the east side of the porch," etc. Experiment showed that the child's ability depended altogether upon correct initial visual orientation. He was easily disoriented when rotated a few times in a dark room.

CHAPTER 10

SOME PSYCHOLOGICAL ASPECTS OF MEASUREMENT
AMONG THE SAULTEAUX

1 Cf. Victor F. Lenzen, "Procedures of Empirical Science," *International Encyclopedia of Unified Science,* I (No. 5, 1938), p. 9, who says that "Measurement is the general procedure of assigning numbers to the properties of objects. A measurable property is usually called a magnitude, but the term quantity is also used."

2 John Dewey, *Logic, The Theory of Inquiry* (New York, 1938), pp. 202, 204, 213.

3 Another way of answering the question "how far" without the use of any units of measurement is illustrated by the experience of Dr. Dorothy Spencer in Fiji. She says, "When I asked how far, or, is it far, to a certain place I would be told it is near to *x*—meaning it is *near* from here to *x* (or nearer to *x*, than *y*), so that I having been to *x* would know that I would have a longer journey to *y*. When I left this time to go from Namalomulo to Nasauoko, Nambuma said, 'It was a *good* path to Bukuya', and I understood her to mean, and rightly, that the journey I was about to undertake would be worse than the one to Bukuya."

4 See Frederick Niven, *Mine Inheritance* (New York, 1940), p. 380. The source material is cited in the bibliography of this excellent historical novel of the founding of the Red River Colony.

5 Processual units of various kinds as measures of distance are very common. Cf. Max Wertheimer, "Über das Denken der Naturvölker," *Zeitschrift für Psychologie,* LX, (1912), p. 375. Some instances he cites are "a cigarette distant," a "pipe of tobacco away."

6 I am following the terminology of J. M. Cooper in his *Snares, Deadfalls and Other Traps of the Northern Algonquins and Northern Athapaskans* (Anthropological Series 5, Catholic University of America [1938]), p. 50 et seq.

7 "A shoemaker of old Pekin makes shoes with no unit of measure and no measuring scale. A strip of blank paper and his thumb nail are his measuring tools. He transfers the foot measures to his paper slip using his thumb nail as a marker. Skilfully he transmutes these measures into perfectly fitting shoes without a unit of length." H. D. Hubbard, "The Romance of Measurement," *Scientific Monthly,* XXXIII (1931), pp. 356-57.

8 An interesting application of the same principle is to be found in Beatrice Blackwood, *Both Sides of Buka Passage* (Oxford, 1935), p. 228. In building a ceremonial structure used in connection with the initiation of boys, certain portions of it were provided by villages other than the one in which it was erected. Special importance is attached to the horizontal ridge poles support-

ing the roof, which must run the full length of the building. In order to have them absolutely correct in length a fibre string of the proper linear dimensions is sent to the village which is to supply the poles. In this case it measured 65'8".

9 I.e., a cubit, in English measure 18".

10 Cf. A. L. Kroeber, *Handbook of the Indians of California* (Bulletin 78, Bureau of American Ethnology [1925]), pp. 160-61, Yuki: "The native did not think, like modern civilized man, of his people owning an area circumscribed by a definite line, in which there might happen to be one or many water courses. This would have been viewing the land through a map, whether drawn or mental; and such an attitude was foreign to his habit. What he did know was that the little town at which he was born and where he expected to die lay on a certain river or branch of a river; and that this stream, or a certain stretch of it, and all the creeks flowing into it, and all the land on or between these creeks, belong to his people; whereas below, or above, or across certain hills, were other streams and tributaries, where other people lived, with whom he might be on visiting terms or intermarried, but who had proprietary rights of their own."

11 The same may be said for Algonkians generally. See my article, "The Size of Algonkian Hunting Territories; A Function of Ecological Adjustment" (1949d).

12 Hogben, *Mathematics for the Million* (New York, 1937), p. 64. I was informed of another method of areal measurement by Ann Fuller (private communication): Among the peasants in Palestine the measure is "enough land to plant 200 vines." This is a more accurate measure than produce since it actually involves *spacing*. A very ancient method of measuring land in the Old World which survived into modern times was based upon the *quantity* of grain required to plant it. These are the so-called "seed-measures." See Edward Nicholson, *Men and Measures: A History of Weights and Measures Ancient and Modern* (London, 1912), pp. 65-66, 90-92, 256-58. Hallock and Wade, *Outlines of the Evolution of Weights and Measures and of the Metric System* (1906), observe, p. 15, that: ". . . Babylonians, in common with other Asiatic nations, also employed for measuring land the amount of seed required to sow a field and statements based on this idea are found in many old Assyrian documents." And, p. 20, "For the measurement of area the Hebrews employed generally the amount of seed required to sow the land, or the amount of ground that could be ploughed by a yoke of oxen, the latter unit being the zemed, which in the *Old Testament* is translated by Acre (1 *Samuel* XIV, 14; *Isaiah* V, 10)."

All these methods of measuring area, it should be noted, are only characteristic of agricultural peoples; it would be impossible for hunters and gatherers to develop them. Hence one would not expect any progress in the development of measures of area among hunting peoples. This appears to correspond with historical facts.

13 Methods of measurement analogous in principle are described by Ruth Bunzel, *The Pueblo Potter* (New York, 1929), p. 50. In this case the problem is to adjust the proportions of the designs to be executed to the size of the area to be painted. "All potters measure the surfaces of their jars in one way or another," although "there is a considerable individual variation in the amount of measuring that is done." One customary measure is the distance between the thumb and the tip of the middle finger when spread apart. The procedure of one expert pottery maker is described as follows: "First she studied carefully for some minutes the undecorated form, turning it around in her hands.

Then she measured hastily with her thumb and middle finger the greatest circumference of the jar. Then she drew in the outlines of the first design, which was to be used four times around the jar. After the first element was completed, she measured it and the remaining space and drew in the second element. The two together occupied a little more than half the space, so the remaining two had to be slightly crowded, but this was hardly perceptible in the finished product." One informant commented: "If I start to paint before it is all measured, then I get nervous that it may not come out right."

CHAPTER 11

TEMPORAL ORIENTATION IN WESTERN CIVILIZATION AND IN A PRELITERATE SOCIETY

1 See M. Sherif, *The Psychology of Social Norms* (New York, 1936), Chap. 3.

2 Cf. M. P. Nilsson, *Primitive Time-Reckoning* (Lund, 1920), p. 15.

3 *Gotik und Renaissance als Grundlagen der Modernen Weltanschauung* (Augsburg, 1929).

4 Helen Huss Parkhurst, "The Cult of Chronology," *Essays in Honor of John Dewey* (New York, 1929), p. 293.

5 Despite the solar basis of our calendar, however, the temporal divisions of the day as conventionally adjusted in terms of Standard Time, adopted by U. S. railroads in 1875 (see Lewis Mumford, *Technics and Civilization,* New York, 1934, p. 198), and Daylight Saving Time transcend "sun-time" and symbolize the importance of the cultural factor in our temporal frame of reference.

6 Mumford, *op. cit.,* p. 16. This author maintains (pp. 14 ff.) that "the clock, not the steam engine, is the key-machine of the modern industrial age." For an historical résumé of time-keeping devices, see A. P. Usher, *A History of Mechanical Inventions* (New York, 1929), Ch. 6, 10, and Bibliography, pp. 379-80.

7 *Op. cit.,* p. 293.

8 Mumford, *op. cit.,* p. 17.

9 *Ibid,* p. 270. "Under capitalism time-keeping is not merely a means of coordinating and inter-relating complicated functions; it is also like money, an independent commodity with a value of its own."

10 Those "masters of regimentation," as Mumford (p. 42) calls the new bourgeoisie of the seventeenth century, "reduced life to a careful, uninterrupted routine: so long for business; so long for dinner; so long for pleasure—all carefully measured out, as methodical as the sexual intercourse of Tristram Shandy's father, which coincided, symbolically, with the monthly winding of the clock. Timed payments; timed contracts; timed work; timed meals; from this period on nothing was quite free from the stamp of the calendar or the clock. Waste of time became for Protestant religious preachers, like Richard Baxter, one of the most heinous sins. To spend time in mere sociability, or even in sleep, was reprehensible."

11 Cf. O. Klineberg, *Race Differences* (New York, 1935), pp. 159-61. This author points out that "the large majority of tests of intelligence depend at least to some extent upon speed." He also stresses the fact that "indifference to speed is cultural and not innate," a conclusion that is supported on the one hand by the absence of any "physiological basis for a racial difference in speed of reaction" and on the other by the fact that "American Indian children who have lived a long time among Whites or who attend a busy and

411

progressive school show a definite tendency to approximate White behavior in this respect . . . ."

12 S. Alexander, *Space, Time and Deity* (London, 1927), Vol. 1, p. 44.

13 *Ibid.*, p. 36. Italics ours.

14 *Time and Western Man* (New York, 1928), Preface, p. xi.

15 *Op. cit.*

16 See George H. Kirby, *Guides for History Taking and Clinical Examination of Psychiatric Cases* (Utica, 1921), p. 69. For abnormalities in the judgment of temporal intervals see P. Schilder, "Psychopathology of Time," *Journal of Nervous and Mental Disorders,* LXXXIII (1936), 530-46; N. Israeli, *Abnormal Personality and Time* (New York, 1936).

17 *Red Virtue* (New York, 1933), pp. 171-72.

18 "The word Saturday is still used, but means not a definite day of the week, but any one of his free days the worker gives to additional voluntary work" (p. 172).

19 Mary Sturt, *The Psychology of Time* (London, 1925). A questionnaire method was employed.

20 F. Lorimer, *The Growth of Reason* (New York, 1929), p. 114.

21 L. Cope, *Calendars of the Indians North of Mexico* (University of California Publications in American Archaeology and Ethnology, XVI [1919]), p. 125.

22 *Op. cit.*, p. 11.

23 A. Radcliffe-Brown, *The Andaman Islanders* (Cambridge, England, 1922), pp. 311 ff.

24 W. Hough, "Time Keeping by Light and Fire," *American Anthropologist,* VI (1893), p. 207.

25 H. Webster, *Rest Days* (New York, 1916), pp. 193 ff.

26 B. Malinowski, "Lunar and Seasonal Calendar in the Trobriands," *Journal of the Royal Anthropological Institute,* LVII (1927).

27 As in Polynesian mythology. See R. B. Dixon, *Mythology of All Races,* IX. *Oceanic* (Boston, 1916).

28 The term *gīzis* is applicable to both sun and moon. Generically, therefore, it may be translated "luminary." In actual use it is defined by its context so that in the English rendering of terms I have used sun or moon. The Saulteaux themselves sometimes use a term which means "night luminary" for the moon. The translations of native words embody the meanings understood by the Indians. They are not based on refined etymological analysis.

29 In the Southwest, on the other hand, nocturnal points of reference are elaborated, as certain songs are customarily sung at certain intervals during the course of ceremonies held at night (Cope, *op. cit.*, p. 126).

30 Our "day" of twenty-four hours is a conventional unit for which we have no specific term. By calling it a "day" we employ the principle of *pars pro toto*. Cf. Nilsson, *op. cit.*, pp. 11 *et seq.* But this author is mistaken when he asserts that reckoning in "nights" among primitive peoples involves the same principle. Since they do not entertain the concept of a day-night period as a unit, "night" cannot be regarded as a symbol of the whole, but simply as a discrete recurring phenomenon that can be counted.

31 Egerton R. Young, *By Canoe and Dog Train Among the Cree and Salteaux Indians* (New York, 1890), pp. 263-64.

32 Cf. J. G. Kohl, *Kitchi-gami* (London, 1860), p. 120: ". . . they add every now and then a thirteenth nameless moon in order to get right with the sun again," and ". . . it is often comical to listen to the old men disputing as to what moon they are in." Cf. Cope, *op. cit.*, pp. 131, 137-39.

33 See the compilations in Cope, *op. cit.*, pp. 165-66, where seven series of names for the lunations are given.

34 *Bird Calendar,* designed and compiled from the records of A. G. Lawrence, Ornithological Secretary.

35 Hallowell, 1935b.

36 *Op. cit.,* p. 136. Italics ours.

37 It is hard to say, of course, whether such practice as notching a stick for every day of the year, carried out by the father of one of Densmore's informants, was a native custom or one suggested by contact with the whites. See Frances Densmore, *Chippewa Customs* (Bulletin, Bureau of American Ethnology, No. 86, 1929), p. 119.

38 Cf. Cope, *op. cit.,* map 2, where the "beginning of the year" among various peoples of native North America is indicated. Cf. Nilsson, *op. cit.,* pp. 267 et seq., for a further discussion of this question.

39 *Op. cit.,* pp. 136-37.

40 Cf. Nilsson, *op. cit.,* p. 105: "Whoever looks back over his past life sees chiefly the more important events, not the dates of the years, and to these he joins the more peripheral events and so finds his way in the labyrinth of memory."

CHAPTER 12

THE NATURE AND FUNCTION OF PROPERTY AS A SOCIAL INSTITUTION

1 Clark Wissler, *Man and Culture* (New York, 1923), p. 74.

2 For example, under Roscoe Pound's definition of law as "social control through the systematic application of the force of politically organized society" adopted by Radcliffe-Brown (see article "Primitive Law" in *Encyclopedia of the Social Sciences,* IX (1933), many primitive peoples have no law. W. Seagle's test of law, the existence of courts, likewise excludes most primitive people (*The Quest for Law* [New York, 1941], p. 34).

3 Seagle, *op. cit.,* p. 51.

4 *Economic Institutions and Cultural Change* (New York, 1941), pp. 33-34.

5 R. Thurnwald, *Economics in Primitive Communities* (International Institution of African Languages and Cultures, [London, 1932]).

6 M. J. Herskovits, *The Economic Life of Primitive Peoples* (New York, 1940).

7 E. Beaglehole, *Property. A Study in Social Psychology* (London, 1931).

8 I have chosen the writing of these two men merely as convenient illustrations since their publications are among the most recent I have seen.

9 H. Cairns, *Law and the Social Sciences* (New York, 1935), p. 59.

10 See, e.g., Henry D. MacLeod, *Elements of Economics* (1881-86) I, pp. 141, 143, 144. "Property," he writes, "in its true and original sense means solely a right, title, interest, or ownership; and consequently, to call material things like land, houses, money, cattle, etc., property is as great an absurdity as to call them right, title, interest or ownership. Neither Bacon, nor, so far as we are aware, any writer of his period calls material goods property, such a use of the word is quite a modern corruption, and we cannot say when it began."

11 W. N. Hohfeld (*Fundamental Legal Conceptions as applied in Judicial Reasoning and other Legal Essays* by W. N. Hohfeld, W. W. Cook [eds.], [New Haven, 1923], p. 28) writing in 1913 selected property as an example of "the ambiguity and looseness of our legal terminology" and goes on to say: "Sometimes it is employed to indicate the physical object to which various legal rights, privileges, etc., relate; then again—with far greater discrimination and

accuracy—the word is used to denote the legal interest (or aggregate of legal relations) appertaining to such physical object. Frequently there is a rapid and fallacious shift from the one meaning to the other. At times, also the term is used in such a 'blended' sense as to convey no definite meaning whatever." He then gives specific citations to support his contention. Cf. R. T. Ely, *Property and Contract in their Relations to the Distribution of Wealth* (New York, 1914), I, p. 108; Morris R. Cohen's essay on "Property and Sovereignty" in *Law and the Social Order* (New York, 1933), p. 45; and C. Reinold Noyes, *The Institution of Property. A Study of the Development, Substance and Arrangement of the System of Property in Modern Anglo-American Law* (New York and Toronto, 1936), pp. 356-57.

12 *Op. cit.,* p. 58.

13 Cf. John R. Commons, *Institutional Economics* (New York, 1934), p. 74. "The term 'property' cannot be defined except by defining all the activities which individuals and the community are at liberty or are required to do or not to do, with reference to the object claimed as property." W. H. Hamilton and Irene Till (in the article on "Property" in the *Ency. Soc. Sciences*) after cautioning that the word "property" "belongs to a culture, to a society, and to a vocabulary" characterize the essence of property as "a conditional equity in the valuables of a community." See also the excellent introductory orientation by L. T. Hobhouse in the symposium, *Property, its Duties and Rights* (London, 1913).

14 E.g., J. Austin, *Lectures on Jurisprudence,* ed. by R. Campbell (3rd ed., rev.; London, 1869), II, pp. 817-18. He says: "Taken in its strict sense, it [property] denotes a right—indefinite in point of user—unrestricted in point of disposition—and unlimited in point of duration—over a determinate thing."

15 Austin clearly recognizes this, for he says (*op. cit.,* p. 824-25), "But though the possible *modes* of property are infinite, and though the indefinite power of user is always restricted more or less, there is in every system of law, some one mode of property in which the restrictions to the power of user are fewer than in others: Or (changing the expression) there is some one mode of property in which the power or liberty of indefinite use is more extensive than in others. *And to this mode of property, the term dominion, property, or ownership is preeminently and emphatically applied.*" (Italics ours.) He also remarks (p. 833), after repeating that "the modes of property are infinite," ". . . that to some of those modes we cannot apply the expression without a departure from established usage." But since they are "modes" of property, they must be property in some sense and, in terms of a more flexible definition, we see from the examples he gives that they are.

16 Seagle, *op. cit.,* p. 51. Cf. R. T. Ely, *Property and Contract in their Relations to the Distribution of Wealth* (New York, 1914), I, pp. 135-36. "The right of property is an exclusive right, but it has never been an absolute right . . . that is, it excluded others; but it was not a right without limitations or qualifications." It has always had a social side. See also R. von Jhering, *Law as a Means to an End,* trans. by I. Husick (New York, 1924), pp. 386, 389. "Jurists and laymen agree in the view that the essence of property consists in the unlimited control of the owner, and that every restriction is essentially an encroachment upon it, which is incompatible with the idea of the institution." Von Jhering (writing in the 70's of the last century) denies this. It is not true "that property involves in its 'idea' the absolute power of disposition. Property in such a form society cannot tolerate and never has tolerated. The 'idea' of property cannot contain anything which is in contradiction with the 'idea' of society. This standpoint is the last remnant of that unhealthy

conception of the Law of Nature which isolated the individual as a being all apart. . . ." M. R. Cohen, *op. cit.*, pp. 57-58, remarks that "lawyers occupied with civil or private law have in any case continued the absolutistic conception of property; and in doing this, they are faithful to the language of the great eighteenth-century codes, the French, Prussian, and Austrian, and even of nineteenth-century codes like the Italian and German, which also begin with a definition of property as absolute or unlimited, though they subsequently introduce qualifying or limiting provisions."

17 Ely, *op. cit.*, p. 137.

18 Cf. Ely, *op. cit.*, p. 263, who says, "Property . . . is not a unity but rather, as we have seen, a bundle of rights. . . ." J. R. Commons, *The Distribution of Wealth* (New York, 1893), p. 92, uses the same figure, as do W. E. Atkins, D. W. McConnell, and others, in *Economic Behavior. An Institutional Approach* (Boston, 1931), II, p. 302; and Noyes, *op. cit.*, pp. 270, 359 et seq.

19 See, e.g., the article by Roscoe Pound, "Legal Rights," in *The International Journal of Ethics,* XXVI (1916). Pound discusses five senses of the word "right" as "used in the law books." He dissects the conventional term "right of owner-ship" into six sub-rights and concludes that "the use of one word for this com-plex and all its constituents has made the term 'right' quite useless for pur-poses of critical reasoning. In jurisprudence, interest, legal interest, power and privilege, are coming into use for the first four of the five meanings of a 'right' set forth above and those who use juridical analogies in other fields would do well to make similar discriminations."

20 See Hohfeld, *op. cit.* His initial paper appeared in the *Yale Law Journal* in 1913. For an evaluaton of Hohfeld's position in the history of Jurisprudence see A. Kocourek, "The Century of Analytic Jurisprudence since John Austin," in *Law. A Century of Progress, 1835-1935,* (New York, 1937) II, p. 207 et seq.

21 E. Adamson Hoebel, "Fundamental Legal Concepts as Applied in the Study of Primitive Law," *Yale Law Journal,* LI (1942), 95-96.

22 R. Firth, *Primitive Polynesian Economy* (London, 1939), p. 257. The author gives specific examples. Cf., also, A. T. and G. M. Culwick, *Ubena of the Rivers* (London, 1935), p. 260 et seq.

23 Firth, *op. cit.*, p. 258.

24 A. S. Diamond, *Primitive Law* (London, 1935), p. 261. This author assumes too close a correspondence between institutionalized forms of property and verbal forms so that he asserts that "primitive law has no such conception as 'ownership.' It knows no name for the relation between a man and his goods."

25 Firth, *ibid.*

26 E.g., W. H. R. Rivers' whole chapter on "Property" in his *Social Organization* (New York, 1924) is organized in these terms. The author says (p. 103), "The main problem with which I shall deal is how far in different societies property is held by social groups, and how far it belongs to the individual." Cf. "The Principle of Polarity" in M. R. Cohen, *Reason and Nature* (New York, 1931). "The principle of polarity," he says (p. xi), "calls attention to the fact that the traditional dilemmas, on which people have for a long time taken opposite stands, generally rest on difficulties rather than real contradic-tions, and that positive gains in philosophy can be made not by simply trying to prove that one side or the other is the truth, but by trying to get at the difficuly and determining in what respect and to what extent each side is justified. This may deprive our results of sweep and popular glamour, but will achieve the more permanent satisfaction of truth." And (p. 166) "The in-determination and consequent inconclusiveness of metaphysical and of a good deal of sociologic discussion results from uncritically adhering to simple al-

ternatives instead of resorting to the laborious process of integrating opposite assertions by finding the proper distinctions and qualifications."

27 E.g., R. H. Lowie, *Primitive Society* (New York, 1920), p. 210. B. Malinowski, *Crime and Custom in Savage Society* (New York, 1926), Chap. 2 and p. 56, "The savage is neither an extreme 'collectivist' nor an intransigent 'individualist,' he is, like man in general, a mixture of both." O. Leroy, *Essai d'introduction critique a l'étude de l'économie primitive* (Paris, 1925), pp. 45-46. M. J. Herskovits, *op. cit.*, writes: "It must be re-emphasized that the entire discussion of communism versus individualism, in so far as reference to primitive societies is concerned, seems to be but shadow-boxing, wherein verbalistic blows are dealt with an inadequate knowledge either of the actual forms taken by economic institutions of primitive groups, or of the significance of the terms 'socialistic' or 'communistic' or, indeed, even 'individualistic.'"

28 Seagle, *op. cit.*, p. 53. Referring to Malinowski he says: "Most anthropologists have attacked primitive communism by garnering evidence from individualistic peoples. But sometimes it is done even with evidence from a communistic people."

29 W. H. R. Rivers, *op. cit.*, p. 106.

30 B. Malinkowski, *Crime and Custom in Savage Society* (London, 1926), pp. 17-21. Cf. R. Firths' analysis of the ownership of canoes in Tikopia (Polynesia), *op. cit.*, pp. 244-50.

31 B. Malinowski, *Coral Gardens and their Magic* (London, 1935), I, Chap. 12, "Land Tenure."

32 *Crime and Custom in Savage Society,* pp. 20-21.

33 Hoebel, *op. cit.*, p. 961.

34 W. Schmidt, *Das Eigentum in den Urkulturen* (Münster in Westfalen, 1937), p. 31 seq. Cf. Sylvester A. Sieber and Franz H. Mueller, *The Social Life of Primitive Man* (St. Louis, 1941).

35 A fairly recent example is to be found in the well-known treatise of Munroe Smith, *The Development of European Law* (New York, 1928), p. 57.

36 *Op. cit.*, p. 291.

37 His first papers on this subject appeared in 1915 ("Basis of American Indian Ownership of the Land," a lecture delivered at the University of Pennsylvania and later published in *Old Penn, Weekly Review of the University of Pennsylvania,* pp. 181-96. "The Family Hunting Band as the Basis of Algonkian Social Organization," *American Anthropologist* [1915], XVII, 289-305.) and were later followed by others too numerous to mention here. For essential items see Cooper's article.

38 For a judicial review of the evidence see John M. Cooper, "Is the Algonquian Family Hunting Ground System Pre-Columbian?" *American Anthropologist,* XLI (1939), 66-90.

39 See Herskovits, *op. cit.*, Chap. 12.

40 MacLeod, *op. cit.*, attacked the classical economists for excluding from "wealth" valuables that were not goods or services. He maintained that rights were wealth as much as goods.

41 Hohfeld, *op. cit.*, writes (p. 29), "In connection with the ambiguities latent in the term 'property' it seems well to observe that similar looseness of thought and expression lurks in the supposed (but false) contrast between 'corporeal' and 'incorporeal' property."

42 See J. R. Commons, *Legal Foundations of Capitalism* (New York, 1924), pp. 18-19. "Property, in the popular usage, the usage of the old common law and the one adhered to in the Slaughter House Cases [1872] and the Munn Case [1876] meant any tangible thing owned. Property in the later decisions,

means any of the expected activities implied with regard to the thing owned, comprehended in the activities of acquiring, using and disposing of the thing . . . The one is property in the sense of things owned, the other is property in the sense of exchange-value of things. One is physical objects, the other is marketable assets. Thus it is that 'corporeal property' in the original meaning of the term, has disappeared . . . consequently, in conformity with the customs and usages of business, there are only two kinds of property, both of them invisible and behavioristic, since their value depends on expected activities on the commodity and money markets. One of these may technically be distinguished as 'incorporeal property,' consisting of debts, credits, bonds, mortgages, in short, of promises to pay; the other may be distinguished as 'intangible property' consisting of the exchange-value of anything whether corporeal property or incorporeal property or even intangible property. The short name for intangible property is *assets.*" Examples: one's reputation, one's horse, house or land, one's ability to work, one's good will, patent right, good credit, stocks, bonds or bank deposit, i.e., "anything that enables one to obtain from others an income in the process of buying and selling, borrowing and lending, hiring and hiring out, renting and leasing, in any of the transactions of modern business." Noyes, *op. cit.,* p. 433, expresses the opinion that Commons has gone too far in identifying property with exchange value. He points out that "the rights of use and enjoyment still remain the origin and much of the content of property. Much property exists which, because exchange does not occur and is not contemplated, is not valued nor considered in the aspect of exchange value." This, of course, is true in primitive societies.

43 R. H. Lowie, *op. cit.,* pp. 235-43, and "Incorporeal Property in Primitive Society," *Yale Law Journal,* XXXVII (1928), p. 551.
44 E.g., Haldsworth, and Pollock and Maitland. See Cairns, *op. cit.,* pp. 28-29.
45 Hoebel, *op. cit.,* pp. 963 ff.
46 See Herskovits, *op. cit.,* pp. 340-343.
47 Seagle, *op. cit.,* p. 52.
48 See in this connection Cairns, *op. cit.,* p. 60 note, where Wigmore is quoted as follows: "The Property-Right is essentially a guarantee of the exclusion of other persons from the use or handling of the thing. Its most absolute form amounts to no other than that. The common mode of definition, therefore, as a right of use *by* the owner himself, is fallacious. Take away the right, and the owner would and could be using it himself, just as well as with the right; unless we add the notion that others are not to interfere or compete in such use, and then that is seen to be the only essential element. Moreover, an owner need not actually make any use of the thing owned. Thus, the exclusion of other persons is the essence of the right." Cf. the remarks of Noyes (*op. cit.,* p. 430 seq.) on property relations viewed in terms of prohibitions, systems of protection and limited permissions.
49 See Chap. 14.
50 See R. T. Ely, *op. cit.,* II, 544-45, and H. Cairns, *op. cit.,* p. 71 et seq.
51 J. R. Commons, *Distribution of Wealth,* p. 109.
52 As a matter of fact, property rights in politically organized states are subject to other sanctions besides the purely legal ones.
53 J. Bentham, *The Theory of Legislation* (Ed. with Introduction and Notes by C. K. Ogen [New York, 1931]), p. 113.
54 E. Westermarck, *The Origin and Development of the Moral Ideas* (London, 1908), II, p. 1.
55 See D. M. Goodfellow, *Principles of Economic Sociology. The Economics of Primitive Life as Illustrated from the Bantu Peoples of South and East*

Africa (Philadelphia, 1939), who writes (p. 61): "The Sociological fact of property, enforced by custom or law, is invariably at the root of economic disposal of resources, and indeed has its necessity in this economic disposal. Nothing is more important to the integration of a culture than the economic utilization of its scarce resources, and it will be found everywhere that this is reflected in very clear formulations of the principles of ownership. True economic disposal could not take place unless social mechanisms guaranteed effective ownership. Conversely, the fact that primitive peoples have been shown to possess well-developed systems of property is a further reason for believing them to dispose of their resources according to economic principles."

56 Ruth Bunzel, "The Economic Organization of Primitive Peoples," *General Anthropology* (ed. Franz Boas), (Boston, 1938), Chap. 8, p. 340.

57 Beaglehole, *op. cit.,* p. 15 (note) says: "It is difficult to know exactly what type of behaviour this instinct embraces. The evidence adduced in its support is usually regrettably vague, while the behaviour it is supposed to explain resolutely refuses to fit into the Procrustes' bed of what smacks at times of an older faculty psychology." See also p. 28. M. R. Cohen (*op. cit.,* p. 366) commenting on Roscoe Pound's chapter, "Property," in the latter's *Introduction to the Philosophy of Law* (1912), observes that "Dean Pound's learning on all related subjects is so accurate and up to date that it is surprising to see him bring in the antiquated notion of an 'instinct of acquisitiveness.' Men's actual desires for acquisition and exclusive possession are certainly not congenital but depend on all sorts of social conditions." This is precisely what the ethnographical data show. See also J. Dewey's remarks on acquisitiveness in relation to the economic order in our culture in *Human Nature and Conduct* (New York, 1930), p. 142 et seq.

58 As Commons points out (*Legal Foundations of Capitalism,* p. 137) the jurists and economists of the eighteenth century oriented their thinking from the standpoint of the *individual.* They did not have the benefit of modern concepts of culture, institutions, customs or what Commons calls "working rules." Society and the individual were dichotomized. The individual is considered as preexistent to "working rules" and "to the individual the important thing is his rights and liberties protected against the infringement by others."

59 D. G. Ritchie, *Natural Rights. A Criticism of Some Political and Ethical Conceptions* (London, 1924), p. 80. The right to vote or to sue in the courts was regarded as means towards the attainment of such fundamental rights as liberty and security and were usually not included.

60 They will be found in Beaglehole, *op. cit.,* Part 1.

61 See the remarks of G. H. Mead, *Mind, Self and Society* (ed. with Introduction by C. W. Morris [Chicago, 1934]), pp. 161-62.

62 This is really all that Beaglehole asserts since he says (p. 251), "From the biological point of view I suggested that these objects might be regarded as primitive property values." His formal definition (p. 15) is that "Property in its most general sense may be taken to mean the exclusive use, enjoyment and control of those things which are of value in so far as, directly or indirectly, they serve to satisfy the fundamental needs of the organism." I have tried to indicate that property considered as a social institution has much broader implications.

63 Cf., Mead, *loc. cit.* "The dog is not taking the attitude of the other dog. A man who says 'this is my property' is taking an attitude of the other person. The man is appealing to his rights because he is able to take the attitude which everybody else in the group has with reference to property, thus arousing in himself the attitude of others."

64 Thomas Hobbes, *Leviathan* (Morley's Universal Library Edition; London, 1894), pp. 64-65.

CHAPTER 13

FEAR AND ANXIETY AS CULTURAL AND INDIVIDUAL VARIABLES IN A PRIMITIVE SOCIETY

1 John Dewey, "Conduct and Experience," in C. Murchison (ed.), *Psychologies of 1930* (Worcester, 1930).

2 Hadley Cantril and W. A. Hunt, "Emotional Effects Produced by the Injection of Adrenalin," *American Journal of Psychology* XLIV (1932), 300-7; Carney Landis and W. A. Hunt, "Adrenalin and Emotion," *Psychological Review*, XXXIX (1932), 467-85.

3 C. A. Ruckmick, "Psychology Tomorrow," *Psychological Review*, XLIV (1937), 138-57.

4 Carney Landis, "The Expression of Emotions," in C. Murchison (ed.), *Handbook of General Experimental Psychology* (Worcester, 1934).

5 Otto Klineberg, *Race Differences* (New York, 1935).

6 So far as tradition is concerned, experiences of this sort are not uncommon. But only a relatively few living individuals seem to have undergone them. In the last analysis, of course, selective factors that involve the personal history of such individuals must be taken into account as well as cultural tradition. Personality differences of this order suggest further problems that need detailed investigation. Cf. W. Morgan, *Human-Wolves among the Navaho* (Yale University Publications in Anthropology, No. 11 [1936]), p. 3. "But Navaho, even within a family, differ so much as individuals that there is no such thing as a uniform fear of these human-wolves. Many of the stories feature a human-wolf climbing upon the adobe roof of the Navaho hogans and looking down through the smoke hole in order to find his victim. Invariably, he knocks some earth loose and it may be heard by those inside the hogan as it rolls off and drops to the ground. When this occurs, it has twice been my experience that a Navaho who is apprehensive about human-wolves will hurry through the door to look around outside. But the man beside him may show little or no interest. This man may have few fears and few worries; or he may have considerable nervous tension but his anxieties have focussed upon some other cultural pattern such as fears of the spirits of the dead. In either case, he will stay where he is sitting or lying on his sheepskins."

7 Karen Horney, *The Neurotic Personality of Our Time* (New York, 1937).

8 *Ibid.*

9 Since dream experiences are believed to be the source of supernatural blessings and esoteric knowledge, such a rationalization is fully accptable to other members of this society. Presumably the giant jack fish, not the ordinary variety, is meant.

10 In August, 1937, I received a letter from one of my Indian informants. He said that J.D. had been "very sick," that some people said he was crazy and that there was talk of sending him to "the hospital or to the asylum." My correspondent added that *he* did not believe J.D. was crazy but that some of the people were afraid of him. "I don't think that the poor man was looked after right," he added.

11 Information, Dr. H. S. Sullivan.

CHAPTER 14

THE SOCIAL FUNCTION OF ANXIETY IN A PRIMITIVE SOCIETY

1 S. Freud, *The Problem of Anxiety*, trans. H. A. Bunker (New York, 1936), pp. 94, 121.

2 *Ibid*, p. 147.

3 *Ibid.*, p. 93.

4 *Ibid.*, p. 94.

5 *Ibid.*, p. 116. Cf. p. 108, "Psychic helplessness is the danger which is consonant with the period of immaturity of the ego, as object loss is the danger appertaining to the state of dependence of early childhood, the danger of castration to the phallic phase, and dread of the superego to the latency period. And yet all these danger situations and anxiety determinants may persist alongside one another and cause the ego to react with anxiety at a later period also than the appropriate one; or several of them may become operative simultaneously."

6 *Ibid.*, p. 94. But Freud rejects O. Rank's theory "that those persons become neurotic who on account of the severity of the birth trauma have never succeeded in abreacting it completely" (p.. 123).

7 Cf. O. H. Mowrer, "A Stimulus-Response Analysis of Anxiety and Its Role as a Reinforcing Agent," *Psychological Review*, XLVI (1939), p. 554*n*.

8 *Ibid.*, p. 563. "Anxiety is thus basically anticipatory in nature and has great biological utility in that it adaptively motivates living organisms to deal with (prepare for or flee from) traumatic events in advance of their actual occurrence, thereby diminishing their harmful effects." According to Mowrer, anxiety may be viewed as "the conditioned form of the pain reaction" (p. 555).

9 Freud, *op. cit.*, p. 147.

10 Freud, *op. cit.*, p. 147. In this paper, reference is made throughout to Freud's revised theory of anxiety. A discussion of the difference between his first and second theories will be found in Chap. 4, *New Introductory Lectures on Psycho-Analysis* (New York, 1933).

11 In Chap. 13 I called attention to this affective differential as an explicit example of how cultural variables not only define situations for the individual but structuralize them emotionally.

12 Cf. Hallowell, 1939a.

13 R. M. MacIver, *Society, its Structure and Changes* (New York, 1931), p. 248.

14 A. R. Radcliffe-Brown, "Sanctions" in *Encyclopedia of the Social Sciences:* "What is called conscience is thus in the widest sense the reflex in the individual of the sanctions of the society."

15 In Radcliffe-Brown's terminology, disease is an example of a diffuse, negative sanction. Curiously enough, he does not mention disease at all in his article, despite the fact that it operates to some degree in many societies. Systematic attention has not been given to it as a sanction.

　　On the basis of the sketch of the Ojibwa given by Ruth Landes in *Cooperation and Competition among Primitive Peoples* (New York, 1937), Margaret Mead concludes (p. 468) that, "Although they know of and sometimes act in reference to concepts of social behavior characteristic of adjacent societies with higher integrations, they [the Ojibwa] lack effective sanctions to enforce any rule, either in mourning obligations or against incest or murder." Although Landes described Ojibwa in a different locale, the belief system and institutional setup is equivalent to that of the Saulteaux. Mead's statement is, to my mind, completely misleading. A closer analysis would show,

I think, that the diseases sanction is both important and effective among all Ojibwa peoples.

16 Cf. Joseph C. Yaskin, "The Psychobiology of Anxiety," *Psychoanalytic Review,* XXIV (1937), Supplement p. 53.

17 Freud, *op. cit.,* p. 149.

18 Cf. Mowrer, *op. cit.,* pp. 563-64, who points out that ". . . experienced anxiety does not always vary in direct proportion to the objective danger in a given situation, with the result that living organisms, and human beings in particular, show tendencies to behave 'irrationally,' *i.e.,* to have anxiety in situations that are not dangerous or to have no anxiety in situations that are dangerous. Such a 'disproportionality of affect' may come about for a variety of reasons, and the analyses of these reasons throws light upon such diverse phenomena as magic, superstition, social exploitation, and the psychoneuroses."

19 While not offered in direct support of our contention, the following remarks of Freud (*op. cit.,* p. 148) seem worth citing: "There are cases in which the attributes of true and of neurotic anxiety are intermingled. The danger is known and of the real type, but the anxiety in regard to it is disproportionately great, greater than in our judgment it ought to be. It is by this excess that the neurotic element stands revealed. But these cases contribute nothing which is new in principle. Analysis shows that involved with the known reality danger is an unrecognized instinctual danger."

20 There seems no doubt that this belief also opens the door wide to the use of suggestion on the part of the native doctor.

21 R. Pettazzoni, reviewing the ethnography of confession (*La Confession des Péchés,* [Paris, 1931]), makes the point that "la confession des primitifs en général n'est pas secrète," pp. 128 ff.

22 Conjuring involves appeal to supernatural entities. The "bad conduct" of a parent may be discovered by this means and sometimes the spirits of the dead may be invoked for consultation if this seems relevant. Cf. Hallowell, 1942a, and Chap. 7.

23 Cf. Mowrer, *op. cit.,* p. 558. "This capacity to be made uncomfortable by the mere prospect of traumatic experiences, in advance of their actual occurrence, (or recurrence), and to be motivated thereby to take realistic precautions against them, is unquestionably a tremendously important and useful psychological mechanism, and the fact that the forward-looking, anxiety-arousing propensity of the human mind is more highly developed than it is in lower animals probably accounts for many of man's unique accomplishments. But it also accounts for some of his most conspicuous failures."

24 Probably seventeen or eighteen years of age. His aunt was not an "old" woman, I was told.

25 The term for father's sister and also for mother-in-law. Because of mother-in-law avoidance there was a double barrier to any erotic behavior.

26 The local English vernacular.

27 Among the Saulteaux there is absolutely no connection between confession and the Supreme Being, so that the disease sanction is not in any sense religious. Attention is drawn to this fact because of P. W. Schmidt's categorical interpretation of certain religious aspects of the *Urkulturen* to which, in his opinion, the Northern Algonkian peoples belong. Cf. Pettazzoni, *op. cit.,* pp. 151-52, who discusses this problem. He stresses the dissociation of confession from supreme deities or supernaturals of lesser rank except in a few cases. After referring to these, he goes on to say that, "dans le reste des cas dont nous avons connaissance—c'est-à-dire le plus souvent—la confession a lieu en dehors de toute intervention directe ou indirecte d'êtres divins."

276—282

28 Cf. R. R. Willoughby, "Magic and Cognate Phenomena: An Hypothesis," in *A Handbook of Social Psychology*, Carl Murchison (ed.), (Worcester, 1935).

29 Cf. O. H. Mowrer, *op. cit.*, p. 564, and his "Preparatory Set (Expectancy): Some Methods of Measurement," *Psychological Monographs*, LII (no. 2, 1940), 1-2, 39; and "Preparatory Set (Expectancy): A Determinant in Motivation and Learning," *Psychological Review*, XLV (1938), 62-91.

CHAPTER 15

AGGRESSION IN SAULTEAUX SOCIETY

1 Frank G. Speck, "Ethical Attributes of the Labrador Indians," *American Anthropologist*, XXXV (1933), 559-94.

2 This and many other psychological observations of Father Le Jeune on the Montagnais-Naskapi that parallel my own observations on the Saulteaux in this paper are to be found in Chapter 6, "Some Psychological Characteristics of the Northeastern Indians."

3 Ruth Landes, writing of the Ojibwa of the Rainy Rivert district—"The Ojibwa of Canada," in Margaret Mead (ed.), *Cooperation and Competition Among Primitive Peoples* (New York, 1937), p. 102—says: "Ojibwa life may be thought of as resting on three orders of hostility. All Ojibwa-speaking persons feel a major hostility towards those of alien speech, epitomized by the Dakota-Sioux. Next in order is the hostility that exists between different local groups of Ojibwa, and the third is the hostility felt by any household toward another whether or not of the same village. Thus the group feeling foisted upon a village by the fact of its separateness from other villages is constantly threatened by the latent hostilities of its constituent households." Landes goes on to emphasize the "atomism" of Ojibwa society by saying that although functionally the household is the irreducible unit, in thought the person is actually the unit. I do not think that Landes sufficiently analyzes the basis for local group and household hostility. On the Berens River, at least, the generalizations made would not hold. Whenever there is hostility between these large units I believe it can be reduced to specific events which have affected the lives of the component individuals. But Lands is quite right in her emphasis upon the individualistic pattern of Ojibwa society. There is a similar "atomism" in the fundamental life patterns of the closely related Saulteaux.

4 Jeannette Mirsky, for example, in her summary of data on the Eskimo of East Greenland in *Cooperation and Competition*, (p. 70) writes: "Murder is of frequent occurrence. The lack of social forms makes it possible for a man to murder within the group without having any punishment visited on him. There is no blood feud, no retaliatory act, either physical or magical, no substitutive procedure, no purification rite, nothing. The man remains within the group and people are careful not to provoke so powerful a person." Among the Eskimo, too, we find the famous "drum matches" which provide a sanctioned vehicle for the exchange of insults or the settlement of disputes (pp. 68-69). Outlets for aggression in Ashanti society are discussed in John Dollard and others, *Frustration and Aggression* (New Haven, 1939), pp. 183 ff. Among other means provided in this culture "there is a peculiar ceremony, held once a year, whose function seems almost entirely that of permitting the expression of aggression. During the ceremony everyone is permitted to tell anyone else, including the king himself, what he thinks of him."

5 Ruth Landes(*op. cit.,* p. 103). "Despite the prescribed friendship and affection existing between households of cross-cousins, a strong feeling of self-consciousness and even hostility exists. For when cross-cousins meet, they must try to embarrass one another. They 'joke' one another, making the most vulgar allegations, by their standards as well as ours. But being 'kind' relatives, no one can take offense. Cross-cousins who do not joke in this way are considered boorish, as not playing the game."

6 Henry R. Schoolcraft pointed out long ago (*History of the Indian Tribes of the United States* [Philadelphia, 1857], Part VI, p. 682) that "The Algonquin language has no words for the expression of oaths; an Algonquin can neither swear nor blaspheme." My own impression of the St. Francis Abenaki is expressed by J. A. Maurault who, on page 15 of the *Histoire des Abenaki,* (Sorel, P. Q., 1866), writes that "they . . . were not wont to show their discontent or hatred by oaths or blasphemies. The same thing may still be noticed among them. They have the greatest horror of imprecations and blasphemies; and there are no words in their language to express these, so often uttered by Canadians."

7 For a summary description of the Saulteaux kinship system see Hallowell, 1937b, in particular pp. 95-110.

8 Ruth Landes (*op. cit.,* p. 103) ". . . a person's behavior toward his prospective parents-in-law is characterized by the most pains-taking respect, the most punctilious diffidence and the greatest efforts to avoid giving offense. And a person behaves in the same way towards his prospective child-in-law (cross-niece and cross-nephew)."

See Louis F. R. Masson, *Les Bourgeois de la Compagnie du Nord-Ouest* (Quebec, 1890), II, p. 262. Cameron's observations are dated 1804.

9 Formerly native games of chance and skill undoubtedly offered a channel for the expression of aggression. But all such games have died out on the Berens River. Landes (*op. cit.,* pp. 115-16) stresses the fact that competitive games may turn into duels between individuals. "When a pair reaches the private duelling stage, they are no longer competing as lacrosse or racing rivals."

In aboriginal days out-group aggression—that is, war—must have been an important institutionalized channel for the displacement and discharge of the suppressed aggressions of individuals. Perhaps this may even explain the ferocity in war exhibited in some cases by the outwardly pacific Algonkians of the northern woodlands, although I have no data on the Saulteaux in this regard. In this connection attention may be called to John Dollard's hypothesis ("Hostility and Fear in Social Life," *Social Forces,* XVII [1938], p. 19): in ". . . direct aggression there is always some displaced aggression accompanying it and adding additional force to the rational attack. Justifiable aggressive responses seem to break the way for irrational and unjustifiable hostilities. This fact is illustrated in any war and probably accounts for the damnable character of the image of the enemy who is hated, and therefore feared, with disproportionate intensity."

What I have termed magic always involves some kind of material substance or "medicine" among the Saulteaux. In fact the term *máckikí* is applied both to the material substance one uses to catch animals or a girl, as well as to plant drugs taken to cure a stomachache. So far as I know, any substances with genuine poisonous properties are unknown to these Indians. Sorcery covers procedures in which *máckikí* is not involved.

10 Ruth Landes (*op. cit.,* p. 109): "Outright murder does not appear to be common. Slashings frequently [*sic*] result from summer hostilities, but do not culminate in murder. Grievances are nursed by one or both individuals and

282—301

avenged shamanistically, by sending bad medicine omens, winter starvation, and attacks of paralysis. When a person dies of winter starvation, or of some insanity, the suspected sorcerer is alleged to be the murderer. Murder might. also, result from trespass upon trapping grounds."

11 John Dollard, *op. cit.*, p. 183.

12 Le Jeune (R. G. Thwaites [ed.], *The Jesuit Relations and Allied Documents* [73 vols., Cleveland, 1937], VIII) relates the story of a young man who was very ill whom he had been called to see. His father had despaired of his conversion and baptism; now, as a last resort, he was converted, but he died. When Le Jeune questioned him about his illness he replied, " 'It is . . . a wicked Algonquian who has given me this disease which sticks in my body, because I was angry at him; and his fear that I would kill him induced him to bargain for my death with the Manitou.' 'And how dost thou know that?' 'I have had the Manitou consulted, and he told me I should make haste and give presents to the Manitousiouekhi,'—these are the jugglers,—'and that he would forestall my enemy, taking his life, and that thus I would be cured; but my misfortune is that I have nothing more,—I have given my Porcelain and my Beavers; and because I cannot continue these presents, I must die.' " (P. 273.)

13 Le Jeune (*op. cit.*, V, p. 179) says, "Although the Savages will give you something for a 'thank you'—this is a word they have learned from the French— you must make them some return for another 'thank you,' otherwise you will be looked upon as ungrateful. They are willing enough to receive without giving; but they do not know what it is to give without receiving. It is true that, if you will follow them into the woods, they will feed you without asking anything of you, if they think that you have nothing. But if they see that you have something, and they want it, they will not stop asking you for it until you have given it."

14 *Op. cit.*, VI, p. 245; V, p. 31.

15 The details of this dream as narrated to me are given in Hallowell, 1936a.

16 Consequently the ground is well prepared in this society for the development of paranoid or pseudo-paranoid trends in individuals. And the genuine paranoid would, no doubt, find it relatively easy to build up a plausible structure of delusions. See the account of J. D. in "Fear and Anxiety as Cultural and Individual Variables in a Primitive Society" (Chap. 13).

17 Another old man once told me that as a boy he had been warned against persons who cover up their motives by laughing in your face while at the same time they are ready to take some action against you.

18 Ruth Landes (*op. cit.*, pp. 113-14) writing of the Manitou Rapids Ojibwa of Ontario says: 'Influential persons who are known or suspected to be sorcerers are recognized in more general ways than in being deferred to professionally. People cower physically before them, shrink away, hush their talk, straighten their faces lest the shaman suspect some intended offense in their behavior. Once a girl and her mother were walking along a road and passed close to where a shaman lay dozing in the grass. They were joking and talking. Yet because of their laughter the shaman became furious and muttered, 'I'll get you! I'll get you!' and the woman soon showed the effects of evil medicine; her mouth became 'twisted' and she became incontinent of urine. One boy became paralyzed shortly after the shaman chose to be offended by his careless laugh. It is perfectly consistent with this attitude that laughing, particularly on the part of women, is not loud but light. Paralysis, incontinence, twisted mouth, and the windigo insanity are sent by shamans who have been offended by casual behavior. . . . The shaman's exquisite sensitiveness to

slights, real or imaginary, is intelligible to the people because it is only an accentuation of the sensitiveness felt by every person."

19 Ruth Landes (*op. cit.*, p. 112) says of Chief George of the Manitou Rapids Band, ". . . he was so feared that few shamans dared to enter shamanistic combat with him when he insulted them with slighting remarks."

20 For further details about this man and the Midewiwin in this area see Hallowell, 1936b.

21 I.e., a *migis*. These shells are objects associated with the Midewiwin. Their projection into a person usually is sufficient to cause death. In the ceremony of the Midiewiwin their lethal effects are demonstrated as well as the power of the midé men to revive victims. A midé would be expected to use such deadly shells in a sorcery duel. Owl's own power was sufficient to counteract the effect of Pazagwigabo's magical weapon and even to eject the shell from his body.

CHAPTER 16

PSYCHOSEXUAL ADJUSTMENT, PERSONALITY, AND THE GOOD LIFE IN A NONLITERATE CULTURE

1 Alfred C. Kinsey, Wardell B. Pomeroy, and Clyde E. Martin, *Sexual Behavior in the Human Male* (Philadelphia, 1948).

2 If we wished to go farther it would be possible to show that in some societies, the cultural evaluation of dreams may be such that interpersonal relations in dream experiences are morally evaluated in the same way as overt acts and the individual may be held responsible for them.

3 Details may be found in Hallowell, 1928b and 1937b. For comparable Ojibwa groups elsewhere see Ruth Landes, *Ojibwa Sociology* (Columbia University Contributions to Anthropology, XXIX [New York, 1937]) and *The Ojibwa Woman* (New York, 1938).

4 Early inquiries I made led to the complete denial of masturbation. I was told that Indian boys knew nothing about it until they were segregated in boarding schools, away from the reservation. Later, confessed cases of masturbation obtained from native doctors, along with other types of sexual transgression, proved the inadequacy of my original approach to the subject. Kinsey's data on the incidence and frequency of masturbation in the American population makes it appear reasonable that if we had quantitative data for these Indians it would be comparable in the pre-marital period at least to lower, rather than upper, level males. For in both groups there are the common factors of a strong tabu on the one hand and the tolerance of heterosexual intercourse on the other.

5 For a brief résumé of the world view and religious belief of these people see Hallowell, 1934a, 1942a, and Chaps. 7, 8.

6 For a few concrete examples see Hallowell, 1939a.

7 However, Ruth Landes, *Ojibwa Sociology*, refers (pp. 54-55) to a reported homosexual relationship between a girl and her aunt, both of them being married.

8 She was the daughter of his deceased first wife by a previous marriage.

9 Comparable in size and shape to a man's penis.

10 Hallowell, 1939a, p. 194.

11 Kinsey, *op. cit.*, p. 371.

12 *Ibid.*, p. 541.

13 See Hallowell, 1938c.

14 *Ibid.*, p. 571.

15 *Ibid.*, p. 572.

307—336

PART IV. THE PSYCHOLOGICAL DIMENSION IN CULTURE CHANGE

INTRODUCTION: PROBLEMS

1 Felix M. Keesing, *Culture Change. An Analysis and Bibliography of Anthropological Sources to 1953* (Stanford Anthropological Series, No. 1 [1953]).

2 Ralph Beals, "Acculturation," in A. L. Kroeber (ed.), *Anthropology Today: An Encyclopedic Inventory* (Chicago, 1953).

3 Erich Fromm, *Escape from Freedom* (New York, 1941).

4 Abram Kardiner, and others, *The Psychological Frontiers of Society* (New York, 1945), Chap. 14, "Basic Personality and History."

5 H. G. Barnett, *Innovation: The Basis of Cultural Change* (New York, 1953), pp. 291-92.

6 See the discussion of "Group Membership Determinants" in Clyde Kluckhohn and Henry A. Murray (eds.), *Personality in Nature, Society, and Culture* (New York, 1953), pp. 57 ff. Although terminology and semantic content have varied, nevertheless comparable phenomena have been brought to attention through the concepts "basic personality structure" (Kardiner), "modal personality structure" (DuBois), "social character" (Fromm), and "national character." For further references see Chap. 3, note 12.

CHAPTER 17

SOCIOPSYCHOLOGICAL ASPECTS OF ACCULTURATION

1 David Bidney, "On the Concept of Culture and Some Cultural Fallacies," *American Anthropologist*, XLVI (1944), 30-44.

2 For a formal definition of acculturation and the history of this term, see Melville J. Herskovits, *Acculturation* (New York, 1938), and Ralph Linton (ed.), *Acculturation in Seven American Indian Tribes* (New York, 1940), particularly Chap. 8.

3 David G. Mandelbaum, "Cultural Changes among the Nilgiri Tribes," *American Anthropologist*, XLIII (1941), 19-26.

4 Ethel J. Lindgren, "An Example of Culture Contact without Conflict; the Reindeer, Tungus and Russian Cossacks of Northwest Manchuria," *American Anthropologist*, XL (1938), 305-621.

5 Robert Redfield, "Culture Contact without Conflict," *American Anthropologist*, XLI (1939), 514-17.

6 Sol Tax, "World View and Social Relations in Guatemala," *American Anthropologist*, XLIII (1941), 37-42.

7 Neal E. Miller and John Dollard, *Social Learning and Imitation* (New Haven, 1941).

8 Ernest Beaglehole, *Some Modern Hawaiians* (University of Hawaii Research Publication No. 19), p. 39.

9 Miller and Dollard, *op. cit.,* Chap. 16, "Copying in the Diffusion of Culture."

10 Richard C. Thurnwald, *Black and White in East Africa: the Fabric of a New Civilization; a Study in Social Contact and Adaptation of Life in East Africa* (London, 1935), p. 174.

11 H. G. Barnett, "Culture Processes," *American Anthropologist*, XLII (1940), 21-48.
12 H. J. Priestly, *The Coming of the White Man, 1492-1848* (New York, 1930), p. 89.
13 Raymond Kennedy, "Acculturation and Administration in Indonesia," *American Anthropoligist*, XLV (1943), 185-90.
14 George Devereux and E. M. Loeb, "Antagonistic Acculturation," *American Sociological Review*, VIII (1943), 133-47.
15 Stephen W. Reed, "The Making of New Guinea," *Memoirs of the American Philosophical Society*, XVIII (1942), p. 524.
16 I. Schapera (ed.), *Western Civilization and the Natives of South Africa; Studies in Culture Contact* (George Routledge and Sons, Ltd., London, 1934), p. 42. Reprinted by permission of the publisher.
17 Beaglehole, *op. cit.*, p. 14.
18 Melville J. Herskovits, "African Gods and Catholic Saints in New World Negro Belief," *American Anthropologist*, XXXIX (1932), 635-43.
19 H. Ian Hogbin, *Experiments in Civilization: the Effects of European Culture on a Native Community of the Solomon Islands* (London, 1939), p. 156; and also Chap. 8, "Native Christianity."
20 *Ibid.*, pp. 181-82.
21 Schapera, *op. cit.*, p. 68. Reprinted by permission of the publishers.
22 Hogbin, *op. cit.*, pp. 153-54.
23 Reed, *op. cit.*, p. 103.
24 Felix M. Keesing, *The South Seas in the Modern World* (New York, 1941), p. 130.
25 Reed, *op. cit.*, p. 102.
26 George Devereux, "The Mental Hygiene of the American Indian," *Mental Hygiene*, XXVI (1942), 71-84.
27 Keesing, *op. cit.*, pp. 66, 149.
28 Hogbin, *op. cit.*, pp. 180-81.
29 Miller and Dollard, *op. cit.*, pp.188 et seq.
30 Reed, *op. cit.*, p. 245.
31 John Gillen, "Acquired Drives in Culture Contact," *American Anthropologist*, LXIV (1942), 550-51.
32 H. G. Barnett, *Year Book of the American Philosophical Society* (1941), p. 216; also, "Personal Conflicts and Cultural Changes," *Social Forces*, XX (1941), 160-71.
33 Ralph Linton, "Nativistic Movements," *American Anthropologist*, LXV (1943), 230-40. See also B. Barber, "Acculturation and Messianic Movements," *American Sociological Review*, VI (1941), 662-67.

CHAPTER 18

BACKGROUND FOR A STUDY OF ACCULTURATION AND THE PERSONALITY OF THE OJIBWA

1 Anthony F. C. Wallace, *The Modal Personality Structure of the Tuscarora Indians, as Revealed by the Rorschach Test* (Bureau of American Ethnology Bulletin 150 [Washington, 1952]).
2 George Spindler, *Sociocultural and Psychological Processes in Menomini Acculturation* (University of California Publications in Culture and Society, V [Berkeley, 1955]).
3 See W. C. McKern, "The First Settlers of Wisconsin," *Wisconsin Magazine of History* (1942), pp. 153-69.

337—365

4 L. Martin, *The Physical Geography of Wisconsin* (Wisconsin Geological and Natural History Survey, Bulletin 36 [1932]). The author points out (p. 414) that "In few parts of the world are there more lakes to the square mile. Parts of the state of Minnesota and of the province of Ontario northwest of Lake Superior and part of Finland east of the Gulf of Bothnia, furnish the only parallels." It is worth noting that the Ojibwa are to be found in the other two regions of North America referred to and that the area east of Lake Winnipeg, although not quite so typical of this kind of habitat, is marginal to the region of Ontario mentioned.

5 William Warren, *History of the Ojibways* (Collection Minnesota Historical Society, No. 5 [1885]). This monograph was completed in 1852-53.

6 Warren, *op. cit.*, pp. 372, 373-76.

7 See Appendix F (p. 442) in Henry R. Schoolcraft, *Narrative Journal of Travels,* etc., ed. by Mentor L. Williams (East Lansing, Michigan, 1953).

8 *Ibid.,* p. 444.

9 Robert F. Fries, "The Founding of the Lumber Industry in Wisconsin," *Wisconsin Magazine of History* (Sept. 1942), p. 34.

10 Ernestine Friedl, *An Attempt at Directed Culture Change. Leadership Among the Ojibwa, 1640-1948.* Doctoral Dissertation, Columbia University, 1950.

11 P. 303.

12 John Gillin, "Acquired Drives in Culture Contact," *American Anthropologist,* XLIV (1942), p. 550.

13 A map showing the "Ownership Status of Land on the Lac du Flambeau Indian Reservation" in 1933 and cited as "an example of a hopelessly checkerboarded reservation" was published in the report of the *National Resources Board* (Washington: U. S. Printing Office, 1934), fig. 63, p. 228. At this time, 32 per cent of the 69,831 acres of the reservation were swamp lands claimed by the State of Wisconsin. Of the remaining 48,000 acres, a little more than 30 per cent had been alienated to white ownership and about 27 per cent tied up in the estates of deceased allottees.

14 Carrie A. Lyford, *The Crafts of the Ojibwa (Chippewa)* (Education Division, United States Office of Indian Affairs [1943], pp. 12-13). This volume contains a map of Ojibwa Reservations in the United States; a photograph of the ceremonial dance ground at Flambeau; Plate 8 illustrates the octagonal type of log dance halls; photographs of native house types are to be found in addition to the material directly illustrating the arts and crafts.

CHAPTER 19

ACCULTURATION AND THE PERSONALITY OF THE OJIBWA

1 Helen H. Davidson, *Personality and Economic Background,* (New York, 1943).

2 Helen H. Davidson, "A Measure of Adjustment Obtained from the Rorschach Protocol," *Journal of Projective Techniques,* XIV (1950), 31-38.

3 In a previous publication (1945b) I referred to what, at first glance, might appear to be comparable figures which are also cited by Melville J. Herskovits, *Man and His Works. The Science of Cultural Anthropology* (New York, 1948), p. 57. While at that time I had the same general problem in mind, the former figures were based on a larger number of signs, some of which have been found to be less reliable than those now used. And the results were grouped into four categories. The tentative conclusions reached at that time are superceded by those stated in this article.

4 Chi-square from such a tabulation equals 12.60, significant at the 1 per cent level of confidence.

CHAPTER 20

VALUES, ACCULTURATION, AND MENTAL HEALTH

1 Jules Henry, "Anthropology in the General Social Science Course," *Journal of General Education* (1949). Cf. also the remarks of C. Kluckhohn (*Mirror for Man* [New York, 1949] pp. 285-86), on the necessity for studying values in relation to behavior.

2 O. H. Mowrer has suggested *integrative* as contrasted with *nonintegrative behavior*. Whereas the former is more psychologically rewarding than punishing, the latter is balanced in the opposite direction since adjustment is achieved "only at the expense of partial psychic self-destruction." O. H. Mowrer and A. D. Ullman, "Time as a Determinant in Integrative Learning," *Psychological Review*, LII (1945), pp. 84, 86. Cf. O. H. Mowrer, "What Is Abnormal Behavior?" in L. A. Pennington and I. A. Berg (eds.), *An Introduction to Clinical Psychology* (New York, 1948).

3 Following a query from Dr. George Spindler, to avoid any confusion with the psychoanalytic "internalized superego" constituted in *social* interaction, the "highly *internalized* conscience" of the original paper has been changed to "highly *internal* conscience."

4 Cf. David Krech and Richard S. Crutchfield, *Theory and Problems of Social Psychology* (New York, 1948). "In general, his psychological field tends spontaneously in the direction of a lower level simplification, which is a reversal of the normal trend toward higher level complexity characteristic of the growth and maturation of the individual" (p. 57).

Bibliography of A. Irving Hallowell

1921 "Indian Corn Hills," *American Anthropologist*, XXIII, 233.

1922 "Two Folk Tales from Nyasaland" (Bantu Texts), *Journal of American Folk Lore*, XXXV, 216-18.

1924 "Anthropology and the Social Worker's Perspective," *The Family*, V, 88-92.

1925 Review, Ivor H. N. Evans, *Studies in Religion, Folk Lore, and Custom in British North Borneo and the Malay Peninsula*, in *Journal of the American Oriental Society*, XLV, 42-43.

1926 a. "Bear Ceremonialism in the Northern Hemisphere," *American Anthropologist*, XXVIII, 1-175.

b. "Following the Footsteps of Prehistoric Man," *The General Magazine and Historical Chronicle*, University of Pennsylvania, XXVIII, 117-22.

1927 Review, H. H. Wilder, *The Pedigree of the Human Race*, in *Saturday Review of Literature*, April 9.

1928 a. "Recent Historical Changes in the Kinship Terminology of the St. Francis Abenaki," *Proceedings, Twenty-second International Congress of Americanists* (Rome), 97-145.

b. "Was Cross-Cousin Marriage Practiced by the North-Central Algonkian?" *Proceedings, Twenty-third International Congress of Americanists* (New York), 519-44.

1929 a. "The Physical Characteristics of the Indians of Labrador," *Journal de la Société des Americanistes de Paris*, Nouvelle Séric. XXI, 337-71.

b. "Anthropology in the University Curriculum," *The General Magazine and Historical Chronicle*, University of Pennsylvania, XXXII, 47-54.

1930 Editorial Comments; the Results of the Safe Harbor "Dig," in *Bulletin, Society for Pennsylvania Archaeology*, I.

1932 a. "Kinship Terms and Cross-Cousin Marriage of the Montagnais-Naskapi and the Cree," *American Anthropologist*, XXXIV, 171-99.

b. Foreword to Henry Lorne Masta, *Abenaki Indian Legends, Grammar and Place Names*, Victoriaville, P.Q., Canada, 9-12.

1934 a. "Some Empirical Aspects of Northern Saulteaux Religion," *American Anthropologist*, XXXVI, 389-404.

b. "Culture and Mental Disorder," *Journal of Abnormal and Social Psychology*, XXIX, 1-9.

1935 a. "The Bulbed Enema Syringe in North America," *American Anthropologist*, XXXVII, 708-10.

b. "Notes on the Northern Range of Zizania in Manitoba," *Rhodora*, XXXVII, 302-4.

c. "Two Indian Portraits," *The Beaver*, No. 3, Outfit 266, 18-19.

d. Review, F. E. Clements, *Primitive Concepts of Disease*, in *American Anthropologist*, XXXVII, 365-68.

e. Review, John M. Cooper, *The Northern Algonquian Supreme Being*, in *American Anthropologist*, XXXVII, 673-74.

1936 a. "Psychic Stresses and Culture Patterns," *American Journal of Psychiatry*, XCII, 1291-1310.

b. "The Passing of the Midewiwin in the Lake Winnipeg Region," *American Anthropologist*, XXXVIII, 32-51.

430

c. "Anthropology—Yesterday and Today," *Sigma Xi Quarterly*, XXIV, 161-69.

d. "Two Indian Portraits," *The Beaver*, No. 1, Outfit 267, 24-25.

e. Review, R. R. Marett, *Head, Heart and Hands in Human Evolution*, in *American Anthropologist*, XXXVIII, 506-7.

f. Review, Hilma Granqvist, *Marriage Conditions in a Palestinian Village*, in *American Sociological Review*, I, 991-93.

g. Review, Fred Kniffen, Gordon MacGregor, Robert McKinnon, Scudder Mekeel, and Maurice Mook (ed. A. L. Kroeber), *Walapai Ethnography*, in *American Sociological Review*, I ,540-41.

1937 a. "Temporal Orientation in Western Civilization and in a Preliterate Society," *American Anthropologist*, XXXIX, 647-70.

b. "Cross-Cousin Marriage in the Lake Winnipeg Area," in D. S. Davidson (ed.), *Twenty-fifth Anniversary Studies* (Philadelphia Anthropological Society), 95-110.

c. Introduction, *Handbook of Psychological Leads for Ethnological Field Workers*, prepared for the Committee on Culture and Personality (Chairman, Edward Sapir), National Research Council. Mimeographed, 60 pp. For printed versions see *Personal Character and Cultural Milieu. A Collection of Readings*, compiled by D. G. Haring (Syracuse, 1948); *The Study of Personality. A Book of Readings* compiled by Howard Brand (New York, 1954).

d. Review, Raymond Firth, *We, the Tikopia*, and W. Lloyd Warner, *A Black Civilization*, in *American Sociological Review*, II, 558-60.

e. Review, Ralph Linton, *The Study of Man*, in *Annals* (American Academy of Political and Social Science), CXC, 249.

f. Review (Yale University Publications in Anthropology, Nos. 1-7): C. Wissler, *Population Changes Among the Northern Plains Tribes;* P. H. Buck, *Regional Diversity in the Elaboration of Sorcery in Polynesia;* L. Spier, *Cultural Relations of the Gila River and Lower Colorado Tribes;* E. Beaglehole, *Hopi Hunting and Hunting Ritual;* W. W. Hill, *Navaho Warfare;* H. S. Mekeel, *The Economy of a Modern Teton Dakota Community;* C. Osgood, *The Distribution of the Northern Athabascan Indians*, in *American Anthropologist*, XXXIX, 140-42.

1938 a. "Fear and Anxiety as Cultural and Individual Variables in a Primitive Society," *Journal of Social Psychology*, IX, 25-47.

b. "Shabwan: A Dissocial Indian Girl," *American Journal of Orthopsychiatry*, VIII, 329-40.

c. "The Incidence, Character and Decline of Polygamy Among the Lake Winnipeg Cree and Saulteaux," *American Anthropologist*, XL, 235-56.

d. "Notes on the Material Culture of the Island Lake Saulteaux," *Journal de la Société des Américanistes de Paris*, Nouvelle Série, XXX, 129-40.

e. "Freudian Symbolism in the Dream of a Saulteaux Indian," *Man*, XXXVIII, 47-48.

f. Review, Tom Harrison, *Savage Civilization* in *Annals* (American Academy of Political and Social Science), CXCVI, 264-65.

g. Review, Franz Boas, *The Mind of Primitive Man* (rev. ed.), in *American Sociological Review*, III, 580.

h. Review, Ruth Landes, *Ojibwa Sociology* and *The Ojibwa Woman*, in *American Sociological Review*, III, 892.

1939 a. "Sin, Sex and Sickness in Saulteaux Belief," *British Journal of Medical Psychology*, XVIII, 191-97.

b. "The Child, the Savage and Human Experience," *Proceedings, Sixth Institute on the Exceptional Child* (The Woods Schools, Langhorne, Pa.),

8-34. Reprinted in *Personal Character and Cultural Milieu. A Collection of Readings*, compiled by D. G. Haring (Syracuse, 1948).

c. "Some European Folktales of the Berens River Saulteaux," *Journal of American Folk Lore*, LII, 155-79.

d. "Anthropology" (with Dorothy M. Spencer), in R. Webster (ed.), *The Volume Library* (The Educators Association, New York), 95-110.

e. "Growing Up—Savage and Civilized," *National Parent-Teacher*, XXXIV, No. 4, 32-34.

f. Reviews: E. C. Parsons, *Pueblo Indian Religion;* F. M. Keesing, *The Menomini Indians of Wisconsin;* Viola E. Garfield, *Tsimshian Clan and Society;* W. Z. Park, *Shamanism in Western North America;* H. P. Junod, *Bantu Heritage;* A. Guillaume, *Prophecy and Divination Among the Hebrews and other Semites;* S. M. Zwemer, *Studies in Popular Islam,* in *American Sociological Review*, IV, 881-83.

1940 a. "Aggression in Saulteaux Society," *Psychiatry*, III, 395-407. Reprinted in Clyde Kluckhohn and H. A. Murray (eds.), *Personality in Nature, Society and Culture* (New York, 1948) and in 2nd ed., 1953.

b. "Spirits of the Dead in Saulteaux Life and Thought," *Journal of the Royal Anthropological Institute*, LXX, 29-51.

c. "Magic: The Role of Conjuring in Saulteaux Society" (Papers Presented before the Monday Night Group [1939-40], Institute of Human Relations, Yale University). (Mimeographed)

d. Review, M. J. Herskovits, *Acculturation,* in *American Anthropologist*, XLII, 690-92.

e. Review, Weston La Barre, *The Peyote Cult,* in *Psychiatry*, III, 150-51.

1941 a. "The Social Function of Anxiety in a Primitive Society," *American Sociological Review*, VII, 869-81. Reprinted in *Personal Character and Cultural Milieu. A Collection of Readings,* compiled by D. G. Haring (Syracuse, 1948).

b. "Psychology and Anthropology," *Proceedings of the Eighth American Scientific Congress* (Washington, D. C.), II, 291-97.

c. "The Rorschach Method as an Aid in the Study of Personalities in Primitive Societies," *Character and Personality*, IX, 235-45.

d. "The Rorschach Test as a Tool for Investigating Cultural Variables and Individual Differences in the Study of Personality in Primitive Societies," *Rorschach Research Exchange*, V, 31-34. (A prospectus written prior to collection of first Rorschach protocols in 1938.)

e. Review, W. Vernon Kinietz, *The Indians of the Western Great Lakes, 1615-1760,* in *American Anthropologist*, XLIII, 645.

1942 a. *The Role of Conjuring in Saulteaux Society* (Philadelphia).

b. "Acculturation Processes and Personality Changes as Indicated by the Rorschach Technique," *Rorschach Research Exchange*, VI, 42-50. Reprinted in Clyde Kluckhohn and H. A. Murray (eds.), *Personality in Nature, Society and Culture* (New York, 1948).

c. "Some Psychological Aspects of Measurement Among the Saulteaux," *American Anthropologist*, XLIV, 62-77.

d. "Some Reflections on the Nature of Religion," *Crozer Quarterly*, XIX, 269-77.

e. "Biological Factors in Family Structure" (with E. L. Reynolds) Howard Becker and Reuben Hill (eds.), *Marriage and the Family* (Boston) 25-46.

f. Review, Karl N. Lewellyn and E. A. Hoebel, *The Cheyenne Way,* in *Annals* (American Academy of Political and Social Science), CCXX, 272-73.

1943   a. "The Nature and Functions of Property as a Social Institution," *Journal of Legal and Political Sociology*, I, 115-38. Reprinted in Morris R. Cohen and Felix S. Cohen, *Readings in Jurisprudence and Legal Philosophy* (New York, 1951).

        b. "Araucanian Parallels to the Omaha Kinship System," *American Anthropologist*, XLV, 489-91.

1945   a. "Sociopsychological Aspects of Acculturation," in Ralph Linton (ed.), *The Science of Man in the World Crisis* (New York), 171-200.

        b. "The Rorschach Technique in the Study of Personality and Culture," *American Anthropologist*, XLVII, 195-210.

        c. " 'Popular' Responses and Culture Differences: An Analysis Based on Frequencies in a Group of American Indian Subjects," *Rorschach Research Exchange*, IX, 153-68.

        d. Review, Abram Kardiner et al, *The Psychological Frontiers of Society*, in *The Scientific Monthly*, LXI, 394-96.

        e. Review, Leo W. Simmons, *The Role of the Aged in Primitive Society*, in *Annals* (American Academy of Political and Social Science), CCXLIV, 229.

        f. Review, *Where the Two Came to Their Father. A Navaho War Ceremonial*, given by Jeff King (text and paintings recorded by Maude Oakes; commentary by Joseph Campbell), in *College Art Journal*, IV, No. 3, 172-74.

1946   a. "Some Psychological Characteristics of the Northeastern Indians," in Frederick Johnson (ed.), *Man in Northeastern North America* (Papers of the R. S. Peabody Foundation for Archeology), III, 195-225.

        b. "Concordance of Ojibwa Narratives in the Published Work of Henry R. Schoolcraft," *Journal of American Folk Lore*, LIX, 136-53.

1947   a. "Myth, Culture, and Personality," *American Anthropologist*, XLXIX, 544-56.

        b. Review, Ruth Underhill, *Papago Indian Religion*, in *Annals* (American Academy of Political and Social Science), CCLIII, 250-51.

1949   a. "The Size of Algonkian Hunting Territories, A Function of Ecological Adjustment," *American Anthropologist*, LI, 35-45.

        b. "Psychosexual Adjustment, Personality, and the Good Life in a Nonliterate Culture," in Paul H. Hoch and Joseph Zubin (eds.), *Psychosexual Development in Health and Disease* (New York), 102-23.

1950   a. "Personality Structure and the Evolution of Man," *American Anthropologist*, LII, 159-73 (Presidential Address, American Anthropological Association, Nov. 18, 1949).

        b. "Values, Acculturation and Mental Health," *American Journal of Orthopsychiatry*, XX, 732-43.

        c. Review, P. A. Schilpp (ed.), *The Philosophy of Ernst Cassirer*, in *American Anthropologist*, LII, 96-99.

        d. Review, David Mandelbaum (ed.), *Selected Writings of Edward Sapir*, in *Scientific Monthly*, LXXII, 349.

        e. Review, Sister Bernard Coleman, *Decorative Designs of the Ojibwa of Northern Minnesota*, in *Journal of American Folk Lore*, LXIII, No. 247, 119-20.

1951   a. "Cultural Factors in the Structuralization of Perception," in J. H. Rohrer and M. Sherif (eds.), *Social Psychology at the Cross Roads* (New York), 164-95.

        b. "The Use of Projective Techniques in the Study of the Sociopsychological Aspects of Acculturation," *Journal of Projective Techniques*, XV,

27-44 (Presidential Address, Society for Projective Techniques, October 8, 1950).

1952 a. "Ojibwa Personality and Acculturation," in Sol Tax (ed.), with an Introduction by Melville J. Herskovits, *Acculturation in the Americas* (Proceedings and Selected Papers of the Twenty-ninth International Congress of Americanists), 105-12.

b. " 'John the Bear' in the New World," *Journal of American Folk Lore,* LXV, No. 258, 418.

1953 a. "Culture, Personality and Society," in A. L. Kroeber (ed.), *Anthropology Today* (Chicago).

b. Review, Alice Joseph and Veronica F. Murray, *Chamorros and Carolinians of Saipan,* in *Journal of Projective Techniques,* XVII, 106-8.

1954 a. "The Self and Its Behavioural Environment," *Explorations,* II (April).

b. "Psychology and Anthropology," in John Gillin (ed.), *For a Science of Social Man* (New York).

c. Comments on Clyde Kluckhohn, "Southwestern Studies of Culture and Personality," *American Anthropologist,* LVI (Southwest Issue), 700-703.

1955 Comments on "Symposium: Projective Testing in Ethnography," *American Anthropologist,* LVII (April, 1955), 262-64.